Communications
in Computer and Information Science

1643

More information about this series at https://link.springer.com/bookseries/7899

Hector Florez · Henry Gomez (Eds.)

Applied Informatics

5th International Conference, ICAI 2022
Arequipa, Peru, October 27–29, 2022
Proceedings

 Springer

Editors
Hector Florez (ID)
Universidad Distrital Francisco Jose de
Caldas
Bogota, Colombia

Henry Gomez (ID)
Universidad Continental
Arequipa, Peru

ISSN 1865-0929 ISSN 1865-0937 (electronic)
Communications in Computer and Information Science
ISBN 978-3-031-19646-1 ISBN 978-3-031-19647-8 (eBook)
https://doi.org/10.1007/978-3-031-19647-8

This Springer imprint is published by the registered company Springer Nature Switzerland AG
The registered company address is: Gewerbestrasse 11, 6330 Cham, Switzerland

Preface

The 5th International Conference on Applied Informatics (ICAI 2022) aimed to bring together researchers and practitioners working in different domains in the field of informatics in order to exchange their expertise and to discuss the perspectives of development and collaboration.

ICAI 2022 was held in blended mode at the Universidad Continental located in Arequipa, Peru, during October 27–29, 2022. It was organized by the Information Technologies Innovation (ITI) research group that belongs to the Universidad Distrital Francisco José de Caldas. In addition, ICAI 2022 was proudly sponsored by Springer and Science Based Platforms.

ICAI 2022 received 90 submissions on informatics topics. Accepted papers covered artificial intelligence, data analysis, decision systems, healthcare information systems, ICT-enabled social innovation, image processing, robot autonomy, software architectures, and software design engineering. The authors of accepted submissions came from the following countries: Argentina, Colombia, Ecuador, Greece, India, Luxembourg, Morocco, Nigeria, Norway, Poland, Russia, Spain, United Arab Emirates, the UK, and USA.

All submissions were reviewed through a double-blind peer-review process. Each paper was reviewed by at least three experts. To achieve this, ICAI 2022 was supported by 58 expert program committee members. The PC members came from the following countries: Argentina, Brazil, China, Colombia, Cyprus, Ecuador, Germany, India, Latvia, Lithuania, Luxembourg, Mexico, Morocco, the Netherlands, Nigeria, Norway, Poland, Portugal, Romania, Spain, and USA. Based on the double-blind review process, 32 full papers were accepted to be included in this proceedings volume of the Communications in Computer and Information Science (CCIS) series, published by Springer.

We would like to thank Jorge Nakahara, Alla Freund, Ramvijay Subramani, and Lekha Shree M from Springer for their helpful advice, guidance, and support in publishing the proceedings.

We trust that the ICAI 2022 proceedings open you up to new vistas of discovery and knowledge.

October 2022

Hector Florez
Henry Gomez

Organization

General Chairs

Hector Florez	Universidad Distrital Francisco José de Caldas, Colombia
Henry Gomez	Universidad Continental, Peru

Steering Committee

Jaime Chavarriaga	Universidad de los Andes, Colombia
Cesar Diaz	OCOX AI, Colombia
Hector Florez	Universidad Distrital Francisco José de Caldas, Colombia
Ixent Galpin	Universidad de Bogotá Jorge Tadeo Lozano, Colombia
Olmer García	Universidad de Bogotá Jorge Tadeo Lozano, Colombia
Christian Grévisse	Université du Luxembourg, Luxembourg
Sanjay Misra	Høgskolen i Østfold, Norway
Ma Florencia Pollo-Cattaneo	Universidad Tecnológica Nacional Facultad Regional Buenos Aires, Argentina
Fernando Yepes-Calderon	Children's Hospital Los Angeles, USA

Organizing Committee

Emma Barrios	Universidad Continental, Peru
Henry Gomez	Universidad Continental, Peru

Workshops Committee

Hector Florez	Universidad Distrital Francisco José de Caldas, Colombia
Ixent Galpin	Universidad de Bogotá Jorge Tadeo Lozano, Colombia
Christian Grévisse	Université du Luxembourg, Luxembourg

Program Committee Chairs

Hector Florez   Universidad Distrital Francisco José de Caldas,
                                 Colombia
Henry Gomez   Universidad Continental, Peru

Program Committee

Fernanda Almeida   Universidade Federal do ABC, Brazil
Francisco Alvarez   Universidad Autónoma de Aguascalientes,
                                 Mexico
Cecilia Avila   Fundación Universitaria Konrad Lorenz,
                                 Colombia
Joseph Bamidele Awotunde   University of Ilorin, Nigeria
Jorge Bacca   Fundacion Universitaria Konrad Lorenz,
                                 Colombia
Alejandra Baena   Universidad Antonio Nariño, Colombia
Carlos Balsa   Instituto Politécnico de Bragança, Portugal
Hüseyin Bicen   Yakin Dogu Üniversitesi, Cyprus
Alexander Bock   Universität Duisburg Essen, Germany
Paola Britos   Universidad Nacional de Río Negro, Argentina
Robert Buchmann   Universitatea Babes-Bolyai, Romania
Santiago Caballero   Universidad Popular Autónoma del Estado de
                                 Puebla, Mexico
Patricia Cano-Olivos   Universidad Popular Autónoma del Estado de
                                 Puebla, Mexico
Ines Casanovas   Universidad Tecnológica Nacional, Argentina
Germán Castañeda   Universidade Estadual de Campinas, Brazil
Robertas Damasevicius   Kauno Technologijos Universitetas, Lithuania
Victor Darriba   Universidade de Vigo, Spain
Luis de-la-Fuente-Valentín   Universidad Internacional de La Rioja, Spain
Saharnaz Dilmaghani   PricewaterhouseCoopers, Luxembourg
Silvia Fajardo   Universidad de Colima, Mexico
Mauri Ferrandin   Universidade Federal de Santa Catarina, Brazil
Hector Florez   Universidad Distrital Francisco José de Caldas,
                                 Colombia
Ixent Galpin   Universidad de Bogotá Jorge Tadeo Lozano,
                                 Colombia
Olmer Garcia   Universidad de Bogotá Jorge Tadeo Lozano,
                                 Colombia
Raphael Gomes   Instituto Federal de Goiás, Brazil
Daniel Görlich   SRH Hochschule Heidelberg, Germany
Aliseri Govardhan   Jawaharlal Nehru Technological University
                                 Hyderabad, India

Jānis Grabis	Rīgas Tehniskā Universitāte, Latvia
Christian Grévisse	Université du Luxembourg, Luxembourg
Guillermo Guarnizo	Universidad Santo Tomas, Colombia
Jens Gulden	Universiteit Utrecht, Netherlands
Alejandro Hossian	Universidad Tecnológica Nacional, Argentina
Monika Kaczmarek	Universität Duisburg-Essen, Germany
Robert Laurini	Knowledge Systems Institute, USA
Marcelo Leon	Universidad Ecotec, Ecuador
Isabel Lopes	Instituto Politécnico de Bragança, Portugal
Rytis Maskeliunas	Kauno Technologijos Universitetas, Lithuania
Sanjay Misra	Høgskolen i Østfold, Norway
Ivan Mura	Duke Kunshan University, China
Hugo Peixoto	Universidade do Minho, Portugal
Diego Peluffo-Ordóñez	Mohammed VI Polytechnic University, Morocco
Tamara Piñero	Hospital Italiano de Buenos Aires, Argentina
Adam Piórkowski	AGH University of Science and Technology, Poland
Ma Florencia Pollo-Cattaneo	Universidad Tecnológica Nacional, Argentina
Filipe Portela	Universidade do Minho, Portugal
Pablo Pytel	Universidad Tecnológica Nacional, Argentina
Juan Camilo Ramírez	Universidad Antonio Nariño, Colombia
Marcelo Risk	Hospital Italiano de Buenos Aires, Argentina
Ben Roelens	Open Universiteit, Netherlands
Enzo Rucci	Universidad Nacional de la Plata, Argentina
José Rufino	Instituto Politécnico de Bragança, Portugal
Alber Sanchez	Instituto Nacional de Pesquisas Espaciais, Brazil
Sweta Singh	Savitribai Phule Pune University, India
Andrei Tchernykh	Centro de Investigación Científica y de Educación Superior de Ensenada, Mexico
Manuel Vilares	Universidade de Vigo, Spain
Gatis Vitols	WeAreDots Ltd., Latvia
Leandro Wives	Universidade Federal do Rio Grande do Sul, Brazil
Fernando Yepes-Calderon	Children's Hospital Los Angeles, USA

Contents

Decision Systems

Health Care Information Systems

ICT-Enabled Social Innovation

Image Processing

Robotic Autonomy

Artificial Intelligence

A Genetic Algorithm for Scheduling Laboratory Rooms: A Case Study

Rafael Fuenmayor[1], Martín Larrea[1], Mario Moncayo[1], Esteban Moya[1],
Sebastián Trujillo[1], Juan-Diego Terneus[1], Robinson Guachi[1],
Diego H. Peluffo-Ordoñez[2,3,4], and Lorena Guachi-Guachi[1,3(✉)]

[1] Department of Mechatronics, Universidad Internacional Del Ecuador,
Av. Simon Bolivar, 170411 Quito, Ecuador
{gufuenmayorso,jalarreafr,mamoncayolo,esmoyata,jutrujillopr,juterneusgo,
roguachigu,loguachigu}@uide.edu.ec
[2] Modeling, Simulation and Data Analysis (MSDA) Research Program,
Mohammed VI Polytechnic University, Lot 660, Hay Moulay Rachid Ben Guerir,
43150 Ben Guerir, Morocco
peluffo.diego@um6p.ma
[3] Smart Data Analysis Systems Group (SDAS Research Group),
Ben Guerir 47963, Morocco
{peluffo.diego,lorena.guachi}@sdas-group.com
[4] Faculty of Engineering, Corporación Universitaria Autónoma de Nariño,
Pasto 520001, Colombia
diego.peluffo@aunar.edu.co
https://sdas-group.com/

Abstract. Genetic algorithms (GAs) are a great tool for solving optimization problems. Their characteristics and different components based on the principles of biological evolution make these algorithms very robust and efficient in this type of problem. Many research works have presented dedicated solutions to schedule or resource optimization problems in different areas and project types; most of them have adopted GA implementation to find an individual that represents the best solution. Under this conception, in this work, we present a GA with a controlled mutation operator aiming at maintaining a trade-off between diversity and survival of the best individuals of each generation. This modification is supported by an improvement in terms of convergence time, efficiency of the results and the fulfillment of the constraints (of 29%, 14.98% and 23.33% respectively, compared with state-of-the-art GA with a single random mutation operator) to solve the problem of schedule optimization in the use of three laboratory rooms of the Mechatronics Engineering Career of the International University of Ecuador.

Keywords: Genetic algorithms · Mutation · Scheduling optimization

1 Introduction

The use of laboratories is critical in professional training because practical sessions supplement theoretical foundations and ensure that concepts are clarified

© The Author(s), under exclusive license to Springer Nature Switzerland AG 2022
H. Florez and H. Gomez (Eds.): ICAI 2022, CCIS 1643, pp. 3–14, 2022.
https://doi.org/10.1007/978-3-031-19647-8_1

and emphasized appropriately. Problems frequently arise in the planning of class schedules and the use of laboratories in various educational facilities. Crossing schedules for students or professors, as well as excessive time for handling constraints, prevent the various initial courses of a career from having access to laboratory facilities, giving priority only to those courses at the end of the careers. These difficulties are typically caused by the laboratory's capacity, the availability of teachers, and the hours during which the laboratory can be used.

Recent research for scheduling problems have introduced the genetic algorithms (GAs) and a combination between GAs and reinforcement learning, as the most widely used and effective techniques for optimizing resources such as time and space availability. For instance, works in [4–8,10,12,13,16–19,21,22] introduce GAs which develop a series of processes from a population of candidate solutions to a specific problem to obtain the best possible solutions. On the other hand, works in [2,14,28], use reinforcement learning algorithms to obtain a solution from the definition of different parameters that represent the starting point of the genetic algorithms. Although there are several works on schedule optimization, each one focuses on a specific problem, and its application in the optimization of schedules for the use of laboratories in the Mechatronics career of the International University of Ecuador demands an adjustment and optimization for the specific conditions of the problem to be solved.

Therefore, in this work, we present the implementation of a GA with a controlled mutation to produce an optimal schedule for the use of laboratories at the International University of Ecuador's Mechatronics Engineering career. The main differences regarding [21], which optimize class scheduling, lie in the control strategy used and the application to the optimization of laboratory practice use.

This paper is structured as follows: Sect. 2 presents a brief overview of the state-of-the-art. The description of the database used for the experimentation is presented, together with the definition of parameters and characteristic operators of the GA in Sect. 3. Then, in Sect. 4, the experimentation process is described together with the metrics used to evaluate the performance of the algorithm. Finally, the obtained results and conclusions are presented in Sects. 5 and 6 which supports that the modification presented in the mutation operator improves the convergence time, efficiency of the results and the fulfillment of the constraints of 41%, 36.36% and 25% respectively, in comparison with [21].

2   Related Works

Evolutionary algorithms are techniques based on various theories of biological evolution in which only the strongest and best adapted individuals within an environment will be able to survive and reproduce; that is, a competition is generated from an initial population of individuals coexisting in a specific environment with limited resources, resulting in a selection of the individuals best adapted to the environment. Through mutation and recombination processes, these individuals become the progenitors of a new generation; these new individuals will now compete among themselves, resulting in an increase in the population's quality.

Taking advantage of these characteristics, several works have used evolutionary algorithms to find an efficient solution for schedule generation problems in various academic and industrial areas. Typically, the generation of schedules or project planning requires the coexistence of multiple factors and resources, which greatly complicates such problems [3–11, 13, 18, 20–23, 25, 27, 29].

For instance, in [13], a genetic algorithm with specific constraints to maximize the fitness value of each individual is proposed, which after several generations arrives at the solution of a research oriented scheduling problem. Hybrid evolutionary algorithms also provide even more optimized solutions. In this regard, [29] offer good results in solving resource-constrained project scheduling problems (RCPSPs) by using the sequential performance of multi-operator algorithms under two sub-populations, which provides a modified forward and backward justification approach to obtain feasible schedules.

Recently, evolutionary algorithms have been used to solve schedule optimization problems is the optimization of resources and labor time in the various involved tasks; for example, the hybridization of artificial intelligence (AI) with GA increases the search capacity for a near-optimal solution while avoiding most premature convergence problems [3, 5–8, 10, 11, 13, 21, 23].Other applications include maximizing the utilization of operating rooms, minimizing the cost of operating time overruns and minimizing the cost of waste due to unused time. The elitist search technique is the most commonly used to optimize this kind of problems, which in minor surgery problems outperforms other applications previously tested. Whilst in complex surgeries, this technique produces satisfactory results [3, 6, 16].

Although evolutionary algorithms have been widely used for scheduling optimization problems, their performance is dependent on different parameter combinations, so they must be redesigned for any extension of the problem [6]. There are cases where the redesigned algorithm may lose diversity and reach a point where it may not converge; as a result, certain stopping conditions, such as a maximum number of generations, population diversity, control of the fitness function, and so on, can be implemented [20].

In order to reduce time-consuming parameter setting tasks, some works have adopted reinforcement learning algorithms, in which a decision is made on various parameters that will provide support to reach an optimal solution to a specific problem [1, 2, 14, 15, 26, 28]. In [24] a technique of waiting time priority genetic algorithms (WTPA) is also implemented for the reduction of the total average time of all the activities of a schedule; obtaining good results and achieving the proposed objective.

3   Materials and Methods

Inspired by [21], a GA for engineering course scheduling, we propose a GA to solve a scheduling generation problem to optimize the use of the laboratories, with the goal of reducing convergence time and restriction compliance.

To solve our problem of laboratory scheduling in the career of Mechatronics in the International University of Ecuador, we used the number of courses, the number of rooms of the laboratory, the number of subjects (electronics, mechanics, ...), and the number of students per subjects as shown in Table 1.

Table 1. Data description of the laboratories of the mechatronics career

Data	Description	Value
Labs	Available labs	3 Labs
Available times	Times in which the labs are available	13 times
Professors	Professors than can impart the subjects	8 Professors
Subjects	Subjects that need to use the laboratories	17 subjects
Students per subject	Number of students that take a certain subject.	Electronics1: 17, Mechanics3: 10, etc.
Lab capacity	Max number of students per lab	Lab1: 25, Lab2: 10, Lab3: 15

The flowchart of the proposed GA is depicted in Fig. 1. It involves three major steps: Initialization, selection & combination, and mutation based on [21].

Initialization of the Population: It creates the first generation of the population which is going to be used for the solution. The first generation is generated randomly using certain parameters, such as which subjects belong to which academic level and which professors can teach which subject. Following that, the fitness score of the population is calculated by taking into account the number of conflicts found on each generated schedule.

Selection: Once the fitness value for each individual in the population has been calculated using the selection operator, the individuals with the highest fitness value are chosen to create the next generation. It allows the algorithm to get closer to the optimal schedule or solution with each generation. Individuals in this application are chosen using a tournament technique to find the fittest individuals. In this work, we set the number of selected individuals to 3 (Tournament selection size = 3).

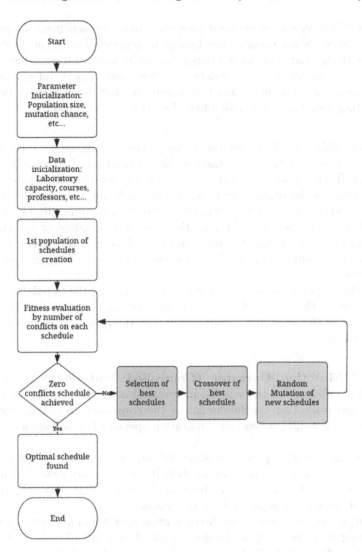

Fig. 1. The genetic algorithm's workflow for generating an optimal schedule for the use of laboratory rooms.

Crossover: The crossover operator uses the parents chosen from the previous generation to create a new one by combining the genetic information of the fittest parents, with the goal of producing populations with higher fitness values. In this work, we use a random number to determine how much genetic information will be taken from each parent involved, randomly mixing the characteristics, and thus creating completely new individuals for the next generation.

Mutation: This is the last operator in the process of implementing the genetic algorithm. Consist in modifying the genetic information of the newly created generation. In this work, a mutation rate of 0.1 is set (mutation rate = 0.1), which determines the probability of an individual being mutated; this value is chosen to ensure the variety of individuals while maintaining its quality. If a random number is less than the mutation rate, the schedule or individual is mutated or generated again. The mutation is used to maintain diversity among individuals in a population, avoiding problems such as the GA not converging quickly enough.

Once these operators are used, a fitness evaluation of the population is performed again. If there is a schedule with no conflicts, the algorithm stops and presents this as the optimal solution. Otherwise, the process is repeated until a solution is found.

Proposed Mutation Operator (Controlled Mutation). In order to improve the efficiency of the results, in terms of convergence, due to increase diversity and respecting the fulfillment of the constraints regarding the algorithm presented in [21], a controlled mutation operator is proposed as depicted in Fig. 2:

In [21], the mutation process was carried out using a single mutation value that was compared with a random number. If the randomly generated number is less than this value, a change is made in the vector that stores the courses, with one of them being replaced by a new course.

In contrast, the proposed controlled mutation operator employs two mutation values (0.05; 0.1), resulting in the generation of two conditionals. In the first one, if the random number is less than 0.05 then one of the first ten courses will be chosen at random and replaced by a new course. In the second one, if the random number is between the mutation rates, a course between position 13 and 17 (of the vector in which the courses are stored) will be randomly chosen to be exchanged with a newly generated course.

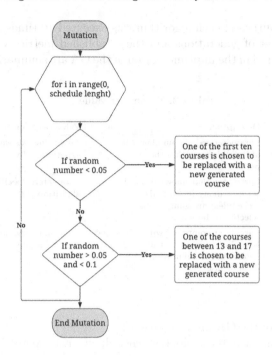

Fig. 2. A controlled mutation operator.

4   Experimental Setup

For the implementation of this algorithm, the Google Colaboratory programming environment with the Python language was used; the environment has 100 GB of storage space and 12 GB of RAM. The Random library was used to maintain randomness in different operators such as mutation and crossover. Prettytable was used to create an appropriate visualization of the results (it provides the possibility of designing a tabular representation of the resulting schedule).

The ability of the proposed GA algorithm with a controlled mutation operator for the use of laboratory rooms was evaluated in terms of the convergence time, effectiveness, and compliance of restrictions.

- **Convergence time:** this metric measures the time required by the algorithm to find an optimal solution free of conflicts.
- **Result effectiveness:** it evaluates the fitness of the individuals of the last generation. While the best individual will always have a fitness value of 1 (there is no conflict), the efficiency is determined by the fitness of the worst individual of the last generation (if the fitness number is lower, then the efficiency will be worse).
- **Compliance of restrictions:** This metric corresponds to the number of conflicts presented by the last generation's individuals. This metric is summarized in the number of conflicts experienced by the worst individual of that generation since the best individual has 0 conflicts.

For comparison purposes, each algorithm was executed 10 times and the execution times, number of generations and the established metrics were registered.
The parameters used in the implementation of the GA are summarized in Table 2.

Table 2. Parameter values.

Parameter	Description	Value	Value selection procedure
Population size	Parameterized the number of individuals within the population	9	This value was determined experimentally.
Selection pressure	Parameter that allows to set how many individuals (schedules) are going to be selected to be parents	1	Parameters specified in base algorithm [18].
Mutation rate	Parameter compared with a random number which determines if a mutation is done or not	0.1 and 0.05	This value was determined experimentally

Python routines of the GA are available at:
https://github.com/mamoncayolo/LabSchedulingGeneticAlgorithm.git

5   Experimental Results

From Table 3, it can be observed the variation of the execution time for the
proposed GA and the base GA with single random mutation [21]. The average
execution time through ten independent executions exhibits that the proposed
GA is faster than the base algorithm with a minimum value of 1.469s and a
maximum value of 2.03s. On the other hand we have the base algorithm with a
minimum time of 1.696s and a maximum time of 3.754s.

Table 3. Execution time required by the proposed GA and the state-of-the-art.

	Execution time (seconds [s.])										MIN	MAX	AVG
	Execution number												
	1	2	3	4	5	6	7	8	9	10			
GA with controlled mutation	1.647	1.48	1.93	1.52	1.775	2.03	1.965	1.469	1.639	1.757	1.469	2.03	1.721±0.21
GA with single random mutation [21]	1.696	2.46	2.27	2.314	2.851	3.055	3.754	1.754	1.605	2.514	1.696	3.754	2.427±0.67

From the Fig. 3, it can be seen that the proposed GA algorithm exhibits
a minimum value of 0.2 (fitness) and a maximum value of 1, being this the
maximum value of an optimal schedule. On the other hand the base algorithm

exhibits a minimum value of 0.167 and a maximum value of 1 as well. However the proposed GA algorithm achieves the highest average value of 0,327 ± 0,0716, against 0,278 ± 0,0756 reached by the base GA algorithm.

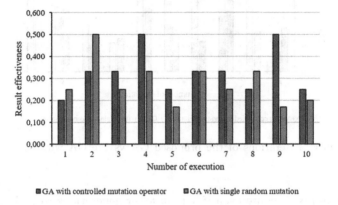

Fig. 3. Result effectiveness of the proposed GA with controlled mutation operator vs GA with single random mutation.

For the constraint compliance metric, the number of conflicts found in the schedules or individuals is taken into account. For this reason, as shown in the Fig. 4, the higher the value, the worse the result. In the proposed GA algorithm there is a minimum value of 1 (number of conflicts) and a maximum value of 4. On the other hand we have the base algorithm with a minimum value of 1 and a maximum value of 5.

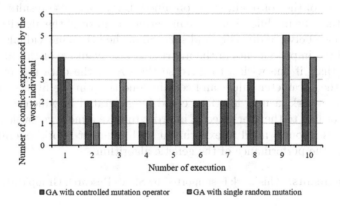

Fig. 4. Compliance of restrictions of the proposed GA vs the GA with a single random mutation.

According to Fig. 5, even though the base algorithm obtains a minimum value of generations less than the proposed GA, this does not imply that the base

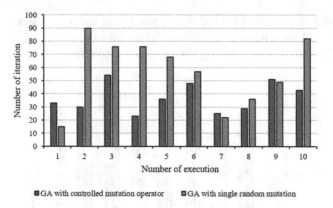

Fig. 5. Number of iterations of the proposed GA vs the GA with a single random mutation.

has better results, because even if it took fewer generations to find an optimal schedule, it took more time to find it.

6   Conclusion

This work presented a genetic algorithm capable of solving the problem of generating an optimized schedule for the use of three laboratory rooms of the Faculty of Mechatronics Engineering. After the experimentation comparing the proposed algorithm with the base algorithm [21], a remarkable improvement in all the analyzed metrics was evidenced. An average improvement of approximately 29% in the convergence time, 14.98% in the efficiency of the results and 23.33% in the fulfillment of the constraints was obtained. Based on these results, it can be concluded that the modification in the mutation operator of the algorithm maintains a balance between diversity and survival of the fittest individuals, which is reflected in the improvements in the metrics. A disadvantage of this application is the fact that, if one wishes to increase the size of the data set, one should reconsider the parameter values and certain conditions in the fitness function.

For future work, a user interface could be generated in which data can be entered according to the user's needs, in order to have a more versatile program. Likewise, it is recommended to experiment with different hybrid operators that can improve the performance of the genetic algorithm.

Acknowledgments. This work is supported by SDAS Research Group (https://sdas-group.com).

References

1. Alhuniti, O., Ghnemat, R., El-Seoud, M.S.A.: Smart university scheduling using genetic algorithms. In: Proceedings of the 2020 9th International Conference on Software and Information Engineering (ICSIE), pp. 235–239 (2020)

2. Alomari, K., Almarashdi, O., Marashdh, A., Zaqaibeh, B.: A new optimization on harmony search algorithm for exam timetabling system. J. Inf. Knowl. Manage. **19**(01), 2040009 (2020)
3. Amindoust, A., Asadpour, M., Shirmohammadi, S.: A hybrid genetic algorithm for nurse scheduling problem considering the fatigue factor. J. Healthcare Eng. **2021** (2021)
4. Amjad, M., Butt, S., Anjum, N., Chaudhry, I., Faping, Z., Khan, M.: A layered genetic algorithm with iterative diversification for optimization of flexible job shop scheduling problems. Adv. Prod. Eng. Manage. **15**(4), 377–389 (2020)
5. Ansari, R., Saubari, N.: Application of genetic algorithm concept on course scheduling. In: IOP Conference series: Materials Science and Engineering, vol. 821, p. 012043. IOP Publishing (2020)
6. Asadujjaman, M., Rahman, H.F., Chakrabortty, R.K., Ryan, M.J.: An immune genetic algorithm for solving NPV-based resource constrained project scheduling problem. IEEE Access **9**, 26177–26195 (2021)
7. Chen, R., Yang, B., Li, S., Wang, S.: A self-learning genetic algorithm based on reinforcement learning for flexible job-shop scheduling problem. Comput. Ind. Eng. **149**, 106778 (2020)
8. Chen, X., Yue, X.G., Li, R., Zhumadillayeva, A., Liu, R.: Design and application of an improved genetic algorithm to a class scheduling system. Int. J. Emerg. Technol. Learn. (iJET) **16**(1), 44–59 (2021)
9. Doğan, A., Yurtsal, A.: Developing a decision support system for exam scheduling problem using genetic algorithm. Eskişehir Tech. Univ. J. Sci. Technol. A-Appl. Sci. Eng. **22**(3), 274–289 (2021)
10. Donoriyanto, D.S., Silfiana, I.Y., Pudji, W.E., Suryadi, A., Widodo, L.U.: Determination of maintenance schedule of loading and unloading pump machine using genetic algorithm method. J. Phys. Conf. Ser. **1569**, 032008 (2020)
11. Ha, V.P., Dao, T.K., Pham, N.Y., Le, M.H.: A variable-length chromosome genetic algorithm for time-based sensor network schedule optimization. Sensors **21**(12), 3990 (2021)
12. Herrera-Granda, I.D., Martín-Barreiro, C., Herrera-Granda, E.P., Fernández, Y., Peluffo-Ordoñez, D.H.: Forthcoming paper icor2020-90b35-01 a hybrid genetic algorithm for optimizing urban distribution of auto-parts by a vertex routing problem
13. Idroes, R., Maulana, A., Noviandy, T., Suhendra, R., Sasmita, N., Lala, A., et al.: A genetic algorithm to determine research consultation schedules in campus environment. In: IOP Conference Series: Materials Science and Engineering, vol. 796, p. 012033. IOP Publishing (2020)
14. Kakkar, M.K., Singla, J., Garg, N., Gupta, G., Srivastava, P., Kumar, A.: Class schedule generation using evolutionary algorithms. In: Journal of Physics: Conference Series, vol. 1950, p. 012067. IOP Publishing (2021)
15. Köksal Ahmed, E., Li, Z., Veeravalli, B., Ren, S.: Reinforcement learning-enabled genetic algorithm for school bus scheduling. J. Intell. Transp. Syst. **26**(3), 269–283 (2022)
16. Li, X., Chen, H.: Physical therapy scheduling of inpatients based on improved genetic algorithm. In: Journal of Physics: Conference Series, vol. 1848, p. 012009. IOP Publishing (2021)
17. Lin, Y.-K., Chou, Y.-Y.: A hybrid genetic algorithm for operating room scheduling. Health Care Manage. Sci. **23**(2), 249–263 (2019). https://doi.org/10.1007/s10729-019-09481-5

18. Liu, J., Liu, Y., Shi, Y., Li, J.: Solving resource-constrained project scheduling problem via genetic algorithm. J. Comput. Civil Eng. **34**(2), 04019055 (2020)
19. Lorente-Leyva, L.L., et al.: Optimization of the master production scheduling in a textile industry using genetic algorithm. In: Pérez García, H., Sánchez González, L., Castejón Limas, M., Quintián Pardo, H., Corchado Rodríguez, E. (eds.) HAIS 2019. LNCS (LNAI), vol. 11734, pp. 674–685. Springer, Cham (2019). https://doi.org/10.1007/978-3-030-29859-3_57
20. Mammi, H.K., Ying, L.Y.: Timetable scheduling system using genetic algorithm for school of computing (tsuGA). Int. J. Innov. Comput. **11**(2), 67–72 (2021)
21. Nugroho, A.K., Permadi, I., Yasifa, A.R., et al.: Optimizing course scheduling faculty of engineering unsoed using genetic algorithms. JITK (Jurnal Ilmu Pengetahuan dan Teknologi Komputer) **7**(2), 91–98 (2022)
22. Pirozmand, P., Hosseinabadi, A.A.R., Farrokhzad, M., Sadeghilalimi, M., Mirkamali, S., Slowik, A.: Multi-objective hybrid genetic algorithm for task scheduling problem in cloud computing. Neural Comput. Appl. **33**(19), 13075–13088 (2021). https://doi.org/10.1007/s00521-021-06002-w
23. Sardjono, W., Priatna, W., Nugroho, D.S., Rahmasari, A., Lusia, E.: Genetic algorithm implementation for application of shifting work scheduling system. ICIC Exp. Lett. **15**(7), 791–802 (2021)
24. Shen, L., Zhang, G.: Optimization design of civil engineering construction schedule based on genetic algorithm. In: Journal of Physics: Conference Series, vol. 1852, p. 032055. IOP Publishing (2021)
25. Shuai, C.J.: Design of automatic course arrangement system for electronic engineering teaching based on monte carlo genetic algorithm. Secur. Commun. Netw. **2021** (2021)
26. Tang, J., Yang, Y., Hao, W., Liu, F., Wang, Y.: A data-driven timetable optimization of urban bus line based on multi-objective genetic algorithm. IEEE Trans. Intell. Transp. Syst. **22**(4), 2417–2429 (2020)
27. Tung Ngo, S., Jafreezal, J., Hoang Nguyen, G., Ngoc Bui, A.: A genetic algorithm for multi-objective optimization in complex course timetabling. In: 2021 10th International Conference on Software and Computer Applications, pp. 229–237 (2021)
28. Xie, L., Chen, Y., Chang, R.: Scheduling optimization of prefabricated construction projects by genetic algorithm. Appl. Sci. **11**(12), 5531 (2021)
29. Zaman, F., Elsayed, S., Sarker, R., Essam, D.: Hybrid evolutionary algorithm for large-scale project scheduling problems. Comput. Ind. Eng. **146**, 106567 (2020)

COVID-19 Article Classification Using Word-Embedding and Different Variants of Deep-Learning Approach

Sanidhya Vijayvargiya[1], Lov Kumar[1], Lalita Bhanu Murthy[1], and Sanjay Misra[2(✉)]

[1] BITS-Pilani Hyderabad, Hyderabad, India
{f20202056,lovkumar,bhanu}@hyderabad.bits-pilani.ac.in
[2] Østfold University College, Halden, Norway
sanjay.misra@hiof.no

Abstract. The COVID-19 pandemic has changed the way we go about our everyday lives, and we will continue to see its impact for a long time. These changes especially apply to the business world, where the market is very volatile as a result. Requirements of the people are changing rapidly, as are the restrictions on transport and trade of goods. Due to the intense competition and struggles brought about due to the pandemic, acting first on profit opportunities is crucial to businesses doing well in the current climate. Thus, getting the relevant news in time, out of the huge number of COVID-19 related articles published daily is of utmost importance. The same applies to other industries, like the medical industry, where innovations and solutions to managing COVID-19 can save lives, and money in other parts of the world. Manually combing through the massive number of articles posted every day is both impractical and laborious. This task has the potential to be automated using Natural Language Processing (NLP) with Deep Learning based approaches. In this paper, we conduct exhaustive experiments to find the best combination of word-embedding, feature selection, and classification techniques; and find the best structure for the Deep Learning model for article classification in the COVID-19 context.

Keywords: COVID-19 · Deep learning · Word embedding

1 Introduction

Article classification is a problem that falls in the domain of text classification in NLP. It involves taking text and converting it into its numerical, vector representation. Features are selected from the vectors which are then fed to the deep learning (DL) models for the final classification step. In the context of this paper, automated article classification can do away with the need for domain experts for manual classification, and improve the efficiency of the organization. While the problem of text classification has been around for a long time, there still exist many problems which result in low accuracy. Some of the problems, as highlighted in [13], are as follows:

- Text Representation: Word embeddings derived using various methods can convert the textual data into its vector representation, and the vector space model is effective and simple. However, based on the word embedding technique used, a lot of semantic information can be lost during the conversion to numerical format. Recently, with the rise of transformers, they can learn a language representation which does a good job of capturing the semantic aspects, but the approach is too time-consuming [8,10,12,18,20,22]. As a result, more research is needed to find a more efficient semantically-based text representation approach.
- Model structure: Deep Learning methods have resulted in more accurate text classification models, but due to technical limitations caused by learning rate, depth of the network, structure of the layers, etc., there is still a lot of room for improvement in terms of optimizing the algorithm and speeding up model training [5,6,11,19,21].

The purpose of this study is to construct extremely accurate article classification models that can be employed in real world scenarios by various industries to get the relevant information at the earliest. The following are the research questions (RQs) that will be used to achieve the objectives.

- RQ1: Which word embedding technique out of the six employed in this work results in the most accurate text representation of the articles?
- RQ2: Does the use of feature selection to get the highly variable features, or the use of dimensionality reduction techniques to remove redundant features help improve the performance of the models?
- RQ3: What is the optimal structure for the DL model which results in the best performance?
- RQ4: What is the difference in the performance when using the title of the article for classification compared to using the content of the article?

To answer the questions thoroughly, multiple performance metrics in the form of accuracy, precision, recall, F-measure, and AUC are used. These metrics thoroughly capture the performance of the models. AUC is the primary metric of comparision as it can handle imbalanced data better than precision and recall metrics. The derived conclusions are backed up using visual representations via box-plots, and statistical testing using Friedman test.

The major contributions of this work are highlighted below.

- This work proposes article classification models that are developed with COVID-19 context that allows them to achieve higher performance and fewer misclassification on COVID-19 related articles.
- To determine which technique is most suitable for the categorization of COVID-19 articles, a detailed comparison of various word embedding strategies for the goal of feature extraction is provided.

- The effect of feature selection strategies on the performance of classification models is investigated in depth.
- Deep learning classifiers are used to improve text classification accuracy over prior research, with modifications in the number of layers and type of layer studied to determine the optimal model out of the eight DL classifiers utilized in this paper.
- The impact on performance of the models when trained on the title of the articles versus the content of the articles is shown. Based on the required use, precision can be traded for higher time efficiency, and lower computing complexity.

The rest of the paper is organized as follows: A literature review of various state-of-the-art approaches to text classification is presented in Sect. 2. The experimental dataset collection, as well as the various machine learning techniques used, are described in Sect. 3. Section 3 also contains an architecture framework to define the research methodology. The findings of the experiments, as well as their analysis, are reported in Sect. 4, which also includes comparison of various sets of models. Finally, Sect. 5 summarizes the results and their analysis and provides study directions.

2   Related Work

2.1   Text Classification

Mironczuk et al. [17] present the pipeline for text classification problems in their work. Starting with data acquisition, one obtains a relevant dataset on which labeling is performed if not previously labeled. The data is pre-processed, and then features are constructed from the unstructured data. To enhance the performance, feature selection techniques are used; followed by training of the classification model, and then the results are evaluated. The two main methods of feature extraction presented are the vector space model, where words are represented as numerical vectors, and the graph representation, where words are represented as nodes, and edges between the nodes represent the relationships between words.

Deng et al. [4] discuss the pros and cons of state-of-the-art feature selection techniques. Despite the fact that there are numerous text categorization classifiers available, one of the most difficult aspects of text categorization is the enormous complexity of the feature space. The authors found Term Frequency-Inverse Document Frequency (TF-IDF), PCA, and Document Frequency to be the most ideal feature selection methods for neural networks.

2.2   Deep Learning Methods

In a variety of text categorization tasks, deep learning-based models have outperformed traditional machine learning approaches. Minaee et al. [16] provide a comprehensive survey of the various deep learning techniques that have been used for text classification purposes. The DL models discussed range from feed forward neural networks that treat text as a bag of words, recurrent neural network-based (RNN-based) models that take text as sequential data, graph neural networks which capture the semantic and syntactic structure of the text, to transformers which allow for more parallelization that RNNs. The authors have also discussed the 40 most popular text classification datasets on which performance is tested.

Cai et al. [3] compared three DL classifiers and evaluated the performance on the Sohu news dataset. The convolutional neural network (CNN) model achieved a precision of 0.8534, the RNN model achieved a precision of 0.8273, and the RNN model with attention mechanism added, achieved a precision of 0.8456. The RNN model was found to be more suitable for short text processing, whereas CNN is preferred for long text processing as it can be highly parallelized.

Wang et al. [24] used a convolutional recurrent neural network (CRNN) to get advantages of the CNN to extract local features from the text, as well as, those of Long Short-Term Memory (LSTM) is memory to connect the extracted features. The proposed method achieved an accuracy of 93.38% on AG's news corpus dataset. The authors also trained the model on two Chinese datasets and were able to outperform existing models.

Khadhraoui et al. [9] surveyed various Bidirectional Encoder Representations from Transformers (BERT)-based models for scientific text classification of COVID-19 related texts and proposed CovBERT to automate the literature review process. Their proposed model is a BERT-based pre-trained language model that was trained on Cov-Dat-20, a huge corpus of scientific text. After training, they used a specific subject linked to COVID-19 to fine-tune the Cov-BERT model. The findings of the study showed that domain-specific models were better at classification than others such as ALBERT or Roberta. Cov-BERT achieved an accuracy of 94%, compared to 84% of SciBERT [2] in the biomedical and scientific domain.

3 Study Design

3.1 Experimental Dataset

The COVID-19 Public Media Dataset[1] contains over 350,000 internet articles from January 1 to December 31, 2020, spanning a year. It includes articles from a variety of domains, culled from more than 60 distinct sources. This dataset is just too vast to be fully analyzed by applying word embedding techniques to transform it to numerical data. As a result, the data examined was confined to March, April, and May. The information was then divided into four groups: finance, business, general, and technology, which were the most common output classes in the dataset. These are the article classification model's output classes. The business class contains the most articles. The dataset was divided into title and content in order to train distinct sets of models, one with the title of the articles as input and the other with the content as input.

---

[1] https://www.kaggle.com/jannalipenkova/covid19-public-media-dataset.

3.2   Word Embedding

Text representation is a key component of the text classification pipeline, where capturing the semantic relationships between words is crucial to achieving high accuracy. While transformers have been shown to give good results when they learn word embeddings from the dataset, the training process is both computationally complex, and time-consuming [8,10,12,13,18,20,22]. Thus, in this work, we have used six different word-embedding techniques which calculate the embeddings reasonably fast, or are pre-trained. The word embeddings used are TF-IDF, FTX, W2V, GLOVE, CBOW, and SKG. These embeddings follow the vector space model. TF-IDF fails to capture the semantic relationships, which others such as FTX, W2V, GLOVE, etc. are capable of doing. Thus a thorough comparision between different embedding techniques for text classification can also be seen in our work.

3.3   Feature Selection and Dimensionality Reduction

One of the biggest challenges posed by DL classifiers is the issue of interpretable DL. It is difficult to understand why a DL model produces extremely good results on a certain dataset, but fails to replicate the performance on others [14]. This paper aims to investigate how the features input to the DL neural network affect the performance of the models; whether DL models can themselves figure out how to achieve maximum performance when given all the original features, or do techniques like dimensionality reduction, or feature selection prevent the redundant and irrelevant features from impacting the performance. This paper compares the performance of models trained on the original set of features with the performance of models trained on a set of features derived after applying Principal Component Analysis (PCA) [1,7], as well as a comparison with models trained on a subset of original features selected using Analysis of Variance (ANOVA) test [15,23,25].

3.4   Deep Learning Models

The dataset is separated into training and testing subsets, and eight deep learning models with a k value of 5 are used to categorize it. The various models' structures are shown below. Every model has an input layer with the same number of neurons as the number of features in the input data. The number of neurons in each consecutive buried layer remains constant. In Deep Learning models, all layers are either Dense layers or Dropout layers [5,6,11,19,21]. Each neuron in a Dense layer receives information from all neurons in the preceding layer. A Dropout layer, on the other hand, picks and omits a specific number of neurons in the layer at random when training the Deep Learning model. A dropout value of 0.2 is employed in this study. Overfitting models can be solved by using dropout layers. Finally, the output layer is made up of four neurons that together represent the projected class's single hot encoding. Except for the output layer, which utilizes a softmax activation function, each layer's activation function is the rectified linear activation function, or ReLU [5,6,11,19,21]. The loss function used is categorical cross entropy, whereas the optimizer is Adam. Figure 1 depicts the architecture of the deep learning system under consideration. The structure shown is for one of the models out of the eight DL models compared. Other models have different number of layers and Dropout layers are also present in some. 5-fold cross-validation with batch size = 30, epochs = 100, and Dropout = 0.2 is used to validate the models mentioned above.

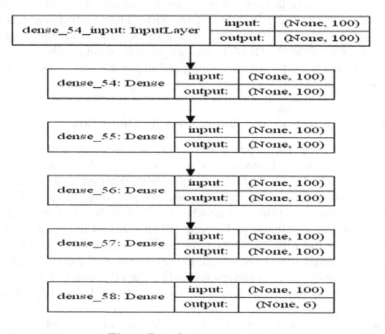

Fig. 1. Deep learning structure

3.5   Research Methodology

The Covid-19 Public Media Dataset is separated into title and content datasets, to analyze the performances due to the different types of inputs. The datasets are limited to the months of March, April, and May. The number of classes is also restricted to the four that are the most common. This is done to avoid classes which have low instances in the dataset, and can adversely affect the performance. Two sets of models are trained on the March data and April data respectively. The testing of the performance is done on the April and May data, respectively, for the two sets of models. The resulting datasets were put through the text classification pipeline mentioned above. The first task was preprocessing the data which included steps such as removing stop-words, tokenization, etc. Features are extracted using six different word embedding techniques from the pre-processed data. Feature selection and dimensionality reduction techniques are employed to select the highly variable features and remove the redundant features, respectively. Then, the data is fed to the DL classifiers which predict the classes (Fig. 2).

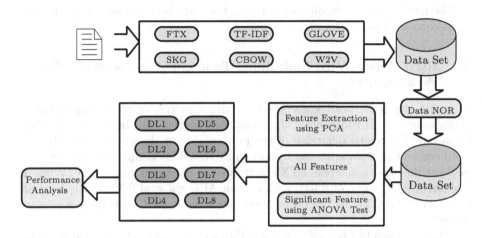

Fig. 2. Research framework

4   Findings and Discussion

The Covid-19 article prediction using different variants of deep-learning and word embedding helps to provide relevant news in time. In this study, we applied six different variants of word embedding techniques to extract numerical features from text. Because the extracted features are used as the input, the predictive ability of the models also depends on the selection of the right sets of features. In this study, we initially used the ANOVA test to remove features that cannot differentiate the types of articles. Thereafter, we applied PCA to a new value of uncorrelated features with better prediction ability. After finding the appropriate sets of features, we applied different variants of deep-learning. The performance of these models was compared using three performance parameters: accuracy, precision, recall, F-measure and Area under ROC curve(AUC) values. In the experiment, we have used two different ways to validate the models such as: M-A (model trained on news published on march and validated using April) and A-M(model trained on news published on April and validated using May). These all experiments conducted on Dell system with 64 GB RAM and Core i3 processor was used. For statistical testing, a p-value of 0.05 is used to back the results. The results achieved by different classifiers on different sets of features are presented in Tables 1, we can infer that:

 - The high value of AUC confirms that the proposed solution have ability to predict types of article based on title or content.

- The models trained on the content of article as an input have better ability of prediction as compared to title.
- The models trained on selected features using ANOVA test have better ability of prediction as compared to all features.
- The models trained using deep-learning two have better ability of prediction as compared to other variants.

4.1   RQ1: Which Word Embedding Technique Results in the Best Performance?

Choosing the right word embedding technique is crucial to getting optimal performance as all consequent ML techniques applied will be on the features extracted. The visual depiction of the performance of the models with the six word embedding techniques can be seen in Fig. 3. GLOVE and W2V clearly outperform the others, whereas FTX's performance is lagging behind. W2V has a maximum AUC value of 0.937, and a mean AUC value of 0.798, with a Q3 of 0.919 AUC. GLOVE on the other hand, has a mean AUC of 0.799, as seen in Table 2.

The Friedman test is used to support the observations made from the descriptive statistics and box-plots. A lower mean rank, shown in Table 3, means better performance. Thus, W2V and GLOVE have the lowest mean ranks of 2.146 and 2.292, respectively. The disappointing performance of FTX is reflected by its mean rank of 5.531, which is the highest among all.

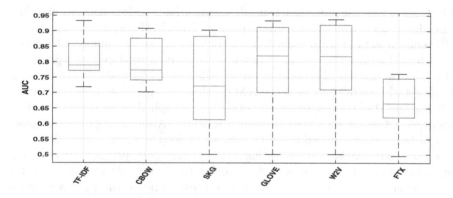

Fig. 3. Word-embedding

4.2   RQ2: What Is the Impact of Feature Selection and Dimensionality Reduction on the Performance?

Based on the box-plot presented in the Fig. 4, it is difficult to infer which set of features, the original set, or the features from ANOVA test, give the best performance. But, it is easy to observe that the features we get from applying

Table 1. AUC values for different variants of deep-learning

	Content								Title							
	DL1	DL2	DL3	DL4	DL5	DL6	DL7	DL8	DL1	DL2	DL3	DL4	DL5	DL6	DL7	DL8
TF-IDF: all features																
M-A	0.86	0.86	0.85	0.86	0.86	0.85	0.86	0.83	0.81	0.81	0.78	0.78	0.78	0.79	0.77	0.77
A-M	0.93	0.93	0.91	0.92	0.92	0.91	0.92	0.91	0.82	0.83	0.80	0.81	0.81	0.80	0.82	0.81
TF-IDF: ANOVA features																
M-A	0.86	0.86	0.85	0.86	0.86	0.84	0.86	0.83	0.81	0.81	0.77	0.77	0.78	0.78	0.78	0.78
A-M	0.92	0.93	0.91	0.92	0.92	0.90	0.92	0.91	0.82	0.83	0.80	0.82	0.81	0.81	0.82	0.80
TF-IDF: PCA features																
M-A	0.93	0.93	0.89	0.92	0.92	0.87	0.92	0.90	0.78	0.79	0.76	0.78	0.77	0.77	0.77	0.77
A-M	0.76	0.72	0.54	0.52	0.50	0.53	0.69	0.51	0.78	0.78	0.66	0.67	0.67	0.67	0.68	0.65
GLOVE: all features																
M-A	0.90	0.91	0.88	0.89	0.88	0.88	0.89	0.89	0.77	0.78	0.74	0.76	0.75	0.74	0.76	0.74
A-M	0.94	0.94	0.92	0.93	0.93	0.92	0.93	0.92	0.84	0.84	0.83	0.82	0.82	0.81	0.83	0.82
GLOVE: ANOVA features																
M-A	0.90	0.91	0.88	0.89	0.88	0.87	0.88	0.85	0.77	0.78	0.74	0.75	0.75	0.74	0.74	0.73
A-M	0.94	0.94	0.92	0.93	0.93	0.92	0.93	0.92	0.84	0.84	0.82	0.83	0.82	0.82	0.83	0.83
GLOVE: PCA features																
M-A	0.87	0.88	0.80	0.80	0.80	0.78	0.77	0.76	0.77	0.77	0.73	0.75	0.73	0.73	0.75	0.71
A-M	0.70	0.69	0.52	0.50	0.51	0.53	0.53	0.50	0.79	0.78	0.67	0.70	0.69	0.68	0.68	0.70
FTX: all features																
M-A	0.90	0.90	0.89	0.89	0.89	0.89	0.88	0.90	0.74	0.75	0.72	0.74	0.75	0.73	0.73	0.71
A-M	0.76	0.75	0.76	0.75	0.75	0.76	0.73	0.75	0.67	0.67	0.64	0.66	0.67	0.63	0.67	0.62
FTX: ANOVA features																
M-A	0.90	0.89	0.89	0.89	0.88	0.90	0.86	0.90	0.73	0.75	0.70	0.73	0.74	0.71	0.74	0.72
A-M	0.76	0.75	0.76	0.75	0.75	0.75	0.70	0.76	0.67	0.67	0.65	0.67	0.67	0.63	0.67	0.62
FTX: PCA features																
M-A	0.50	0.50	0.50	0.50	0.50	0.50	0.50	0.50	0.69	0.68	0.60	0.60	0.59	0.57	0.59	0.61
A-M	0.70	0.73	0.50	0.67	0.63	0.63	0.65	0.55	0.60	0.64	0.56	0.51	0.61	0.50	0.51	0.55
CBOW: all features																
M-A	0.75	0.76	0.72	0.73	0.74	0.73	0.74	0.73	0.82	0.82	0.79	0.79	0.79	0.78	0.78	0.79
A-M	0.93	0.93	0.91	0.92	0.92	0.92	0.93	0.92	0.84	0.85	0.81	0.83	0.83	0.82	0.83	0.82
CBOW: ANOVA features																
M-A	0.75	0.76	0.73	0.74	0.74	0.72	0.74	0.73	0.81	0.81	0.78	0.78	0.77	0.79	0.78	0.79
A-M	0.93	0.93	0.91	0.92	0.92	0.90	0.92	0.92	0.84	0.85	0.82	0.83	0.82	0.81	0.84	0.82
CBOW: PCA features																
M-A	0.92	0.92	0.89	0.91	0.91	0.88	0.91	0.88	0.80	0.80	0.77	0.79	0.79	0.78	0.79	0.79
A-M	0.63	0.76	0.53	0.58	0.70	0.58	0.71	0.60	0.78	0.79	0.63	0.66	0.68	0.66	0.69	0.67
SKG: all features																
M-A	0.89	0.90	0.87	0.87	0.88	0.88	0.88	0.87	0.75	0.76	0.72	0.73	0.74	0.73	0.74	0.73
A-M	0.93	0.93	0.91	0.92	0.92	0.91	0.93	0.91	0.82	0.83	0.80	0.81	0.81	0.79	0.82	0.80
SKG: ANOVA features																
M-A	0.89	0.90	0.86	0.88	0.88	0.87	0.88	0.87	0.75	0.76	0.73	0.74	0.74	0.72	0.74	0.73
A-M	0.93	0.93	0.92	0.92	0.92	0.91	0.93	0.91	0.82	0.83	0.79	0.80	0.80	0.81	0.81	0.79
SKG: PCA features																
M-A	0.87	0.88	0.80	0.78	0.79	0.75	0.80	0.78	0.75	0.76	0.72	0.73	0.73	0.71	0.72	0.70
A-M	0.74	0.75	0.53	0.50	0.50	0.73	0.50	0.72	0.79	0.77	0.68	0.70	0.67	0.66	0.69	0.68

Table 2. Descriptive statistics: word-embedding

	Min	Max	Mean	Median	Q1	Q3
TF-IDF	0.719	0.933	0.810	0.789	0.772	0.858
CBOW	0.702	0.908	0.800	0.773	0.741	0.876
SKG	0.500	0.903	0.725	0.721	0.613	0.882
GLOVE	0.501	0.933	0.799	0.820	0.701	0.912
W2V	0.501	0.937	0.798	0.818	0.710	0.919
FXT	0.495	0.762	0.665	0.665	0.621	0.746

Table 3. Pairwise rank-sum test with Friedman test: Word-Embedding

	TF-IDF	CBOW	SKG	GLOVE	W2V	FXT	Rank
TF-IDF	1.00	0.09	0.00	0.22	0.21	0.00	3.13
CBOW	0.09	1.00	0.00	0.08	0.09	0.00	3.27
SKG	0.00	0.00	1.00	0.00	0.00	0.00	4.64
GLOVE	0.22	0.08	0.00	1.00	0.67	0.00	2.29
W2V	0.21	0.09	0.00	0.67	1.00	0.00	2.15
FXT	0.00	0.00	0.00	0.00	0.00	1.00	5.53

PCA result in a drastic drop in performance. As per Table 4, the original set of features have a mean AUC of 0.809, a Q3 of 0.889 AUC, and a max of 0.937 AUC.

To differentiate between the performance of the original set of features, and those from the ANOVA test, we compare the mean ranks presented in Table 5. The original set of features marginally outperformed the ANOVA features with a mean rank of 1.510 compared to a mean rank of 1.729 for the ANOVA features. The features from PCA had a mean rank of 2.760, which fits the observations made from the box plot. Thus, we can conclude that using feature selection or dimensionality reduction techniques only regresses the performance of the models.

Table 4. Descriptive statistics: feature selection

	Min	Max	Mean	Median	Q1	Q3
ALL_FEAT	0.59	0.94	0.81	0.81	0.75	0.89
ANOVA	0.59	0.94	0.81	0.81	0.74	0.88
PCA	0.50	0.93	0.68	0.69	0.58	0.77

Table 5. Pairwise rank-sum test with friedman test: feature selection

	ALL_FEAT	ANOVA	PCA	Rank
ALL_FEAT	1.00	0.82	0.00	1.51
ANOVA	0.82	1.00	0.00	1.73
PCA	0.00	0.00	1.00	2.76

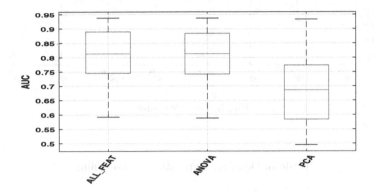

Fig. 4. Feature selection

4.3 RQ3: Which of the Eight Structures for the DL Neural Network Is the Most Suitable for Text Classification?

The box-plots can be seen in Fig. 5. DL-1 and DL-2 give better results than all the other DL models. The descriptive statistics presented in Table 6 show that DL-2 has a mean AUC of 0.797, max AUC of 0.937, and Q3 AUC of 0.880. Neural networks with less hidden layers have performed better than more complex ones for this task.

The Friedman test, whose results are shown in Table 7, helps decide which DL model is the most suitable for the task. DL-2 has the lowest mean rank of 1.674, whereas DL-1 has a mean rank of 2.160. The other DL models lag behind considerably with DL-6 having the highest mean rank of 6.118. The difference between DL-1 and DL-2 is the presence of a Dropout layer in the latter which potentially performs better as it is able to deal with overfitting better.

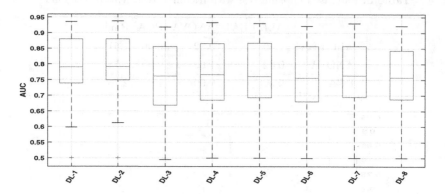

Fig. 5. Deep-learning

Table 6. Descriptive statistics: deep-learning

	Min	Max	Mean	Median	Q1	Q3
DL1	0.50	0.94	0.79	0.79	0.74	0.88
DL2	0.50	0.94	0.80	0.79	0.75	0.88
DL3	0.50	0.92	0.75	0.76	0.67	0.86
DL4	0.50	0.93	0.76	0.77	0.69	0.87
DL5	0.50	0.93	0.76	0.76	0.69	0.87
DL6	0.50	0.92	0.75	0.76	0.68	0.86
DL7	0.50	0.93	0.76	0.76	0.70	0.86
DL8	0.50	0.92	0.75	0.76	0.69	0.84

Table 7. Pairwise rank-sum test with Friedman test: deep-learning

	DL1	DL2	DL3	DL4	DL5	DL6	DL7	DL8	Rank
DL1	1.00	0.72	0.05	0.11	0.11	0.04	0.10	0.04	2.16
DL2	0.72	1.00	0.03	0.06	0.05	0.02	0.05	0.02	1.67
DL3	0.05	0.03	1.00	0.59	0.56	0.95	0.59	1.00	5.89
DL4	0.11	0.06	0.59	1.00	0.95	0.64	1.00	0.60	4.84
DL5	0.11	0.05	0.56	0.95	1.00	0.57	0.95	0.55	4.70
DL6	0.04	0.02	0.95	0.64	0.57	1.00	0.64	0.95	6.12
DL7	0.10	0.05	0.59	1.00	0.95	0.64	1.00	0.60	4.51
DL8	0.04	0.02	1.00	0.60	0.55	0.95	0.60	1.00	6.11

4.4 How Do the Performances of the Models Trained on the Title Dataset Compare with Those Trained on the Content Dataset?

As shown in the box-plot in Fig. 6, the content dataset models vastly outperform those trained on the title dataset. More specifically, the title dataset has a mean AUC of 0.733, while the content dataset has a mean AUC of 0.799. The max AUC is 0.850, and 0.937 respectively for the two datasets. Based on these descriptive statistics in Table 8, one can sacrifice performance for less training time and computational complexity if the accuracy achieved by the models trained on the title dataset is acceptable depending on the use.

The Friedman test shows that the content dataset models do better, with a mean rank of 1.208. The title dataset models achieve a mean rank of 1.792 (Table 9).

Table 8. Descriptive statistics: content and title

	Min	Max	Mean	Median	Q1	Q3
Title	0.50	0.85	0.73	0.74	0.67	0.79
Content	0.50	0.94	0.80	0.86	0.74	0.91

Table 9. Pairwise rank-sum test with Friedman test: content and title

	Title	Content	Rank
Title	1.00	0.00	1.79
Content	0.00	1.00	1.21

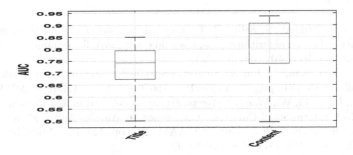

Fig. 6. Content and title

5   Conclusion

The purpose of this study is to generate COVID-19 context-based article classification models with maximum possible accuracy using Deep Learning methods. Different ML techniques such as word embedding, feature selection, and dimensionality reduction are applied to find the best input to the DL models which results in the best performance. Various structures for the DL models are experimented with to find the optimal structure for the task. A comparison of performance when training the models titles of the articles, which require less training time and computational power, versus training them on the content of the articles, which result in higher accuracy, is provided. In future work, there is scope to compare this performance using a transformer with attention mechanism, and also try an undersampling approach on the dataset. Due to the variety of online articles covered in the dataset used. The findings should be generalizable to a large extent to other such article datasets. The main conclusions are as follows:

– W2V is the best word embedding technique for the task of article classification, with GLOVE as a good alternative.
– The performance of the models regressed when a set of features derived from PCA, or a subset of features selected using ANOVA test were used. The original set of features worked best with the DL models.
– The optimal structure for the DL model was that of DL-2, which included a single Dense layer, followed by a Dropout layer. Adding further layers only led to a regression in performance.
– Based on the results of the models trained on the title dataset and the content dataset, one can use the set of models that fits the requirements of accuracy, time, and computational resources.

References

1. Anowar, F., Sadaoui, S., Selim, B.: Conceptual and empirical comparison of dimensionality reduction algorithms (pca, kpca, lda, mds, svd, lle, isomap, le, ica, t-sne). Comput. Sci. Rev. **40**, 100378 (2021)
2. Beltagy, I., Cohan, A., Lo, K.: Scibert: pretrained contextualized embeddings for scientific text. arXiv preprint arXiv:1903.10676 vol. 1, no. 1.3, p. 8 (2019)
3. Cai, J., Li, J., Li, W., Wang, J.: Deeplearning model used in text classification. In: 2018 15th International Computer Conference on Wavelet Active Media Technology and Information Processing (ICCWAMTIP), pp. 123–126 (2018). https://doi.org/10.1109/ICCWAMTIP.2018.8632592
4. Deng, X., Li, Y., Weng, J., Zhang, J.: Feature selection for text classification: a review. Multimedia Tools Appl. **78**(3), 3797–3816 (2018). https://doi.org/10.1007/s11042-018-6083-5
5. Dong, S., Wang, P., Abbas, K.: A survey on deep learning and its applications. Comput. Sci. Rev. **40**, 100379 (2021)

6. Gupta, H., Kulkarni, T.G., Kumar, L., Neti, L.B.M., Krishna, A.: An empirical study on predictability of software code smell using deep learning models. In: Barolli, L., Woungang, I., Enokido, T. (eds.) AINA 2021. LNNS, vol. 226, pp. 120–132. Springer, Cham (2021). https://doi.org/10.1007/978-3-030-75075-6_10

7. Ji, H., Qin, W., Yuan, Z., Meng, F.: Qualitative and quantitative recognition method of drug-producing chemicals based on sno2 gas sensor with dynamic measurement and pca weak separation. Sens. Actuators, B Chem. **348**, 130698 (2021)

8. Kalouptsoglou, I., Siavvas, M., Kehagias, D., Chatzigeorgiou, A., Ampatzoglou, A.: An Empirical evaluation of the usefulness of word embedding techniques in deep learning-based vulnerability prediction. In: Gelenbe, E., Jankovic, M., Kehagias, D., Marton, A., Vilmos, A. (eds.) Security in Computer and Information Sciences, EuroCybersec 2021, Communications in Computer and Information Science, vol. 1596, pp. 23–37. Springer, Cham (2022). https://doi.org/10.1007/978-3-031-09357-9_3

9. Khadhraoui, M., Bellaaj, H., Ammar, M.B., Hamam, H., Jmaiel, M.: Survey of bert-base models for scientific text classification: Covid-19 case study. Appl. Sci. **12**(6) (2022). https://doi.org/10.3390/app12062891, https://www.mdpi.com/2076-3417/12/6/2891

10. Kumar, L., Baldwa, S., Jambavalikar, S.M., Murthy, L.B., Krishna, A.: Software functional and non-function requirement classification using word-embedding. In: Barolli, L., Hussain, F., Enokido, T. (eds.) AINA 2022. LNNS, vol. 450, pp. 167–179. Springer, Cham (2022). https://doi.org/10.1007/978-3-030-99587-4_15

11. Kumar, L.: Deep-learning approach with DeepXplore for software defect severity level prediction. In: Gervasi, O., et al. (eds.) ICCSA 2021. LNCS, vol. 12955, pp. 398–410. Springer, Cham (2021). https://doi.org/10.1007/978-3-030-87007-2_28

12. Kumar, L., Kumar, M., Murthy, L.B., Misra, S., Kocher, V., Padmanabhuni, S.: An empirical study on application of word embedding techniques for prediction of software defect severity level. In: 2021 16th Conference on Computer Science and Intelligence Systems (FedCSIS), pp. 477–484. IEEE (2021)

13. Li, Q., et al.: A survey on text classification: from traditional to deep learning. ACM Trans. Intell. Syst. Technol. **13**(2) (2022). https://doi.org/10.1145/3495162

14. Li, X., et al.: Interpretable deep learning: interpretation, interpretability, trustworthiness, and beyond (2021). https://doi.org/10.48550/ARXIV.2103.10689, https://arxiv.org/abs/2103.10689

15. Liu, Q., Wang, L.: t-test and Anova for data with ceiling and/or floor effects. Behav. Res. Methods **53**(1), 264–277 (2021)

16. Minaee, S., Kalchbrenner, N., Cambria, E., Nikzad, N., Chenaghlu, M., Gao, J.: Deep learning-based text classification: a comprehensive review. ACM Comput. Surv. **54**(3) (2021). https://doi.org/10.1145/3439726

17. Mirończuk, M.M., Protasiewicz, J.: A recent overview of the state-of-the-art elements of text classification. Exp. Syst. Appl. **106**, 36–54 (2018). https://doi.org/10.1016/j.eswa.2018.03.058, https://www.sciencedirect.com/science/article/pii/S095741741830215X

18. Nguyen, H.N., Teerakanok, S., Inomata, A., Uehara, T.: The comparison of word embedding techniques in RNNs for vulnerability detection. In: ICISSP, pp. 109–120 (2021)

19. Niu, Z., Zhong, G., Yu, H.: A review on the attention mechanism of deep learning. Neurocomputing **452**, 48–62 (2021)

20. Selva Birunda, S., Kanniga Devi, R.: A review on word embedding techniques for text classification. In: Raj, J.S., Iliyasu, A.M., Bestak, R., Baig, Z.A. (eds.)

Innovative Data Communication Technologies and Application. LNDECT, vol. 59, pp. 267–281. Springer, Singapore (2021). https://doi.org/10.1007/978-981-15-9651-3_23

21. Shorten, C., Khoshgoftaar, T.M., Furht, B.: Deep learning applications for covid-19. J. Big Data 8(1), 1–54 (2021)
22. Tummalapalli, S., Kumar, L., Murthy Neti, L.B., Kocher, V., Padmanabhuni, S.: A novel approach for the detection of web service anti-patterns using word embedding techniques. In: Gervasi, O., et al. (eds.) ICCSA 2021. LNCS, vol. 12955, pp. 217–230. Springer, Cham (2021). https://doi.org/10.1007/978-3-030-87007-2_16
23. Tummalapalli, S., Kumar, L., Neti, L.B.M., Krishna, A.: Detection of web service anti-patterns using weighted extreme learning machine. Comput. Stand. Interfaces **82**, 103621 (2022)
24. Wang, R., Li, Z., Cao, J., Chen, T., Wang, L.: Convolutional recurrent neural networks for text classification. In: 2019 International Joint Conference on Neural Networks (IJCNN), pp. 1–6 (2019). https://doi.org/10.1109/IJCNN.2019.8852406
25. Yu, Z., Guindani, M., Grieco, S.F., Chen, L., Holmes, T.C., Xu, X.: Beyond t test and ANOVA: applications of mixed-effects models for more rigorous statistical analysis in neuroscience research. Neuron **110**(1), 21–35 (2021)

Crop Classification Using Deep Learning: A Quick Comparative Study of Modern Approaches

Hind Raki[1,4(✉)], Juan González-Vergara[4], Yahya Aalaila[1,4],
Mouad Elhamdi[1,4], Sami Bamansour[2,4], Lorena Guachi-Guachi[3,4],
and Diego H. Peluffo-Ordoñez[1,4,5]

[1] Modeling, Simulation and Data Analysis (MSDA) Research Program,
Mohammed VI Polytechnic University, Lot 660, Hay Moulay Rachid Ben Guerir,
43150 Ben Guerir, Morocco
{hind.raki,yahya.aalaila,mouad.elhamdi,peluffo.diego}@um6p.ma
[2] University Cadi Ayyad, Marrakech, Morocco
sami.bamansour@um6p.ma, sami.bamansour@edu.uca.ma
[3] Department of Mechatronics, Universidad Internacional del Ecuador,
Av. Simon Bolivar, 170411 Quito, Ecuador
loguachigu@uide.edu.ec
[4] Smart Data Analysis Systems Group (SDAS Research Group),
47963 Ben Guerir, Morocco
{hind.raki,juan.gonzalez,yahya.aalaila,mouad.elhamdi,sami.bamansour,
lorena.guachi,diego.peluffo}@sdas-group.com
[5] Faculty of Engineering, Corporación Universitaria Autónoma de Nariño,
Pasto 520001, Colombia
diego.peluffo@aunar.edu.co
https://sdas-group.com/

Abstract. Automatic crop classification using new technologies is recognized as one of the most important assets in today's smart farming improvement. Investments in technology and innovation are key issues for shaping agricultural productivity as well as the inclusiveness and sustainability of the global agricultural transformation. Digital image processing (DIP) has been widely adopted in this field, by merging Unmanned Aerial Vehicle (UAV) based remote sensing and deep learning (DL) as a powerful tool for crop classification. Despite the wide range of alternatives, the proper selection of a DL approach is still an open and challenging issue. In this work, we carry out an exhaustive performance evaluation of three remarkable and lightweight DL approaches, namely: Visual Geometry Group (VGG), Residual Neural Network (ResNet) and Inception V3, tested on high resolution agriculture crop images dataset. Experimental results show that InceptionV3 outperforms VGG and ResNet in terms of precision (0,92), accuracy (0,97), recall (0,91), AUC (0,98), PCR (0,97), and F1 (0,91).

Supported by SDAS Research Group (https://www.sdas-group.com).

Keywords: Deep learning · Smart farming · Convolutional neural networks

1   Introduction

Through the process of plant domestication, the wild plants evolved into crop plants using artificial selection. Other than houseplants which are used for decoration purposes, crops are destined for food consumption. For example, the family of *Pocaceae* (including maize, wheat, rice, sugarcane, etc.) is an economically important flowering family. In China, maize, rice, and wheat are considered as the three major cereal crops, ensuring national food safety [23]. To this end, automatic crop classification using new technologies is recognized as one of the most important assets in today's smart farming improvement. Investments in technology and innovation are key issues for shaping agricultural productivity as well as the inclusiveness and sustainability of the global agricultural transformation [13,24].

Nowadays, these advancements play a salient role in the generation of crop maps, due to the digital systems using satellite platforms or unmanned aerial vehicles (UAVs). The collected datasets, in the form of images, are highly valuable for identifying suitable crop areas and collecting precise information [15,17]. Digital image processing (DIP) has been widely adopted in this field, by merging UAV-based remote sensing and deep learning (DL) as a powerful tool for crop classification. The recent Convolutional Neural Network-based (CNN or ConvNet) methods applied to precise and automatic crop classification has been reviewed [3,15], with emphasis on the UAV-based remote sensing image analysis for farming applications. The adoption of a certain technique should be wise and precise, while taking into consideration the crop class, the output of interest and the dataset type [3].

CNNs made an impressive breakthrough on DIP. Deeper convolutional networks were investigated by pushing the depth to 16/19 weight layers, such as Visual Geometry Group (VGG). VGG16 and VGG19 models made a significant improvement regarding accuracy, especially on large-scale image classification [18]. On the other hand, He et al. [9] argue that an extreme increase of the depth for a higher accuracy is limited when using standard ConvNets, hence the accuracy of the model gets saturated and starts degrading rapidly. Purposely, Residual Neural Network (ResNet) model introduces shortcut connections between convolutional blocks that allow the gradients to flow more easily in the network. Nonetheless, the Inception network comes with a lower cost whilst maintaining high performance vision networks, empowering two grand factors, computational efficiency and low parameter. The Inception module comprises a concatenation layer, in which a series of outputs and feature maps from the conv filters are merged to create a single output [21].

Although, Deep architectures have been widely exploited in the last years [14], with various applications in various industries. An up-to-date evaluation of said architectures in agriculture is needed-especially in crop classification settings.

In this work, we carry out an exhaustive comparison between three major DL tools, VGG, ResNet and Inception V3. To do so, the agriculture crop images dataset is used [11], which holds a total of 999 labelled images, from five crops classes, namely, jute, wheat, rice, sugarcane and maize.

The rest of this manuscript is structured as follows: Sect. 2 briefly outlines works and studies related to our research. Section 3 presents the proposed experimental framework along with the dataset description, NNs architectures considered in this study and the evaluation process. Thereof, Sect. 4 gathers the results and the discussion. Finally, Sect. 5 draws concluding remarks and states future work lines.

2 Related Works

One latter published study has been conducted utilizing the same dataset [10]. They propose a fuzzy logic-based learning rate scheduler, which takes the current epoch as the input and changes the momentum during the training for higher accuracy results. Purposely, the main objective of our research is the establishment of a comparative study between various DL techniques. In the recent literature, several studies tackled the aforementioned problematic. In a recent paper [16], GoogLeNet and VGGNet were also adopted for two distinct datasets, using Transfer Learning (TL) approach by varying the number of 'frozen' layers. The crop types classification was successful with high overall accuracy for both models. In fact, TL adoption allows the implementation of deep neural networks even with limited labelled data. It is efficient for satellite and UAV images for crop classification purposes, while acquiring timely and accurate results [4,7]. Multiple studies conducted comparative analysis of various TL strategies, deploying deep CNNs such as ResNet50, VGG16, VGG19, Xception, and MobileNetV2, whilst using the ImageNet pretrained weights. They were experimented in weeds classification [4,7] for crops diseases management, intercropping identification, and early mapping of croplands [8,24]. Algorithms are mainly evaluated based on their accuracy, precision and F1 score, hence their strengths and limitations [20].

3   Methodology

To better understand the article's workflow, Fig. 1 presents a graphical explanation throughout the Cross-industry standard process for data mining (CRISP-DM) methodology.

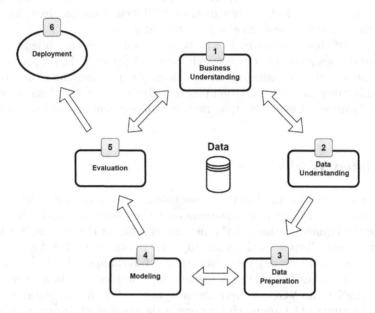

Fig. 1. Data mining workflow explained using CRISP-DM methodology [12]

3.1   Data Understanding and Preparation

In this research, the data was acquired from the Kaggle database under the name Agriculture crop images [11]. The primary dataset sub-file contains around 40 images of each crop. Hence, the data quality has been enhanced by providing an additional data under the name of *kag2*. This secondary dataset has been generated by data augmentation techniques: horizontal flip, rotation, horizontal shift, and vertical shift. A supplementary file has also been included, "Cropdetails.csv", which contains 999 labelled data points of all images with their accordingly path and crop labels. The images vary from aerial to ground view of the different periods of these crops' life cycles. Although maize, wheat and rice are considered cereals, they possess some major differences as of their morphological traits (Fig. 2).

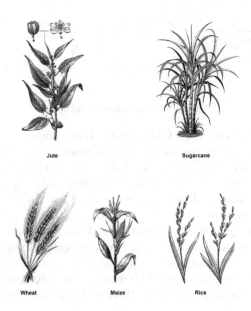

Fig. 2. The morphology of the five crops classes.

For the here proposed comparison, the 804 images of *kag2* are used. The dataset is well-balanced, having 160 samples for jute, maize, rice, sugarcane and 164 for wheat. Then, the data is split in 80% for training, and 20% for testing. That is, 32 samples for jute, maize, rice, sugarcane and 33 for wheat. Validation data is taken as the 30% of the training data. Furthermore, for each of the samples, pixels are normalized by 255.

3.2   Modeling

Deep CNN-based architectures are widely used for image classification tasks, where multiple models are available to experiment with. Consequently, pre-trained models can serve as a shortcut for transferring the accumulated knowledge gained from a particular classification quest. In essence, such method is referred to as *Transfer Learning*. It consists of re-using a pre-trained model and its optimized weights for a different classification task [22].

Therefore, using `Keras` library [5], three well-known architectures have been chosen from its API reference. The loaded models have been pre-trained with weights learned from classifying the ImageNet database [6]. By the end of each architecture, four layers of fully connected neurons were added, in order to classify the crop images properly, Fig. 3. Hence, the chosen loss function is Categorical Hinge, and the optimizer is ADAM with a learning rate of 1×10^{-4}. The processes were repeated for 50 epochs. In order to provide a better understanding of the results obtained by each model, the studied CNN-based models are briefly summarized as the following:

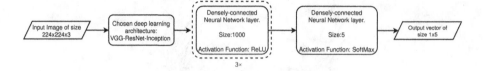

Fig. 3. Experimental setup

Visual Geometry Group (VGG): VGG-16 is a convolution neural network that is considered as one of the excellent vision model architectures in the present date [18]. The input to VGG-16 is a fixed-size 224×224 RGB image. Its architecture is composed of convolution layers of 3×3 filter with a stride 1, consistently using the same padding and max pooling layer of 2×2 filter of stride 2. VGG-16 has numerous hyperparameters that focus on using 3×3 filters uniformly. It follows this arrangement of convolution and max pooling layers consistently throughout the whole architecture. In the end, the model has two fully connected layers followed by a soft-max output. All hidden layers are equipped with the rectification (ReLU) non-linearity. The number 16 (resp. 19) in VGG-16 (resp. VGG-19) refers to the 16 layers (resp. 19 layers) that have weights in the model (Fig. 4).

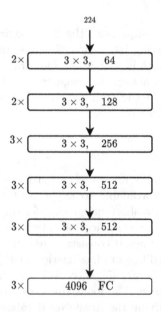

Fig. 4. VGG-16 architecture

ResNet: Deep Convolutional Neural Networks (CNN) is a pioneer approach to deal with image classification, due to the high/mid/low integration of features, which is enriched by the number of stacked layers (depth). However, extensive use of depth counterintuitively leads to performance limitations due to vanishing gradients and degradation issues [1,9]. Inspired by the *highway networks* [19], Residual Neural Network (ResNet) remedies this problem by approximating the residual function $\mathcal{F}(x)$ instead of the underlying mapping function $\mathcal{H}(x)$ [2,9]. $\mathcal{F}(x)$ represents what the network learns "differently" than the input x which can, in some cases, tend to zero (Fig. 3.2). Using this shortcut connections, ResNet was able to increase the depth without loosing accuracy, as well as substantial decrease in the number of FLOPS [9].

The overall architecture of ResNet, as summarized in Fig. 6 has an input of 224×224 with 3 channels, a convolution and pooling step, followed by 16 2-layers blocks of the same nature as Fig. 3.2. Every block performs 3×3 convolution with fixed number of feature filters 64, 128, 256 and 512, respectively. A key step in the proposed method is the pass from low to high dimensional channels. Since the input's dimension, in this case, is double the output. The original paper proposed three techniques to deal with this, the second of which was adopted in modern DL techniques. Namely, a shortcut projection of the form $\mathcal{F}(x) + W_s x$ as to increase the dimension (Fig. 5).

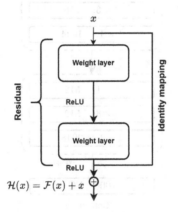

Fig. 5. Residual connection block

This approach was initially presented with 34-layer depth, but later on was increased in ResNet50 (ResNet) and ResNet152 (ResNetV2) to reach 50 and 152, respectively. These two variants were substantial improvement over Resnet34. In fact, ResNet152 won the ImageNet context in 2016 competition with an 3.67% error rate. ResNet50 and Resnet152 are a testament that deeper CNN architectures do not necessarily have to perform worse than their shallower counterpart. Also, a 3-layer *Bottleneck* blocks were used instead of the 2-layer blocks in Resnet34 as to avoid computational burden as shown in Fig. 6.

Inception V3: In recent years, there has been an increasing interest to develop various DL architectures as to deal with image classification tasks. Inception V3

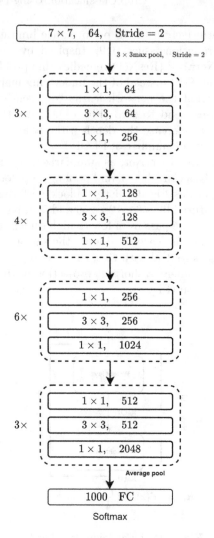

Fig. 6. Resnet architecture with 50-layers depth.

is considered to be one of the most used methods due to its performance and efficiency levels in various applications.

Inception V3 is an extended network of GoogleNet [21], aiming to decrease the computational issues and to reduce the model parameters by concatenating multiple different sized convolutional filters into one filter. The power of inception V3 was obtained mostly by using dimensionality reduction. This can be seen as a special case of factorizing convolution efficiently in terms of computations. One key aspect of this architecture is the factorization into smaller convolutions, which reduces the parameters by sharing the weights between adjacent tiles. For instance, a 5×5 can be replaced with two layer of 3×3 convolutions (Fig. 8(a)).

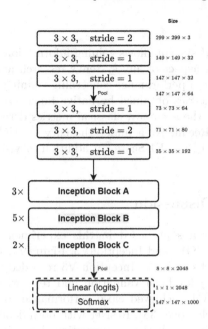

Fig. 7. InceptionV3 basic architecture

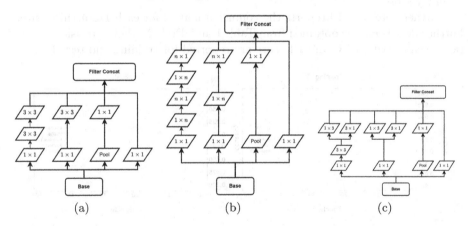

Fig. 8. The three building blocks of inceptionV3 architecture. (*a*) Block A, (*b*) block B, (*c*) block C

Also, The Spacial Factorization into Asymmetric Convolutions has become a ubiquitous factorization method to disentangled parameters and therefore with faster training. This method consist of replacing $n \times n$ by a $1 \times n$ convolution, followed by a $n \times 1$ convolution (Fig. 8(*b*)). The overall architecture of this approach (Fig. 7) takes advantage of the aforementioned techniques as inception blocks, namely Block A, B and C (Fig. 8(*a*), 8(*b*) and 8(*c*), respectively)

3.3   Evaluation

The evaluation of an AI system allows gaining information about its behaviour, which is a determining aspect of any system's research and design process. In order to measure our data performance concerning training, validation and testing, we used several metrics obtained by native functions of a previous paper [5]. Besides calculating the accuracy, classical metrics derived from a confusion matrix are obtained: Recall, Area under the curve (AUC) - Score, Precision Recall Curve - Score (PRC), F1-Score. In addition, a visual representation of the results is provided.

4   Results and Discussion

Various CNN architectures are used in this experiment, namely ResNet50, ResNet152, VGG16, VGG19 and InceptionV3. Figure 9 details the accuracy of each approach as Epochs increase. Inception V3 recorded the highest accuracy score (just over 97.5%) for both validation and test, with under 10 Epochs. Both VGG16 and VGG19 achieved close performance to InceptionV3 with a higher number of Epochs (over 35). ResNet with both depth 50 and 152 underperformed in comparison with the aforementioned architectures around 81% accuracy score.

Furthermore, Fig. 10 reports the confusion matrix for each DL architecture. Further details can be obtained from Table 1 and Table 2, where precision, accuracy, recall, AUC, PRC and F1-score are reported for training and test data.

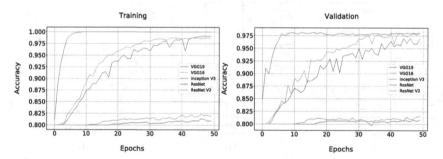

Fig. 9. Accuracy of the architectures in training and validation process.

Table 1. Performance metrics for training data.

	Precision	Accuracy	Recall	AUC	PRC	F1
Inception V3	0,99	0,99	0,98	1	1	0,99
VGG16	0,96	0,99	0,96	0,98	0,97	0,96
VGG19	0,96	0,99	0,96	0,99	0,98	0,96
ResNet50	0,73	0,81	0,09	0,75	0,47	0,17
ResNet152	0,93	0,82	0,11	0,8	0,54	0,19

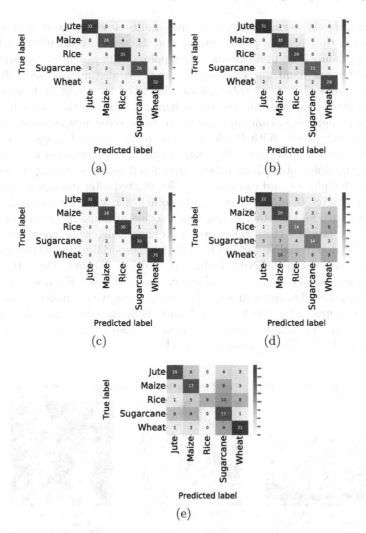

Fig. 10. Resulting multi-class confusion matrices for testing data with respect to: (a) InceptionV3, (b) VGG16, (c) VGG19, (d) ResNet152, (e) ResNet50.

Table 2. Performance metrics for test data.

	Precision	Accuracy	Recall	AUC	PRC	F1
Inception V3	0,92	0,97	0,91	0,98	0,97	0,91
VGG16	0,88	0,95	0,88	0,95	0,9	0,88
VGG19	0,9	0,96	0,89	0,96	0,93	0,89
ResNet50	0,68	0,81	0,09	0,74	0,47	0,16
ResNet152	0,85	0,82	0,11	0,79	0,53	0,19

To quantify the segmentation outcomes, multi-class confusion matrices are considered as they provide precise insights on the data classification, highlighting both right labels and misclassified data points. Noteworthy observations are as follows: On one hand, the jute crop was easier to distinguish, being different from other crops. Jute is morphologically described as a long, soft, shiny bast fibre with strong threads. On the other hand, it appears that with Inception and VGG models, sugarcane and maize are more often misclassified and confused with each other. With ResNet152, the most confused crops were wheat and maize, also rice and wheat. We might explain, that for wheat and rice they can hardly be differentiated, especially from aerial pictures, during the growing and vegetative phases, and can only be differentiated after full ripening of their fruits. For ResNet50, most training data points of rice were misclassified, and confounded with all the other crops, which seems incomprehensible. For example, it falsely labelled most rice pictures as sugarcane, while they are plainly different. By design CNNs various formulations, especially the deeper architectures, are beneficial in detecting high, mid, and low features. The latter being of the up most significance in Crop classification-type tasks. For instance, wheat and rice are generally similar in 80% of the crop cycle, which makes it difficult to differentiate between the two, thus misclassify them. Inception and VGG method exude promising preliminary results without prepossessing step, while it seems to be a requisite for ResNet models (Fig. 11).

Fig. 11. Classification performed by inception V3

5   Conclusions and Future Works

In this paper, we conducted a comparative analysis of three deep learning methods (InceptionV3, VGG and ResNet) for crop classification images, including wheat, maize, rice and jute. As a result, Inception V3 outperforms the others in every measurement, achieving high quality performance without any hyperparameter tuning. The VGG models also achieve quality results, but rather with more epochs. Meanwhile, the ResNet techniques scored lower results regarding the two previous architectures. These outcomes might suggest that the dimensionality reduction technique employed by Inception works better than the one used by VGG and a lot better than the residual function approximation of ResNet. On the other hand, we propose the inclusion of a profound pre-processing step before training ResNet, to benefit from its architecture in maintaining a low error rate. A great deal of future work can still be directed toward expanding the relevant crop types that are of strategic economic importance. Indeed, more comparative research papers are needed in crop identification using deep learning methods in order to map crops intelligently for sustainable agriculture development.

Acknowledgments. This work is supported by SDAS Research Group (https://sdas-group.com).

References

1. Bengio, Y., Simard, P., Frasconi, P.: Learning long-term dependencies with gradient descent is difficult. IEEE Trans. Neural Networks **5**(2), 157–166 (1994)
2. Bishop, C.M., et al.: Neural Networks for Pattern Recognition. Oxford University Press, Oxford (1995)
3. Bouguettaya, A., Zarzour, H., Kechida, A., Taberkit, A.M.: Deep learning techniques to classify agricultural crops through UAV imagery: a review. Neural Comput. Appl. **34**, 9511–9536 (2022). https://doi.org/10.1007/s00521-022-07104-9
4. Chew, R., et al.: Deep neural networks and transfer learning for food crop identification in UAV images. Drones **4**(1), 7 (2020)
5. Chollet, F., et al.: Keras. https://keras.io (2015)
6. Deng, J., Dong, W., Socher, R., Li, L.J., Li, K., Fei-Fei, L.: Imagenet: a large-scale hierarchical image database. In: 2009 IEEE Conference on Computer Vision and Pattern Recognition, pp. 248–255. IEEE (2009)
7. Gadiraju, K.K., Vatsavai, R.R.: Comparative analysis of deep transfer learning performance on crop classification. In: Proceedings of the 9th ACM SIGSPATIAL International Workshop on Analytics for Big Geospatial Data, pp. 1–8 (2020)
8. Gupta, K., Rani, R., Bahia, N.K.: Plant-seedling classification using transfer learning-based deep convolutional neural networks. Int. J. Agric. Environ. Inf. Syst. (IJAEIS) **11**(4), 25–40 (2020)
9. He, K., Zhang, X., Ren, S., Sun, J.: Deep residual learning for image recognition. In: Proceedings of the IEEE Conference on Computer Vision and Pattern Recognition, pp. 770–778 (2016)

10. Hosseinzadeh, M., Khoramdel, J., Borhani, Y., Najafi, E.: A new fuzzy logic based learning rate scheduling method for crop classification with convolutional neural network. In: 2022 8th International Conference on Control, Instrumentation and Automation (ICCIA), pp. 1–5. IEEE (2022)
11. Jaiswal, A.: Agriculture crop images (2021)
12. Kordon, A.K.: Applying data science: How to create value with artificial intelligence. Springer Nature (2020)
13. Lu, B., Dao, P.D., Liu, J., He, Y., Shang, J.: Recent advances of hyperspectral imaging technology and applications in agriculture. Remote Sens. **12**(16), 2659 (2020)
14. Moreno-Revelo, M.Y., Guachi-Guachi, L., Gómez-Mendoza, J.B., Revelo-Fuelagán, J., Peluffo-Ordóñez, D.H.: Enhanced convolutional-neural-network architecture for crop classification. Appl. Sci. **11**(9), 4292 (2021)
15. Moreno-Revelo, M.Y., Gómez-Mendoza, J.B., Peluffo-Ordoñez, D.H.: Satellite-image-based crop identification using unsupervised machine learning techniques: preliminary results. Revista Ibérica de Sistemas e Tecnologias de Informação **E22**, 337–348 (2019)
16. Nowakowski, A., et al.: Crop type mapping by using transfer learning. Int. J. Appl. Earth Obs. Geoinf. **98**, 102313 (2021)
17. Pech-May, F., Aquino-Santos, R., Rios-Toledo, G., Posadas-Durán, J.P.F.: Mapping of land cover with optical images, supervised algorithms, and google earth engine. Sensors **22**(13), 4729 (2022)
18. Simonyan, K., Zisserman, A.: Very deep convolutional networks for large-scale image recognition. arXiv preprint arXiv:1409.1556 (2014)
19. Srivastava, R.K., Greff, K., Schmidhuber, J.: Highway networks. arXiv preprint arXiv:1505.00387 (2015)
20. Srivastava, S., Divekar, A.V., Anilkumar, C., Naik, I., Kulkarni, V., Pattabiraman, V.: Comparative analysis of deep learning image detection algorithms. J. Big Data **8**(1), 1–27 (2021). https://doi.org/10.1186/s40537-021-00434-w
21. Szegedy, C., Vanhoucke, V., Ioffe, S., Shlens, J., Wojna, Z.: Rethinking the inception architecture for computer vision. In: Proceedings of the IEEE Conference on Computer Vision and Pattern Recognition, pp. 2818–2826 (2016)
22. Tammina, S.: Transfer learning using VGG-16 with deep convolutional neural network for classifying images. Int. J. Sci. Res. Publ. (IJSRP) **9**(10), 143–150 (2019)
23. Wang, Y., Gao, F., Gao, G., Zhao, J., Wang, X., Zhang, R.: Production and cultivated area variation in cereal, rice, wheat and maize in china (1998–2016). Agronomy **9**(5), 222 (2019)
24. Zhao, H., Chen, Z., Jiang, H., Jing, W., Sun, L., Feng, M.: Evaluation of three deep learning models for early crop classification using sentinel-1a imagery time series-a case study in zhanjiang, china. Remote Sens. **11**(22), 2673 (2019)

Internet of Things (IoT) for Secure and Sustainable Healthcare Intelligence: Analysis and Challenges

Sunday Adeola Ajagbe[1](✉) ⓘ, Sanjay Misra[2] ⓘ, Oluwaseyi F. Afe[3],
and Kikelomo I. Okesola[3] ⓘ

[1] Department of Computer Engineering, Ladoke Akintola University of Technology,
LAUTECH, Ogbomoso, Nigeria
saajagbe@pgschool.lautech.edu.ng
[2] Østfold University College, Halden, Norway
sanjay.misra@hiof.no
[3] Department of Computer Science, Lead City University, Ibadan, Nigeria
{afe.seyi,okesola.kikelomo}@lcu.edu.ng

Abstract. Many medical errors are caused by inadequate critical patient-related medical data. The use of information and communication technologies (ICTs) has the potential to improve medical data accessibility, and it is critical for patient safety. Meanwhile, the introduction of computing technologies that are IoT-enabled on data will result in significant changes in the healthcare environment. There is an emerging large and multifaceted architecture of technology and applications for ubiquitous computing. Mobile phones, laptops, Wi-Fi, Bluetooth, and a variety of digital, Radio Frequency Identification (RFID), wireless sensor network (WSN) technologies, and other sensing devices are now widely used in the healthcare industry as parts of artificial intelligence contributions to healthcare. This paper is aimed at analyzing the IoT for Secure and Sustainable Healthcare Intelligence with a view to exposing the IoT exploration of smart health. The paper described IoT-enabled technologies, IoT applications for intelligent healthcare, the effects of IoT on quality and affordable healthcare delivery, secured IoT for healthcare error reduction and optimization, and research trends. We concluded the paper and highlight the problems in making IoT a reality as future work.

Keywords: Artificial intelligence · Healthcare intelligence · Internet of things IoT · Internet-enabled system · Internet of medical things · Security

1 Introduction

The internet of things (IoT) is a special type of network that is based on the connectivity that exists among sensor-based devices and Radio Frequency Identification (RFID) such that a ubiquitous sensing environment is created in a way that a complete solution is provided [1, 2]. The first time the term "IoT" was coined was in 1999 by Kevin Ashton

© The Author(s), under exclusive license to Springer Nature Switzerland AG 2022
H. Florez and H. Gomez (Eds.): ICAI 2022, CCIS 1643, pp. 45–59, 2022.
https://doi.org/10.1007/978-3-031-19647-8_4

[3]. Analyzing each term in this concept will lead to a better understanding of what the IoT is all about. Internet is defined as a globally interconnected communication of computer networks over a communication bandwidth. While "Things" refers to any physical (machines, objects, animals, humans) or virtual (business procedures) that can be made intelligent by providing a means of unique identification, connectivity to the internet, and passing data over a network without human interference [4].

Data format generated from these varying sensors differs depending on the type of device and targeted mode of processing for specific analysis. Basically, IoT technology functions based on the information supplied by sensors on devices. It converts electrical signals from these sensors into mechanical parameters such as pressure, motion, temperature, and others. The ability to make meaning out of these signals without human interference is what is being regarded as intelligence in this discourse. Internet of things has brought a dynamic change to the internet environment in a way that has generated a novel community referred to as a smart environment in which the vast volume of generated data can be accessed and processed for automated utilization [5]. Virtually every aspect of human life has been revolutionized through the impact of IoT, ranging from home to work environment, industries, governance, healthcare delivery, and others [6]. The general goal of IoT is to provide services that can enhance and improve the human way of life, by making connectivity available anytime with anything, anywhere over any network [7]. IoT functionalities are achievable due to the availability of cloud computing services, and this makes many services intelligence-based [8].

IoT has wide application areas as its embraces the integration of other emerging technologies, which are described in this paper as IoT-enabling technologies. This has resulted in IoT being deployed in automation, home automation and monitoring, heavy machinery, factories, transportation, electricity, energy, smart cities, and appliances such as television, and smartphones just to mention a few, as the list is endless [9, 10]. The major application area of IoT is depicted in Fig. 1. The focus of this paper is to;

i.   Analyse IoT-enabled technologies with respect to sustainable healthcare;
ii. Discuss IoT applications for intelligence healthcare;
iii. Enumerate sustainable IoT techniques for error reduction, optimizations and challenges (security) in healthcare intelligence delivery

This paper has the basic element of the IoT environment in Sect. 2, IoT application for intelligence healthcare in Sect. 3, sustainable IoT techniques for error reduction, optimizations and challenges (security) in healthcare intelligence delivery 4 and conclusion and future suggestion in Sect. 5.

2   Basic Elements of IoT Environment

The six basic elements required to provide IoT functionalities as itemized by [11] are identifiers, sensing devices, communication devices, compute devices, services IoT and semantics. These elements are responsible for the six fundamental operations involved in IoT actualization, which are identification, sensing, communication, computation,

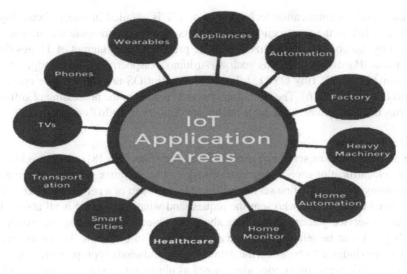

Fig. 1. Application areas of IoT

services and semantics. This section will explore details of the basic elements of IoT from the perspective of the six itemized fundamental operations.

Identification

There is an explicit identification for each object within the IoT network. There are two procedures in identification: naming and addressing. The naming refers to the object's title or name, while the addressing clarifies the object's location or address within the network. These two processes are completely different; even though two or more objects may have the same name, yet every object is within the IoT network is distinct. A number of ways of speeding up the naming of IoT network objects have been identified [12]. Initially, Internet Protocol version 4 called IPv4 was used to allocate the address, but it was impossible to meet the demand due to a large number of IoT devices; nevertheless, IPv6 is widely used today because it uses a 128-bit addressing system. Every object in IPv6 has its own unique address, which makes every object on the IoT network distinct.

Sensing

This IoT operation entails gathering data from the environment through the use of IoT sensing devices and sending it to a local or cloud-based database. Intelligent and portable sensors and actuators can all be identified. The information gathered is sent to the storage medium. RFID tags, portable sensors, smart sensors, wearable, actuators and other detection devices are used to gather data on objects [13].

Communication and Computation

Communication is one of the key purposes of the IoT, in which diverse devices connect and communicate with one another. Communication devices can send and receive messages, documents, and other data over the communication layer. IoT communication techniques communicate heterogeneous artefacts to achieve smart services. Further explanation of communication technologies of IoT is entailed in under Technologies Enabling of IoT in the next section [14]. Sensors are used to compute the information acquired by the objects. It is utilized to create processing for Internet of Things (IoT) applications. Hardware platforms such as Arduino, Raspberry Pi, and Gadgeteer are used, while Android, Tiny OS [15], Lite OS and Riot OS are some of the operating systems that are used [16]. The operating system is crucial in the processing of software platforms that can ensure sustainable healthcare delivery in an IoT environment.

Services IoT

There are four types of services provided by applications [17, 18], which are identity service or identification service, aggregation service, collaborative service, and pervasive or ubiquitous service. The first service is linked to an object or a person's identification. It is utilized to figure out who sent the request and what the request is all about. The aggregation service gathers all the data about the objects and handles the processing accordingly. It can be referred to as the aggregation of information. The collaborative service makes judgments based on the data collected and sends appropriate responses to the devices. The pervasive service also known as ubiquitous service is used to replace equipment without regard for time or location. These are the four services carried out by IoT to actualize its functionalities in healthcare intelligence and every other field of its application.

Semantics

It is the IoT's goal to make it easier for users to complete their jobs. It is the most critical component of IoT in order to fulfil its tasks. It serves as the brain of the IoT. It takes in all of the data and makes the necessary decisions about how to respond to the devices or make inferences based on the data collected [11].

The IoT basic elements and their features that make IoT productive for healthcare intelligence are shown in Fig. 2.

Classification of IoT Technologies

The IoT technology application can be classified into three different categories by different authors [3, 19], the most mentioned categories are: healthcare delivery, smart cities, environmental, commercial, industrial, and general aspect. There are three known classes of IoT-enabled technologies in healthcare, namely identification, communication, and location technologies. These IoT-enabled applications in healthcare include Preferred Reporting Items for Systematic reviews and Meta-Analyses (PRISMA), and this is discussed in the next session. Figure 3 shows PRISMA Flow Chat HIoT-Enable Technologies in healthcare, it shows the interactions between healthcare IoT technologies, identification, communication, and location technologies.

i. Identification Technologies

To be useful, an IoT system must allow authorized nodes (sensors) to access patient data remotely. A healthcare network's node and sensor identification are required. In order to establish identification and enable clear data exchange, each authorized entity must be assigned a unique identifier (UID). A UID is associated with nearly every healthcare

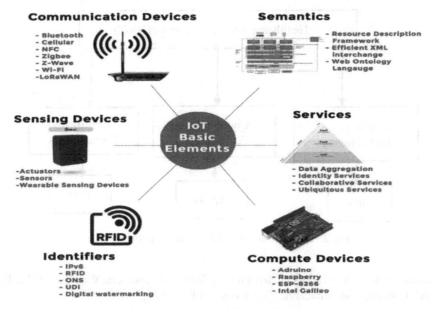

Fig. 2. Basic elements of IoT environment

resource (hospital, doctor, nurse, caregiver, medical device, etc.). This ensures digital resource identification and connectivity. The literature lists numerous identification standards. The open science framework (OSF) developed one of the identifiers (the universally unique identifier- UUID and a globally unique identifier- GUID), while the other is a GUID [20]. The UUID does not require centralized coordination. Identifying and addressing a healthcare network's sensors and actuators is critical to system performance. Because IoT-based technologies are constantly evolving, the component's unique identifier may change. The device/system must be able to update this information to maintain its integrity [21]. A possible explanation is that the change in configuration affects both the tracking of network components and the diagnosis of the change. A global directory search for efficient IoT service discovery is required using the UUID scheme.

ii. **Communication Technology**

In an IoT-based healthcare network, various devices can communicate with each other through the use of communication technologies. Short-range (within a limited range of some meters) communication, and medium-range communication (which supports long distance communication) are the two main categories of these technologies. For example, communication within a body area network uses a short-range communication protocol, while the base station can connect to a BAN's central node via medium-range communication protocols, such as Wi-Fi. Most healthcare IoT applications use short-range communication technology [21]. Wireless communication technologies such as RFID, Zigbee, and Wi-Fi are among the most commonly used. The IoT Communication

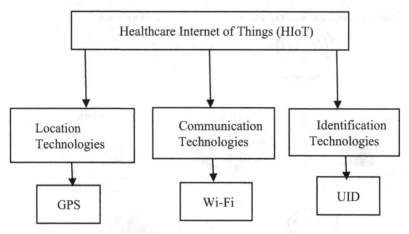

Fig. 3. PRISMA flow chat HIoT-enabled technologies

technologies include Wireless fidelity (Wi-Fi), WiMAX, Low-Rate Wireless PAN (LR-WPAN), Mobile communication, Bluetooth and WSN [22].

iii. **Location Technologies**

These technologies are used to track and identify an object's location within the healthcare network. Real-time location system technologies are employed, which track the treatment process based on resource distribution. Global Positioning System (GPS) is one of the most frequently used technologies in this category. It keeps an eye on things through the use of satellites. GPS can track an object's location as long as there is a clear line of sight between it and at least four satellites. This technology has a variety of applications in IoT-based healthcare delivery, including locating a patient's healthcare team or an ambulance. As a result, GPS's use in indoor applications is limited, as the surrounding infrastructure can act as a communication barrier. In these instances, a local positioning system network can be used effectively to track an object by deploying an array of receivers that detect the radio signal emitted by the traveling object [21]. Additionally, the local positioning system can be implemented via Zigbee, Wi-Fi, RFID, and other near-field communication technologies. Ultra-wideband (UWB) radio is preferred over conventional radios due to its superior temporal resolution. This method enables the determination of an accurate arrival time. Several authors have used UWB-based tracking systems that rely on the time difference of arrival. Future smart healthcare networks may include GPS and other high-bandwidth connection technologies [23].

3 IoT Applications for Healthcare Intelligence

The advancement in technology has been extended in recent times to the healthcare industry with the use of IoT-enabled devices. Social and technological advancements are combining to push the deployment of IoT in therapeutic settings. Health care costs are rising far faster than inflation as a result of the aging population in developed nations and the associated burden on clinical facilities [24]. Healthcare businesses are well-positioned to take advantage of the expanding availability of high-bandwidth connectivity, low-cost cloud storage and processing, and massive data analytics [25, 26]. This gives room to sophistication and improvement in several healthcare services and applications resulting in healthcare intelligence. Figure 4 is the general application of IoT in healthcare, it is all about monitoring and improving the health conditions of the patient.

IoT-based devices include wearable sensors, drug dispensers, remote monitoring, activity trackers, smart sensors, and the integration of smart medical devices. Because of recent technological advancements, it is now possible to diagnose numerous ailments and keep track of one's health with small, wearable gadgets like smartwatches [27], thereby transforming healthcare delivery from a hospital-centered system to patient-centered system. Examples include the ability to undertake clinical analyses (such as blood pressure and oxygen) without the assistance of a healthcare provider. Clinical data can also be transferred via high-speed telecommunications from remote sites to healthcare centers [28].

In conjunction with fast increasing technology (such as machine learning, wireless sensing, cloud computing, big data analysis, IoT, and mobile computing), the utilization of such communication services has made healthcare facilities more accessible [21] such that required medical and health data can be collected and the collected information is transferred to a physician or to a cloud platform using real-time monitoring through smart medical devices (e.g. smartphones, tablets, computers, and nearly anything else with a sensor) which are connected using the internet connectivity [29]. It serves as a decision-support system [30]. The IoT device captures and transmits health information such as oxygen, temperature, weight, blood pressure, blood sugar levels, pulse rate as well as Electrocardiogram (ECG). Currently, there are 20.35 billion connected devices which is predicted to hit 75.44 billion in 2025 globally [31].

The tremendous impact of IoT in the medical field has been ever-increasing due to advancements in smartphone technology, the transition from common sensors to intelligent sensors, and unequivocal progress made in software applications over the last few years. This undeniable impact of IoT is felt in the medical field to the extent that a new groundbreaking field emerged known as the internet of medical things (IoMT) [32].

3.1 Types of IoT Applications in Healthcare

With the trend of deployment of IoT technologies to healthcare delivery, there has been massive number of systems with varying capabilities [33]. Basically, the essence of these applications is to be able to introduce intelligence into the use of these devices, such that data gathered can be used in a way to sense impending health issues [34]. These systems can be grouped into two broad categories lone system and composite system and they could be in form of wearable devices, monitoring system, and drug dispenser [27, 34] grouped the wearable devices into 2 different classes: those used by medics and those that can be used individually without the assistance of the medics.

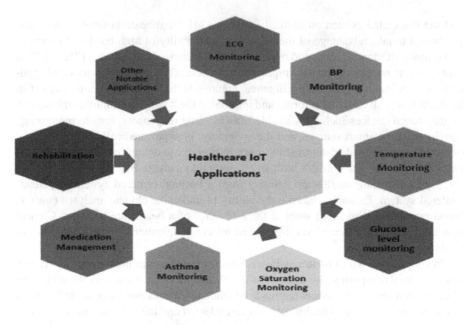

Fig. 4. IoT applications in healthcare delivery

i. **Lone System**

Systems in this category are those that focus on monitoring specific health situations by accepting singular input which is evaluated for generating output. Examples of this are glucose level monitoring, blood pressure monitoring, seizure monitoring, temperature monitoring, oxygen saturation monitoring, and electrocardiogram (ECG) monitoring, asthma monitoring [27, 35].

ii. **Composite System**

In this category, multiple sensor inputs are analysed to give a correct and adequate situation report of patient condition. In addition, communication is two-way such that the patient being monitored can have feedback based on the outcome of analysed sensor inputs data [21]. Rehabilitation systems, Medication management, wheelchair management, smartphone healthcare solutions, and Future IoT – embedded healthcare solutions are in this category [35]. Some of the systems in this category are discussed briefly in the next section. Basically, IoT can be applied to provide solutions to healthcare services. Some of these services include but are not limited to; Measurable (Quantitative) Healthcare, Preventive Care, Patient's Homecare and Monitoring, and Healthcare Data Management.

Measurable (Quantitative) Healthcare
IoT has increased human independence while simultaneously broadening the range of ways in which they can engage with their surroundings. A substantial part of the IoTs' contribution to global communication was made possible thanks to cutting-edge protocols and algorithms. It connects a vast number of items to the Internet, including wireless

sensors, home appliances, and electrical devices. These devices can continuously measure and monitor a set of predetermined health status parameters being worn by the patient [36].

Preventive and Clinical Care

Patient-centered care and digital transformation in healthcare necessitate efficient clinical workflows, safer patient experiences, and improved preventative care. Distributed analytics can be used to gain meaningful insights from data of IoT devices generated by physician-patient encounters and wearables, which are generating vast amounts of data [37]. Medical technology has come a long way since the introduction of the first remedial treatment a decade ago. But the focus is now on preventing sickness through the use of IoT devices in healthcare settings. It boosts productivity efficiency. It enhances resource utilization. Continual monitoring of key physiological indicators is required for certain types of chronically unwell patients. In most cases, such individuals are admitted to hospital intensive care units (ICUs). This type of monitoring can be done utilizing sensors that collect full physiological information relevant to the different important body characteristics of patients, thanks to IoT-driven noninvasive monitoring technologies. The data obtained by these sensors is relayed to close family and caregivers via gateways and wireless networks, allowing them to take necessary action to care for the patient. [38]. This IoT technology takes the place of traditional in-person continuous monitoring by health care personnel and doctors in hospitals. Chronically ill people can receive better automated health care at home at a low cost with this technology. Other clinical care for patients in healthcare intelligence includes medication intake tracking, drug tracking, medical inventory and equipment tracking, smart hospital space and body position measurement.

Patient's Homecare and Monitoring

Using the IoT in healthcare delivery improves patient care by making it stronger, healthier, and more convenient. As a result of the IoT, doctors will spend less time travelling, diagnosing illnesses, and communicating with patients, allowing for a more efficient healthcare delivery system. Patients with chronic conditions, such as epilepsy, and those at risks, such as children and the "elderly," can be monitored remotely using IoT technologies and wearables without direct contact of the clinician with the patient [39, 40]. Wearable medical devices are those devices placed on the surface of the human body or in close contact with the human body. Environment-embedded devices make use of sensors embedded in strategic positions within the environment. Body position measurement, patient location, and overall monitoring of unwell patients in hospitals and at home are all possible applications of these healthcare devices.

Healthcare Data Management

Healthcare sensors that are powered by the IoT can be used for clinical exams and self-monitoring of one's own health. In the absence of direct contact with the patients, they assist remote clinicians in determining the best course of treatment for their patients [39, 40]. It is through the IoT that large volumes of data may be processed into actionable activities by connecting sensors and applying complicated rules and workflows. Also, the information gathered by these wearable sensors is stored in a distributed ledger indefinitely. They also keep track of the patient's progress, so that healthcare workers can see how the patient's condition changes over time [36] Patients' medical histories can be accessed while they are being tested, for example, using automated blood pressure, or digital thermometers [41].

4 Sustainable IoT Techniques for Error Reduction, and Challenges (Security) in Healthcare Delivery

In the United States alone, medical errors are a leading cause of death based on a study by researchers from Johns Hopkins, and these medical errors could be fatal. Examples of such include surgical complications that go unnoticed, as well as medication mix-ups and other data-related issues [42]. An incident to affirm this occurred in 2010 where a Singaporean couple, who conceived through in-vitro fertilization, were shocked when their baby was born with a skin tone that was obviously different from theirs as the parents, and it was also discovered that the baby's blood type differed from theirs. Undergoing a DNA test, it was confirmed that they were victims of a medical blunder. That is, the mother's eggs had been fertilized by a genetic specimen from a stranger. The specimens were handled by two embryologists who were found culpable of displaying lapses in procedure and human error. A solution to this problem is provided by the introduction of IoT which creates a world where components like sensors, barcodes, and RFID tags fixed to objects and linked to the internet give them a digital voice.

4.1 Healthcare Error Reduction Using Secured IoT Solutions

Wrong Blood Sample for Patients: Errors sometimes happen when blood samples are being taken in the wards. These human errors can be eliminated by utilizing IoT devices through scanning of patients' wristbands to validate their identity by nurses using IoT-enabled communication technology, and nurses can be directed through the blood collection process and print barcode labels using mobile printers attached to the sample [43]. Failure to Monitor Patient's Heart Rate: Heart attacks have claimed the lives of many people in recent years. When the heart's blood supply is cut off, a heart attack can ensue. Medical experts have found it difficult to save the lives of many people because of the lack of early diagnosis and detection of a heart attack, especially in developing nations. However, the advent of IoT solutions in healthcare with attention to error reduction has reduced this risk by monitoring the patient's heart rate [44].

4.2 Healthcare Optimization Using IoT

The Internet of Things (IoT) has the potential to spur the creation of smart systems that aid in the delivery of healthcare and biomedicine. The use of biomedical equipment in smart hospitals and the real-time monitoring of patient's physiological data can help diagnose clinical deterioration earlier, identify and track patients automatically, and track drug-patient correlations [45]. Errors happen when blood samples are taken in the wards. These human errors can be eliminated by utilizing IoT devices. Patients' wristbands can be scanned to validate their identity by nurses using these devices, and nurses can be directed through the blood collection process and print barcode labels using mobile printers attached to the sample using mobile printers [46].

4.3 Security Challenges in Healthcare Intelligence Delivery

Numerous benefits are attached to the deployment of IoT technology in the healthcare delivery sector. With these benefits arises the challenges that can entirely discourage the use of this novel technology. Basically, the challenges related to IoT-based healthcare delivery are general limitations of IoT technologies. Some of the challenges that have been identified in IoT applications and healthcare delivery inclusive are: Data management in terms of loss of privacy, system security, absence of stakeholder collaboration and interoperability. Security challenges that are related to IoT in general are also directly applicable and critical to IoT in healthcare, such as lack of access control/ privacy, software system susceptibility, infected programs affecting IoT network, entity recognition, android security challenge and lightweight cryptographic systems and security protocols [47]. Table 1 presents the analysis of these security challenges in intelligence healthcare delivery.

In the Table 1 present some IoT-based technologies with their limitation/challenges for an improved healthcare delivery.

Table 1. Healthcare IoT-based study, descriptions and challenges

S/N	References	Description	Challenges
1	[24]	Generation of applicable knowledge from multi-facetted/heterogeneous record by proposing the introduction of business analytics technique, i.e. (interoperability) Also, architectural reliability is address by proposing the implementation of a mess topology. While Network security and power consumption were addressed by implementing device- level authentication and link encryption	Encryption technique introduced to handle data confidentiality can hinder the system from accessing full potential of business analytics technique. The system has limited functionalities
2	[35]	A physical medication box enhanced with IoT technology to help individuals to stick to timely and correct usage of medication	Power consumption is high, hence faster power drainage. Needs enhanced security measure like second level authentication accessing the box. Also, needs more sensor to get more health details

(continued)

Table 1. (*continued*)

S/N	References	Description	Challenges
3	[34]	A monitoring model for epileptic patients using a cloud-based health IoT system was proposed. DWT-SVD based watermarking was applied on time-frequency domain EEG data to enhance data security	Further studies can be done on feature extraction and classification with watermark extraction from EEG data in the cloud, to detect or predict epileptic seizures in the patient. Other machine learning algorithms can also be used
4	[14]	This article highlights the description of the major aspects of wireless body area networks (WBAN)-based telemedicine such as research issues, characteristics, and its challenges in telemedicine systems for patient monitoring in different circumstances. The authors designed a framework to integrate BAN on telemedicine systems	The major challenges are bandwidth limitations, power consumption, and skin or tissue protection
5	[11]	The classification function of the wound by the monitoring system into three classes was based on the decision tree	Other health issues that could affect the healing rate of the wounds were not put into consideration, as well as the environment condition around the wound area
6	[48]	The paper presented a review of challenges faced in IoT-connected healthcare and information security in developing nations. The study began by providing an overview of IoT connectedness in healthcare in developing nations. An analysis of how this portends a threat to security was provided	The challenges of healthcare delivery in developing nations evolve security and corruption

5 Conclusion and Future Direction

This paper discusses the novelty of IoT in healthcare delivery, viz-a-viz IoT-enabled technologies, basic elements and classifications of IoT environment and technologies respectively. The IoT applications for healthcare intelligence were x-ray including medical image processing that was done with the help of AI tools. The effects of IoT on quality and affordable healthcare delivery. The penultimate section explains sustainable IoT techniques for error reduction, optimizations and security in healthcare intelligence delivery with a view to unveilling the challenging area of IoT technology in healthcare for possible qualitative healthcare delivery. The future direction in the area of secure and sustainable healthcare intelligence is to address the challenges of confidentiality, privacy, security and ensure a robust and healthcare intelligence system. This includes but is not limited to:

i. Address the issue of data anonymization, a desire for cryptography system protection and relational data concealment has arisen. The homomorphic encryption technique could be employed in research to find a suitable solution to the privacy concern and it is a liable tool for intelligence and sustainable healthcare delivery.

ii. Further studies are needed to address feature extraction and classification with watermark extraction from EEG data in the cloud, to detect or predict epileptic seizures in the patient. Other machine learning algorithms can also be used.

iii. The challenges of data security in the healthcare sector and corruption in funding healthcare section in the developing nation need to be addressed

References

1. Kassab, W., Darabkh, K.A.: A–Z survey of Internet of Things: architectures, protocols, applications, recent advances, future directions and recommendations. J. Netw. Comput. Appl. **163**(2), 102663 (2020)
2. Aman, A.H., Yadegaridehkordi, E., Attarbashi, Z., Hassan, R., Park, Y.J.: A survey on trend and classification of internet of things reviews. IEEE Access **8**, 111763–111782 (2020)
3. Al-Emran, M., Malik, S.I., Al-Kabi, M.N.: A survey of Internet of Things (IoT) in education: opportunities and challenges. In: Hassanien, A.E., Bhatnagar, R., Khalifa, N.E.M., Taha, M.H.N. (eds.) Toward Social Internet of Things (SIoT): Enabling Technologies, Architectures and Applications. SCI, vol. 846, pp. 197–209. Springer, Cham (2020). https://doi.org/10.1007/978-3-030-24513-9_12
4. Patel, K., Keyur, S.: Internet of Things-IOT: definition, characteristics, architecture, enabling technologies, application & future challenges. Int. J. Eng. Sci. Comput. **6**, 6122–6131 (2016)
5. Hajjaji, Y., Boulila, W., Farah, I.R., Romdhani, I., Hussain, A.: Big data and IoT-based applications in smart environments: a systematic review. Comput. Sci. Rev. **39**, 100318 (2021)
6. Asghari, P., Rahmani, A.M., Javadi, H.: Internet of Things applications: a systematic review. Comput. Netw. **148**, 241–261 (2019)
7. Nóbrega, L., Gonçalves, P., Pedreiras, P., Pereira, J.: An IoT-based solution for intelligent farming. Sens. (Switz.) **19**(3), 1–24 (2019)
8. Kaur, C.: The cloud computing and Internet of Things (IoT). Int. J. Sci. Res. Sci. Eng. Technol. **7**, 19–22 (2020)
9. Hernandez, J., Daza, K., Florez, H., Misra, S.: Dynamic interface and access model by dead token for IoT systems. In: Florez, H., Leon, M., Diaz-Nafria, J.M., Belli, S. (eds.) ICAI 2019. CCIS, vol. 1051, pp. 485–498. Springer, Cham (2019). https://doi.org/10.1007/978-3-030-32475-9_35
10. Olowu, M., Yinka-Banjo, C., Misra, S., Florez, H.: A secured private-cloud computing system. In: Florez, H., Leon, M., Diaz-Nafria, J.M., Belli, S. (eds.) ICAI 2019. CCIS, vol. 1051, pp. 373–384. Springer, Cham (2019). https://doi.org/10.1007/978-3-030-32475-9_27
11. Ali, S., Ansari, M., Alam, M.: Resource management techniques for cloud-based IoT environment. In: Alam, M., Shakil, K., Khan, S. (eds.) Internet of Things (IoT), pp. 63–87. Springer, Cham (2020). https://doi.org/10.1007/978-3-030-37468-6_4
12. Barik, K., Misra, S., Konar, K.F.-S.L., Murat, K.: Cybersecurity deep: approaches, attacks dataset, and comparative study. Appl. Artif. Intell. Int. J. **36**, 1–24 (2022)

13. Sharif, M., Sadeghi-Niaraki, A.: Ubiquitous sensor network simulation and emulation environments: a survey. J. Netw. Comput. Appl. **93**, 150–181 (2017)
14. Cao, Q., Abdelzaher, T., Stankovic, J., He, T.: Proceedings of the International Conference on Information Processing in Sensor Network (2008)
15. Levis, P., et al.: TinyOS: an operating system for sensor networks. In: Weber, W., Rabaey, J.M., Aarts, E. (eds.) Ambient Intelligence. Springer, Heidelberg (2005). https://doi.org/10.1007/3-540-27139-2_7
16. Baccelli, E., Hahm, O., Günes, M., Wählisch, M., Schmidt, T.: RIOT OS: towards an OS for the Internet of Things. In: Proceedings IEEE Conference on INFOCOM WKSHPS (2013)
17. Gigli, M., Koo, S.: Internet of things: services and applications categorization. Adv. Internet Things **1**, 27–31 (2011)
18. Xing, X., Wang, J., Li, M.: Services and key technologies of the Internet of Things. ZTE Commun. **2**, 1–11 (2010)
19. Awotunde, J.B., et al.: An improved machine learnings diagnosis technique for COVID-19 pandemic using chest X-ray images. In: Florez, H., Pollo-Cattaneo, M.F. (eds.) ICAI 2021. CCIS, vol. 1455, pp. 319–330. Springer, Cham (2021). https://doi.org/10.1007/978-3-030-89654-6_23
20. Oyeniyi, J., Ogundoyin, I., Oyediran, O., Omotosho, L.: Application of Internet of Things (IoT) to enhance the fight against Covid-19 pandemic. Int. J. Multidiscip. Sci. Adv. Technol. **1**(3), 38–42 (2020)
21. Pradhan, B., Bhattacharyya, S., Pal, K.: IoT-based applications in healthcare devices. J. Healthc. Eng. **2021**, 1–18 (2021)
22. Ahmadi, H., Arji, G., Shahmoradi, L., Safdari, R., Nilashi, M., Alizadeh, M.: The application of internet of things in healthcare: a systematic literature review and classification. Univ. Access Inf. Soc. **18**(4), 837–869 (2018). https://doi.org/10.1007/s10209-018-0618-4
23. Saha, H., Mandal, A., Sinha, A.: Recent trends in the Internet of Things. In: 2017 IEEE 7th Annual Computing and Communication Workshop and Conference (CCWC) (2017)
24. Satpathy, S., Mohan, P., Das, S., Debbarma, S.: A new healthcare diagnosis system using an IoT - based fuzzy classifier with FPGA. J. Supercomput. **76**, 5849–5861 (2020). https://doi.org/10.1007/s11227-019-03013-2
25. Habibzadeh, H., Dinesh, K., Shishvan, O.R., Boggio-Dandry, A., Sharma, G., Soyata, T.: A survey of Healthcare Internet of Things (HIoT): a clinical perspective. IEEE Internet Things J. **7**(1), 53–71 (2020)
26. Mikac, M.: Networking case study in stem education - application layer protocol labs. In: EDULEARN 2021 Proceedings, pp. 2938–2947 (2021)
27. Gandhi, D.A., Ghosal, M.: Intelligent healthcare Using IoT: a extensive survey. In: Proceedings of the International Conference on Inventive Communication and Computational Technologies (ICICCT) (2018)
28. Swamy, T.J., Murthy, T.N.: ESmart: an IoT based intelligent health monitoring and management system for mankind. In: 2019 International Conference on Computer Communication and Informatics, ICCCI 2019 (2019)
29. Krishna, C.S., Sampath, N.: Healthcare monitoring system based on IoT. In: 2nd International Conference on Computational Systems and Information Technology for Sustainable Solutions, CSITSS 2017 (2018)
30. Chatterjee, P., Cymberknop, L.J., Armentano, R.L.: IoT-based decision support system for intelligent healthcare - Applied to cardiovascular diseases. In: Proceedings of 7th International Conference on Communication Systems and Network Technologies CSNT 2017 (2018)
31. Katre, S., Dakhole, P., Patil, M.: IoT based healthcare monitoring systems: a review. J. Adv. Res. Dyn. Control Syst. **12**(6), 51–57 (2020)
32. Baker, S.B., Xiang, W., Atkinson, I.: Internet of things for smart healthcare: technologies, challenges, and opportunities. IEEE Access **5**, 26521–26544 (2017)

33. Nord, J.H., Koohang, A., Paliszkiewicz, J.: The Internet of Things: review and theoretical framework. Expert Syst. Appl. **133**, 97–108 (2019)
34. Banerjee, A., Chakraborty, C., Kumar, A., Biswas, D.: Emerging trends in IoT and big data analytics for biomedical and health care technologies. In: Handbook of Data Science Approaches for Biomedical Engineering (2019)
35. Islam, S., Kwak, D., Kabir, M., Hossain, M., Kwak, K.S.: The internet of things for health care: a comprehensive survey. IEEE Access **3**, 678–708 (2015)
36. Frikha, T., Chaari, A., Chaabane, F., Cheikhrouhou, O., Zaguia, A.: Healthcare and fitness data management using the IoT-based blockchain platform. J. Healthc. Eng. **2021**, 1–12 (2021)
37. Maktoubian, J., Ansari, K.: An IoT architecture for preventive maintenance of medical devices in healthcare organizations. Heal. Technol. **9**(3), 233–243 (2019). https://doi.org/10.1007/s12 553-018-00286-0
38. Raj, P., Raman, A.C.: The Internet of Things: Enabling Technologies, Platforms, and Use Cases. CRC Press, London (2017)
39. Wang, D.H.: IoT based clinical sensor data management and transfer using blockchain technology. J. ISMAC **2**(3), 154–159 (2020)
40. Keerthi, H.S., Patil, K.B., Shetty, M.U., Mandhara, G., Bhuvaneswari, P.: Health monitoring and secured data management using IOT. Int. J. Adv. Res. Innov. Ideas Educ. (IJARIIE) **2**(5), 74–78 (2017)
41. Bilal, M., Shin-Gak, K.: An authentication protocol for future sensor networks. Sensors **5**(17), 979 (2017)
42. Ajagbe, S.A., Oladipupo, M.A., Balogun, E.O.: Crime belt monitoring via data visualization: a case study of folium. Int. J. Inf. Secur. Priv. Digit. Forensic **4**(2), 35–44 (2020)
43. Adebisi, O.A., Busari, O., Oyewola, Y., Adeaga, I.: Automatic classification of lung nodules on computed tomography images using a pre-trained convolutional neural network. Int. J. Eng. Sci. Invent. (IJESI) **9**(1), 63–66 (2020)
44. Dang, L., Piran, M., Han, D., Min, K., Moon, H.: A survey on internet of things and cloud computing for healthcare. Electronics **8**(7), 768 (2019)
45. Busari, O., Adebisi, O.A., Oyewola, Y.: A comprehensive study of independent component analysis (ICA) in the characterisation of human faces. Int. J. Sci. Eng. Res. (IJSER) **6**(7), 775–781 (2015)
46. Mrabet, H., Belguith, S., Alhomoud, A., Jemai, A.: A survey of IoT security based on a layered architecture of sensing and data analysis. Sens. (Switz.) **20**(13), 1–20 (2020)
47. Neeli, J., Patil, S.: Insight to security paradigm, research trend & statistics in internet of things (IoT). Glob. Transit. Proc. **2**, 84–90 (2021)
48. Naqvi, K.H., Markus, E.D., Muthoni, M., Abu-Mahfouz, A.: A critical review of IoT-connected healthcare and information security in South Africa. In: Zhang, Y.-D., Senjyu, T., So-In, C., Joshi, A. (eds.) Smart Trends in Computing and Communications. LNNS, vol. 286, pp. 739–746. Springer, Singapore (2022). https://doi.org/10.1007/978-981-16-4016-2_70

Multiple Colour Detection of RGB Images Using Machine Learning Algorithm

Joseph Bamidele Awotunde[1](✉) (ID), Sanjay Misra[2] (ID), David Obagwu[1],
and Hector Florez[3] (ID)

[1] University of Ilorin, Ilorin, Nigeria
awotunde.jb@unilorin.edu.ng
[2] Østfold University College, Halden, Norway
[3] Universidad Distrital Francisco Jose de Caldas, Bogota, Colombia
haflorezf@udistrital.edu.co

Abstract. Colour detection is the act of identifying the name of any colour. Color detection is required for object recognition, and it is also utilized in a variety of picture editing and sketching programs. Machine Learning (ML) has been proof useful in this area, and lot of researches have been done. This has been utilized in fields of neural networks and digital image processing recently. RGB images multiple colour recognition are powerful tools for various images for images and sketches. There have been several suggested regression models that use crop image characteristics and image indices, however, they have not been properly tested for accuracy and adaptation effectiveness for multiple colors. Therefore, this paper proposes K- Nearest Neighbour (KNN) classifier for efficient colour detection of RGB images. The KNN algorithm is a prominent ML technique and neural network classification technique. The KNN classifier is utilized to segregate distinct colors in the RGB images. The paper utilized colour histogram for feature extraction to find the features that most relevant pattern that define certain colours. The feature extraction further improved the efficacy and accuracy of KNN classifier's in the classification of RGB images.

Keywords: Machine learning · Feature extraction · Colour histogram · RGB images · Colour detection · Object recognition

1 Introduction

Within the actual world, the human eye is capable of detecting and distinguishing colours based on predetermined identification or conventional learning, after which the colour can be seen by the eyes and interpreted by the mind. The colour detection or colour sensation mechanism in computer vision is nearly identical to that in the eyes of humans, however, it must be designed with algorithms and logic processes that enable the CPU to take a piece of colour and do the necessary mathematical and logical operations to identify what colour that piece includes based on its recognition of all colour names [1].

The method of detecting the name of any colour is known as colour detection. This is an exceedingly simple task for people, however, computers are not so straightforward.

© The Author(s), under exclusive license to Springer Nature Switzerland AG 2022
H. Florez and H. Gomez (Eds.): ICAI 2022, CCIS 1643, pp. 60–74, 2022.
https://doi.org/10.1007/978-3-031-19647-8_5

Humans' eyes and brains collaborate to transform light into colour. Light receptors in our eyes transmit the signal to the brain. The colour is then recognized by our brain [2]. There has been the mapping of lights with their colour labels since we were children. To detect colour names, we'll use an approach that's similar to this one. Colour detection is used in a range of industries to help with the production and packaging process. Colour may be used as a quality control metric in the food industry, for example. Colour detecting sensors can be used in various sectors, such as the car, textile, and paint industries, to categorize goods or input materials based on their colours. Furthermore, during the bottling of items, Colour detection is employed to distinguish between those that have a bottle cap and those that do not.

Artificial Intelligence (AI) and Machine Learning (ML) are currently active research subjects with practical applicability [3]. ML is a method of generating predictions using computers based on a set of data or prior experience. Using supervised and unsupervised learning techniques from ML, these can manage massive volumes of data and solve classification issues [4, 5]. ML now is not the same as machine learning in the past, thanks to advances in computer technology. Pattern recognition and the idea that computers could learn to execute tasks without being explicitly taught how to do so inspired AI researchers to investigate if computers could learn from data. ML's iterative feature is crucial since models can expand autonomously when exposed to new data. They use past computations to make dependable, repeatable judgments and results. It isn't a new science, but it is receiving renewed interest. Machine learning is a subset of AI that teaches a machine how to learn. AI is a general word for the study of simulating human abilities [6].

Over the years, colour images have taken over our lives through the medium of television, books, newspapers and photography [7]. With this technological breakthrough, colour televisions, colour scanners among others are now an integral part of our personal and professional environment. However, recognition of colour objects has evolved as a big challenge in computer vision [8]. Colour recognition, particularly in professional settings, colour management is required across all equipment in the manufacturing process, many of which use RGB [9, 10]. During a normal production cycle, multiple transparent conversions between device-independent and device-dependent colour spaces emerge from colour management, ensuring colour consistency throughout the process. Therefore, this study use the K Nearest Neighbour classifier trained with the RGB Histogram to detect RGB images colours.

The paper develops a model to detect multiple colours in RGB images using ML algorithm. The specific contributions of this paper are to:

i.   design a model that is able to detect colours in images using KNN classifier;
ii.   Perform feature extraction to select relevant pattern for the detection of RGB colour in RGB images, before training and testing the model using a dataset; and
iii. evaluate the performance of the designed model.

The remaining part of this paper is organized as follows: section presents some relevant literature in multiple colour detection and prediction using machine learning. Section 3 discusses the methodology used in the paper. The results and discussion is presented in Sect. 4 while Sect. 5 conclude the study with future work and scope.

2 Related Work

ML aims to teach a computer how to learn. We'll also need to provide the machine the ability to react to user input. The main difference between traditional programming and machine learning is that instead of instructions, we must provide data. Machine learning algorithms also try to aid the machine in learning how to respond rather than presenting a predefined answer [11].

According to authors in [12], When dealing with large volumes of data, when dealing with big volumes of data, a basic model may function for short training sets but is less adaptive when dealing with large amounts of data. This is referred to as underfitting. If your model is underfitted to the data, it isn't capturing enough information and so delivers an incorrect forecast. On the other side, we may build a model that is flexible enough to operate with the dataset but is extremely complicated and difficult to comprehend. This is referred to as overfitting. Advanced techniques to solving the challenge of colour detection include machine learning algorithms.

Machine vision is a difficult field to work with. Neural network techniques are particularly beneficial for a number of challenges when compared to standard procedures. A traditional strategy for colour recognition is the K-Nearest Neighbors Machine Learning algorithm with feature extraction. In addition to feature extraction, other characteristics such as the Color Histogram, Color Correlogram, and Color Moments can be used [13]. The K-Means technique is a standard machine learning strategy for extracting colours from pictures and Colour space values are used to categorize each image in a collection. Any colour space can be utilized, including RGB, CYMK, HSV, and so on.

In [14], the authors suggested a colour recognition method using K-Nearest Neighbors Machine Learning classification algorithm trained on colour histogram features. They presented a colour recognition method using KNN classifier which is trained by RGB color histogram. The training dataset plays a very important role in classification accuracy. It can classify eight different colours namely White, Black, Orange, Green, Yellow, Red, Blue, and Violet. For classification of more colours and for increasing the accuracy large training dataset can be used. Authors in [15] suggested using Python and OpenCv for RGB image colour detection. The major goal of this application was to develop a mechanism for recognizing colour hues and making a precise forecast of their names. The OpenCv platform is used to implement many processes. The advantage of this approach is that it can differentiate monochromatic colors.

In [16], the authors study based on human facial recognition proposes one set of clever skin tone gathering methodologies. It starts with color photographs of the face and then uses FACE++ to determine the face's facial location in the image as a human facial recognition result. Based on the facial characteristics of the human face, it also determines the skin colour point for the human face collection. Programs that identify face colour have been developed as a result of this study. The clever approach allows it to calculate large amounts of data and even complex situations. This colour-selecting approach may be used to calculate large amounts of data. As a result, the gathered data may be used to construct a skin color trend.

Authors in [17] proposed colour identification using colour histogram feature extraction and the K-nearest neighbor classifier. Twelve distinct colours are distinguished using the KNN classifier. The colors utilized include blue, brown, green, navy, orange, forest green, pink, black, red, violet, yellow, and white. To extract characteristics that identify the colours, the colour histogram feature extraction approach is applied. With K = 5, the most accurate colors are black and pink (90%). Violet and yellow, on the other hand, have the best ROC curve values. The findings suggest that a strong training dataset and well-chosen K values are crucial for classification accuracy, and that accuracy improves with them.

In [18], the authors published a paper called "Combing Colour Detection and Neural Networks for Gland Detection", they developed a new method that blends a statistical colour identification model with a neural network. In a pre-processing stage, colours at gland borders are recognized and enhanced. A neural network model based on Faster R-CNN is then trained to detect glands using these colour pixels as input.

A color detection technique is implemented using fuzzy logic and a predetermined dataset that has a table of colour names that are related. The image's colours are compared to the table, and the comparison is successful if the table finds values for the image's colours that match the desired colour to be detected by providing the colour name. In addition, there are three more functions: most dominant color identification, conversion of HSV and HSI color models, and 3D histogram visualization.

In [19], the authors suggested employing digital image processing to determine soil colour. The procedure is coded in MATLAB. The database was created using photos from Munsell soil charts. To separate the soil part from the backdrop of a given input picture, the HSV segmentation technique is utilized. Images are categorized using KNN and annotated with Munsell soil notation depending on their RGB values. The Munsell soil notation is used to obtain the result.

The authors in [20] suggested a method for identifying 2-D pictures utilizing colour thresholds and the RGB colour model to detect colours. The colours identified here are red, green, blue, magenta, cyan, and yellow. The provided 3-D colour image is transformed to a Grey-Scale image, then the two pictures are subtracted to produce a two-dimensional black and white image. Unwanted noise is eliminated from the image using median filtering. Digital pictures are tagged in the connected region after being detected using a linked component. The measure for each marking area is determined by the bounding box and its properties. The RGB value of each pixel is used to determine the shade of each picture element.

In [21], the authors proposed multi-scale fuzzy colour recognition and colour image segmentation. This work proposes a multi-scale fuzzy colour detection and picture segmentation technique based on the HSV colour space in a visual environment. The method in this study allows it to quickly distinguish image color by classifying a wide range of multi-scale fuzzy colours in a visual scene picture into the nine colour ranges' subspace. The image's multi-scale segmentation is completed by obtaining picture edge information using the recognized colour information. A significant number of detail components were slowly segmented after the multi-scale fuzzy operation, resulting in a relatively good segmentation result. The recognition and segmentation result of this algorithm avoids colour duplication and improves desired recognition performance and delayed image response time, enabling convenience for sequential environment knowledge, navigating, planning, and behavioural patterns, as well as a novel notion for obtaining rapid and expanded automatic environmental awareness based on colour and edge information.

Colour Face Recognition Using KNN Classification Algorithm and PCA was proposed by authors in [22]. The KNN algorithm is used to classify colour face photos. Initially, the classification was done using a k-NN classifier. Later, characteristics of colour face photographs are extracted and the image data is simplified using a combination of Principal Component Analysis (PCA) and the k-NN classifier. Different colour space models and k values are evaluated in the apps. HSV, YCbCr, RGB, and YIQ are the colour space models. Finally, the outcomes of the experiments are compared. According to the classification accuracies of KNN and classification accuracies of PCA and KNN in the two tables provided, increasing the k value lowers the classification accuracies. Furthermore, in certain cases, changing the k value has little effect on categorization accuracy.

In [23], the authors proposed the segmentation of colour images using Feedforward Neural Networks with FCM. For color pictures, they presented a hybrid image segmentation approach. They employed feedforward networks and FCM (Fuzzy C-Means). They provided two innovative approaches for identifying the number of clusters, comprising a method for determining the number of clusters based on co-occurrence and validation of clusters using a silhouette index. This will be very beneficial for clustering algorithms. The FCM clustering approach to the CIE L*a*b* colour reduction image is a standout element of their work. The feed forward network is trained using the Levenberg-Marquardt back-propagation approach with the labels obtained from FCM.

The authors in [24] suggested a method for picture segmentation based on k-means and a subtractive clustering algorithm. They used the k-clustering technique to segment a picture and to create the initial centroid used a subtractive cluster. The segmented image is improved with the median filter, while the original image is improved by partially contrast stretching. We may establish that the recommended clustering approach gives superior segmentation after comparing the final segmented output to the k-means clustering technique. The output photos are also customizable by changing the hyper sphere cluster radius, and we can deduce that by changing the hyper sphere cluster radius, we can get a range of results.

A colour pattern identification of multiclass fruits using a histogram-based feature selection method was proposed by authors in [25], they proposed using chi-square feature selection to create a colour pattern for multiclass fruit photos. The colour pattern is made up of a variety of intensity values from the R, G, and B channels of RGB photographs. In [26], the authros proposed a technique for raw arecanut categorization. Colour properties are used to classify objects. The raw arecanut is classified using colour moments and colour histograms, as well as the KNN method. To investigate the impact, this model employs a KNN classifier and four distance measurements. Using K closest neighbor with K value 3 and Euclidean distance metric for colour histogram characteristics, a result of 98.13% was obtained. Accuracy of 20% was achieved using a theoretical technique.

The authors in [27] published an article titled "An Image Processing Technique for Colour Detection and Distinguishing Patterns of Similar Colour: An Aid for Colour

Blind People". The suggested approach of determining a given image's colour and edges achieves the work's goal. LabVIEW IMAQ vision and vision aid are used as a development tool to determine the colour and edge of a colour picture. The entire work setting is determined to be low-cost, practicable, adaptable, and efficient.

In [28], the authors presented novel real-time colour identification capabilities for vision-based human–computer interaction, such as extracting fundamental colours. They worked on colour-based picture segmentation and vision-based color identification in order to solve these problems. Colour detection was proposed by using a statistical technique. It starts with picture capture and object boundary detection to separate it from the backdrop [7, 29]. The iterative procedure was used to acquire the binary values of various layers. A pixel-by-pixel Region of Interest (ROI) was employed to process the data. The threshold that aids in colour detection of an item is determined using a statistical technique. The threshold approach is applied to the ROI obtained, and the colour of the provided item is detected.

3 Methodology

3.1 Overall Framework

The major phases in the implementation of the colour detecting algorithm are depicted in Fig. 1.

Fig. 1. Framework of colour detection

Image Acquisition
Image acquisition is the process of capturing the photos that will be used in further processing. Because no processing can be done without a photo, this is the first step in the process. Various photos are gathered here. The images are unedited when they are taken.

Filtering
Noise is an essential factor to consider when processing digital images. Whenever a picture is taken, it is possible that it will be filled with noise in some way. When an image has noise, it appears irregular, rough, uneven, or white. As a result, we need to employ appropriate filters to remove noise from the image. For filtering purposes, the

median filter is utilized. It's a spatial nonlinear filter. For filtering, this filter employs a square window.

Segmentation

Image segmentation is commonly used to remove a portion of an image that has similar qualities or properties, or dividing an image into many segments with similar qualities or properties. There are several methods for segmenting a photograph. Techniques for segmentation include edge-based, clustering, region-based, and thresholding. The threshold approach of segmentation may be further broken down into other ways. The picture is initially transformed from RGB to HSV in this step. The hue component's upper and lower limits are then set. The image is returned to its original RGB colour space and presented after the hue is thresholded to see the results.

Classification

In image processing, machine learning techniques are becoming more popular. There are three types of machine learning techniques: Supervised, Unsupervised and Reinforcement. Supervised techniques use labeled inputs and outputs to train the algorithm. The system is educated using information that is neither categorized nor labeled in unsupervised learning. Reinforcement involves an agent capable of perceiving and interpreting its environment, acting on its findings, and learning through trial and error.

3.2 K-Nearest Neighbour (KNN)

K-Nearest Neighbor is a supervised machine learning algorithm (KNN) used to classify things. KNN is well-known for its speed and ease of usage. KNN compares the k most similar examples from an instance to find which class is the most common in the set (x). The instance class is assumed to be the one that appears the most frequently (x). In order to select the closest instance, the KNN system uses a distance metric. There are a variety of distance metrics that may be utilized, including Euclidean, which will be used in this research.

By comparing the test picture features to characteristics in the dataset, the Euclidean distance is determined. The identification rate is determined by the minimal distance between the test picture feature value and feature values contained in the dataset. The Euclidean distance is based on the following formula:

$$D = \sqrt{\sum_{i=1}^{n} (hist1_i - hist2_i)^2}$$

Pseudocode For KNN

1. Load the test and training data

  2. Determine the value of K.

  3. For each point in the test data, do the following:

  - Calculate the Euclidean distance between all of the training data points.

  - Create a list of Euclidean distances and sort it

  - Pick the top k points

  - depending on the majority of classes contained in the chosen points, assign a class to the test point

  4. End

3.3 RGB Colour Histogram

In image processing, an image's histogram is a histogram of pixel intensity values. The histogram is a graph that shows how many pixels are in a picture at each different intensity value. For an 8-bit grayscale image, there are 256 distinct intensities, so the histogram will graphically display 256 numbers that represent the distribution of pixels among those grayscale values. Colour pictures may also be histogrammed, either as separate red, green, and blue channel histograms, or as a three-dimensional histogram with the three axes indicating the red, blue, and green channels, with intensity at each point reflecting the pixel count. The actual outcome of the operation is decided by the implementation. It may be a picture in a suitable image format showing the required histogram, or it could be a data file providing the required histogram statistics in some fashion. Figure 2 displayed the RGB colour Histogram samples.

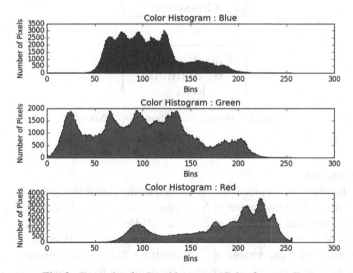

Fig. 2. Example of colour histogram (Color figure online)

Pseudocode for RGB Colour Histogram

1. Load the source image.
2. Separate the source image in its three R,G and B planes. For this we use the OpenCV function cv2.split().
3. Establish the number of bins.
4. Set the range of values (between 0 and 255).
5. Proceed to calculate the histogram by using the OpenCV function cv2.calcHist().
6. Create an image to display the histogram.
7. Display the histogram.

3.4 Colour Classification Using KNN

Colour classification is done by applying K-Nearest Neighbor algorithm. The general steps involved are stated in Fig. 3:

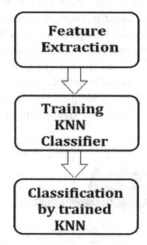

Fig. 3. Colour classification using KNN

Feature Extraction
The colour distribution of a picture is represented by the colour histogram. In the digital realm, the term "colour histogram" refers to the number of pixels in a picture that are made up of colours from a set of colour ranges divided by the image's colour space which is a collection of all conceivable colour values. An input image's RGB colour histogram can be obtained. The highest value of pixel count for RGB as an attribute is combined with the bin number of histogram to produce the dominant RGB values for constructing

feature vectors for training. Because the KNN classifier is a supervised learning system, the RGB values for each training image are acquired using colour histogram and labelled.

Training KNN Classifier
RGB colour Histogram measurements are used to train the KNN classification algorithm.

Classification by Trained KNN
A classifier is an algorithm that performs classification in a concrete execution. The term "classifier" refers to a mathematical function that plots supplied data into a group using a classification technique. The KNN method saves all of the cases it encountered, and fresh cases are classified using the similarity measure. The classification processes are shown in Fig. 4.

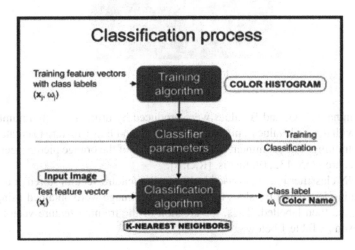

Fig. 4. Classification process

Pseudocode to Implement The KNN Classification
Given a new item:

1. Determine the distances between the new item and the rest of the objects.
2. Select a set of k lesser distances.
3. In these k distances, choose the most prevalent class.
4. That is the class in which the new item will be classified.

4   Implementation and Results

This paper focuses on colour detection using a KNN that has been trained using RGB colour histograms. Black, blue, green, orange, red, violet, white, and yellow are among the eight (8) colors it can identify. Colours are introduced in photographs on unsplash.com, and each colour includes numerous training data, which are utilized to construct datasets for all the colours. The data set may be enlarged to accommodate more operations. The application employs the KNN algorithm, which was developed using digital image processing technologies.

4.1 Feature Extraction

Here, we got the colour histogram of our test image by finding the peak pixel values for RGB in Fig. 5.

Fig. 5. Test image

The dominant R, G, and B values were produced by utilizing the bin number of a histogram with the peak value of pixel count for R, G, and B as a feature to create feature vectors for training. The prominent R, G, and B values of the orange picture seen above, for example, are [255, 132, 0], that is, [R,G,B].

The KNN classifier is a supervised learner using feature vectors stored in a csv file, the dominating R, G, and B values for each training image were obtained using Color Histogram and then labelled. Thus, the creation of the training feature vector dataset which is given in Table 1 below:

Table 1. Table listing the training feature vector dataset/ RGB Histogram values (bins)

Red	Yellow	Green	Orange	White	Black	Blue	Violet
139, 0, 0	255, 255, 0	159, 217, 140	252, 79, 19	249, 255, 241	9, 0, 0	3, 91, 188	127, 0, 255
204, 22, 0	255, 242, 39	125, 194, 75	255, 102, 0	253, 251, 251	28, 29, 33	0, 0, 254	111, 0, 255
206, 0, 25	249, 217, 94	37, 202, 38	255, 127, 0	242, 233, 228	27, 32, 35	0, 0, 255	82, 24, 250
220, 0, 3	252, 234, 4	0, 166, 82	255, 128, 0	242, 233, 228	36, 29, 33	1, 119, 193	63, 0, 255
254, 0, 0	255, 183, 9	64, 189, 85	255, 103, 0	250, 240, 230	0, 0, 0	0, 48, 143	138, 43, 226

(continued)

Table 1. (*continued*)

Red	Yellow	Green	Orange	White	Black	Blue	Violet
61, 13, 3	247, 224, 23	0, 128, 1	255, 122, 1	243, 239, 227	49, 54, 57	0, 0, 154	160, 32, 240
128, 24, 24	254, 242, 0	35, 67, 17	254, 101, 33	255, 237, 231	47, 47, 47		
174, 32, 26	246, 191, 39	123, 252, 1	255, 153, 0	229, 224, 221	40, 39, 45		
254, 0, 2	255, 215, 12	0, 255, 0	255, 103, 0	248, 249, 254	37, 37, 37		
209, 23, 23	255, 166, 0	33, 83, 54		238, 228, 220	10, 18, 13		
		125, 232, 88			28, 28, 28		

Training the KNN Classifier

The Classifier is trained using the RGB Colour Histogram measurements in the table above. It stores the training data in memory for future classification. To get k, we counted our classes which is the eight colours and to avoid getting a tie in the voting stage we make k odd, therefore k = 3.

Classification by Trained KNN

1. Obtaining training data is the first step.
2. Obtaining test image characteristics
3. Euclidean distance calculation
4. Obtaining the k closest neighbors.
5. Voting of neighbors.
6. Prediction of colour.

When the picture is loaded, the model reads it and then looks for training data. If the data for training is ready, it loads the classifier and if the training data is not ready, it creates a training data for the image. It then gets the detected colour and displays it.

The results of the model reveal that when the KNN algorithm is paired with digital image processing technology, it is possible to detect colours in pictures as shown in Fig. 6.

4.2 Comparison

In previous works, they were able to detect more colours but their accuracy was low especially for red, yellow and violet. Some also converted RGB images to HSV colour model to detect colours. In this work, RGB the default colour model of images was used and the accuracy of the above mentioned colours were improved.

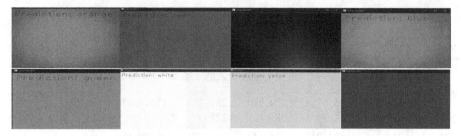

Fig. 6. Detected colors (Color figure online)

5 Conclusion

The findings imply that training data and K value are both important factors in determining accuracy, and that using more relevant training data might improve accuracy. Lighting and shadows are another crucial component; the photographs should be taken in appropriate lighting conditions. All eight colours were detected, so the aim of goals of this project was achieved. White has the highest possibility of being detected while violet has the lowest. Based on the findings of this study, Colour Detection in RGB Images can be enhanced by: (i) accounting for light intensity in the surroundings; (ii) the performance of this proposed methodology being compared to other techniques; (iii) conducting other studies using other Machine Learning algorithms or using Neural Networks; (iv) using a computer system with higher systems configurations in order to handle much larger datasets because training the model on a system with lower configurations takes longer time to accomplish, and (v) developing softwares that detects colour in images automatically.

References

1. Gonzalez, R.C., Woods, R.E., Eddins, S.L.: Morphological reconstruction. Digital image processing using MATLAB, MathWorks (2010)
2. Praveen, P.: Color detection using OpenCV Python. Medium, 17 July 2020. https://medium.com/programming-fever/color-detection-using-opencv-python-6eec8dcde8c7. Accessed 23 Nov 2021
3. Folorunso, S.O., Awotunde, J.B., Adeniyi, E.A., Abiodun, K.M., Ayo, F.E.: Heart disease classification using machine learning models. In: Misra, S., Oluranti, J., Damaševičius, R., Maskeliunas, R. (eds.) ICIIA 2021. CCIS, vol. 1547, pp. 35–49. Springer, Cham (2022). https://doi.org/10.1007/978-3-030-95630-1_3
4. Awotunde, J.B., Abiodun, K.M., Adeniyi, E.A., Folorunso, S.O., Jimoh, R.G.: A deep learning-based intrusion detection technique for a secured IoMT system. In: Misra, S., Oluranti, J., Damaševičius, R., Maskeliunas, R. (eds.) ICIIA 2021. CCIS, vol. 1547, pp. 50–62. Springer, Cham (2022). https://doi.org/10.1007/978-3-030-95630-1_4
5. Oladipo, I.D., AbdulRaheem, M., Awotunde, J.B., Bhoi, A.K., Adeniyi, E.A., Abiodun, M.K.: Machine learning and deep learning algorithms for smart cities: a start-of-the-art review. In: Nath Sur, S., Balas, V.E., Bhoi, A.K., Nayyar, A. (eds.) IoT and IoE Driven Smart Cities. EAI/Springer Innovations in Communication and Computing, pp. 143–162. Springer, Cham (2022). https://doi.org/10.1007/978-3-030-82715-1_7

6. Awotunde, J.B., Misra, S.: Feature extraction and artificial intelligence-based intrusion detection model for a secure internet of things networks. In: Misra, S., Arumugam, C. (eds.) Illumination of Artificial Intelligence in Cybersecurity and Forensics, vol. 109, pp. 21–44. Springer, Cham (2022). https://doi.org/10.1007/978-3-030-93453-8_2

7. Kar, S.K., Mohanty, M.N.: Statistical approach for color image detection. In: 2013 International Conference on Computer Communication and Informatics, pp. 1–4. IEEE, January 2013

8. Swain, M.J., Ballard, D.H.: Color indexing. Int. J. Comput. Vision 7(1), 11–32 (1991)

9. Sarraf, S.: Hair color classification in face recognition using machine learning algorithms. Am. Acad. Sci. Res. J. Eng. Technol. Sci. 26(3), 317–334 (2016)

10. Yousif, M.A., Awouda, A.A.: Design and implementation of colour detection technique using fuzzy logic. Int. J. Soc. Sci. Technol. (IJSSTR) 4(5), 46–58 (2019). ISSN: 2415-6566. http://www.ijsstr.com/data/frontImages/5._October_2019.pdf

11. Awotunde, J.B., et al.: An improved machine learnings diagnosis technique for COVID-19 pandemic using chest X-ray images. In: Florez, H., Pollo-Cattaneo, M.F. (eds.) ICAI 2021. CCIS, vol. 1455, pp. 319–330. Springer, Cham (2021). https://doi.org/10.1007/978-3-030-89654-6_23

12. Koehrsen, W.: Overfitting vs. Underfitting: A Complete Example. Medium (2021). https://towardsdatascience.com/overfitting-vs-underfitting-a-complete-example-d05dd7e19765. Accessed 23 Nov 2021

13. Kayhan, N., Fekri-Ershad, S.: Content based image retrieval based on weighted fusion of texture and color features derived from modified local binary patterns and local neighborhood difference patterns. Multimedia Tools Appl. 80(21–23), 32763–32790 (2021). https://doi.org/10.1007/s11042-021-11217-z

14. Pooja, K.S., Shreya, R.N., Sree Lakshmi, M., Yashika, B.C., Rekha, B.N.: Color recognition using K-nearest neighbors machine learning classification algorithm trained with color histogram features. Int. Res. J. Eng. Technol. (IRJET) 8(1), 1935–1937 (2017)

15. Raguraman, P., Meghana, A., Navya, Y., Karishma, S., Iswarya, S.: Color detection of RGB images using Python and OpenCV. Int. J. Sci. Res. Comput. Sci. Eng. Inf. Technol., 109–112 (2021). https://doi.org/10.32628/cseit217119

16. Yen, C.-H., Huang, P.-Y., Yang, P.-K.: An intelligent model for facial skin colour detection. Int. J. Opt. 2020, 1–8 (2020)

17. Bayraktar, R., Akgul, B.A., Bayram, K.S.: Colour recognition using colour histogram feature extraction and K-nearest neighbour classifier. New Trends Issues Proc. Adv. Pure Appl. Sci. (12), 08–14 (2020). https://doi.org/10.18844/gjpaas.v0i12.4981

18. Shu, J., Lei, J., Gao, Q., Zhang, Q.: Combing colour detection and neural networks for gland detection. In: Proceedings of the 2nd International Conference On Artificial Intelligence And Pattern Recognition - AIPR 2019 (2019). https://doi.org/10.1145/3357254.3357280

19. Maniyath, S., Hebbar, R., Akshatha, K.N., Architha, L.S., Subramoniam, S.: Soil color detection using KNN classifier. In: 2018 International Conference on Design Innovations for 3Cs Compute Communicate Control (ICDI3C) (2018). https://doi.org/10.1109/icdi3c.2018.00019

20. Sudharshan Duth, P., Mary Deepa, M.: Color detection in RGB-modeled images using MATLAB. Int. J. Eng. Technol. 7(2.31), 29 (2018). https://doi.org/10.14419/ijet.v7i2.31.13391

21. Liu, C., Wang, L.: Multi-scale fuzzy color recognition and segmentation of color image. In: 2016 12th International Conference on Natural Computation, Fuzzy Systems and Knowledge Discovery (ICNC-FSKD) (2016). https://doi.org/10.1109/fskd.2016.7603312

22. Eyupoglu, C.: Implementation of color face recognition using PCA and k-NN classifier. In: 2016 IEEE NW Russia Young Researchers in Electrical and Electronic Engineering Conference (EIConRusNW) (2016). https://doi.org/10.1109/eiconrusnw.2016.7448153

23. Arumugadevi, S., Seenivasagam, V.: Color image segmentation using feedforward neural networks with FCM. Int. J. Autom. Comput. **13**(5), 491–500 (2016). https://doi.org/10.1007/s11633-016-0975-5
24. Dhanachandra, N., Manglem, K., Chanu, Y.J.: Image segmentation using K-means clustering algorithm and subtractive clustering algorithm. Procedia Comput. Sci. **54**, 764–771 (2015)
25. Rachmawati, E., Khodra, M.L., Supriana, I.: Histogram based color pattern identification of multiclass fruit using feature selection. In: 2015 International Conference on Electrical Engineering and Informatics (ICEEI), pp. 43–48. IEEE, August 2015
26. Siddesha, S., Niranjan, S., Manjunath Aradhya, V.: Color features and KNN in classification of raw arecanut images. In: 2018 Second International Conference on Green Computing and Internet of Things (ICGCIOT) (2018). https://doi.org/10.1109/icgciot.2018.8753075
27. Navada, B.R., Santhosh, K.V., Prajwal, S., Shetty, H.B.: An image processing technique for color detection and distinguish patterns with similar color: an aid for color blind people. In: International Conference on Circuits, Communication, Control and Computing, MSRIT, Bangalore, India, pp. 333–336 (2014)
28. Senthamaraikannan, S.S., William, J.: Real time color recognition. Int. J. Innov. Res. Electr. Electron. Instrum. Control Eng. **2**(3), 1251–1253 (2014)
29. Velosa, F., Florez, H.: Edge solution with machine learning and open data to interpret signs for people with visual disability. In: ICAI Workshops, pp. 15–26. 2020

Neural Model-Based Similarity Prediction for Compounds with Unknown Structures

Eugenio Borzone[✉], Leandro Ezequiel Di Persia, and Matias Gerard

Research Institute for Signals, Systems and Computational Intelligence (sinc(i)),
FICH-UNL/CONICET, Ciudad Universitaria UNL, S3000 Santa Fe, Argentina
eborzone@sinc.unl.edu.ar
http://www.sinc.unl.edu.ar

Abstract. Compounds similarity analysis is widely used in many areas related to cheminformatics. Its calculation is straightforward when compounds structures are known. However, there are no methods to get similarity when this information is not available. Here we propose a novel approach to solve this problem. It generates compound representations from metabolic networks, and are use a neural network to predict similarity. The results show that generated embeddings preserve the neighborhood of the original metabolic graph, i.e. compounds participating into the same reactions are close together in the embedding space. Results for compounds with known structures show that the proposal allows to estimate the similarity with an error of less than 10%. In addition, a qualitative analysis of similarity shows that the prediction for compounds with unknown structure provides promising results using the generated embeddings.

Keywords: Neural networks · Molecular similarity · Embeddings

1 Introduction

Similarity evaluation is widely used in a wide range of applications and fields of research. Recommender systems [6,15], social networks [17], clustering algorithms [21], and so on take advantage of this. To evaluate similarities, numerical vectors summarize all the available information of the objects to be compared.

Molecular similarity [12,20] has been extensively used in cheminformatics and related areas such as medicinal chemistry and drug discovery. Its applications include property prediction [5], virtual screening [12], similarity searching [20], and the design of metabolic pathways through the use of compounds molecular structure to guide the search [11,14]. In practice, molecular descriptors called fingerprints are used to calculate the similarity between compounds. These fingerprints are created from the structures present in the compounds [7]. However, if molecular structure is not available, similarity calculation cannot be performed.

Embedding techniques are a family of methods able to represent objects and their components as numerical vectors. There are two well-known approaches

© The Author(s), under exclusive license to Springer Nature Switzerland AG 2022
H. Florez and H. Gomez (Eds.): ICAI 2022, CCIS 1643, pp. 75–87, 2022.
https://doi.org/10.1007/978-3-031-19647-8_6

for graph embeddings. One method is based on neural networks to generate embeddings. An example of this approach is the case of Structural Deep Network Embedding [19]. The other approach uses random walks to travel the graph and describe its components from this information. It builds a representation of each node by sampling its neighborhood through random walks, and combining information of the retrieved paths. This is the case of DeepWalk [13], and in particular Node2Vec [8], which is a modification of the previous one. It has hyperparameters to control the importance between a microscopic view around each node, and a more general view of the whole graph. Based on these ideas, if a metabolic pathway is modeled as a compound graph, its elements can be described as vertex embeddings according to the information of their neighborhoods. This, allow to represent compounds without needing their molecular structures, since compounds embeddings could be constructed directly from the graph structure.

Neural networks have demonstrated an incredible ability to predict physical and chemical properties [16] in several research fields. In a previous work [4], we successfully tested the ability of a Multi-Layer Perceptron (MLP) to predict the similarity between compounds with known structure. We now propose to extend this work by predicting similarity also for compounds with unknown structures, for witch traditional approaches cannot be applied. In fact, we have no knowledge of other methods that could be able to calculate similarity between compounds without having the molecular structures of both compounds.

This work is organized as follow. In Sect. 2, we describe the algorithm used to build embeddings, the neural model, and how the dataset was created. In Sect. 3 we present the experiments and their results. Finally, we present conclusions in Sect. 4.

2   Materials and Methods

This section presents the theoretical concepts and materials used in this work. First, we describe the embedding algorithm. Then, we show the neural model used and its components finally, we describe the process to build the dataset.

2.1   Embeddings Construction

In order to build the embeddings, the Node2Vec algorithm was used. This is a graph-based algorithm that generates embedding by condensing the neighborhood information of each node. It is a supervised method that combines two classical and opposite sampling strategies: Breadth-First Sampling (BFS), that restrict the neighborhood of each node to those which are immediate neighbors of the source one; and Depth-First Sampling (DFS) that takes the neighborhood from sequentially samples of nodes, increasing the distances from the source node. Node2Vec uses randomized walks to incorporate information from a smooth interpolation between BFS and DFS. The balance between both methods is controlled by these hyperparameters, and must be adjusted according to each specific application.

To generate embeddings, this method performs a number of random walks (*numwalk*) starting from each node of the graph. In each step, the information of the neighborhood is combined, and nodes that are taken into account for this process depend of the size of the window (*window*) considered. Given a source node, the algorithm chooses the next one based on hyperparameters p and q, witch control the probabilities to select a new node or to return to a previously selected node. Finally, the information collected from all steps (*lenwalk*) is used to generate an embedding of a specified size (*size*), by using an approach based on Word2Vec [8]. The algorithm has six important tunable hyperparameters that need to be optimized, in order to adequately characterize the compounds and calculate similarity between them.

2.2   Neural Model

To perform similarity prediction, a multilayer perceptron [9] (MLP) was trained. As shown in Fig. 1, input x corresponds to a couple of concatenated embeddings, one for each compound to be compared, and their similarity as a target output y, is the similarity between considered compounds. In this model, the activation function used in the hidden layers is the ReLU, defined as:

$$ReLU(x) = max(0, x),\tag{1}$$

where x is the linear output of each layer, and max is a function that takes two arguments and return the biggest one. The output layer uses the sigmoid function, defined as:

$$Sigmoid(x) = \frac{1}{1 + e^{-x}},\tag{2}$$

where x is the linear output of the layer. This function is used to scale the output of the model to values between 0 and 1. Dropout [18] was used as a regularizer with a unique probability p_d for all hidden layers.

We also explored a variable number of hidden layers. According to this description, the neural model has six tunable hyperparameters to be explored: the size of layers 1, 2 and 3; the dropout probability; the learning rate; and the batch size.

2.3   Dataset Construction

For this study, two datasets were prepared. Figure 2 shows how the dataset building process was carried out. The entire glycolysis metabolic pathway[1] was used. This pathway is composed of 52 reactions, involving a total of 60 compounds n, of which only 47 have known structure. Data were extracted from KEGG[2] (v95.2). For each compound, the molecular structure was downloaded in SMILES

---

[1] https://www.genome.jp/pathway/map00010.
[2] https://www.genome.jp/kegg/.

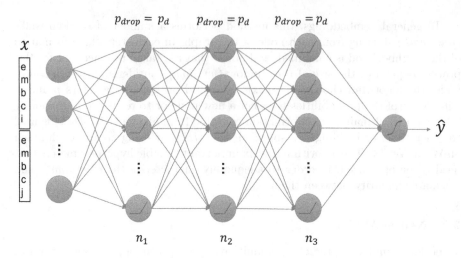

Fig. 1. Model architecture. embci and embcj corresponds to the concatenation of embeddings for compound i and j, respectively.

format, when available from PubChem[3] database. Through the RDKit[4] library was used to calculate MACC keys [7] fingerprints for all the compounds with know structure. Then, Tanimoto coefficient [1] was used to calculate similarity between compounds, according to:

$$T(\mathbf{c}_i, \mathbf{c}_j) = \frac{\sum_k (\mathbf{c}_i^k \wedge \mathbf{c}_j^k)}{\sum_k (\mathbf{c}_i^k \vee \mathbf{c}_j^k)} \tag{3}$$

where $\wedge$ and $\vee$ are the binary operators *and* and *or*, respectively, and $\mathbf{c}_i$ and $\mathbf{c}_j$ are binary representations of the structures of compounds i and j. The Tanimoto coefficient takes values in the range $[0, 1]$ and calculates the proportion of shared features between the two structures.

In total, 1081 patterns were defined resulting from the pairwise combinatorics of the 47 compounds with known structure. As shown in Fig. 3, each x input to the neural model results from the concatenation of embeddings for both compounds between which similarity is to be calculated.

3   Results

Creation of embeddings is not a trivial task; both, the algorithm for constructing embeddings from the graph and the neural model have several hyperparameters that must be tuned. Since the embedding algorithm involves six hyperparameters, and the neural network six more, the number of possible combinations to explore is too large. To avoid this, we split the search in two stages. The first

---

[3] https://pubchem.ncbi.nlm.nih.gov/.
[4] https://www.rdkit.org.

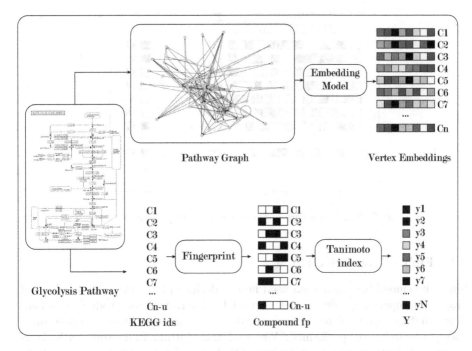

Fig. 2. Dataset pipeline. Where n is the total number of compounds in the Glycolysis pathway, u is the number of unknown structure compounds, and N is the pairwise combinatorics of the compounds with known structure $\frac{(n-u)!}{2!(n-u-2)!} = 1081$.

one was carried out to perform an exploration on the hyperparameters for the embedding algorithm. In order to determine if the embeddings were correctly capturing the information needed to characterize compounds, a neural network model with a manually defined set of hyperparameters was trained. The second step was the neural network hyperparameters exploration. It was also done in two steps. Initially, a grid search was performed using the best five embeddings previously found to calculate evaluate the performance. Then, the embeddings and the best hyperparameters found were keep fixed and the hidden layers number was explored.

Clearly, this two-step procedure allows an important reduction in the number of experiments to perform, specially if it is compared with the number required for a full grid search considering all the hyperparameters involved. Thus, although suboptimal configuration could be obtained, the number of experiments is reduced from hundreds of thousands to thousands.

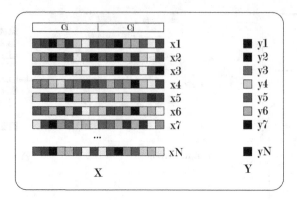

Fig. 3. Final structure of the dataset for the neural network.

3.1   Embeddings Selection

Since the embedding algorithm used here is designed to works with any kind of graph, appropriate hyperparameters must be determined for producing embeddings that can be used to correctly predict the Tanimoto index. To determine them, a search was performed. We used the Optuna framework with Tree-structured Parzen Estimator sampler[5] (TPE) [2,3]. A total of 2,500 combinations of hyperparameters were analyzed: hyperparameters q and p between 0.1 and 1 with a step of 0.1; embedding $size = \{47, 64, 128, 256\}$; $window$ sizes $= \{2, 5, 10, 15\}$; $numwalk$ between 100 and 500, with a step of 100, and $lenwalk$ between 5 and 20, with a step of 5 were explored. To determine the quality of each embedding, an MLP with architecture [2*$size$,145,20,1] was trained using cross-validation with 5 folds, and a validation portion of 10%. The Mean Square Error (MSE) was used as loss function. Table 1 shows the best five combinations of hyperparameters resulting from the search. The square root of MSE (RMSE) was included in the table since it has the same magnitude order as the Tanimoto index.

Table 1. Hyperparameter values corresponding to the five embeddings with lower cross-validation error.

q	p	$lenwalk$	$numwalk$	$size$	$window$	RMSE
1	**0.8**	**10**	**300**	**47**	**10**	**0.1124**
1	0.6	10	300	64	15	0.1125
0.8	0.4	10	300	64	2	0.1126
0.9	0.5	20	300	47	5	0.1131
0.9	0.2	15	300	128	5	0.1131

---

[5] https://optuna.readthedocs.io/en/stable/reference/generated/optuna.samplers.
TPESampler.html.

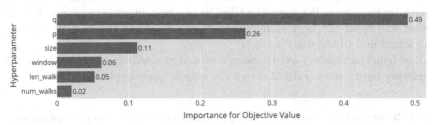

Fig. 4. Embedding algorithm hyperparameter importance analysis

The effect of the embedding algorithm's hyperparameters over similarity prediction was analyzed using FAnova [10]. Results of are presented in Fig. 4. As it can seen, the hyperparameter q is the most important in terms of influence on the model error, followed by the hyperparameter p.

3.2   Optimization of the Neural Architecture

In this section we seek to optimize the architecture of the neural network. Two MLP architectures were considered: one involving 3 hidden layers and another including 4 hidden layers. The experiments were carried out using 6000 training epochs, and 1000 epochs for early stopping. Cross-validation with 5 folds and a validation percentage of 10% was used. The model was implemented using Pytorch 1.9. Training was performed using Adam optimizer, and MSE as cost function.

Since there are multiple hyperparameters that can affect the performance of the model, two grid search were carried out. The first was done with the hyperparameters listed in Table 2. Furthermore, the five best embeddings from the previous experiment were taken as an additional search hyperparameter. Combinatorics performed between the hyperparameters of the Table 3 and each set of embedding. The second grid search was a fine tunning of the layers sizes with the best embedding, learning rate, and batch size found in the previous experiment.

Table 2. Hyperparameters explored during architecture optimization.

Hyperparamer	Range
Learning rate	$1 \cdot 10^{-5}$, $3 \cdot 10^{-4}$ and $1 \cdot 10^{-3}$
Batch size	10, 50 and 100
P dropout	0.2, 0.3 and 0.5
Layer 2 size	120, 145 and 180
Layer 3 size	20, 30 and 50
Layer 4 size	0, 10, 20, 80

As a result of the grid search, learning rate of $3 \cdot 10^{-4}$, batch size of 100, and dropout probability of 0.3 were identified as the best hyperparameters. We also selected and fixed the best embeddings, which provided the best predictions, being found in 4 of the top 5 models.

Once hyperparameters were chosen, a second grid search was carried out only considering layers sizes. Table 3 shows the search space explored.

Table 3. Range of values used in the grid search for hyperparameter exploration.

Hyperparamer	Range	Step
Layer 2 size	100–200	5
Layer 3 size	50–200	5
Layer 4 size	50–200	5

Table 4. Error obtained in the cross-validation for the selection of neural architecture hyperparameters.

Layer2	Layer3	Layer4	RMSE
195	**110**	**110**	**0.0928**
185	195	190	0.0932
200	200	150	0.0944
200	185	75	0.0950
185	105	190	0.0955

Table 4 shows the five best results of the grid search. The best model was obtained with the following hyperparameters set: learning rate of $5 \cdot 10^{-4}$, batch size of 100, dropout probability of 0.3, and [1] neurons in each layer respectively. The cross-validation $RMSE$ was 0.0928 and, the Pearson coefficient R^2 was 0.92 for the test set. These results indicate a good performance of our model, given that the average absolute error was 9.2%, and the distribution of real and predicted similarity values among compounds was similar. Figure 5 shows the real Tanimoto indices (targets) compared to those predicted by in the neural network one of the best folds. Additionally, trend lines were added for each partition set. We can observe that most of the points are located on the 45° line for all sets, indicating that our model performs good predictions. Futhermore, it can be seen that real and predicted Tanimoto values are similar.

3.3   Similarity Prediction in Compounds of Unknown Structure

The embedding method we used does not require the molecular structure of compounds, since it uses the metabolic graph structure to generate compound

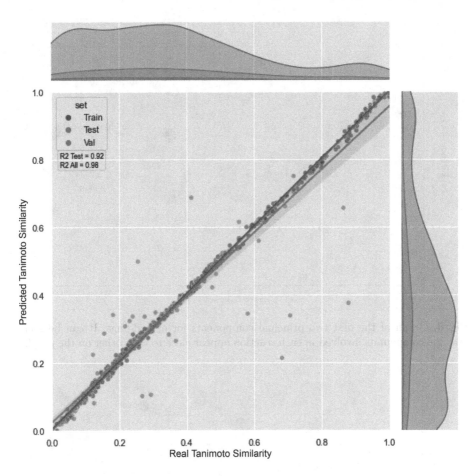

Fig. 5. Real vs predicted Tanimoto similarity are plotted above. R2 indicates to the square correlation coefficient of Pearson for the test set and for all the dataset, respectively. The training values are shown in blue, the test values in orange and the validation values in green. (Color figure online)

embeddings. That allow the embedding construction for all compounds, even those for which molecular structure is unknown. To evaluate the quality of the results, a principal component analysis (PCA) for the best embeddings was performed. Figure 6 shows the projection of the embeddings in the first 2 principal component directions. In particular, the compounds belonging to the reaction R03270: C05125 + C15972 ⟷ C16255 + C00068 are marked with green, and those belonging to the reaction R07618: C15973 + C00003 ⟷ C15972 + C00004 + C00080 with red. It can be seen how the compounds participating in each reaction are actually close to each other. This is most evident in reaction R03270.

Figure 7 shows the PCA in the area around the reaction R07618. Despite molecular structure of compounds C15972 and C15973 is clearly known, note

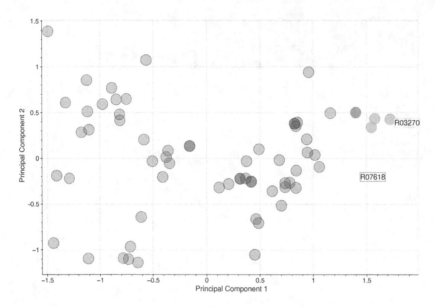

Fig. 6. Graph of the first two principal components for embeddings. It can be seen that the compounds involved in each reaction appear close to each other on the graph.

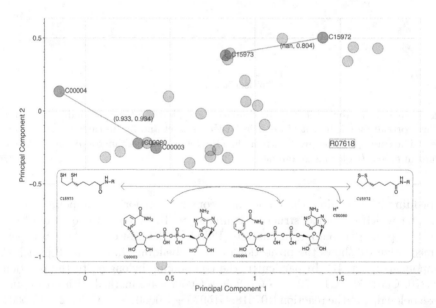

Fig. 7. Enlargement of a region of the figure around reaction R07618. A yellow line joins certain selected compounds to be compared. On the left are shown the target values and on the right the values predicted by the neural model. (Color figure online)

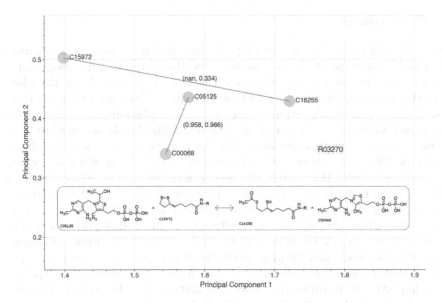

Fig. 8. Enlargement of a region of the figure around reaction R03270. A yellow line joins certain selected compounds to be compared. On the left are shown the target values and on the right the values predicted by the neural model. (Color figure online)

this includes generic substituent "-R" in both cases. In consequence, similarity can be only subjectively estimated since this information cannot be processed to build fingerprints. This situation does not affect our approach, since it uses embeddings learned from the graph topology of the metabolic network to represent compounds. As a result, predicted similarity (0.804) is in accordance wit visual analysis, since both compounds share a high proportion of their molecular structures. Furthermore, predicted similarity for compounds C00004 and C00003 is 0.934, that is in accordance with the real value (0.933).

Figure 8 shows an excerpt of the PCA projection, in the area around reaction R03270. This reaction involves the compounds C15972 and C16255 with no known structure. This reaction decomposes the substrates C05125 and C15972 into the products C16255 and C00068. As expected, the similarity between C05125 and C00068 shows high similarity (real: 0.958, predicted: 0.966) since they share a large part of their structures. On the other hand, predicted similarity for the C15972 and C16255 is 0.334, indicating that they do not share an important proportion of their structures. However, we can appreciate from structures in chemical equation that it is not correct. Examples like this indicate that more information needs to be incorporated into the model in order to get more accurate predictions for unknown structures.

4 Conclusions

This work addresses the problem of predicting similarity between compounds when molecular structure is not available. For this purpose, a metabolic pathway was modeled as a graph, where each node is a compound and the edges connect compounds that are substrates and products of the same chemical reaction. Using a general algorithm to generate node embeddings, descriptors for compounds were generated according to their neighborhoods and used to train a neural model to predict similarity. For the construction of the embeddings, a total of 2500 combinations of hyperparameters of the embedding algorithm were explored. From this search, the best 5 were selected to explore together with these the hyperparameters of the MLP through a grid search. Finally, the best set of embeddings and the hyperparameters that gave the best results were selected to explore the network architecture through another grid search. The results clearly shows that it is possible to predict similarity between compounds using neural networks and the proposed embedding strategy. Moreover, this approach allows to obtain an average error close to 10%. The proposal is expected to be improved by incorporating more information, in order to generate more robust descriptors to predict the similarity between compounds.

References

1. Bajusz, D., Rácz, A., Héberger, K.: Why is Tanimoto index an appropriate choice for fingerprint-based similarity calculations? J. Cheminformatics **7**(1), 1–13 (2015). https://doi.org/10.1186/s13321-015-0069-3
2. Bergstra, J., Bardenet, R., Bengio, Y., Kégl, B.: Algorithms for hyper-parameter optimization. In: Advances in Neural Information Processing Systems, vol. 24. Curran Associates, Inc. (2011)
3. Bergstra, J., Yamins, D., Cox, D.: Making a science of model search: hyperparameter optimization in hundreds of dimensions for vision architectures. In: Dasgupta, S., McAllester, D. (eds.) Proceedings of the 30th International Conference on Machine Learning. Proceedings of Machine Learning Research, vol. 28, pp. 115–123. PMLR, Atlanta, Georgia, USA, 17–19 June 2013
4. Eugenio, B., Gerard Matias, D.P.L.: Evaluación de un modelo neuronal para la estimación de similaridad entre compuestos a partir de representaciones one-hot. In: 52st JAIIO Jornadas Argentinas de Informática - ASAI (2022)
5. Brown, R.D., Martin, Y.C.: Use of structure-activity data to compare structure-based clustering methods and descriptors for use in compound selection (1996)
6. Covington, P., Adams, J., Sargin, E.: Deep neural networks for youtube recommendations. In: Proceedings of the 10th ACM Conference on Recommender Systems, pp. 191–198. ACM, Boston Massachusetts USA, September 2016. https://doi.org/10.1145/2959100.2959190
7. Durant, J.L., Leland, B.A., Henry, D.R., Nourse, J.G.: Reoptimization of MDL keys for use in drug discovery. J. Chem. Inf. Comput. Sci. **42**(6), 1273–1280 (2002). https://doi.org/10.1021/ci010132r
8. Grover, A., Leskovec, J.: node2vec: scalable feature learning for networks. In: Proceedings of the 22nd ACM SIGKDD International Conference on Knowledge Discovery and Data Mining, pp. 855–864. ACM, San Francisco California USA, August 2016. https://doi.org/10.1145/2939672.2939754

9. Haykin, S.: Neural Networks: a Comprehensive Foundation. Prentice Hall PTR, Hoboken (1994)

10. Hutter, F., Hoos, H., Leyton-Brown, K.: An efficient approach for assessing hyper-parameter importance. In: Xing, E.P., Jebara, T. (eds.) Proceedings of the 31st International Conference on Machine Learning. Proceedings of Machine Learning Research, vol. 32, pp. 754–762. PMLR, Bejing, China, 22–24 June 2014

11. McShan, D.C., Rao, S., Shah, I.: PathMiner: predicting metabolic pathways by heuristic search. Bioinformatics 19(13), 1692–1698 (2003)

12. Muegge, I., Mukherjee, P.: An overview of molecular fingerprint similarity search in virtual screening. Expert Opin. Drug Discov. 11, 137–148 (2016). https://doi.org/10.1517/17460441.2016.1117070

13. Perozzi, B., Al-Rfou, R., Skiena, S.: DeepWalk: online learning of social representations. In: Proceedings of the 20th ACM SIGKDD International Conference on Knowledge Discovery and Data Mining, pp. 701–710, August 2014. https://doi.org/10.1145/2623330.2623732, arXiv:1403.6652 [cs]

14. Rahman, S.A., Advani, P., Schunk, R., Schrader, R., Schomburg, D.: Metabolic pathway analysis web service (pathway hunter tool at CUBIC). Bioinformatics 21(7), 1189–1193 (2005)

15. Steck, H., Baltrunas, L., Elahi, E., Liang, D., Raimond, Y., Basilico, J.: Deep learning for recommender systems: a Netflix case study. AI Mag. 42(3), 7–18 (2021). https://doi.org/10.1609/aimag.v42i3.18140, number: 3

16. Thomsen, J.U., Meyer, B.: Pattern recognition of the 1H NMR spectra of sugar alditols using a neural network. J. Magn. Reson. (1969) 84(1), 212–217 (1989). https://doi.org/10.1016/0022-2364(89)90021-8

17. Tiwari, S.P.: Social media based recommender system for e- commerce platforms. Int. J. Res. Eng. Sci. (IJRES) 87–98 (2021)

18. Wager, S., Wang, S., Liang, P.S.: Dropout training as adaptive regularization, p. 9 (2013)

19. Wang, D., Cui, P., Zhu, W.: Structural deep network embedding. In: Proceedings of the 22nd ACM SIGKDD International Conference on Knowledge Discovery and Data Mining, KDD 2016, pp. 1225–1234. Association for Computing Machinery, New York (2016). https://doi.org/10.1145/2939672.2939753

20. Willett, P., Barnard, J.M., Downs, G.M.: Chemical similarity searching. J. Chem. Inf. Comput. Sci. 38, 983–996 (1998). https://doi.org/10.1021/ci9800211

21. Xie, J., Girshick, R., Farhadi, A.: Unsupervised deep embedding for clustering analysis. In: Balcan, M.F., Weinberger, K.Q. (eds.) Proceedings of The 33rd International Conference on Machine Learning. Proceedings of Machine Learning Research, vol. 48, pp. 478–487. PMLR, New York, 20–22 June 2016

Data Analysis

Classifying Incoming Customer Messages for an e-Commerce Site Using Supervised Learning

Misael Andrey Albañil Sánchez$^{(\boxtimes)}$ and Ixent Galpin

Facultad de Ciencias Naturales e Ingeniería, Universidad de Bogotá – Jorge Tadeo
Lozano, Bogotá, Colombia
{misaela.albanils,ixent}@utadeo.edu.co

Abstract. Throughout the world, the provision of online goods and services has increased significantly over the last few years. We consider the case of Tango Discos, a small company in Colombia that sells entertainment products through an e-commerce website and receives customer messages through various channels, including a webform, email, Facebook and Twitter. This dataset comprises 29,970 messages collected from 2019 to 2021. Each message can be categorized as being either being a *sale*, *request* or *complaint*. In this work we evaluate different supervised classification models to automate the task of classifying the messages, viz. decision trees, Naive Bayes, linear Support Vector Machines and logistic regression. As the data set is unbalanced, the different models are evaluated in combination with various data balancing approaches to obtain the best performance. In order to maximize revenue, the management is interested in prioritizing messages that may result in potential sales. As such, the best model for deployment is one that minimizes false positives in the *sales* category, so that these are processed in a timely fashion. As such, the best performing model is found to be the Linear Support Vector Machine using the Random Over Sampler balancing technique. This model is deployed in the cloud and exposed using a RESTful interface.

Keywords: E-commerce · Message classification · Supervised learning · Support vector machine · Balancing techniques

1 Introduccion

In Colombia there are approximately 307,679 micro-enterprises registered [5] that offer their products and services on the Internet. During 2020, according to the BlackSip report [3] online sales increased 113% over the previous year in this business sector. Although the volume of online transactions and sales in Colombia has been increasing year-on-year, 2020 represented the highest growth over last five preceding years (see Fig. 1). This trend has been further punctuated during the COVID-19 pandemic, during which many goods and services were made available online.

© The Author(s), under exclusive license to Springer Nature Switzerland AG 2022
H. Florez and H. Gomez (Eds.): ICAI 2022, CCIS 1643, pp. 91–105, 2022.
https://doi.org/10.1007/978-3-031-19647-8_7

Fig. 1. Growth of online retail of some Latin American countries 2017–2021 [3].

For this work we consider Tango Discos[1], a small company in Colombia, as a case study. This company has over 20 year's experience in the sale of entertainment products such as music discs, books and accessories for audio equipment. In 2019, they decided to open their online store to the public and offer their catalog of products through an e-commerce website. Subsequently, the ubiquity of social networks led to the opening of new channels of communication with customers. This, in turn, led to a substantial increase in incoming message traffic with requests, complaints or questions about the products. The high volume of requests has proved challenging due to the finite capacity of the customer service department. An important concern for the management was knowing that a significant percentage of incoming messages had the purpose of requesting information about products. Such interactions have a high probability of resulting in a subsequent sale. Due to inefficiency in the handling of incoming messages, there is concern that potential sales are being lost.

The main contribution of this paper is to evaluate various approaches to classifying client messages in an automated fashion. We use a dataset of incoming messages in Spanish from various sources provided by the company. Each free-text message in the data set is labelled to indicate whether it is a *sale*, *request*, or *complaint*. Classification models are trained using supervised techniques such as decision trees, Naive Bayes, linear Support Vector Machines (LSVMs) and logistic regression. These are couple with various techniques used to mitigate the fact that the data is unbalanced. Using confusion matrices, Receiver Operating Characteristic (ROC) curves, and metrics such as accuracy and recall, the best performing models are identified. The best performing model is subsequently deployed exposing a RESTful interface on a Heroku server, available for the business to use so that it may prioritize messages according to its requirements.

We broadly follow the well-established CRISP-DM methodology for data mining projects [17], and this is reflected in the paper structure. The *business understanding* phase is covered in this section, as well as Sect. 2, which presents related works with a brief survey of message classification approaches

---

[1] https://tangodiscos.com.co/.

used in various domains. The *data understanding* and *data preparation* phases are described in Sects. 3 and 4. Section 5 corresponds to the *modelling* phase, and presents the models and balancing techniques implemented, which are evaluated subsequently in Sect. 6 (*evaluation* phase). The *deployment* phase is presented in Sect. 7. Finally, Sect. 8 draws conclusions and proposes future work.

2 Related Work

One of the earliest works that address the issue of message classification is proposed by Busemann *et al.* [4], who present an approach to classify customer emails using various approaches including Naive Bayes and Support Vector Machines. The aim of the approach is to identify the client's issue thus partially automating the technical support process.

Considerable work in message classification addresses the issue of detecting spam emails. An early proposal is that of Duan [6] *et al.*, who describe a binary classification model to determine whether an email is spam, using a KNN classification algorithm. More recently, Alghoul *et al.* [2] address the issue of spam email classification using an artificial neural network. A comprehensive survey of machine learning approaches in this domain is given by Mansoor *et al.* [9]. Furthermore, Osho *et al.* [14] focus on compare various approaches for detecting phishing URLs.

The widespread use of social networks like a Twitter, Facebook and Instagram by teenagers has led to the phenomenon of *cyberbullying*. Menini [11] *et al.* propose a natural language processing (NLP) approach to allow the detection of different forms of abusive language by means of a classification model. Cyberbullying is also the focus of other proposals [15, 18].

In the e-commerce domain, which is the focus of our paper, the role of message classification has also been shown to be invaluable [1,10,13]. For example, work by Nkansah underlines how in Ghana, e-commerce is becoming an important sales channel for many companies. The work proposes an approach whereby users interact with other users and products. The result is a convenient, intuitive and contextually relevant e-shopping system that, based on user messages, identifies categories of products. This is complemented with a recommendation algorithm to provide customers with a personalized list of product recommendations available in the online store [13].

3 Integration of Data Sources

The dataset used in our case study contains 29,970 records (incoming messages) from different sources over a period of three years (March 2019 to December 2021). For each source, scripts were developed using different technologies to automate the extraction and loading of messages and corresponding metadata into a MySql[2] database, summarized in Fig. 2. The messages are loaded to the database from each source as follows:

---

[2] https://www.mysql.com/.

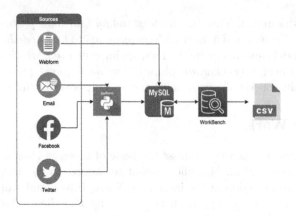

Fig. 2. Information sources diagram

- **Webform** The form on the e-commerce website[3]. This form is developed in PHP and interacts directly with the databas using SQL scripts.
- **Email** The company has a corporate email available to the public. A script was developed in Python 3.9 using version 0.1.2 of the imaplib library[4], and version 0.1.0 of the email[5] library, to extract the messages and send them to the database.
- **Facebook** The account on this social network has a chat for users to send messages. A script was developed in Python and working with Facebook Messenger Graph API[6] the messages are captured and sent it to the database.
- **Twitter** The account on this social network allows the company to receive tweets or mentions from their users. A script was developed in Python using version 1.7.1 of the tweepy[7] library to capture the tweets and send then to the database.

Table 1. Number of messages per source between 2019 to 2021.

Source	Percentage of messages	Message count
Webform	64	19,181
Email	15	4,496
Facebook	13	3,896
Twitter	8	2,398
Total	100	29,970

---

[3] https://tangodiscos.com.co/webform/contacto.
[4] https://pypi.org/project/secure-imaplib/.
[5] https://pypi.org/project/email/.
[6] https://developers.facebook.com/docs/graph-api.
[7] https://pypi.org/project/tweepy.

The figures presented in Table 1 show the number of messages received during the three-year period from the different sources. Once the message records were loaded to the database, the open source Workbench[8] software was used to connect to the MySql database and export the records to CSV format for further processing. The message records obtained have the following attributes:

- Id: Primary key generated automatically by the database;
- Source: Identifier of the message source;
- Submitted Time: Date and time the message was sent;
- IP address: IP address of the device from which the message is sent;
- Name and Last name: Name and surname of the sender of the message;
- Email: Email Contact of the sender;
- Phone: Telephone number of the sender;
- Comment: Message text;
- Type: Classification or label manually assigned by the customer service agent (either *sale*, *request*, *complaint* or *spam*).

4 Data Preparation

As an initial step, messages from the Trash category are filtered out, leading to the removal of 4,140 spam messages or those that had irrelevant information. The resulting data set has 25,830 messages, manually classified on three remaining labels (*Sale*, *Request* and *Complaint*). Table 2 shows the count of messages classified by each of those labels.

Table 2. Number of messages per label.

Labels	Messages count
Sales	15,400
Request	9,020
Complaints	1,410
Total	25,830

In this study, the message text is the focus of analysis. To extract the relevant information of each message, we apply the following steps, which are well-established in text-mining [8]:

1. *Tokenization* [16], whereby the text is split into words. For this, we use the Python spaCy[9] library.
2. *Cleaning*, whereby elements that do not contribute semantics of the message such as emoticons, hashtags, URLs etc. are removed.

---

[8] https://www.mysql.com/products/workbench/.
[9] https://spacy.io.

3. *Stop-word removal*, where words that do not provide much information are removed. Examples of such words include conjunctions or prepositions. The spaCy library provides us a dictionary of stop-words[10] in Spanish with a list of these words that can be filtered.
4. *Normalization* of the text [8], whereby the tokenizer recognizes words equivalent words, e.g., by ignoring capitalization (thus 'buy', 'Buy' y 'BUY' would be considered the same word).
5. *Lemmatization* [8], a process which obtains the root of a word according to its lexical component. For example, "buys", "would buy", "bought" would all map to to "buy". By applying lemmatization, it is possible to reduce the number of unique words (Fig. 3).

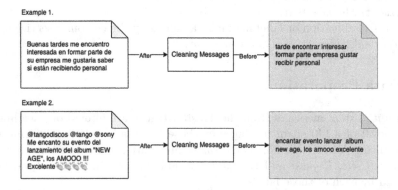

Fig. 3. Example application of the message cleaning workflow.

Table 3 presents an example of applying these five steps. After cleaning, the tokenized elements within a new list are shown in Table 3. Next, we proceed to the generation of the TF-IDF matrix. The TF-IDF matrix [8] is a technique used to quantify words within a document, this value is calculated for each word and represents the relevance in the document and overall corpus .

$$tfidf(t, d, D) = tf(t, d)idf(t, D) \qquad (1)$$

Table 4 presents a fragment of the obtained values of the TF-IDF matrix. Each value represents the weight of the word not only with respect to the vocabulary index and also considering all documents.

As previously noted in Table 2, the data is clearly unbalanced. If the classification methods are applied directly to the data set, the model is likely to favor the label with the greatest number of observations. To avoid this bias, we apply one of the following balancing techniques (at a time) over the dataset:

– *Ramdom Oversampler* [12], which involves randomly duplicating instances of the minority class and adding them to the training dataset.

---

[10] https://spacy.io/models/es.

Table 3. Example snippet list of words normalized by label

Sales	Requests	Complaints
Querer	Preguntar	Mirar
Comprar	Realizar	Desconfiar
Tener	Entregar	Atrazar
Pedir	Enviar	Necesitar
Informar	Estudiante	Consignar
Album	Manifestar	Pasar
Disco	Formar	Esperar
Producto	Ayudar	Concertar
Interesar	Aclarar	Hacer

Table 4. Matrix of TF-IDF matrix

Message ID	Sales	Requests	Complaints
840	0.158	0.154	0.170
841	0.167	0.123	0.393
842	0.112	0.021	0.235
843	0.331	0.154	0.152
844	0.124	0.238	0.136
845	0.245	0.275	0.086
846	0.331	0.188	0.241
847	0.016	0.473	0.247
848	0.231	0.148	0.108

- *Random Undersampler* [12], which conversely has the effect of reducing the number of instances in the majority class.
- *Smote*, a synthetic minority oversampling technique which analyzes minority samples and artificially synthesizes new samples based on minority samples, and adds them to the data set.
- *Nearmiss* [7], a undersampling technique whose objective is based on reducing the number of samples with the majority label. Its choice for the elimination of the instances employs the k-nearest neighbors approach .
- *Weight*, works as an equalizer between the different labels so that the classification model is as equitable as possible between them. For the present study, we use the Sci-kit Learn library[11] to calculate each label weight.

---

[11] https://scikit-learn.org/stable/index.html.

5 Modeling

In this section, we evaluate combinations of the balancing techniques described in the previous section with various models, namely:

- *Decision Tree Classifier*, one of the predictive modeling approaches that uses a decision tree to work on the observations on an item (represented in the branches) and obtain predictions about the target value of the item (represented in the leaves).
- *Naive Bayes*, a probabilistic machine learning model based on Bayes' theorem, where we can find the probability that A occurs, given that B has occurred. Here, B is the evidence and A is the hypothesis. The assumption made here is that the predictors/features are independent. That is, the presence of one particular feature doesn't affect the other. That is why it is referred to as naive.
- *Linear Support Vector Machine*, an algorithm that determines the best decision between vectors that belong to the same group (or category) and the vectors that do not belong to the same category. It can be applied to any type of vectors encoding any type of data. To take advantage of this classification method, messages must to be transformed into vectors.
- *Logistic Regression*, a type of statistical model is often used for classification and predictive analysis where the probability of an event occurring is estimated based on a given data set of independent variables. Since the result is a probability, the dependent variable is limited between 0 and 1. In logistic regression, a "logit" transformation is applied over the probability, that is, the probability of success divided by the probability of failure.

For each combination of classification model and balancing method, the following metrics are computed to evaluate performance:

- *ROC Curve*, the representation of the proportion of true positives (VPR = True Positives) versus the proportion of false positives (FPR = False Positives). Interpretation is based on comparison of the area under the curve (AUC) of the tests. This area has a value between 0.5 and 1, where 1 represents a perfect diagnostic value and 0.5 is a test without diagnostic discriminatory capacity.
- *Confusion matrix*, whereby each column of the matrix represents the number of predictions of each class, and each row represents the instances in the actual class.
- *Precision*, a metric which enables the quality of the machine learning model in classification process to be measured. In this case of study, it refers to the fact that precision is the answer to the question: ¿What percentage of messages were True Positives (VPR)?
- *Recall*, which calculates how many of the Actual Positives the model capture through labeling it as Positive (True Positive). Applying the same understanding, we know that Recall shall be the model metric we use to select our best model when there is a high cost associated with False Negatives.

- *F-Value*, or *F1-value* is used to combine the precision and recall measures into a single value, using the harmonic mean of these two values.
- *Accuracy*, measures the fraction of cases which are correct.

For the development of the analysis in this study, we use the Anaconda Navigator 2.1.4, Spyder 5.1.5 and Python 3.9.0. To perform the data balancing, we use the imbalanced-learn[12] library, which provides methods corresponding to each balancing technique presented at the end of Sect. 4. The classification models are implemented using the sklearn[13] library. In addition, we use the numpy and pandas libraries for data extraction and analysis, as well as matplotlib and scikitplot for result visualization. The Python code and anonymized version of the data set we use is available on GitHub[14]. As an illustrated example, we explain the steps carried out for the DecisionTreeClassifier and the data set balanced with the smote technique:

- The data set is obtained from the source file in CSV format, as shown in Fig. 2). Subsequently, data set is divided into training and test partitions using the train-test-split[15] library.
- After splitting the dataset, the next step involves feature engineering. The text messages will be converted into a count matrix of tokens (CountVectorizer), and then will be transformed into a count matrix in a normalized TF-IDF representation (TF-IDF transformer).
- The Smote balancing technique is implemented to obtain a balanced data set (see the result in Fig. 4).
- We use a function with the algorithm that implements the classification model on the balanced data set. This function is parameterized by balancing method.
- The classification model performance metrics are obtained and stored for later analysis (see precision, recall, F1-score in Table 5, and the ROC curve and confusion matrix in Fig. 5).

6   Evaluation

This section reports the results obtained for the combinations of classification model and balancing method. The accuracy and recall for each combination are shown in Tables 6 and 7. In Figs. 6 and 7, confusion matrices and ROC curves are shown respectively. Note that due to space constraints, we do not show the results for all combinations, only the ones that we deem to be most "interesting" or representative.

We observe that if the results are only evaluated by taking the accuracy criterion into account, the "best" combination would be the Linear Support Vector

[12] https://imbalanced-learn.org/stable/index.html.
[13] https://scikit-learn.org/stable/modules/classes.html.
[14] https://github.com/malbanil/MIAD-Classifying-Messages.git.
[15] https://scikit-learn.org/stable/modules/generated/sklearn.model_selection. train_test_split.html.

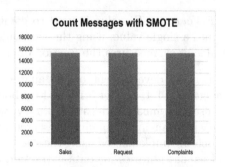

(a) Unbalanced data set.   (b) Balanced data set with Smote.

Fig. 4. Data set comparison before and after applying the Smote balancing technique.

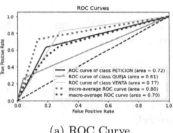
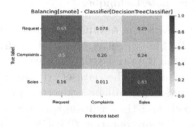

(a) ROC Curve.   (b) Confusion matrix.

Fig. 5. Graphs resulting from the process using the DecisionTreeClassifier classification model and the balanced data set with Smote.

Table 5. Results of the classification model over the test data.

-	Precision	Recall	F1-score	Support
Sales	0.58	0.49	0.53	278
Requests	0.16	0.29	0.20	38
Complaints	0.76	0.78	0.77	459
-	-	-	-	-
Accuracy	-	-	0.50	775
Macro avg	0.50	0.52	0.50	775
Weighted avg	0.67	0.65	0.66	775

Machine with no data balancing, as the accuracy value is the highest at 0.7896. However, taking into account the confusion matrix in the analysis (see Fig. 6(c)), we observe that this combination underperforms when classifying "Complaint" messages. Therefore, business requirements may deem it to be inadequate for deployment.

If we take as reference the confusion matrices (see Fig. 6(a)) and ROC curves (see Fig. 7(a)), we may conclude that the combination that best classifies the three labels is Naive Bayes with smote data balancing. This is reflected by the fact that the values of the confusion matrix diagonal are the highest and most balanced. Thus, if all three labels are deemed to be equally important according to business requirements, this would be the best combination for deployment.

However, if we consider the concern exposed in the business understanding phase, where those messages that correspond to sales are more important than other types of messages, the best combination for deployment would be the Linear Support Vector Machine classification model coupled with the Random Over Sampler data balancing technique (see Fig. 6(b)).

Table 6. Balancing technique vs. model accuracy

Balancing technique	Decision tree classifier	Naive Bayes	LSVM	Logistic regression
Unbalanced	0.74	0.78	**0.79**	0.76
Over sampler	0.66	0.74	0.79	0.76
Smote	0.71	0.75	0.77	0.77
R.UnderSampler	0.51	0.62	0.66	0.67
NearMiss	0.45	0.68	0.62	0.64
Weight	0.69	-	0.78	0.77

Table 7. Balancing technique vs. model recall

Balancing technique	Decision tree classifier	Naive Bayes	LSVM	Logistic regression
Unbalanced	0.51	0.52	0.54	0.57
Over sampler	0.52	**0.69**	0.67	0.57
Smote	0.57	**0.71**	0.62	**0.69**
R.UnderSampler	0.52	**0.69**	0.64	0.64
NewMiss	0.5	0.57	0.58	0.58
Weight	0.58	-	0.62	0.58

7 Deployment

For the deployment phase, the model exposes an interface via a REST API that has two input parameters, the message content and source, and returns the predicted message class:

- Input: `Message(String)`, `Source(String)`. Sender message and source of the message.
- Output: `Label(String)`. The classification label that the model predicts.

This solution is hosted in a Heroku cloud server instance, back-end framework with Python 3.1.9 and Flask 2.1[16] library to create a RESTful services, as shown in the implementation architecture in Fig. 8.

---

[16] https://flask.palletsprojects.com/en/2.1.x/.

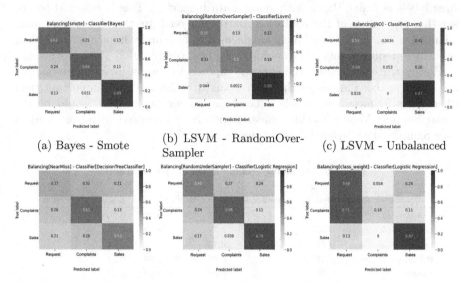

(a) Bayes - Smote

(b) LSVM - RandomOver-Sampler

(c) LSVM - Unbalanced

(d) DecisionTreeClassifier - Nearmiss

(e) Logistic Regression - RandomUnderSampler

(f) Logistic Regression - Weight

Fig. 6. Confusion matrix results graphs.

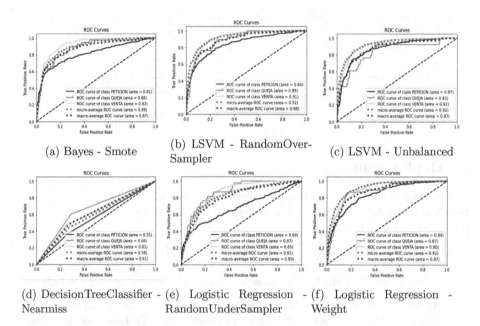

(a) Bayes - Smote

(b) LSVM - RandomOver-Sampler

(c) LSVM - Unbalanced

(d) DecisionTreeClassifier - Nearmiss

(e) Logistic Regression - RandomUnderSampler

(f) Logistic Regression - Weight

Fig. 7. ROC curve results graphs.

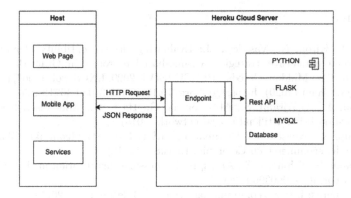

Fig. 8. Deployment implementation architecture.

8   Conclusions and Future Work

As this case study demonstrates, varying classification models alone, in some scenarios, is insufficient to obtain a good result. The data preparation and balancing techniques played an important part in improving model performance. Furthermore, in addition to the technical process, it was necessary to evaluate the results of applying different classification models in combination with balancing techniques. With this information, concepts from data analytics together with the business objectives were used to determine the best model. For example, if all message labels are deemed to be equally important, Naive Bayes with smote data balancing would be the selected model for deployment.

This work paves the way for future studies that seek to understand how e-commerce clients communicate with businesses to make requests, complaints or ask about products (which potentially result in sales). It is envisaged that this can facilitate the development of tools that enhance help desks or customer management services. Future work could usefully include: (1) Evaluation of the selected model with a naturally balanced data set; (2) The evaluation of other classification methods such as neural networks, genetic algorithms to compare their performance with the results obtained; (3) Incorporation of a sentiment analysis algorithm to improve classification accuracy; (4) Integrating message classification with a recommender system to give website visitors personalized product recommendations; (5) Integration of the message classification model into the call center work flow, by capturing voice messages, converting them to text so that inbound calls can be classified automatically; and finally (6) enabling support for multiple languages, including English.

References

1. Adaji, I., Kiron, N., Vassileva, J.: Evaluating the susceptibility of e-commerce shoppers to persuasive strategies. A game-based approach. In: Gram-Hansen, S.B., Jonasen, T.S., Midden, C. (eds.) PERSUASIVE 2020. LNCS, vol. 12064, pp. 58–72. Springer, Cham (2020). https://doi.org/10.1007/978-3-030-45712-9_5
2. Alghoul, A., Al Ajrami, S., Al Jarousha, G., Harb, G., Abu-Naser, S.S.: Email classification using artificial neural network (2018)
3. BlackSip, V., Nielsen, P., Credibanco, M.L., Rappi, B.: Icommkt: BlackIndex: reporte del ecommerce en Colombia. BlackSip (2019)
4. Busemann, S., Schmeier, S., Arens, R.G.: Message classification in the call center. arXiv preprint cs/0003060 (2000)
5. Confecamaras: https://confecamaras.org.co. (13 de Enero de 2022)
6. Duan, L., Li, A., Huang, L.: A new spam short message classification. In: 2009 First International Workshop on Education Technology and Computer Science, vol. 2, pp. 168–171. IEEE (2009)
7. Fang, W., Luo, H., Xu, S., Love, P.E., Lu, Z., Ye, C.: Automated text classification of near-misses from safety reports: An improved deep learning approach. Adv. Eng. Inform. 44, 101060 (2020)
8. Manning, C., Raghavan, P., Schütze, H.: Introduction to information retrieval. Nat. Lang. Eng. 16(1), 100–103 (2010)
9. Mansoor, R., Jayasinghe, N.D., Muslam, M.M.A.: A comprehensive review on email spam classification using machine learning algorithms. In: 2021 International Conference on Information Networking (ICOIN), pp. 327–332. IEEE (2021)
10. Masterov, D.V., Mayer, U.F., Tadelis, S.: Canary in the e-commerce coal mine: Detecting and predicting poor experiences using buyer-to-seller messages. In: Proceedings of the Sixteenth ACM Conference on Economics and Computation, pp. 81–93 (2015)
11. Menini, S., Moretti, G., Corazza, M., Cabrio, E., Tonelli, S., Villata, S.: A system to monitor cyberbullying based on message classification and social network analysis. In: Proceedings of the Third Workshop On Abusive Language Online, pp. 105–110 (2019)
12. Mohammed, R., Rawashdeh, J., Abdullah, M.: Machine learning with oversampling and under sampling techniques: overview study and experimental results. In: 2020 11th international conference on information and communication systems (ICICS), pp. 243–248. IEEE (2020)
13. Nkansah, E.A.: Kayayo: An e-commerce site with recommendations and text messaging (2013)
14. Osho, O., Oluyomi, A., Misra, S., Ahuja, R., Damasevicius, R., Maskeliunas, R.: Comparative evaluation of techniques for detection of phishing URLs. In: Florez, H., Leon, M., Diaz-Nafria, J.M., Belli, S. (eds.) ICAI 2019. CCIS, vol. 1051, pp. 385–394. Springer, Cham (2019). https://doi.org/10.1007/978-3-030-32475-9_28
15. Özel, S.A., Saraç, E., Akdemir, S., Aksu, H.: Detection of cyberbullying on social media messages in Turkish. In: 2017 International Conference on Computer Science and Engineering (UBMK), pp. 366–370. IEEE (2017)
16. Webster, J.J., Kit, C.: Tokenization as the initial phase in NLP. In: COLING 1992 volume 4: The 14th international conference on computational linguistics (1992)

17. Wirth, R., Hipp, J.: Crisp-dm: Towards a standard process model for data mining. In: Proceedings of the 4th International Conference on the Practical Applications of Knowledge Discovery and Data Mining, vol. 1, pp. 29–39. Manchester (2000)
18. Zois, D.S., Kapodistria, A., Yao, M., Chelmis, C.: Optimal online cyberbullying detection. In: 2018 IEEE International Conference on Acoustics, Speech and Signal Processing (ICASSP), pp. 2017–2021. IEEE (2018)

Comparison of Machine Learning Models for Predicting Rainfall in Tropical Regions: The Colombian Case

Carlos Andres Rocha-Ruiz[✉], Ixent Galpin[ORCID], and Olmer García-Bedoya[ORCID]

Universidad de Bogota Jorge Tadeo Lozano, Bogotá, Colombia
{carlosa.rochar,ixent.galpin,olmer.garciab}@utadeo.edu.co

Abstract. In this work, we compare various machine learning models for weather forecasting in tropical regions. We take the Colombian case as an example, using a dataset with monthly rainfall levels obtained from the Institute of Hydrology, Meteorology and Environmental Studies (IDEAM) from 1980 to 2018 for each meteorological station installed in the country. We identify six kinds of time series according to results of an augmented Dickey-Fuller test and evaluate seven machine learning models. Overall, we find that the decision trees, long short-term memory, random forest, and support vector machine models perform best. However, our main finding is that the best performing model depends on the category of time series that a particular weather station is associated with. We envisage that this segmentation proposed in this paper for weather forecasting in tropical regions may be beneficial for the deployment of instruments that mitigate against agricultural production loss risk caused by the weather.

Keywords: Machine learning · Time series forecasting · Weather · Rainfall · Tropics

1 Introduction

The ability to make accurate climate predictions is of paramount importance for economies in transition, where agricultural production is a historically important sector [9]. While agricultural production largely depends on the natural resources present in the area, climate also has a huge impact on the success or failure of a crop harvest. Farmers often have to contend with a high degree of uncertainty, often compounded by the unpredictability of climate change. A higher or lower than expected increase in rainfall can have a negative impact and lead to a loss of production. As such, predictions of future rainfall levels are likely to be useful for a farmer, as these may inform his or her decision about whether to produce (or not) a certain agricultural product. Indeed, such information may lead a farmer to grow more resilient crops in face of climate adversity. It can include hydroponic crops like is presented in [7].

H. Florez and H. Gomez (Eds.): ICAI 2022, CCIS 1643, pp. 106–120, 2022.
https://doi.org/10.1007/978-3-031-19647-8_8

Tropical regions, that is, regions that are around the Equator, have the peculiarity of not having established and differentiated seasons as in temperate regions of the world. However, precipitation levels in tropical regions typically have a seasonal component in the year that reveals trends in rainfall levels. In this study, we obtain a dataset comprising monthly rainfall levels reported by 2,091 meteorological stations installed throughout Colombia, for the period 1980 to 2018. This level of temporal granularity enables a medium and long-term vision to be obtained, in which it is possible to predict, on average, what the level of rainfall is going to be at a certain point a time. Subsequently, we propose and evaluate various machine learning models that enable year per year predictions of rainfall levels to be provided for tropical regions, taking Colombia as a case study. In this way, it is possible to obtain a medium and long-term vision of the potential that the implementation of these models has in this sector.

We note that existing models used to predict rainfall levels involve a high degree of use of computational resources [12]. This limits the possibility of deploying such models in low-income areas (which typically rely on agricultural production as the main economic driver). For example, the Weather Research and Forecast (WRF) model has been widely used to predict the trajectory of hurricanes to take preventive measures against natural disasters [10]. However, in central and tropical regions, far from the coasts where these phenomena do not occur, climate prediction has been shown to be less accurate [19]. Consequently, the implementation of a machine learning model for climate prediction may be a low-cost tool with high accuracy.

This would benefit small local agricultural producers who do not have access to sophisticated weather prediction systems. As well as being beneficial for agricultural producers directly, the development of models that allow a medium- or long-term vision with regards to level of rainfall may also inform the design of financial instruments that contend with risk (such as insurance for agricultural production), or other protection mechanisms that may assist farmers in the event of sudden or unexpected increases or decreases in rainfall levels.

A total of six types of time series were identified, according to the Dickey-Fuller tests, in which most of the information focuses on random walks without drift and trend and stationery without unit root. Within the first group, about 73% of the data are found, so that emphasis was placed on this group, making forecasts of a subsample of four series within this group based on a model trained with a fifth series. This is done to determine a degree of generalization between the trained models and the series belonging to said group.

The article is structured as follows: Sect. 2 presents a literature review in which related work is presented. Sections 3, 4 and 5 broadly correspond to steps in the CRISP-DM methodology widely used in data mining projects [21]: In Sect. 3, we describe the dataset used. Section 4 presents the data preparation steps required for the machine learning model training. In Sect. 5, the model evaluation is presented. In Sect. 6, a discussion is provided. Finally, Sect. 7 concludes.

2   Literature Review

Numerous machine learning algorithms and models have been developed in recent times. Additionally, different metrics have been developed in parallel for the comparison of different models to quantify the status and prioritization of different factors that each model has. On the one hand, the existing balance between variance and bias within the models means that, at first, the comparison of different models focuses on prioritizing one factor, but sacrificing another [13]. This means that each model has different nuances on the one hand, that it has some strengths, but in turn, it has some weaknesses on the other hand.

For the prediction of climate there are various methodologies and approaches by which it has been developed [2]. However, the method used from the WRF methodology is the most developed methodology and for which much research has been done. Studies such as a comparison in the performance of WRF models in tropical cyclone simulation in India [14], another study uses WRF models in the prediction of temperature in the western United States [4]. However, it requires a high computational cost [17]. This model is based on the physical modeling of a process in which there are different initial conditions that determine the system, and from the physical laws that intervene in the process, the path by which the physical system behaves is simulated [17].

The implementation of machine learning models and statistical learning have also been implemented for the prediction of the weather [1,8]. However, there is less development in the implementation of these methodologies for tropical areas such as Colombia. Similarly, the comparison between these models has not been explored in as great depth. On the other hand, the analysis of climate prediction has focused on multivariate models of spatially distributed time series [20].

The implementation of stochastic models for the prediction of the climate has been based on the modeling and simulation of this process based on the probabilities of occurrence, as is the case with Markov Chains [16]. However, the comparison of the models for the prediction of the climate has not had a great development within the field. On the other hand, there have been different comparison studies between algorithms and models that allow, through different metrics, to find the algorithm with the greatest general benefit. In the same way, there are different studies which compare the models themselves within a classification of old and new models [3] in which they compare the algorithms within a balance between accuracy and training time.

First, it should be noted that there has been majority of development for forecast of rainfall on seasonal regions and not in tropical regions. Similarly, most studies focus on physical techniques and mathematical models to forecast weather [8].

Various studies develop weather prediction methodologies around variables such as rainfall, temperature, and wind speed, among others. These studies can be divided into two large groups, the first is the use of climate simulation models [12,14,22], away from the machine learning approach, and the second are models based on statistics that are they can in turn divide into two groups. One of statistical stochastic simulation models (such as Markov chains) [3] and another in the implementation of supervised models such as Long short-term memory (LSTM), linear regression, support vector machines (SVMs), among others [15].

Within the approaches explored for the prediction of the level of rainfall, there are results of relatively simple models of linear regression and functional regression that seek the forecast of the climate based on the level of rainfall and temperature, obtaining forecasting difficulties in the short term, but with strengths in the medium and long term [19]. For its part, another approach, in which a SVM model is compared against a multilayer perceptron, finding better results in the SVM, using rainfall and temperature as climatic variables [15]. Likewise, other approaches oriented to the use of LSTM and CovLSTM models for the prediction of precipitation prediction, found that there is a superiority in the CovLSTM models compared to the other Deep Learning models implemented in the study [18].

On the other hand, *Galanis et al.* [6,11], propose a climate forecast methodology based on the implementation of a Kalman filter with the use of non-linear functions and make a numerical simulation of the climate, in which takes variables such as temperature and wind speed. On the other hand, [17] and [3], propose a methodology based on stochastic Markov chain processes, in which they use variables such as solar radiation or wind speed to make estimates of the climate.

Within the framework in which the aforementioned previous studies have been developed, they share that they are studies in which the regions where it is attempted to forecast climatic variables are non-tropical regions, with seasons. This makes a substantial difference given that the seasonality of the climate (as happens in the northern or southern hemisphere of the planet), gives relative stability in terms of rainfall levels, temperature, or any climatic behavior. For its part, despite continuing to have a relatively predictable behavior, rainfall levels in tropical regions tend to be more diverse and unpredictable.

An attempt to forecast the climate in tropical regions is the implementation of the ETA model, which consists of a deterministic model in which physical relationships are used in such a way that the climate is predicted from its location [4]. However, machine learning models have not been widely used for predicting climatic variables within a tropical region.

3   Data Understanding

For the prediction of the climate, the levels of rainfall reported by the meteorological stations installed throughout Colombia are considered (shown in Fig. 1). This information is collected by the Institute of Hydrology, Meteorology and Environmental Studies (IDEAM)[1], the Colombian government entity responsible for managing scientific, hydrological, meteorological, and environmental information in the country.

The variable considered in this study collected by the meteorological stations is the amount of liquid water rain particles with a diameter greater than 0.5 mm,

---

[1]   http://www.ideam.gov.co/.

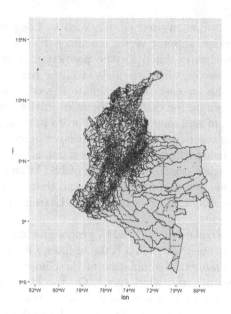

Fig. 1. Distribution map of meteorological stations in Colombia, Source: IDEAM

measured in millimeters per square meter in the measurement area. This information is available as a monthly average reported by the station. In addition, the installed meteorological stations collect the average temperature reported in the sector monthly.

Likewise, in a country like Colombia, whose economy has had historical importance in agriculture, a significant part of the population is dependent on the primary sector of the economy [9]. Given that this sector has a close relationship with the exogenous factors, such as the climate, the level of rainfall is decisive in the type of agricultural production and the way in which it is produced. For this reason, it is beneficial for this sector to have tools that allow knowing the medium and long-term trend in the levels of rainfall in the regions where the different agricultural products of the country are produced. Within this framework, the decisions made about whether to produce a particular product, insure it or have a long-term vision regarding its production are closely related to the behavior of the climate and specifically to the levels of rainfall.

3.1 Descriptive Statistics

Given the information reported by IDEAM, Fig. 2 shows the level of rainfall per square meter and the annual average until 2018 of all meteorological stations installed in Colombia. The increasing trend of the level of rainfall from year to year in is clear through the confidence bands.

On the other hand, Fig. 3 shows how the average level of rainfall in each month for all years in all meteorological stations installed in Colombia. This

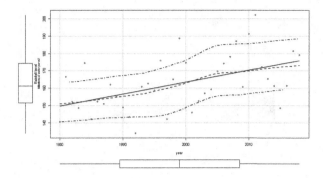

Fig. 2. Rainfall level per year

graph shows, on average, which are the months with the highest level of rainfall, in such a way that it allows to identify the annual cycle in the rainfall levels.

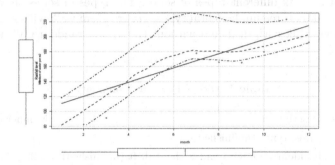

Fig. 3. Monthly rainfall level for period 1980–2018

The trend in the year is to start with relatively dry months and end with high levels of rainfall. However, the increase in the level of rainfall is constant until June to August, when the level of rainfall reaches its maximum in the year, and then shows a slight decrease in the level of rainfall.

Finally, Fig. 4 shows the relationship between the monthly rainfall level reported by the meteorological stations and the altitude at which it is installed. Colombia has a varied geography, so the different climates that the different regions of Colombia can present can be very varied. For this reason, height can be a factor of fixed effects that affect changes in rainfall levels for each region. In general, the meteorological stations present rainfall levels with a greater dispersion at the lowest points and less dispersion at the highest points.

Due to the high number of meteorological stations, a time series classification was carried out to identify the presence of unit roots and determine whether the series correspond to 1) a random walk with drift, 2) a random walk without drift, or 3) a random walk with drift and trend. This was achieved by employing

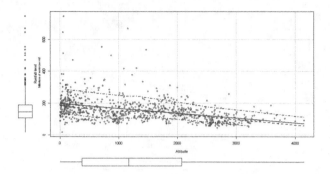

Fig. 4. Altitude vs. Rainfall level for the period 1980–2018

augmented Dickey-Fuller test [5], a statistical test that determines the presence of a unit root for the cases mentioned above, where the null hypothesis is the presence of a unit root. Table 1 shows the results of the tests, in which the series are grouped into six different types of series. The types of series shown in the table are based on three fundamental types, *viz.*, random walk without drift and trend, random walk with drift and without trend, and random walk with drift and trend.

Table 1. Dickey-Fuller test summary

Series type	Description	Number of series
1	Three types (unfinished)	15
2	Random walk with and without drift (unfinished)	25
3	Random walk with and without trend (unfinished)	22
4	Random walk without drift and trend	1547
5	Random drift and trending walk	4
6	None	478

Most of the series in Table 1 are Type 4, which correspond to series with a random walk without drift and trend and series without unit root. Additionally, 478 series are deemed to be series with a random walk, drift or trend (Type 6). Furthermore, the first three categories in Table 1 comprise 62 series that yield ambiguous results regarding the type of series. In the first case (unfinished with the three types of series) they seem like series that have both components. However, this may be given that the trend component may or may not be present in different time periods. The second case (unfinished in drift) has ambiguous results since both tests refer to opposite series. In the third case (unfinished in drift) it is ambiguous in terms of drift but not in the trend of the series.

4   Methodology

Different machine learning techniques for weather forecasting were proposed. Said information is collected as time series. Time series and supervised learning methodologies were proposed for the prognosis of the series. However, for the development of supervised learning models, the input and output information explained above are required. However, by the nature of the time series, it is historical information in which the input data are the same as the output data over time. For this reason, for the implementation of supervised learning models, it is necessary to carry out a transformation to the data that allows its implementation in such a way.

4.1   The Model

Time series are defined as collected data that meet an order (over time) at regular intervals (daily, monthly, yearly, etc.). These data are recorded in a periodic and discrete manner such that $x = x_t, x_{t-1}, x_{t-2}, \ldots, x_1, x_0$. a time series is made up of a T $\times$ 1 vector.

For the implementation of a supervised learning model, a transformation is required in such a way that the time series is represented in a $n * k$ matrix in input data with a $k * 1$ vector of output data. For this reason, the organization of the proposed time series is made up of a $n * k$ matrix where each column k corresponds to the time series a period lagged to the next column of the matrix. To do this, it is necessary to define the dimensions n of the matrix where the number of columns corresponds to the number of lags defined in a sliding window row by row. That said, the input data matrix corresponds to the time series where each column is the vector of the time series and each row is the rolling window of the predefined number of lags. The matrix corresponds to the following shape given of twelve lags in the rolling window.

$$
\begin{bmatrix}
x_0 & x_1 & x_2 & \cdots & x_{12} \\
x_1 & x_2 & x_3 & \cdots & x_{13} \\
x_2 & x_3 & x_4 & \cdots & x_{14} \\
\vdots & \vdots & \vdots & \ddots & \vdots \\
x_{t-12} & x_{t-11} & x_{t-10} & \cdots & x_{t-1} \\
x_{t-11} & x_{t-10} & x_{t-9} & \cdots & x_t
\end{bmatrix}
\tag{1}
$$

With the structure of the data matrix, 12 lags were chosen because the natural period of the data corresponds to 12 months (since a year corresponds to 12 months). Having said matrix constructed, the vector corresponding to column 12 was taken as output data in such a way that the data of the matrix $11 * k$ correspond to the input data and the vector $n * 1$ correspond to the output data such that:

$$\begin{bmatrix} x_0 & x_1 & x_2 & \cdots & x_{11} \\ x_1 & x_2 & x_3 & \cdots & x_{12} \\ x_2 & x_3 & x_4 & \cdots & x_{13} \\ \vdots & \vdots & \vdots & \ddots & \vdots \\ x_{t-13} & x_{t-12} & x_{t-11} & \cdots & x_{t-2} \\ x_{t-12} & x_{t-11} & x_{t-10} & \cdots & x_{t-1} \end{bmatrix} \Rightarrow \begin{bmatrix} x_{12} \\ x_{13} \\ x_{14} \\ \vdots \\ x_{t-1} \\ x_t \end{bmatrix} \tag{2}$$

Given the previous data structure, the implementation can implement different supervised learning models adapted to the time series forecasting problem with the transformations that this requires. That said, the implementation of a supervised learning model with the previous data structure requires the tuning of the hyperparameters that make up each model.

On the other hand, the time series with a monthly frequency of information present a high amount of variance that hinders the efficient implementation of a predictive model. For this reason, each time series is decomposed into each of its seasonal, trend and noise elements. The seasonal components of the series refer to the frequent component of the series that repeats itself in a predictable period. In them it is found that there are months in which the rains increase their level and are due to seasonal climatic factors but not to endogenous factors of a trend increase in the level of rainfall. Likewise, the trend component refers to the long-term trend in which a medium or long-term increase (or decrease) is established in the level of rainfall independent of the predictable level of rainfall of the seasonal component. Figure 5 shows the decomposition of the series in question.

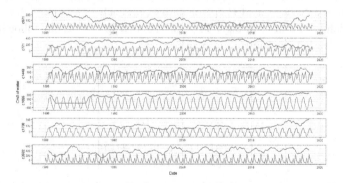

Fig. 5. Decomposition of the time series sample

Based on the above, the trend component of the time series is used to implement the proposed models since, by isolating the components and separating the random component from the noise to the original series, the statistical gain in the confidence of the forecasts of the time series, in addition to allowing the classification of the series according to its allied components.

5 Model Evaluation

In the approach to the supervised models and the time series model, the results obtained are presented within the framework of the six types of time series found according to the statistical tests described in Sect. 3. In such a way that the comparison of the models was made according to the same series under the same conditions that, based on a common metric, the ability of each one to forecast new values is evaluated and thus also evaluate its ideal forecast horizon.

Within the time horizon for the validation of the models, two forecasting approaches were considered, in which each model presents a particular performance. Within the two approaches, there is 1) a one-step forecast, in which the model is evaluated with real data and the forecast of the immediately subsequent value is compared, and 2) a recursive forecast in which forecasts greater than a higher window a 1, correspond to the prediction of the model based on previous forecasts.

The first approach establishes, for its part, that the value corresponding to each predicted month is established with real data and, therefore, the accumulation of the error from a period far from the last training period corresponds to the nature of the problem itself, that is, for the variable effects of each meteorological station. However, the forecast horizon established does not exceed the one immediately after and limits decision-making in a long- or medium-term period.

For its part, the second approach, the forecast horizon for the calculation of new values can exceed the immediately subsequent period, in such a way that, based on the current data, a forecast horizon is established and those values higher than the immediately higher period. The predicted values are going to use as input, previous predicted values. This implies that, as the forecast horizon moves away from the latest available real data, these forecasts will accumulate an error, corresponding to the sum of errors of the forecasts of previous periods. However, to find medium or long-term trends, this accumulation of error is inevitable.

Table 2 shows the results of the normalized mean square error (RMSE) in which, for each station in the sample, the results of the best model are relative to the type of sample. This means that, for each of the series presented, the model varies and there is no consistency between the models that can be used for all the series. The foregoing may mean that the universal development of a single machine learning model, which allows forecasting the weather for all places where weather stations are located.

Therefore, the dependence of each location on the type of model may be the reason why scaling a model to forecast rainfall levels in all regions requires a prior analysis of each series. However, according to the previous results, the classification of the series on all the meteorological stations in Colombia allows giving a type of generalization that can establish a general rule for its forecast. Among the results obtained, the Decision Trees, LSTM, Random Forest (RF) and Vector Support Machines (SVM) models are the best models within the analysis. For their part, the KNN, Linear and XGBoost models are models where they do not have the slightest error for any case.

It should be noted that the SVM model is the one that turns out to be the best model in 3 of 6 series, which implies that this model may have the potential to be a model that allows a forecast in a significant percentage of the time series.

Table 2. Mean squared error normalized by model and weather station

Stations	Decision tree	KNN	Linear	LSTM	RF	SVM	XGBoost
c1738	**0.1186**	0.1957	0.1284	0.1298	0.1461	01463	0.1351
c1655	0.1551	0.1387	0.1324	0.1462	0.1389	**0.1139**	0.1747
c771	0.0931	0.2218	0.1388	0.2229	0.1338	**0.0917**	0.0980
c2032	0.1442	0.1421	0.1509	**0.1330**	0.1382	0.1528	0.1388
c671	0.1459	0.1506	0.1386	0.1381	**0.1330**	0.1491	0.1447
c1448	0.1747	0.1570	0.1206	0.2303	0.1120	**0.0765**	0.1288

Similarly, the results obtained from the best model for each series are shown in Fig. 5. In general terms, the models fail to capture those periods where there is a sudden increase in rainfall levels, in such a way that the periods of unexpected rains are periods with great difficulties to forecast. The models presented show that they forecast a trend in the medium and long term, since the forecasts are centered around the mean of the period in which it is located.

Likewise, depending on the series, the model has a higher error than the other series. This is mainly due to the unusual number of unexpected increases (or decreases) in rainfall levels in given periods of time. For this reason, some series may have greater prognostic difficulties compared to others.

For this reason, the implementation of predictive models of the rainfall levels of each of the meteorological stations results in that, for certain stations, an ideal forecast success percentage is achieved compared to other stations. As such, in certain stations, the error to be assumed in the forecast of the stations that present a greater degree of unexpected random events will be associated with the risk in which this may be incurred. In other words, there are certain places, whose level of rainfall is more difficult to forecast, so in these stations, the error in the forecasts will be greater.

The best model for each region may be relative to the degree of efficiency that is expected from it. However, within the established prediction metric, it can be said that the model also depends on the nature of the time series. For this reason, the individual prediction of each region is subject to a specific model but not a general one that allows predicting any region. However, within the information division that was made based on data from the meteorological stations installed in Colombia, six types of series were detected that share common components, most of which are random walks without drift and with a trend. This allows giving a vision in which, for this group, taking the series randomly, the best

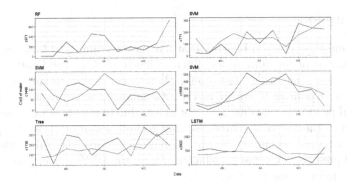

Fig. 6. Forecasts for each series based on your best model.

resulting model was LSTM. However, this model (like the other models) fails to capture an unexpected rise in rainfall levels, but it does manage to capture a medium and long-term trend (Fig. 6).

This assumes that those random and unexpected events of an increase or decrease will not be able to be captured satisfactorily, but a trend can be captured that allows defining moments in time where a systematic event in rainfall levels is anticipated and allows giving a vision for decision making.

Based on this, the trained LSTM model with the series corresponding to the random walk without drift and trend was used to make forecasts of four different series belonging to said group, but outside the training data. Figure 7 shows the one-step forecasts of these series, in which the forecasts fail to capture the sudden rises or falls in rainfall levels, but they do capture the trend of the series. It should be noted that the forecasts are based on a model trained for another series belonging to this same group. This suggests that a model can be used to forecast another series if it meets the same characteristics.

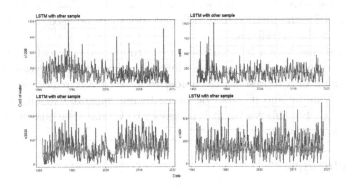

Fig. 7. Predictions based on the LSTM model trained with the sample series in the random walk without drift and trend

6   Discussion

The need and the potential benefits that having a medium and long-term vision on the behavior of the climate for different fields, such as the levels of rainfall within a region, can bring. This could allow decisions based on public information such as policies to ensure or create a financial instrument that protects agricultural production against a potential loss due to a sudden increase in rainfall. Likewise, the use of machine learning techniques to address this problem may have potential scalability benefits in remote regions where the existence of traditional prediction mechanisms (such as from the WRF model) may not be a viable local information solution.

On the other hand, despite the potential benefits, the implementation of a machine learning model carries with it a degree of uncertainty where the models may have difficulties in predicting moments where there is an unusual increase or decrease in rainfall levels, which would lead to a wrong decision in the medium and long-term trend. However, regardless of the model used, this uncertainty will always be present given the nature of the problem, so low in this context, the use of predictive models, regardless of their nature, carries an associated risk.

The historical economic importance shared by several countries makes the use of available decision-making tools relevant, even more so in countries where rainfall levels may not be stable over time given their position within the tropics, such as the Colombian case. Similarly, the use of information within an agricultural context where the transition in decision-making to change from one crop to another within the same land may be late, having a medium and long-term vision of the levels of rainfall can facilitate the decision to favor a crop whose probability of loss is minimized if an increase in rainfall levels is expected within the region of interest.

Based on the above, the separation and categorization of the time series by groups according to their type can generate benefits in terms of the forecasting methodology since, as shown in Fig. 7, the forecasts made based on a model trained by one series to another subsample, they show that the creation of a general model for the prediction of different series can be used, as long as they meet the same characteristics.

Further, segmentation into time series by groups allows to calculate a model per region or kind of time series according with their characteristics. However, a generalization of a representative model to forecast any region depends on a time series dynamic and it could be prone to not capture exogenous shock as global warming. For this reason, it is necessary to validate the quality of forecast into an implementation.

7   Conclusions

The climate in the different regions of the world is diverse. Regions further from the tropics tend to have a more marked seasonal component than in regions closer to the tropics. The existence of seasons makes a substantial difference to the stability of occurrence of climatological events. However, the onset of climate change has been shown to impact such stability. Most of the climate prediction studies are oriented to temperate regions, meaning that climate prediction approaches are less mature.

Likewise, the development of tools and techniques that inform decision makers, particularly in economies that depend on exogenous factors such as the climate, is of paramount importance. Considering that often economies in transition have a high reliance on the agricultural sector, such techniques and tools are relevant and can provide a medium-term vision to enable decisions to be made regarding potential investments in the agricultural sector for a specific region.

Within this context, we have presented a comparison of various machine learning models using a dataset from meteorological stations located within Colombia. Since this country is close to the Equator, it is harder to establish a clear pattern in rainfall levels compared to countries in the North or South of the planet.

The dataset comprised monthly rainfall levels from 2,091 meteorological stations, from 1980 to 2018 and were grouped according to their statistical nature. Using a Dickey-Fuller test, which allows the presence of a unit root to be detected, six categories of time-series were identified. Of the six categories identified, the category with the highest number of time series corresponds to those with random walks without drift and with a trend component.

Various machine learning models were evaluated for each category. Results were found to differ according to category. Overall, the best performing models are decision trees, LSTM, Random Forest, and SVMs. It is worthy mention that SVMs are found to be the best model on more than one occasion. However, for Type 4 series, which is the category that most of the timeseries belong to, the best model is LSTM. However, all models have in common that they cannot predict unexpected random events (for example, unexpected increases or decreases in rainfall levels). As such, the implementation of a prediction model for this problem manages to capture a medium and long-term trend, but it fails to predict specific events of interest in time.

References

1. Abrahamsen, E.B., Brastein, O.M., Lie, B.: Machine learning in python for weather forecast based on freely available weather data (2018)
2. Balsa, C., Rodrigues, C.V., Lopes, I., Rufino, J.: Using analog ensembles with alternative metrics for hindcasting with multistations. ParadigmPlus. **1**(2), 1–17 (2020). https://doi.org/10.55969/paradigmplus.v1n2a1, https://journals. itiud.org/index.php/paradigmplus/article/view/11
3. Carpinone, A., Giorgio, M., Langella, R., Testa, A.: Markov chain modeling for very-short-term wind power forecasting. Elect. Power Syst. Res. **122**, 152–158 (2015)
4. Chou, S., Bustamante, J., Gomes, J.: Evaluation of eta model seasonal precipitation forecasts over south America. Nonlinear Process. Geophys. **12**(4), 537–555 (2005)
5. Dickey, D.A., Fuller, W.A.: Distribution of the estimators for autoregressive time series with a unit root. J. Am. Statist. Assoc. **74**(366a), 427–431 (1979)

6. Galanis, G., Louka, P., Katsafados, P., Pytharoulis, I., Kallos, G.: Applications of Kalman filters based on non-linear functions to numerical weather predictions. In: Annales Geophysicae, vol. 24, pp. 2451–2460. Copernicus GmbH (2006)
7. Hernandez, J., Daza, K.: Implementation of an irrigation system to estimate water in hydroponic crops through evapotranspiration. ParadigmPlus. 2(1), 20–39 (2021). https://doi.org/10.55969/paradigmplus.v2n1a2, https://journals.itiud.org/index.php/paradigmplus/article/view/32
8. Holmstrom, M., Liu, D., Vo, C.: Machine learning applied to weather forecasting. Meteorol. Appl. 10, 1–5 (2016)
9. Kalmanovitz, S., et al.: La agricultura en colombia entre 1950 y 2000. Banco de la Republica de Colombia, Technical report (2003)
10. Klemp, J.: Prediction of landfalling hurricanes with the advanced hurricane WRF model. Mon. Weather Rev. 136(6), 1990–2005 (2008). https://doi.org/10.1175/2007mwr2085.1
11. Louka, p, et al.: Improvements in wind speed forecasts for wind power prediction purposes using Kalman filtering. J. Wind Eng. Indust. Aerodyn. 96(12), 2348–2362 (2008)
12. Maity, S., Bonthu, S., Sasmal, K., Warrior, H.: Role of parallel computing in numerical weather forecasting models. In: IJCA Special Issue on International Conference on Computing, Communication and Sensor Network CCSN 2012, vol. 4, pp. 22–27 (2013)
13. Mohri, M., Rostamizadeh, A., Talwalkar, A.: Foundations of Machine Learning. MIT Press, Cambridge (2018)
14. Pattanayak, S., Mohanty, U.C.: A comparative study on performance of MM5 and WRF models in simulation of tropical cyclones over Indian seas. Current Sci. 923–936 (2008)
15. Radhika, Y., Shashi, M.: Atmospheric temperature prediction using support vector machines. Int. J. Comput. Theory Eng. 1(1), 55 (2009)
16. Ross, S.M., et al.: Stochastic Processes, vol. 2. Wiley, New York (1996)
17. Shainer, G., et al.: Weather research and forecast (WRF) model performance and profiling analysis on advanced multi-core HPC clusters. In: 10th LCI ICHPCC (2009)
18. Shi, X., Chen, Z., Wang, H., Yeung, D.Y., Wong, W.K., Woo, W.: Convolutional LSTM network: a machine learning approach for precipitation nowcasting. Adv. Neural Inf. Process. Syst. 28, 1–9 (2015)
19. Subramanian, A.C., Palmer, T.N.: Ensemble super parameterization versus stochastic parameterization: a comparison of model uncertainty representation in tropical weather prediction. J. Adv. Model. Earth Syst. 9(2), 1231–1250 (2017)
20. Wang, J., Chameides, B.: Global warming's increasingly visible impacts. Environ. Defense (2005)
21. Wirth, R., Hipp, J.: CRISP-DM: towards a standard process model for data mining. In: Proceedings of the 4th International Conference on the Practical Applications of Knowledge Discovery and Data Mining. vol. 1, pp. 29–39. Manchester (2000)
22. Yang, H., Li, Y., Lu, L., Qi, R.: First order multivariate Markov chain model for generating annual weather data for Hong Kong. Energy Build. 43(9), 2371–2377 (2011)

Deep Mining Covid-19 Literature

Joshgun Sirajzade(✉) ⓘ, Pascal Bouvry ⓘ, and Christoph Schommer ⓘ

Department of Computer Science, University of Luxembourg, Belval, 6 avenue de la
Fonte, 4264 Esch-sur-Alzette, Luxembourg
{joshgun.sirajzade,pascal.bouvry,christoph.schommer}@uni.lu
https://wwwen.uni.lu/recherche/fstm/dcs

Abstract. In this paper we investigate how scientific and medical
papers about Covid-19 can be effectively mined. For this purpose we use
the CORD19 dataset which is a huge collection of all papers published
about and around the SARS-CoV2 virus and the pandemic it caused.
We discuss how classical text mining algorithms like Latent Semantic
Analysis (LSA) or its modern version Latent Drichlet Allocation (LDA)
can be used for this purpose and also touch more modern variant of
these algorithms like word2vec which came with deep learning wave and
show their advantages and disadvantages each. We finish the paper with
showing some topic examples from the corpus and answer questions such
as which topics are the most prominent for the corpus or how many percentage of the corpus is dedicated to them. We also give a discussion
of how topics around RNA research in connection with Covid-19 can be
examined.

Keywords: CORD19 · SARS-CoV-2 · Covid-19 · Pandemic · Topic
modeling · Latent Drichlet Allocation · word2vec

1 Introduction

The Covid-19 virus and the pandemic it caused hit the world very hard in many
aspects, including the economy, political and social life as well as health care
systems of different countries. As answer to that, in many countries around the
world a huge effort has been put in order to fight against the pandemic; the virus
was studied profoundly, vaccines were developed and many measures against the
spread of the virus were taken. Despite that, the pandemic is still going on as
of September 2022 and many aspects of it, especially the best ways of fighting
it, are still not very well understood, yet. At the same time, the nations around
the world gained a great experience in fighting a pandemic and are prepared like
never before. The huge portion of this experience and knowledge is hidden in
the scientific and medical publications around the world. The number of these
publications is meanwhile increasing to a six digit figure and it is very hard or
sometimes impossible to keep the overview. Time needed for reading or reviewing
that much publications has grown out of a life span of an human being long time
ago. This is where the digital organisation and techniques of information retrieval

H. Florez and H. Gomez (Eds.): ICAI 2022, CCIS 1643, pp. 121–133, 2022.
https://doi.org/10.1007/978-3-031-19647-8_9

and text mining come in handy. We believe that with the help of intelligent text mining techniques one can create a good overview of the existing papers about Covid-19. In this paper we discus how the algorithms like LDA or Word2Vec can be used in order to extract topics from Covid-19 literature. We shed light into the inner workings of the algorithms and into the history and the future of extracting topics. Then we investigate how it can be best adapted for Covid-19 literature in the example of the CORD19 dataset.

2   Dataset

Cord19 (COVID-19 Open Research Dataset) is a big and open source dataset consisting of scientific publications about and around Covid-19 pandemic gathered by the Allen Institute for AI in collaboration with the White House Office of Science and Technology Policy (OSTP), the National Library of Medicine (NLM) and many other institutions and research organisations[1]. Its aim is to centralize all the research papers about SARS-CoV-2 virus, the disease it causes, the pandemic and its prevention as well as its impact from social, political and economical view [16]. This dataset is constantly growing as new papers are published. In the time of this paper (September 2022) the data comprises of slightly under half a million papers over 30 GB as pure JSON files.

3   Related Work

3.1   Search Engines

From the moment the data was published Allen Institute announced competitions in different tasks in Kaggle[2]. Shortly after several information retrieval systems were built for the dataset. As one of the projects worth mentioning is a neural search engine which was developed by the Amazon Web Services AI team[3]. This search engine is publicly available online and uses traditional scalable information retrieval methods combined with natural language querying possibilities [1]. It is based on Amazon Kendra which utilises deep learning techniques for search engines. The search engine performs document ranking, passage ranking, question answering and FAQ matching and leverages knowledge graphs and topic modeling for better structuring the search. Although also a classical topic modeling technique like Z-label LDA was applied, the developers reduced the topics generated by the algorithm to the following ten after the consultation of medical professionals: Vaccines/immunology, Genomics, Public health Policies, Epidemiology, Clinical Treatment, Virology, Influenza, Healthcare, Industry, Pulmonary Infections and (human) Lab Trials [1]. After that the whole corpus was multi-label classified with the mentioned topics.

---

[1] https://allenai.org/data/cord-19.
[2] https://www.kaggle.com/allen-institute-for-ai/CORD-19-research-challenge.
[3] https://cord19.aws/.

Another search engine was developed by the joint effort of researchers from the Universities of Waterloo, Delaware, New York and Canadian Institute for Advanced Research. The creators of this engine called it Covidex[4]. It also uses the classical keyword search in the core of their platform which was supplemented with the sequence to sequence transformer models for reranking and feedback [18]. The algorithm used for the latest is the so called doc2query [12] which, in its turn, is an extension to the well known BERT model. Also the search engine built by google ai labs[5] is worth mentioning.

3.2 Mining of Cord19

Besides the efforts of building a search engine there has been also some attempts to analyse, study and mine the cord19 dataset. These are mostly based on finding topics in the dataset or applying other machine and deep learning technologies to the dataset. Otmakhova et al. [13] have an interesting approach by applying Latent Drichlet Allocation (LDA) to the documents which were transformed into an unordered set of Unified Medical Language System (UMLS) concepts. Worth mentioning is also the work of Karami et al. [7] who applied descriptive statistics and topic modeling to a small corpus of 9298 articles about Covid-19. Here the terms were pre-annotated as "chemical" or "disease" and were incorporated into the analysis.

4   Text Mining

Text Mining is a fast growing sub discipline, historically inspired from Data Mining as being its special form. Its aim is to discover and extract information from large text data why it is also called Text Data Mining. This information is mostly either hidden and can not be spotted by the reader immediately or the text data at hand is so huge that it would take a lot of time to read and be analyzed by a human. The spilt of Text Mining from Data Mining is mostly due to the fact that text data has a different structure (also known as unstructured data) compared to well structured data that Data Mining is using. In this regard Text Mining is closely related to Natural Language Processing (NLP). Usually, apart from the traditional data mining techniques, the topics in this field are Word Association Mining, Text Clustering, Text Categorisation, Text Summerization, Topic Analysis, Opinion Mining and Sentiment Analysis [17].

4.1   Classical Topic Modelling with Bag of Words: From LSA to LDA

Generating Term Document Frequencies and Vector Space Model dominated the IR and Text Mining research for a long time. Compressing the text documents

---

[4] https://github.com/castorini/covidex.
[5] https://covid19-research-explorer.appspot.com/.

to the topics with the help of Singular Value Decomposition (SVG) opened a new research field that is also called Latent Semantic Analysis (LSA) [5]. In its basic form it is usually formulated as $A_{mn} = U_{mk}\Sigma_{kk}V_{kn}^{\top}$ where A stands for the Document Term Matrix, U and V are orthogonal matrices of left and right singular vectors (columns) respectively, and Σ is a diagonal matrix of the corresponding singular values. The expressing of a (usually large and sparse) document term matrix in 3 components can be interpreted as U and V expressing document to term or term to document relationship respectively and Σ being a reduced form of Document Term Matrix to topics. Note that, the shape of Σ or the number of topics can be freely defined. Usually, it depends on the size of the text collection and is a number somewhere between 40 up to 300 in the real life LSA applications.

In the late 90s this process was formulated probabilistically which was called Probabilistic Latent Semantic Analysis (PLSA) [6]. It formulates the topics, thus the latent variable as $z \in Z = \{z_1, ..., z_k\}$ assuming that the documents $d \in D = \{d_1, ..., d_N\}$ are composed of topics Z, which is an unobserved variable, and the topics are composed of terms $w \in W = \{w_1, ..., w_M\}$. This way, the whole model is defined as mixture of

$$P(d, w) = P(d)P(w|d), P(w|d) = \sum_{z \in Z} P(w|z)P(z|d). \tag{1}$$

Here z is designed as bottleneck since its cardinality is smaller than the number of documents or words. The whole model can also be rewritten as

$$P(d, w) = \sum_{z \in Z} P(z)P(d|z)P(w|z), \tag{2}$$

where our diagonal matrix Σ will be equivalent to $diag(P(z_k))_k$, so PLSA is very similar to LSA. Model Fitting here happens with the help of EM Algorithm where the posterior probabilities for the words and documents given the topic are calculated

$$P(w|z) \propto \sum_{d \in D} n(d, w)P(z|d, w), \tag{3}$$

$$P(d|z) \propto \sum_{w \in W} n(d, w)P(z|d, w), \tag{4}$$

$$P(z) \propto \sum_{d \in D} \sum_{w \in W} n(d, w)P(z|d, w). \tag{5}$$

With the development of PLSA the research was paying more attention to the fact that all these approaches did not consider the order of words in a text. This is known as the so called Bag-Of-Words approach which has a great advantage and flexibility in terms of mapping of all documents and queries to one fix number of dimension, usually the total number of words in all documents. However, this approach has also some shortcomings. These were more apparent when PLSA was further developed to Latent Drichlét Allocation (LDA). First, in PLSA the number of parameters in the model grows linearly with the corpus size. Secondly, it was not yet clear how to assign probability to a document outside of the training set [2]. This problem was solved by adding the uncertainty of the topic coverage distribution for a document and entire collection in the form of an integral. It assumes that each document in a collection is generated by a random mixture of latent topics which is chosen from a Dirichlet distribution $\theta \sim Dir(\alpha)$. By plugging in all the variables we get the marginal distribution of a document:

$$p(\mathbf{w}|\alpha, \beta) = \int p(\theta|\alpha) \left(\prod_{n=1}^{N} \sum_{z_n} p(z_n|\theta) p(w_n|z_n, \beta) \right) d\theta. \tag{6}$$

The probability of a corpus is then obtained as product of the marginal probabilities of single documents:

$$p(\mathbf{D}|\alpha, \beta) = \prod_{d=1}^{M} \int p(\theta_d|\alpha) \left(\prod_{n=1}^{N_d} \sum_{z_{d}n} p(z_{d}n|\theta_d) p(w_{d}n|z_{d}n, \beta) \right) d\theta_d. \tag{7}$$

One of the main advantages of LDA, which is basically a Bayesian formulation of PLSA, is that by addressing and adding the topic mixture the parameters of the model are reduced to $k + kV$ which avoids the theoretical overfitting problem of PLSA. However, the most important detail here is the dilemma of using the power of bag-of-words approach – indeed LDA takes advantage of the *exchangebility* of words, topics and the documents – on one hand and on the other hand the reflection on the shortcoming of it by adding the notion of n-grams to topic modeling. In fact, Blei et al. [2] suggests that LDA can be used as mixture model of larger structural units such as n-grams or even paragraphs. In probabilistic language modeling the usage of n-grams has a rich tradition and LDA makes an attempt to combine these two.

4.2   Beyond Bag of Words: Text Classification and Clustering with Word Embeddings

Traditionally, regarding the word order the probabilistic language modeling was the opposite of bag-of-words approach. It considers the order of words (or characters), usually in form of *bi-* or *tri*-grams, but initially they do not capture and ignore the whole context or document. Language models were successfully applied in various tasks and are especially handy for example when dealing with unknown words in pos-tagging or in guessing/building the next word in automatic speech recognition. One of the famous algorithms used in this context was the so called Hidden Markov Models. With the time, the usage of artificial neural networks (ANN) would play a central role in NLP and Text Mining. Many ANN architectures were inspired by the traditional probabilistic language modelling. However, with the development and success of special architectures like Convolutional Neural Networks (CNN) or Long Term Short Term Memory (LSTM) a new approach emerged. Using many layers in (more or less) complex architectures with an embedding layer, delivered good results in solving many tasks. That is why, using some additional semantic information or word embeddings made sense and became popular. This again was an attempt to combine the context of documents and the order of words or other units. Despite the fact that this idea was around for some time, the real brake through came with the development of the word2vec algorithm by Mikolov [9,10]. All word2vec does is to generate vectors for words from a window with the help of a logistic regression (or a so called shallow network because it has only one hidden layer). Usually, this window is a small number like 5 words to the left and right of the word for which the vectors needs to be generated. The window in a way imitates a sentence and the created vectors capture the semantic representation of words. The success of wordvec was not only due to the fact that it could capture semantically related words well, but due to fact that the handy embedding vectors could be used for other tasks like text classification.

4.3   Topic Analysis with Deep Architectures

In our opinion the developments in deep learning had several impacts on topic modelling. First, using topics – especially probabilistic topic modelling – for search engines became less popular although it was the very thing that made topics popular. Instead, modern deep learning architectures seem to deliver better results in information retrieval tasks. The reason for that lies probably in the nature of the topic phenomenon. Term distributions as topics usually create a more general linguistic description of text collections, especially when word order does not matter. This might be great for text mining purposes in order to see what a text collection is about, however in a search one might want to receive more concrete results. In fact, the recent developments in DL based NLP widened the application and retrieval possibilities which are getting more sophisticated. They are meanwhile far beyond of search and find and resemble more human like communication. These are tasks like sentence completion, textual entailment, question answering etc. to name a few [15]. New models like BERT support these all functionalities [4]. The intuition behind it is that the searching of documents will be and is more like asking questions or beginning a sentence and hoping the search engine can complete it for you. And getting a much precise, concrete and narrowed down answer is priority.

While these developments are astonishing, they result in the fact that the questions asked also need to be concrete. The elegance of the classical topic modeling lies in the fact that one could understand a text collection even without having a question. It is the possibility to brake down many documents into few topics. However, there is also some debate on how interpretive word distributions are as topics, especially the ones which are generated by the bag-of-words approach [3]. Despite this fact, the expressive power of topics should be investigated and similar approaches further developed.

Reviewing the recent research one can observe two main approaches; the first one tries to combine algorithms and techniques from topic modeling with language technologies from ANN/DL research. Moody [11] tries for example to bring LDA and word verctors together. The second group of research tries to formulate the whole Bayesian inference process of topic modeling (like LDA) with the help of deep neural networks, also using of additional information or embedding layers [19].

5   Experiments

5.1   Preparing the Data

Text files in the dataset are delivered in two folders – pdf_json and pmc_json. Every paper resides inside one file with some metadata. First, every file was read, cleaned and appended into one file. Metadata about authors, date etc. was removed and only the content of json text element was kept. Also, some non unicode characters were removed as far as they would obviously confuse the analysis, especially the ones contained in the formulas or in the name of chemical elements. After cleaning the data the size of pure text dropped to under 10GB. Of course the link to the metadata.csv file which is additional table with the information such as author names, title, publishing data etc. was kept in order to be able to identify every paper.

In the experiments two prominent libraries – gensim [14] and mallet [8] – were used, both have implementions of above mentioned algorithms like LSA, PLSA and LDA. Gensim was implemented in python and has support of multi-core and even distributed computing for some of the algorithms. However, the data pre-processing pipeline supports only one core running which means it takes a lot of time for datasets bigger than 10GB. During our experiments we needed go back, in order to remove some unwanted stop words like *et al.* which appears a lot in the corpus. Mallet was written in Java. It is unfortunately not very well scalable, nonetheless it is very easy to use and produces well dependable results. It is also very well utilizing the type safety in the programming language Java. In dealing with big datasets both libraries require huge amount of memory, we recommend to use more than 50 GB.

5.2   Finding the Most Prominent Topics

We run LDA with the help of mallet and gensim libraries. Since the dataset is relatively huge, the number of topics was set to 400. It is wort mentioning that the output of the algorithm is twofold; $P(w_i|z_i)$ the probability distribution of each word in each topic and $P(z_i|d_i)$ the probability of each topic in each document:

$$Words \begin{matrix} & Topics \\ & \begin{bmatrix} P(w_1|z_1) & \cdots & P(w_1|z_n) \\ \vdots & \ddots & \vdots \\ P(w_n|z_1) & \cdots & P(w_n|z_n) \end{bmatrix} \end{matrix} \tag{8}$$

$$Topics \begin{bmatrix} P(z_1|d_1) & \cdots & P(z_1|d_n) \\ \vdots & \ddots & \vdots \\ P(z_n|d_1) & \cdots & P(z_n|d_n) \end{bmatrix} \quad (9)$$

In both cases the result is a matrix where the values of rows in a column always add up to the number 1 because these are probabilities. This means the sum of the probabilities of all topics for every document is 1, however some topics for a document have higher probability than others. The first 15 topics and their respective keywords are shown in Table 1. We see from the topics that some are really related to infections like number 9 or studies to active cases like in 2 or restrictions put on schools like in 7.

Table 1. The first 15 topics from mallet

0	stroke cerebral brain ischemic eeg neurological epilepsy cognitive ich seizures seizure hemorrhage icp neurolo gy tbi mri intracranial acute scale outcome
1	cns demyelination disease myelin eae astrocytes spinal cord lesions brain oligodendrocytes demyelinating autoimmune microglia mbp sclerosis multiple encephalomyelitis matter tmev
2	patients results methods study years age conclusion months treatment patient cases clinical data therapy performed aim analysis background disease conclusions
3	food products consumption foods production meat safety consumers milk agricultural nutrition foodborne eating diet vegetables dietary agriculture fresh produce farmers
4	animal animals farms veterinary livestock farm production cattle sheep meat fmdv farmers disease control risk goats btv poultry veterinarians zoonotic
5	fig data number table values analysis observed shown results high average similar total calculated time based set higher compared range
6	article rights protected copyright reserved accepted reservedthe elsevier reserved.the reserved.accepted the this hrcs edx nicorandil gie reserved.in andthis b.v cecs
7	school household schools households closure closures students childcare teachers closed attack members home secondary reopening absenteeism classrooms children elementary classroom
8	opioid drug gambling overdose substance cocaine opioids vcp illicit cannabis injection addiction drugs buprenorphine methadone heroin reward abuse taar harm
9	fever infection infections cases measles illness hepatitis risk symptoms transmission infected blood transmitted days united exposure endemic children contact skin
10	infection hand hygiene mrsa infections control ipc nosocomial prevention compliance healthcare hospital hai ha is hospitals rates catheter practices vre patient
11	cells xbe patients expression response mbl human ifn-g cell immune results bacteria iga protein responses blood levels complement increased production
12	lasv lcmv arenavirus arenaviruses tfr junv gpc lassa macv fever stt world mopv thermometer pcn-dosed dbs hemor rhagic forehead mixing candid
13	n/a airbnb leprosy dot ulcerans bms bmp donkeys leprae globin nans-p ahr ecn hookworm ccdab hipab rental epz besnoitia rfhgst-s
14	health public care services system population medical national insurance coverage healthcare systems people private access prevention community service diseases social

In the Table 2 the 20 topics containing the term "rna" can be seen. These can be interpreted as topics from the papers which do a research on a rna vaccine or the sequencing of the genome of the virus. Whether all these topics can be accumulated to one, needs to be further investigated.

Table 2. The 20 topics containing the search phrase "rna"

41	viral virus protein proteins host replication viruses cell cells infection cellular rna genome infected membrane entry cycle interaction antiviral virions
66	hcv hbv hepatitis patients chronic liver genotype hbsag hcc therapy viral infection core svr dna rna treatment huh ribavirin weeks
107	frameshifting structure trna sequence frameshift pseudoknot stem base rna codon prf ribosome mrna ribosomal structures loop site frame sequences translation
128	sars-cov sars spike viral coronavirus anti-sars-cov sars-cov-infected coronaviruses epi_isl nucleocapsid vero pandemic mers-cov gisaid rna respiratory syndrome orf patient global
152	samples viral positive detection detected rna swabs sample specimens virus collected negative swab rt-pcr pcr load tested results sampling clinical
162	cells expression cell human growth protein gene proliferation mrna results increased role induced levels endothelial tissue mice receptor differentiation factor
177	rna replication genome rnas synthesis sequence viral transcription end genomic fig polymerase mrna strand region helicase nucleotides structure template subgenomic
187	tlr activation rig-i signaling innate immune irf mda mavs response dsrna trim rna tlrs ifn traf sting nlrp antiviral dna
206	ifn-l nmd upf tcv ifnlr sst tudor-sn pemv smg heo hou ifn-a/b cob elephants balb/cv sgrna pvx-gfp mmtv prokunina-olsson gfp-l
221	hpv cas editing cervical crispr ifi crispr-cas crispr/cas sgrna crrna crrnas target sgrnas hts types vrti eri lvs grna acrs
227	sirna mir sirnas rnai mirnas mirna target rna silencing gene expression mrna targeting antisense rnas dsrna sequence shrna dicer genes
233	india indian lncrnas lncrna delhi kerala states state till pradesh maharashtra bengal neat mumbai nrav west gujarat tamil nadu districts
239	mrna translation eif rna mrnas initiation rnase ires pkr splicing sgs stress utr cap transcripts cleavage ribosome ribosomal synthesis translational
251	plant mosaic tmv coat dsrna plants baculovirus tbsv insect yeast movement cpmv pvx leaves ctv benthamiana protoplasts baculoviruses orf symptoms
310	virus viruses viral rna family human dna genome genus species host acid nucleic capsid families hepatitis members group related infect
317	nsp orf activity rna plp nsps exon cap domain conserved replication mtase replicase nidoviruses nidovirus eav capping mhv cov complex
335	sars-cov coronavirus coronaviruses cov sars human virus respiratory mers-cov covs protein viruses spike viral ncov host humans rna receptor syndrome
337	pcr rna samples primers min primer kit rt-pcr dna performed reverse table reaction gene cdna xce/xbcl extracted usa positive study
347	rdrp polymerase nucleotide template rdrps incorporation importin-a ntp remdesivir motif polymerases thumb fidelity rna palm active fingers atp triphosphate motifs
366	bortezomib cml imatinib chl wolters kluwer hoct kir lymphoma survivors unauthorized abl lines mutation reproduction gltscr qol mrna ppl picts

One of the most interesting results of the mining process can be found in the Table 3. Here, the 15 most prominent topics in the entire collection are shown. We use the sum of the topics in the documents and we see here that the corpus is indeed representative for doing Covid-19 research. While the most prominent topic, 311 is about clinical cases the second most prominent topic, 117 focuses on the social measures done by the government such as lockdown. In the figure1

Table 3. The 15 most used topics

311	covid patients sars-cov severe disease infection respiratory acute risk clinical syndrome viral coronavirus reported mortality injury data ards higher severity
117	covid pandemic health people social measures lockdown public virus distancing spread coronavirus march countries due government outbreak world impact home
320	time case important make long number made fact part large point form means problem system general result good process small
300	results based study case considered number analysis order due important present studies specific method high table main data level information
5	fig data number table values analysis observed shown results high average similar total calculated time based set higher compared range
183	covid care pandemic staff patients time health patient clinical team services providers healthcare resources provide support access including crisis virtual
344	covid symptoms sars-cov cases patients infection disease respiratory coronavirus confirmed reported asymptomatic clinical fever positive infected severe virus case china
38	patients study patient hospital data clinical days table reported performed admission median included years time admitted group disease medical received
89	cells immune inflammatory response cytokines inflammation production cytokine activation macrophages levels role increased expression responses cell effects receptor shown disease
340	risk studies study reported found increased evidence factors data higher compared high increase recent significant potential disease important including exposure
336	e.g. potential provide including important studies multiple include critical approach impact systems current ability significant future understanding additional strategies specific
399	infection patients patient ppe transmission risk room contact equipment staff care protective isolation respiratory medical control procedures protection precautions workers
329	study age table higher found reported significant prevalence studies years data number compared analysis cases total group groups significantly differences
37	disease clinical diagnosis cases patients common acute treatment infection chronic include present severe syndrome therapy symptoms reported diagnostic including infections
114	global health development countries public national international community support policy local government systems capacity response including resources world research approach

the proportion of the most prominent topics are shown. The y-axis stands for the percentage cover of the topic in the collection. The most prominent topic 311 occupies 2% of the collection and with every other topic this number drops.

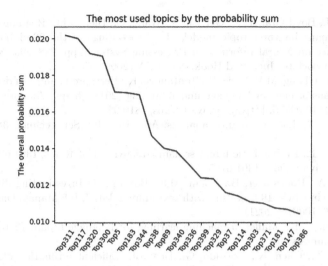

Fig. 1. The proportion of the most prominent topics in the dataset.

6   Conclusion

Almost three years passed since the Covid-19 pandemic hit the planet. Still, we fight against it and try to understand how our society can respond to it. In this paper we show that topic modeling can be very helpful in achieving this goal.

Topic modeling was gaining a lot of attention since LDA was first published in 2004. Despite the fact that the recent research on language technologies introduced many kinds of new algorithms, with BERT being the culmination, it is not clear, yet how these technologies can be optimally and efficiently used for topic extraction. BERT indeed outperforms many other existing algorithms in tasks like sentiment analysis, question answering or just semantic search querying, because it creates a very detailed and contextualized language representation. However, when we do topic modeling, we do not ask a specific question to our corpus, but we try to extract clear and easy understandable information about its content. LDA delivers more or less understandable results where topics created from the dataset are abstract enough for a quick distant reading and at the same time concrete enough, in order to capture the slight semantic differences in the topics or documents. In the future, we want to investigate how topics can be extracted and presented in a similar manner with the help of newer algorithms.

References

1. Bhatia, P., et al.: AWS CORD-19 search: a neural search engine for COVID-19 literature. http://arxiv.org/abs/2007.09186
2. Blei, D.M., Ng, A.Y., Jordan, M.I.: Latent Dirichlet allocation. J. Mach. Learn. Res. **3**, 993–1022 (2003)

3. Chang, J., Boyd-Graber, J., Gerrish, S., Wang, C., Blei, D.M.: Reading tea leaves: How humans interpret topic models. In: Proceedings of the 22nd International Conference on Neural Information Processing Systems, pp. 288–296. NIPS 2009, Curran Associates Inc., Red Hook, NY, USA (2009)

4. Devlin, J., Chang, M.W., Lee, K., Toutanova, K.: Bert: pre-training of deep bidirectional transformers for language understanding (2018). https://doi.org/10.48550/ARXIV.1810.04805, https://arxiv.org/abs/1810.04805

5. Dumais, S.T.: Latent semantic analysis. Ann. Rev. Inf. Sci. Technol. **38**, 188–230 (2005)

6. Hofmann, T.: Probabilistic latent semantic analysis. CoRR abs/1301.6705 (2013). http://arxiv.org/abs/1301.6705

7. Karami, A., Bookstaver, B., Nolan, M.S., Bozorgi, P.: Investigating diseases and chemicals in Covid-19 literature with text mining. Int. J. Inf. Manag. Data Insights **1**, 100016–100016 (2021)

8. McCallum, A.K.: Mallet: a machine learning for language toolkit (2002). http://mallet.cs.umass.edu

9. Mikolov, T., Chen, K., Corrado, G., Dean, J.: Efficient estimation of word representations in vector space. In: Bengio, Y., LeCun, Y. (eds.) 1st International Conference on Learning Representations, ICLR 2013, Scottsdale, Arizona, USA, 2–4 May 2013, Workshop Track Proceedings (2013). http://arxiv.org/abs/1301.3781

10. Mikolov, T., Sutskever, I., Chen, K., Corrado, G., Dean, J.: Distributed representations of words and phrases and their compositionality. CoRR abs/1310.4546 (2013). http://arxiv.org/abs/1310.4546

11. Moody, C.E.: Mixing Dirichlet topic models and word embeddings to make LDA2vec. CoRR abs/1605.02019 (2016). http://arxiv.org/abs/1605.02019

12. Nogueira, R., Yang, W., Lin, J., Cho, K.: Document expansion by query prediction. arXiv preprint arXiv:1904.08375 (2019)

13. Otmakhova, Y., Verspoor, K., Baldwin, T., Šuster, S.: Improved topic representations of medical documents to assist COVID-19 literature exploration. In: Proceedings of the 1st Workshop on NLP for COVID-19 (Part 2) at EMNLP 2020. Association for Computational Linguistics (2020). https://doi.org/10.18653/v1/2020.nlpcovid19-2.12, https://www.aclweb.org/anthology/2020.nlpcovid19-2.12

14. Řehůřek, R., Sojka, P.: Software framework for topic modelling with large corpora. In: Proceedings of the LREC 2010 Workshop on New Challenges for NLP Frameworks, pp. 45–50. ELRA, Valletta, Malta, May 2010. http://is.muni.cz/publication/884893/en

15. Wang, A., Singh, A., Michael, J., Hill, F., Levy, O., Bowman, S.R.: GLUE: a multitask benchmark and analysis platform for natural language understanding (2018). https://doi.org/10.48550/ARXIV.1804.07461, https://arxiv.org/abs/1804.07461

16. Wang, L.L., et al.: Cord-19: The COVID-19 open research dataset. ArXiv (2020)

17. Zhai, C., Massung, S.: Text Data Management and Analysis: A Practical Introduction to Information Retrieval and Text Mining, 1st edn. ACM Books, San Rafael (2016). OCLC: ocn957355971

18. Zhang, E., et al.: Covidex: neural ranking models and keyword search infrastructure for the COVID-19 open research dataset. In: Proceedings of the First Workshop on Scholarly Document Processing, pp. 31–41. Association for Computational Linguistics (2020). https://doi.org/10.18653/v1/2020.sdp-1.5, https://www.aclweb.org/anthology/2020.sdp-1.5

19. Zhao, H., Phung, D., Huynh, V., Jin, Y., Du, L., Buntine, W.: Topic modelling meets deep neural networks: a survey (2021). https://doi.org/10.48550/ARXIV.2103.00498, https://arxiv.org/abs/2103.00498

Keyword-Based Processing for Assessing Short Answers in the Educational Field

Javier Sanz-Fayos[(⊠)] ⬤, Luis de-la-Fuente-Valentín[(⊠)] ⬤, and Elena Verdú[(⊠)] ⬤

Universidad Internacional de La Rioja, UNIR, Logroño, Spain
{javier.sanz,luis.delafuente,elena.verdu}@unir.net

Abstract. When grading open-ended engineering exam responses, it is assessed to what extent its content and quality suit the requirements and accomplish the objectives of the test. This is a time consuming and subjective task. The support of a software tool that identifies the correctness of the response and provides useful feedback to both student and teacher may alleviate its complexity. In this work, a semi-automatic evaluation method based on augmented Spanish keyword recognition is presented.

This assessment is based on the occurrence of a set of keyterms that the teacher expects to appear in a good response. The evaluation is based on an augmented catalogue of terms, automatically created from the teacher selected keyterms, resulting in an ad hoc thesauri. The method uses state-of-the-art techniques, but also ad hoc procedures developed from the Spanish corpus Wikicorpus, for pre-processing the texts.

The results, tested using real anonymized data from engineering exam topics such as database techniques and bigdata, indicate good performance in the thesauri creation and keyword matching. Besides, the keyterms strategy allows simple individualized feedback. However, the relationship found between automatic and human grading indicates that further research is required.

Keywords: Dictionary · Feedback · Keyterms · Natural language processing · Semi-automatic evaluation

1 Introduction

The evaluation of exams is one of the most important tasks in the educational field. It is time demanding and susceptible to random errors in the judgment of the questions. Specifically, open-ended responses are those that most compromise accuracy as they are more linked to subjectivity factors, due to the difference in correction criteria among the teaching staff [10,15]. This variability, even if it is mitigated with the use of rubrics, could penalize or benefit certain students [3].

This work is partially funded by the PLeNTaS project, "Proyectos I+D+i 2019", PID2019-111430RB-I00.

For this reason, it is intended to research and develop a software application, based on Natural Language Processing (NLP), that contributes to the development and improvement of the currently existing approaches for automatic/semi-automatic content evaluation. Specifically, the study focuses on exploring the suitability of a keyword-based approach for conducting such evaluation. In differ to other studies, our assessment is based on the occurrence of an automatically augmented set of keyterms (which were created from a group of words that the teacher selected as crucial aspects in the ideal response). Therefore, during this process, we will try to answer these research questions:

- RQ1: How valid is a keyterm-based evaluation to determine the quality of any student response? Is there a correlation between the criteria used by examiners and the one used and proposed in this method?
- RQ2: Is it possible to generate competent feedback with this method to justify both content errors and guesses in the responses?

This work is one of the modules considered by the PLeNTaS project, whose objective is the development of a semantic-based automatic grading tool for short answers (which do not exceed 200 words). In PLeNTaS, outputs of multiple methods that evaluate different aspects of the student's response will be combined to design an evaluation format based on a weighted rubric of the different analyzed areas. The aim is to achieve a general and reasoned qualification of said response. In this project, then, the viability of one approach to partially or totally evaluate the semantic part of a response within the rubric will be assessed.

2   State of the Art

In the educational area, NLP seeks to extract, modulate and transform human expert knowledge of a certain domain into assets that allow machines to emulate it on a computational level. This scenario contributes to the possibility of improving current online education [9]. *Assisted Study*, for example, is a tool that provides the student with an automatically created set of open-ended training exams so that he/she can practice while he/she is being guided. The system also assists teachers to assess the syntactic and semantic evaluation of them, providing certain feedback of the student's performance [15].

There are other dialogue-based systems as AutoTutor, for example, which is a natural language tutoring system capable of dialoguing and guiding one student by building a student's model, which is perfected through the interaction with the system [12]. Other tutoring model examples are: *Why2*, *CIRCSIM-Tutor*, *GuruTutor*, *DeepTutor*, or *MetaTutor*. These are also based on adaptive learning mechanisms and offer guarantees of effectiveness like those that could provide a human person [16]. The goal of the above described systems is the support of the students during their study and practice time, but they are not used for the accuracy evaluation of a response.

There are also systems that provide a series of analyzable indexes that serve to obtain metrics that are useful to better evaluate the responses. Westera et al. [18] manage to generate up to 200 indexes to evaluate the student's pass or fail. Another solution is ReaderBench [4], which allows to evaluate the complexity of texts, summaries and explanations, integrating the indexes provided by the systems *E-rater* [14], *iSTART* [11] and *CohMetrix* [5].

Systems, such as the one proposed by Panaite et al. [13], are nourished by the knowledge provided by this type of indexes to perform the qualification of short answers. Another similar system, focused more on training the student in writing essays, is *Writing Pal*, which uses NLP to assess the quality of student's writing and to provide feedback of it, including evaluation indexes to identify the complexity, cohesion, rhetoric and linguistics of the text. On the other hand, automated scoring engines could also be used to fulfil the same purpose, such as *C-rater* [8].

In Automatic Short Answer Grading (ASAG), the techniques that are achieving one of the best performances in the field, managing to resolve certain issues of more or less simplicity, are those based on deep learning. These techniques do not literally process words but, instead, work with representation vectors that are known as word embeddings [7]. Initially, these word embedding models such as Word2vec or Fast Text were static, so they provided the same vector for the same word regardless of the context [1]. However, new models such as ELMo or BERT manage to assign different representations depending on the context, thus improving the performance of algorithms [2]. Anyway, it cannot be assumed that the student is comfortable being evaluated by a machine. For this reason, studies are recently emerging to measure student acceptance of being evaluated by intelligent software [17].

To the best of our knowledge, there is not a complete solution to the proposed problem, that is the automatic evaluation of student's responses, despite the present development of expert knowledge automatic abstraction methods. In addition, although we are aware of the existence of some keyword matching approaches that are generally used for assessing free-text short responses [6,19], we consider there is no keyword-based approach that implements an automatically augmented catalogue of terms and assesses the content of a response without great error. There is still more research to be done in this area to improve algorithms, especially the ones that are related to NLP, in order to get better semantic identification and extraction techniques so that better knowledge and evaluation models could be built [21].

3   Methodology

3.1   Automated Scoring

The prime focus of this work, as mentioned in RQ1, is the research of methods for semi-automated evaluation of a student's response to a specific question. The assessment will be based on the occurrence of a set of keyterms that the teacher expects to appear in a good response. Instead of just matching words in the text, the evaluation is based on an augmented catalogue of keyterms, automatically created from the teacher selected keyterms. For that, the first step is the creation of a corpus for the Word Sense Disambiguation (WSD) task. Then, a thesauri is used to obtain synonyms and antonyms of each keyterm. Finally, both the augmented catalogue of keyterms and the student response are processed with the WSD corpus so that different forms of the same keyterm can be detected, as well as the syntactical form of each of the words (e.g. a word that can be a verb and a noun scores better when it appears in the catalogue and in the text in the same form). To create the corpus, a representative, random, balanced and not too specific corpus in Spanish will be formed so that it will not be mainly composed of words from a certain domain. This approach makes general informative extraction from the language possible, which is useful to develop WSD techniques.

Taking all this criteria into consideration, a wide variety of texts from *Wikicorpus* were selected, so that the composed corpus was made up to 32 texts and 60 880 634 words. After its processing, a dictionary of lemmas structured by levels (word, grammatical category and lemma) was created in order to facilitate both pre-processing and WSD tasks. Whereas serving as the lemmatization engine of the project, with the combination of the Spanish pipeline of *Stanza*[1], it also allows to store or calculate the grammatical category of words, which is the key in which the WSD of the project is based, as there are words that should be reduced to one canonical form or another depending on that.

Therefore, the implemented strategy for WSD was to elaborate a *Markov* hidden model (HMM), decoded using the *Viterbi* algorithm, in order to build a part-of-speech (POS) tagger. Given the vast set of data handled, program interruptions appeared during the calculation of probability tables. To solve this, each corpus text was approached separately, assuming equal representation and quality in all of them, so that the final probability tables were obtained from a mean that was relative to the number of occurrences of each token.

Dates, numbers and proper names were also filtered. Unlike the first two, the elimination of proper names does lead to the loss of significant information. Consequently, a new token was created (called *tokenseliminados*) to collect and store the mentioned discarded information, just like a buffer. Then, if a new word appears when using *Viterbi*, it will be considered as "*tokenseliminados*". Probability values of this token (which are combined with an introduced penalty to the less probable categories) are thus used to label the unknown word.

The collection used for the empirical validation was formed by a group of 3 datasets that were composed of real responses with less than 200 words. These responses were collected in engineering examinations taken at university level. The first one had 144 samples about the subject of *capture methods*, the second one had 96 about *business intelligence*, and the third one had 47 about *computer technology*, all of which are subjects related to the field of database management and bigdata. All the samples were the response of different students to the same group of questions about the corresponding subject. The responses catalogue of

---

[1] https://stanfordnlp.github.io/stanza/.

the 3 subjects, in JSON format, contains for each response the exam question, the set of keyterms that the teacher considered should be in the response, the actual text response and the scores assigned by the teacher during its evaluation. With this information, the empirical validation approach will be to use the keyterms and the text response for the semi-automatic grading, and then to compare the results with the human-assigned score.

From the mentioned keyterms, two thesaurus were formed augmenting those keyterms with its synonyms and antonyms, respectively, which are obtained through the web scraping of *WordReference* [20]. To provide additional information, one more level was added to the two thesauri. One of its indexes indicates whether the word is itself a keyword or is a significant unit of a compound keyterm. The remaining indexes allow, on the one hand, access to the correspondent information obtained with *WordReference* and, on the other hand, access to the grammatical category of the keyword.

The mentioned instrument will be analyzed to identify whether the student's response includes keyterms or those words close to them in terms of meaning. The developed strategy consists in going over the phrase to check if the variable-size n-gram matches any keyterm. Before proceeding with the keyword matching, all responses are pre-processed and segmented into simpler phrases to facilitate the use of certain NLP techniques and to analyze the appearance distribution of keyterms throughout the response. A tokenization process is also applied to each of these sentences, followed by the previous explained lemmatization process.

Keyword matching is repeated for each keyterm available, for each window size and for each set of study (keyterms-synonyms-antonyms). Based on the relationship between the total number of keyterms defined by the teacher and the number of independent matches in the student's response, the score of the method is adjusted (Eq. 1). All keyterms are weighted equally, regardless of how they appear (literally or by its synonyms/antonyms). At the end of the matching stage, the score is compared with the human-assigned score.

$$score = \frac{number\ of\ identified\ keywords}{number\ of\ keywords} \tag{1}$$

3.2 Effective Feedback

The need of explaining the given grade is to be considered, so that both student and teacher could explicitly understand that output, as mentioned in RQ2. The implemented feedback system is based on a set of informative sentences that serve to show the adequacy of the identified words within the expected context. For each type of matching that can be found (exact matching, synonym, etc.), a templated-sentence is constructed. The feedback module selects the appropriate sentence for each matching (or absence) keyterm and constructs the final feedback. That is a brief but precise feedback of the selection nature of each keyterm, with the student words copied within the explanation. For the evaluation, expert teachers validate if the constructed sentences are suitable as real feedback for the students.

4   Results

The corpus, code and datasets used for this study are published and available in GitHub[2] for research purposes.

4.1   Program Functioning

The morphosyntactic tagger functioning was assessed to perform accurately. According to results, the tagger is robust to new words and does not make the program to interrupt when analyzing words that are not collected in the dictionary, so it can be used for the WSD of any sentence. However, it is appreciated that words considered as *"tokenseliminados"*, due to their formation process, are quite conditioned to be substantive, which sometimes might cause the analysis not to be entirely correct. Despite this factor, the error will not extend beyond a low-size n-gram and all the keyterms, that are the words that are supposed to be disambiguated, will appear in the dictionary, so the impact of it will not be severe.

As for the functioning of the feedback generator, the set of sentences was built so that each phrase could be triggered when it is supposed to, configuring them with variables (the words that are not written between quotation marks) so that the meaning of them could match the exact analyzed information. Some of the cited sentences are shown below:

"La palabra clave" + keyword + "aparece correctamente utilizada en el texto". *(Spanish for: "The keyword" + keyword + "appears correctly used in the text").*

"En el texto aparece la palabra " + element + ", que es sinónima del lema de la palabra clave " + keyword. *(Spanish for "The word" + element + "appears in the text, which is synonymous with the lemma of the keyword" + keyword).*

"La palabra " + component + " aparece en el texto y es una forma de expresar la palabra clave " + keyword + ", pero su significado puede no ser el adecuado". *(Spanish for: "The word" + component + "appears in the text and is a way of expressing the keyword" + keyword + ", but its meaning may not be adequate").*

Although being supervised by experts, the accuracy of the keyword matching system and its integrated feedback generator has not been empirically validated. It is true that, apparently, the tests made show great results, but further investigations should be done before assuring its good results with confidence. RQ2, thus, will be totally approached in the future, but the actual performance is shown below:

Response sentence:

''- arbitro: encargado de nombrar al nodo secundario que comienza a actuar en caso de que el primario deje de tener disponibilidad.'' (''- *arbitrator: in charge of naming the secondary node that begins to act in the event that the primary node is no longer available.''*)

---

[2] https://github.com/jasanfa/Keyword-based-Processing-for-Assessing-Short-Answers-in-the-Educational-Field.git.

Generated feedback:

``La palabra clave arbitrar aparece en el texto, pero no con la categoría gra-
matical buscada, por lo que su sentido podría ser inadecuado'', ``La palabra
clave disponibilidad aparece correctamente utilizada en el texto'', ``En el
texto aparece la palabra actuar, que es sinónima del lema de la palabra clave
arbitrar''. (``The keyword arbitrate appears in the text, but not with the
grammar category searched for, so its meaning could be inappropriate '', ``
The keyword availability appears correctly used in the text'', ``In the text
the word act appears, which is synonymous with the lemma of the keyword arbitrate''.)

As it can be seen, both keywords and their synonyms/antonyms in the proposed example are accurately identified. The implemented filtering and lemmatization strategies ensure that the identification is robust to the many possible
ways of writing the words. For example, it correctly processes the word "arbitro", which has a dot attached and may not be identified in a word-for-word
comparison. On the other hand, the generated feedback clearly describes each
situation encountered, which facilitates the understanding of each algorithm's
decision.

4.2 Relationship Between Calculated and Real Mark

The comparison between both student's real mark (obtained in his/her exam)
and the calculated mark of this work (based on keyterms) is shown in Figs. 1,
2 and 3. On the ordinate axis (Y), the score from 0 to 1 achieved by both
methods is represented and, on the other hand, each unit of the abscissa axis
(X) represents a different student. The values of these graphs are ordered by the
increasing value of the real mark, showing a growing difference between them
from a real mark of 0.6.

From the previous figures, the existing deviation between samples, which is
obtained from the calculation of the absolute error between them, is calculated.
In order to consider the samples to be similar, when plotting an histogram most
of them should be located near zero deviation, so that the generated Gaussian
had little variance. At first glance, it can be seen in Figs. 1, 2 and 3 that there is
significant difference between both methods. In fact, the obtained distribution
of the samples of all 3 datasets is flattened and is shifted to the right in the
histogram, with a maximum formed around 0.5–0.6 deviation, which means that
the error obtained is very considerable, since it implies not having the ability
to even identify passing or failing grades. It is also observed that generally the
calculated score is lower than the real one because the deviation obtained is
positive and not negative.

4.3 Influence of Each Keyterm on the Mark

To complement the analysis, it is considered important to also represent the
influence of each pair of keyterms, on each other, with respect to the grade. The

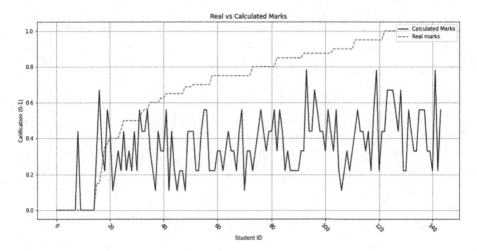

Fig. 1. Relationship between the calculated and real marks of the first dataset (ordered from lowest to highest real mark)

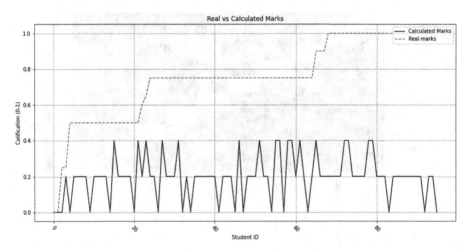

Fig. 2. Relationship between the calculated and real marks of the second dataset (ordered from lowest to highest real mark)

intention was to verify the existence of a possible binding relationship between them in order to better weigh the calculated grade. As it can be seen in Figs. 4, 5 and 6, because of the weakness of these relationships, no evidence can be drawn to claim that the relationship is significant enough, neither between them nor with the grade. For example, in the Fig. 4, the two keywords that are most related to each other and most related to the mark are "disponibilidad" and "arbitrar". However, the maximum score obtained, that is 0.6, stills being quite low.

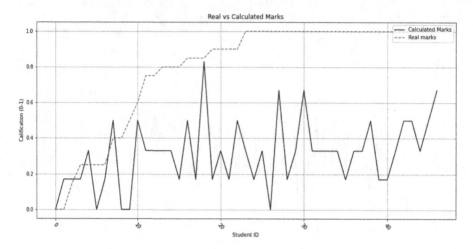

Fig. 3. Relationship between the calculated and real marks of the third dataset (ordered from lowest to highest real mark)

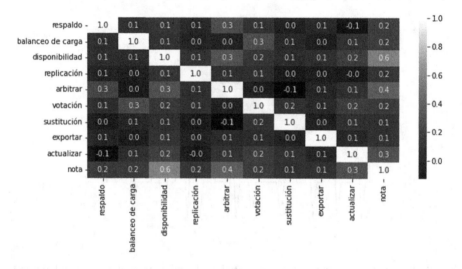

Fig. 4. Correlation matrix of the worked variables of the first dataset

It is also worth mentioning that the recognition of specific and single terms is better achieved, as it can be seen in Fig. 5, where the method is only capable of distinguishing two keyterms because all of them are compound terms and have more or less abstract meaning. From this statement, future work should focus on making the students responses as specific as possible from the question itself, thus facilitating any type of upcoming analysis.

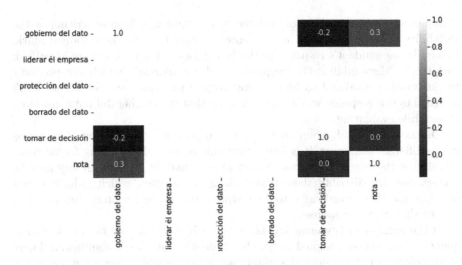

Fig. 5. Correlation matrix of the worked variables of the second dataset

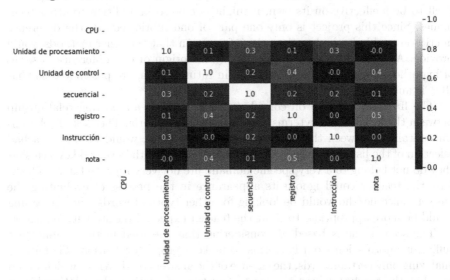

Fig. 6. Correlation matrix of the worked variables of the third dataset

5   Discussion

The results show, with clear evidence, that there is no relationship between the found number of keyterms and the student's received final mark. For example, there are students who achieved the maximum mark including fewer keyterms in their response than some who failed. The possible relationship between the different keyterms and the marks is also discarded, despite having observed a certain tendency for students to include certain pairs of keyterms. This frequency of appearance seems to be more related to the student's form of writing or the suitability of those keyterms in the context rather than to the obtained mark. In fact, in one student's response of the first dataset, 4 keywords were identified: "arbitrar", "disponibilidad", "respaldo" and "actualizar", which are precisely the keywords considered to be the most important. However, the actual mark assigned to this response was zero, evidencing that the teacher did not considered them while evaluating.

On the other hand, when analyzing the appearance distribution of keyterms in the different sentences, it is found that this is not a determining factor while calculating the mark. Keyterms do not appear mainly grouped in any specific phrase, but are distributed naturally along the answer, which indicates that students use these words as a tool to explain the learned content and not as a way to shorten the response.

If the number of keyterms has no weight while calculating the mark, consequently, the method designed to get the student's mark is not significant. There is, therefore, a not considered variable when rating which has influence in the difference of criteria that have both techniques. While this method has proven itself to be ineffective on its own, it might not be so in addition to other techniques. Since this project is only one part of one rubric section, the difference in criteria could also be based on the information that the other methods would provide. As there are no means to identify the origin of this difference, a series of hypotheses, which should be refuted in future works, are postulated so that RQ1 is answered:

The first one is based on considering that there is an existing relationship between the number of keyterms and the teacher's criteria. The lack of relationship obtained between the two methods, consequently, would be due to a bad selection of the list of keyterms. Ergo, it is possible that the selected keyterms, as they do not belong to a very specific domain, are not very representative. Therefore, the teacher could ignore its appearance in the process of evaluating the answer, since he/she would be looking for other types of words whose meaning would be more appropriate to what the teacher expected the student to answer.

The second one is based on considering that the used method cannot get sufficient information from keyterms to make a proper evaluation. That is, by analyzing only certain words, the essence of the answer could be lost, which would be what the teacher valued the most. The type of writing, the relationship of concepts and the use of descriptive language are very important resources when evaluating, and all that go completely unnoticed with this approach. Moreover, in the text there might not be a direct reference of a keyterm, but there might be a reference to its meaning or what it represents. The search for keyterms, therefore, should be complemented, since the list of keyterms would be considered as a set of abstract indexes that the student should not explicitly cite. What the student should do is to explain its meaning in other words or express that idea applied to another specific point in the domain.

The last one would be based on the combination of the previous mentioned hypotheses. Regardless of them, it can be assured that the results obtained from keyterm extraction in combination with the individualized feedback are encouraging. The created sentences are so clear, precise and simple, that they manage to inform without overwhelming the reader, which makes them ideal to be consulted quickly during the performance of an exam or task. For future work, instead of matching the teacher's keyterms in the responses, one approach that is thought to be of interest might be to generate some terms that summarize the content of each response, in order to see if there is notable difference between them and the ones the teacher highlighted.

6   Conclusions

This paper has argued whether keyterms can be suitable for automatic grading and feedback generation or not. Although the current study is based on a relatively small sample of participants per dataset, the findings suggest that the designed evaluation method, in this case, is not adequate to provide useful information about the student's mark provided the obtained difference between both grading methods. However, investigation and experimentation into RQ1 reversing the implemented procedure is strongly recommended, that is generating the keyterms from the text itself, as it could be a good approach to better extract the essence of the answer.

In addition, this study has identified that the procedure for obtaining the augmented catalogue of terms has proven useful in expanding the concept of words in a keyword-based study. It's like augmenting its dimensionality. Given this premise, we would recommend to use and combine it with the proposed keyterm generation if it were to be approached in the future. Along with the augmented catalogue of terms, the morphosyntactic tagger was empirically validated to perform adequately, and can be an optimal tool to determine the grammatical category of unknown words, specially in cases in which the corpus has low extension.

Finally, whilst this study did not confirm RQ2, it did partially substantiate that the extraction of keywords from the student's response might be interesting for generating sufficiently clear and particular feedback, meaning that this could be a fruitful area for further work.

References

1. Arumugam, R., Rajesh, Shanmugamani: Hands-On Natural Language Processing with Python: A Practical Guide to Applying Deep Learning Architectures to your NLP Applications (2018)
2. Beseiso, M., Alzahrani, S.: An empirical analysis of Bert embedding for automated essay scoring. Int. J. Adv. Comput. Sci. App. **11**, 204–210 (2020). https://doi.org/10.14569/IJACSA.2020.0111027
3. Brame, C.J.: Rubrics: Tools to Make Grading More Fair and Efficient, pp. 175–184. Science Teaching Essentials, Academic Press (2019)
4. Dascalu, M.: ReaderBench (1) - Cohesion-Based Discourse Analysis and Dialogism (2014)

5. Graesser, A.C., McNamara, D.S., Kulikowich, J.M.: Coh-metrix. Educ. Res. **40**(5), 223–234 (2011)
6. Jordan, S., Mitchell, T.: E-assessment for learning? The potential of short-answer free-text questions with tailored feedback. Br. J. Edu. Technol. **40**(2), 371–385 (2009)
7. Khodeir, N.: Bi-GRU urgent classification for MOOC discussion forums based on Bert. IEEE Access 1 (2021). https://doi.org/10.1109/ACCESS.2021.3072734
8. Leacock, C., Chodorow, M.: C-rater: automated scoring of short-answer questions. Comput. Hum. **37**(4), 389–405 (2003)
9. Maldonado, L.F., Londoño, O.L., Gómez, J.P.: Sistemas ontológicos en el aprendizaje significativo: estado del arte. Actualidades Investigativas en Educación **17**(2), 1–18 (2017)
10. McNamara, D.S., Crossley, S.A., Roscoe, R.D., Allen, L.K., Dai, J.: A hierarchical classification approach to automated essay scoring. Assess. Writ. **23**, 35–59 (2015)
11. McNamara, D.S., Levinstein, I.B., Boonthum, C.: iSTART: interactive strategy training for active reading and thinking. Behav. Res. Methods, Instruments, Comput. **36**(2), 222–233 (2004)
12. Nye, B.D., Graesser, A.C., Hu, X.: Autotutor and family: a review of 17 years of natural language tutoring. Int. J. Artif. Intell. Educ. **24**(4), 427–469 (2014)
13. Panaite, M., et al.: Bring it on! challenges encountered while building a comprehensive tutoring system using ReaderBench. In: Penstein Rosé, C., et al. (eds.) AIED 2018. LNCS (LNAI), vol. 10947, pp. 409–419. Springer, Cham (2018). https://doi.org/10.1007/978-3-319-93843-1_30
14. Ramineni, C.: Automated essay scoring: psychometric guidelines and practices. Assess. Writ. **18**(1), 25–39 (2013)
15. Rodrigues, F., Oliveira, P.: A system for formative assessment and monitoring of students' progress. Comput. Educ. **76**(4), 30–41 (2014)
16. Rus, V., D'Mello, S., Hu, X., Graesser, A.: Recent advances in conversational intelligent tutoring systems. AI Mag. **34**(3), 42–54 (2013)
17. Sánchez-Prieto, J., Cruz-Benito, J., Therón, R., García-Peñalvo, F.: Assessed by machines: development of a tam-based tool to measure AI-based assessment acceptance among students. Int. J. Interact. Multimed. Artif. Intell. **6**(4), 80–86 (2020)
18. Westera, W., Dascalu, M., Kurvers, H., Ruseti, S., Trausan-Matu, S.: Automated essay scoring in applied games: Reducing the teacher bandwidth problem in online training. Comput. Educ. **123**, 212–224 (2018)
19. Willis, A.: Using NLP to support scalable assessment of short free-text responses. In: Proceedings of the Tenth Workshop on Innovative Use of NLP for Building Educational Applications, pp. 243–253, June 2015
20. WordReference: Diccionario de sinónimos y antónimos (2021). https://www.wordreference.com/sinonimos/
21. Zouaq, A., Gasevic, D., Hatalar, M.: Towards open ontology learning and filtering. Inf. Syst. **36**(7), 1064–1081 (2011)

Statistical Characterization of Image Intensities in Regions Inside Arteries to Facilitate the Extraction of Center Lines in Atherosclerosis Frameworks

Fernando Yepes-Calderon[1,2,3(✉)] (iD)

[1] Science Based Platforms, 405 Beact CT, Fort Pierce, FL 34950, USA
fernando.yepes@strategicbp.net
[2] GYM Group SA, Cra 78A No. 6-58, Cali, Colombia
[3] Universidad del Valle - Facultad de Medicina, Cl. 4b 36-00, Cali, Colombia

Abstract. The center line algorithms in atherosclerosis follow the random directions that arteries and vessels take and are devoted to providing information that scientists use to establish parallel planes where quantifications could be accomplished with accuracy. Unfortunately, during the center line construction, high-intensity regions representing pathologies such as atheromas and calcifications mislead algorithms and thus medical verdicts. Physicians and developers assume that Computer Tomography intensities measured in Hounsfield units are stable and reproducible among scanners. However, experiments presented in this document suggest significant variabilities in the magnitudes obtained by four different institutions. The current work provides a methodology to dynamically estimate the thresholds to separate the various structures within arteries and present enough evidence of segmentation separability in the four studied institutions. Furthermore, the proposed methods are easily translated to other centers.

Keywords: Carotid artery imaging · Artery lumen intensity · Artery calcification intensity · Computer tomography imaging · Atherosclerosis

1 Introduction

Atherosclerosis is a disease that manifests itself through an alteration of the arterial wall and a progressively growing atheroma that blocks the blood fluid [9,13]. The pathology has diverse consequences depending on its location and the degree of channel obstruction [7].

The medical ramifications associated with these arterial pathologies (stenosis and aneurysms) are highly insidious. Mortality from cardiovascular diseases is 28.7% (125.6 per 100,000 inhabitants), the second cause of death. Considering only the case of coronary artery stenosis, its direct consequence, myocardial infarction, represents one of the leading causes of mortality worldwide [1].

© The Author(s), under exclusive license to Springer Nature Switzerland AG 2022
H. Florez and H. Gomez (Eds.): ICAI 2022, CCIS 1643, pp. 147–157, 2022.
https://doi.org/10.1007/978-3-031-19647-8_11

Coronary heart disease produces 12.3% of healthy years of life lost due to non-communicable disease (265,119/2,149,099) and is the second leading cause of death after homicides and violence [18]. By 1995, ischemic heart disease represented the leading cause of healthy years lost due to illness, surpassing nearly double that of homicides, which is the second leading cause [5]. Cerebral infarction, on the other hand, is not an essentially fatal entity, but it consumes a significant post-hospital amount of resources. Approximately 750,000 people experience an ischemic cerebrovascular event each year in the United States, with an estimated 40 billion USD in direct and indirect costs. Twenty-five percent of these events are related to occlusive disease of the extracranial carotid arteries [16].

Medical imaging has emerged as a crucial assisting tool for diagnosis and is capable of displaying results in 3D models that greatly facilitate the work of the experts [2]. However, in the case of arteries and vessels, it is still challenging to determine the stenosis degree at a glance due to the natural random directions that blood conduits take within the human body. A good starting strategy to overcome this difficulty is to determine the tube's Central Line (CL) and refer quantifications to planes parallel to the previously extracted CL [19]. Different geometries of the modeled tube and inside it can be quantified by integrating the areas in the parallel planes. Determining the CL is crucial, and automation struggles to succeed in this aim when atheromas are present due to the intensity of the obstructions that violate the rationale used in the CL extraction algorithms [10].

In this work, we provide statistical ranges of intensities for each zone found in CT images of the carotid artery where background, lumen, and calcification have been manually gathered on images acquired in four distinct institutions. Here we demonstrate the existence of significant intensity discrepancies among institutions, and although it is possible to segment intra-institutionally with the statistically found thresholds, the values are not traceable between centers. The above remains true, although Hounsfield units are highly stable.

The best ranges to assert separability of regions inside the carotide artery in the four studied institutions are (presented as bakground, lumen, calcification): (-4,105), (193,340), (342, 1612) for institution 1; (-12,93), (196, 502), (519, 1809) for institution 2; (14, 121), (318,535), (697, 1661) for institution 3 and (27,90), (163, 461), (381, 1192) for institution 4.

2   Materials and Methods

2.1   Statistically Estimating Level of Intensities for Pathogenic Arteries

In the design of the experiments, we cared for the possibility of human-induced noise (errors) by reducing operator intrusion and implementing standard exporting formats between specialized applications such as Mysql [8] and python [6]. From the images, raw intensities and coordinates were recovered in comma-separated data files (CSV extension) [11]. These formats are 100% compatible with import mechanisms in DB Engines like Mysql or analyzing platforms like Pandas. The use of CSV files assures that information travels from one application to another without risk of being modified, lost, or corrupted [3]. The use of a database engine ensures accurate selectiveness.

Sample Acquisition Methodology. The acquisition protocol is graphically explained in Fig. 1.

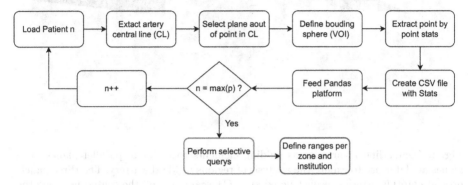

Fig. 1. Data acquisition protocol. The strategy gathers information within a VOI with predefined dimensions in milimiters that renders resolution differences introduced by the distinct imaging protocols ineffective. Also, human invervention is fully precluded to avoid errors.

– A set of patients' images in DICOM format is randomly selected using python.
– The volume of interest (VOI) is defined to encompass the carotid artery using the CL algorithm yet with errors detection. See Fig. 2.
– Within each plane containing a CL point, the automation triggers the following functions:
  • Determine the number of pixels framing a squared area of 2.25 mm^2 where the seed point is in the isocenter of the geometry. The study area is empirically selected and obeys common axial regions of carotid arteries.
  • Extract a circular shape that fits inside the created squared shape.
  • Determine the intensity of each point, obtain the average, variance, deviation standard, all this, in the ROI (in-plane VOI).
  • Create a CSV file, adding the generated data in the previous step and including the intensity values and coordinates of each point x,y, and z within the ROI.
  • Jump to the next plane where the selection of a new point will be executed.

Sample Size. Previous experiments have attempted to define threshold ranges using information from a single seed point selected by the specialist. As suggested in [17] and [15]. Due to the variability in intensities in the same image slice, we decided to define an ROI and make an average of intensities in that ROI to determine later a range of thresholding based on the data presented in the

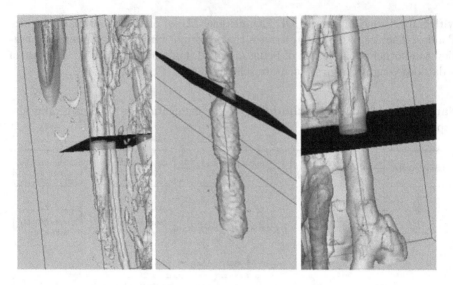

Fig. 2. Center line in arteries as guiding elements to estimate parallel planes. The planes are later use to excute the analysis of regions inside the artery. The three panels present carotide arteries reconstructed after CT scanning and the centerline along the traject.

selected area. This exercise suggests that thresholding is not absolute but a range of numbers created after statistics. Therefore, the extracted limits become more representative while we gather more data. In the current implementation, we estimate the range as points separated by n standard deviations from the mean until the estimated range covers 90.

Influence of the Acquisition Protocol in Each Entity. Since we work with clinical data and judging by the significant variability of the data inside the same institution, we assume that data has not been acquired with a rigorous protocol. However, since the CT systems work based on the absorption of the ionizing radiation, the resulting Hounsfield units are expected to be highly stable [20]. The differences between laboratories could be attributed to the different configurations and acquisition protocols. The current experiments keep the analysis separated by institution – as shown in Fig. 3 – aiming to find theoretically unexpected differences in the Hounsfield units. In case these inter-institutional differences appear, we are intended to provide accurate ranges for separating each region inside healthy and abnormal arteries for each contributing institute.

3   Results

The Table 1 presents the technical sheet of the developed experiment. You can see the number of records collected, the discrimination of these records by areas of interest (lumen, calcifications, and background), and the number of institutions evaluated.

Table 1. Technical records of the experiment

Institution	Samples (19397)		
	Lumen	Calcification	Background
1	1531	314	1837
2	2273	1408	2914
3	1907	668	2111
4	1924	540	1970
Total	7635	2930	8832

The following tables present the ranges for each zone discriminated by laboratory. We display the tables until range $mean \pm std$ covers 90% – at least – of the points gathered for a given region and, in case of overlapping, it is allowed to happen once.

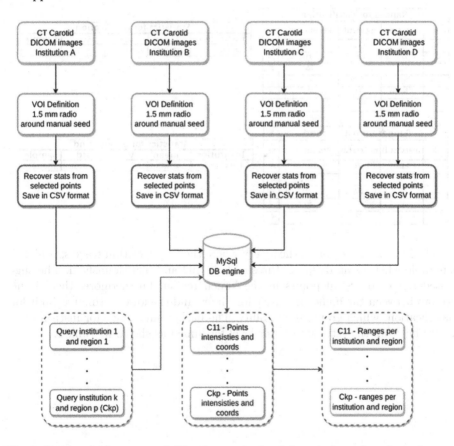

Fig. 3. Data gathering protocol. The data gathering is kept independent for each analyzing institution, and areas are set in mm^2 to avoid the influence of resolution in the number of pixels. The data is saved in CSV format and later moved to Mysql, where we query the database engine to recover the data accurately. The expression C_{kp} refers to the combinatory between the regions and the institutions

3.1   Institution 1. Statistical Values for Lumen, Calcifications and Background

Table 2. Statistical ranges of intensities in Hounsfield units for the studied regions in Institution 1.

Ranges for lumen				
X	m+(x*std)	m-(x*std)	Pts out (PO)	%
1,0	273	425	823	36
1,2	257	440	556	24
1,4	242	455	363	16
1,6	227	470	190	8
1,8	212	486	34	1
2,0	197	501	20	1

Statistics for lumen				
Institution	Mean	Var	Std	Sample
Institution 1	348,6410	5784,7725	76,0577	2273

Ranges for calcification				
X	m+(x*std)	m-(x*std)	Pts out (PO)	%
1,0	842	1486	463	33
1,2	778	1550	344	24
1,4	713	1615	254	18
1,6	649	1679	178	13
1,8	584	1743	81	6
2,0	520	1808	38	3

Statistics for calcification				
Institution	Mean	Var	Std	Sample
Institution 1	1163,9063	103676,1660	321,9878	1408

Ranges for background				
X	m+(x*std)	m-(x*std)	Pts out (PO)	%
1,0	12	69	1305	45
1,2	6	75	1061	36
1,4	1	80	699	24
1,6	-5	86	56	2
1,8	-11	92	11	0

Statistics for background				
Institution	Mean	Var	Std	Sample
Institution 1	40,5110	804,6379	28,3661	2914

The lumen, the region in the artery where the CL algorithm travels, is highly separable when using dynamic thresholds in 192 and 339 Hounsfield. The suggested range covers all points in the lumen region. Furthermore, there is no overlap between the higher intensity for lumen and the lower estimated limit for classification, which grants separability. The background range for institution 1 is also far from the estimated lower level for lumen as shown in Table 2.

3.2   Institution 2. Statistical Values for Lumen, Calcifications and Background

Table 3. Statistical ranges of intensities in Hounsfield units for the studied regions in Institution 2.

Ranges for lumen				
X	m+(x*std)	m-(x*std)	Pts out (PO)	%
1,0	273	425	823	36
1,2	257	440	556	24
1,4	242	455	363	16
1,6	227	470	190	8
1,8	212	486	34	1
2,0	197	501	20	1

Statistics for lumen				
Institution	Mean	Var	Std	Sample
Institution 2	348,6410	5784,7725	76,0577	2273

Ranges for calcification				
X	m+(x*std)	m-(x*std)	Pts out (PO)	%
1,0	842	1486	463	33
1,2	778	1550	344	24
1,4	713	1615	254	18
1,6	649	1679	178	13
1,8	584	1743	81	6
2,0	520	1808	38	3

Statistics for calcification				
Institution	Mean	Var	Std	Sample
Institution 2	1163,9063	103676,1660	321,9878	1408

Ranges for background				
X	m+(x*std)	m-(x*std)	Pts out (PO)	%
1,0	12	69	1305	45
1,2	6	75	1061	36
1,4	1	80	699	24
1,6	-5	86	56	2
1,8	-11	92	11	0

Statistics for background				
Institution	Mean	Var	Std	Sample
Institution 2	40,5110	804,6379	28,3661	2914

In institution 2, the range for lumen was found between 197 and 501 Hounsfield to cover 99% of the points in the region. The broader range of intensities for calcifications starts in 520, which grants separability. The dynamically estimated range for background pushed the lower limit to negative values when subtracting more than 1.6 times the standard deviation from the mean. Although a negative intensity is unfeasible in the CT framework, setting these limits in a segmentation program does not lead to failures. Plase, review these values and analysis in Table 3.

3.3 Institution 3. Statistical Values for Lumen, Calcifications and Background

Table 4. Statistical ranges of intensities in Hounsfield units for the studied regions in Institution 3.

Ranges for lumen				
X	m+(x*std)	m-(x*std)	Pts out (PO)	%
1,0	359	493	239	12
1,2	346	507	200	10
1,4	332	520	185	10
1,6	319	534	176	9

Statistics for lumen				
Institution	Mean	Var	Std	Sample
Institution 3	426,2209	4514,4988	67,1900	1924

Ranges for calcification				
X	m+(x*std)	m-(x*std)	Pts out (PO)	%
1,0	938	1419	179	33
1,2	890	1467	130	24
1,4	842	1515	97	18
1,6	794	1564	61	11
1,8	746	1612	37	7
2,0	698	1660	19	4

Statistics for calcification				
Institution	Mean	Var	Std	Sample
Institution 3	1178,6759	57876,9356	240,5763	540

Ranges for background				
X	m+(x*std)	m+(x*std)	Pts out (PO)	%
1,0	41	94	247	13
1,2	36	99	159	8
1,4	31	104	131	7
1,6	25	110	108	5
1,8	20	115	89	5
2,0	15	120	87	4

Statistics for background				
Institution	Mean	Var	Std	Sample
Institution 3	67,5330	692,3882	26,3133	1970

The third institution presented a high dispersion in all the regions. Recall that this automation stops reporting the ranges when there is overlap between the study regions. Although the 90% inclusion while keeping separability is feasible with the CT data generated in this institution, the best case scenario will leave 9% of the points out of the lumen to reach a good separation of calcifications that leaves 4% of points out. For the records, the background, lumen, and calcification, ranges for the third institution are [15–120], [319–534], and [608–1660], respectively. Plase, see Table 4 to corroborate the mentioned findings.

3.4   Institution 4. Statistical Values for Lumen, Calcifications and Background

Table 5. Statistical ranges of intensities in Hounsfield units for the studied regions in Institution 4.

Ranges for lumen				
X	m+(x*std)	m-(x*std)	Pts out (PO)	%
1,0	255	369	323	17
1,2	244	380	259	14
1,4	232	392	257	13
1,6	221	403	253	13
1,8	209	415	249	13
2,0	198	426	227	12
2,2	187	437	188	10
2,4	175	449	89	5
2,6	164	460	39	2

Statistics for lumen				
Institution	Mean	Var	Std	Sample
Institution 4	312,0288	3247,3208	56,9853	1907

Ranges for calcification				
X	m+(x*std)	m-(x*std)	Pts out (PO)	%
1,0	497	1075	181	27
1,2	440	1133	135	20
1,4	382	1191	79	12

Statistics for calcification				
Institution	Mean	Var	Std	Sample
Institution 4	786,2605	83462,1719	288,8982	668

Ranges for background				
X	m+(x*std)	m-(x*std)	Pts out (PO)	%
1,0	44	74	540	26
1,2	40	77	390	18
1,4	37	80	275	13
1,6	34	83	160	8
1,8	31	86	117	6
2,0	28	89	84	4

Statistics for background				
Institution	Mean	Var	Std	Sample
Institution 4	58,5599	226,7006	15,0566	2111

In the fourth institution, the 90% of inclusion was violated for calcification, and the reader could see the overlapping condition in action. Observe how the lower range of intensity in calcification overlaps the higher level for lumen. Such a situation forced the reporting automation to stop and display the best case separability scheme for this dataset, with 12% of the points in calcification not classified inside the calculated range. For the records, the found values for background, lumen, and calcification are [28–89], [164–450], and [382–1191], respectively. Please, review Table 5.

4   Discussion

A detailed review of the results for each institution shows that the acquisition protocol applied in each center has significant implications for the intensities, a claim already presented even in phantoms [14]. Authors have not found consensus regarding the doses to be used in CT for the best artery visualization [12]. The given reference and evidence justifies the different results obtained among the studied institutions. The ideal solution to avoid image heterogeneity is strictly using a standard image acquisition protocol. This suggestion could be utopic since setup imaging in hospitals obeys medical necessities and not the needed uniformity aimed by developers [4]. Achieving uniformity is even more challenging inter-institutionally suggesting the need to propose alternative tools. An acceptable good approach could be that image processing platforms gain specification by identifying the centers and setting the dynamic Housfiled limits accordingly. Such functionality is feasible after finding the center's name in the DICOM header of every CT slide. This proposal is supported in the provided numbers, where the reader can observe that the ranges for lumen, calcification, and background in the same laboratory do not overlap and that these areas, far from being closely linked, leave a window of between 3% and 8% of the maximum intensity found for the particular institution. The only exception to this rule happened in institution 4 where overlap between the areas of calcification and lumen exists. The high variability in this data makes the standard deviation grow, and thus the lower limit for calcification quickly finds the upper limit for lumen, and even so, the experiment continues to show 7% of the points outside the range for calcification. A less hasty analysis allows us to see that this 7% overlapping is due to points on top of the calcification threshold and not at the bottom where the issue with lumen takes place. We registered the gathered data in Mysql and performed SQL queries to guarantee the repeatability of the experiment. new queries they can be generated to cross or verify the registered information.

5   Conclusions

Although Hounsfield units are supposed to be stable among scanners, setup variables accessible by technicians influence the degree of separability among zones in the resulting image. Those factors include but are not limited to the power of ionizing radiation, contrast concentration, distances between the x-ray source, collimator, the patient, and the detector array. According to the findings presented in this work, automatic algorithms must be adaptable to consider the different schemes of intensities produced by various possible setups that can happen intra-institutionally. The fact that Hounsfield units are reproducible through scanners has been misleading scientists, and automatic segmentation in an initially non-complex scenario has become cumbersome to accomplish. Artificial intelligence is handly, but a supervised exercise will require data augmentation to provide the learning device with a representative sample that could cover all possible variations with their outcomes in the image.

References

1. Barquera, S., et al.: Global overview of the epidemiology of atherosclerotic cardio-vascular disease. Arch. Med. Res. **46**(5), 328–338 (2015)

2. Dey, N., Bhateja, V., Hassanien, A.E.: Medical Imaging in Clinical Applications. Algorithmic and Computer-Based Approaches. SCI, vol. 651. Springer, Cham (2016). https://doi.org/10.1007/978-3-319-33793-7

3. DuBois, P.: MySQL Cookbook. O'Reilly Media, Inc., Sebastopol (2003)

4. Hendee, W.R., et al.: Addressing overutilization in medical imaging. Radiology **257**(1), 240–245 (2010)

5. Jensen, R.V., Hjortbak, M.V., Bøtker, H.E.: Ischemic heart disease: an update. In: Seminars in Nuclear Medicine, vol. 50, pp. 195–207. Elsevier (2020)

6. Kelly, Sloan: What is python? In: Python, PyGame and Raspberry Pi Game Development, pp. 3–5. Apress, Berkeley, CA (2016). https://doi.org/10.1007/978-1-4842-2517-2_2

7. Koskinas, K.C., Ughi, G.J., Windecker, S., Tearney, G.J., Räber, L.: Intracoronary imaging of coronary atherosclerosis: validation for diagnosis, prognosis and treatment. Eur. Heart J. **37**(6), 524–535 (2016)

8. Krogh, Jesper Wisborg: MySQL workbench. In: MySQL 8 Query Performance Tuning, pp. 199–226. Apress, Berkeley, CA (2020). https://doi.org/10.1007/978-1-4842-5584-1_11

9. Libby, P.: Atherosclerosis: the new view. Sci. Am. **286**(5), 46–55 (2002)

10. Libby, P.: The changing landscape of atherosclerosis. Nature **592**(7855), 524–533 (2021)

11. Mitlöhner, J., Neumaier, S., Umbrich, J., Polleres, A.: Characteristics of open data CSV files. In: 2016 2nd International Conference on Open and Big Data (OBD), pp. 72–79. IEEE (2016)

12. Oh, J.H., Choi, S.P., Wee, J.H., Park, J.H.: Inter-scanner variability in Hounsfield unit measured by CT of the brain and effect on gray-to-white matter ratio. Am. J. Emerg. Med. **37**(4), 680–684 (2019)

13. Ross, R.: The pathogenesis of atherosclerosis-an update. N. Engl. J. Med. **314**(8), 488–500 (1986)

14. Sande, E.P.S., Martinsen, A.C.T., Hole, E.O., Olerud, H.M.: Interphantom and interscanner variations for Hounsfield units-establishment of reference values for HU in a commercial QA phantom. Phys. Med. Biol. **55**(17), 5123 (2010)

15. dos Santos, F.L.C., Joutsen, A., Terada, M., Salenius, J., Eskola, H.: A semi-automatic segmentation method for the structural analysis of carotid atherosclerotic plaques by computed tomography angiography. J. Atheroscler. Thromb. **21**(9), 930–940 (2014)

16. Shepard, D., VanderZanden, A., Moran, A., Naghavi, M., Murray, C., Roth, G.: Ischemic heart disease worldwide, 1990 to 2013: estimates from the global burden of disease study 2013. Circ. Cardiovasc. Q. Outcomes. **8**(4), 455–456 (2015)

17. Wesarg, S., Firle, E.A.: Segmentation of vessels: the corkscrew algorithm. In: SPIE Medical Imaging (2004)

18. Yamagishi, M., et al.: JCS 2018 guideline on diagnosis of chronic coronary heart diseases. Circ. J. **85**(4), 402–572 (2021)

19. Zreik, M., Van Hamersvelt, R.W., Wolterink, J.M., Leiner, T., Viergever, M.A., Išgum, I.: A recurrent CNN for automatic detection and classification of coronary artery plaque and stenosis in coronary CT angiography. IEEE Trans. Med. Imaging **38**(7), 1588–1598 (2018)

20. Zurl, B., Tiefling, R., Winkler, P., Kindl, P., Kapp, K.S.: Hounsfield units variations. Strahlentherapie und Onkologie **190**(1), 88–93 (2013). https://doi.org/10.1007/s00066-013-0464-5

Text Encryption with Advanced Encryption Standard (AES) for Near Field Communication (NFC) Using Huffman Compression

Oluwashola David Adeniji[1]([✉]) [ID], Olaniyan Eliais Akinola[1],
Ademola Olusola Adesina[2] [ID], and Olamide Afolabi[1]

[1] Computer Science Department, University of Ibadan, Ibadan, Nigeria
od.adeniji@ui.edu.ng, olamide@touchandpay.me
[2] Department of Mathematical Sciences, Olabisi Onabanjo University, OOU, Ago-Iwoye,
Nigeria
ademola.adesina@oouagoiwoye.edu.ng

Abstract. The combination of Huffman Code with some Cryptographic Algorithms such as symmetric encryption algorithms will guarantee multi-level security. Huffman code can access both the code wordlist with the encoded bits in order to decode the message. In this way, improper error correction algorithms with encoded bits can be damaged resulting in total loss of information. However, code wordlist and code bit sent to the receiver require a high-level of transmission time. There is a need to provide countermeasures techniques to secure and fix the damaged encoded bit. The challenge, therefore, is to protect the original wordlist from intrusion without damaging the existing code bit. Data of Personally Identifiable Information must not be compromised which requires data encryption. The focus of the study is to mitigate against intrusion in the levels of communication transaction between the card and the reader. In this research, a Mifare classic 1k and Radio Frequency Identification (RFID) were used during the simulation because of the vulnerability status of the card. The Advanced Encryption Standard (AES) of varying bytes with a number of Unique Characters was simulated.

Keywords: Advanced Encryption Standard · Cryptographic Algorithms · Huffman · NFC RFID · Security

1 Introduction

The use of a functional human identification system has been built from the draft for use of Radio Frequency Identification (RFID) in human identification from demography and health survey (DHS) Emerging Applications. Therefore, the Application of RFID in human tracking and identification is important in areas such as enterprise-module applications and supply-chain systems. The use of RFID tags across these areas requires different entities of privacy. The protocol implementation in the transfer of ownership in mobile applications normally considers handheld components from readers to the

© The Author(s), under exclusive license to Springer Nature Switzerland AG 2022
H. Florez and H. Gomez (Eds.): ICAI 2022, CCIS 1643, pp. 158–170, 2022.
https://doi.org/10.1007/978-3-031-19647-8_12

backend server. To secure and provide counterfeit-measure transactions of RFID systems where tags with limited resources is very important [1]. New optional modes of ownership transfer are developed which has led to improvement and maintenance specific application. This application is very from Ubiquitous Computing, Logistics Management, and Traceability. Privacy and Authentication are the major concern in RFID systems. Cryptanalysis has been implemented to protocols using the electronic product code generation 2 (EPC-C1G2) standard thereby analyzing the level of security. The passive tag such as ultra-high frequency (UHF) EPC-C1G2 class 1 was approved by ISO 18,000-4C.ALHO algorithm. The focus of the algorithm when was tested is to reduce collision and use Time-division multiplexing. The implication of this is major to correct robust protocol error correction codes. Encryption is a technology for protecting sensitive data, most algorithm used in encryption combines both Public and Private Key [2]. Basically, encryption usually hides sensitive data of users which are used for information retrieval. Data Encryption Standard (DES) can encryption and decryption using the shared secret key in form of blocked ciphers. Round are 16 identical stages of processing the permutation of plaintext bits. Advanced Encryption Standard (AES) encrypts all 128 bits in one iteration. AES is fast and flexible, to crack the cipher during operation requires the use of different multiple keys. AES system may not be configured appropriately and the attack can be a related-key attack [3, 4, 14]. An attack can be known if the decryption and encryption of the key are defined. Such attacks can be known. Also, there could be a major risk in an AES attack where information is gathered when the cryptographic operation mode is performed. This type of attack is known as a side-channel attack.

In this study, the authors release that there is a need to provide countermeasures techniques to secure and fix the damaged encoded bit. The challenge, therefore, is to protect the original wordlist from intrusion without damaging the existing code bit. Data of personally identifiable information must not be compromised which requires data encryption. Therefore, the objective of this paper is to mitigate against intrusion in the levels of communication transaction between the card and the reader.

2 Literature Review

The categories of lossless compression algorithms and canonical Huffman coding associated with a given system with limited computational and energy resources are due to low complexity and high compression efficiency [1, 5]. A proposal by [5] on Authentication Protocol with Group Tags Ownership and using RFID and Web-Based Application for Academic Sector. Transport tracking using RFID can equally be used in the internet of things (IoT) [6] global system for mobile (GSM)-based technique. The review in [7] presents the application of Huffman encoding to images, video and files. The performance analysis of the Huffman code was discussed in [8]. Symmetric Key Block Cipher Algorithms were developed thereby describing the analysis of the cipher algorithm. Huffman coding is a concept that determines the frequency occurrence of a data item which may differ according to the type of data which may be video, image, text or other file formats [9]. However, the use of Huffman coding in the representation symbol, resulting in a prefix-free code is required, which means the bit string representing a particular symbol is never a prefix of the bit string representing any other symbol. The observation is that characters with shorter strings of bits are used for less common source symbols. Huffman in his study designed an efficient compression method which can map individual source symbols to unique strings. The significant roles of encryption algorithms are numerous and essential in information security by [10] in Comparative Study of Symmetric Cryptography Mechanism. The encryption process using AES cryptography consists of a six-step process which are key expansion, Initial transformation, Substitute bytes, Shift rows, Mix columns and adding a round key. This strategy attempts to detect only known attacks based on predefined attack characteristics was proposed in [11]. A Secured Text Encryption with Near Field Communication (NFC) using Huffman Compression was proposed [12]. There are two methods for system design in which a hybrid of online-offline with minimum information is stored on the tag although the online system is required to verify the information. Also, a proposal on the tradeoff between the two protocols can provide a significant impact on the networks was presented in [13]. Character Proximity for RFID Smart Certificate System was designed to curb Forgery Menace in [2]. A review in [14] shows a system that allows quick access to infant medical history, mortality status and integration with other neonatal-care sessions.

3 Methodology

- The Design Architecture in this research are the Information System Module (ISM), card Interactor Module (CIM) and Middleware Module(MM). ISM is the center of the system and consists of three modules which are Core, Infrastructure and WebAPIs. The core is the center of the system, it implements the entities and business rules and makes sure data is securely accessed. Infrastructure layer handles external concerns on the database, calling an external endpoint, and sending emails. WebAPIs is the interface that provides the ISM to securely access the core through HTTP requests.
- Card Interactor Module (CIM) is the second part of the design architecture. Basically, the CIM is the hardware. In CIM the API communicates with the card through the interfaces provided through dependency injection.
- Interactor/ Middleware is the third stage which consists of Repository, Logic, Security and Interface. The Repository is the storage mechanism that hosts both structured or unstructured information. During the simulation, the logic layer ensures that the information created or updated is in conformity with the set of canonical rules before approval. The logic layer ensures integrity. Below the logic layer is the security which ensures that the information system is secure from unauthorized action and data theft. The security control Anti-Collision feature, Mutual pass authentication and Random ID support GUI and API are combined to build the Interface. The simulation was implemented using a reader ACR1311, which supports both Bluetooth and USB 2.0 connection. The near field communication (NFC) card is a Mifare Classic 1k. The testbed for the simulation is shown in Fig. 1.
- The interface was connected together with the NFC Card and the reader. After which the two hardware interacted during communication as shown in Fig. 2. The algorithm used in the simulation of the developed model is shown in Fig. 3.

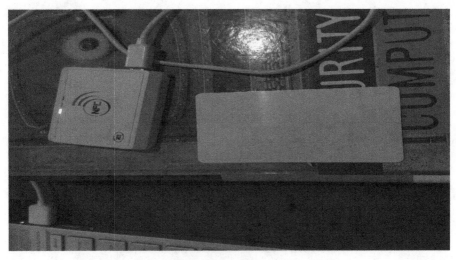

Fig. 1. Interface of NFC card and reader

Fig. 2. Interaction between NFC card and reader

The user information keeps the reference of encoded data which includes the binary object and character map. This information checks for AES mode. The unique character register is configured while the payload is writing to the buffer. If the unique character register is not properly configured at the AES mode, another reconfiguration is done but if it is properly configured, the unique character mode is generated. The subkey to unique character mode is also generated. At this stage, another write is done to the buffer. An interrupt of a unique character is registered and the algorithm is terminated as shown in Fig. 3.

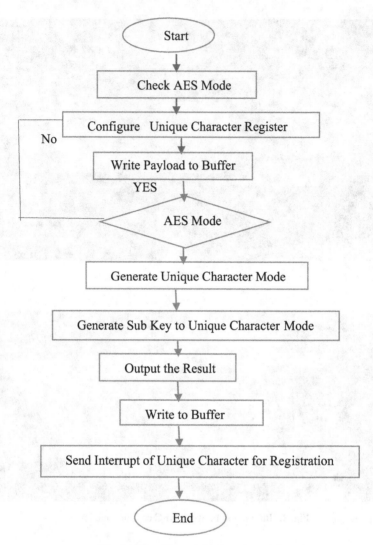

Fig. 3. Algorithm of developed model

The developed model was implemented was C# and run on visual studio IDE. The script was captured during the simulation as depicted in Fig. 4.

Fig. 4. Simulation of the developed model.

The Repository storage constraint considers the final data size of the encryption. The encryption algorithm AES was used. AES output size is dependent on the input size and the key size. From the figure below, the output size is consistently a multiple of 128 which is the block size of the algorithm, this result is the same for both cipher modes was tested. The Huffman Time function was defined as:

$$T(n) = N\lceil n + \log(2n - 1)\rceil + S \times n \tag{1}$$

The Huffman Time function was used to identify and categorise the symbols. Basically, symbols are not independent and identically distributed. The compression in Huffman is constructed with the aim of getting the optimal compression. The priority queue data structures require $0 \, (\log n)$ time per insertion. The Complexity of the Huffman Time function is given as: $0 \, (N^2)$. Huffman coding tree is a complete binary tree, this algorithm operates in $0(n \times \log^n)$ time, where n is the total number of characters. If a given message of byte N, when n is denoted has the total number of unique characters in equation one (1). It was observed that less compression was achieved as n increased. The maximum compression ratio is achieved when n = 1 for the same value of N. The lossless technique compresses a given data without losing the original data and quality of the content. İt was observed that the lossless data compression leads to a reduction in file size while retaining the original quality of the data. The Interface Showing Card interactor window when No card was detected and when the card was detected is shown in Figs. 5 and 6.

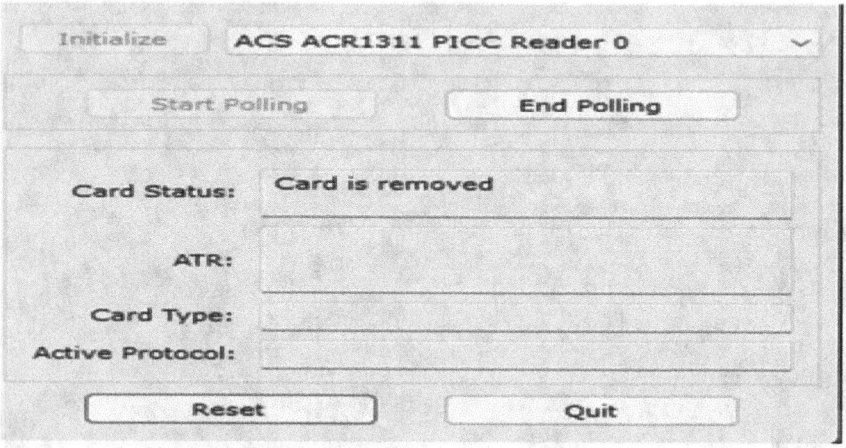

Fig. 5. Interactor window no card detected.

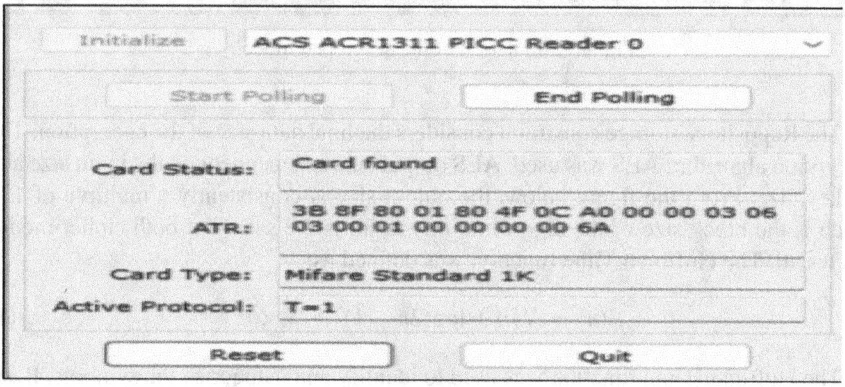

Fig. 6. Interactor window card detected.

4 Result and Discussion

The results from the model investigate the importance of entropy, S. The password entropy predicts how difficult a given password would be to crack through brute force or guessing.

$$L_c = |C| \tag{2}$$

$$L_k = |K| \tag{3}$$

$$Z = L_c^{L_k} \tag{4}$$

$$S = \log_2 Z \tag{5}$$

With the above Eq. (4) it will be difficult to guess the password. It is important that at least one character is chosen from each of the three sets. This 6-character key is further separated and hashed for better security. AES algorithm was deployed on the raw code of Huffman. The higher the entropy of the initial text the more accommodating the output size to change in the value of N. There is also a direct correlation between the value of N and the output size as seen in Figs. 7, 8, 9 and 10. When AES Encrypted Byte of N = 50, the result was obtained as shown in Fig. 7.

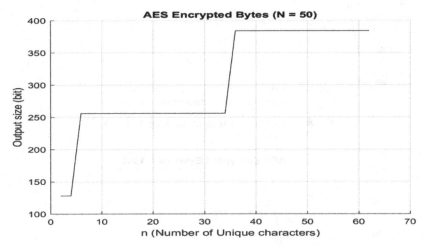

Fig. 7. Output size vs. unique character N = 50

There is an indication that the complexity of symbol-by-symbol coding in the result is determined by the factor responsible for the performance. The unique character increases in the output as compression reduces. In a related experiment when N = 100 for AES Encrypted Byte, the output size and number of the unique character increases with less compression. Also, when N = 150 for AES Encrypted Byte and when N = 200 for AES Encrypted Byte as shown in the figures below a similar result was examined.

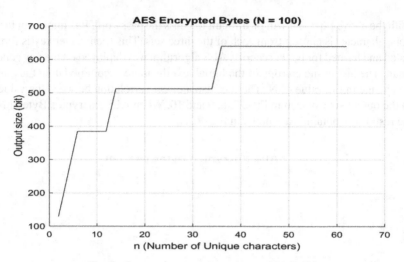

Fig. 8. Output size vs. unique character N = 100

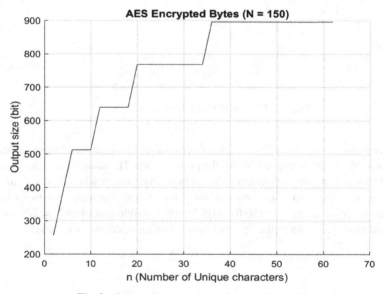

Fig. 9. Output size vs. unique character N = 150

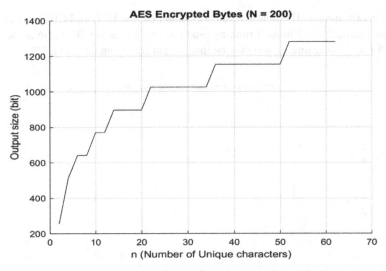

Fig. 10. Output size vs. unique character N = 200

Performance Evaluation to determine the time required for encryption was conducted during the study. Time performance for both cipher Block Chaining (CBC) and electronic code book (ECB) at N = 50 was analysed during the experiment. Figure 11 shows the result obtained.

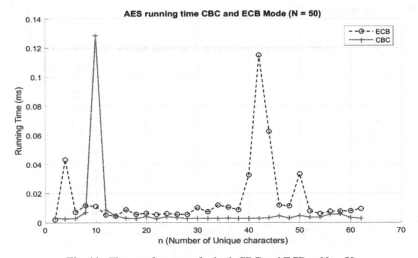

Fig. 11. Time performance for both CBC and ECB at N = 50

The performance time with a number of the unique characters of 2 when N = 50, CBC and ECB at AES running mode shows that CBC optimal 0.13 ms and ECB 0.12 ms at optimality. Then symbol-by-symbol restriction is dropped with known input distribution. The Time performance for both CBC and ECB at N = 100 was analysed during the experiment. The below result was obtained, the ECB and CBC of a number of unique characters at 2 in AES running mode were 0.13 ms at CBC optimal and ECB was 0.05 ms. Also, a single code may be insufficient for optimality (Fig. 12).

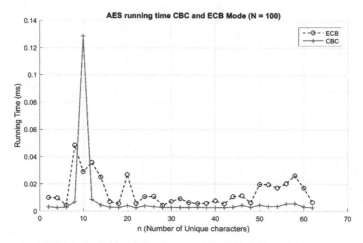

Fig. 12. Time performance for both CBC and ECB at N = 100

The ECB and CBC of a number of unique characters at 1 in AES running mode with 0.025 ms at CBC optimal and ECB 0.05 ms when N = 150. Also, a single code may be insufficient for optimality (Fig. 13).

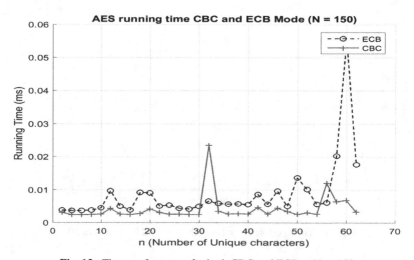

Fig. 13. Time performance for both CBC and ECB at N = 150

The experiment when N = 200 was conducted and the result below was obtained. The number of unique characters at 0.5 in AES running mode with 0.023 ms at CBC optimal and ECB 0.023 ms. The important performance determinant is the time required for encryption, AES was implemented in both ECB and CBC cipher-modes to compare performance as shown in Fig. 14.

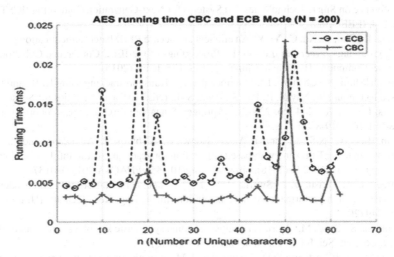

Fig. 14. Time performance for both CBC and ECB at $N = 200$

The result obtained in all the experiments provides the advantage of converting the binary object to hexadecimal which can then be written to the card while the middleware software in the third stage of implementation will store the character map against the card Serial number during the simulation.

5   Conclusion

The use of the application protocol data unit (APDU) as a medium of communication unit between a smart card reader and a smart card contains a mandatory byte header. Redundancy and patterns of stored contents with less space are assured. The unique character has a different location on the tree, the characters may not represent the same number of bit lengths. The developed model in the research using AES Techniques is to secure and fix the unique number character at a different location on the tree with N denoted in the simulation. The symbol-by-symbol cipher mode can determine the correlation running time thereby protecting the levels of communication transaction between the card and the reader.

References s

1. Konstantinides, J.M., Andreadis, I.: Performance analysis for canonical Huffman coding with fixed window size. Electron. Lett. **52**(7), 525–527 (2016)
2. Ajagbe, S.A., Adesina, A.O., Oladosu, J.B.: Empirical evaluation of efficient asymmetric encryption algorithms for the protection of electronic medical records (EMR) on web application. Int. J. Sci. Eng. Res. **10**(5), 848–871 (2019)

3. Ajagbe, S.A., Adesina, A.O., Odule, T.J., Aiyeniko, O.: Evaluation of computing resource consumption of selected symmetric-key algorithms. J. Comput. Sci. Appl. **26**(2), 64–67 (2019)

4. Padmapriya, N., Tamilarasi, K., Kanimozhi, P., Ananth Kumar, T., Ajagbe, S.A.: A secure trading system using high-level virtual machine (HLVM) algorithm. In: 2022 International Conference on Smart Technologies and Systems for Next-Generation Computing (ICSTSN), pp. 1–4. IEEE (2022)

5. Zhang, R., Zhu, L., Xu, C., Yi, Y.: An efficient and secure RFID batch authentication protocol with group tags ownership transfer. In: Proceedings of the IEEE Conference Collaboration Internet Computing Hangzhou, China, pp. 168–175. IEEE (2015)

6. Subbulakshmi, N., Chandru, R., Manimegalai, R.: Transport tracking using RFID and GSM based technique. In: Nayak, P., Pal, S., Peng, S.-L. (eds.) IoT and Analytics for Sensor Networks. LNNS, vol. 244, pp. 225–234. Springer, Singapore (2022). https://doi.org/10.1007/978-981-16-2919-8_20

7. Rjeib, H.D., Ali, N.S., Al Farawn, A., Al-Sadawi, B., Alsharqi, H.: Attendance and information system using RFID and web-based application for academic sector. Int. J. Adv. Comput. Sci. Appl. **9**(1), 266–274 (2018). https://doi.org/10.14569/IJACSA.2018.090137

8. Shireesha, T., Thrisul, K.J., Swarna, L.E.: FPGA implementation of huffman encoder and decoder for high-performance data transmission. Int. J. Eng. Res. Technol. (IJERT) **3**(2), 745–749 (2014)

9. Mankotia, S., Sood, M.: A critical analysis of some symmetric key block cipher algorithms. Int. J. Comput. Sci. Inf. Technol. **6**(1), 495–499 (2015)

10. Logunleko, K.B., Adeniji, O.D., Logunleko, A.M.: A comparative study of symmetric cryptography mechanism on DES, AES, and EB64 for information security. Int. J. Sci. Res. Comput. Sci. Eng. **8**(1), 45–51 (2020)

11. Adeniji, O.D., Akinola, O.E.: A secured text encryption with near field communication (NFC) using Huffman compression. Int. J. Eng. Appl. Comput. Sci. **4**(2), 14–18 (2022)

12. Adeniji, O.D., Olatunji, O.O.: Zero-day attack prediction with parameter setting using bi direction recurrent neural network in cyber security. Int. J. Comput. Sci. Inf. Secur. (IJCSIS) **18**(3), 111–118 (2022)

13. Yang, M., Fu, M., Zhang, Z.: The adoption of digital technologies in supply chains: Drivers, process and impact. Technol. Forecast. Soc. Change **169**, 120795 (2021)

14. Olowu, M., Yinka-Banjo, C., Misra, S., Florez, H.: A secured private-cloud computing system. In: Florez, H., Leon, M., Diaz-Nafria, J., Belli, S. (eds.) ICAI 2019. CCIS, vol. 1051, pp. 373–384. Springer, Cham (2019). https://doi.org/10.1007/978-3-030-32475-9_27

Decision Systems

A Systematic Review on Phishing Detection: A Perspective Beyond a High Accuracy in Phishing Detection

Daniel Alejandro Barreiro Herrera[✉] and Jorge Eliecer Camargo Mendoza[✉]

Universidad Nacional de Colombia, Bogotá, Colombia
{dabarreiroh,jecamargom}@unal.edu.co
https://unal.edu.co/

Abstract. Phishing is one of the cyberattacks most feared by users who use transactional services over the Internet, although there are a lot of studies focused on detecting phishing attacks showing high accuracy, those have problems acting with the effectiveness required to prevent people to fall into these attacks in the early stages. In this article, a state-of-the-art overview of phishing detection is shown using a systematic literature review methodology for studies addressed between 2016 and 2022, such as other survey papers between 2020 and 2022, focused on the different detection stages, information sources, phishing characterization, and different methods used in the literature. Found that 83% of applications works selected are focused on the mitigation stage, where the methodologies act in reactive ways using statics features that provides high accuracy but turn the models fail through time. Finally, conclusions will be presented to highlight the importance of using brand information and mixing different methods to improve stage detection and assure durability in the detection model. The article's contribution is focused on establishing another perspective that encourages future research and future related works to consider their models beyond a high accuracy and start thinking about how these models can to provide effective solutions that could be integrated into production environments to protect the users.

Keywords: Phishing · State of the art · Detection · Stages · Systematic review

1 Introduction

Our environment and how we interact as a society has lived a great transformation in recent years. Technology and especially advances in communications have been largely responsible for this, providing alternatives to carry out actions that previously were carried out in physical sites consuming a lot of time on a daily basis, and now they can be carried out with just one click. The portfolio of services available on the web every day is more diverse and complete, after

© The Author(s), under exclusive license to Springer Nature Switzerland AG 2022
H. Florez and H. Gomez (Eds.): ICAI 2022, CCIS 1643, pp. 173–188, 2022.
https://doi.org/10.1007/978-3-031-19647-8_13

the pandemic episode it is not just an alternative, this issue has accelerated the digital transformation of many organizations, retail and small business, which has been motivated to publish via web site their services, for that reason safety for people who interact with them is a subject of great importance.

In this field there are two main actors, providers that offer services to increase the number of clients who make use of them, seeking a good experience that ensures continued use on posterity, and on the other hand, there are the users of these services who despite the comfort that these services can provide, they are not willing to sacrifice security in their transactions that may affect them monetarily or violate their data privacy. According to studies such as [1] Anti-Phishing Working Group in Q4 of 2021, phishing as an attack is one of the most suffered by users on the web, this study shows an amount of 316,747 attacks in December 2021 and it is the month with the most count of phishing attacks in the history. This report also mentions that the number of attacks at the end of 2021 has tripled the number of early attacks in the early months of 2020. It also makes an analysis most targeted industry sectors and found that the financial sector is one of the most suffered (23.2%) followed closed by SAAS/Web-mail (19.5%) and e-commerce/retail services (17.3%)

The same previous analysis was done by [2] and [3] in his introduction 2 and 4 years ago respectively and surprisingly these stats have continued growing in the following years. That shows that, although the research on phishing detection is varied and not especially a recent topic, the application of mechanisms that allow not only mitigating but preventing users from falling into the early stages of phishing should be strengthened. This review paper intends to conduct a study of the state of the art in detecting phishing and establish key points where research still has shortcomings.

In [4]it is described a review of research related to phishing and what it calls security challenges, Fig. 1 shows the aspects that this article wants to highlight.

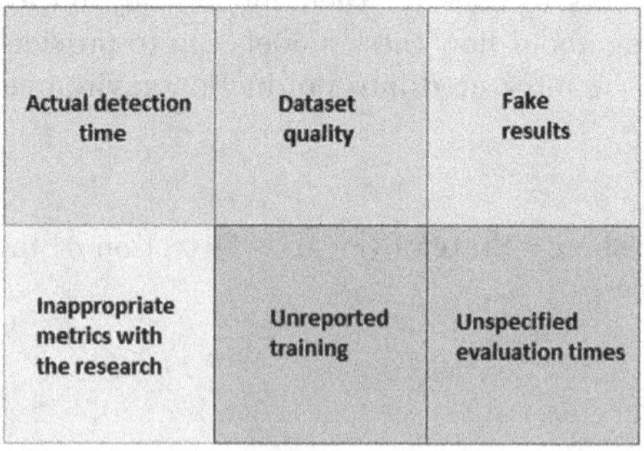

Fig. 1. Challenges in phishing detection models

The reality is that some research, especially engineering research, should be concerned with innovating previously unused methods, looking for different configurations that provide better results, or trying new approaches, it should also prioritize risks and reevaluate objectives. Phishing detection research is not particularly new and targeting efforts to detect as many malicious URLs as possible might seem like a good goal, seeking to remove the manual effort from security SOCs and ranking potentially dangerous URLs rather than a list of websites that are not. Far from the purpose of this article is to point out that this objective is bad or unnecessary, otherwise, it is considered very important and it is proposed a thought related to changing the approach in which the detection of phishing must act by mixing various methods, various actors in the process and overall considering of vital importance to act in the stage of prevention.

Another aspect to consider is the change of the characteristics of phishing in the time [4]. Phishing of 2022 is different from the phishing of 2018 in just 4 years the attackers have found ways to steal the information of the users through forms, hacked sites, free hosting services, and tunneling of local sites. For that reason, it is necessary to consider characteristics that could give us not only high accuracy in the detection currently if else also can achieve mechanisms that can be adapted to different techniques and that can identify key elements of the features of phishing to act in the early stages allowing to keep the performance of the solution for an acceptable time after the implementation.

This paper will check the studies related to phishing detection, taking into account the chronology of the different studies, and identifying the stages in which they act. The article is structured with an initial explanation of the methodology used, with the research questions formulation, and next with the literature selection to build a frame in phishing detection that allows analysis and synthesis using 4 pillars found in the review. Finally, the findings will enable it to reflect on the features identified in state of the art and adjust a model proposal for phishing identification that manages to act in the early stages of detection.

2   Methodology

2.1   Research Question Formulation

Let's launch a premise: "It is necessary to avoid that phishing attacks catch the people". So, there are many ways to be approached a possible solution, but particularly we are thinking here in some collection of programs, algorithms, and validations that alert previously a user that could fall on the attack. So the following guiding questions were raised taking into account the phishing detection broad topic:

- What are the characteristics of a phishing attack?
- What are the currently used mechanisms to identify phishing?
- What are the characteristics found in the literature used in phishing detection?
- When phishing attacks are found?
- What characteristics are attributable to the brand affected by phishing and which are typical of a generic phishing attack?
- What are the challenges and/or gaps in phishing detection?

2.2 Sourcing of Relevant Literature

The chosen articles were obtained from a search equation based on the research questions: TITLE-ABS-KEY ("Characteristics of a phishing" OR "mechanisms to identify phishing" OR "extract features phishing" OR "features brand phishing" OR "features generic phishing" OR "Machine learning phishing detection") Bibliographic database such as IEEE explorer where used in this literature search. Finally another articles where added from the citations of the first articles, taking into account some review articles and organizations mentioned in the first articles such as AWPG.

2.3 Literature Selection

Based on the research question formulation, search equations were executed to reach a reference frame that allowed identifying 4 pillars of this research, these are: When? (detection stage), Where? (information sources), What? (Phishing features), How? (Phishing methods detection). 244 research articles were collected from the first decade of 2000 up to date. However, in the first review, it was found that more recent works already covered previous studies taking as global categories detection methods as List, Heuristically, Machine learning and it was also necessary to consider a great variation in the techniques used by cyber-criminals. The same happens concerning the technologies and procedures used in the implementation of web pages. So 57 articles were identified as key in phishing detection literature in recent years, taking into account that the objective given by the thematic is identifying the 4 pillars in the articles, identifying the point of action of each one of the investigations, identifying the information sources, the characterization of the attack and the methodology used for detection.

3 Phishing Detection Stages, When?

To understand when the studies of phishing attacks are acting, it is important to identify different types of approaches in the literature that deal with the problem, and according to that analyze and present their results. Lets to show it through an example:

Lets to analyze different studies acting in completely different detection stage, studies such as [5] focuses its efforts on validating phishing from an already deployed URL, it is a mean which already exists the attack. Probably some people already also has received the same URL and some of them have fallen into phishing, meanwhile, some others have been instructed to avoid falling into it. On the other side studies such as [6] focus on creating domain generation algorithms that allow it to act in zero time; it is mean that this algorithm could identify a potential attack of phishing even before this attack would be deployed.

Although both of them are aimed at detecting phishing, they differ greatly on: methodology, stage detection, sources, and techniques used. Considering the result [6] presents accuracy less than 5% and [5] accuracy above 90%, however in where no person had to have fallen on fraud, while the accuracy can cover a wider range of brands taking into account that cost can not be quantified on how many people might fall on the attack before it is being detected. Taking this into account here a proposal of the stages for phishing detection will be proposed:

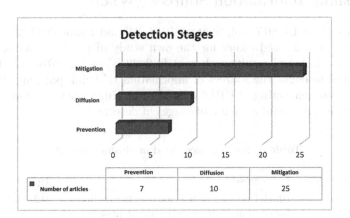

Fig. 2. Description of the detection stage in which the reviewed papers are located

3.1 Prevention Stage

Where there are jobs for generating domains such as nakamura 2019 [6], Buber 2017 [7], Adil 2020 [8], Spaulding 2016 [9], Starov 2019 [10], Ginsberg 2018 [11] and Li 2016 [12] based on features extracted, this stage is perfect pipelining for applications that actually prevent the spread of phishing before reaching a user or a propagation medium.

3.2 Diffusion Stage

In this stage there are works such as Ya 2019 [5], Li 2017 [13], Li 2020 [14], Eshmawi 2019 [15], Balim 2019 [16], Dalgic 2018 [17], Yan 2020 [18], Sahoo 2018 [19], Baykara 2018 [20], Lingam 2018 [21] and Lingam 2019 [22] related to identify mechanisms in which phishing reaches end users; this is how analyzes are presented on social networks or email dissemination, among others.

3.3 Mitigation Stage

Final stage of action on which 83% models studied act based on community databases or reported URLs such as Phishtank or Openphish.

Currently, the 35 articles and investigations here studied have focused on the last two stages, seeking to identify and study the means by which phishing spreads and how it is dispersed or analyzing the final URL in which users have already fallen.

For practical purposes throughout this paper, we will refer to these 3 previous stages as prevention, propagation, and mitigation, as it is depicted in Fig. 2.

4   Phishing Information Sources ¿Where?

In studies such as Li 2017 [13], Sharma 2017 [23] and Pande 2017 [24] different sources were found, used either for the own study of phishing characteristics, or for the validation of results such as Adil 2020 [8] and Li 2016 [12]. For this, it is essential to count the sources of information that link phishing sites or at least that allow extracting of URLs related to phishing features. Here are some sources considered useful at different stages of detection:

Table 1. Some sources used in phishing search

Source name	Description	Ref
Phishtank	PhishTank is a collaborative clearinghouse for data and information about phishing on the Internet	[12, 23, 24, 33]
APWG/ecx APWG	Different types of anti-phishing working group tools focused on the detection and centralization of information about phishing	[4]
Openphish	OpenPhish provides cyber-threat intelligence services	

Table 1 shows some sources found on the web to obtain websites reported by the community or specialized teams, where usually researchers can put together their data sets and make a preliminary analysis of the characteristics of phishing attacks. However, it is necessary to mention that these types of sources present different types of utilities for different users involved in the detection. However, although it is a good way to centralize information regarding active phishing, acting with these data for the detection of phishing would help only in the mitigation stage. Thus, it is possible to highlight what stage of detection certain investigations are at, based on the choice of their data sources. An investigation that wants to act in stages of dissemination, will look for sources related to social networks, emails, or web advertising, while a mitigation stage would use sources related to Table 1 that would allow automating classification processes where it would help in more systematized processes to classify URLs with more elements; while for early stages it would be ideal to act within the domain registry itself, where clues begin to be given that the domain is focused on impersonating another web page.

Table 2 shows some sources focused on domain detection from its prevention stage. They are sources that, based on a keyword, can allow searches for recently

Table 2. Some sources that can be used in prevention stages

Source name	Description	Ref
Domainwatch	Useful tool to search information of a domain from a keyword. Provides historical and current information	[25]
Urlscan	urlscan.io is a service for scanning and analyzing websites that can search for domains using a keyword	[26]

registered domains, as well as displaying whois, associated security certificates, and other domains.

5 Phishing Characterization What?

5.1 Challenges for Feature Selection

In studies such as Zhu 2018 [27] and Yang 2019 [28] authors seek to diversify the characteristics used in searching for higher detection accuracy. However, the more characterized phishing today is more susceptible to future attack changes. Within the features mentioned in the literature such as Aung 2019 [29], Eshmawi 2019 [15], McGahagan 2019 [30] and Yuan 2018 [31] as a phishing alarm, a wide variety of options are presented. They are considered to act at different stages since some depend on whether the URL is already deployed with a phishing attack, while others, such as those extracted in heuristic methods, know what they are specifically looking for and this could allow them to identify these characteristics in early stages, These features have different extraction mechanisms and different requirements to be able to quantify them. Ideally, a complete system should encompass the extraction of characteristics in all possible stages, although the ideal would be to identify in the prevention stage, so the greatest number of possible features in the first stage would be ideal. However, features of this type should be searched in the sources shown in Table 2. It is difficult to search in these sources if it is not sure what it is looking for, it is at this point where features related to the brand can help us search in the great number of domains registered every second and can help us validate phishing before it is in a diffusion stage.

6 Phishing Detection How?

6.1 Surveyed Papers for Detecting Phishing

It is considered important to start with the current approaches in phishing detection since it will give a general idea of what is being implemented and possible approaches to these methods (Fig. 3).

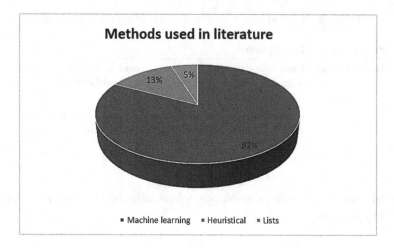

Fig. 3. Distribution of methods used in the literature.

6.2   Blacklist-Whitelist Approach

It is inevitable to mention the topic corresponding to the use of stored data for blocking IP or domains already detected as fraudulent since in articles as Buber 2017 [7], Mondal 2019 [32] and Patil 2018 [3] they are considered important features to take into account in more structured systems, where they can help mitigate an attack, being the most relevant fact of this model has a very effective mitigation potential if there is a system of interconnected information browsers. [33]

These types of strategies are still useful because they allow acting where the other validation systems have failed and although in lesser numbers, they may be able to act in early stages based on notorious precedents, such as past attacks reactivation or malicious IPs blocking.

6.3   Heuristic Approaches

The heuristic approaches depend on the quality of the features that are extracted some articles such as Ali 2019 [34], Huang 2019 [35], nakamura 2019 [6], Nathezhtha 2019 [36], Baral 2019 [37]. In these works results allow visualizing expected behaviors, that is, in the case of these implementations, it is necessary to know what is being looked for and based on this build the algorithms that allow the identification of these expected characteristics. This type of implementation can act in any of the three stages depending on the approach for which it is designed as in [6], where it is used for early detection. But it can also be used in mitigation stages since it can be based on features of a URL of phishing already deployed. In this type of method, it is important to have information about keywords and patterns that can be effective in the prevention stage. The biggest disadvantage is the static detection that results in evaluating additional non-obvious aspects.

6.4   Machine Learning

The other mechanism is the use of tools that monitor URLs and seek to give a risk based on characteristics detected on a certain web page. The tools that use machine learning have proven to have the best results in recent years [38]. Based on this risk, decisions can be made to mitigate the impact of fraud [33].

Although machine learning detection algorithms give the best results, there is still a gap in differentiating between phishing detection and validation. And the difference between these two concepts lies in the stage where the tests of these models are implemented. In 25 models studied, tests are performed on deployed URLs, so rather than detection, they are phishing validation systems acting in the mitigation stages. There is a general absence of evaluating results, being implemented in real environments and over a long period of time, to evaluate the accuracy that machine learning algorithms give against the changes that attackers show in their attacks.

6.5   Detection Phishing Methods

The methods used in the detection phishing process describe a set of phases to structure the design, the technical implementation, the results analysis and also the context of the application, and the best conditions for use it is considered. In a General classification, there are three big methods used in current research these are based list detection, heuristics detection, and machine learning detection.

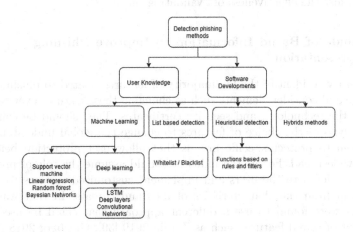

Fig. 4. Distribution of methods used in the literature.

The Fig. 4 can provide a review of methods used in detection phishing researches.

7   Opportunities for Future Researches

7.1   Identifying Challenges in the Review

An important aspect to consider is the pattern found in most of the studied identification systems. It is important to have in mind that there are studies [4] that have identified different challenges in each one of these processes and for the case of this work are considered appropriate to mention.

1. Source extraction stage: This stage presents the obtaining information challenge that is not biased to a certain group of threats, as well as obtaining the information in real-time, in general, shortening the gap that limits the quality of the data and the ideal development of research.
2. Data analysis and relevant data extraction: At this stage, there are still quite a few challenges to explore. [4] raises two main ones that are related to the quality of the data from which these characteristics are extracted and the time scaled since the attack is active.
3. Training and/or adjustment of the system: At this stage, the challenge of configuring the appropriate features are posed so that while the system learns it can be adaptable not only to the data which it was trained-configured but also could help with attacks that come to the future.
4. System evaluation: There are challenges in that proper evaluation parameter must be sought that not only depend on a correct interpretation of the results but also depends on the quality of the past stages to provide information beyond just the effectiveness of "validating phishing".

7.2   Include of Brand Information to Improve Phishing Representation

It is necessary to identify the big majority of features related to phishing at an early stage and consider elements such as changing these features over time, the change in the technology, and security certificates. They should be considered in the analysis of the choice of features to change the global understanding of the problem to protect specific brands that allow user protection before the attack is widespread. For it, the industry should assume the role of protecting the service offered to the users and implement customized systems to address the problem from the characteristics of its fraud threats. In that way, some researchers were found to use a different approach that could be used under the concept of brand features such as Zuraiq 2019 [39], Ginsberg 2018 [11] and Concone 2019 [40]. Related work was found as an example of email-phish with high similarity, demonstrating recurrent neural networks with an accuracy of more than 98% [5]. Figure 5 presents features that can be extracted in each stage.

Additionally [41] shows how from NLP-W2V-based feature extraction it is possible to run a model that can be tracked in real-time. However, a connection is not established with phishing prevention stages, so it is not possible to determine that it can work in previous stages, but it shows how it could be used for the extraction of possible brand features and their vector representation.

Another approach [42] provides results using the extraction characteristics of logos showing an accuracy of 97%. So consideration should be given to using image validation from early stages.

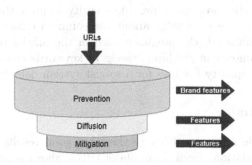

Fig. 5. Features extraction diagram and its importance in the different stages

7.3   How Patterns and Brand Features Can be Used in Prevention Stages

The most valuable improvement that the new research can develop is the capability to increase the detection in prevention stages according to Fig. 2. Additionally, these must increase the accuracy in this stage, the majority of methods used in this stage are associated with heuristics and list methods but Machine Learning methods are low. The machine learning methods need a number of relevant features that can teach the model to learn the characteristics of phishing attacks. But what kind of features can a model take of a recently registered domain? the answer is probably none with the current approach. A recent domain just has a sequence of chars associated and probably information through a WHOIS request.

Here is where a new approach can appear taking into account the patterns and the acknowledgment of the brands, although it could sound like a start of heuristics methods, a machine learning model that can learn the patterns and features associated with a brand could be powerful recognizing phishing for a specific brand. So the importance of studying these features could be of vital importance in developing a detection phishing system in the prevention stage. Here are described global features to be taken into account for this proposal:

Attacker Characterization. A domain recently registered can detect a number of features related to the WHOIS record, such as registrant data, registrar, hosting, country, and actives services as possible MX record, as also can be detected ssl certified and his respective organization.

Character Analysis. Generally, the domains can contain the name of the affected brand or similar chars [6] that can be processed with just the domain considering additionally features as [12] and involving methods such as Ya 2019 [5], McGahagan 2019 [30] and Xiang [43].

Brand Characterization. As in Sect. 5.1 described knowledge about the brand can provide a detection system to provide security to users that want to access the offered services, the knowledge about the common colors used, the official domain or IPs associated, the language used in the official pages, as also the patterns used commonly in phishing attacks as keywords and patterns in paths could provide high-quality features for a robust system detection.

8   Conclusions

After reviewing the research, although there are good results regarding phishing "detection-validation" from a sample of URLs, showing accuracy detection above 90%, in most cases, there are still many challenges that suggest trying other approaches from different perspectives to achieve comprehensive action in the 3 stages described in this paper. Although some approximations may be appropriated for a certain group of threats, it might be good to review the methodologies used to be more effective in seeking benefits applicable to reality. There is a problem in providing models that act in the early stages where the objective is not mitigation, but prevention. Acting from the domain registry itself is not possible if it is not known what is being searched in the registered domains or what content within the domain can help to identify a potential threat. Additionally, the implemented model is required to have adaptability over time, an aspect that was not found in the results of any of the related works. The industry should understand that it should protect the service offered to the users by implementing custom systems to address the problem from its own features. For this reason, a particular approach to avoid phishing from the affected brand should be considered. Identifying particular brand features could help to be focused on early detection.

References

1. apwg: Phishing activity trends report Q4 2021 (2022). http://www.apwg.org
2. Athulya, A.A.: Towards the detection of phishing attacks Praveen K TIFAC-CORE in cyber security Amrita Vishwa Vidyapeetham (2020). ISBN 9781728155180
3. Patil, V., Thakkar, P., Shah, C., Bhat, T., Godse, S.P.: Detection and prevention of phishing websites using machine learning approach. In: 2018 Fourth International Conference on Computing Communication Control and Automation (ICCUBEA), pp. 1–5 (2018). https://doi.org/10.1109/ICCUBEA.2018.8697412
4. Das, A., Baki, S., Aassal, A.E., Verma, R., Dunbar, A.: SoK: a comprehensive reexamination of phishing research from the security perspective. IEEE Commun. Surv. Tutor. **22**(1), 671–708 (2020). https://doi.org/10.1109/COMST.2019.2957750. ISSN 1553-877X VO - 22

5. Ya, J., Liu, T., Zhang, P., Shi, J., Guo, L., Gu, Z.: NeuralAS: DeepWord-based spoofed URLs detection against strong similar samples. In: 2019 International Joint Conference on Neural Networks (IJCNN), pp. 1–7 (2019). ISBN 2161-4407 VO. https://doi.org/10.1109/IJCNN.2019.8852416

6. Nakamura, A., Dobashi, F.: Proactive phishing sites detection. In: IEEE/WIC/ACM International Conference on Web Intelligence, Series WI 2019, pp. 443–448. Association for Computing Machinery, New York (2019). https://doi.org/10.1145/3350546.3352565. ISBN 9781450369343

7. Buber, E., Demir, Ö., Sahingoz, O.K.: Feature selections for the machine learning based detection of phishing websites. In: 2017 International Artificial Intelligence and Data Processing Symposium (IDAP), pp. 1–5 (2017). https://doi.org/10.1109/IDAP.2017.8090317. ISBN: VO

8. Adil, M., Khan, R., Ghani, M.A.N.U.: Preventive techniques of phishing attacks in networks. In: 2020 3rd International Conference on Advancements in Computational Sciences (ICACS), pp. 1–8 (2020). https://doi.org/10.1109/ICACS47775.2020.9055943. ISBN: VO

9. Spaulding, J., Upadhyaya, S., Mohaisen, A.: The landscape of domain name typosquatting: techniques and countermeasures. In: 2016 11th International Conference on Availability, Reliability and Security (ARES), pp. 284–289 (2016). https://doi.org/10.1109/ARES.2016.84. ISBN: VO

10. Starov, O., Zhou, Y., Wang, J.: Detecting malicious campaigns in obfuscated JavaScript with scalable behavioral analysis. In: 2019 IEEE Security and Privacy Workshops (SPW), pp. 218–223 (2019). https://doi.org/10.1109/SPW.2019.00048. ISBN: VO

11. Ginsberg, A., Yu, C.: Rapid homoglyph prediction and detection. In: 2018 1st International Conference on Data Intelligence and Security (ICDIS), pp. 17–23 (2018). https://doi.org/10.1109/ICDIS.2018.00010. ISBN: VO

12. Li, X., Geng, G., Yan, Z., Chen, Y., Lee, X.: Phishing detection based on newly registered domains. In: 2016 IEEE International Conference on Big Data (Big Data), pp. 3685–3692 (2016). https://doi.org/10.1109/BigData.2016.7841036. ISBN: VO

13. Li, J., Wang, S.: PhishBox: an approach for phishing validation and detection. In: 2017 IEEE 15th International Conference on Dependable, Autonomic and Secure Computing, 15th International Conference on Pervasive Intelligence and Computing, 3rd International Conference on Big Data Intelligence and Computing and Cyber Science and Technology Congress(DASC/PiCom/DataCom/CyberSciTech), pp. 557–564 (2017). https://doi.org/10.1109/DASC-PICom-DataCom-CyberSciTec.2017.101. ISBN: VO

14. Li, Q., Cheng, M., Wang, J., Sun, B.: LSTM based phishing detection for big email data. IEEE Trans. Big Data 1 (2020). https://doi.org/10.1109/TBDATA.2020.2978915. ISSN 2332-7790 VO

15. Eshmawi, A., Nair, S.: The roving proxy framewrok for SMS spam and phishing detection. In: 2019 2nd International Conference on Computer Applications & Information Security (ICCAIS), pp. 1–6 (2019). https://doi.org/10.1109/CAIS.2019.8769562. ISBN: VO

16. Balim, C., Gunal, E.S.: Automatic detection of smishing attacks by machine learning methods. In: 2019 1st International Informatics and Software Engineering Conference (UBMYK), pp. 1–3 (2019). https://doi.org/10.1109/UBMYK48245.2019.8965429. ISBN: VO

17. Dalgic, F.C., Bozkir, A.S., Aydos, M.: Phish-IRIS: a new approach for vision based brand prediction of phishing web pages via compact visual descriptors. In: 2018 2nd International Symposium on Multidisciplinary Studies and Innovative Technologies (ISMSIT), pp. 1–8 (2018). https://doi.org/10.1109/ISMSIT.2018.8567299. ISBN: VO

18. Yan, X., Xu, Y., Xing, X., Cui, B., Guo, Z., Guo, T.: Trustworthy network anomaly detection based on an adaptive learning rate and momentum in IIoT. IEEE Trans. Ind. Inform. 1 (2020). https://doi.org/10.1109/TII.2020.2975227. ISSN 1941-0050 VO

19. Sahoo, P.K.: Data mining a way to solve phishing attacks. In: 2018 International Conference on Current Trends towards Converging Technologies (ICCTCT), pp. 1–5 (2018). https://doi.org/10.1109/ICCTCT.2018.8550910. ISBN: VO

20. Baykara, M., Gürel, Z.Z.: Detection of phishing attacks. In: 2018 6th International Symposium on Digital Forensic and Security (ISDFS), pp. 1–5 (2018). https://doi.org/10.1109/ISDFS.2018.8355389. ISBN: VO

21. Lingam, G., Rout, R.R., Somayajulu, D.V.L.N.: Detection of social botnet using a trust model based on spam content in Twitter network. In: 2018 IEEE 13th International Conference on Industrial and Information Systems (ICIIS), pp. 280–285 (2018). https://doi.org/10.1109/ICIINFS.2018.8721318. ISBN 2164-7011 VO

22. Lingam, G., Rout, R.R., Somayajulu, D.V.L.N.: Deep Q-learning and particle swarm optimization for bot detection in online social networks. In: 2019 10th International Conference on Computing, Communication and Networking Technologies (ICCCNT), pp. 1–6 (2019). https://doi.org/10.1109/ICCCNT45670.2019.8944493. ISBN: VO

23. Sharma, H., Meenakshi, E., Bhatia, S.K.: A comparative analysis and awareness survey of phishing detection tools. In: 2017 2nd IEEE International Conference on Recent Trends in Electronics, Information & Communication Technology (RTEICT), pp. 1437–1442 (2017). https://doi.org/10.1109/RTEICT.2017.8256835. ISBN: VO

24. Pande, D.N., Voditel, P.S.: Spear phishing: diagnosing attack paradigm. In: 2017 International Conference on Wireless Communications, Signal Processing and Networking (WiSPNET), pp. 2720–2724 (2017). https://doi.org/10.1109/WiSPNET.2017.8300257. ISBN: VO

25. DomainWatch, DomainWatch - Domain WHOIS Search, Website Information. https://domainwat.ch/

26. urlscan, URL and website scanner. https://urlscan.io/

27. Zhu, E., Ye, C., Liu, D., Liu, F., Wang, F., Li, X.: An effective neural network phishing detection model based on optimal feature selection. In: 2018 IEEE International Conference on Parallel & Distributed Processing with Applications, Ubiquitous Computing & Communications, Big Data & Cloud Computing, Social Computing & Networking, Sustainable Computing & Communications (ISPA/IUCC/BDCloud/SocialCom/SustainCom), pp. 781–787 (2018). https://doi.org/10.1109/BDCloud.2018.00117. ISBN: VO

28. Yang, P., Zhao, G., Zeng, P.: Phishing website detection based on multidimensional features driven by deep learning. IEEE Access 7, 15 196–15 209 (2019). https://doi.org/10.1109/ACCESS.2019.2892066. ISBN: 2169-3536 VO - 7

29. Aung, E.S., Yamana, H.: URL-based phishing detection using the entropy of non-alphanumeric characters. In: Proceedings of the 21st International Conference on Information Integration and Web-Based Applications & Services, iiWAS2019, v. Association for Computing Machinery, New York (2019). https://doi.org/10.1145/3366030.3366064. ISBN 9781450371797

30. McGahagan, J.. Bhansali, ,D, Gratian, M., Cukier, M.: A comprehensive evaluation of HTTP header features for detecting malicious websites. In: 2019 15th European Dependable Computing Conference (EDCC), pp. 75–82 (2019). https://doi.org/10.1109/EDCC.2019.00025. ISBN 2641-810X VO

31. Yuan, H., Chen, X., Li, Y., Yang, Z., Liu, W.: Detecting phishing websites and targets based on URLs and webpage links. In: 2018 24th International Conference on Pattern Recognition (ICPR), pp. 3669–3674 (2018). https://doi.org/10.1109/ICPR.2018.8546262. ISBN 1051-4651 VO

32. Mondal, S., Maheshwari, D., Pai, N., Biwalkar, A.: A review on detecting phishing URLs using clustering algorithms. In: 2019 International Conference on Advances in Computing, Communication and Control (ICAC3), pp. 1–6 (2019). https://doi.org/10.1109/ICAC347590.2019.9036837. ISBN: VO

33. Megha, N., Babu, K.R.R., Sherly, E.: An intelligent system for phishing attack detection and prevention. In: 2019 International Conference on Communication and Electronics Systems (ICCES), pp. 1577–1582 (2019). https://doi.org/10.1109/ICCES45898.2019.9002204. ISBN: VO

34. Ali, W., Ahmed, A.A.: Hybrid intelligent phishing website prediction using deep neural networks with genetic algorithm-based feature selection and weighting. IET Inf. Secur. **13**(6), 659–669 (2019). https://doi.org/10.1049/iet-ifs.2019.0006. ISSN 1751-8717 VO - 13

35. Huang, Y., Qin, J., Wen, W.: Phishing URL detection via capsule-based neural network. In: 2019 IEEE 13th International Conference on Anti-counterfeiting, Security, and Identification (ASID), pp. 22–26 (2019). https://doi.org/10.1109/ICASID.2019.8925000. ISBN 2163-5056 VO

36. Nathezhtha, T., Sangeetha, D., Vaidehi, V.: WC-PAD: web crawling based phishing attack detection. In: 2019 International Carnahan Conference on Security Technology (ICCST), pp. 1–6 (2019). https://doi.org/10.1109/CCST.2019.8888416. ISBN 2153-0742 VO

37. Baral, G., Arachchilage, N.A.G.: Building condence not to be phished through a gamified approach: conceptualising user's self-efficacy in phishing threat avoidance behaviour. In: 2019 Cybersecurity and Cyberforensics Conference (CCC), pp. 102–110 (2019). https://doi.org/10.1109/CCC.2019.000-1. ISBN: VO

38. Anand, A., Gorde, K., Moniz, J.R.A., Park, N., Chakraborty, T., Chu, B.: Phishing URL detection with oversampling based on text generative adversarial networks. In: 2018 IEEE International Conference on Big Data (Big Data), pp. 1168–1177 (2018). https://doi.org/10.1109/BigData.2018.8622547. ISBN: VO

39. Zuraiq, A.A., Alkasassbeh, M.: Review: phishing detection approaches. In: 2019 2nd International Conference on new Trends in Computing Sciences (ICTCS), pp. 1–6 (2019). https://doi.org/10.1109/ICTCS.2019.8923069. ISBN: VO

40. Concone, F., Re, G.L., Morana, M., Ruocco, C.: Assisted labeling for spam account detection on Twitter. In: 2019 IEEE International Conference on Smart Computing (SMARTCOMP), pp. 359–366 (2019). https://doi.org/10.1109/SMARTCOMP.2019.00073. ISBN: VO

41. Yazhmozhi, V.M., Janet, B.: Natural language processing and machine learning based phishing website detection system. In: 2019 Third International conference on I-SMAC (IoT in Social, Mobile, Analytics and Cloud) (I-SMAC), pp. 336–340 (2019). https://doi.org/10.1109/I-SMAC47947.2019.9032492. ISBN: VO

42. Yao, W., Ding, Y., Li, X.: LogoPhish: a new two-dimensional code phishing attack detection method. In: 2018 IEEE Intl Conf on Parallel & Distributed Processing with Applications, Ubiquitous Computing & Communications, Big Data & Cloud Computing, Social Computing & Networking, Sustainable Computing & Communications (ISPA/IUCC/BDCloud/SocialCom/SustainCom), pp. 231–236 (2018). https://doi.org/10.1109/BDCloud.2018.00045. ISBN: VO
43. Xiang, G., Hong, J., Rose, C.P., Cranor, L.: CANTINA+: a featurerich machine learning framework for detecting phishing web sites (2011)

Application of Duality Properties of Renyi Entropy for Parameter Tuning in an Unsupervised Machine Learning Task

Sergei Koltcov$^{(\boxtimes)}$

Laboratory for Social and Cognitive Informatics, National Research University Higher School of Economics, 55/2 Sedova Street, St. Petersburg 192148, Russia
skoltsov@hse.ru

Abstract. This work demonstrates the possibility of applying the duality properties of a statistical collection of texts to determine the optimal number of topics/clusters. In a series of numerical experiments on text data, it was demonstrated that Renyi entropy of topic models, expressed in S_q form (based on the escort distribution), as a function of the number of topics, is the most effective in terms of determining the optimal number of topics. At the same time, S_{2-Q} and $S_{1/q}$ forms are not suitable for determining the number of topics.

Keywords: Duality · Renyi entropy · Tsallis entropy · Topic modeling

1 Introduction

To date, the concept of statistical system and the respective entropic approaches have been mainly applied to the analysis of physical phenomena. At the same time, in human societies the proliferation of the Internet that generates huge amounts of data has led to the emergence of datasets comparable in size with mesoscopic physical systems. This opens a possibility to apply the concepts from statistical physics to different machine learning tasks existing for these datasets by viewing the latter as statistical systems.

A statistical system is a mesoscopic ensemble of elements that interact with one another. The character of the interaction determines the behavior of the elements in the phase space. In complex systems, in contrast to simple systems, the phase space is determined by a small fraction of elements, whose behavior, additionally, may change a lot with the change of external parameters.

The results of the project "Modeling the structure and socio-psychological factors of news perception", carried out within the framework of the Basic Research Program at the National Research University Higher School of Economics (HSE University) in 2022, are presented in this work.

H. Florez and H. Gomez (Eds.): ICAI 2022, CCIS 1643, pp. 189–203, 2022.
https://doi.org/10.1007/978-3-031-19647-8_14

Different formulations of statistical systems are caused by the application of various deformed functions and the escort distribution [33], which lead to the substitution of standard Shannon entropy by Tsallis and Renyi entropies. Another important factor that affects the behavior of such statistical systems is the group properties of deformed functions, notably by their duality [12,14]. Among different types of dualities, 2-Q duality has been found the one of most appropriate for the formulation of physical systems.

Unlike Shannon entropy which has been already applied for machine learning tasks (e.g. in decision tree learning, Bayesian learning, and classification [1,5,10]) the potential of deformed entropies stays relatively underresearched. It is only in the last five years that a series of works discussing the application of deformed functions for machine learning tasks [16,17,21,23,28,29,34] has appeared. Of them, two [16,17] are devoted to topic modeling, but not to 2-Q duality, and only one considers 2-Q duality, but for another unsupervised machine learning task [34].

This work generalizes the results of our previous research [16,17] to the three types of deformed entropies by examining the role of their grouping properties in model parameter optimization. Specifically, we propose the formulation of q, $2 - Q$, and $1/q$ versions of our entropic approach to the task of finding an optimal number of clusters in topic models. At present, this task stays largely unresolved as most topic modeling algorithms offer their users to set the number of clusters manually without providing any criteria for such decisions. At the same time, the number of topics is important because it determines the level of topic granularity and, ideally, should signal the algorithm user how diverse the collection is. The latter is only possible if this number can be inferred from the data instead of being arbitrarily pre-set by a user.

The rest of this work consists of the following parts. Section 2.1 briefly describes the assumptions and the problems of topic modeling. Section 2.2 establishes a link between topic modeling and statistical physics. Section 2.3 describes the earlier developed entropic approach [16] for topic modeling. Section 3 considers q, $2 - Q$, and $1/q$ versions of the entropic approach in topic modeling. Section 4.1 describes our English- and Russian-language datasets and the experiments conducted on them. Sections 4.2 and 4.3 analyze the obtained results for the three versions of the entropic approach. Section 5 summarizes our findings.

2   The Entropic Approach to Topic Modeling

2.1   Introduction into Topic Modeling

Topic modeling (TM), although it has been developed for finding topics in texts, is in fact an advanced version of fuzzy cluster analysis suitable for grouping very diverse types of data, including mass spectra [8], images [24], and social media news [7]. A special feature of topic modeling is the ability to co-cluster both observations and features by latent variables, e.g. words by topics and documents by topics, simultaneously. Mathematically, topic modeling is a family of algorithms, which are based on the following statements [13]:

1. Let D be a collection of text documents, W be the set (vocabulary) of all unique words. Each document $d \in D$ represents a sequence of words $w_1, ..., w_{n_d}$ from the vocabulary W. By $|W|$ we will denote the size of the vocabulary.
2. Assume that there exists a finite number of topics $|T|$, and each entrance of word w in document d is associated with some topic $t \in T$. A topic is a set of words that often (in the statistical sense) appear together in a large number of documents.
3. The document collection is considered a random and independent sample of triples (w_i, d_i, t_i), $i = 1, ..., n$ from a discrete distribution $p(w, d, t)$ on a finite probability space $W \times D \times T$. Words and documents are observable variables, while topics are latent (hidden) variables.
4. It is assumed that the order of words in documents is not important for topics identification ('bag of words' model). The order of documents in the collection is neither important.

In TM, it is assumed that probability $p(w|d)$ of word w in document d can be expressed through the product of distributions $p(w|t)$ and $p(t|d)$. According to the formula of total probability and the hypothesis of conditional independence, we obtain the following expression [13]:

$$p(w|d) = \sum_{t \in T} p(w|t)p(t|d) = \sum_{t \in T} \phi_{wt}\theta_{td}, \qquad (1)$$

where $p(w|t) \equiv \phi_{wt}$ is the distribution of words by topics, $p(t|d) \equiv \theta_{td}$ is the distribution of topics by documents.

Thus, to construct a topic model of a dataset means to solve an inverse problem where one has to find the set of hidden topics based on observable variables d and w, i.e., to find the set of one-dimensional conditional distributions $p(w|t) \equiv \phi_{wt}$ for each topic t, which constitute matrix Φ (distribution of words by topics) and the set of one-dimensional distributions $p(t|d) \equiv \theta_{td}$ for each document d, which form matrix Θ (distribution of documents by topics). In the literature, one can find three main types of models that allow solving this inverse task: 1) a E-M based family of models which unites pLSA [13], variational LDA [6], BigARTM [35] and some others, where the hidden distributions are searched for by means of E-M algorithm; 2) Gibbs sampling based models [30], including the initial Gibbs sampling algorithm [11] and its extensions, such as GLDA [20], among others; 3) non-parametric hierarchical topic models, where Chinese restaurant franchise is used for model inference [32]. An overview of the principles of topic model construction and the problems of model stability is given in work [9]. For the models based on the E-M algorithm and Gibbs sampling procedure, the problem of determining the optimal number of topics has not been solved yet. The authors of the non-parametric model claim that this model allows selecting the optimal number of topics automatically, however, this model has a set of parameters whose values significantly influence the inferred number of topics. An analysis of hierarchical models in terms of the entropic approach was made in work [19]. In the current work, we will consider only the models based on the E-M algorithm and Gibbs sampling procedure.

2.2 Free Energy of a Textual Collection

A large textual collection can be considered an open statistical system that can reside in different degrees of order. At the initial moment (when the clustering procedure has not been performed yet), such a system resides in a state with a large value of entropy. This occurs because initially matrices Φ and Θ either have flat (uniform) distributions when all the probabilities are equal and constant (for models based on Gibbs sampling procedure), or are filled with random values in the range $[0, 1]$ (for models based on E-M algorithm). Clustering is a procedure of ordering, where the results significantly depend on model parameters. It is thus both possible and important to investigate clustering solutions as statistical systems in terms of the degree of their orderliness and its relation to different parameters, including the number of clusters (topics).

Since the sum of all probabilities in matrix Φ equals the number of topics, one can view the number of topics as the temperature of an open statistical system. The size of matrix Φ is $|W| \times |T|$. Thus, this matrix defines the total number of microstates in a textual statistical system. Each element of the matrix is a microstate characterized by the probability of belonging of a word to a topic. Correspondingly, the energy of a microstate can be expressed as $\epsilon_{wt} = -\ln(\phi_{wt})$. A small part of words (about 3–5%) is assigned high probabilities resulting from clustering, while a larger part of words has small probabilities. Thus, the major contribution to the energy and entropy of such a system is made by words with high probabilities. Based on ideas of Klimontovich, Mora, and Walczak from works [15, 25], one can express the density of states function through the Heaviside step function $(H(\cdot))$ as follows:

$$\rho = \frac{\sum_{t \in T} \sum_{w \in W} H(\phi_{wt} - 1/|W|)}{|T| \cdot |W|}. \tag{2}$$

If probability ϕ_{wt} is above the threshold $1/|W|$, then Heaviside function $H(\phi_{wt} - 1/|W|)$ equals one, otherwise it is zero. The value of the threshold $1/|W|$ corresponds to the initial distribution of probabilities in matrix Φ, i.e., the flat distribution. The relative Gibbs-Shannon entropy of the system can be expressed as:

$$S(E) = \ln(\rho) = \ln(\sum_{t \in T} \sum_{w \in W} H(\phi_{wt} - 1/|W|)) - \ln(|T| \cdot |W|) \tag{3}$$

Equation 3 characterizes the difference between the entropies of the initial distribution and the distribution obtained as a result of topic modeling. The internal relative energy of the ensemble of words in a text collection is expressed as follows: $E = -\ln(\frac{\sum_{t \in T} \sum_{w \in W} \phi_{wt} \cdot H(\phi_{wt} - 1/|W|)}{|T|}) = -\ln(\tilde{P})$. Thus, the relative free energy of a text collection as a function of the number of topics can be expressed as:

$$\Lambda_F = F(T) - F_0 = (E(T) - E_0) - T \cdot (S(T) - S_0) = -\ln(\tilde{P}) - T\ln(\rho), \tag{4}$$

where F_0, E_0, S_0 are the free energy, internal energy, and entropy of the initial state, while $F(T), E(T), S(T)$ are the free energy, internal energy, and entropy of the state after clustering [16].

2.3   Renyi and Tsallis Entropies for Textual Collections

The partition function of a textual collection can be expressed through the density of states function ρ, internal energy and escort distribution as $Z_q = \exp(-qE + S) = \rho \tilde{P}^q$, where $q = 1/T$. Thus, q version of Renyi entropy for a textual collection can be expressed as follows:

$$S_q^R = \frac{\ln(Z_q)}{q-1} = \frac{\ln(\rho \tilde{P}^q)}{q-1} = \frac{\ln(\rho) + q \ln(\tilde{P})}{q-1}. \tag{5}$$

In turn, Renyi entropy can also be expressed in terms of Tsallis entropy by means of the following relation [4]: $Z_q = \exp((q-1)S_q^R)$, which implies $S_q^T = \frac{1-\exp((q-1)S_q^R)}{q-1}$.

The idea of Renyi entropy application in TM is based on the information-theoretic approach, according to which the information maximum of a system corresponds to the entropy minimum. Thus, Renyi entropy approach allows us to partially solve the problem of determining the number of topics in TM; namely, to find the optimal model parameters, one has to find the Renyi entropy minimum. In works [16,17], the behavior of different topic models (pLSA, variational LDA, LDA Gibbs sampling, GLDA) was analyzed under variation of the number of topics and other model hyper-parameters. Document collections with human topical mark-up were used as test datasets. It was demonstrated that the minimum of q version of Renyi entropy is located in the region of the number of topics that coincides with the human markup. However, these works have not considered the role of duality $(2 - Q$ and $1/q)$.

3   The Duality of Topic Modeling

Both Tsallis and Renyi entropies can be expressed in terms of deformed logarithm, which is defined as follows [4,36]: $\ln_q(x) = \frac{x^{1-q}-1}{1-q}$. A '$2-q$' duality property is a well known feature of deformed logarithms, namely of those expressed as $-\ln_q(x^{-1}) = \ln_{2-q}(x)$. This property has been widely discussed in the literature [2,4,36] in the framework of non-extensive statistical physics. However, in the field of machine learning, it has not been investigated. Based on the definition of deformed logarithm, Renyi and Tsallis entropies in topic modeling can be expressed in two forms, q and $2 - Q$. By means of group properties [12], one can transform q versions of Renyi and Tsallis entropies into $2 - Q$ forms:

$$S_{2-Q}^R = \frac{\ln(Z_{2-Q})}{1-Q} = \frac{\ln(\rho \tilde{P}^{2-Q})}{1-Q} \tag{6}$$

$$S_{2-Q}^T = \frac{1 - \exp((1-Q)S_{2-Q}^R)}{1-Q}. \tag{7}$$

The inverse number of topics $(1/T)$ is considered the deformation parameter q or Q. Correspondingly, for $\hat{q} = 1/q$, we obtain the following expressions:

$$S_{\hat{q}}^R = \frac{\ln(Z_{\hat{q}})}{\hat{q}-1} = \frac{\ln(\rho \tilde{P}^{\hat{q}})}{\hat{q}-1} = \frac{\ln(\rho) + \hat{q}\ln(\tilde{P})}{\hat{q}-1} \tag{8}$$

$$S_{\hat{q}}^T = \frac{1 - \exp((\hat{q}-1)S_{\hat{q}}^R)}{\hat{q}-1}. \tag{9}$$

The choice of q, $2 - Q$, or $1/q$ formulation for machine learning applications can be made by comparing Renyi/Tsallis entropy curves as functions of the number of topics, i.e., of the deformation parameter q under different versions of duality.

Let us note that the obtained expressions for Renyi and Tsallis entropies in terms of $2 - Q$ and $1/q$ duality are the particular cases of a triplet relation $\nu(1 - \mu) + 1 = q$ [31], where for $\nu = 1$, one obtains $\mu = 2 - q$ duality. However, a complete research of different variations of parameters q, μ, ν for the purposes of cluster analysis is currently complicated due to the following reason. In such research, one has to assign the parameters μ, ν meanings in terms of a machine learning task being solved. For instance, the inverse number of topics $(q = 1/T)$ can be used as the first parameter (q). The second parameter (μ) can be reserved for Jaccard coefficient that measures the change in the composition of words in similar topics of different solutions under variation of the number of topics, as proposed in [18]. This allows to estimate the degree of orderliness in a cluster solution by means of Sharma-Mittal entropy. However, for the third parameter, no interpretation exists yet.

Let us also note that the formulation of Renyi entropy may differ by its sign. For instance, in Beck notation [4], the coefficient of Renyi entropy is $1/(q-1)$ while in Tsallis notation [33], the coefficient is $1/(1-q)$. The choice of Renyi entropy formulation is determined by the fact that entropy has to be positive both for a small number of topics/clusters and a large number of topics/clusters in numerical experiments. This is related to the fact that for a small number of clusters (e.g., one or two), the information value of such a model is minimal; correspondingly, the entropy of the model is maximal. On the other hand, for a large number of topics or clusters, the distribution of words by topics tends to uniform distribution, which, in turn, corresponds to a large value of entropy and a small information value of the model.

In work [22], it was demonstrated that Tsallis entropy is more stable than Renyi entropy. It leads to the fact that, for text collections, a valley of Tsallis entropy curve containing the minimum value is rather wide which makes it difficult to determine the exact position of the minimum [16]. Thus, the lack of Lesche stability in the Renyi entropy turns out to be useful for revealing local minima necessary for unsupervised models. Based on the above observations, we consider only different versions of Renyi entropy formulations in this work.

An example of comparing Tsallis and Renyi entropy in topic models is given in work [16]. Specifically, we compare the behavior of Renyi entropy curves for its q, $2 - Q$ and $1/q$ versions, which are calculated based on the results of topic modeling for three different datasets, two of which have a human markup on topics.

4 Results and Discussion

4.1 Description of Numerical Experiments

To demonstrate the effect of q, $2 - Q$ and $1/q$ duality for determining the optimal number of topics/clusters, we conducted a set of computer experiments on the three following datasets.

- 'Lenta' dataset in the Russian language (8630 documents containing 23297 unique words). The documents of the dataset were manually classified by assessors into 10 topics. However, some of these topics can be considered as subclusters of larger topics. Thus, this dataset can be described by 7–10 topics.
- '20 NewsGroups' dataset is a well-known and widely used dataset in the field of topic modeling. The dataset is available at http://qwone.com/~jason/20Newsgroups/. It contains 15425 news articles in English with 50965 unique words. Each news article is assigned one of 20 topic groups. In works [3,16], it was demonstrated that this collection can be represented by 14–20 topics.
- 'LiveJournal' dataset in Russian language. This dataset contains 101481 posts with 172939 unique words from 'LiveJournal' blog platform. This collection has no human markup.

In the framework of this work, the following topic models were tested: 1) pLSA model with E-M inference algorithm [13], 2) LDA model with Gibbs sampling procedure (LDA GS) [30], and 3) LDA model with variational E-M algorithm (VLDA) [6]. The number of topics was varied in the range of 2–50 topics for Lenta and 20 NewsGroups datasets, and in the range of 2–50 for LiveJournal dataset.

4.2 Renyi Entropy of Topic Models with E-M Algorithms (pLSA and VLDA Models)

Figures 1, 2, 3, 4, 5 and 6 show the results of the calculation of Renyi entropy in the three different versions of its formulation. Each figure plots all types of Renyi entropy as the functions of the number of topics modeled by one of the two types of algorithms (E-M or Gibbs sampling) on one of the three aforementioned datasets. $1/q$ type of Renyi entropy lines are omitted in the figures devoted to the LiveJournal dataset for the reason addressed further below.

As both tested E-M models (pLSA and VLDA) produce nearly identical outputs, we do not report all the resulting graphs in this section. Instead, Figs. 1

and 2 plot the pLSA-based results for Lenta and 20NewsGroups datasets, respectively, while Fig. 3 plots VLDA-based results for LiveJournal dataset, as an illustration.

From Figs. 1 and 2 it can be seen that both $2 - Q$ and $1/q$ formulations of Entropy functions (red and green lines) are monotonically increasing without producing any visible extrema. The functions of q formulation of Entropy, on the contrary, start with a relatively sharp decrease and, after reaching a minimum, demonstrate a gradual increase on both figures. The difference between the figures is in the location of the minima. For Lenta dataset (Fig. 1), the minimum is seven topics which is close to the human mark-up lying between 7 and 10 topics. For 20NewsGroups dataset (Fig. 2) the minimum is found at 14 topics which also lies within the range given by the human mark-up (14–20). For VLDA models that are not reported in the figures the observed minima produced by q formulation of Entropy are 10 and 18 topics, respectively.

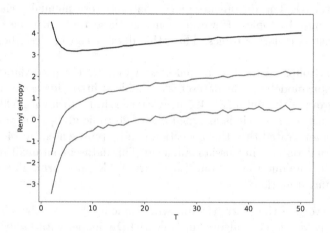

Fig. 1. Three versions of Renyi entropy for Lenta dataset (pLSA model). Black: S_q^R; green: $S_{1/q}^R$; red: S_{2-Q}^R. (Color figure online)

Figure 3 demonstrates Renyi entropy curves for 'LiveJournal' dataset. This dataset has no human markup, but, as it has been previously shown [16], in addition to the global entropy minimum, some (but not all) algorithms identify a number of local minima in it, at the topic numbers significantly higher than that of the global minimum. This suggests that LiveJournal dataset, being very large, is likely to have an hierarchical topical structure. If so, the global minimum should correspond to the number of topics of the first, that is, the most general level, while other minima may indicate the optimal number of topics for lower levels of the hierarchy. Work [27] also suggests that, for some desired levels of topic granularity, the reasonable number of topics for this dataset may be very high. On Fig. 3, however, we can see that VLDA model finds only one minimum around 14 topics. The behavior of pLSA (not shown) is similar.

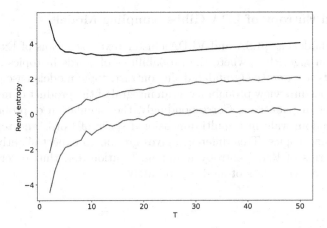

Fig. 2. Three versions of Renyi entropy for 20 NewsGroups dataset (pLSA model). Black: S_q^R; green: $S_{1/q}^R$; red: S_{2-Q}^R. (Color figure online)

We do not provide the curve of Renyi entropy in $1/q$ formulation since for large numbers of topics (about 80 and more), the partition function becomes infinitely large which does not allow calculating Renyi entropy. Entropy in $2 - Q$ formulation, as earlier, demonstrates no clear minimum. Both trends are true for pLSA as well.

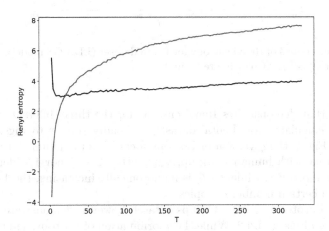

Fig. 3. Two versions of Renyi entropy for LiveJournal dataset (VLDA model). Black: S_q^R; red: S_{2-Q}^R. (Color figure online)

4.3   Renyi Entropy of LDA Gibbs Sampling Model

Such topic models as pLSA and VLDA cluster texts by means of Expectation-Maximization algorithm, where the probabilities of words in topics and topics in documents are iteratively updated. In contrast, topic models based on Gibbs sampling procedure view probability as an integral of the product of multinomial and Dirichlet distributions. Correspondingly, the calculation of probabilities is based on random walk in a multi-dimensional space of words and topics, or of documents and topics. This difference gives ground to expect slightly different results in terms of Renyi entropy minimum location and thus determines the necessity to test this class of models separately.

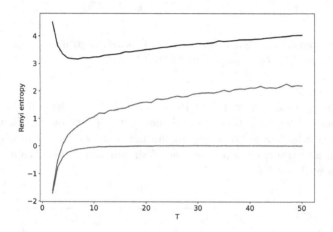

Fig. 4. Three versions of Renyi entropy for Lenta dataset (LDA GS model). Black: S_q^R; green: $S_{1/q}^R$; red: S_{2-Q}^R. (Color figure online)

Figure 4 that demonstrates Renyi entropy for the three different versions of formulation calculated for 'Lenta' dataset is broadly similar to Figs. 1 and 2. Just like in Fig. 1, the q version of Entropy locates its minimum at the number of 7, consistent with human mark-up, but neither $2 - Q$ nor $1/q$ demonstrate any minima; moreover, while $2 - Q$ is monotonically increasing, the $1/q$ version is flat after a certain number of topics.

Figure 5, devoted to 20NewsGroups dataset, however, demonstrates a certain difference from Figs. 1 and 2. While the q formulation of Entropy, again, matches the human mark-up at the number of 17, and $1/q$ version has no clear minimum, the $2 - Q$ version of entropy does have an extremum, but it turns to be a maximum there where the q version shows the minimum. As one can swap the sign when formulating Renyi entropy, this maximum, in fact, may be interpreted as a minimum. However, even when viewed like this, the $2 - Q$ version identifies an optimal number of topics far from human mark-up (5 against 14–20).

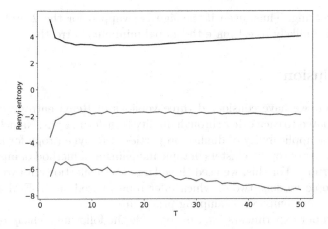

Fig. 5. Three versions of Renyi entropy for 20 NewsGroups dataset (LDA GS model).
Black: S_q^R; green: $S_{1/q}^R$; red: S_{2-Q}^R. (Color figure online)

Finally, comparing the results of VLDA and LDA GS models for the Live-Journal dataset (Figs. 3 and 6) one can see several important trends. First, for neither models $1/q$ formulation of Entropy can be calculated. Second, one can see that the model based on Gibbs sampling is more sensitive than the those based on E-M algorithm since its q version has not only the global minimum at 12 topics, but also the local minima at 116 and around 200 topics which is in line with the assumed hierarchical structure of this dataset. The $2 - Q$ version also shows fluctuations around the numbers of the local minima - 116 and 200, but they look more like local maxima than minima, while in the area of the global minimum, as identified by the q version, the $2 - Q$ version is monotonically and

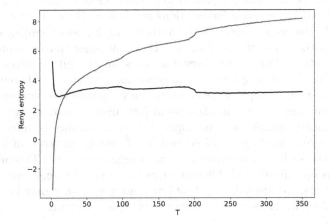

Fig. 6. Two versions of Renyi entropy for LiveJournal dataset (LDA GS model). Black: S_q^R; red: S_{2-Q}^R. (Color figure online)

rapidly increasing. Thus, even if the sign is swapped for the $2 - Q$ version of entropy, it is unlikely to estimate the global minimum correctly.

5   Conclusion

In this paper, we have considered three versions of Renyi entropy calculation which are related to each other through duality transformations. Namely, we have estimated the applicability of duality properties of Renyi entropy for finding the optimal number of topics/clusters in topic modeling as a method of unsupervised machine learning. For this, we used three large text collections in two languages and three topic models, two of which infer topics based on an E-M algorithm, and the third one employs a sampling procedure.

Based on our experiments, we can conclude the following. The q formulation of Renyi entropy based on escort distribution allows finding the global minimum of Renyi entropy as a function of the number of topics, consistent with human mark-up. Additionally, this formulation turns out to be sensitive enough to identify local minima when the tested range of the topic numbers is large. This suggests that this formulation of entropy might be also applicable to topic number optimization in hierarchical models. We, therefore, conclude that, in line with our previous research, the q formulation of Renyi entropy is able to optimize the work with unsupervised models in machine learning. However, $2 - Q$ and $1/q$ transformations of Renyi entropy produce monotone decreasing/increasing curves (depending on the entropy sign) whose behavior is in fact similar to a simple logarithm function. Thus, these two formulations of entropy are not recommended for topic number optimization in topic models. The data that support the findings of this study are openly available in GitHub: https://github.com/hse-scila/duality-renyi.

Work [12] shows that the q type of entropy is a result of entropy reconstruction based on Tsallis-Souza approach [33] which involves escort distributions, while $2 - Q$ and $1/q$ entropy formulations result from Hanel-Thurner approach (developed in the earlier works of the authors of [12]) which employs ordinary constraints without escort distributions. Both entropies can be expressed one through the other. This opens several avenues for the future development of this work. One is an adaptation of a generalized version of thermostatistics [26,36] to the task of topic number optimization where the number of topics is included into the model's mathematical formalism as parameter to be optimized. Another promising way to improve the performance of topic modeling lies through expressing a generalized version of entropy in terms of incomplete gamma functions with multiple parameters, as suggested in [12]. This might allow simultaneous optimization of different properties required from topic modeling by its end users. Additionally, all best-performing entropies may be tested for the applicability to datasets with hierarchical topic structure.

References

1. Aggarwal, C.C.: Machine Learning for Text, 1st edn. Springer, Heidelberg (2018). https://doi.org/10.1007/978-3-319-73531-3
2. Baldovin, F., Robledo, A.: Nonextensive Pesin identity: exact renormalization group analytical results for the dynamics at the edge of chaos of the logistic map. Phys. Rev. E **69**, 045202 (2004). https://doi.org/10.1103/PhysRevE.69.045202
3. Basu, S., Davidson, I., Wagstaff, K. (eds.): Constrained Clustering: Advances in Algorithms, Theory, and Applications. Chapman & Hall/CRC Data Mining and Knowledge Discovery Series, 1st edn. Taylor & Francis Group, Boca Raton (2008)
4. Beck, C.: Generalised information and entropy measures in physics. Contemp. Phys. **50**(4), 495–510 (2009)
5. Bishop, C.M.: Pattern Recognition and Machine Learning. Information Science and Statistics, Springer, Heidelberg (2006)
6. Blei, D.M., Ng, A.Y., Jordan, M.I.: Latent Dirichlet allocation. J. Mach. Learn. Res. **3**, 993–1022 (2003). https://doi.org/10.1162/jmlr.2003.3.4-5.993
7. Bodrunova, S., Koltsov, S., Koltsova, O., Nikolenko, S., Shimorina, A.: Interval semi-supervised LDA: classifying needles in a haystack. In: Castro, F., Gelbukh, A., González, M. (eds.) MICAI 2013. LNCS (LNAI), vol. 8265, pp. 265–274. Springer, Heidelberg (2013). https://doi.org/10.1007/978-3-642-45114-0_21
8. Chernyavsky, I., Alexandrov, T., Maass, P., Nikolenko, S.I.: A two-step soft segmentation procedure for maldi imaging mass spectrometry data. In: GCB, pp. 39–48 (2012)
9. Daud, A., Li, J., Zhou, L., Muhammad, F.: Knowledge discovery through directed probabilistic topic models: a survey. Front. Comput. Sci. China **4**(2), 280–301 (2010). https://doi.org/10.1007/s11704-009-0062-y
10. Goodfellow, I., Bengio, Y., Courville, A.: Deep Learning. The MIT Press, Cambridge (2016)
11. Griffiths, T.L., Steyvers, M.: Finding scientific topics. Proc. Natl. Acad. Sci. **101**(Supplement 1), 5228–5235 (2004). https://doi.org/10.1073/pnas.0307752101
12. Hanel, R., Thurner, S., Gell-Mann, M.: Generalized entropies and logarithms and their duality relations. Proc. Natl. Acad. Sci. **109**(47), 19151–19154 (2012). https://doi.org/10.1073/pnas.1216885109
13. Hofmann, T.: Probabilistic latent semantic indexing. In: Proceedings of the 22nd Annual International ACM SIGIR Conference on Research and Development in Information Retrieval, SIGIR 1999, pp. 50–57. Association for Computing Machinery, New York (1999). https://doi.org/10.1145/312624.312649
14. Jeldtoft Jensen, H., Tempesta, P.: Group entropies: from phase space geometry to entropy functionals via group theory. Entropy **20**(10), 804 (2018). https://doi.org/10.3390/e20100804
15. Klimontovich, Y.L.: Problems in the statistical theory of open systems: criteria for the relative degree of order in self-organization processes. Sov. Phys. Uspekhi **32**(5), 416 (1989)
16. Koltcov, S.: Application of Rényi and Tsallis entropies to topic modeling optimization. Phys. A **512**, 1192–1204 (2018). https://doi.org/10.1016/j.physa.2018.08.050
17. Koltcov, S., Ignatenko, V., Boukhers, Z., Staab, S.: Analyzing the influence of hyper-parameters and regularizers of topic modeling in terms of Renyi entropy. Entropy **22**(4), 394 (2020). https://doi.org/10.3390/e22040394

18. Koltcov, S., Ignatenko, V., Koltsova, O.: Estimating topic modeling performance with Sharma-Mittal entropy. Entropy **21**(7), 660 (2019). https://doi.org/10.3390/e21070660
19. Koltcov, S., Ignatenko, V., Terpilovskii, M., Rosso, P.: Analysis and tuning of hierarchical topic models based on Renyi entropy approach (2021)
20. Koltcov, S., Nikolenko, S.I., Koltsova, O., Bodrunova, S.: Stable topic modeling for web science: Granulated LDA. In: Proceedings of the 8th ACM Conference on Web Science, WebSci 2016, pp. 342–343. ACM (2016). https://doi.org/10.1145/2908131.2908184
21. Lee, K., Kim, S., Lim, S., Choi, S., Oh, S.: Tsallis reinforcement learning: a unified framework for maximum entropy reinforcement learning (2019)
22. Lesche, B.: Instabilities of rényi entropies. J. Stat. Phys. **27**, 419–422 (1982)
23. Lima, C.F.L., de Assis, F.M., de Souza, C.P.: A comparative study of use of Shannon, Rényi and Tsallis entropy for attribute selecting in network intrusion detection. In: Yin, H., Costa, J.A.F., Barreto, G. (eds.) IDEAL 2012. LNCS, vol. 7435, pp. 492–501. Springer, Heidelberg (2012). https://doi.org/10.1007/978-3-642-32639-4_60
24. Misra, H., Goyal, A.K., Jose, J.M.: Topic modeling for content based image retrieval. In: Swamy, P.P., Guru, D.S. (eds.) Multimedia Processing, Communication and Computing Applications. Lecture Notes in Electrical Engineering, vol. 213, pp. 63–76. Springer, New Delhi (2013). https://doi.org/10.1007/978-81-322-1143-3_6
25. Mora, T., Walczak, A.M.: Renyi entropy, abundance distribution and the equivalence of ensembles (2016)
26. Naudts, J.: Generalized thermostatistics based on deformed exponential and logarithmic functions. Phys. A **340**(1), 32–40 (2004). https://doi.org/10.1016/j.physa.2004.03.074
27. Nikolenko, S.I., Koltcov, S., Koltsova, O.: Topic modelling for qualitative studies. J. Inf. Sci. **43**(1), 88–102 (2017). https://doi.org/10.1177/0165551515617393
28. Oh, S., Baggag, A., Nha, H.: Entropy, free energy, and work of restricted Boltzmann machines. Entropy **22**(5), 538 (2020). https://doi.org/10.3390/e22050538
29. Palamidessi, C., Romanelli, M.: Feature selection with Rényi min-entropy. In: Pancioni, L., Schwenker, F., Trentin, E. (eds.) ANNPR 2018. LNCS (LNAI), vol. 11081, pp. 226–239. Springer, Cham (2018). https://doi.org/10.1007/978-3-319-99978-4_18
30. Steyvers, M., Griffiths, T.: Probabilistic Topic Models, pp. 427–448. Lawrence Erlbaum Associates (2007)
31. Suyari, H., Wada, T.: Multiplicative duality, Q-triplet and (μ, ν, q)-relation derived from the one-to-one correspondence between the (μ, ν)-multinomial coefficient and Tsallis entropy s_q. Phys. A **387**(1), 71–83 (2008). https://doi.org/10.1016/j.physa.2007.07.074
32. Teh, Y.W., Jordan, M.I., Beal, M.J., Blei, D.M.: Hierarchical Dirichlet processes. J. Am. Stat. Assoc. **101**(476), 1566–1581 (2006)
33. Tsallis, C.: Introduction to Nonextensive Statistical Mechanics: Approaching a Complex World. Springer, New York (2009). https://doi.org/10.1007/978-0-387-85359-8

34. Venkatesan, R.C., Plastino, A.: Deformed statistics free energy model for source separation using unsupervised learning (2011)
35. Vorontsov, K.V.: Additive regularization for topic models of text collections. Dokl. Math. **89**(3), 301–304 (2014). https://doi.org/10.1134/S1064562414020185
36. Wada, T., Scarfone, A.: Connections between Tsallis' formalisms employing the standard linear average energy and ones employing the normalized Q-average energy. Phys. Lett. A **335**(5), 351–362 (2005). https://doi.org/10.1016/j.physleta.2004.12.054

Preliminary Study for Impact of Social Media Networks on Traffic Prediction

Valeria Laynes Fiascunari[✉] and Luis Rabelo

Industrial Engineering and Management Systems, University of Central Florida, Orlando, FL 32816, USA
valeria.laynes@knights.ucf.edu, luis.rabelo@ucf.edu

Abstract. While smart cities have the required infrastructure for traffic prediction, underdeveloped cities lack the budget and technology to perform an accurate model. Current research uses data mining of tweets and specific posts to provide population trends, but there is no work done in social network analysis for the same end. This paper proposes an applied informatics application with social network usage to aid in the lack of data due to nonexistent traffic sensors. The Twitter API was used to download a network of users that follows traffic updates accounts and then, use a model of information diffusion (independent cascade model) to retrieve a variable that holds a metric of how the information regarding current traffic has traveled through the network. Finally, an updated traffic dataset with the new social network variable is used to train and validate an LSTM neural network to show if the new variable can be a predictor for traffic. Results show that a deterministic independent cascade model ran on a New York City-based 2-tier social network marginally improved the prediction by 0.4%. This proposal can be replicated in other information diffusion models.

Keywords: Social network · Traffic prediction · Deep learning · Applied informatics

1 Introduction

For some time now, smart cities have been implementing new technologies and growing their online platforms. They work by having a technological base, a physical infrastructure, and usage and adoption by the population. A big part of it is Intelligent Transportation Systems (ITS). A survey on big data in ITS summarizes the architecture in three layers: data collection, data analytics, and application [1]. The authors specified the data collection as the basis for a successful ITS system since it feeds data from Internet of Things (IoT) devices like GPS, sensors, videos, etcetera. Usually, smart cities have an IoT-enabled ITS, used for traffic management and control by enabling access and communication between physical and virtual worlds [1,2]. However, this presents a financial and resource issue for Latin America and underdeveloped countries.

H. Florez and H. Gomez (Eds.): ICAI 2022, CCIS 1643, pp. 204–218, 2022.
https://doi.org/10.1007/978-3-031-19647-8_15

Latin America is the most urbanized region in the world due to rural exodus [3]. However, cities in this region are behind in applied informatics (AI) for Intelligent Transportation Systems despite having chaotic traffic. Bogota in Colombia, Lima in Peru, and Mexico City in Mexico are some examples, having the second, third, and ninth places, respectively, for the cities with the worst traffic congestion in the world. Furthermore, Lima and Bogota experienced an increase of 42% and 55% in travel times in 2021 (with respect to non-congested conditions), respectively [4]. On the other hand, cities in the United States have at most an increase of 35% (New York), dropping to 28% only at the third place (Miami) [4].

The growth in urbanization and in congestion calls for an enhanced ITS. Despite the cities' needs for an update, there are still challenges that prevent Latin America improve the system: lack of long-term mobility policies, resistance by transport operators to system integration, limited infrastructure, lack of financial resources, and limited use of bank accounts by the population [5]. Unfortunately, some of these challenges are correlated. For example, if a city lacks financial resources, it cannot have a high-end infrastructure.

The main hypothesis of this paper is the potential complementing of lacking traffic management infrastructure with social networks data. Platforms such as Twitter, Instagram, and Facebook have millions of posts daily that can provide information about the population, its trends, and how they react to traffic updates. Considering the lack of resources for Latin American countries and the demand for a good ITS to alleviate traffic-related issues, there is a need for a method that develops traffic predictions with limited data availability. This paper concentrates on a proposal that uses social networks and information diffusion methodologies to show a possible traffic predictor.

The following sections are as follows: Sect. 2 summarizes the current research on traffic prediction and its use of social media, Sect. 3 presents the methods and techniques used for the experiments and the experimental setting, Sect. 4 includes the experiments, results, and validation, and Sect. 5 gives a summary and future research venues to enhance the proposal.[1]

2   Background

Traffic prediction uses many data types like sensor data, GPS in vehicles, social networks, and others. Traditional data for this area of research is collected in highways/freeways with static and dynamic sensors, and advanced cities go a step further using cellular networks (communications) and crowd-sourced data [6]. These records feed different types of prediction models described below.

One of the most used methods for traffic prediction is the Long-Short Term Memory (LSTM) neural network [7], which is a kind of recurrent neural network that processes time series using feedback from previous time-frames. A

---

[1] Misra. (2021). A Step by Step Guide for Choosing Project Topics and Writing Research Papers in ICT Related Disciplines. In Information and Communication Technology and Applications (pp. 727–744). Springer International Publishing.

study used this tool to predict the traffic congestion level in an app to help the user identify which roads to avoid [8]. The traffic level was determined using real-time images collected from drones to extract road speed information and volume. Then, an LSTM network processed the features as a classification problem. Another use of this network was for a forecasting problem using a floating car dataset collected from sensors in a highway [9]. They compared it against Support Vector Regression (SVR) and showed that LSTM has higher accuracy and better robustness under non-recurrent traffic congestion.

Other methods used are Multilayer Perceptron (MLP), classical forms of Recurrent neural networks (RNN), and non-deep learning methods like decision trees. A tailored MLP neural network with a batch training method help reduce training times for traffic flow prediction in a highway [10]. However, the study lacked special events and other external variables. A Bayesian Combination Model was used in an article to fuse sub-predictors and reduce the phenomena of error magnification but used a deep learning method, RNN, to make an advanced regression model for highway traffic prediction. A study used integration of a tree method and Lasso regression for feature selection, then Gradient Boosted Regression Trees for highway traffic prediction [11]. Finally, the use of a recursive leas squares-extended Kalman filter also aided in the prediction of average speed [12] with floating car data. Unfortunately, none are applicable in urban areas or underdeveloped countries due to the limited sensor data or lack of a road network analysis.

Models targeted for urban scenarios are also available. Two studies that use highway/freeway and urban data from sensors for an LSTM NN model training [13,14] take advantage of the sequence to sequence (seq2seq) feature of LSTM. Both studies highlight the importance of using traffic-related features for the predicted road, such as neighboring traffic lanes and past time-frame correlations with current traffic prediction.

These features are in techniques that consider the spatial relation of different roads in a traffic network. Another deep learning tool, Graph Convolutional Network (GCN), takes advantage of the similarities between a multidimensional graph and a road network. The most natural application is converting the road network into a road graph and feeding it to a seq2seq model [15]. This study classified the roads into seven categories to use as an extra feature in the regression model. A more advanced application for GCN is transforming prediction locations into nodes and adjacency to other roads as edges and then feeding this model into an LSTM NN for short-term prediction [16]. This research explains that the model's accuracy is not highly dependent on the graph size, meaning that the GCN can take small portions of urban areas and make individual predictions for each.

All the studies presented until this section only consider traffic-related datasets, like historical data, holidays, dates, and timestamps. However, traffic prediction gets more challenging when sensor or GPS data is not widely available. Underdeveloped countries with increasing populations could offset the lack of traffic data with social media.

2.1   Social Media and Traffic Prediction

Traffic prediction studies that use social media address the issue of inaccurate urban predictions due to the lack of sensors. Twitter seems to be a popular hub for "human sensors", where a geocoded tweet can impact traffic. Twitter API implementation helped create an augmented traffic network using spatial features and its dependency to overcome the sparsity issue of the merged dataset [17]. This algorithm can make predictions even in regions without historical data. Another study highlights the correlation between tweets and traffic conditions [18], but cannot replace historical data. The application's performance has three steps: segmentation of the dataset to a custom section of the city, static network creation at each time step, and application of weights to the edges of the network depending on traffic information. But the use of these networks is not merged with traffic dataset features, and the routes achieved a 60% accuracy compared with Google Maps, which seems redundant to the user.

Highway traffic prediction in the United States rarely needs social media to increase accuracy. Since fatalities in road accidents are on the rise [19], however, some studies use event detection for a dynamic and real-time forecast using online information like tweets and weather [20,21]. These two studies are the only ones with a complete set of variables (climate, traffic information, timestamp, social media) influencing traffic congestion.

GCN and LSTM are applied in research with social media by using user queries and analysis of travel [22]. Users searched for Points of Interest or routes, and travel time to the destination was analyzed, which affected traffic flow at a future point in time. The model predicted traffic in an urban setting using a seq2seq model and a three-part dataset including queries, road network, and traffic flow. However, frameworks that incorporate social media use data mining of tweets without using the full capabilities of the social network. No known research includes social media network analysis to improve accuracy or aid in the lack of traffic sensors.

Social networks have shown to predict online behavior and interactions. Using network analysis, like centrality measures [23], characteristics of a network can be extracted and used as a scalar variable in prediction models [24]. A Twitter network, for example, has been shown to discover co-occurrences patterns in congestion [25], and correlation between the social network and traffic [26]. Both are indicators of social networks' influence on traffic. Furthermore, sparse geolocated tweets have aided in the prediction of traffic [17], but there is a minimal percentage of tweets with coordinates attributes and it does not give information about the network itself. Hence, the prediction capabilities of a network's behavior are still unknown. In summary, the hypothesis is that social networks can aid in predicting vehicular traffic when data is scarce due to a lack of resources. The main contributions are as follows:

(1) A systematic literature review presenting a gap in novel traffic prediction methods for underdeveloped cities. (2) A preliminary study for traffic prediction in cities with ITS that cannot hold a significant amount of sensor data. (3) Proposition of future research venues where this method can be applied.

3   Method and Experimental Setting

As mentioned before, the main focus of this work is to show the predictor capability of the social network instead of the individual posts (tweets). For this, a similar feature network extraction presented in [24] will be developed. A dataset is needed such that it can hold the known traffic predictors (date, time of day, day of week, etc.), the target variable (traffic count) and variables corresponding to the social networks at each time step. A general workflow of the overall methodology for this feature extraction is presented in Fig. 1.

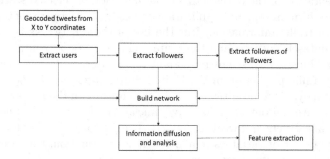

Fig. 1. Flowchart of methodology used to extract feature from a social network of a specific location.

Geo-coded posts (tweets) are going to be downloaded using a specific set of coordinates, depending on the city. Examine dataset and extract users that have a high amount/frequency of postings using location. Then, the network is built with two tiers of followers. Meaning, initial users, their followers, and their followers' followers. This network might be heavily connected (small world network) or might have influential nodes (scale-free network). An aggregation function then is developed to have a metric for each network per time step. In this paper, the metric will be an information diffusion model. The resulting dataset will then have an entry per network per time step that can be easily be fed into a deep learning algorithm for traffic prediction. A sample dataset can be seen in Table 1.

3.1   Information Diffusion Model

Information diffusion models are a way to analyze how the information travels in a network by interactions. The model used in this paper is the Independent Cascade Model (ICM). For any diffusion model, there are three types of nodes: infected or active, nodes that currently hold the information; susceptible, nodes that have a probability of becoming infected by a direct neighbor node; and inactive, nodes that have been previously infected or are not susceptible by an immediate neighbor.

Table 1. Sample table of target variable and predictor variables after feature extraction

Time step	Traffic count	Variables	Network 1	Network 2	Network M
1	4245	...	Agg(N11)	Agg(N21)	Agg(NM1)
2	3361	...	Agg(N12)	Agg(N22)	Agg(NM2)
3	2852	...	Agg(N13)	Agg(N23)	Agg(NM3)
...	...	...	...	...	...
t	94	...	Agg(N1t)	Agg(N2t)	Agg(NMt)

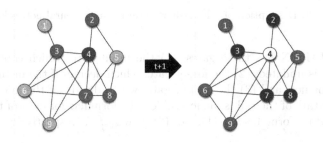

Fig. 2. Example of information diffusion by Deterministic Independent Cascade Model.

The directed network is defined as $G = (N, E)$, where G is the network graph, N is the set of nodes (users) and E is the set of edges (connections between users). A node n_i can have a predecessor n_h and a successor n_j. The edge $e_{h,i}$ means that node i follows node h, and edge $e_{i,j}$ means that node i is followed by node j.

At each time step t, there is a defined set of active nodes A_t, a set of susceptible nodes S_t, and a set of inactive nodes I_t within the network. For the time step t, an active node a_i can infect susceptible node s_j with a probability associated with edge $e_{i,j}$, which we will call $p_{i,j}$. For a deterministic ICM, $p_{i,j} = 1$ for all edges, meaning that any neighboring node of an active node will be infected in the time step t+1. An example of the deterministic ICM is show in Fig. 2. In this figure, at time t (left graph), $A_t = (4)$, $S_t = (2, 3, 7, 8)$, and $I_t = (1, 5, 6, 9)$. At the next time step (t+1), $A_t = (2, 3, 7, 8)$, $S_t = (1, 5, 6, 9)$, and $I_t = (4)$.

Since the methodology to merge the ICM model with the dataset calls for only one number per time step, the sum of all infected nodes for a specific t will be used. Hence, for Table 1, the aggregated function $Agg(t) = length(I_t)$.

3.2   Prediction Model

Following the state of the art for traffic prediction, a simple LSTM neural network is used as the deep learning model. Long-Short Term Memory (LSTM) Neural Networks are a type of Recurrent Neural Network (RNN) that avoids the backpropagated error to be blown up or decayed exponentially by inserting an LSTM cell, illustrated in Fig. 3, instead of just a tanh layer.

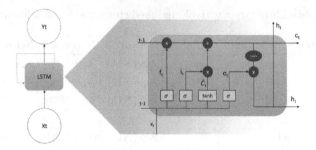

Fig. 3. Description of a long-short term memory neural network.

The LSTM NN has three gates: (1) the input gate, which controls if the memory cell is updated, (2) the forget gate, which decides if the memory has to be set to 0 or not, and (3) the output gate, which decides if the information of the current state of the cell is made visible. The formulas for each of these gates can be found in Formulas Eq. (1), Eq. (2), and Eq. (3) respectively.

$$i^{(t)} = \sigma(W^i[h^{(t-1)}, x^t] + b^i) \tag{1}$$

$$f^{(t)} = \sigma(W^f[h^{(t-1)}, x^t] + b^f) \tag{2}$$

$$o^{(t)} = \sigma(W^o[h^{(t-1)}, x^t] + b^o) \tag{3}$$

The validation of the prediction model will be done by using Mean Absolute Error (MAE) loss function, which is a method of evaluating how well the model is for the dataset, and R^2 accuracy metric. MAE formula is shown in Eq. (4), and shows the distance between the prediction and the real value.

$$MAE = \frac{\sum_{i=1}^{n} |y_i - x_i|)}{n} \tag{4}$$

3.3 Experimental Setting

Traffic data for underdeveloped regions, such as Latin America, is limited to published statistical analysis or nonexistent. However, social networks are active within these cities, with 82% of the population using one of the six most important social networks: Whatsapp, Facebook (Meta), Youtube Instagram, Twitter, Tiktok [27]. Their urban design is core-oriented, as well as New York City [28,29], where the population of latino community is as much as the white population [30]. New York City is one of the most touristic and congested cities in USA, and has the highest increase in travel times within the US. Effective traffic management and prediction is a must in the region, and therefore effective data collection has been established in the city. This city was chosen for the study due to its urban design, demographics, and traffic congestion similarity with Latin American cities and its data availability.

Using the Twitter API, a total of 80567 tweets were identified within a radius of 12 miles from the point latitude = 40.776435 and longitude = -73.971891 between the years 2014 and 2021. Most of the geo-coded tweets (80415) were from 10 accounts belonging to 511NYC, New York Traffic and Commuter Information. The mapped tweets are shown in Fig. 4. Information and a description of the accounts can be found in Table 2.

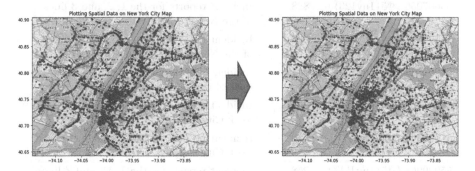

Fig. 4. Tweets locations from 2014 to 2021 within specified radius in New York City. Map on the left shows tweets from all users using coordinates, while map on the right shows tweets only from traffic updates accounts.

The traffic dataset used (downloaded from the NYC DOT website) only had the timestamp and traffic count. Two variables were included: peak, defined peak hours from 8:00 am to 18:00 pm, and day, defined from Monday to Sunday using integers from 1 to 7 respectively. This data had traffic count for the months of February and March of 2016. The twitter networks data for each of the case studies was adjusted according to these dates.

4   Evaluation and Validation

As a baseline, the prediction model with the LSTM neural network was ran only with the traffic dataset, using a moving window of 1 h. Meaning, the traffic count at t-1 will be used as an extra variable to predict traffic at t. The parameters used for the network were 50 neurons in the first layer, 1 neuron in the last layer, loss function calculated was mean absolute error (MAE), the optimizer used was Adam. The model ran for 100 epochs, using 72 as batch size. The training-test data split was 70-30, a summary of these parameters can be found in Table 3. After running the model, an R^2 of 0.690 was achieved. The loss function can be seen in Fig. 5. It does not show any signs of over-fitting, both losses (train and test) stay near each other, between 0.050 and 0.75 by the end of the 100 epochs.

Table 2. Account information for 511NYC users at the time of this research

User ID (screen name)	Followers	Description
50706690 (@511NY)	3,685	Traffic updates for all of New York State
51149096 (@511nyNJ)	2,277	Traffic updates for New Jersey
55005906 (@511nyACE)	685	Incident reports for the A, C, and E lines of the New York City subway
55007056 (@511ny123)	828	Incident reports for the 1, 2, and 3 lines of the New York City subway
55007804 (@511ny456)	699	Incident reports for the 4, 5, and 6 lines of the New York City subway
55008355 (@511nyBDFV)	744	Incident reports for the B, D, F and V lines of the New York City subway
55008759 (@511ny7)	357	Incident reports for the 7 line of the New York City subway
55009342 (@511nyG)	320	Incident reports for the G line of the New York City subway
55009968 (@511nyJMZ)	258	Incident reports for the J, M, and Z lines of the New York City subway
55346033 (@511nyLS)	389	Incident reports for the L and S lines of the New York City subway

Table 3. Summary of hyperparameters used for the model.

Hyperparameter	Value
First layer	50 neurons
Last layer	1 neuron
Loss function	MAE
Optimizer	Adam
Epochs	100
Batch size	72
Training-test split	70-30

Three case studies were developed: (1) Network of 10 511NYC accounts and their followers, (2) Network of one user from 511NYC (user id: 55009968 - Incident reports for the J, M, and Z lines of the New York City subway) and its followers, and (3) a merged network including the two previous cases. Due to the Twitter API download rate limits, only one specific 511NYC account was studied on case study 2.

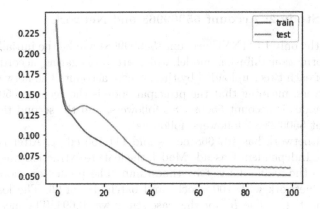

Fig. 5. Loss function for traffic dataset.

4.1 Case Study 1: All of 511NYC Accounts and Followers

In this case, the 10 511NYC accounts will be the initially infected, and the information diffusion model will start propagating according to the timestamp of each tweet uploaded by them.

The total network has 7,503 nodes and 10,242 edges. After running the Deterministic Independent Cascade Model, the feature extraction was performed and added to the traffic dataset by timestamp. The prediction model was ran using LSTM network with 100 epochs and batch size of 96. The loss function can be seen in Fig. 6. The R^2 for this case study was 0.692. The mean absolute error (MAE) loss function stays consistent with the baseline of traffic dataset, with an improvement of 0.2% in accuracy. Just like in the baseline prediction, Case Study 1 does not show signs of over-fitting.

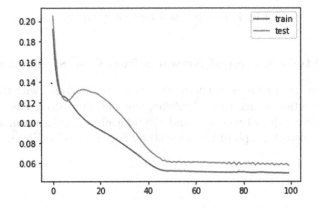

Fig. 6. Loss function for Case Study 1.

4.2   Case Study 2: Account 55009968 and Network

In this case, the only 1 511NYC account (55009968) will be the initially infected, and the information diffusion model will start propagating according to the timestamp of each tweet uploaded by this specific account. The network has two tiers of followers, meaning that the principal node is the account 55009968, the first tier of nodes is account 55009968's followers, and the second tier of nodes is the account 55009968's followers' followers.

The total network has 107,668 nodes and 111,105 edges. After running the Deterministic Independent Cascade Model, the feature extraction was performed and added to the traffic dataset by timestamp. The prediction model was ran using LSTM network with 100 epochs and batch size of 96. The loss function can be seen in Fig. 7. The R^2 for this case study was 0.694. The mean absolute error (MAE) loss function stays consistent with the baseline and Case study 1, with an improvement of 0.2% from Case Study 1, and 0.4% from the baseline prediction accuracy. Case Study 2 does not show signs of over-fitting.

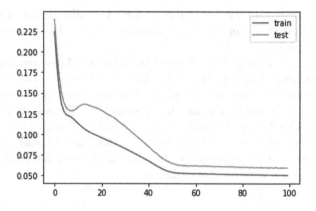

Fig. 7. Loss function for Case Study 2.

4.3   Case Study 3: Merged Networks from Case Studies 1 and 2

In this case, the the previous two networks are merged into one, with the principal point of connection being user 55009968, the initially infected nodes are the same as in the previous two cases, and the information diffusion model is held. A simplified network graph of this case study is portrayed in Fig. 8.

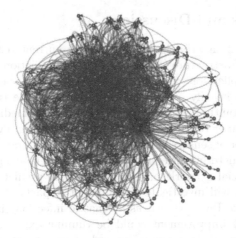

Fig. 8. Merged network from cases 1 and 2. Network with users that have 8 or more connections (degree ≥ 8). The number of nodes in this simplified network is 252 and 1,720 edges.

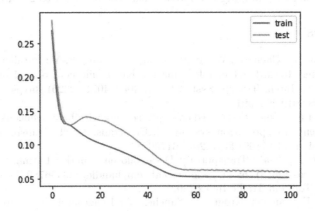

Fig. 9. Loss function for Case Study 3.

The total network has 114,301 nodes and 121,089 edges. After running the Deterministic Independent Cascade Model, the feature extraction was performed and added to the traffic dataset by timestamp. The prediction model was ran using LSTM network with 100 epochs and batch size of 96. The loss function can be seen in Fig. 9. The R^2 for this case study was 0.686. The loss function does not show signs of over-fitting. However, by the end of the 100 epochs, the MAE seems to be higher than in the previous cases, between 0.05 and 0.1. This shows a sign of more prediction errors, which might be attributed to a more complicated social network and an imbalanced structure, since Case Study 2 had a two-tiered follower network while Case Study 1 had a one-tiered follower network.

5   Conclusions and Discussion

Latin America has high urbanization rates, and current technologies are not tailored for their infrastructure types. Most traffic prediction research uses sensor data and AI applications with other variables (weather or event calendar). However, this relies heavily on expensive additions to the transportation system. Since it is constantly being updated by users, social media holds millions of data points. This paper researches the possibility of using Twitter in countries that lack the number of sensors necessary to yield an accurate traffic prediction. Results show that a deterministic independent cascade model ran on a New York City-based 2-tier social network marginally improved prediction by 0.4%.

Further research will investigate the different impacts of other information diffusion models, like Bass, as well as stochastic infection times and infection probability. Another improvement could be running experiments using traffic data with vehicle speed data points instead of vehicle count since the latter could be biased by the characteristics of the road segment and not by the traffic congestion itself. Another area of research would concentrate on the LSTM prediction model by changing the moving window from 1 h to 24, 48, or 72 h.

References

1. Zhu, F., Lv, Y., Chen, Y., Wang, X., Xiong, G., Wang, F.-Y.: Parallel transportation systems: toward IoT-enabled smart urban traffic control and management. IEEE Trans. Intell. Transp. Syst. **21**(10), 4063–4071 (2020). https://doi.org/10.1109/TITS.2019.2934991
2. Feng, X., et al.: Time-constrained ensemble sensing with heterogeneous IoT devices in intelligent transportation systems. IEEE Trans. Intell. Transp. Syst. (2022) https://doi.org/10.1109/TITS.2022.3170028
3. Estupiñán, N., et al.: Transporte y Desarrollo en América Latina, vol. 1, no. 1. CAF, Caracas (2018). http://scioteca.caf.com/handle/123456789/1186
4. TomTom, Tomtom Traffic Index (2021)
5. Martinez, E., van der Krogt, A., Sanchez, J.: Image and signal processing. In: ICVISP 2020, 9–11 December 2020, Bangkok, Thailand, p. 7p. ACM, New York (2020) https://doi.org/10.1145/3448823.3448860
6. Ashwini, B.P., Sumathi, R.: Data sources for urban traffic prediction: a review on classification, comparison and technologies. In: 2020 3rd International Conference on Intelligent Sustainable Systems (ICISS), pp. 628–635 (2020). https://doi.org/10.1109/ICISS49785.2020.9316096
7. Nagy, A.M., Simon, V.: Survey on traffic prediction in smart cities. Pervasive Mob. Comput. **50**, 148–163 (2018). https://doi.org/10.1016/j.pmcj.2018.07.004. ISSN 1574-1192
8. Huang, F., Wang, C., Chao, C.: Traffic congestion level prediction based on recurrent neural networks. Paper Presented at the 2020 International Conference on Artificial Intelligence in Information and Communication (ICAIIC), 19–21 February 2020 (2020)
9. Zhao, J.D., Gao, Y., Bai, Z.M., Lu, S.H., Wang, H.: Traffic speed prediction under non-recurrent congestion: based on LSTM method and BeiDou navigation satellite system data. IEEE Intell. Transp. Syst. Mag. **11**(2), 70–81 (2019). https://doi.org/10.1109/mits.2019.2903431

10. Qu, L.C., Li, W., Li, W.J., Ma, D.F., Wang, Y.H.: Daily long-term traffic flow forecasting based on a deep neural network. Expert Syst. Appl. **121**, 304–312 (2019). https://doi.org/10.1016/j.eswa.2018.12.031

11. Chen, X., Zhang, S.C., Li, L.: Multi-model ensemble for short-term traffic flow prediction under normal and abnormal conditions. IET Intel. Transp. Syst. **13**(2), 260–268 (2019). https://doi.org/10.1049/iet-its.2018.5155

12. Zhu, D.F., Shen, G.J., Liu, D.Y., Chen, J.J., Zhang, Y.J.: FCG-ASpredictor: an approach for the prediction of average speed of road segments with floating car GPS data. Sensors **19**(22), 4967 (2019). https://doi.org/10.3390/s19224967

13. Ma, Y., Zhang, Z., Ihler, A.: Multi-lane short-term traffic forecasting with convolutional LSTM network. IEEE Access **8**, 34629–34643 (2020). https://doi.org/10.1109/ACCESS.2020.2974575

14. Zhao, Z., Chen, W.H., Wu, X.M., Chen, P.C.Y., Liu, J.M.: LSTM network: a deep learning approach for short-term traffic forecast. IET Intel. Transp. Syst. **11**(2), 68–75 (2017). https://doi.org/10.1049/iet-its.2016.0208

15. Xie, Z., Lv, W., Huang, S., Lu, Z., Du, B., Huang, R.: Sequential graph neural network for urban road traffic speed prediction. IEEE Access **8**, 63349–63358 (2020). https://doi.org/10.1109/ACCESS.2019.2915364

16. Zhang, Y., Cheng, T., Ren, Y.B., Xie, K.: A novel residual graph convolution deep learning model for short-term network-based traffic forecasting. Int. J. Geogr. Inf. Sci. **34**(5), 969–995 (2020). https://doi.org/10.1080/13658816.2019.1697879

17. Liu, X., Kong, X., Li, Y.: Collective traffic prediction with partially observed traffic history using location-based social media. Paper Presented at the 25th ACM International Conference on Information and Knowledge Management, CIKM 2016, 24–28 October 2016, Indianapolis, IN, USA (2016)

18. Santos, B.P., Rettore, P.H.L., Ramos, H.S., Vieira, L.F.M., Loureiro, A.A.F.: Enriching traffic information with a spatiotemporal model based on social media. Paper Presented at the 2018 IEEE Symposium on Computers and Communications, ISCC 2018, 25–28 June 2018, Natal, Brazil (2018)

19. National Highway Traffic Security Administration: Newly released estimates show traffic fatalities reached a 16-year high in 2021. NHTSA, 17 May 2022. https://www.nhtsa.gov/press-releases/early-estimate-2021-traffic-fatalities. Accessed 18 Aug 2022

20. Soua, R., Koesdwiady, A., Karray, F.: Big-data-generated traffic flow prediction using deep learning and Dempster-Shafer theory. In: 2016 International Joint Conference on Neural Networks, pp. 3195–3202. IEEE (2016)

21. Zhou, T., Gao, L.X., Ni, D.H.: Road traffic prediction by incorporating online information. Association for Computing Machinery (2014)

22. Liao, B.B., Zhang, J.Q., Wu, C., McIlwraith, D., Chen, T., Yang, S.W.: Deep sequence learning with auxiliary information for traffic prediction. Association for Computing Machinery, New York (2018)

23. Kumar Behera, R., Kumar Rath, S., Misra, S., Damaševičius, R., Maskeliūnas, R.: Distributed centrality analysis of social network data using MapReduce. Algorithms **12**(8), 161 (2019)

24. Zandian, Z., Keyvanpour, M.: Feature extraction method based on social network analysis. Appl. Artif. Intell. **33**(8), 669–688 (2019)

25. Shen, D., Zhang, L., Cao, J., Wang, S.: Forecasting citywide traffic congestion based on social media. Wirel. Pers. Commun. **103**(1), 1037–1057 (2018). https://doi.org/10.1007/s11277-018-5495-x

26. Bichu, N., Panangadan, A.: Analyzing social media communications for correlation with freeway vehicular traffic. In: 2017 IEEE SmartWorld, Ubiquitous Intelligence & Computing, Advanced & Trusted Computed, Scalable Computing & Communications, Cloud & Big Data Computing, Internet of People and Smart City Innovation (SmartWorld/SCALCOM/UIC/ATC/CBDCom/IOP/SCI), pp. 1–7 (2017). https://doi.org/10.1109/UIC-ATC.2017.8397565
27. Carrasquilla, A.: A marketer's handbook to social media usage in Latin America. Colibri Content, 4 April 2022. https://www.colibricontent.com/social-media-latin-america/
28. Buzai, G.D.: Urban models in the study in Latina American cities, pp. 271–288. Universität Innsbruck (2016)
29. Florida, R.L., Institue, M.P.: The divided city: and the shape of the new metropolis. Martin Prosperity Institute (2014)
30. Cuza, B.: Hispanics closing in on whites as New York City's largest racial group. Spectrum News NY1, 14 October 2021. https://www.ny1.com/nyc/all-boroughs/local-politics/2021/10/13/hispanics-closing-in-on-whites-as-new-york-city-s-largest-racial-group

Website Phishing Detection Using Machine Learning Classification Algorithms

Mukta Mithra Raj[✉] and J. Angel Arul Jothi[✉]

Department of Computer Science, Birla Institute of Technology and Science Pilani Dubai
Campus, Dubai International Academic City, Dubai, UAE
{f20190134,angeljothi}@dubai.bits-pilani.ac.in

Abstract. The growth and development of internet technology have made life
a lot better and easier. It has increased the convenience of performing essential
transactions with the click of a button using smart devices. Convenience comes
with a price, the menace of cybercrimes. In recent years, the incidence of phishing
websites has been one of the serious cyber security threats as it leads to the leak-
age of sensitive personal information. Phishing attacks have become a matter of
major concern, and diligent actions and measures must be taken to curtail them.
Detection of malicious websites can prevent phishing attacks to a great extent. In
this paper, a URL feature-based website phishing detection technique is proposed
to predict whether the websites are phishing or not with high accuracy. For this,
we explored eight existing machine learning classification algorithms like extreme
gradient boosting (XGBoost), random forest (RF), adaboost, decision trees (DT),
K-nearest neighbours (KNN), support vector machines (SVM), logistic regression
and naïve bayes (NB) to detect malicious websites. From the results it is obvious
that XGboost exhibited the highest accuracy of 96.71%. Therefore, based on the
implementation outcomes on the phishing website dataset, XGBoost performs better than the other classification algorithms in classifying the websites as phishing
or legitimate.

Keywords: URL features · Data mining · Machine learning · Classification
algorithms · Phishing website detection

1 Introduction

Website phishing [1] is the unethical method of creating mirror websites that look similar
to legitimate websites and are used to extract sensitive information and data by faking as
real. The vast leap in technological advancement has made the Internet an indispensable
part of our life. The recent years, especially since the advent of the pandemic, have seen
a sudden rise in online financial transactions, data, and information storage. This has
provided a breeding ground for the ever-mushrooming phishing websites. The vulnerable
customers are caught unawares and tricked to click on the fake URLs that appear cloned
and genuine. Such malicious phishing attacks rob them of their private sensitive data and
credentials. Huge financial losses are incurred. Organisations and customers are equally
at risk.

According to the data breach report published by IBM in 2021 [2], 85% of phishing attacks were to steal user credentials. This will lead to further infiltrations and damaging attacks. It is very difficult for an unsuspecting naïve user to identify the URL of a phishing website. To counter the vicious threats, a state-of-the-art phishing automatic detection system is a prerequisite. Phishing activities can be detected by models built into web browsers. Moreover, if website attributes are combined with the input dataset from a large number of websites, automated phishing detection models can become more effective.

Machine Learning is one of the easiest and fastest methods to detect phishing websites. Classification algorithms are initially trained using the training data in the machine learning method. It even works well with less training data to train the classifier and comparatively less time than the deep learning approach. It also does not require specific hardware like Graphics Processing Units (GPU) used for the implementation of deep learning. Hence, the motivation of this paper is to use machine learning methods to identify phishing websites in less time with high accuracy. The URL features of the dataset are employed and tested with 8 different classification algorithms namely extreme gradient boosting (XGBoost), random forest (RF), adaboost, decision trees (DT), K-nearest neighbours (KNN), support vector machines (SVM), logistic regression and naïve bayes (NB) to detect malicious URLs. The research also explores the impact of using fewer features on the classification performance of the classifiers.

The remainder of the paper is arranged as follows: Literature review is discussed in Sect. 2. Dataset description is given in Sect. 3. The methodology and the classification algorithms are specified in Sect. 4. Implementation details are elaborated in Sect. 5. Results and Discussion are presented in Sect. 6. Conclusion and future work are given in Sect. 7.

2 Literature Review

There exist several approaches to prevent website phishing attacks. In this study we review several related works focusing on single and hybrid classification algorithm-based methods employed for data extraction and website phishing detection.

2.1 Single Classification Algorithm

M. Thaker et al. [3] proposed a cloud-based model for the detection of website phishing. Data mining is used to detect phishing websites by extracting the URL features of the website. The extracted features through the URL would be the test data for the classifier trained using the random forest algorithm on the server-side and Chrome extension added on the client side. They tested using SVM, naïve bayes, neural network, J48, RF, and IBK Lazy classifiers and found that the accuracy of the random forest classifier is the maximum.

Andrei Butnaru et al. [4] experimented, configured, and optimised RF, SVM, and multi-layer perceptron algorithms on the URL dataset and found that RF was the best performing algorithm. They worked on an imbalanced dataset and evaluated it over time without model retraining. The detection capability of their model remains the same even if it is evaluated against a dataset that is available several months later.

H. Yousif et al. [5] also conducted a study by integrating C4.5 (J48), decision table, RF, SVM and bayes net classifiers also found that RF performed better on the dataset collected. When the user clicked on the link, system data base (SDB) started functioning. It detected whether the URL was legitimate or phishing and took proper action. The classification is implemented and trained using WEKA. Random forest outperformed C4.5 (J48), decision table, bayes net, and support vector machine in identifying phishing and legitimate websites in terms of speed and accuracy.

Similar result was obtained by Buket Geyik et al. [6] on executing RF, NB, J48, and logistics regression on the URL dataset, to detect whether the webpage is phishing or not. After data pre-processing and 5-fold validation they made it available on WEKA. The random forest algorithm is found to work better with a higher accuracy rate. They observed that a balanced and enhanced dataset increased the accuracy of algorithms.

In the paper by Jitendra Kumar et al. [7] classification algorithms like logistic regression, RF, KNN, NB classifier, and DT were tested on the dataset. Experimental results showed that naïve bayes and random forest achieved an accuracy of 98%.

Jan Bohacik et al. [8] suggested a Chrome plugin with a decision tree model for the detection of web page phishing. They use the C4.5 algorithm of data mining, on the collected data of legitimate and phishing webpages, to create the decision tree. The detection is done using a Chrome plugin written in JavaScript which contains the decision tree. Different attributes of the URL are checked. They confirmed the results by doing the 10-fold cross-validation and found it highly promising. They tried several other data mining models and found that the use of the decision tree model in the Chrome plugin during internet browsing is simple and highly accurate for the detection of website phishing.

Abdullateef O. Balogun et al. [9] proposed an optimised decision forest (ODF) method which comprised a genetic algorithm (GA) to produce a subtree from optimally diverse individual trees in a forest, with high efficiency for detecting phishing websites. Experimental outcomes proved the superiority of the proposed method over the other baseline classification methods like decision tree, NB, SVM, MLP, BN in terms of high accuracy, F-score and low false positive rate.

Moreover, a novel methodology was proposed by P.A. Barraclough et al. [10] that combined machine learning classification algorithms with blacklist, web content and heuristic based methods. The experimental analysis is done by testing the dataset using ANFIS, NB, PART, J48, JRip. All the classifiers are found to obtain an accuracy of 99% and higher. Among all the classifiers PART achieved the best speed with an accuracy of 99.33%. The proposed methodology can detect phishing websites in real time and can deduce new phishing website attacks.

In the study proposed by Yazan A. Al-Sariera et al. [11] four Artificial Intelligence (AI) based meta learner models namely adaboost-extra tree, bagging-extra tree, rotation forest-extra tree and logitboost-extra tree are put forth. Each of them is tested using the phishing website dataset and their performances are measured. The proposed models outdid the existing models achieving an accuracy of 97% and very low false positive rate.

2.2 Hybrid Classification Algorithms

A. Pandey et al. [12] came up with a random forest-support vector machine (RF-SVM) hybrid model. Their experimental results show that the RF-SVM hybrid model outweighs random forest and support vector machine in terms of accuracy. The dataset is trained using random forest by dividing it into multiple units. The final decision unit is obtained by bagging each subunit. The subunit of RF is then reclassified using SVM to enhance the accuracy. The SVM and RF results are bagged to merge the results. The hybrid model can detect the phishing websites with a high success rate.

The efficiency of ensemble model in detecting phishing websites is also evident in the SVM, decision tree, and random forest ensemble model proposed by Hesham Abusaimeh et al. [13] Additionally, they use the classification models individually to compare with the proposed model, after which the proposal is executed and analysed using the dataset. The outcome indicates that the three models display a minute difference in their outcome, however, all the models show lesser accuracy than the ensemble.

Two stacking models were proposed by Ammara Zamir et al. [14]. The first model is an ensemble of random forest, neural network, and bagging. The second model consists of random forest, KNN and bagging. The application of principal component analysis (PCA) improved the accuracy of the proposed models. When compared to the individual classifiers and the second stacking model, the first stacking model attained the highest accuracy of 97.4%.

A machine learning framework was put forth by Aaisha Makkar et al. [15] for the detection of phishing websites. Ten models namely bagged adaboost, bayesian generalised linear model, naïve bayes, linear SVM with class weights, ensembles of generalised linear models, monotone multilayer perceptron neural network, quadratic discriminant analysis, multilayer perceptron, neural networks with feature extraction, and oblique RF are tested and an ensemble of the best three in terms of accuracy is then subjected to ten rounds of cross-validation. The models tested exhibit an overall accuracy of 97.27%.

In this study, we use 8 different machine learning classification algorithms used in the various reviewed papers and test them on a different dataset other than the ones used by them. The accuracy rate and F1 score are evaluated using 30, 15, 10 and 5 URL features.

Table 1. URL attributes, types and values

Attribute	Attribute type	Value
UsingIP, ShortURL, Symbol@, Redirecting//, PrefixSuffix-, DomainRegLen, Favicon, NonStdPort, HTTPSDomainURL, RequestURL, InfoEmail, AbnormalURL, StatusBarCust, DisableRightClick, UsingPopupWindow, IframeRedirection, AgeofDomain, DNSRecording, PageRank, GoogleIndex, StatsReport	Categorical	$\{-1, 1\}$
LongURL, SubDomains, HTTPS, AnchorURL, LinksInScriptTags, ServerFormHandler, WebsiteTraffic, LinksPointingToPage	Categorical	$\{-1, 0, 1\}$
WebsiteForwarding	Categorical	$\{0, 1\}$

3   Dataset Description

For this study, the phishing website dataset available in Kaggle [16] is used. It comprises URLs of 11,000 plus websites. Each URL has 30 attributes. Values 1 and -1 are used to classify the websites as legitimate and phishing respectively. The attributes of a URL, its types and values are given in Table 1. Values vary according to the attributes, from 2 values to 3 values depicting their range of strength from low to high.

4   Methodology

One of the methods to identify a phishing website is to analyse the different features of the URL of the website. Figure 1 illustrates the method used in this work to classify the websites. Definite features that constitute each URL are selected. The selected features are then utilised for training and testing in which 70% of the samples in the dataset are used for training, and 30% for testing. Thereafter, each classification model is trained to classify whether the website is phishing or not.

The algorithms applied for the classification of the websites are extreme gradient boosting (XGBoost), RF, SVM, NB, logistic regression, KNN, decision tree and adaboost. The following subsections explain these classification algorithms.

4.1   XGBoost

The supervised-learning technique XGBoost is widely used for regression and classification on huge datasets. It provides reliable results by using successively created shallow decision trees and a highly scalable training strategy that minimises overfitting. The algorithm is optimized by the hyperparameters. The significant hyperparameters are the maximum depth per tree, learning rate, the number of trees, the fraction of columns that are randomly sampled, gamma, etc. The performance increases with depth, but it increases the complexity and overfitting. The learning rate determines the rate at

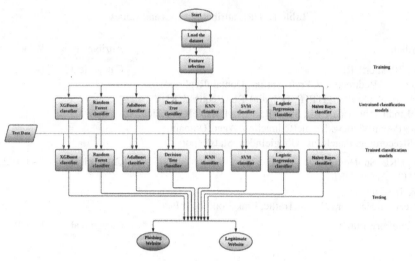

Fig. 1. Architectural diagram

which the model learns. The fraction of columns improves overfitting. Gamma is a regularisation parameter. Regularisation increases with increase in the value of gamma [17].

4.2 Random Forest (RF)

RF classifier is an algorithm that consists of an ensemble of various decision trees. The trees in it are not pruned and are grown fully. This algorithm makes use of randomness to construct each of the individual trees that are then merged to produce a prediction. The results produced by the classifier vary with time as they are irreproducible. This algorithm is more efficient than single decision trees for large dataset and produces lesser variance comparatively. They also approximate missing data almost precisely. The hyperparameters taken are the number of trees, the minimum number of data objects needed to split an internal node, the minimum number of samples required to be present in the leaf node and the number of jobs that will run simultaneously [18].

4.3 Support Vector Machine (SVM)

SVM is an algorithm that is used for either classification or regression problems. It consists of a hyperplane that divides the attribute space into two categories: phished or legitimate websites. This hyperplane is otherwise also known as the margin. After training the algorithm with the dataset, it sets the legitimate websites on one side and the phished websites on the other side of the plane, which leads to the classification of the websites. It helps in reducing the potential errors, which are generated because of over-training. The type of algorithm to be utilised is specified by the kernel hyperparameter and the probability hyperparameter to enable the probability estimates [19].

4.4 Naïve Bayes (NB)

NB classification algorithm is a probabilistic classifier, based on Bayes' Theorem. It makes predictions based on an object's probability. The type of NB classifier used in this work is Bernoulli naïve bayes where the features used are boolean variables. The presence of one particular feature does not affect the other as the features are assumed to be independent. Here the number of classes is the only parameter which cannot be changed [19].

4.5 Logistic Regression

Logistic regression is a machine learning algorithm that is used for classification as well as regression. It is extensively used when the classification problem considered is binary. The sigmoid function is used in logistic regression to compute the probability of a label [19].

4.6 K-Nearest Neighbours (KNN)

The K-nearest neighbours (KNN) algorithm is a supervised machine learning algorithm that is mainly used for classification even though it can be used for regression problems. It uses a similarity or distance measure between two data objects to classify them. K is the number of neighbours and the value of K used in this work is 5. Some of the important hyperparameters are the number of neighbours, the distance metrics for deciding on the composition of the neighbourhood and the weight function used for prediction [17].

4.7 Decision Tree (DT)

DT is a supervised learning method that builds a tree structure to solve classification and regression problems. The attribute with the highest information gain is taken as the splitting attribute or the decision node. The leaf nodes in the decision tree represent the class label. The stopping criteria of a decision tree is when the child node has homogeneous class. The most important hyperparameter used is the number of trees [17].

4.8 AdaBoost

Adaboost, an ensemble technique can be used to boost the performance of any machine learning algorithm. It is best when used with weak learners like decision trees. The adaboost used here has 50 decision trees with a learning rate of 1. The important hyper-parameters are choosing the weak learner to train the model, the number of weak learners to train and the weights of the weak learners that contributes to the learning rate [20].

5   Implementation

This work was developed using the Jupyter Notebook accessed from Anaconda with Python version 3.10.4. The in-built machine learning library scikit-learn was utilised to build the eight classification models. The models were built by using 70% of the dataset for training and the rest 30% for testing. The confusion matrix is formed by considering the samples that fall into the predicted and actual classes and is used to formulate the evaluation metrics. The evaluation metrics used to compare the algorithms are accuracy, error rate, recall, specificity, precision and F1 score given in Table 2. These metrics are calculated using True Positive (TP), False Negative (FN), False Positive (FP) and True Negative (TN). When a legitimate website is correctly predicted as legitimate it is TP, whereas if the prediction is false, then it is FN. When a phishing website is rightly identified as phishing, it is TN, while if it is incorrect, it is FP.

Table 2. Evaluation metrics

True positive rate (TPR)/Recall/Sensitivity	$TP/(TP + FN)$
True negative rate (TNR)/Specificity	$TN/(FP + TN)$
Accuracy	$(TP + TN)/(TP + FP + TN + FN)$
Error rate	$(1 - Accuracy)$
Precision	$TP/(TP + FP)$
F1 score	$2 * Precision * Recall/(Precision + Recall)$

6   Results and Discussion

In our work, phishing detection was carried out with an imbalanced dataset. We experimented with different number of attributes to investigate the importance of feature selection on the classification models.

To begin with, the performance of each of the classifiers has been analysed for all the 30 attributes excluding the 'index' attribute since it does not contribute for the classification of the websites. The experiment was repeated with the most important 15, 10 and 5 attributes for different classification models as given in Table 3. The selection of features in adaboost, RF, DT, KNN and XGBoost was determined by the average impurity decrease computed from each decision tree [21, 22]. Similarly, the feature selection in logistic regression and SVM was obtained by assigning coefficients to the dataset attributes and in NB by measuring the predictive value of a feature and this is achieved by how the prediction error rises when a feature is unavailable.

The comparison of the performance of the classifier models for the various evaluation metrics for 30, 15, 10 & 5 attributes are given in Tables 4, 5, 6 and 7 respectively. The performance of the random forest classifier was optimised by estimating the best value for the number of decision trees built. It was done by finding the averages of predictions and by calculating the number of data objects predicted correctly for a given dataset sample, where the set of random values range between 40 and 300. The best value for

Table 3. Attributes used

Algorithms	15 Attributes	10 Attributes	5 Attributes
AdaBoost, Decision Tree	HTTPS, AnchorURL, WebsiteTraffic, LinksInScriptTags, SubDomains, PrefixSuffix, ServerFormHandler, LinksPointigToPage, PageRank, RequesstURL, GoogleIndex, DomainRegLen, AgeofDomain, UsingIP, LongURL	HTTPS, AnchorURL, WebsiteTraffic, LinksInScriptTags, SubDomains, PrefixSuffix, ServerFormHandler, LinksPointigToPage, PageRank, RequesstURL	HTTPS, AnchorURL, WebsiteTraffic, LinksInScriptTags, SubDomains
KNN	HTTPS, AnchorURL, WebsiteTraffic, SubDomains, LinksInScriptTags, PrefixSuffix-, RequestURL, ServerFormHandler, LinksPointingToPage, AgeofDomain, DomainRegLen, UsingIP, GoogleIndex, DNSRecording, PageRank	HTTPS, AnchorURL, WebsiteTraffic, SubDomains, LinksInScriptTags, PrefixSuffix-, RequestURL, ServerFormHandler, LinksPointingToPage, AgeofDomain	HTTPS, AnchorURL, WebsiteTraffic, SubDomains, LinksInScriptTags
Logistic Regression	AnchorURL, PrefixSuffix-, HTTPS, WebsiteFowarding, ServerFormHandler, LinksPointingToPage, LinksInScriptTags, GoogleIndex, SubDomains, WebsiteTraffic, UsingIP, NonStdPort, HTTPSDomainURL, ShortURL, DNSRecording	AnchorURL, PrefixSuffix-, HTTPS, WebsiteFowarding, ServerFormHandler, LinksPointingToPage, LinksInScriptTags, GoogleIndex, SubDomains, WebsiteTraffic	AnchorURL, PrefixSuffix-, HTTPS, WebsiteFowarding, ServerFormHandler

(*continued*)

Table 3. (*continued*)

Algorithms	15 Attributes	10 Attributes	5 Attributes
Naïve Bayes	HTTPS, PrefixSuffix-, AnchorURL, SubDomains, WebsiteTraffic, UsingIP, GoogleIndex, DNSRecording, AgeofDomain, PageRank, RequestURL, ServerFormHandler, LinksPointingToPage, HTTPSDomainURL, WebsiteForwarding	HTTPS, PrefixSuffix-, AnchorURL, SubDomains, WebsiteTraffic, UsingIP, GoogleIndex, DNSRecording, AgeofDomain, PageRank	HTTPS, PrefixSuffix-, AnchorURL, SubDomains, WebsiteTraffic
Random Forest	HTTPS, AnchorURL, WebsiteTraffic, SubDomains, PrefixSuffix-, LinksInScriptTags, RequestURL, ServerFormHandler, LinksPointingToPage, DomainRegLen, AgeofDomain, UsingIP, DNSRecording, GoogleIndex, PageRank	HTTPS, AnchorURL, WebsiteTraffic, SubDomains, PrefixSuffix-, LinksInScriptTags, RequestURL, ServerFormHandler, LinksPointingToPage, DomainRegLen	HTTPS, AnchorURL, WebsiteTraffic, SubDomains, PrefixSuffix-

(*continued*)

Table 3. (*continued*)

Algorithms	15 Attributes	10 Attributes	5 Attributes
SVM	AnchorURL, PrefixSuffix-, HTTPS, WebsiteFowarding, LinksPointingToPage, LinksInScriptTags, ServerFormHandler, SubDomains, GoogleIndex, UsingIP, ShortURL, NonStdPort, WebsiteTraffic, InfoEmail, HTTPSDomainURL,	AnchorURL, PrefixSuffix-, HTTPS, WebsiteFowarding, LinksPointingToPage, LinksInScriptTags, ServerFormHandler, SubDomains, GoogleIndex, UsingIP	AnchorURL, PrefixSuffix-, HTTPS, WebsiteFowarding, LinksPointingToPage
XGBoost	HTTPS, AnchorURL, PrefixSuffix-, ServerFormHandler, WebsiteTraffic, LinksInScriptTags, SubDomains, GoogleIndex, ShortURL, DomainRegLen, PageRank, LinksPointingToPage, AgeofDomain, UsingIP, InfoEmail	HTTPS, AnchorURL, PrefixSuffix-, ServerFormHandler, WebsiteTraffic, LinksInScriptTags, SubDomains, GoogleIndex, ShortURL, DomainRegLen	HTTPS, AnchorURL, PrefixSuffix-, ServerFormHandler, WebsiteTraffic

the number of decision trees were found as: 200 for all 30 attributes, 120 for 15 attributes, 280 for 10 attributes, and 80 for 5 most important attributes.

According to Table 4 for 30 attributes, it is evident that XGBoost is the best among the eight classifiers since it has the highest accuracy of 96.71% and F1 score of 96.27%. Whereas the naïve bayes classifier ranks the lowest in performance because of its high error rates and low F1 score. XGBoost shows high accuracy and F1 score though its specificity and precision value are low when compared to RF and adaboost. This is due to XGBoost having higher FP rates than FN rates when compared to RF and Adaboost. This is a fair trade-off because frequent false positives would simply annoy users when phishing websites are mistakenly labelled as legitimate sites. A high false negative rate, on the other hand, would imply that the algorithm had failed to detect phishing attempts, which could result in a security breach. It is also observed that accuracy, F1 score,

Table 4. Evaluation metric values for 30 attributes

Classifier models	Accuracy	Error rate	Recall	Specificity	Precision	F1 score
Naïve Bayes	0.9089	0.0910	0.9010	0.9150	0.8925	0.8967
Logistic Regression	0.9291	0.0708	0.9141	0.9408	0.9236	0.9188
SVM	0.9309	0.0690	0.9141	0.9441	0.9275	0.9207
KNN	0.9378	0.0621	0.9223	0.9500	0.9352	0.9287
Decision Tree	0.9556	0.0443	0.9505	0.9596	0.9485	0.9495
AdaBoost	0.9659	0.0340	0.9539	0.9752	0.9679	0.9609
Random Forest	0.9662	0.0337	0.9567	0.9736	0.9660	0.9613
XGBoost	0.9671	0.0328	0.9677	0.9666	0.9578	0.9627

Table 5. Evaluation metric values for 15 attributes

Classifier models	Accuracy	Error rate	Recall	Specificity	Precision	F1 score
Naïve Bayes	0.9095	0.0904	0.8983	0.9183	0.8958	0.8971
SVM	0.9240	0.0759	0.9045	0.9392	0.9209	0.9126
Logistic Regression	0.9261	0.0738	0.9127	0.9365	0.9184	0.9156
KNN	0.9333	0.0666	0.9182	0.9451	0.9291	0.9236
Decision Tree	0.9496	0.0503	0.9498	0.9494	0.9363	0.9430
AdaBoost	0.9538	0.0461	0.9484	0.9580	0.9465	0.9475
Random Forest	0.9586	0.0413	0.9553	0.9613	0.9507	0.9530
XGBoost	0.9589	0.0410	0.9587	0.9591	0.9483	0.9535

Table 6. Evaluation metric values for 10 attributes

Classifier models	Accuracy	Error rate	Recall	Specificity	Precision	F1 score
Naïve Bayes	0.9101	0.0898	0.9045	0.9145	0.8922	0.8983
SVM	0.9134	0.0865	0.8756	0.9430	0.9232	0.8988
Logistic Regression	0.9240	0.0759	0.9059	0.9382	0.9198	0.9128
KNN	0.9427	0.0572	0.9148	0.9645	0.9527	0.9334
Random Forest	0.9469	0.0530	0.9395	0.9527	0.9395	0.9395
XGBoost	0.9475	0.0524	0.9471	0.9478	0.9342	0.9406
AdaBoost	0.9478	0.0521	0.9375	0.9559	0.9433	0.9404
Decision Tree	0.9481	0.0518	0.9443	0.9511	0.9379	0.9411

Table 7. Evaluation metric values for 5 attributes

Classifier models	Accuracy	Error rate	Recall	Specificity	Precision	F1 score
SVM	0.9068	0.0931	0.8592	0.9441	0.9232	0.8900
Decision Tree	0.9083	0.0916	0.9065	0.9097	0.8870	0.8967
Naïve Bayes	0.9089	0.0910	0.9237	0.8973	0.8756	0.8990
Logistic Regression	0.9119	0.0880	0.8729	0.9425	0.9223	0.8969
XGBoost	0.9179	0.0820	0.9526	0.8909	0.8723	0.9107
KNN	0.9261	0.0738	0.9114	0.9376	0.9196	0.9154
Random Forest	0.9291	0.0708	0.9423	0.9188	0.9008	0.9211
AdaBoost	0.9303	0.0696	0.9086	0.9473	0.9310	0.9197

precision and recall values of other classification models are lower when compared to XGBoost, RF and adaboost.

In Table 5 for 15 attributes, XGBoost has the highest accuracy of 95.89% and F1 score of 95.35% while naïve bayes classifier ranks the lowest. Results of Table 6 for 10 attributes show that decision tree tops the list with an accuracy of 94.81% and F1 score of 94.11% meanwhile naïve bayes has the lowest performance. Table 7 for 5 attributes shows that adaboost has the highest accuracy of 93.03% and F1 score of 91.97%. At the same time, SVM ranks the lowest.

According to the findings from all the tables, XGBoost exhibited the best performance in most cases. Also, it is clearly visible that feature selection did not improve the classification performance. It can be observed that the performance of the classifiers is the most efficient with more attributes, here 30 attributes for the dataset used, and reduces noticeably by decreasing the number of attributes. The dataset used does not contain any noise or irrelevant data and hence all attributes are considered to obtain a good result. It should be emphasised, however, that the number of attributes is not as crucial in obtaining better results as the importance of the attributes in the dataset.

Table 8 presents the comparison of the best results reported in this work with the previous work [14]. The previous work used a dataset [23] which contained 11,055 whereas the proposed work uses 11,054 records i.e., the datasets are the same except for one record. [14] used a stacking classifier comprising RF, NN and bagging which achieved the highest performance of 97.4%. Moreover, PCA was applied to reduce the features before classification. It can be seen from Table 8 that [14] obtained an accuracy of 97.4%, precision of 96%, recall of 98.1% and a F1 score of 97% while the proposed work is able to attain an accuracy of 96.71%, precision of 95.78%, recall of 96.77% and a F1 score of 96.27%. The better performance of the model reported in [14] may be due to the use of a stacking classifier along with PCA.

An unbalanced dataset is used to train the classifiers in this paper. However, the accuracy of such models can be deceptive. To overcome this issue, the dataset used in this research can be improved using sampling techniques.

Table 8. Comparison with previous work

Method	Accuracy	Precision	Recall	F1 score
[14] (Stacking classifier with PCA)	0.974	0.960	0.981	0.970
Proposed (XGBoost)	0.9671	0.9578	0.9677	0.9627

7 Conclusions

Phishing attacks have detrimental effects on both website owners and end users. When hackers conduct a cyberattack and users of the website lose sensitive information, the integrity of website owners is at stake. Due to its widespread use, phishing cannot be eliminated in a single day. To tackle the challenge, intensive research must be done. Timely detection of phishing websites using classification algorithms can safeguard users from malicious attacks. Therefore, an analysis of ML-based methods for phishing website detection is done in this research. In this paper, 8 classification models, i.e., naive bayes, logistic regression, SVM, KNN, decision tree, adaboost, random forest and XGBoost were implemented and compared to predict whether a website is phishing or legitimate based on URL features.

Furthermore, in contrast to earlier studies in the literature, we assessed the work using an imbalanced dataset, where the proportion of legitimate URLs is significantly higher than that of phishing URLs. Due to the higher likelihood of legitimate URLs in real systems, this allowed us to assess the protection provided in a realistic environment. All the classification models are trained and tested using the dataset. According to the results obtained XGBoost classification algorithm gives the best accuracy, precision and F1 score. Hence, XGBoost can be utilised for better prediction of phishing websites. The ensemble model created using various high-performing classification algorithms for the detection of phishing websites is intended for future work.

References

1. Fruhlinger, J.: What is phishing? examples, types, and Techniques. CSO Online, 12 April 2022
2. Cost of a data breach report 2021 (n.d.-b). Dataendure.com
3. Thaker, M., Parikh, M., Shetty, P., Neogi, V., Jaswal, S.: Detecting phishing websites using data mining. In: 2018 Second International Conference on Electronics, Communication and Aerospace Technology (ICECA), pp. 1876–1879. IEEE, March 2018
4. Butnaru, A., Mylonas, A., Pitropakis, N.: Towards lightweight URL-based phishing detection. Future Internet **2021**, 1, 1 (2019)
5. Yousif, H., Al-saedi, K.H., Al-Hassani, M.D.: Mobile phishing websites detection and prevention using data mining techniques. Int. J. Interact. Mob. Technol. **13**(10) (2019)
6. Geyik, B., Erensoy, K., Kocyigit, E.: Detection of phishing websites from URLs by using classification techniques on WEKA. In: 2021 6th International Conference on Inventive Computation Technologies (ICICT), pp. 120–125. IEEE, January 2021

7. Kumar, J., Santhanavijayan, A., Janet, B., Rajendran, B., Bindhumadhava, B.S.: Phishing website classification and detection using machine learning. In: 2020 International Conference on Computer Communication and Informatics (ICCCI), pp. 1–6. IEEE, January 2020
8. Bohacik, J., Skula, I., Zabovsky, M.: Data mining-based phishing detection. In: 2020 15th Conference on Computer Science and Information Systems (FedCSIS), pp. 27–30. IEEE, September 2020
9. Balogun, A.O., et al.: Optimized decision forest for website phishing detection. In: Silhavy, R., Silhavy, P., Prokopova, Z. (eds.) CoMeSySo 2021, pp. 568–582. LNNS, vol. 231. Springer, Cham (2021). https://doi.org/10.1007/978-3-030-90321-3_47
10. Barraclough, P.A., Fehringer, G., Woodward, J.: Intelligent cyber-phishing detection for online. Comput. Secur. **104**, 102123 (2021)
11. Alsariera, Y.A., Adeyemo, V.E., Balogun, A.O., Alazzawi, A.K.: Ai meta-learners and extra-trees algorithm for the detection of phishing websites. IEEE Access **8**, 142532–142542 (2020)
12. Pandey, A., Gill, N., Sai Prasad Nadendla, K., Thaseen, I.S.: Identification of phishing attack in websites using random forest-SVM hybrid model. In: Abraham, A., Cherukuri, A., Melin, P., Gandhi, N. (eds.) ISDA 2018 2018. AISC, vol. 941, pp. 120–128. Springer, Cham (2020). https://doi.org/10.1007/978-3-030-16660-1_12
13. Abusaimeh, H., Alshareef, Y.: Detecting the phishing website with the highest accuracy, vol. 10, pp. 947–953 (2021)
14. Zamir, A., et al.: Phishing web site detection using diverse machine learning algorithms. Electron. Libr. **38**(1), 65–80 (2020)
15. Makkar, A., Kumar, N., Sama, L., Mishra, S., Samdani, Y.: An intelligent phishing detection scheme using machine learning. In: Giri, D., Buyya, R., Ponnusamy, S., De, D., Adamatzky, A., Abawajy, J.H. (eds.) Proceedings of the Sixth International Conference on Mathematics and Computing. AISC, vol. 1262, pp. 151–165. Springer, Singapore (2021). https://doi.org/10.1007/978-981-15-8061-1_13. Kaggle.com, Kaggle
16. Website Phishing, 28 February 2020. Kaggle.com; Kaggle. https://www.kaggle.com/code/eswarchandt/website-phishing/data
17. Korkmaz, M., Sahingoz, O.K., Diri, B.: Detection of phishing websites by using machine learning-based URL analysis. In: 2020 11th International Conference on Computing, Communication and Networking Technologies (ICCCNT), pp. 1–7. IEEE, July 2020
18. Shaik, A.B., Srinivasan, S.: A brief survey on random forest ensembles in classification model. In: Bhattacharyya, S., Hassanien, A., Gupta, D., Khanna, A., Pan, I. (eds.) International Conference on Innovative Computing and Communications. LNNS, vol. 56, pp. 253–260. Springer, Singapore (2019). https://doi.org/10.1007/978-981-13-2354-6_27
19. Popat, R.R., Chaudhary, J.: A survey on credit card fraud detection using machine learning. In: 2018 2nd International Conference on Trends in Electronics and Informatics (ICOEI), pp. 1120–1125. IEEE, May 2018
20. Subasi, A., Kremic, E.: Comparison of adaboost with multiboosting for phishing website detection. Procedia Comput. Sci. **168**, 272–278 (2020)
21. Feature importances with a forest of trees (n.d.). Scikit-Learn
22. Bujokas, E.: Feature importance in decision trees. Towards Data Science, 2 June 2022. https://towardsdatascience.com/feature-importance-in-decision-trees-e9450120b445
23. Kumar, A.: Phishing website dataset (2018)

Health Care Information Systems

AESRSA: A New Cryptography Key for Electronic Health Record Security

Sunday Adeola Ajagbe[1]([✉]) [iD], Hector Florez[2] [iD],
and Joseph Bamidele Awotunde[3] [iD]

[1] Ladoke Akintola University of Technology, Ogbomoso, Nigeria
saajagbe@pgschool.lautech.edu.ng
[2] Universidad Distrital Francisco Jose de Caldas, Bogota, Colombia
haflorezf@udistrital.edu.co
[3] University of Ilorin, Ilorin, Nigeria
awotunde.jb@unilorin.edu.ng

Abstract. When compared to old paper record systems, privacy concerns are likely the most significant impediment to the adoption of electronic health record (EHR) systems, which are regarded as more efficient, less error-prone, and more available. Patients will not accept the EHR system unless the security of the healthcare information system (HIS) is ensured, and the exposure of sensitive data, which is difficult to achieve without the patients' consent, is damaging to patient care. This study proposes AESRSA cryptography key for EHR data security, and the proposed cryptography technique is based on two efficient existing cryptography keys Advance Encryption Standard (AES) and Rivest-Shamir-Adleman (RSA) which are private and public cryptography keys respectively. The new system was implemented alongside the existing techniques (AES and RSA) using XAMPP, Apache Web server, MySQL database, PHP programming language, Hypertext markup language (HTML), and Javascript for EHR data. The three cryptography keys were evaluated using computing time, computing memory, processor consumption, and power consumption. The results show that hybridizing cryptography keys (public and private cryptography keys) is possible and improves the security of EHR data. Although the results of both encryption and decryption of the proposed cryptography key were slightly increased than the two existing cryptography keys but guaranteed improved security of EHR on the system prototype that was implemented, which was transmitted securely between the local server and the web server This was discovered to be a safe healthcare record system on the web that addressed user concerns about security and ensured the confidentiality, security, and privacy of patients' health records.

Keywords: Cryptography · Clinical decision support · Electronic health record (ehr) · Information security · Advanced Encryption Standard (AES) · Rivest-Shamir-Adleman (RSA) · AESRSA

1   Introduction

The past decades have witnessed an explosion in the number of digital information systems. As the world population increases by the day, Information and Communication Technology (ICT) resources become more available to support all facets of human endeavors, such as governance (eGovernance), agriculture, economy (eCommerce), education (eEducation), retail services, engineering (which gave birth to ICT), and most importantly, health (eHealth). It becomes increasingly interesting to map the ICT resources available to medical personnel for their day-to-day activities in the hospitals. The use of electronic medical records (EMR), a type of healthcare information system (HIS), is becoming more popular among medical practitioners and consumers of health information systems. Electronic health records (EHR), electronic patient records (EPR), computerized physician order entries (CPOE), and EMR are all from HIS. All HIS products are used mostly for record-keeping and they have been available for many years, though they are yet to be embraced in most hospitals in underdeveloped and developing countries [6,9]. The common paper-based record with different flaws still dominates the healthcare record-keeping system in hospitals and clinics, especially in underdeveloped and developing countries [6,16].

EHR is contributing in no small measure to the advancement of healthcare delivery, by easing the job of healthcare experts and reducing the time that patients spent when checking paper-based records and referral processes. EHR also helps because it contains legal, valuable, and digitized health records from a range of sources in many industrialized nations, it was on the verge of becoming widely adopted as one of the ways for increasing patient awareness of their condition health. A patient's EMR accumulates significant data over time, including identifying information, hospital visits and dates/times, physician progress notes, laboratory data, radiology reports, surgery, allergies, immunizations, vital signs, prescriptions, sexual preference, psychological profiles, treatments, and other relevant data that defines a medical record [13,22].

However, just like many other sectors such as governance, economy, education, engineering, and health, it is been faced with many challenges that are limiting its acceptability by some healthcare providers, practitioners as well as patients. EHR data was implicated in information confidentiality, privacy, and security issues identified by health organizations over the years [17,21]. Several studies have shown patients' growing concern over the confidentiality, privacy, and security of their personal and sensitive data stored in EHR, and has been a contributing factor to the slow adoption of EHR technology.

A patient's relationship would not be encouraged to be enrolled on EHR or once the details are revealed, he/she is willing to reveal the genuine state of his/her health of his/her special illness, such as mental disorder, HIV/AIDS, or hepatitis, is disclosed to his/her employers through EHR, resulting in him/her being fired, divorced, stigmatized, and eventually losing his/her life. Although some researchers have provided solutions to EHR, the issues are yet to be addressed. As a result, it is necessary to design an improved security system using cryptography keys to safeguard data on EHR so that it remains incomprehensible even when accessed. Therefore, the goals of this study are:

- Implementing an EHR security based on AES and RSA cryptography keys
- Designing a new cryptography algorithm for EHR security named AESRSA based on AES and RSA cryptography keys hybridization
- Evaluating the algorithms using computing time, computing memory, processor consumption, and power consumption

This is how the rest of the paper is structured: Sect. 2 presents the background to cryptography keys. Section 3 presents the related work. The approach to the study is presented in Sect. 4, while the results and discussion are contained in Sect. 5. Finally, Sect. 6 presents the conclusions and future study considerations.

2 Background

2.1 Cryptography Keys

The history of cryptography is long and fascinating. Cryptography has a long history, dating back to the Egyptians around 4000 years ago when it was used to determine the outcome of global battles. Military, diplomatic, banking, commercial, and government sectors are the primary consumers of cryptography systems. In the mid-1960s, as computers and communications systems became more common, there was a demand from the commercial sector for ways to protect digital information and provide security services [11,12].

Initially, cryptography was utilized to safeguard national secrets and strategy, but later, it is been adopted in other areas majorly for security purposes. The Data Encryption Standard, or DES, is a well-known symmetric key cryptography algorithm that has been utilized by the US military for many years. The general public was unaware of it at the time. However, it has now been removed from their list. Many financial institutions, military organizations, governments, and other organizations around the world use DES to safeguard electronic transactions.

The underlining theories behind cryptography keys have to do with the encryption and decryption of data. Plaintext is data that can be read and understood without the assistance of any additional software. Encryption is a means of hiding the content of plaintext by concealing its appearance. When plaintext is encrypted, the outcome is ciphertext, which is unintelligible gibberish. Encryption is used to keep information secret from anyone who isn't supposed to see it, including those who can see the encrypted data [19]. The process of converting ciphertext to plaintext is known as decryption. The process of converting plaintext to ciphertext is known as encryption. Figure 1 illustrates the encryption and decryption process.

A cryptography algorithm, also called a cipher, is a mathematical function for encrypting and decrypting data. A cryptography approach is used in conjunction with a keyword, number, or phrase to encrypt plaintext. The same plaintext encrypts to various ciphertexts with different keys. The strength of the cryptography method and the secrecy of the key determine the security of encrypted data. Basically, a cryptography algorithm uses either a public or private key for its operations. In the following subsections, we review common public and private cryptography keys and some related studies.

2.2 Common Cryptography Keys

Cryptography algorithms are the act of encoding or changing a message in such a way that it becomes incomprehensible to anyone who does not have the key to decode. It is also known as the cryptography method. Symmetric Encryption (or Cryptography Key) and Asymmetric Encryption are the two forms of encryption or cryptography technologies used to secure information (or Cryptography Key) [1].

Public Cryptography Keys. Asymmetric public key cryptography encrypts data using a pair of keys: a public key for encryption and a private key (secret key) for decryption. The public keys are usually made available to the public while keeping private keys private is often called asymmetric keys. Anyone who has a copy of the public key can encrypt data that can only be viewed, only those who have the private keys can decrypt the data. Common examples of public keys include Digital Signature Algorithm (DSA), RSA and Elliptic-Curve Cryptography (ECC) [14].

- **Digital Signature Algorithm (DSA)** was proposed by the National Institute of Standards and Technology (NIST) in 1991 to use as digital signatures. The specified FIPS 186 was adopted in 1993. When it comes to signature verification, It's not quite as efficient as RSA, but it's close. The Secure Hash Algorithm (SHA-1) hash function is used only by DSS to construct message digests, according to the standard [3]. The fixed subgroup size is the biggest issue with DSA that reduces the security to about 80 bits.
- **Rivest-Shamir-Adleman (RSA)** was designed in 1978 by Ron Rivest, Adi Shamir, and Leonard Adleman. The encryption key was named after the trio. It is a public-key encryption method that uses a pair of keys and is the industry standard for encrypting data delivered over the internet. In Ubuntu and Launchpad programs, one of the ways used in fairly good privacy security is RSA. The output of RSA encryption was a massive jumble of gibberish that takes a long time and a lot of processing power to crack. This cryptography key has the advantage of being one of the most commonly researched and utilized cryptography keys, as well as being simple, well-tested, and incredibly elegant [4].
- **Elliptic-curve cryptography (ECC)** is based on the algebraic structure of elliptic curves over finite fields and is one of the public-key encryption approaches. To guarantee equal security, ECC requires fewer keys than non-EC encryption. Digital signatures, key agreements, and other jobs can all

benefit from elliptic curves. By combining the key agreement with a symmetric encryption algorithm, they can be used for encryption indirectly [3].

Private Cryptography Keys. In private keys, one key is used for both encryption and decryption. Private keys are also known as traditional cryptography, secret-key, or symmetric-key encryption. DES is an example of a traditional cryptosystem used extensively by the United States government. Other common examples of private keys are Advanced Encryption Standard (AES), and BLOWFISH [4].

- **Advanced Encryption Standard (AES)** is otherwise known as Rijndael. This was a block cipher developed by Vincent Rijmen and Joan Daemen and was announced in 2001 by the NIST to be trusted as a standard algorithm. AES just like DES counterpart, DES, is a symmetric block cipher, using a shared secret key to encrypt a data stream one block at a time [20]. AES is known to be a fast and compact cipher, it uses keys such as 128, 192, or 256 bits long [20].
- **Blowfish**. Bruce Schneier devised Blowfish, a quick, simple, and compact block encryption technique. The method works with keys up to 448 bits long and is optimized for both 32-bit and 64-bit machines. The algorithm has been released into the public domain because it is unpatented. Many programs, including secure shell, take advantage of it. For individual encryptions, this symmetric cipher divides messages into blocks of 64 bits. Many argue that Blowfish has never been vanquished because of its incredible speed and overall effectiveness. However, vendors have taken full advantage of the public domain's free availability. It was designed to replace DES [8].
- **Data Encryption Standard (DES)** is a block cipher that uses a 56-bit key and has a number of various working modes depending on the application. DES was designed by IBM in 1974 and the government of the U.S. adopted DES as a standard in 1977 and the American National Standards Institute standard in 1981. The DES was considered to be a strong encryption algorithm, but today the short key length limits its usage [14].

3   Related Work

As cryptography keys are applicable for the security of digital information in other fields, it is equally applicable for the security of medical information. In this subsection, we review medical information security based on cryptography keys with a view to identify open issues in the area and propose a possible solution.

The Ciphertext Policy Attribute-Based Encryption (CPABE) and Elliptic Curve Digital Signature Algorithm approaches were developed as a way to safeguard medical data [10]. Because the patient has access to the data that has been uploaded, and the privileges based on attributes incorporated during the data encryption process, the solution can protect data centers from unauthorized access. Before being delivered to the data center, encrypted data was appended to the digital signature to pass the authentication process. The outcomes of the studies were used to provide efficient system security and minimal computing time security. However, the efficiency of the proposed approach cannot be determined as evaluation metrics were mainly encryption and decryption time.

Using the uniqueness of fingerprint and iris characteristic characteristics to secure cryptography keys in a bio-cryptography framework, this study proposes the construction of a privacy and security solution for cryptography-based EHR. The results of the system evaluation revealed that this method of cryptography-based EHR improved significantly in terms of time efficiency. The false acceptance rate (FAR) for both the fuzzy vault and the fuzzy commitment was 0%, reducing the chances of imposters gaining successful access to the keys protecting patients' sensitive health information. This research also demonstrates the viability of using a fuzzy key binding method in real-world applications, particularly fuzzy vault, which performed better during key reconstruction [18].

On mobile devices, a self-protecting EMR was created and deployed using attribute-based encryption. Unlike past techniques, the solution was created to keep the EMR accessible even when providers are unavailable. The system was developed to enable fine-grained encryption and the ability to protect individual objects within an EMR, where each encrypted item may have its own access control policy, to balance the needs of emergency treatment and patient privacy. We built a novel key- and ciphertext-policy attribute-based encryption library, which we used to build a prototype system. The study was implemented on an iPhone app that enables customizable and automatic policy formulation while storing and managing EMRs offline. The ABE library used in the design performs well, has reasonable storage requirements, and is practical and useable on modern smartphones, according to a study of the design [7]. The efficiency of the proposed solution cannot be determined as it was limited to mobile apps and the study has based the evaluation on any state-of-the-art metric in the study area but used only encryption and decryption time.

For EMR security, a system with PHP as the backend, HTML, and CSS as the frontend, Apache as the server, and MySQL as the database, was created by [5]. The proposed solution lowered patient information access rates and improved information integrity by encrypting patient information stored in the EMR, such that data may only be accessed by authorized individuals who have obtained the patient's permission. However, the proposed system was not evaluated hence, its efficiency cannot be ascertained.

El Rifai and Verma proposed a self-contained, ultra-secure router-to-router communication system, and [20] gave a comparative review of different encryption algorithms for use in it. The original concept used a discrete logarithm-based encryption solution that was compared to the encryption methods RSA, AES, and ECC. RSA certificates have long been popular in the business, but they require a secure key generation and delivery infrastructure. AES and ECC have advantages in key length, processing requirements, and storage space while retaining a high level of security. Each of the four methods was adapted for usage in a self-contained router-to-router environment system, and then they were compared in terms of features supplied and data transfer needs, encryption/decryption efficiency, and key generation requirements. The study implemented a different bit of cryptography key successfully but the keys were not evaluated by any state-of-the-art metrics to evaluate their performances.

To protect EMR data, AES-256 was used by [15]. Because biometric fingerprints are difficult to misplace, they were also employed as a patient's unique identifier. As a result, when compared to using the administrative system and manually writing medical record data, this system saves 61% of the time. Additionally, Because the EMR data was encrypted, the technology safeguarded the patient's EMR data from unauthorized access. with AES 256, making it impossible to read directly. On the other hand, AES has some limitations in terms of computing resource consumption and security [4].

Based on the review works, it is clear that researchers are contributing to the development of a secured EHR system. However, the security of information on EHR is yet to be guaranteed and users' lives and information remain unsaved. Hence, it is an open issue and the need to develop a new security system that will offer improved security to EHR data. The selection of the cryptography keys in this research was based on their advantages and efficiencies as spelled out by various scholars including [1,4].

The authors in [15] presented a safeguard medical information in the IoMT context using the Crypto-Stegno model. The study tested the system on healthcare data sets and found remarkable results in terms of perceptibility quality, data loss resistance, and data integrity. The proposed system's extreme embedding capability and security made it an authentic approach for insightful and efficient healthcare data on the IoTM platform. In [2], the authors proposed a New Lightweight Speck Cryptography Algorithm to Improve Healthcare Data Security in High-Performance Computing. In comparison to the cryptography methods usually used in cloud computing, the recommended methodology's investigative results revealed a high level of security and a noticeable enhancement in terms of the time it takes to encrypt data and the amount of confidentiality achieved.

4   Approach for EHR Security Based on Improved Cryptography

This section explains how the research's three unique objectives were met. These include the data acquisition, execution environment, implementation, and performance evaluation. Figure 1 depicts the proposed architecture for the security of EHR based on cryptography keys.

4.1   Data Source

The software OpenMRS was one of the online databases that received special attention. The OpenMRS community is a global network of volunteers from

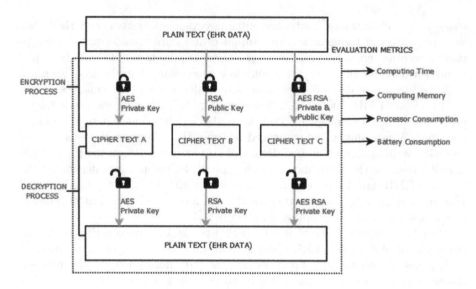

Fig. 1. Proposed architecture for EHR security based on new cryptography key

a variety of backgrounds, including technology and healthcare, who are working together to create the world's most flexible technology and largest platform to support healthcare in some of the world's most difficult environments. The anonymized EHR dataset used for this experiment was acquired from https://wiki.openmrs.org/display/RES/Demo+Data. Patients' EHRs containing observations, vital signs, past medical history, laboratory data, radiological reports, prescriptions, and so on are included in the data. To accommodate the study environment, the EHR dataset was preprocessed in HTML format and other relevant information such as unique id, email, username, and password were included for implementation and communication purposes. All these information were in addition to bio-data and other patients' records such as birth date, age, sickness, diseases diagnosed, medical laboratory reports and name of doctor that were already available on the acquired EHR datasets.

4.2   Implementation Environment

This study was carried out using the following hardware and software execution environment.

- **Hardware.** The following hardware devices were used for the study: The Intel Core 2 Duo Processor, 3 GB RAM on Dell machine, 320 GB Hard Drive, and Operating system -Windows 10.
- **Software.** The following software devices were used for the study: XAMPP, Apache Web server, MySQL database, PHP programming language, Hypertext (HTML), CSS, and Javascript.

4.3   Implementation

The implementation of this study is divided into four algorithms: private key encryption, private key decryption, public-key encryption, and public key decryption. The system prototype was implemented using a XAMPP local server and between the local server and the web server, it was safely transmitted. The research methodologies highlighted were used for each encryption and decryption of both private, public, and hybrid cryptography keys.

The procedure for private key encryption algorithms is as follows:

1. Start
2. Configure the encryption environment with the type of encryption algorithm to use
3. Retrieve encryption secret password from a file
   (a) Create the corresponding prime number N using a random number generator, then choose a fixed prime number.
   (b) Separate the corresponding messages into EHR plaintext and organize them into groups.
   (c) Create a random number R.
   (d) Utilize private cryptography key $C = \sum_1 C_1 = \sum_1 (m_1 + N + NQR)$ figure out the ciphertext $C = c_1, c_2, \ldots, c_n$.
4. Encrypt patient's data using the retrieved password
5. Store the encrypted patients' records in the database
6. Stop

The procedure for private key decryption algorithms is as follows:

1. Start
2. Get the patient's encrypted record from the database
3. Retrieve encryption secret password from a file
   (a) Following receipt of ciphertext C to obtain ciphertext C, users form a group $C = c_1, C_2, \ldots c_n$
   (b) Calculate m_1, use key N and the decryption technique $m_1 = c_1 mod(n)$
   (c) Obtain the message in plaintext $M = m_1, m_2, \ldots m_n$
4. Decrypt patient's data using the retrieved password
5. Return the decrypted data to the doctor
6. Stop

The procedure for public key encryption algorithms was as follows:

1. Start
2. Set up the encryption environment with the encryption algorithm you want to use
3. Both the private and public keys should be generated
4. Save the private key to a file so you may use it again
   (a) Create the corresponding prime number N using a random number generator, then choose a fixed prime number.

(b) Separate the corresponding messages into EHR plaintext and organize them into groups.

(c) Create a random number R

(d) Utilize private cryptography key $C = \sum_1 C_1 = \sum_1 (m_1 + N + NQR)$ figure out the ciphertext $C = c_1, c_2, \ldots, c_n$.

5. Using the public key, encrypt the patient's record
6. Add the patient's information to the database
7. Stop

The procedure for public key decryption algorithms was as follows:

1. Start
2. Get the patient's encrypted record from the database.
3. Request that the patient grants you access to his or her medical records.
4. The private key can be retrieved from a file
5. Verify that the public and private keys are the same.
   (a) Following receipt of ciphertext C to obtain ciphertext C, users form a group $C = c_1, C_2, \ldots c_n$
   (b) Calculate use key N and the decryption technique = mod n.
   (c) Obtain the message in plaintext $M = m_1, m_2, \ldots m_n$
6. Decrypt the data of the patient with the private key
7. Return the decrypted data to the doctor
8. Stop

4.4   Performance Evaluation

These performance measures were automated in the experiment using an EHR ciphertext of 500 Kb. The efficiency of each cryptography key was evaluated based on the performance metrics: computing time, processor consumption, and power consumption. Graphical illustrations of the results were generated for the three cryptography keys.

Computing Time. Computing time is the time taken (in seconds) by the system to encrypt/decrypt EHR cipher-text using each cryptography key. The execution time or processing time are other names for computing time.

Processor Consumption. Another computing resource to measure the performance of cryptography keys is called processor consumption. It measures the percentage used by the system to encrypt or decrypt EHR data using each cryptography key.

Power Consumption. The power consumption used by the system during encryption or decryption of EHR data using each cryptography key. This can also be referred to as power usage and it was measured in watts (W).

5   Experimental Result and Analysis

The achieved experimental findings for each of the defined performance measures, as well as certain features of the email notification system prototype, are presented in this section. Basically, three separate cryptography keys were measured; They are AES, RSA, and developed AESRSA. The efficiency was tested using the performance keys that had been proposed by [1,4].

5.1   Result of EHR Data Encryption Evaluation

Table 1 reports the results of EHR cryptography encryption performance in this study, the performance metrics are computing time, computing memory, processor consumption, and power consumption, the report of the EHR cryptography encryption is graphically represented in Fig. 2. The same size of EHR plaintext was encrypted (500 Kb), the EHR plaintext comprises age, blood group, sickness, diseases diagnosed, medical laboratory reports, and so on.

Table 1. Cryptography encryption performance

EHR data size	Cryptography keys	Computing time (s)	Computing memory (Kb)	Processor consumption (%)	Battery consumption (W)
500 Kb	AES	0.024	2.37	0	1.56E−05
	RSA	5.487	2.08	0.7	0.004141
	AESRSA	5.502	4.17	0.7	0.005091

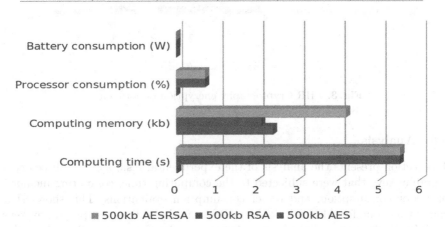

Fig. 2. Cryptography encryption performance

5.2 Result of EHR Data Decryption Process Evaluation

Table 2 reports the results of EHR cryptography decryption performance in this study, the performance metrics are computing time, computing memory, processor consumption, and power consumption, the report of the EHR cryptography encryption is graphically represented in Fig. 3.

Table 2. EHR Cryptography encryption performance

Cryptography keys	Computing time (s)	Computing memory (kb)	Processor consumption (%)	Battery consumption (W)
AES	0.022	2.32	0	1.50E−05
RSA	5.48	2.03	0.6	0.00411
AESRSA	5.5	4.12	0.6	0.00502

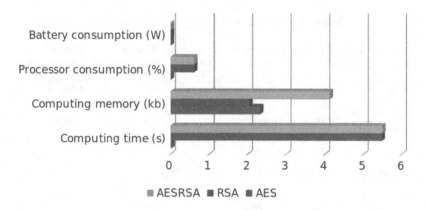

Fig. 3. EHR Cryptography encryption performance

5.3 Analysis

The section presents the analysis of the experimental results of the three cryptography keys that were subjected to the computing time, computing memory, processor consumption, and power consumption evaluations. This shows that computing time for AES is lesser than RSA and hybridizing cryptography keys (AESRSA) also have a slight increase in computational time than RSA. A similar result of that nature was repeated in both the encryption and decryption processes of the EHR dataset. Meanwhile, the computing time for AESRSA for both encryption and decryption was lesser than the addition of the two computing times and provides more efficient security.

In computing memory, AES consumes higher than RSA and AESRSA also consumes slightly higher than AES. A similar result of that nature was repeated in both the encryption and decryption processes of the EHR dataset. Meanwhile, the computing memory for AESRSA for both encryption and decryption was lesser than the addition of the two computing memories and provides more efficient security.

In processor consumption, AES consumes 0% of the processor for the 500 Kb EHR dataset experimented, but RSA and AESRSA consumed 0.7% processor. A similar result of that nature was repeated in both the encryption and decryption processes of the EHR dataset but slightly reduced to 0.6%. Meanwhile, the processor consumption for AESRSA for both encryption and decryption was equal to the addition of the two processor consumption and provides more efficient security.

In power consumption, AES consumes lesser power than RSA for the 500 Kb EHR dataset experimented and AESRSA consumed more than RSA. A similar result of that nature was repeated in both the encryption and decryption processes of the EHR dataset but slightly reduced. Meanwhile, the power consumption for AESRSA for both encryption and decryption was lesser than the addition of the two power consumption and provides more efficient security.

6 Conclusions and Future Work

The adoption of an EHR system is gaining traction in the health industry around the world, but the security of patient medical records is endangering its acceptance. In this paper, we experimented with two existing cryptography keys (AES and RSA) and developed and novel cryptography key (AESRSA). The three cryptography keys were successfully used to encrypt and decrypt the EHR plaintext comprising age, blood group, sickness, diseases diagnosed, medical laboratory reports, and so on.

The three cryptography keys were subjected to the following evaluation metrics; computing time, computing memory, processor consumption, and power consumption. The shows that hybridizing cryptography keys (public and private cryptography keys) is possible and it improves the security of EHR data. Although the results of all the performance metrics (computing time, computing memory, processor consumption, and power consumption) were slightly increased AES and RSA were lesser than the summation of the two cryptography keys in all cases.

On EHR, a system prototype was implemented, which is securely exchanged between the local server and web server. Our contribution includes the development of new encryption techniques to secure sensitive information. This was discovered to be a safe healthcare record system on the web that addressed user concerns about security and ensured the confidentiality, security, and privacy of patients' health records. Security and privacy-related issues are thus becoming even more important in such a cross-organization and the patient who owns the information has to be given a role in the disclosure of his/her medical records because such information can lead to the death of such patient. As a suggestion for future work, it is also expected to implement encrypted medical records on mobile apps (both on Android, iOS, etc.) and wireless devices notification for the system.

References

1. Abdulraheem, M., Awotunde, J.B., Jimoh, R.G., Oladipo, I.D.: An efficient lightweight cryptographic algorithm for IoT security. In: ICTA 2020. CCIS, vol. 1350, pp. 444–456. Springer, Cham (2021). https://doi.org/10.1007/978-3-030-69143-1_34

2. AbdulRaheem, M., et al.: An enhanced lightweight speck system for cloud-based smart healthcare. In: Florez, H., Pollo-Cattaneo, M.F. (eds.) ICAI 2021. CCIS, vol. 1455, pp. 363–376. Springer, Cham (2021). https://doi.org/10.1007/978-3-030-89654-6_26

3. Agarwal, A., Saraswat, R.: A survey of group signature technique, its applications and attacks. Int. J. Eng. Innovative Technol. (IJEIT) **2**(10), 28–35 (2013)

4. Ajagbe, S., Adesina, A., Odule, T., Aiyeniko, O.: Evaluation of computing resources consumption of selected symmetric-key algorithms. J. Comput. Sci. Appl. **26**(2), 64–76 (2019)

5. Ajagbe, S.A., Adesina, A.O.: Design and development of an access control based electronic medical record (EMR). Centrepoint J. **2020008**, 26108 (2020)

6. Ajagbe, S.A., Adesina, A., Oladosu, J.: Empirical evaluation of efficient asymmetric encryption algorithms for the protection of electronic medical records (emr) on web application. Int. J. Scientific Eng. Res. (IJSER) **10**(5), 848–871 (2019)

7. Akinyele, J.A., Pagano, M.W., Green, M.D., Lehmann, C.U., Peterson, Z.N., Rubin, A.D.: Securing electronic medical records using attribute-based encryption on mobile devices. In: Proceedings of the 1st ACM Workshop on Security and Privacy in Smartphones and Mobile Devices, pp. 75–86 (2011)

8. Awotunde, J., Ameen, A., Oladipo, I., Tomori, A., Abdulraheem, M.: Evaluation of four encryption algorithms for viability, reliability and performance estimation. Niger. J. Technol. Dev. **13**(2), 74–82 (2016)

9. Awotunde, J.B., et al.: An improved machine learnings diagnosis technique for COVID-19 pandemic using chest x-ray images. In: Florez, H., Pollo-Cattaneo, M.F. (eds.) ICAI 2021. CCIS, vol. 1455, pp. 319–330. Springer, Cham (2021). https://doi.org/10.1007/978-3-030-89654-6_23

10. Fitri, N.A., Al Rasyid, M.U.H., Sudarsono, A.: Medical health record protection using ciphertext-policy attribute-based encryption and elliptic curve digital signature algorithm. EMITTER Int. J. Eng. Technol. **7**(1), 151–175 (2019)

11. Fonseca-Herrera, O.A., Rojas, A.E., Florez, H.: A model of an information security management system based on NTC-ISO/IEC 27001 standard. IAENG Int. J. Comput. Sci **48**(2), 213–222 (2021)

12. Hernandez, J., Daza, K., Florez, H., Misra, S.: Dynamic interface and access model by dead token for IoT systems. In: Florez, H., Leon, M., Diaz-Nafria, J.M., Belli, S. (eds.) ICAI 2019. CCIS, vol. 1051, pp. 485–498. Springer, Cham (2019). https://doi.org/10.1007/978-3-030-32475-9_35

13. Higgins, D., Madai, V.I.: From bit to bedside: a practical framework for artificial intelligence product development in healthcare. Adv. Intell. Syst. **2**(10), 2000052 (2020)

14. Naser, S.: Cryptography: from the ancient history to now, it's applications and a new complete numerical model. Int. J. Math. Stat. Stud. **9**(3), 11–30 (2021)
15. Ogundokun, R.O., Awotunde, J.B., Adeniyi, E.A., Ayo, F.E.: Crypto-Stegno based model for securing medical information on IOMT platform. Multimedia Tools Appl. **80**(21), 31705–31727 (2021)
16. Ogunseye, E.O., Adenusi, C.A., Nwanakwaugwu, A.C., Ajagbe, S.A., Akinola, S.O.: Predictive analysis of mental health conditions using AdaBoost algorithm. ParadigmPlus **3**(2), 11–26 (2022)
17. Olowu, M., Yinka-Banjo, C., Misra, S., Florez, H.: A secured private-cloud computing system. In: Florez, H., Leon, M., Diaz-Nafria, J.M., Belli, S. (eds.) ICAI 2019. CCIS, vol. 1051, pp. 373–384. Springer, Cham (2019). https://doi.org/10.1007/978-3-030-32475-9_27
18. Omotosho, A., Emuoyibofarhe, J., Meinel, C.: Ensuring patients' privacy in a cryptographic-based-electronic health records using bio-cryptography. Int. J. Electron. Healthc. **9**(4), 227–254 (2017)
19. Onwutalobi, A.C.: Overview of cryptography. SSRN Electron. J. 1–9 (2011). https://doi.org/10.2139/ssrn.2741776
20. Parmar, N.J., Verma, P.K.: A comparative evaluation of algorithms in the implementation of an ultra-secure router-to-router key exchange system. Secur. Commun. Netw. **2017**, 1–14 (2017). https://doi.org/10.1155/2017/1467614
21. Rabelo, L., Ballestas, A., Valdez, J., Ibrahim, B.: Using delphi and system dynamics to study the cybersecurity of the IoT-based smart grids. ParadigmPlus **3**(1), 19–36 (2022)
22. Sinha, S., Singh, A., Gupta, R., Singh, S.: Authentication and tamper detection in tele-medicine using zero watermarking. Procedia Comput. Sci. **132**, 557–562 (2018)

Detection of COVID-19 Using Denoising Autoencoders and Gabor Filters

Jayalakshmi Saravanan[1] , T. Ananth Kumar[1] , Andrew C. Nwanakwaugwu[2] ,
Sunday Adeola Ajagbe[3](✉) , Ademola T. Opadotun[3] , Deborah D. Afolayan[3] ,
and Oluwafemi O. Olawoyin[2]

[1] IFET College of Engineering, Tamil Nadu, Villupuram 605108, India
tananthkumar@ifet.ac.in
[2] Department of Data Science, University of Salford, Greater Manchester M5 4WT, UK
o.o.olawoyin@edu.salford.ac.uk
[3] Department of Computer Engineering, Ladoke Akintola University of Technology,
Ogbomoso, Nigeria
saajagbe@pgschool.lautech.edu.ng, atopadotun@oyscatech.edu.ng,
adediran.damilola@polyibadan.edu.ng

Abstract. As of 2019, COVID-19 is the most difficult issue that we are facing. Till
now, it has reached over 30 million deaths. Since SARS-CoV-2 is the new virus,
it took time to investigate and examine the influence of Coronavirus in human.
After analyzing the spreading and infection of COVID-19, researchers applied
Artificial Intelligence (AI) techniques to detect COVID-19 quickly to balance the
rapid spreading of the virus. Image segmentation is a critical first step in clinical
implementations, is a vital role in computer - aided diagnosis that relies heavily
on image recognition. Image segmentation is used in medical MRI research to
determine the proportions of different anatomical areas of the tissue, as well as
how they change as the disease progresses. CT scans are often used to aid with
diagnoses. Computer-assisted therapy (CAD) using AI is a particularly significant
research area in intelligent healthcare. This paper presents the detection of COVID-
19 at an early stage using autoencoders algorithm and Generative Adversarial
Networks (GAN) using deep learning approach with more accurate results. The
images of Chest Radiograph (CRG) and Chest Computed Tomography (CCT) are
used as a trained dataset to detect since SARS-CoV-2 first affect the respiratory
system in humans. We achieved a ratio of 1.0, 0.99, and 0.96, the combined dataset
was randomly divided into the train, validation, and test sets. Although the early
detection of Coronavirus is still a question since the accuracy of the deep learning
approach is still under research.

Keywords: Chest radiograph · Computed tomography · Datasets · Denoising
autoencoders · Gabor filters · COVID-19

1 Introduction

In emergency units, the most simple and effective response technique is early isolation
of potential patients by early detection [1–3]. Chest radiography, also known as CR, is a

H. Florez and H. Gomez (Eds.): ICAI 2022, CCIS 1643, pp. 252–266, 2022.
https://doi.org/10.1007/978-3-031-19647-8_18

quick and inexpensive imaging modality that can be used to locate abnormalities in the lungs. Most countries have failed to fill the distance between the size of the epidemic and the size of the monitoring with traditional PCR testing [4]. So, CRG and CT scan reports are used to detect the disease.

1.1 Artificial Intelligence (AI)

In the medical industry, artificial intelligence focuses on the processing and evaluation of large data sets to support physicians in making better decisions, efficiently handling patient data, designing customized medicine programmes from complicated data sets, and developing new medicines. The term "artificial intelligence" (AI) refers to the intelligence that can be demonstrated by robots, in contrast to the "natural intelligence" that can be demonstrated by humans and animals, which includes awareness and obsessiveness. Artificial intelligence's application in medicine has led to the development of complex algorithms that streamline the performance of specific tasks. When academics, medical professionals, and other scientists feed data into machines, the recently developed algorithms will analyze, categorize, and possibly even suggest solutions to complex health problems.

1.2 Chest Radiograph (CRG)

CRG is the basic scan that is considered to detect the disease. It is available even in a small clinic and is also cost-efficient. All the disease detection method using the Artificial Intelligence (AI) technique uses CRG for image processing. But the images are not clear enough to detect accurately.

- These include ground-glass opacities (GGO), diffuse air space disorder (DASD), bilateral lower lobe consolidations, and peripheral air space opacities, which are all prevalent Radiographic findings on COVID-19. These are primarily dorsosacral in both lungs [5, 6]. Figure 1b shows the GGO (arrows) of the lungs.
- Fig. 1a shows the CRG of the healthy lung. In CRG, air appears black, but when the lungs are healthy and stable, they can appear dark as well: not completely black, since there is still tissue present, but dark nevertheless.
- Fig. 1c shows the CRG of other pneumonia-infected persons which are also considered for the training dataset in algorithm.

1.3 Computed Tomography (CT) Scan

Through the use of computed tomography (CT) scans, the morphological patterns of lung lesions that are associated with COVID-19 have been identified [1, 7]. Chest radiographs can be used to diagnose COVID-19, but the accuracy of this method is highly dependent on the radiologist. Deep learning approaches have also been investigated as a method for automating and assisting in detection.

- In a CT scan, a normal lung will appear fully black. A CT scan of the upper lungs is shown in Fig. 1d. We can see internal tissue of lung clearly in CT scan.

- Fig. 1e represent the CT scan of COVID-19 infected lungs. More than 70% of COVID-19 cases that an RT-PCR test has proved have ground-glass opacities, vascular enlargement, bilateral anomalies, lower lobe involvement, and a preference for the back of the chest [8].
- In Fig. 1f, a CT scan shows consolidation in the alveoli and gives a prominent picture of the airway (trachea and bronchi). This information can help figure out if pneumonia is caused by something wrong with the airway. This finding shows that people with pneumonia have symptoms like abscesses, pleural effusions, and swollen lymph nodes.

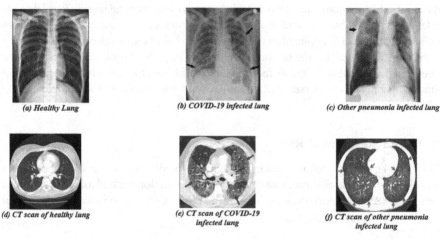

(a) Healthy Lung   (b) COVID-19 infected lung   (c) Other pneumonia infected lung

(d) CT scan of healthy lung   (e) CT scan of COVID-19 infected lung   (f) CT scan of other pneumonia infected lung

Fig. 1. CRG scan to detect the disease

2 Related Work

Devinder Kumar et al. propose using an autoencoder to research and classify unsupervised pulmonary nodule characteristics [11]. In [12], the spectrum was sampled in the region directly in the middle of the lung nodule using FFT to develop the function. The dictionary was constructed using all of its features, and the function of a lung nodule was depicted using BOVW mode. According to Chun Chet Tan et al. [13], mammogram images suggested substantial compression. This strategy suggests selecting a single patch instead of an entire image for training purposes in order to reduce the amount of time required for system testing. This algorithm considers the mean square error and the SSIM as its efficiency metrics. In order to condense high-dimensional input data into a more manageable code space, a multilayer autoencoder is also recommended for use in the proposed method.

In contrast to the Restricted Boltzmann Machine, the proposed method employs Multi-Time Backpropagation (MBP), also known as "multiple times backpropagation"

(RBM). The journal [14] demonstrates in depth that deep learning models can function effectively in high-resolution implementations. They suggested employing a three-dimensional convolutional network with PSNR and SSIM scores of 37.51 and 0.9735, respectively, to improve resolution by a factor of two. Li et al. [15] identified COVID-19 identification from CXR images as a cost-sensitive learning challenge to manage the high misdiagnosis cost of COVID-19 cases due to their visual similarity to other pneumonia cases. This was done to prevent incorrect diagnosis of COVID-19 cases. In order to solve the problem of feature similarity between COVID-19 and other instances of pneumonia, they proposed a conditional center-loss that takes class-conditional knowledge into account when determining the centre points for each class. This action was taken to address the problem. Health specialists created the cost matrix to reduce the number of incorrect diagnoses. This method also requires sufficient data for COVID-19 outbreaks, which may be challenging to obtain in the early stages of a pandemic.

In the study referenced by [16], a deep convolutional neural network was trained using COVID-19-positive chest CT images, pneumonia bacterial CT images, pneumonia viral CT images, and standard CT images. Moreover, the model's average rate of accuracy was 89.5%. [18] It has 76 favorable PA perspectives compared to 26 negative ones. These photographs were created using an assortment of tools sourced from around the globe. COVID-19 Chest X-ray Dataset Initiative is another instance of a COVID-19 dataset. Avin et al. [19] hypothesized that X-Ray categorization could be achieved by combining a local patch representation of the X-Ray image material with a bag of features. Through the use of machine vision, neural networks have contributed significantly to the advancement of medical research. It has been demonstrated that deep learning approaches are practical, but they require enormous data sets to function properly. The absence of these datasets and the length of time required for these networks to practice have hampered the application of deep learning in medical diagnosis. These two factors have contributed to the lack of advancement. Several proposals have been made regarding applying deep neural networks to the artificial recognition of covid-19 [20]. Initial classification in [21] was performed using a supervised procedure and a SIFT descriptor of length 128. Then, a weighted Clique was constructed by applying a 4-length likelihood vector against the four distinct nodule groups. We utilized the overlap between the various types of lung nodules to improve the accuracy of the final classification. These strategies involve the use of standard architectural components. Despite being considered mid-level abstractions of lung nodules with limited versatility, these methods outperform the standard low-level functionality. The system presented by Haisheng Fu et al. [22] employs a convolutional neural network to generate a condensed representation of the input signal. This representation is then encoded with the FLIF codec to produce the best possible image representation.

The literature survey reveals some methodological flaws and shortcomings of the existing works, one of them is the lack of effective noise removal techniques for the detection of COVID-19 at an early stage is still an open issue to be addressed by both the researcher and the experts in the field. Hence, the paper proposes two main filters for removing the noise in the image; the first one is Denoising Autoencoders and the second one is feature extraction using the Gabor filter.

3   Existing Framework

This section represents the list the algorithm that are already exist to detect the COVID-19 in Deep Learning. Researchers still working in deep learning algorithm to detect diseases for more accurate.

3.1 DeepCoroNet

Fatih Demir [9] suggested The DeepCoronet, a deep LSTM architecture, was used to learn from processed CRG files. The DeepCoroNet's output was improved by processed images generated using the MCWS (Modified marker-controlled watershed) algorithm. Figure 2 represents Fatih Demir's proposed system of COVID-19 detection using DeepCoroNet.

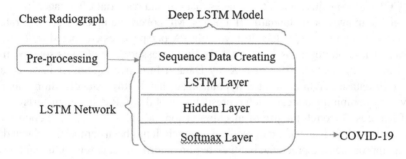

Fig. 2. COVID-19 detection using DeepCoroNet

- *Limitations:* The suggested method's computational time is increased by using the MCWS algorithm. For real-world implementations, a deep LSTM-based solution necessarily requires a lot of memory bandwidth.

3.2 Deep Belief Networks (DBN)

The authors [10] suggested a Deep Belief Networks algorithm to detect COVID-19 which is shown in Fig. 3. First, the noise from the image is removed by using a Gaussian filter. After that, segmentation software separated the essential lungs from the rest of the medical images. Furthermore, after the segmentation process, the grey pixels and the white pixels were clearly distinguished from one another, and it was also clear that the number of grey pixels in normal lungs was significantly higher than in lungs infected with Covid-19. Then, DBN was used to extract features from the segmented image.

- *Limitations:* DBNs do not consider the two-dimensional structure of an input image, which can significantly affect the effectiveness and applicability of these algorithms in the context of computer vision and multimedia processing issues.

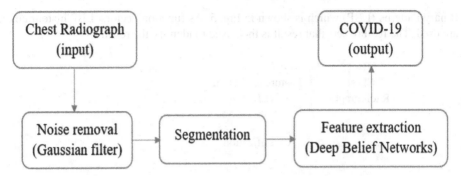

Fig. 3. COVID-19 detection using DBN

3.3 Multilayer Perceptron (MLP)

They started by having to teach a deep convolutional neural network, or CNN, the imaging characteristics of COVID-19 patients using the patients' initial CT scans [17]. The researchers then classified COVID-19 patients using multilayer perceptron (MLP) classifiers based on their collected clinical data. In the end, they created a model based on neural networks to determine the status of COVID-19 by using radiological and clinical evidence. Figure 4 represents the COVID-19 identification using MLP.

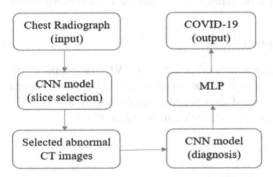

Fig. 4. COVID-19 detection using MLP

- *Limitations:* This analysis has a significant flaw because it does not have a large enough sample size. Even though the application of the AI model to screen COVID-19 patients yielded positive results, additional research is required to determine whether or not the AI model applies to patient populations other than COVID-19 patients. Owing to the small sample size, there are also problems with model training.

3.4 Local Binary Patterns (LBP)

[23] The chest X-Ray scans are initially visible in grayscale. The images are transferred to the feature extraction function, which extracts features from the images using Local

Binary Patterns (LBP) which is shown in Fig. 5. As function vectors, LBP histograms are used. The feature sets that result is then used to identify the results.

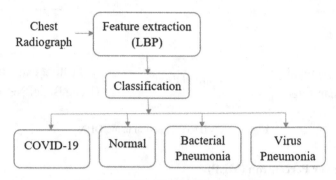

Fig. 5. COVID-19 detection using LBP

- *Limitations:* Because LBP generates very long histograms, the recognition speed is decreased, especially when working with large databases. They bypass the regional structure, and in some instances, they do not even account for the influence that the middle pixel can have. They create binary data that is noise-sensitive.

3.5   Issue Description

All the above existing framework detect the COVID-19, but the accuracy is the common issue and still a question mark. Datasets available for COVID-19 is small. So, the accurate detection is not possible. This paper proposes the detection of COVID-19 more precisely by using the Autoencoders algorithm in deep learning.

4   Datasets

COVID-19 diagnostic systems with significant clinical utility cannot currently be developed using currently available CRG image collections because the quality is not high enough [29]. Covid-19 Image Data Collection is currently being used to teach COVID-19 class. The COVID-19 Chest X-ray Dataset Initiative is yet another dataset created by COVID-19 [30]. Chest Xray images (CR, DX) and computed tomography (CT) scans of patients who did not have COVID-19 are included in the BIMCV-COVID19-dataset, along with their radiographic findings, pathologies, polymerase chain reaction (PCR) results, immunoglobulin G (IgG) and immunoglobulin M (IgM) diagnostic antibody tests, and radiographic reports. An open research dataset compiled by the Allen Institute for Artificial Intelligence (AI) in response to the COVID-19 pandemic has been made available (CORD-19). If you are a researcher looking for information on COVID-19 and the coronavirus family of viruses, you will find a wealth of information here. [32]. The POCOVID-Net Dataset contains 654 COVID-19 scan images, 277 scan images with pneumonia infection, and 172 scan images with no findings [33]. These scans' contrast, brightness, size, and shape are different. According to this dataset, which was provided by the National Institutes of Health (NIH), all of the images are 1024×1024 pixels in a portrait mode and have the exact dimensions as the COVID-19 dataset. COVID-19 dataset images are compared to the usual COVID-19 images The COVID-CT Dataset, made available to the public [34–39], contained CRG and CT scans from patients with and without the COVID-19 mutation.

5 Proposed Framework

The proposed system contains two main sections. They are, removing the noise in the image using Denoising Autoencoders and feature extraction using the Gabor filter. Figure 6 represents the overall architecture of the proposed system.

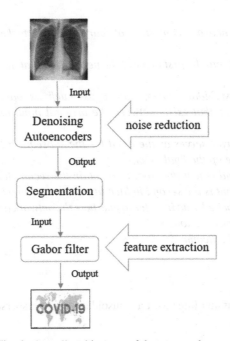

Fig. 6. Overall architecture of the proposed system

5.1 Denoising Autoencoders

[24] The Denoising Autoencoder is a variant on the traditional autoencoder. Denoising autoencoder tries to corrupt input data at random. The autoencoder is a convolutional layer whose output is similar to the initial data. The encoder transforms the data into a secret representation, while the decoder reconstructs the initial input values. Figure 7

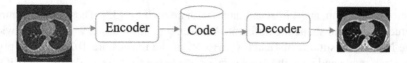

Fig. 7. Structure of Denoising Autoencoders

represents the structure of Denoising Autoencoders. It consists of three main components. They are encoder, code and decoder. The code consists of many hidden layers to
reduce noise in the images.

Algorithm
Input: Chest Radiograph or Computed Tomography Scan
   Output: Noise removed Chest Radiograph or Computed Tomography Scan
   Steps:

1. *Construct a deep network consisting of four layers of stacked denoising autoencoders.*
2. *The data are input into the first layer of the network so that the output and the input
   are equal.*
3. *To obtain the first hidden layer, reduce as much as possible the amount of
   reconstruction error that exists between the original input and the reconstructed
   output.*
4. *The first hidden layer serves as the input for the subsequent layer, and the output
   and the input make up the final layer.*
5. *Return to step 3 and repeat the process to obtain the second hidden layer.*
6. *The classifier's input is the second hidden layer that was previously created.*
7. *Make use of the labelled data in order to fine-tune the network and reduce the amount
   of error in the reconstruction.*
8. *Obtain the desired outcome.*

5.2 Gabor Filter

A Gabor filter is a gaussian filter with a sinusoidal term interspersed. In 2 dimensions,
a Gabor filter is

$$g(x, y; \lambda, \theta, \psi, \sigma, \gamma) = \exp\left(-\frac{x'2 + \gamma^2 y'2}{2\sigma^2}\right) \cos\left(2\pi \frac{x'}{\lambda} + \psi\right) \tag{1}$$

$$X' = xcos(theta) + ysin(theta); \tag{2}$$

$$Y' = -xsin(theta) + ycos(theta); \tag{3}$$

Figure 8 represents the structure of Gabor Filter. The weights are provided by the gaussian, and the directionality is provided by the sinusoidal [25].

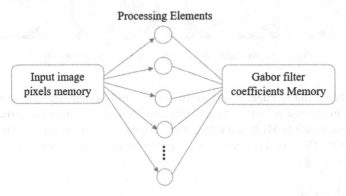

Fig. 8. Structure of Gabor Filter

Algorithm

1. *Split the query image into subblocks measuring 16 by 16.*
2. *Compute the features of four distinct scales using eight distinct angles, resulting in eight distinct angles for each scale.*
3. *Determine the mean and standard deviation of the Gabor features vector using the appropriate formulas.*

5.3   Architecture Explanation of Proposed Framework

Figure 6 represents the overall architecture of the planned framework. The main step of the algorithm includes these steps:

Noise Reduction
An encoder is a mapping function, denoted by f, that transforms an input vector into a hidden representation, denoted by y. Its definition is as follows:

$$y = f(x) = \sigma_e(W * x + b) \tag{4}$$

where W represents the weight matrix from input to hidden layer, b represents the Bias vector and σ_e represents the activation function for the encoder.

Segmentation
The methods of segmentation based on partial differential equations are the quickest. These are suitable for time-sensitive applications. The PDE method produces blurred edges and borders, which can be moved with close operators.

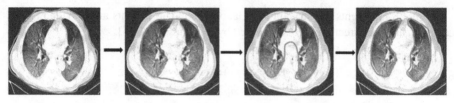

Fig. 9. Segmentation of computer tomography using PDE

[28] When a blurry edge, strong noise, and intensity inhomogeneity appear in an image, a conventional active contour model fails to segment contours, particularly in medical images such as MRIs and ultrasounds. So, noise should be removed before segmentation using Denoising Autoencoders. Figure 9 shows the segmentation of Computed Tomography using PDE.

Feature Extraction
A group of Gabor filters with varying frequencies and orientations may help extract useful characteristics from an image. The two-dimensional Gabor filters are given in the discrete domain. Figure 10 represents the feature extraction using Gabor filter.

$$G_c[i,j] = Be - \frac{(i^2 + j^2)}{2\sigma^2} \cos(2\pi f(i \cos \theta + j \sin \theta)) \tag{5}$$

$$G_s[i,j] = Ce - \frac{(i^2 + j^2)}{2\sigma^2} \sin(2\pi f(i \cos \theta + j \sin \theta)) \tag{6}$$

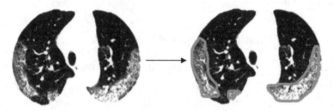

Fig. 10. Feature extraction using Gabor filter

6 Experimental Outcome

6.1 Overall Performance

The proposed implementation was put to the test on 168 Covid and 1596 non-Covid pictures. F1-Score, Precision, Recall, Sensitivity, Accuracy, and Specificity were measured to evaluate the proposed implementation's results. Figure 11 represents the overall performance of the proposed system.

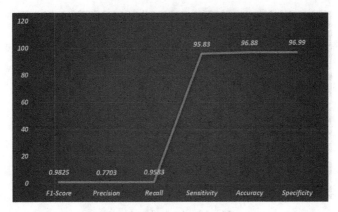

Fig. 11. Overall performance

6.2 Datasets for Training

The precision, recall and F1- Score obtained by training a dataset in represented in the given chart. Since the dataset available for COVID-19 is minimum, it is difficult to train. However, we achieved a ratio of 1.0, 0.99, and 0.96, the combined dataset was randomly divided into train, validation, and test sets. Figure 12 represents the results obtained by training a dataset.

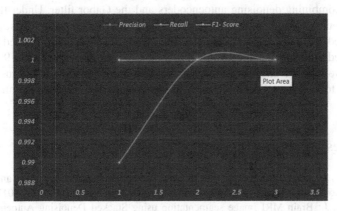

Fig. 12. Training datasets

6.3 Data Analysis

The final data analysis of the trained dataset is shown in the given chart. The precision and F1-score are still 1 the value of Recall is 0.86. Total datasets are divided into Covid-19 positive, normal and other pneumonia affected images. Figure 13 shows the data analysis of the trained dataset. The proposed method is able to detect the COVID-19 positive cases that have been reported accurately. The accuracy of the system that is being proposed is 98.5%.

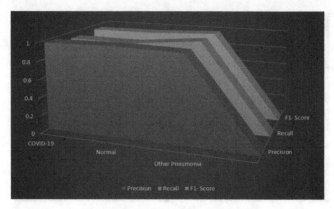

Fig. 13: Analyzing data

7 Conclusion

The ability to detect COVID-19 from chest radiograph images is essential for both medical professionals and patients in order to minimize the amount of time spent testing and the associated costs. Artificial intelligence and deep learning could recognize images from a chest radiograph or CT scan if they are associated with the appropriate activities. This paper proposes an efficient method for analyzing COVID-19 extracted from medical images by combining denoising autoencoders and the Gabor filter. Under the current conditions, our proposed system is able to detect the COVID-19 positive cases that have been reported accurately. The accuracy of the system that is being proposed is 98.5%. The proposed model can also be utilized to diagnose patients with Covid-19 promptly, thereby preventing the onset of pneumonia brought on by the Covid-19 virus. It would be essential to stop the COVID-19 outbreak, manage it, and break the communication chain.

References

1. Chen, M., Shi, X., Zhang, Y., Wu, D.: Deep features learning for medical image analysis with convolutional autocoder neural network. https://doi.org/10.1109/TBDATA.2017.2717439
2. Bandaria, J.: Brain MRI image segmentation using Stacked Denoising Autoencoders, 18 October 2017
3. Jang, S.B., et al.: Deep-learning algorithms for the interpretation of chest radiographs to aid in the triage of COVID-19 patients: a multicenter retrospective study. https://doi.org/10.1371/journal.pone.0242759
4. Pandit, M.K., Banday, S.A., Naaz, R., Chishti, M.A.: Automatic detection of COVID-19 from chest radiographs using deep learning. https://doi.org/10.1016/j.radi.2020.10.018
5. Jacobi, A., Chung, M., Bernheim, A., Eber, C.: Portable chest X-ray in coronavirus disease-19 (COVID-19): a pictorial review. Clin. Imaging **64**, 3542 (2020). https://doi.org/10.1016/j.clinimag.2020.04.001.Crossref,Medline
6. Wong, H.Y.F., Lam, H.Y.S., Fong, A.H.T., et al.: Frequency and distribution of chest radiographic findings in COVID-19 positive patients. Radiology (2020). Accessed Apr 2020

7. Silva, P., et al.: COVID-19 detection in CT images with deep learning: a voting-based scheme and cross-datasets analysis. https://doi.org/10.1016/j.imu.2020.100427

8. Adams, H.J.A., Kwee, T.C., Yakar, D., Hope, M.D., Kwee, R.M.: Chest CT imaging signature of coronavirus disease 2019 infection: in pursuit of the scientific evidence. Chest (2020). https://doi.org/10.1016/j.chest.2020.06.025. Accessed 6 June 2020

9. Demir, F.: DeepCoroNet: a deep LSTM approach for automated detection of COVID-19 cases from chest X-ray images. https://doi.org/10.1016/j.asoc.2021.107160

10. Abdulrahman, S.A., Salem, A.-B.M.: A efficient deep belief network for detection of corona virus disease COVID-19. https://doi.org/10.5281/zenodo.3931877

11. Kumar, D., Wong, A., Clausi, D.A.: Lung nodule classification using deep features in CT images. In: 12th IEEE Conference on Computer and Robot Vision (CRV), pp. 133–138 (2015)

12. Ciompi, F., Jacobs, C., Scholten, E.T., et al.: Bag-of-frequencies: a descriptor of pulmonary nodules in computed tomography images. IEEE Trans. Med. Imaging **34**(4), 962–973 (2015)

13. Tan C.C., Eswaran, C.: Using autoencoders for mammogram compression. J. Med. Syst. **35**(1), 49–58 (2011). https://doi.org/10.1007/s10916-009-9340-3

14. Pham, C.-H., Ducournau, A., Fablet, R., Rousseau, F.: Brain MRI super-resolution using deep 3D convolutional networks. In: 2017 IEEE 14th International Symposium on Biomedical Imaging (ISBI 2017) (2017). https://doi.org/10.1109/isbi.2017.7950500

15. Li, T., et al.: Robust screening of COVID-19 from chest X-ray via discriminative cost-sensitive learning. arXiv preprint arXiv:2004.12592. Cited by: §2

16. Khan, A.L., Junaid, L.S.: CoroNet: MB a deep neural network for detection and diagnosis of COVID-19 from chest X-ray images. Comput. Methods Programs Biomed. **196**(11), 105581 (2020). https://doi.org/10.1016/j.cmpb.2020.105581

17. Mei, X., Lee, H.-C., Yang, Y.: Artificial intelligence–enabled rapid diagnosis of patients with COVID-19, 19 May 2020

18. Figure 1 COVID-19 chest X-ray dataset initiative (2020). https://github.com/agchung/Figure1-COVID-chestxray-dataset

19. Avni, U., Sharon, M., Goldberger, J.: X-ray image categorization and retrieval using patch-based visual words representation. In: Proceeding of the International Conference on Biomedical Imaging, pp. 350–353 (2009)

20. Ozturk, T., Talo, M., Yildirim, E.A., Baloglu, U.B., Yildirim, O., Rajendra Acharya, U.: Automated detection of COVID-19 cases using deep neural networks with X-ray images [published online ahead of print, 2020 Apr 28]. Comput. Biol. Med., 103792 (2020). https://doi.org/10.1016/j.compbiomed.2020.103792

21. Zhang, F., Cai, W., Song, Y., Lee, M.-Z., Shan, S., Dagan, D.: Overlapping node discovery for improving classification of lung nodules. In: Proceedings of the 35th Annual International Conference of the IEEE Engineering in Medicine and Biology Society (EMBC 2013), Osaka, Japan, pp. 5461–5464, July 2013

22. Fu, H., et al.: Improved hybrid layered image compression using deep learning and traditional codecs. Signal Process. Image Commun. **82**(2019), 115774 (2020)

23. Thepade, S.D., Jadhav, K., Sange, S., Das, R.: COVID19 identification from chest X-ray using local binary patterns and multilayer perceptrons (2020)

24. Manju, D., Seetha, M., Sammulal, P.: Frame prediction-noise removal using denoising autoencoders. Int. J. Innov. Technol. Explor. Eng.

25. Ansari, M.A.: Gabor filter algorithm. Int. J. Comput. Appl. (2015)

26. Chandra, B., Sharma, R.K.: Adaptive noise schedule for denoising autoencoder. In: Loo, C.K., Yap, K.S., Wong, K.W., Teoh, A., Huang, K. (eds.) ICONIP 2014. LNCS, vol. 8834, pp. 535–542. Springer, Cham (2014). https://doi.org/10.1007/978-3-319-12637-1_67

27. Kaur, D., Kaur, Y.: Various image segmentation techniques: a review. Int. J. Comput. Sci. Mob. Comput. **3**, 809–814 (2014)

28. Wei, J., Chan, L.: An image segmentation method based on partial differential equation models (2016)
29. Jayalakshmi, S., Hemalatha, P.: Measuring the water quality in bore well using sensors and alerting system. In: 2019 IEEE International Conference on System, Computation, Automation and Networking (ICSCAN), pp. 1–4. IEEE (2019)
30. Jayalakshmi, S., Sangeetha, N., Swetha, S., Ananth Kumar, T.: Network slicing and performance analysis of 5G networks based on priority. Int. J. Sci. Technol. Res. **8**(11), 3623–3627 (2019)
31. Born, J., et al.: POCOVID-Net: automatic detection of COVID-19 from a new lung ultrasound imaging dataset (POCUS) (2020). arXiv:2004.12084
32. Wang, X., et al.: Chest X-ray8: hospital-scale chest x-ray database and benchmarks on weakly-supervised classification and localization of common thorax diseases. In: Proceedings of the IEEE Conference on Computer Vision and Pattern Recognition (CVPR), Honolulu, HI, USA, pp. 3462–3471. IEEE (2017). https://doi.org/10.1109/CVPR.2017.369
33. Nih dataset (2020). https://www.nih.gov/newsevents/news-releases/nih-clinical-center-provides-one-largest-publiclyavailable-chest-x-ray-datasets-scientific-community
34. Zhao, J., Zhang, Y., He, X., Xie, P.: COVID-CT-dataset: a CT scan dataset about COVID-19 (2020). arXiv:2003.13865
35. BIMCV COVID-19-: A large annotated dataset of RX and CT images from COVID-19 patients
36. COVID-19 Open Research Dataset (CORD-19). Version YYYY-MM-DD. COVID-19 Open Research Dataset (CORD-19) (2020). Accessed YYYY-MM-DD. https://doi.org/10.5281/zenodo.3715505
37. Kumar, A.T., Rajmohan, R., Pavithra, M., Ajagbe, S.A., Hodhod, R., Gaber, T.: Automatic face mask detection system in public transportation in smart cities using IoT and deep learning. Electronics **11**(6), 904 (2022). https://doi.org/10.3390/electronics11060904
38. Awotunde, J.B., et al.: An improved machine learnings diagnosis technique for COVID-19 pandemic using chest X-ray images. In: Florez, H., Pollo-Cattaneo, M.F. (eds.) ICAI 2021. CCIS, vol. 1455, pp. 319–330. Springer, Cham (2021). https://doi.org/10.1007/978-3-030-89654-6_23
39. Fernandes, A., Lima, R., Figueiredo, M., Ribeiro, J., Neves, J., Vicente, H.: Assessing employee satisfaction in the context of COVID-19 pandemic. ParadigmPlus **1**(3), 23–43 (2020)

Development of a Mobile Application to Save Lives on Catastrophic Situations

Rocío Rodriguez-Guerrero$^{(\boxtimes)}$ ⓘ, Alvaro A. Acosta ⓘ, and Carlos A. Vanegas ⓘ

Universidad Distrital Francisco Jose de Caldas, Bogota, Colombia
{rrodriguezg,cavanegas}@udistrital.edu.co,
aaacostam@correo.udistrital.edu.co

Abstract. The development of mobile applications for the care of human beings has increased. Topics such as individual health, modifying habits, monitoring an ailment, or simply storing significant data, are important elements in the design and implementation of new apps. This article describes the creation of a mobile application that allows people to consult information on earthquakes reported in the Colombian Geological System. The application uses a scraping technique to notify and send the last location of users to their contacts. It also reports the location of health centers, and hospitals and provides information on security protocols that will improve the response to this type of natural disaster.

Keywords: Mobile applications · Individual health · Earthquake · Scraping · Natural disaster

1 Introduction

Nowadays new strategies have been developed using information technologies. These strategies allow professionals to study and later mitigate earthquakes affectations; for example, the production of a seismic vulnerability map could help disaster management organizations to develop and implement a plan to promote awareness of earthquake vulnerability and implementation of seismic vulnerability [7]. The simulation can calculate the appropriate behavior of evacuees in order to avoid tsunami damage in these situations [6]. Other strategies have been based on the development of mobile applications for simulations and disaster attention. We developed primarily an assistant app aimed at emergency cases, specifically for likely events in a natural disaster. Our proposal is to educate Colombian citizens about seismic events or the consequences related to them.

The rest of the paper is structured as follows. Section 2 introduces the seismics hazards in Colombia. Section 3 explains the natural emergencies in Colombia. Section 4 presents the Colombian geological service. Section 5 presents our mobile-based approach. Section 5.1 discusses the tests and operations of the mobile app built in this project. Finally, Sect. 6 concludes the paper.

ⓒ The Author(s), under exclusive license to Springer Nature Switzerland AG 2022
H. Florez and H. Gomez (Eds.): ICAI 2022, CCIS 1643, pp. 267–277, 2022.
https://doi.org/10.1007/978-3-031-19647-8_19

2   Seismic Hazards in Colombia

Colombia is located in the "Pacific Ring of Fire" [2] as presented in Fig 1. The volcanic activity in Colombia is generated by the subduction of the Nazca plate under the South American plate [4]. This generates great seismic and volcanic activity and the zone concentrates the subduction areas most important in the world [5]. For this reason, Colombia is considered a country at high seismic risk. Figure 2 shows the Structural Geology of Western Colombia - Seismic hazard in Colombia for an event with a return period of 475 years.

Some estimations made in the last census of 2018 carried out by the National Administrative Department of Statistics DANE[1] and the 165 seismic hazard maps in Colombia [9] determined that approximately 5.5 million people are exposed to volcanic hazards in the country.

3   Natural Emergencies in Colombia

Natural emergencies occur continuously in Colombia due to its geographical characteristics. Inundation, landslides, forest fires, gales, and earthquakes represent the natural emergencies that happen more constantly.

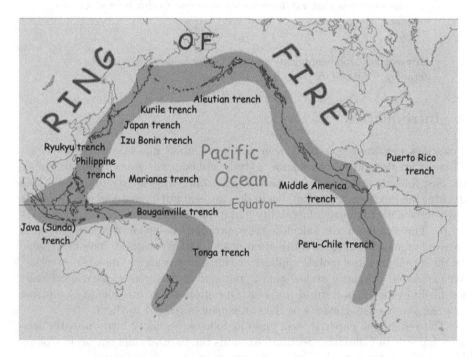

Fig. 1. Plate tectonics and the ring of fire [10]

---

[1] https://www.dane.gov.co/.

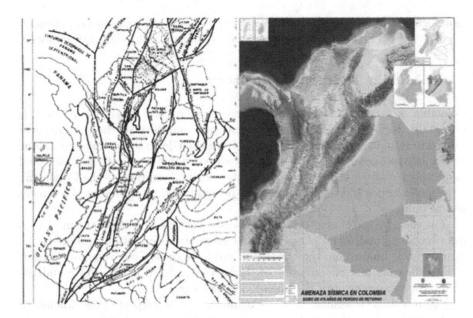

Fig. 2. Structural geology of western Colombia - seismic hazard in Colombia for an event with a return period of 475 years [2]

According to the National Seismological Network of the Colombian Geological Service, there are areas of the country where these telluric movements are more frequent and occur with greater intensity. Places such as the Pacific Coast (Nariño, Cauca, Valle del Cauca, and Chocó), the Caribbean Coast, and the places around the mountain ranges.

4   Colombian Geological Service

Starting in the 1980s, the Colombian State has assigned to the National Institute of Geological Mining Research INGEOMINAS[2] as responsible for the basic studies related to natural disasters of geological origin. The assignment was created due to the disasters caused by the Popayan earthquake in 1983 and the eruption of the Nevado del Ruiz volcano in 1985. This entity was in charge of the creation and operation of the National Seismological Network and the country's volcanological observatories [3].

The risk related to lose and damage was one of the reasons why the National System for Disaster Prevention and Attention (SNPAD)[3] was created in 1988. In 2011, INGEOMINAS became the Colombian Geological Service. This entity investigates and delivers to the country reports related to the tracking and

---

[2] https://www.igac.gov.co/.
[3] https://portal.gestiondelriesgo.gov.co/.

monitoring of threats of geological origin, and subsoil information management, among others. These reports are generated as open data through its web portal.

5   A Mobile Technology Strategy

Colombia is a country with a high presence of natural emergencies, so it is important, to create mechanisms that mitigate and address the consequences related to seismic events. For this reason, from open data, the scraping technique and mobile technology were proposed to create a mobile application to warn and inform people about the seismic events in Colombia reported by the Colombian Geological Service and the location of the hospitals and medical attention centers in real time.

The effective use of open data can generate multiple benefits that can be seen from economic and social perspectives. It allows transformation processes with transparency, innovation, the creation of products or services, the improvement in the efficiency and effectiveness of the services offered by the State and the predictive measurement of the impact of policies [8].

Figure 3 shows a seismic event in Colombia. This is a report of the Colombian Geological Service web portal in the open data format.

According to the information provided in the open data format of the web portal of the Colombian Geological Site for the mobile application, the diagram of Fig. 4 was created based on the estimated requirements, such as the alert generator, emergency area report module, consultation of protocols in case of emergencies and user configuration [1,11–13].

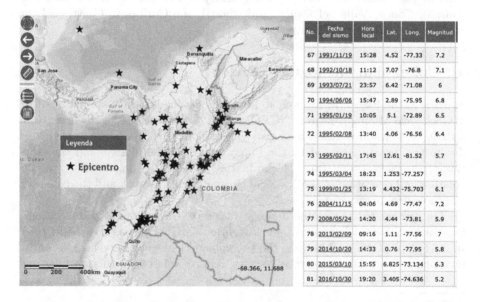

No.	Fecha del sismo	Hora local	Lat.	Long.	Magnitud
67	1991/11/19	15:28	4.52	-77.33	7.2
68	1992/10/18	11:12	7.07	-76.8	7.1
69	1993/07/21	23:57	6.42	-71.08	6
70	1994/06/06	15:47	2.89	-75.95	6.8
71	1995/01/19	10:05	5.1	-72.89	6.5
72	1995/02/08	13:40	4.06	-76.56	6.4
73	1995/02/11	17:45	12.61	-81.52	5.7
74	1995/03/04	18:23	1.253	-77.257	5
75	1999/01/25	13:19	4.432	-75.703	6.1
76	2004/11/15	04:06	4.69	-77.47	7.2
77	2008/05/24	14:20	4.44	-73.81	5.9
78	2013/02/09	09:16	1.11	-77.56	7
79	2014/10/20	14:33	0.76	-77.95	5.8
80	2015/03/10	15:55	6.825	-73.134	6.3
81	2016/10/30	19:20	3.405	-74.636	5.2

Fig. 3. Open data web portal Colombian geological Service

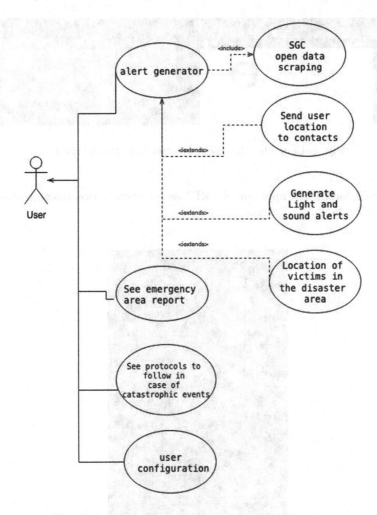

Fig. 4. Case diagram mobile app for earthquake alert

The application was created for smartphones with the Android operating system. Two different development environments were used IntelliJ IDEA[4] for the data collector and the official android development environment Android Studio[5].

Firebase[6] was implemented as a database service for applications provided by Google. SQLite[7] was used as a lightweight database engine incorporated

---

[4] https://www.jetbrains.com/idea/.

[5] https://developer.android.com/.

[6] https://firebase.google.com/.

[7] https://www.sqlite.org/index.html.

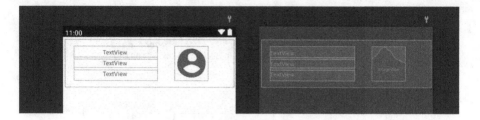

Fig. 5. Contacts interface to interact with the database

by Android for mobile apps and GIMP[8] as an open-source image editor and programming language Python.

Fig. 6. Emergency message

---

[8] https://www.gimp.org/.

The development methodology used was Scrum. The proposed and executed sprints are listed below:

– Sprint No 1. Implemented firebase service where the last recorded earth-quake was stored, for which, a scraping module was created for the SGC and created the login interface to be used by the firebase service.
– Sprint No 2. The Design and implementation of the local database were created to store the last earthquake and show it in notifications. Also, the contacts interface to interact with the database was created (see Fig. 5).
– Sprint No 3. The implementation of the services related to permissions, text messages, and maps. This service was implemented to request permissions, creating a task that automatically sends a text message and implements the Application Programming Interface (API) of the google maps service (see Fig. 6).
– Sprint No 4. Development of the service to show the location of the last earthquake in the activity maps and creates the configuration interface of the application (see Fig. 7).

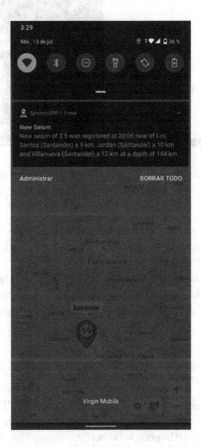

Fig. 7. Location of the last earthquake

Fig. 8. Markers for new emergencies, emergency information, and description editable field.

- Sprint No 5. In this sprint, a form to display emergency information related to an earthquake was designed and implemented. Also, it was the toolbar to access the configuration that was created (see Fig. 8).
- Sprint No 6. In this sprint, the module that uses the components of the telephone to start the location routine and the creation of the educational module of protocols to follow in the event of an earthquake was designed and implemented.

5.1 Test and Operations

For the first testing process, the login views were verified. The validation of email and password fields was tested. The authentication with the "access" buttons and the authentication with google accounts using the "google" button were verified.

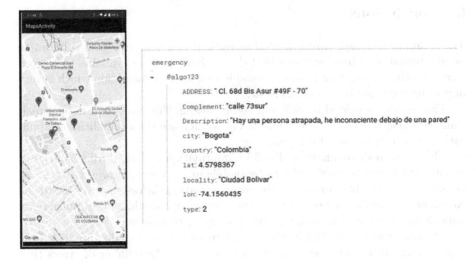

Fig. 9. Notification and epicenter marker

The test verifies that the application requests the necessary permissions for its operation of the location permissions, camera, contacts, storage, and SMS. After the permissions were obtained, the firebase real-time database listening service started. The phone settings were opened and finally, the processes that run in the background were seen in the "SeismicAPP", because the service was running. The next step in the tests was the execution of the process that the application showed when a new earthquake was registered in the database. The notification showed basic information such as magnitude, time, and populations near the epicenter. Then the location of this earthquake should have been visible on the activity maps in the app.

To test the contacts module, two dummy contacts were added to the phone's contacts application and then added to the contact list in the "SeismicAPP" application. In the Maps activity, adding markers was tested to indicate new emergencies, related to collapsed structures, trapped people, gas or water leaks, collapsed roads, etc. These emergencies were uploaded to the Firebase database after allowing the user to modify parameters or add a description (see Fig 9).

The basic configuration for the operation of the application consisted of a switch button in which the user indicated if he wanted his location to be sent to his contacts. Then the user has a space where he can edit the message that he wants to send to his contacts. Also, the app has a button to edit the message and save it. Finally, a Slidebar defined the value for the Richter scale from which the notification is triggered.

For the last test, the notification asks the user if he is okay. If the user does not interact with the notification, a routine is activated and the app uses the camera flash and the phone's speaker to make their position visible.

6   Conclusions

The scraping technique implemented in python is a very practical solution to obtain official data from agencies that do not have services available to be consumed by the public. This makes it possible to massify information which is very important for emergency management.

The services provided by different companies; in this case, the Firebase real-time database can be used very effectively to increase the capabilities of applications that can be used for human care.

The need to disseminate and collect information before, during, and after an emergency can be very well met by mobile applications. However, these can be limited by possible damage to the communications infrastructure due to the emergency. A restrictive bot policy on the agency page would make it much more difficult to collect information through a scraping technique.

The use of available API in the market to create the mobile app allows the app to have an accurate performance and to reduce the number of errors that can take place during the execution. This allows the app to be reliable. The sound and light alert implementation can make the localization of people that can be affected after an earthquake faster and easier.

The emergency map can facilitate the task of coordination and prioritization relative to the possible consequences of an earthquake.

References

1. Cantor, J.E., Montoya, G.A., Lozano-Garzon, C.: Establishing best pedestrian paths considering SARS-CoV-2 contagions: mathematical optimization model and mobile application approach. ParadigmPlus **2**(3), 14–36 (2021)
2. Duque Escobar, G.: Terremotos en el occidente colombiano (2019). https://repositorio.unal.edu.co/handle/unal/69670
3. Espinosa, A.: Breve historia del servicio geológico colombiano (2018). https://www2.sgc.gov.co/Nosotros/AcercaDelSgc/Paginas/Historia.aspx
4. Gosteva, T.P., Correa, M., Ramírez, J.P.: Determinación de la energía geotérmica hidrotermal y los impactos ambientales en el departamento de caldas, colombia. Desarrollo e Innovacion en Ingenieria, p. 97 (2021)
5. IDEAM: Estudio nacional de la degradacion de suelos por erosion en colombia (2015). http://documentacion.ideam.gov.co/openbiblio/bvirtual/023646/Sintesis.pdf
6. Ishida, R., Izumi, T., Nakatani, Y.: Simulation system of tsunami evacuation behavior during an earthquake around JR Osaka station area. In: Zlatanova, S., Peters, R., Dilo, A., Scholten, H. (eds.) Intelligent Systems for Crisis Management. Lecture Notes in Geoinformation and Cartography, pp. 67–78. Springer, Heidelberg (2013). https://doi.org/10.1007/978-3-642-33218-0_6
7. Khamespanah, F., Delavar, M.R., Alinia, H.S., Zare, M.: Granular computing and dempster-shafer integration in seismic vulnerability assessment. In: Zlatanova, S., Peters, R., Dilo, A., Scholten, H. (eds.) Intelligent systems for crisis management. Lecture Notes in Geoinformation and Cartography, pp. 147–158. Springer, Heidelberg (2013). https://doi.org/10.1007/978-3-642-33218-0_11

8. Ministerio de Tecnologías de la Información y las Comunicaciones: Guía para el uso y aprovechamiento de datos abiertos en colombia (2018). https://herramientas.datos.gov.co/sites/default/files/Guia%20de%20Datos%20Abiertos%20de%20Colombia.pdf
9. Molina, C.R.: La gestión del riesgo volcánico en colombia: una historia eruptiva con importantes lecciones aprendidas. Revista Fasecolda **185**, 40–44 (2022)
10. National Geographyc: Plate tectonics and the ring of fire (2022). https://education.nationalgeographic.org/resource/plate-tectonics-ring-fire
11. Rodriguez G., R., Castang M., G., Vanegas, C.A.: Information encryption and decryption analysis, vulnerabilities and reliability implementing the RSA algorithm in python. In: Florez, H., Pollo-Cattaneo, M.F. (eds.) ICAI 2021. CCIS, vol. 1455, pp. 391–404. Springer, Cham (2021). https://doi.org/10.1007/978-3-030-89654-6_28
12. Sanchez, D., Florez, H.: Model driven engineering approach to manage peripherals in mobile devices. In: Gervasi, O., et al. (eds.) ICCSA 2018. LNCS, vol. 10963, pp. 353–364. Springer, Cham (2018). https://doi.org/10.1007/978-3-319-95171-3_28
13. Wanumen, L., Moreno, J., Florez, H.: Mobile based approach for accident reporting. In: Botto-Tobar, M., Pizarro, G., Zúñiga-Prieto, M., D'Armas, M., Zúñiga Sánchez, M. (eds.) CITT 2018. CCIS, vol. 895, pp. 302–311. Springer, Cham (2019). https://doi.org/10.1007/978-3-030-05532-5_22

Internet of Things with Wearable Devices and Artificial Intelligence for Elderly Uninterrupted Healthcare Monitoring Systems

Joseph Bamidele Awotunde[1] , Sunday Adeola Ajagbe[2(✉)] , and Hector Florez[3]

[1] University of Ilorin, Ilorin, Nigeria
awotunde.jb@unilorin.edu.ng
[2] Ladoke Akintola University of Technology, Ogbomoso, Nigeria
saajagbe@pgschool.lautech.edu.ng
[3] Universidad Distrital Francisco Jose de Caldas, Bogota, Colombia
haflorezf@udistrital.edu.co

Abstract. The advent of recent pandemics has changed the priority given to the healthcare system by each country, and this has changed the thinking of many towards the management of health-related illnesses. The Internet of Things (IoT) interconnects with smart devices in today's Internet and has changed the trend in the next-generation technologies. This comes with various advantages like the connectivity of smart devices with several services to amass a huge amount of data and connectivity. These have revolutionized modern healthcare by assuring economic, social, and technological prospects. There has been an increase in the number of elderly people living or staying alone, and the need of monitoring them remotely increasing exponentially. Hence, the use of IoT-based systems can be used to leverage these challenges. The combination of IoT-wearable devices enabled by Artificial Intelligence can be used to solve some of these problems by monitoring elderly persons remotely and allowing them to conduct their day-to-day activities without any fear. Therefore, this paper proposed IoT-wearable enabled AI to remotely monitor elderly persons in real-time. Various wearable sensors were used to capture elderly physiological signs, the IoT-based cloud database was used to store the captured data, and the AI model was to process the data for effective decision-making. The health status of the elderly gets to the healthcare workers in real-time, thus enabling them to give precautionary advice to save lives. The system will also reduce the workload of medical personnel by monitoring elderly persons in real-time and remotely.

Keywords: Internet of Things · Artificial Intelligence · Wearable body sensor · Machine-to-machine · Modern healthcare · Internet connectivity

H. Florez and H. Gomez (Eds.): ICAI 2022, CCIS 1643, pp. 278–291, 2022.
https://doi.org/10.1007/978-3-031-19647-8_20

1   Introduction

In most countries, advances in clinical research and technological advancements have boosted life expectancy. Surprisingly, this has led to an increase in the number of persons suffering from age-related degenerative illnesses, what's more, this has prompted an increment in the expenses and tension on medical care frameworks [13]. Besides, in many areas of the planet, the old populace is extending at a more noteworthy rate than the more youthful gatherings. According to the latest figures, there were 703 million persons aged 65 and up in 2019, and by 2050 the population of the elderly is predicted to grow to 1.5 billion, more than twice the current figure [34]. The number of elderly people above 65 years and more settled in New Zealand will moreover generally twofold from 711,200 in 2016 to someplace in the scope of 1.3 and 1.5 million by 2046. This expansion, thus, comes down to advanced age medical care frameworks and emotionally supportive networks and expands the number of retirees that each functioning age individual needs to help [24].

When compared to previous decades, life expectancy has improved significantly. Women's life expectancy, on the other hand, is generally higher than men's, and hence, the majority of older individuals live alone [1,12]. The Countries in the middle east have seen an upsurge in the number of old individuals, thus causing an escalation in elderly people with increasing concern [9,11]. The health of the elderly is deteriorating, including the importance of maintaining gait balance, neurological issues, and heart function. Medical care and security perception of the aging people is ending up being the most recent examination issue that requires research solutions [14].

A significant worry of continuously expanding old people in a few countries is the proficient stockpile of Medicare which is much of the time dangerous because of the declining state in their neurological state. Diseases like diabetes, high blood pressure, Dementia, Alzheimer's, and other health-related issues in the elderly necessitate the use of a health-monitoring system. The IoT monitoring systems can be used in this direction and plays a vital role in elderly people, and their life is saved, and the patient is alerted to the danger of death [6,8,33]. The IoT-based adaptive system comprises a series of wearable sensors and AI-based models that are connected to experts over the Internet [1]. The use of IoT-based healthcare monitoring systems allows elderly people to obtain information about their health status remotely and in real-time services without leaving their homes [9,16].

The IoT is the technology in the cutting edge innovations, which interconnects the brilliant gadgets in the present Internet structure with more related advantages. The significant benefit of the framework incorporates the availability of these shrewd gadgets with the administration surpassing the conventional methods [27]. IoT assumes a significant part in building savvy unavoidable outlines. An assortment of use of IoT-based systems in various fields has changed many things most especially in healthcare-related environments. The IoT upheaval is reexamining current medical services by guaranteeing mechanical, social, and financial possibilities. Progressions as far as observing them dis-

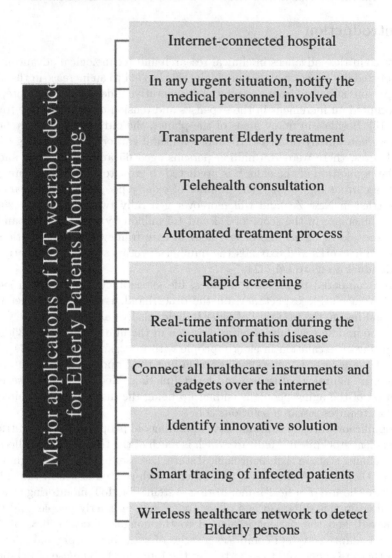

Fig. 1. Applicability of IoT-based enabled diseases monitoring systems for Elderly Patients

tantly are the need of time, and IoT development has utilized something similar. Older people face a ton of difficulties in directing their everyday life, the difficulties range from cognitive decline, vulnerability to infections, and debilitation making them live in an endurance mode.

The applicability of IoT-based enabled wearable sensors for monitoring elderly patients is displayed in Fig. 1.

IoT-based devices can be conveyed for older persons detecting with the guide of cell phones, crucial sign screens, wearables sensors, sound video sensors, shrewd gadgets, and keen TV. IoT techniques joined with Big Data and Cloud can be utilized successfully to give various answers to the issue of detached elderly people [25,26]. The IoT-based remote checking frameworks can be used to screen older individuals with for all intents and purposes different medical services concerns. These can be recorded progressively and distantly by sending caught information to the cloud data set for executions utilizing AI models [10]. There are currently procedures in place to aid self-care and increase the autonomy of the elderly. Assistive living systems are a common name for such systems. The services' major goals are to allow elderly citizens to live independently at home for longer, to improve living quality, and to save money for the community and social healthcare systems. Assisted living tools can enhance older people with daily duties, allowing them to remain alive and healthy while living comfortably.

When compared to previous decades, life expectancy has improved significantly. Women's life expectancy, on the other hand, is generally higher than men's, and hence, the majority of older individuals live alone. The Countries in the middle east have seen an upsurge in the number of old individuals, thus causing an escalation in elderly people with increasing concern. The well-being of the older is falling apart, including their significance of keeping up with step balance, neurological issues, and heart work [15]. Clinical consideration and security impression of the maturing individuals are winding up being the latest assessment issue that requires research arrangements. A significant worry of continuously expanding old people in a few countries is the proficient stockpile of Medicare which is much of the time dangerous because of the declining state in their neurological state. Diseases like diabetes, high blood pressure, Dementia, Alzheimer's, and other health-related issues in the elderly necessitate the use of a health monitoring system [1]. The IoT-based checking frameworks can be utilized toward this path and assumes an indispensable part in old individuals, and their life is saved, and the patient is made aware of the risk of death. The IoT-based adaptive system comprises a series of wearable sensors and AI-based models that are connected to experts over the Internet [8,26]. The use of IoT-based healthcare monitoring systems allows elderly people to obtain information about their health status remotely and real-time services without leaving their homes.

Therefore, the study proposes an elderly healthcare monitoring system using IoT-based through wearable devices enabled with an AI-based model. IoT-based wearable sensors were used to collect various physiological signs from elderly persons with the help of a variety of accessories that are linked to the internet and mobile devices. The data collected is stored in the cloud database continuously from wearable and mobile devices. The Deep feed-forward Neural Network (DFFNN) was for the analysis process, the data stored by the cloud database was processed using the DFFNN classifier. The key contributions of the paper are as follows:

– The integration of IoT-based wearable devices for capturing elderly persons' physiological signs and activities. The captured data was processed using a DFFNN-based classifier to improve the accuracy of the elderly person's physiological signs and activities. The elderly medical data was trained and enhanced using the AI model and thereby improving the previous healthcare history examination process using various metrics for performance evaluation.

2   Materials and Methods

This section explains the proposed IoT-based wearable devices enabled with an AI model for monitoring elderly persons using the UCI dataset. The proposed system consists of five steps namely: (i) wearable devices layer; (ii) Gateway layer (iii) IoT-Cloud based (Data) layer; (iv) AI-model (data processing) layer, and (v) the Alert Monitoring Platform For Elderly Patients (Hospital Layer). The physiological data of the elderly are collected from the wearable devices and sensors layer, the physiological devices are linked with the IoT-Cloud database

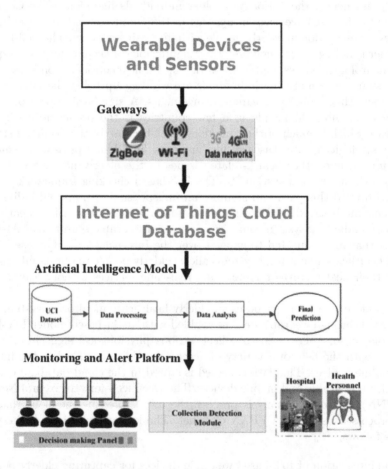

Fig. 2. Proposed framework for the monitoring system

by the gateway layer, and the captured data will be stored using the IoT-based Cloud database. The data processing using the captured data from the elderly physiological status is done in the AI model. The monitoring platform layer gives the medical expert the opportunity of tracking the sensory data of an elderly patient in real-time, thus monitoring the elderly remotely without being physically present at any hospital. The physicians study the processed data using the AI models to be able to take action or give proper advice to elderly patients. The unwanted data are automatically deleted from the cloud database, and the application replicates data in real-time immediately after it arrives at the IoT Cloud server. This gives the medical experts access to update information concerning each elderly patient and make an immediate decision in case of any emergency, hence, prevent worsens cases, and prevent congested hospital admission. Figure 2 displayed the framework for the proposed elderly persons monitoring system.

2.1 Pre-processing

The pre-processing stage is provided the data set, which consists mostly of two approaches. Data conversion and data normalization are two of them. For processing, the data conversion converts nominal features to numeric features. The data normalization process reduces the huge disparity in attribute values to a reasonable range of values. We employed the minimum-to-maximum scaling strategy, which is described mathematically by Eq. 1.

$$Y = \frac{Y - min(Y)}{max(Y) - min(Y)} \tag{1}$$

where Y specifies the data set's feature value, which is in the range $[0, 1]$.

2.2 Deep Feed-Forward Neural Network (DFFNN)

The feedforward networks have been the essential noteworthy learning models called the feedforward neural memories or multi-layer perceptrons (MLPs). A feedforward association's inspiration is too unpleasant a limit f^x. For example, $y = f^x(x)$ moves data x with y a classifier for characterization. The $y = f(x)$ is used by a best-limited gauge in a feedforward network learns to have potential gains of the limits result. Since information travels through the limit being surveyed from x, the momentary assessments are imperative to describe f to ultimately yield y by feedforward network models. Feedforward neural connections that have been lightened up to link processing relationships are known as disjointed neural connections. In general, a DFFNN is described as an ANN technique using a perceptron, a couple of mystery centers, and a yield neuron that is generally clearly related without the usage of a cycle [30].

The mysterious surface of every hub thinks about indistinguishable properties subordinate to the first stage's showcase, which is progressively figured and handled in numerous layers to create yields. This procedure is prepared to utilize a stochastic incline plunge back-engendering system [7]. You can give a more profound feed-forward neural organization the capacity to catch more convoluted portrayals by making a more profound feed-forward neural organization. On the off chance that the intricacy is reasonable, this could be advocated. It enjoys the benefit of having the option to promptly address more complicated capacities. This calculation preparing information approach depends on the arbitrary possibility of neural organization variable actuation, which brings about the format being placed in minima arrangements with helpless standardization [7]. To further develop the union rate and the consequences of directed learning, pre-preparing solo techniques, explicitly an AE can be utilized to construct the initiation details [7].

2.3 Deep Auto-Encoder (DAE)

A DAE is a feed-forward neural organization procedure for quick unaided registering execution [32]. It explores the assessment of a novel assignment, where the outcome (x) is equivalent to the info $(\hat{x})$ to develop a meaning of an assortment of information, that is $(x \to \hat{x})$, x. Its schematic portrayal comprises vectors $(x^{(i)})$ in the information hubs and a few disguised units of non-straight commencement ascribes. To learn smaller provisions of the information, the separated components utilize fewer neurons than the information hubs. Therefore, it knows the main credits and brings down spatial size, and perspectives of the info information as a reflection. Toward the finish of the technique, the yield layer $(\hat{x}^i)$ is displayed as a nearby portrayal of the info layer presented in Eq. 2.

$$T(t) = \frac{1 - e^{-2t}}{1 + e^{-2t}} \tag{2}$$

The AE calculation has two major parts encoder and decoder [5], and deterministic planning called an encoder technique $(f\theta)$ is utilized [23] to change the information vector $(x^{(i)})$ into a secret layer portrayal $(z^{(i)})$ and the right number of codes is diminished, and represented by a dimensionality $(x^{(i)})$ as presented in Eq. 3.

$$f\theta(x^{(i)}) = T(W_{x^{(i)}} + b) \tag{3}$$

where the weighted network is represented by $W = d^0 x d^h, d^h$, Tanhinitiation utility is represented by T, the plan boundaries are represented by θ, $[W, b]$, the disguised level neurons dh is represented by $(d^0 < d^h)$, and b is the predisposition vector. The visualization of the hidden layer's output is projected, The deterministic plotting determines the interpretation technique for $(g\theta')$ as a guess $(\hat{x}^i)$ to rebuild the contribution as an estimate $(\hat{x}^i)$ as presented in Eq. 4

$$g\theta'(x^{(i)}) = T(W'_{z^{(i)}} + b') \tag{4}$$

The weight framework W' is represented by $d^0 x d^h$, planning boundaries is addresses in $[W', b']$ by θ', and b is a predisposition vector.

The data in that packed portrayal is then utilized as contributions to recreate the first data in the wake of being changed to fit the mysterious surface.

The change botch (i.e., the modification between the crude archive and its low-dimensional propagation) for a norm or little cluster preparing set (s) is determined by the preparation interaction presented in Eqs. 5 and 6.

$$E(x, \hat{x}) = \frac{1}{2} \sum_{i}^{s} ||x^{(i)} - \hat{x}^{(i)}||^2 \qquad (5)$$

$$\theta = [W, b] = argmin_\theta E(x, \hat{x}) \qquad (6)$$

2.4   The UCI Dataset

The evaluations have been done with a party of 30 volunteers ages 19 to 48 years. Every individual performed six exercises (WALKING, WALK-ING_UPSTAIRS, WALKING_DOWNSTAIRS, SITTING, STANDING, LAY-ING) wearing a phone on the mid-locale. Using its introduced accelerometer and whirligig, we got a 3-critical direct speed increment and 3-center jaunty speed at a consistent speed 50 Hz. The examinations have been video-recorded to check the data truly. The sensor signals (accelerometer and gyroscope) were pre-arranged by applying commotion diverts and subsequently analyzed in fixed-width sliding windows of 2.56 sec and a half to get more than (128 readings/window). The sensor speed increment signal, which has gravitational and body development parts, was confined using a Butterworth low-pass channel into body speed increment and gravity. The gravitational force is relied upon to have quite recently low-repeat parts, subsequently, a channel with a 0.3 Hz cutoff repeat was used. From each window, a vector of parts was gotten by determining factors from the time and repeat region [3, 4, 21]. 1: Walking, 2: Walking steps, 3: Walking the first floor, 4: Sitting, 5: Standing, 6: Laying.

The proposed model was implemented in the R programming language, and the performance of the model was tested using various evaluation metrics. The activity monitoring recognition dataset with seamless characteristics, and contains six activities for elderly physiological monitoring activities. The dataset was divided into ratios of 70:30 for training and testing respectively, this was done by splitting the dataset into vectors. The DFFNN model was used as a classifier for the training and testing of the proposed model. Six major elderly activities used in label index class are sitting, standing, walking, laying, walking downstairs, and walking upstairs. the generated vectors from the dataset have the same values and were added together. The test dataset was used for the performance evaluation of the proposed model.

3   Experimental Results and Evaluation

Experiments were conducted on the UCI dataset using 70% for training and 30% for testing the dataset. A customary segment of the dataset into preparing and test sets were utilized except if expressed in any case. The synopsis of the acquired outcomes for exercise acknowledgment is introduced in Table 1. The

Table 1. The performance of the proposed model

Activities	Accuracy	Precision	Recall	F-Measure	ROC
A1	98.40%	99.00%	99.10%	98.80%	98.60%
A2	96.70%	97.30%	97.10%	96.90%	96.60%
A3	97.40%	97.30%	96.80%	98.60%	97.90%
A4	98.30%	98.80%	98.70%	98.50%	98.80%
A5	98.90%	97.20%	97.60%	98.40%	98.70%
A6	99.70%	99.30%	99.10%	100.00%	100.00%
Average	98.23%	98.15%	98.07%	98.53%	98.43%

proposed classifier on the dataset demonstrates an accuracy of 98.23%, thus outperforming the existing classifiers on the same dataset. The classification system produces results for the seven physical activities designated as A1-A7 for the sake of simplicity. A1 = Walking, A2 = Walking upstairs, A3 = Walking downstairs, A4 = Sitting, A5 = Standing, and A6 = Laying.

Figure 3 presents a 10-cross-over customer-based cross-endorsement to investigate the ebb and flow of findings in the dataset The accuracy was running someplace in the scope of 97.54% and 98.54% with a typical worth with a mean of 97.47% and an error margin of 1.92%, and this is similar results obtained in the traditional ML techniques used on the dataset.

The UCI dataset has effectively been parted into preparing and testing proportion of 70:30 dependent on a few members, henceforth has a rendition that is as divided into training and testing sets, each including data from different members, consequently, in this dataset, the client autonomous choice won out. The greater part of the chips away at the UCI dataset utilized mama chine

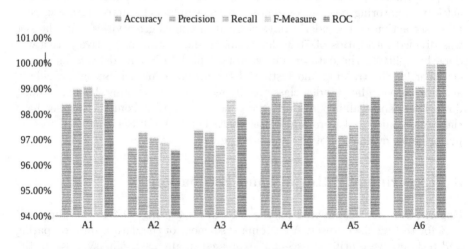

Fig. 3. Performance evaluation of the proposed model

learning with highlight determination like in [2,20,31], in any case, a couple of significant learning methods were furthermore proposed [19,22,28,29]. In Seto et al. [31], Deep Boltzmann Machines were adapted to independent component extraction, and in any case, they are not assigned to getting close by their presentation which was preferable to the following hand-made blueprints due to data arrangement. One more encouraging arrangement with the low computational expense, the authors in [28] depend on the RNN technique. However, because of another exclusive split of the dataset into training and testing parts, it's difficult to compare its accuracy to previous methods. The best results for the UCI dataset were achieved using 561 features in [21], which produced the greatest outcomes, as well as many classifiers on top of them. The accuracy of the proposed model was compared with the existing models using the UCI dataset in Table 2.

Utilizing the UCI dataset, Table 2 shows the total presentation measures for the proposed framework and different techniques. The precision of the proposed strategy is better than that of different strategies. In general, the suggested elderly activities monitoring method has a 98.23% accuracy, which is 0.6% greater than the second-highest accuracy, CNN + Stat. features + data centering. The suggested model outperformed other strategies on all assessment metrics when compared to the UCI dataset. Given its strong element determination and rule-based wellness calculation, the recommended strategy has hardly any more prominent exactness.

Table 2. Comparison of the proposed model accuracy with existing models for UCI dataset

Method	Accuracy
Handcrafted features + Dropout [2]	76.26
Handcrafted features + Random Forest [2]	77.81
Hidden Markov Models [20]	83.51
Dynamic Time Warping [31]	89
Hidden Markov Models [28]	91.76
PCA + SVM [22]	91.82
Stacked Autoencoders + SVM [22]	92.16
Recurrent Neural Network [18]	95.03
Convolutional Neural Network [19]	95.18
Handcrafted features + SVM [4]	96.37
CNN + Stat. features + data centering [17]	97.63
CNN + Stat. features [17]	96.06
Proposed Method	98.23

The proposed model varies from earlier geriatric activity monitoring classification models in that it use DFFNN models with adequate input to achieve classification that is both effective and efficient. Furthermore, because of the reduced hidden layer, the model understands and analyses high-level functioning, automatically reduces data dimensionality, and effectively displays significant properties. As a result, the suggested model is best suited for categorization in healthcare businesses that deal with large amounts of unlabeled and unstructured data, such as medical data.

4   Conclusions

According to the World Health Organization, the global population of persons aged 60 and more will reach 2 billion in 2050 from its current 841 million. Human longevity is predicted to become the norm because of recent improvements in information technologies that make treatment available to everybody. Hence, providing a convenient platform for senior patients has drawn the attention of numerous researchers from diverse fields, thus making the smart healthcare system a desirable option for many. Advances in IoT, cloud computing, and wearable devices, have aided in bringing healthcare closer to rural areas and improving aged care around the world. Therefore, this paper proposed IoT-based wearable devices for capturing elderly persons' physiological signs and activities, and an AI model was used for the processing of the captured data. From the results, the proposed system performs better when compared with other existing models using the UCI dataset to test the performance of their models. The system has an accuracy of 98.23% with an increase of 0.6% better than the closest model. The IoT-based enabled wearable sensors for the elderly can accommodate various types of devices and any number of sensors, but it must be with the advice of an expert. The proposed model allows the monitoring of elderly patients in real-time, and remotely without physically being in the hospital for checkups. The model reduces the workload of medical experts and the cost of admission in a hospital, eliminates medical faults, and minimizes pressure on medical doctors. Future work can make use of other datasets to test the performance of this model and make comparisons and recommendations. The use of feature selection techniques may also be considered in a similar dataset especially when there are large features or irrelevant features. It is also hoped that the trial with a geriatric cohort will be implemented and compare the results with the cohort analyzed as a control group of baseline clinical and demographic characteristics.

References

1. Adeniyi, E.A., Ogundokun, R.O., Awotunde, J.B.: IoMT-based wearable body sensors network healthcare monitoring system. In: Marques, G., Bhoi, A.K., Albuquerque, V.H.C., K. S., H. (eds.) IoT in Healthcare and Ambient Assisted Living. SCI, vol. 933, pp. 103–121. Springer, Singapore (2021). https://doi.org/10.1007/978-981-15-9897-5_6

2. Ajagbe, S.A., Amuda, K.A., Oladipupo, M.A., Oluwaseyi, F.A., Okesola, K.I.: Multi-classification of Alzheimer disease on magnetic resonance images (MRI) using deep convolutional neural network (DCNN) approaches. Int. J. Adv. Comput. Res. **11**(53), 51 (2021)

3. Anguita, D., Ghio, A., Oneto, L., Parra, X., Reyes-Ortiz, J.L.: Human activity recognition on smartphones using a multiclass hardware-friendly support vector machine. In: Bravo, J., Hervás, R., Rodríguez, M. (eds.) IWAAL 2012. LNCS, vol. 7657, pp. 216–223. Springer, Heidelberg (2012). https://doi.org/10.1007/978-3-642-35395-6_30

4. Anguita, D., Ghio, A., Oneto, L., Parra Perez, X., Reyes Ortiz, J.L.: A public domain dataset for human activity recognition using smartphones. In: Proceedings of the 21th International European Symposium on Artificial Neural Networks, Computational Intelligence and Machine Learning, pp. 437–442 (2013)

5. Awotunde, J.B., Ayoade, O.B., Ajamu, G.J., AbdulRaheem, M., Oladipo, I.D.: Internet of things and cloud activity monitoring systems for elderly healthcare. In: Internet of Things for Human-Centered Design, pp. 181–207. Springer, Singapore (2022). https://doi.org/10.1007/978-981-16-8488-3_9

6. Awotunde, J.B., Bhoi, A.K., Barsocchi, P.: Hybrid cloud/fog environment for healthcare: an exploratory study, opportunities, challenges, and future prospects. In: Kumar Bhoi, A., Mallick, P.K., Narayana Mohanty, M., Albuquerque, V.H.C. (eds.) Hybrid Artificial Intelligence and IoT in Healthcare. ISRL, vol. 209, pp. 1–20. Springer, Singapore (2021). https://doi.org/10.1007/978-981-16-2972-3_1

7. Awotunde, J.B., Chakraborty, C., Adeniyi, A.E.: Intrusion detection in industrial internet of things network-based on deep learning model with rule-based feature selection. Wireless Commun. Mobile Comput. (2021)

8. Awotunde, J.B., Folorunso, S.O., Bhoi, A.K., Adebayo, P.O., Ijaz, M.F.: Disease diagnosis system for IoT-based wearable body sensors with machine learning algorithm. In: Kumar Bhoi, A., Mallick, P.K., Narayana Mohanty, M., Albuquerque, V.H.C. (eds.) Hybrid Artificial Intelligence and IoT in Healthcare. ISRL, vol. 209, pp. 201–222. Springer, Singapore (2021). https://doi.org/10.1007/978-981-16-2972-3_10

9. Awotunde, J.B., Jimoh, R.G., AbdulRaheem, M., Oladipo, I.D., Folorunso, S.O., Ajamu, G.J.: IoT-based wearable body sensor network for COVID-19 pandemic. In: Hassanien, A.-E., Elghamrawy, S.M., Zelinka, I. (eds.) Advances in Data Science and Intelligent Data Communication Technologies for COVID-19. SSDC, vol. 378, pp. 253–275. Springer, Cham (2022). https://doi.org/10.1007/978-3-030-77302-1_14

10. Awotunde, J.B., Ogundokun, R.O., Misra, S.: Cloud and IoMT-based big data analytics system during COVID-19 pandemic. In: Chakraborty, C., Ghosh, U., Ravi, V., Shelke, Y. (eds.) Efficient Data Handling for Massive Internet of Medical Things. IT, pp. 181–201. Springer, Cham (2021). https://doi.org/10.1007/978-3-030-66633-0_8

11. Awotunde, J.B., Oluwabukonla, S., Chakraborty, C., Bhoi, A.K., Ajamu, G.J.: Application of artificial intelligence and big data for fighting COVID-19 pandemic. In: Hassan, S.A., Mohamed, A.W., Alnowibet, K.A. (eds.) Decision Sciences for COVID-19. ISORMS, vol. 320, pp. 3–26. Springer, Cham (2022). https://doi.org/10.1007/978-3-030-87019-5_1

12. Chan, A., Visaria, A., Gubhaju, B., Ma, S., Saito, Y.: Gender differences in years of remaining life by living arrangement among older Singaporeans. Eur. J. Ageing **18**(4), 453–466 (2021). https://doi.org/10.1007/s10433-020-00594-3

13. Cho, J.: Current status and prospects of health-related sensing technology in wearable devices. J. Healthc. Eng. (2019)
14. Fonseca-Herrera, O.A., Rojas, A.E., Florez, H.: A model of an information security management system based on NTC-ISO/IEC 27001 standard. IAENG Int. J. Comput. Sci. **48**(2), 213–222 (2021)
15. Gallardo, J., Bellone, G., Risk, M.: Ultra-short heart rate variability and Poincaré plots. ParadigmPlus **2**(3), 37–52 (2021)
16. Hernandez, J., Daza, K., Florez, H., Misra, S.: Dynamic interface and access model by dead token for IoT systems. In: Florez, H., Leon, M., Diaz-Nafria, J.M., Belli, S. (eds.) ICAI 2019. CCIS, vol. 1051, pp. 485–498. Springer, Cham (2019). https://doi.org/10.1007/978-3-030-32475-9_35
17. Ignatov, A.: Real-time human activity recognition from accelerometer data using convolutional neural networks. Appl. Soft Comput. **62**, 915–922 (2018)
18. Inoue, M., Inoue, S., Nishida, T.: Deep recurrent neural network for mobile human activity recognition with high throughput. Artif. Life Robot. **23**(2), 173–185 (2017). https://doi.org/10.1007/s10015-017-0422-x
19. Jiang, W., Yin, Z.: Human activity recognition using wearable sensors by deep convolutional neural networks. In: Proceedings of the 23rd ACM international conference on Multimedia, pp. 1307–1310 (2015)
20. Kim, Y.J., Kang, B.N., Kim, D.: Hidden markov model ensemble for activity recognition using tri-axis accelerometer. In: 2015 IEEE International Conference on Systems, Man, and Cybernetics, pp. 3036–3041. IEEE (2015)
21. Kolosnjaji, B., Eckert, C.: Neural network-based user-independent physical activity recognition for mobile devices. In: Jackowski, K., Burduk, R., Walkowiak, K., Woźniak, M., Yin, H. (eds.) IDEAL 2015. LNCS, vol. 9375, pp. 378–386. Springer, Cham (2015). https://doi.org/10.1007/978-3-319-24834-9_44
22. Li, Y., Shi, D., Ding, B., Liu, D.: Unsupervised feature learning for human activity recognition using smartphone sensors. In: Prasath, R., O'Reilly, P., Kathirvalavakumar, T. (eds.) MIKE 2014. LNCS (LNAI), vol. 8891, pp. 99–107. Springer, Cham (2014). https://doi.org/10.1007/978-3-319-13817-6_11
23. Marques, G., Miranda, N., Kumar Bhoi, A., Garcia-Zapirain, B., Hamrioui, S., de la Torre Díez, I.: Internet of things and enhanced living environments: measuring and mapping air quality using cyber-physical systems and mobile computing technologies. Sensors **20**(3), 720 (2020)
24. de Meijer, C., Wouterse, B., Polder, J., Koopmanschap, M.: The effect of population aging on health expenditure growth: a critical review. Eur. J. Ageing **10**(4), 353–361 (2013). https://doi.org/10.1007/s10433-013-0280-x
25. Olowu, M., Yinka-Banjo, C., Misra, S., Florez, H.: A secured private-cloud computing system. In: Florez, H., Leon, M., Diaz-Nafria, J.M., Belli, S. (eds.) ICAI 2019. CCIS, vol. 1051, pp. 373–384. Springer, Cham (2019). https://doi.org/10.1007/978-3-030-32475-9_27
26. Padikkapparambil, J., Ncube, C., Singh, K.K., Singh, A.: Internet of things technologies for elderly health-care applications. In: Emergence of Pharmaceutical Industry Growth with Industrial IoT Approach, pp. 217–243. Elsevier (2020)
27. Rabelo, L., Ballestas, A., Valdez, J., Ibrahim, B.: Using delphi and system dynamics to study the cybersecurity of the IoT-based smart grids. ParadigmPlus **3**(1), 19–36 (2022)
28. Ronao, C.A., Cho, S.B.: Human activity recognition using smartphone sensors with two-stage continuous hidden markov models. In: 2014 10th international conference on natural computation (ICNC), pp. 681–686. IEEE (2014)

29. Ronao, C.A., Cho, S.B.: Human activity recognition with smartphone sensors using deep learning neural networks. Expert Syst. Appl. **59**, 235–244 (2016)
30. Satapathy, S.K., Bhoi, A.K., Loganathan, D., Khandelwal, B., Barsocchi, P.: Machine learning with ensemble stacking model for automated sleep staging using dual-channel EEG signal. Biomed. Signal Process. Control **69**, 102898 (2021)
31. Seto, S., Zhang, W., Zhou, Y.: Multivariate time series classification using dynamic time warping template selection for human activity recognition. In: 2015 IEEE Symposium Series on Computational Intelligence, pp. 1399–1406. IEEE (2015)
32. Srinivasu, P.N., SivaSai, J.G., Ijaz, M.F., Bhoi, A.K., Kim, W., Kang, J.J.: Classification of skin disease using deep learning neural networks with mobilenet V2 and LSTM. Sensors **21**(8), 2852 (2021)
33. Tun, S.Y.Y., Madanian, S., Parry, D.: Clinical perspective on internet of things applications for care of the elderly. Electronics **9**(11), 1925 (2020)
34. United Nations: World population ageing 2017: Highlights. https://www.un-ilibrary.org/content/books/9789213627457 (2018)

ICT-Enabled Social Innovation

A Wayuunaiki Translator to Promote Ethno-Tourism Using Deep Learning Approaches

Rafael Negrette[(✉)] [ID], Ixent Galpin [ID], and Olmer Garcia [ID]

University of Bogota Jorge Tadeo Lozano, Bogotá, Colombia
{olmer.garciab,ixent.galpin,rafael.negrettea}@utadeo.edu.co
https://www.utadeo.edu.co/es/facultad/ciencias-naturales-e-ingenieria
/programa/bogota/maestria-en-ingenieria-y-analitica-de-datos

Abstract. The Guajira region in Colombia is renowned by ethno-tourists, who immerse themselves in a unique cultural experience by interacting with the Wayúu indigenous peoples. Such tourism is deemed to bring benefits to the region. To further foster tourism, we implement a Spanish-Wayuunaiki translator to facilitate communication between visitors and the Wayúu. We used the well-established CRISP-DM methodology for data mining projects. As a first step, we collect a Spanish-Wayuunaiki corpus of data from a variety of sources. This corpus is used to train the deep learning model employed, which is a recurrent neural network which implements an autoencoder with an attention-based mechanism. Our intention is to integrate the symbolic elements of the Wayúu culture with the traditional activities of ethno-tourism and offer it as a commercial product that provides a unique experience to the visitor. In this way, the natural and cultural resources available in the region are leveraged. Together with the participation of the Wayúu community, it is sought that tourism be an instrument to preserve culture. We implement an application has been deployed in Angular as a frontend on the GitHub Pages service. This application consumes the service deployed in the Heroku Docker Instance, resulting in the application with a translation service on the web. This work aims to contribute to the promotion of the Wayúu culture. Our software is available under an open-source model and approach may be replicated for other indigenous languages.

Keywords: Ethno-tourism · Wayúu · Deep learning · Attention · Translation

1 Introduction

La Guajira in Colombia is home to the Wayúu people, who comprise 20% of Colombia's indigenous population. As such, it is an ideal location to develop ethno-tourism, both at a domestic and international level. Ethno-tourism has the potential to provide benefits for the community, such as promoting the culture

H. Florez and H. Gomez (Eds.): ICAI 2022, CCIS 1643, pp. 295–307, 2022.
https://doi.org/10.1007/978-3-031-19647-8_21

and generating employment. In this work, we propose a Spanish-Wayuunaiki translation tool to facilitate communication between visitors and the Wayúu indigenous people.

Several authors consider the importance of languages in the context of tourism. For example, Bobanovic and Grzinic [5] highlight the importance of knowing another language in the hospitality sector, and the approach that employees give to bilingualism, who has a vocabulary focused on their work activities. Clark [9] studies the relevance of language tourism in tourist resorts using a qualitative-quantitative or mixed approach, where the benefits of language tourism are evidenced. This work also carries out a study on the relevance of language tourism in tourist resorts using a qualitative-quantitative or mixed approach, where the benefits of language tourism are evidenced. Bobanovic and Grzinic [5] highlight the importance of knowing another language and the perception of hotel sector employees regarding communication difficulties with tourists who speak other languages, their research has shown that employees have a vocabulary focused on the development of your work activities but that can still be limited at times.

Other authors highlight the importance of language in the field of tourism as a cultural identity. Hall-Lew *et al.* [15] base their research on various studies on sociolinguistics, where the authors have considered language of vital importance in the tourist sector. Furthermore, they state that understanding linguistic variations and language use in tourism is essential to discovering how tourist destinations are marketed and how attractive tourist experiences are created. Bobanovic and Grzinic [5] consider the importance of knowing another language, and the perception of hotel sector employees regarding communication difficulties with tourists who speak other languages. Their research has shown that employees have a vocabulary focused on the development of your work activities but that can still be limited at times. Russell and Leslie [26] show how the lack of linguistic skills negatively affects the tourism sector in the UK. At the same time, the ability to understand other languages is an advantage for employees of companies that provide tourism services and makes clear the need to regularly reinforce these skills for the well-being of tourism in the UK.

In this work, we apply the well-established CRISP-DM methodology for data mining projects [28] to collect a corpus from reliable sources, and use this to train and evaluate two neural network models. As part of the first step of CRISP-DM (*business understanding,* see Sect. 4.1), we consider [22] which shows little access to knowledge networks, and the lack of resources and technological infrastructure to meet the demand of tourists who visit the department in high seasons. Existing sources of texts in Wayúunaiki include literary works such as The Little Prince, The New Testament, magazines of the Jehovah's Witnesses group, magazines, and education books.

The article is structured as follows: Sect. 2 presents the theoretical framework, with the main concepts necessary to understand the technical content of the article. In Sect. 3, related work is described. Section 4 describes the steps undertaken by applying the CRISP-DM methodology, which include steps from data collection to application deployment. Section 5 features discussions and Sect. 6 concludes.

2   Preliminaries

2.1   Wayúunaiki in Tourism

Wayúunaiki, which is part of the Arawak linguistic trunk, is the mother tongue of the Wayúu indigenous people who have approximately 600,000 speakers among the inhabitants of the territories of Colombia and Venezuela. As such, it has become one of the most spoken and important languages of South America [19]. The territory of La Guajira received in the year 2019 a flow of tourists of 3,015[1]. One of the most notable problems about the language is that few translated materials exist that can serve as learning for the model of translation implemented in this project. However, [2] presents a collection of works that explain the grammar of the language and translate phrases and words from Spanish to Wayúunaiki. These works have been helpful to know some of the grammatical rules that we will consider in the development of the model. Fundamentally, two dialects are handled in Wayúunaiki, arribero in *Wipumüin* and abajero in *Wopumüin* with minimal dialectal differences notable when using the article of the third person in the feminine singular. However, these differences do not affect the communication between the Wayúu of both dialects [2].

2.2   Artificial Neural Networks in Translation

Artificial Neural Networks (ANNs) have been used in automatic language translation, text-to-speech conversion, and automatic speech recognition. Due to recent technological advances, the possibility of developing ANN models for the translation of languages without deterioration in intermediate stages is much stronger every day. One of the most important contributions of the ANN-based approach is the possibility of designing and training end-to-end systems [13].

Recurrent neural networks (RNN) have nodes interconnected sequentially. The training procedure, known as *backpropagation*, consists of repeatedly adjusting the weights of the connections in the network to minimize a loss function. As a result of weight adjustment, 'hidden' internal units that are not part of the input or output come to represent important features of the task domain, and the interactions of these units capture regularities in the task [25].

Attention neural networks define an attention function that can be described as assigning a query and a set of key-value pairs to an output. The output is calculated as a weighted sum of the values, where a query compatibility function calculates the weight assigned to each value with the corresponding key [29].

Transformer ANNs prevent recurrence and instead rely entirely on an attention mechanism for drawing global dependencies between input and output (see Fig. 1). The transformer allows significantly greater parallelization and can achieve state of the art translation quality [8].

---

[1] CITUR: Tourist Information Center of Colombia, responsible for collecting national statistics of tourist numbers.

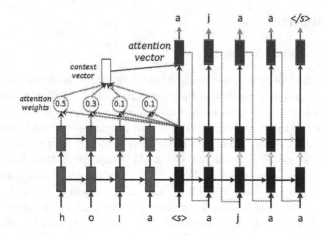

Fig. 1. Automatic translation with an ANN model.

Transformers include input and output *encoder* and *decoder* mechanisms, which are circuits of combinational logic, where logic is implemented using Boolean algebra. *Encoders* convert the active data signal into an encoded message format; it is an RNN that reads each symbol from an input sequence sequentially. The hidden state of the RNN changes after reading the end of the sequence. The hidden state of the RNN is a summary of the entire input sequence. *Decoders* perform the inverse operation to encoders, and have other RNNs trained to generate the output sequence by predicting the following symbol [8].

3   Related Work

Esfehani *et al.* [12] focus on the concept of cross-language in the context of tourism and hospitality. In this study, the difficulties of understanding a language are addressed. The authors carry out a case study focused on the translation of the English language into Persian. The study develops a model to perform translations using humans (unlike our work, computer techniques are not used) and has a special focus on the translation of complex (non-literal) concepts relevant to tourism and hospitality. The epistemology, methodology, and ethics were considered when carrying out the translation process.

Several works explore the role of technology in promoting tourism [18]. In particular, some projects seek to provide automatic translators for indigenous or minority languages. One of the earliest projects [10] seeks to implement a tool that translates words and sentences from the Spanish language to Aymara, which is an indigenous language belonging to the Aymara people in Bolivia, Chile, Peru, and Argentina. Using natural deduction and a syntactic tree viewer for the translation of sentences, the result of the study showed 84% of translations are correct with an error of 16% [10]. Another project based on language translation is the mintzai project [13], a research project to investigate and develop neural machine translation systems for speech, with particular emphasis on translation between Basque and Spanish. The mintzai project produced the first satisfactory results for its researchers, who focused on extending and improving the systems developed and on validating the results obtained. It is noteworthy because Euskera is, like Wayúunaiki, an indigenous native language. Also of interest is Velosa *et al.* [30] to translate sign language for people with visual disabilities.

A number of projects, all of which were discontinued, and do not have corpus information available, focus on translation for the Wayúunaiki language. The *Iwana* translator was a project developed using the Java language [4]. The rule-based automatic translation software by Transfer had software available on the page of the LEXICÓN group [14]. Iguarán Fernández *et al.* [16] present an API that exposes translation services using web technologies. The project was fed with phrases in Wayuunaiki for evaluation. Sinchi *et al.* [17] propose a low-cost approach for language translation using Raspberry Pis with touch screens that do not require an Internet connection. This project is novel given its offline approach in remote areas, and the issues raised by Lisseth *et al.* [22] about the lack of resources and technological infrastructure to meet the demand of tourists who visit the area in high seasons. The Pepper Social Robot Project [24], developed with the model transformation methodology, aims to recognize voice commands in Wayúunaiki. Results expected include the generation of new knowledge and the appropriation of knowledge that benefits researchers to continue with the project. However, the training corpus is not available for this project either.

Unlike the Wayúunaiki language translation projects mentioned above, this project uses an ANN for machine translation. In addition, a corpus constructred from Internet Sources and complemented with native Wayúunaiki translators, described in Sect. 4.2, is publicly available for researchers who wish to develop related projects.

4   Methodology

We use CRISP-DM as a reference model for data mining projects, in which the project life cycle is divided into phases [28]. The development of each phase is described in this section.

4.1   Business Understanding

The department of La Guajira is a territory with enormous natural wealth that makes it suitable for various kinds of tourism including ethnotourism. La Guajira is an ancestral territory inhabited by the Wayúu ethnic group, the largest indigenous population in Colombia. The majority of the population speak Wayúunaiki, only 32% speak Spanish, implying that La Guajira is a multilingual and multicultural territory [1]. In this work, we hope to integrate the symbolic elements of the Wayúu culture with the traditional activities of tourism and offer it as a commercial product that provides a unique experience to the tourist. In such a way that the natural and cultural resources available are taken advantage of, and together with the participation of the Wayúu community, it is sought that tourism is an instrument to help preserve culture. We aim to facilitate a positive exchange between visitors and the Wayúu population, thus enabling La Guajira to be strengthened as a tourist destination.

Samala *et al.* [27] seeks to solve the problem presented by the language barrier and help tourists to communicate with the indigenous Wayúu through a translation application from Wayúunaiki to Spanish and vice-versa, based on a neural network model. In the same way, it is intended to be of help to the tourism sector in general, since agencies and tourist guides obtain using the translation application a tool to achieve not only effective communication with members of the Wayúu ethnic group as well an instrument to generate publicity promoting and offering bilingual services. The trends in tourist activities for this 2021 are nature tourism, national tourism, rural tourism, and, in general, destinations close to home; considering the above, La Guajira is positioned as an ideal destination according to trends. Additionally, the technology plays a fundamental role in the reactivation of tourism [7]. Based on this, we count on the fact that this project on a wayúunaiki translation application - Spanish and Spanish - Wayúunaiki will be of help to the entire tourism sector while it encourages an increase in ethno-tourism in the department of La Guajira.

4.2   Data Understanding

Wayúunaiki is an ancient language that has not had a written form until relatively recently. There are differences in dialects, as is the case of the "arribero" dialect spoken in the northern part of La Guajira, and the "abajero" spoken in the South. There are also some morphological and lexical differences between the different regions, such as the case of the wayúunaiki word "juya" which can be translated as "rain" and as "year" in Spanish. Both translations are accepted, and the interpretation given to it will depend on the context in which the word is used. These factors have contributed to making the translation process more challenging in projects that have been carried out date. The grammatical rules of the Wayúu language are unfamiliar to a Spanish speaker. Sentences do not follow the same grammatical order as European languages, e.g., in Wayúunaiki, the sentence structure is verb-subject-object. Another difficulty is that some words have no translation as happened during the translation of "The Little Prince" where words were found that had to be adapted and even lexical creations [11].

Table 1 presents the Internet sources found with phrases in Spanish and Wayuunaiki that could be used to train a Spanish–Wayuunaiki translator. In total, this initial corpus consists of 84,089 pairs of Spanish–Wayuunaiki phrases. This data set was complemented with data acquired through the native Wayúu translators. This was integrated into a single data set.

Table 1. Internet sources that comprised the corpus data.

Source	Number of phrases	Description
Fernández Paz and Rodríguez on manythings.org	26,000	*Manual translation of Tatoeba public database*
Wayúu language manual [3]	1,000	*Wayúu speaking learning manual for Spanish speakers*
Abridged Wayúu language grammar [2]	1,000	*Grammatical rules of Wayúunaiki*
Pürinsipechonkai and the Jean-Marc Probst Foundation [11]	1,665	*Translation in Wayúunaiki of the book The Little Prince by Antoine de Saint-Exupéry*
Lozano and Mejía [20]	550	*Trilingual cartoon illustrated by students of the Universidad Libre de Colombia*
Jintulu Wayúu–Guajirita magazine with translations, Ministry of Education in Colombia [23]	566	*Illustrated primer in Spanish and Wayúunaiki*
JW300 corpus compiled for the Opus project	52,039	*Bible New Testament of the Jehovah's Witness denomination*
Captain and Captain [6]	1,269	*Illustrated bilingual dictionary with Spanish and Wayúunaiki words*
Total	**85,089**	

4.3   Data Preparation

The following steps were carried out to process the integrated data set described in the previous section:

1. *Data Cleaning:* The phase of filtering the inconsistency of previously selected data is carried out using Python, as follows:
   - All letters are made lowercase, punctuation marks and trailing spaces are removed
   - Text strings are normalized from UTF-8 to ASCII (except for vowels with accents and "u" with umlauts)
   - Other non-alphanumeric characters are removed.
   - Phrases with less than 15 words are removed.
   - The sentences whose difference in the number of words between Spanish and Wayuunaiki is greater than 5 are also filtered.

After the cleaning process, we obtain 40,797 sentences in our final corpus.

2. *Tokenization:* We use a separate tokenizer for sequences in Spanish and sequences in Wayúunaiki. We use the *Keras Tokenize* class to assign words to integers, as needed for modeling. During the tokenization process, we obtained 28,189 words in Wayuunaiki and 16,293 words in Spanish.

3. *The division between test data and training data:* Initially, the data for feeding the translation model contains around 10,000 sentences, mostly short sentences. This is a sufficient number for developing a small translation model as the complexity of the model increases as vocabulary, sentences, and sentence size grow.

When running the training models, different files are created that contain all the data that we can use to define the parameters of the model, such as the maximum length of the sentences, the vocabulary, and the test data set. While a larger corpus was being compiled, the final number of sentences was increased, leaving 36,717 of training data and 4,080 of test data approximately.

4.4   Modeling

The following models were developed for evaluation:

1. *Model 1:* An improved RNN with an attention mechanism. We use an LSTM codec model. In this architecture, the input stream is encoded by a front-end model called an encoder and then decoded word for word by a back-end model called a decoder.

2. *Model 2:* This is a model of neural networks with an attention mechanism, this is modified to facilitate the deployment of the model and that in turn can be consumed by other applications, with the use of TensorFlow-text, a library that facilitates the training and inference of NPL models. We trained the model for 15 epochs; each epoch takes on average 1153 s on 1xNVIDIA Tesla k80 hardware (2 GPUs).

4.5   Evaluation

In the training Model 1, the loss function shows a slightly different training and test graph as seen in Fig. 2a, in this case, given that it was trained with 25 epochs, the jump between each of the epochs is observed. The epochs keep a certain correlation between the values of the loss function. This relationship varies a little more the result because of adding the database of other sources and other translators, this corpus is broader with a variety of vocabulary. It was performed on a server on the SaturnCloud 9: 32 cores - 128 GB RAM - 1 GPU (Nvidia Tesla T4-8XLarge) - 10Gi Disk. Subsequently, a laptop with an Nvidia rtx 2026 GPU was used. Model 1 is compiled in the same way, in an inverse way to achieve the objective of translating in the opposite direction, that is, from Wayúunaiki to Spanish, trained with 38,551 thousand sentences. In the evaluation, a 0.340795 coefficient of BLEU-1 was obtained.

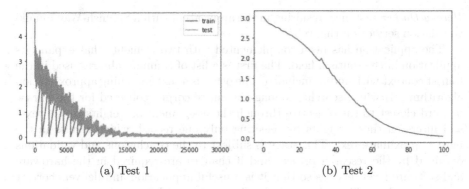

(a) Test 1   (b) Test 2

Fig. 2. Epoch vs. Loss function.

For model 2, a comparison was used through a survey with native Wayuu-naiki speakers who collaborated on the project. Contrary to what the graphical representation of the decrease of the test function shows, Fig. 2b. The results of the human evaluation indicate that model 1 can translate more accurately than model 2.

Tests were carried out with the help of the main translator Leonardi Fernández belonging to the Jinnu Clan, who is one of the main collaborators of the Wikipedia in Wayúunaiki to determine translation efficiency. According to Fernández, the translation of model-1 is very close to being able to translate correctly. Considering their opinion and with the results obtained from the survey, we find that the model is the one that gives the best results, providing the most probable answers in the evaluated cases. The learning process regarding the potential of the application of tools makes it necessary to continue working, adjusting the model, adding new variables that allow the results to be further adjusted.

4.6   Deployment

Several tests were made for the implementation of Model 1, all of them consisting of the exposure of an HTTP *Endpoint* which is a function that predicts the results, among we have:

- Hosting services in *Docker* with *Heroku* using the *Flask Framework.*
- Static web page hosting on *GitHub* Pages.

We also tried to use a machine learning pipeline from *Google, AWS,* and *Azure* [34] which consists of an executable workflow independent of a task, but these tools require preparation time to be used correctly and associated costs because these tools were not finally discarded because they did not have the time resource. Currently, an application has been deployed in *Angular* as a frontend in the *GitHub* Pages service, this application consumes the service deployed in the

Heroku Docker Instance, resulting in the application with a Spanish-Wayúunaiki translation service on the web[2].

The application has been complemented with two elements that expand its application in the tourism field. The first is a list of common phrases used in the tourist context with audios included. The other is a text-matching approximation algorithm [21] which searches among the entire corpus collected for the phrase or word closest to the objective through the assignment of weights to the texts and filters on these weights by selecting only one record, which results in the most approximate text. This stage is subject to the conclusions and validations obtained by the research project and if changes are required in the hardware and software level services so that it is a useful application and delivers correct and quality data efficiently for those who need or wish to use it.

5   Discussion

In this work, a recurrent neural network model is employed for the translation of Spanish to Wayúunaiki and vice-versa. A challenge we faced was the shortage of available translated phrases. In addition, there is inconsistent grammar throughout the translations in the corpus. For example, in the New Testament the tests of the loss function registered values greater than 0.4.

An evaluation with three human translators using a multiple-choice survey to identify the model with the best translation capacity showed that the subset of the model used for training affects translation quality. The corpus containing sentences of no more than fifteen words led to better translations than the model trained with the total corpus. The corpus was subsequently supplemented with sixty common phrases in the context of tourism to improve model performance. Overall, the evaluators considered that the sentences are understandable, even if at times they are not entirely correct.

Future work proposals include supporting the model with a dictionary of common tourism phrases, enabling audio translations, and developing a lightweight model for an offline application that does not require Internet connectivity, given that parts of La Guajira do not have Internet access.

6   Conclusion

The artifacts resulting from this work are:

- To date, a corpus of new translations of more than 26,000 common phrases. We have collected through *web scraping* approximately another 10,000 which, added to the Bible corpus, leaves a total corpus of approximately 80,000 phrases. Our corpus is publicly[3].

---

[2] https://rafanegrette.github.io/wayuunaiki-translator-angular/.
[3] https://osf.io/6kbze/?view_only=e66b22fbd73f4c11852730be0002a495.

– Source code of both applications, comprising the presentation layer[4] and the server with the models[5]. The application, capable of translating from Spanish to Wayúunaiki and from Wayúunaiki to Spanish, is hosted open source on GitHub. In the *Heroku Free Layer*, two models are deployed, one to translate from Spanish to Wayúunaiki and the other model to translate from Wayúunaiki to Spanish.

While preliminary results have been satisfactory, as the corpus is expanded it is expected that model performance will improve. As such, we consider that the results of this work have significant potential to promote ethnotourism in the La Guajira region in Colombia.

References

1. Población indígena creció 36% y llegó a 1,9 millones de personas según el dane (2019). https://www.larepublica.co/economia/poblacion-indigena-crecio-36-y-llego-a-19-millones-de-personas-2909134. Accessed 23 June 2021
2. Alvarez, J.: Lear: Compendio de la gramática de la lengua wayuu (2017). http://lear.unive.it/jspui/handle/11707/7828. Accessed 23 June 2021
3. Álvarez, J.: Manual de la lengua wayuu. karalouta atüjaaya saa'u wayuu-naikikuwa'ipa (2017)
4. Barrera, E.: Diseño e implementación de una aplicación de traducción automática móvil español-wayúunaiki -español (2012)
5. Bobanovic, M.K., Grzinic, J.: The importance of english language skills in the tourism sector: a comparative study of students/employees perceptions in croatia. Almatourism J. Tourism Cult. Territorial Dev. **2**(4), 10–23 (2011). https://doi.org/10.6092/issn.2036-5195/2476, https://almatourism.unibo.it/article/view/2476. Accessed 03 Sep 2022
6. Captain, D.M., Captain, L.B.: Diccionario Basico: Ilustrado. Wayuunaiki-Espanol; Espanol-Wayuunaiki. Edit, Fundación para el Desarrollo de los Pueblos Marginados (2005)
7. Castaño, M.A.: ¿cuáles son las tendencias del turismo para el 2021? — el espectador (2021). https://www.elespectador.com/turismo/cuales-son-las-tendencias-del-turismo-para-el-2021-article. Accessed 23 June 2021
8. Cho, K., et al.: Learning phrase representations using RNN encoder-decoder for statistical machine translation. In: Proceedings of the 2014 Conference on Empirical Methods in Natural Language Processing (EMNLP), pp. 1724–1734. Association for Computational Linguistics, Doha, Qatar (2014). https://doi.org/10.3115/v1/D14-1179, https://www.aclweb.org/anthology/D14-1179. Accessed 03 Sep 2022
9. Clark, C.: Turismo idiomático: La importancia del idioma como recurso turístico. Master's thesis, Universidad nacional del sur departamento de geografía y turismo. Bahía Blanc (2014). http://repositoriodigital.uns.edu.ar/handle/123456789/3216. Accessed 03 Sep 2022

---

[4] https://github.com/rafanegrette/wayuunaiki-translator-angular/tree/feature/way-to-spa.
[5] https://github.com/rafanegrette/translator-guc-spa-api.

10. Condori Canaviri, W.B.: Traductor del idioma español-aymara utilizando deducción natural. Master's thesis, Universidad Mayor de San Andrés (2009). https://repositorio.umsa.bo/bitstream/handle/123456789/103/T.1454.pdf. Accessed 03 Sep 2022

11. Dorado, J.A.J.F.E.M.A.: Purinsipechonkai. The Jean-Marc Probst Foundation (2016). https://petit-prince-collection.com/lang/show_livre.php?lang=en& id=4119. Accessed 23 June 2021

12. Esfehani, M.H., Walters, T.: Lost in translation? cross-language thematic analysis in tourism and hospitality research. Int. J. Contemp. Hosp. Manag. **30**(11), 3158–3174 (2018)

13. Etchegoyhen, T., et al.: Mintzai: Sistemas de aprendizaje profundo e2e para traducción automática del habla. Procesamiento del Lenguaje Natural, pp. 97–100 (2020). https://doi.org/10.26342/2020-65-12

14. GARCÍA, E.L.: Software traductor de español a lengua wayuu (J2013). https://www.researchgate.net/profile/Ernesto-Llerena-Garcia/publication/342674307_software_traductor_de_espanol_a_lengua_wayuu/links/5f005d9292851c52d616f547/software-traductor-de-espanol-a-lengua-wayuu.pdf. Accessed 03 Sep 2022

15. Hall-Lew, L.A., Lew, A.A.: Speaking heritage. In: The Wiley Blackwell Companion to Tourism, pp. 336–348. John Wiley & Sons, Ltd. (2014). https://doi.org/10.1002/9781118474648.ch27

16. Iguarán Fernández, D.P., Molina Atencia, J.G., Quintero Gamboa, O.I.: Diseño e implementación de API web para traducción automática de pares de lenguas de grupos étnicos colombianos: caso Español-Wayuunaiki. Master's thesis (2013). http://repository.unipiloto.edu.co/handle/20.500.12277/1105. Accessed 03 Sep 2022

17. Jara Sinchi, J.J.: Prototipo de un dispositivo traductor de idiomas basado en tecnología Raspberry. Master's thesis, Universidad de Guayaquil. Facultad de Ingeniería Industrial. Carrera de … (2019). http://repositorio.ug.edu.ec/handle/redug/46699. Accessed 03 Sep 2022

18. Kysela, J.: Analysis of usability of various geosocial network POI in tourism. In: Florez, H., Leon, M., Diaz-Nafria, J.M., Belli, S. (eds.) ICAI 2019. CCIS, vol. 1051, pp. 32–42. Springer, Cham (2019). https://doi.org/10.1007/978-3-030-32475-9_3

19. Loukotka, Č., Wilbert, J.: Classification of South American Indian Languages. (Reference Series. Latin American Center. University of California), Latin American Center, UCLA (1968). https://books.google.com.co/books?id=m58uAAAAYAAJ. Accessed 23 June 2021

20. Lozano, J., Mejía, J.: Wayuunkeera. Universidad Libre of Colombia, Trilingual cartoon illustrated (2007)

21. Navarro, G.: A guided tour to approximate string matching. ACM Comput. Surv. **33**(1), 31–88 (2001). https://doi.org/10.1145/375360.375365

22. Paola, L., Castañeda Vega, L., Quintero, S.: AnÁlisis de las políticas de ctei aplicadas al sector turismo en el departamento de la guajira desde la teoría de la gobernanza. In: 5° Congreso Internacional de Gestión Tecnológica y de la Innovación, Bucaramanga (2016)

23. Peláez, A.: Jintulu Wayuu, 1st edn. Río de letras. Territorios Narrados PNLE, Ministerio de Educación Nacional Colombia (2014)

24. Rojas, A.M., Amaya, S.P.: Inclusión de la lengua wayuunaiki en el reconocimiento de comandos de voz del robot social pepper empleando la metodología de transformación de modelos (2019). https://repository.usta.edu.co/handle/11634/22652. Accessed 03 Sep 2022

25. Rumelhart, D.E., Hinton, G.E., Williams, R.J.: Learning representations by back-propagating errors. Nature **323**(6088), 533–536 (1986). https://doi.org/10.1038/323533a0
26. Russell, H., Leslie, D.: Foreign languages and the health of UK tourism. Int. J. Contemp. Hospitality Manag. **16**, 136–138 (2004). https://doi.org/10.1108/09596110410520025
27. Samala, N., Katkam, B.S., Bellamkonda, R.S., Rodriguez, R.V.: Impact of AI and robotics in the tourism sector: a critical insight. J. Tourism Futures **8**(1) (2022). https://doi.org/10.1108/jtf-07-2019-0065
28. Shearer, C.: The crisp-DM model: the new blueprint for data mining. J. Data Warehousing **5**(4), 13–22 (2000)
29. Vaswani, A., et al.: Attention is all you need. In: Proceedings of the 31st International Conference on Neural Information Processing Systems, p. 6000–6010. NIPS'17, Curran Associates Inc., Red Hook, NY, USA (2017)
30. Velosa, F., Florez, H.: Edge solution with machine learning and open data to interpret signs for people with visual disability. In: ICAI Workshops, pp. 15–26 (2020)

Rating the Acquisition of Pre-writing Skills in Children: An Analysis Based on Computer Vision and Data Mining Techniques in the Ecuadorian Context

Adolfo Jara-Gavilanes[ID], Romel Ávila-Faicán[ID],
Vladimir Robles-Bykbaev[✉][ID], and Luis Serpa-Andrade[ID]

GI -IATa, Cátedra UNESCO Tecnologías de Apoyo Para la Inclusión Educativa,
Universidad Politécnica Salesiana, Cuenca, Ecuador
{ajarag2,ravilaf1}@est.ups.edu.ec, {vrobles,lserpa}@ups.edu.ec

Abstract. Pre-writing skills are a set of essential skills to learn to write. Commonly, in South America's public schools, a teacher has a class with approximately 30 or more students. As a result, the teacher has the challenging task to detect if a child has difficulties in pre-writing essential activities. In light of the above, in this paper, we present an analysis to determine the feasibility of using computer vision and data mining techniques to determine if a child fails to meet, meets few, or meets a pre-writing skill. We conducted the process with the open corpus "UPS-Writing-Skills," containing the HU moments and the shape signature descriptors extracted from a collection of 358 images drawn by children.

Keywords: Pre-writing skills · Education · Data mining · Shape signatures · Hu moments · Naïve Bayes · Adaboost · Random Forest

1 Introduction

The sensorimotor skills are considered one of the fundamental pillars when learning the skill to write in a child. These skills are called "pre-writing skills." They contribute to a child holding and using a pencil and can draw, copy and color basic strokes, thicken a line and pattern, thicken shapes and others [15]. In this line, it is important to mention that failure to attain handwriting competency during the school-age years commonly has far-reaching negative effects for children in two areas: academic success and self-esteem [4]. Several researches claim that there is a direct link between the development of language, verbal skills for expression and achievements of the child in learning and writing [11].

In developing countries such as Ecuador this situation becomes more complicated due to the lack of appropriate educational and diagnostic strategies as well as the few technological tools to support the children monitoring and educational accompaniment. Nowadays it's really important to develop new tools to detect the lack of this set of skills to prevent the negative effects of it. Therefore it can help with the right development of children in school.

For these reasons, in this paper we present a research where we used different classifiers based on data mining to improve the classification of two tasks: predict which figure was drawn by the children, and the score of the figure. This with the goal to create a system that can help educators and therapists to detect children with the lack of this skill. Therefore they don't waste their time scoring the geometric shapes drawn by children and they can focus on giving children the right therapy to improve this skill.

To this aim, we have used the corpus "UPS-Writing-Skills," which consists of 358 images drawn by Ecuadorian children of Cuenca city (115 triangles, 129 squares, and 114 circles). A team of experts in special education has evaluated each image considering the following criteria:

(a) The skill is not reached. The team assigned 0 points in these cases: the figure is not closed or is not predominantly circular (circle), has no 4 corners (square), or has no 3 corners (triangle).
(b) The skill is under development. The team assigned 1 point in these cases: the figure is not closed (circle), the figure is not a square but has 4 corners and 4 angles, and the lines are not straight/the vertex is not at the center of the triangle base.
(c) The skill is achieved. The team assigned 2 points when the circle is closed, the square has 4 corners with angles between 80 and 100°C, and the triangle has 3 corners with 3 proportional sides. The lines do not present undulations in any case.

The teachers use these scores to determine whether exists a gap between the child's development age and his/her chronological age. Similarly, they can determine the best strategies to assist children through reinforcement exercises or therapy sessions. However, it is essential to note that in Latin American countries, it is a challenging task for a teacher to assess and monitor more than 30 or 40 students per scholar period. In light of the above, this type of tool can be used in schools to help teachers in the early identification of children with issues with pre-writing skills development.

The paper is organized as follows. Section 2 presents some relevant contributions related to diagnostic tools based on fine motor qualification and graphological characterization. Then, Sect. 3 depicts the methodology used in this proposal. Section 4 describes the algorithms and experiments carried out. Finally, Sects. 5 and 6 present the limitations of this research and the conclusions, respectively.

2   Related Work

In [14], the researchers created an automated system to grade the pre-writing skills of children with and without special educational needs. This system receives images of three geometrical shapes: triangle, square, and circle. First, the image is pre-processed in order to obtain the 7 Hu moments and the 12 Fourier shape signature values. They are fed to the neural network, which is a Multi-Layer Perceptron(MLP). The MLP was trained to grade the image: 0(not learned), 1(on learning process), and 2(learned); and to classify the figure as circle, triangle, or square. For the grading task, the MLP obtains a 75% accuracy using the shape signature, and for the classifier task, the MLP obtains a 98% accuracy using the same parameters [14].

In [2], the authors present a system to classify 4 geometric shapes in photographs: circle, rectangle, square and triangle. They used 3 machine learning techniques: Random Forest, Decision Trees and SVM (Support Vector Machines) that are fed on 9 different geometrical features. The size of the dataset that they worked with, contains 250 images. Random Forest yielded the best results with an accuracy of 96% [2].

In [8], the researchers applied computer vision techniques, Electro-MyoGraphy (EMG) signal processing, and an Artificial Neural Network to predict if an individual has or not Parkinson's Disease. They implemented two methodologies: the first is based on extracting four features from an individual's handwriting: execution time, execution average linear speed, density ratio, and height ratio. In this case, their methodology achieved 95.81% accuracy. For the second method, they only extracted two features: execution time and execution average linear speed. In this case, their methodology achieved 95.52% of accuracy [8].

In [10], the authors developed a smart mirror that assists children with ASD (Autism Spectrum Disorder) in evolving their handwriting, math, speech, and attention skills. They created this smart mirror with games that are basically for tracing and connecting dots, counting, identifying and writing the name of shapes, learning the alphabet, identifying alphabets and objects, and spelling words. During the game, the mirror takes pictures of the children's work. They are passed to a CNN to grade their work and to determine if the game should level up or not. The results showed an accuracy of 85% in predicting the children's grades [10].

In [16], the authors created an intervention program for children to unveil the correlation between visual-motor and fine motor skills in their handwriting. The program consisted of various activities to support the development of those skills during ten weeks and 20 sessions. Before and after the program, children took a test divided into two sections: first, they wrote their names on a tablet to extract the following features: pen movement frequency, pressure on the digitizer surface, and writing automaticity. Second, the children were asked to draw some geometrical shapes that were projected on a screen to determine their tracing and visual skills. Using Pearson's correlation, it was determined that the frequency of written traces changes from negative to positive, after the program, for the visual abilities, and for the fine motor control skills [16].

Following in Table 1, there is a comparison between all these related works and this study. Thus the differences can be appreciated easily. The related works in the table are placed in the same order as they were described in this section.

Table 1. Comparison between related works and this study.

Author	Year	Figure prediction	Evaluation prediction (skills rating)	Detection of difficulties in pre-writing skills (according to an educational scale)	Easiness to use the tool in developing countries	Technique (approach)
Serpa-Andrade et al.	2021	Yes	Yes	Yes	Yes	ANN
Soma Debnath et al.	2018	Yes	No	No	No	Machine Learning
Claudio Loconsole et al.	2017	Yes	No	No	No	Computer Vision
R.S. Najeeb et al.	2020	No	No	Yes	No	CNN
Livia Taverna et al.	2020	Yes	No	No	No	Machine Learning
Jara-Gavilanes et al.	2022	Yes	Yes	Yes	Yes	Data mining

3   Methodology

The study aims to present the difference between the accuracies of four types of classifiers: Naïve Bayes model with k-folds, Random Forest, Adaboost (Adaptive Boosting) and Adaboost CV (Adaptive Boosting with Cross-Validation). Those are explained later. The reason for choosing these classifiers is because they yield great results while working with small datasets. Also, they are among the best techniques with the goal for classifying. The goal was to recognize and evaluate three geometrical shapes: circle, triangle and square, which are related to the acquisition of pre-writing skills.

To train and test the classifiers, we used 358 images drawn by children with and without special needs (from corpus "UPS-Writing-Skills"). These drawings were preprocessed to extract two descriptors to feed the classifiers: Hu moments, and Shape Signature. The steps for the preprocessing were the following (Fig. 1):

- First, the noise in the images was removed by applying the median filter. Then, the images were converted to HSV color space. In this stage we define the range for later performing the binarization. The values according to each channel are the following: Hue $[107, 140]$, Saturation $[20, 255]$ and Value $[20, 255]$.
- Second, an empty border is placed in the region where the geometrical shape is. This is done with the goal to save time looking for the first pixel of the image and because there are many images that contain strokes that are in the frontiers of the shape too.
- Third, the system adds an empty border around the Region of Interest (ROI) to later determine if the shape is opened or closed. Then the system transforms the image to a binary image by applying color threshold binarization using the Eq. 1.

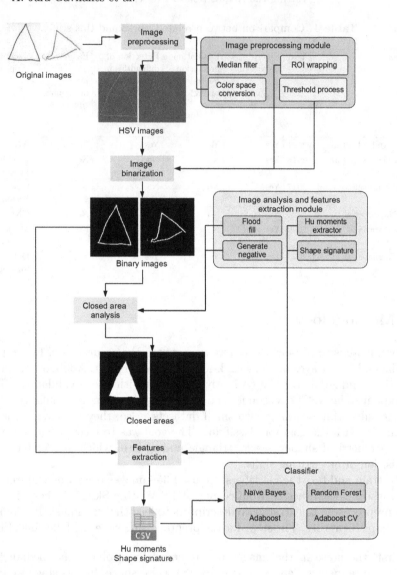

Fig. 1. The steps carried out to extract the images' features and perform the two classification tasks with the data mining approach.

$$newValue(i,j) = \bigcap_{c=1}^{N} lowerBound_c \leq pixel(I(i,j))_c \leq upperBound_c$$

$$newImage(i,j) = \begin{cases} 1, \text{if } newValue(i,j) = TRUE \\ 0, \text{otherwise} \end{cases} \quad (1)$$

Where:

- i, j are the coordinates of each pixel in the image whereas c represents the channel for a given number of channels N. In our case the images have three channels (HSV).
- $pixel(I(i, j))$ is the function used to obtain a three-component pixel given the coordinates i, j of the image I.
- $lowerBound_c$ and $upperBound_c$ represent the minimum and maximum values defined in the first stage. With these values we can capture the range of blue colors used by children when they trace the figures.
- $newValue$ contains the result of performing the logical AND (intersection) between each channel value given a pixel. If the $newValue$ is $TRUE$, the result pixel for the new image will be 1, and 0 otherwise.

- Fourth, the system determines whether the shape is opened or closed using the flood fill function [7]. Next, the seven Hu moments are extracted from the binary images, which are used to describe the shape that is drawn into an image. The Hu moments are invariant to translation, rotation and scaling, therefore Hu moments are greatly applied to describe the shape characteristics of objects in images [13]. Equation 2 shows how the Hu central moments are calculated, whereas the Eq. 3 is used to obtain the 7 moments [14]:

$$\mu_{p,q} = \sum_{x=0}^{N-1} \sum_{y=0}^{M-1} (x - x_c)^p \cdot (y - y_c)^q \cdot f(x, y) \tag{2}$$

$$\eta_{p,q} = \frac{\mu_{p,q}}{\mu_{0,0}^\delta} \quad \delta = \frac{p+q+2}{2} \tag{3}$$

Where:

- x_c and y_c represent the coordinates of the centroid.
- p and q are the order of the moments to be calculated, while N and M are the rows and columns of the image.
- μ is the central moment.
- $\eta_{p,q}$ is the Hu moment of order p, q.

In this case the objects are the geometric shapes. They are really important in this work to be able to feed the classifiers with accurate data and therefore obtain great results.

- Fifth, the shape signature of the binary image is extracted. There are seven shape signatures that can be used: Complex coordinates, centroid distance function, tangent angle (turning angles), curvature function, area function, triangle-area representation and chord length function [14]. In this case, the centroid distance function is used to obtain a description of the shape that is drawn into an image. The system uses Eq. (4) to obtain the Fourier descriptor of the shape signature [9], while Eq. (5) is the Fast Fourier Transform (FFT) of this set of points. It is essential considering that the values inferred with the FFT must be normalized (through the DC component and the absolute value) to obtain invariance to rotation, translation and scaling. [9].

$$r(k) = \sqrt{(x_k - x_c)^2 + (y_k - y_c)^2} \tag{4}$$

$$a_n = \frac{1}{N} \cdot \sum_{k=0}^{N-1} r(k) \cdot e^{\frac{-j2\pi kn}{N}} \tag{5}$$

Where:

- x_c and y_c represent the coordinates of the centroid.
- x_k and y_k represent the coordinates of each point on the contour.
- $r(k)$ is the k-th element of a set of values for the shape signature.
- a_n is each coefficient of the FFT ($n = 0, 1, \ldots, N - 1$).

After these steps, the Hu moments and the shape signature are used to feed the four classifiers that are explained below.

Naïve Bayes model with k-folds

Naïve Bayes is a probabilistic classifier based on Bayes Theorem. It supposes that all the variables are independent of the classification variable [12]. It uses k-folds, which is a technique to split the training set into k numbers of subsets to evaluate the model. This aids the model to reach a higher accuracy. For this model, the data was split into training and test sets: 70%-30%, 80%-20%, 85%-15%, and 90%-10% respectively. The values that were assigned to k were: 10, 7, and 5 with the aim to try different numbers of models and choose the best. These values are the most commonly used because of their effectiveness to reach higher accuracy. To determine the probability of getting the class or the evaluation given a set of image features, we have used the Eq. 6:

$$P(\mathcal{C}|\mathcal{F}_i, \ldots, \mathcal{F}_k) = \frac{P(\mathcal{C}) \cdot P(\mathcal{F}_i, \ldots, \mathcal{F}_k|\mathcal{C})}{P(\mathcal{F}_i) \cdot P(\mathcal{F}_{i+1}) \cdot \cdots \cdot P(\mathcal{F}_k)} \tag{6}$$

where:

- $P(\mathcal{C}|\mathcal{F}_i, \ldots, \mathcal{F}_k)$: represents the probability of getting a figure class or an evaluation given a set of features.
- $\mathcal{C}$: represents the figure or the evaluation given to a features set depending on the task (figure classification or figure evaluation).
- $\mathcal{F}_i$: represents each feature of the Hu Moments and the Shape Signature descriptors. For Hu Moments we used 7 features whereas for Shape Signature we extracted 12 normalized features (invariant to rotation, scale and translation).
- k: is the total features used (7 for Hu Moments and 12 for Shape Signature).

Random Forest

Random forest is a machine learning technique used for classification and regression problems. It produces many decision trees forming a forest, hence the reason why it is called a random forest. The forest makes use of bagging and random forest to provide uncorrelated decision trees. In this way, the model assumes that the decision trees are distinct. In the end, it sums up all the outputs of the decision trees, and the prediction highly voted is the result [17]. The model generated 500 decision trees with the goal to obtain a higher accuracy, and the data was split in the same way as the Naïve Bayes model to select the best dataset split. There is an important feature in Random Forest: Gini Index. This feature is computed by deducting 1 from the sum of square probabilities of each class. Its value varies between 0 and 1. This is really important at the time of building a decision tree because the features with a lower Gini Index value are most likely to be chosen to build a decision tree [1]. To determine the Gini of each branch on a node we have used the Eq. 7:

$$Gini = 1 - \sum_{i=0}^{C} (p_i)^2 \tag{7}$$

where:

- *Gini*: determines which of the branches is more likely to occur.
- *C*: represents the number of classes according to the task (circle, square, and triangle for image classification, and 0, 1, and 2 for image evaluation). In this case C will be 3 for both tasks, however, can be extended to use more figures.

Adaboost(Adaptive Boosting)

Adaboost is a statistical classification and regression algorithm. In contrast with the Random Forest technique, it generates stumps that are smaller than decision trees. Adaboost uses iterative training for the "weak learners". It means that it recognizes the misclassified data and produces a new classifier, and it repeats this process many times. In the end, it uses all those "weak learners" to create a robust classifier [6]. In this model, 50 iterations were generated with the goal to obtain a robust classifier and the data was split in the same way than the Naïve Bayes model with the aim to select the best dataset split. The output of weak classifier is determined using the Eq. 8:

$$H\left(\mathcal{F}_i, \ldots, \mathcal{F}_k\right) = sign\left(\sum_{s=1}^{S} \alpha_s \cdot h_s\left(\mathcal{F}_i, \ldots, \mathcal{F}_k\right)\right) \tag{8}$$

where:

- $H\left(\mathcal{F}_i, \ldots, \mathcal{F}_k\right)$: represents the output given by the weak classifier s for the input $\left(\mathcal{F}_i, \ldots, \mathcal{F}_k\right)$.

- α_s: is weight assigned to classifier. This value is calculated using this formula: $\alpha_t = 0.5 \cdot \ln\left(\frac{1-E}{E}\right)$. The parameter E is the error rate.
- $\mathcal{F}_i$: represents each feature of the Hu Moments and the Shape Signature descriptors (similarly to the case of Naïve Bayes classifier).

Adaboost(Adaptive Boosting) with Cross-Validation

Adaboost with Cross-Validation has the same fundamentals as Adaboost. The key difference is that Cross-Validation resamples the training set into a training and a validation set, which are applied in many iterations. Thus producing a more accurated model [3]. This model was defined in 3 ways: the first model had 5 stumps and 10 validation sets, the second had 8 stumps and 7 validation sets, and the third had 10 stumps and 5 validation sets. In this way is assured to obtain different results and select the model with higher accuracy. Besides, these are commonly used models based on the accuracy they reach.

4   Experiment and Preliminary Results

As can be seen in Fig. 2, Multidimensional Scaling (MDS) was applied to represent the 7 Hu moments, and the 12 shape signature to 2 features. Thus with the goal to observe the distribution of the images from the dataset both for classifying the figure and grading the figure. As can be seen, many points overlap each other, consequently both tasks are complex to perform.

To perform the MDS analysis for the two datasets (Hu and Shape Signature), we have considered the following parameters:

- Number of components: 2 (to use a 2D graph).
- Metric: metric MDS
- Maximum number of Iterations: 300
- Relative tolerance: 1e-3
- Random state: 0 (in order to make a reproducible experiment).

On the other hand, once we have trained the classifiers, we carried out an evaluation to determine the precision of each of them. The percentage of accuracy of the four classifiers is explained below.

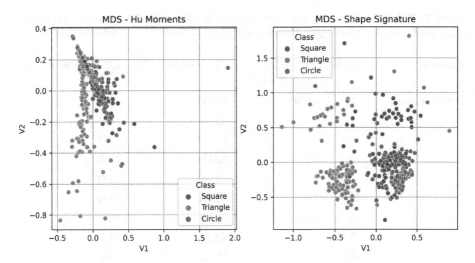

Fig. 2. A 2D representation of the Hu moments and shape signature features. As it can be seen, several samples are highly overlapped, turning the classification task harder.

4.1 Naïve Bayes with K Folds

In this classifier, as can be seen in Table 2, the best descriptor for classifying the figure was shape signature. It achieved 89.71% of accuracy. The number of folds was set to 5, and the dataset was split into 80% for training and 20% for testing. In contrast to Hu moments that achieved 55.41% of accuracy. In this case, the number of folds was set to 10, and the dataset was split in the same way as shape signature.

When classifying the evaluation of the figure, the best descriptor was also the shape signature. It reached 81.17% of accuracy. The number of folds was set to 5, and the dataset was split into 90% for training and 10% for testing. In contrast to Hu moments that reached 49% of accuracy. In this instance, the dataset was split into 85% for training and 15% for testing (Table 2).

4.2 Random Forest

In this classifier, as can be seen in Table 3, the best descriptor for classifying the figure was shape signature with 92.45% of accuracy. The dataset was split into 85% for training and 15% for testing. In contrast to Hu moments that achieved 75% of accuracy. For this model, the dataset was split into 75% for training and 25% for testing.

For the classification of the evaluation of the figure, the best descriptor was shape signature too. It achieved 88.23% of accuracy. The dataset was split into 90% for training and 10% for testing. As opposed to Hu moments that reached 71.15% of accuracy. In this instance, the dataset was split into 85% for training and 15% for testing (Table 3).

Table 2. Results obtained by the Naïve Bayes classifier with Hu moments and shape signature for both tasks: Figure Prediction (FP) and Evaluation Prediction (EP).

Features	Folds	Dataset split (train/test)	FP accuracy (%)	EP accuracy (%)
Hu moments	5	70/30	52.60	47.0
	7		52.86	44.0
	10		52.69	43.0
	5	75/25	50.00	41.0
	7		52.66	42.0
	10		50.54	44.0
	5	80/20	52.68	46.0
	7		55.10	48.0
	10		55.41	48.0
	5	85/15	54.66	49.0
	7		54.83	48.0
	10		54.70	47.0
	5	**90/10**	**55.30**	45.0
	7		53.50	47.0
	10		53.53	**50.0**
Shape Signature	5	70/30	89.42	62.77
	7		88.84	68.33
	10		86.26	73.10
	5	75/25	71.16	70.19
	7		69.20	64.53
	10		70.97	56.05
	5	**80/20**	**89.71**	76.13
	7		86.06	79.22
	10		88.72	72.43
	5	85/15	71.90	71.04
	7		74.82	73.17
	10		69.88	72.40
	5	**90/10**	70.43	**81.17**
	7		72.93	67.87
	10		70.43	79.81

Table 3. Results obtained by the Random Forest classifier with Hu moments and shape signature for both tasks: Figure Prediction (FP) and Evaluation Prediction (EP).

Features	Dataset split	FP accuracy (%)	EP accuracy (%)
Hu moments	70/30	71.69	65.71
	75/25	75	64.04
	80/20	**74.28**	64.28
	85/15	60.37	**71.15**
	90/10	73.52	55.88
Shape Signature	70/30	90.56	80.95
	75/25	88.63	82.02
	80/20	87.14	77.14
	85/15	**92.45**	80.76
	90/10	88.23	**88.23**

Table 4. Results obtained by the Adaboost classifier with Hu moments and shape signature for both tasks: Figure Prediction (FP) and Evaluation Prediction (EP).

Features	Dataset split	FP accuracy (%)	EP accuracy (%)
Hu moments	70/30	71.69	69.52
	75/25	72.72	59.55
	80/20	**78.57**	60
	85/15	75.47	57.69
	90/10	76.47	**64.7**
Shape Signature	70/30	90.56	75.23
	75/25	94.31	**80.89**
	80/20	92.85	75.71
	85/15	**96.22**	75
	90/10	91.17	79.41

4.3 Adaboost

In this classifier, as can be seen in Table 4, the best descriptor for classifying the figure was shape signature. It achieved 96.22% of accuracy. The dataset was split into 85% for training and 15% for testing. In contrast to Hu moments that achieved 78.57% of accuracy. In this instance, the dataset was split into 80% for training and 20% for testing.

Once again the shape signature was the best descriptor when classifying the evaluation of the figure. It achieved 80.89% of accuracy. The dataset was split into 75% for training and 25% for testing. In contrast to Hu moments that achieved 69.52% of accuracy. In this case the dataset was split into 70% for training and 30% for testing (Table 4).

4.4 Adaboost CV

In this classifier, the best descriptor for classifying the figure was shape signature. It achieved 91.89% of accuracy. It contained 10 cross-validation subsets. On the other hand Hu moments achieved 70.39% of accuracy with the same number of cross-validation subsets.

Once more, the best descriptor was shape signature for classifying the evaluation of the figure when compared to the results of the Hu moments. It achieved 75.97% of accuracy with 10 cross-validation subsets. Whereas Hu moments achieved a maximum of 62.29% of accuracy with 7 cross-validation subsets (Table 5).

Table 5. Results obtained by the Adaboost with cross-validation classifier with Hu moments and shape signature for both tasks: Figure Prediction (FP) and Evaluation Prediction (EP).

Features	CV subsets	FP accuracy (%)	EP accuracy (%)
Hu moments	5	68.99	58.93
	7	68.71	**62.29**
	10	**70.39**	54.74
Shape Signature	5	91.06	74.3
	7	90.5	73.18
	10	**91.89**	**75.97**

5 Limitations

The main limitation in this study is the size of the dataset. It contained 358 images and it affected the training and testing of the classifiers used in this research. If the dataset were to be bigger, the classifiers would perform better and obtain more accurate results. This problem is due to the cost and the time that it would take to recollect more data. To restrain this problem, a data augmentation technique could be applied to the original dataset.

The main goal of this technique, as its name describes, is to increase the number of data without affecting the original objects. This is reached by applying different kinds of transformations to the original data. In this manner the dataset would acquire more data for better results. The main transformations used in the state of the art are the following: rotation, translation, inclination, and adding Gaussian noise [5]. The advantages of using this technique is the low computational cost and the little time that it takes to apply it. This technique is not only used in small datasets, like the one used in this study, but it can be used in bigger datasets too. Thus to obtain a better performance in machine learning and deep learning methods [18].

6 Conclusions

After analyzing the results from the different classifiers, it's worth mentioning that the best image descriptor for image classification and skill rating tasks is the shape signature. This technique throws better results in both tasks: figure prediction and evaluation prediction. Therefore, shape signature is a better image descriptor. Also, as can be seen in Table 2, 3, 4 and 5 the best classifier for figure prediction was AdaBoost Classifier, achieving a 96.22% of FP accuracy. For this case, the best dataset split was 85% for training and 15% for testing. As mentioned in the Methodology section, this classifier was trained with 50 iterations. For the other task of evaluation prediction, the Random Forest outperformed the other classifiers obtaining an EP accuracy of 88.23%. The dataset split that suited this accuracy was 90% for training and 10% for testing. As mentioned in the Methodology section, this classifier contained a forest of 500 decision trees. It's worth pointing out that this is not the best dataset split that should be used to train and test a classifier. The same problem happens with the Naïve Bayes classifier, therefore the best classifier would be Adaboost with an accuracy of 80.89%. The dataset was split into 75% for training and 25% for testing. Otherwise, the results of this paper shows a little lower accuracy regarding the classification task with previous systems, especially with [14], while it shows higher accuracy for the rating task regarding [14]. The key difference was that they used a MLP while we used Adaboost, therefore the difference is in the classifier used.

As future work, we propose the following lines:

- To develop a bigger dataset through a data augmentation technique and therefore achieve better results.
- To implement the latest machine learning classifiers techniques like: CatBoost, XGBoost and LightGBM. In this way we can compare which classifier achieves better results.
- To apply hyperparameter tuning to the classifiers to minimize the loss function and consequently obtain better results.

Acknowledgments. This work has been funded by the "Sistemas Inteligentes de Soporte a la Educación (v5)" research project, the Cátedra UNESCO "Tecnologías de apoyo para la Inclusión Educativa" initiative, and the Research Group on Artificial Intelligence and Assistive Technologies (GI-IATa) of the Universidad Politécnica Salesiana, Campus Cuenca.

References

1. Algehyne, E.A., Jibril, M.L., Algehainy, N.A., Alamri, O.A., Alzahrani, A.K.: Fuzzy neural network expert system with an improved gini index random forest-based feature importance measure algorithm for early diagnosis of breast cancer in Saudi Arabia. Big Data Cognitive Comput. **6**(1) (2022). https://www.mdpi.com/2504-2289/6/1/13

2. Debnath, S., Changder, S.: Automatic detection of regular geometrical shapes in photograph using machine learning approach. In: 2018 10th International Conference on Advanced Computing, ICoAC 2018. pp. 1–6 (2018). www.scopus.com

3. Duan, F., Yin, S., Song, P., Zhang, W., Zhu, C., Yokoi, H.: Automatic welding defect detection of x-ray images by using cascade adaboost with penalty term. IEEE Access **7**, 125929–125938 (2019)

4. Kadar, M., Wan Yunus, F., Tan, E., Chai, S.C., Razaob@Razab, N.A., Mohamat Kasim, D.H.: A systematic review of occupational therapy intervention for handwriting skills in 4-6 year old children. Australian Occup. Ther. J. **67**(1), 3–12 (2020). https://doi.org/10.1111/1440-1630.12626

5. Karadağ, Ö.Ö., Erdaş Çiçek, Ö.: Experimental assessment of the performance of data augmentation with generative adversarial networks in the image classification problem. In: 2019 Innovations in Intelligent Systems and Applications Conference (ASYU), pp. 1–4 (2019)

6. Kumar, K., Kishore, P., Kumar, D.A., Kumar, E.K.: Indian classical dance action identification using adaboost multiclass classifier on multifeature fusion. In: 2018 Conference on Signal Processing And Communication Engineering Systems (SPACES), pp. 167–170. IEEE (2018)

7. Lee, J., Kang, H.: Flood fill mean shift: A robust segmentation algorithm. Int. J. Control Autom. Syst. **8**(6), 1313–1319 (2010). https://doi.org/10.1007/s12555-010-0617-6

8. Loconsole, C., Trotta, G.F., Brunetti, A., Trotta, J., Schiavone, A., Tatò, S.I., Losavio, G., Bevilacqua, V.: Computer vision and EMG-based handwriting analysis for classification in parkinson's disease. In: Huang, D.-S., Jo, K.-H., Figueroa-García, J.C. (eds.) ICIC 2017. LNCS, vol. 10362, pp. 493–503. Springer, Cham (2017). https://doi.org/10.1007/978-3-319-63312-1_43

9. Lozhnikov, P., Sulavko, A., Eremenko, A., Volkov, D.: Methods of generating key sequences based on parameters of handwritten passwords and signatures. Information **7**(4), 59 (2016)

10. Najeeb, R., Uthayan, J., Lojini, R., Vishaliney, G., Alosius, J., Gamage, A.: Gamified smart mirror to leverage autistic education - aliza. In: 2020 2nd International Conference on Advancements in Computing (ICAC), vol. 1, pp. 428–433 (2020). https://doi.org/10.1109/ICAC51239.2020.9357065

11. Ozkan, H.B., Aslan, F., Yucel, E., Sennaroglu, G., Sennaroglu, L.: Written language skills in children with auditory brainstem implants. Eur. Arch. Oto-Rhino-Laryngology **279**, 1–9 (2022). https://doi.org/10.1007/s00405-022-07359-x

12. Reddy, A.V.N., Krishna, C.P., Mallick, P.K.: An image classification framework exploring the capabilities of extreme learning machines and artificial bee colony. Neural Comput. Appl. **32**(8), 3079–3099 (2019). https://doi.org/10.1007/s00521-019-04385-5

13. Ren, Y., Yang, J., Zhang, Q., Guo, Z.: Ship recognition based on Hu invariant moments and convolutional neural network for video surveillance. Multimedia Tools Appl. **80**(1), 1343–1373 (2020). https://doi.org/10.1007/s11042-020-09574-2

14. Serpa-Andrade, L.J., Pazos-Arias, J.J., López-Nores, M., Robles-Bykbaev, V.E.: Design, implementation and evaluation of a support system for educators and therapists to rate the acquisition of pre-writing skills. IEEE Access **9**, 77920–77929 (2021)

15. Shah, L.J., Bialek, K., Clarke, M.L., Jansson, J.L.: Study of pre-handwriting factors necessary for successful handwriting in children. Int. J. Educ. Pedagogical Sci. **10**(3), 707–714 (2016)

16. Taverna, L., Tremolada, M., Tosetto, B., Dozza, L., Renata, Z.S.: Impact of psycho-educational activities on visual-motor integration, fine motor skills and name writing among first graders: a kinematic pilot study. Children **7**(4), 27 (2020)

17. Yap, F.Y., et al.: Shape and texture-based radiomics signature on CT effectively discriminates benign from malignant renal masses. Eur. Radiol. **31**(2), 1011–1021 (2020). https://doi.org/10.1007/s00330-020-07158-0

18. Zhang, X., Wang, Z., Liu, D., Ling, Q.: Dada: Deep adversarial data augmentation for extremely low data regime classification. In: ICASSP 2019–2019 IEEE International Conference on Acoustics, Speech and Signal Processing (ICASSP), pp. 2807–2811 (2019)

Study Techniques: Procedure to Promote the Comprehension of Texts in University Students

Eilen Lorena Pérez-Montero$^{(\boxtimes)}$ (iD) and Yolanda Díaz-Rosero$^{(\boxtimes)}$ (iD)

Corporación Universitaria del Huila – CORHUILA, Neiva, Colombia
{eilen.perez,Yolanda.diaz}@corhuila.edu.co

Abstract. The objective of this study was to assess the students' appropriation level of studying techniques to strengthen text comprehension at the University Corporation of Huila, through the use of learning worksheets on underlining, summarizing, and the main idea. The study was carried out due to the unsatisfactory results in reading comprehension, the low use, and lack of knowledge of techniques to address the academic activities of university students. The type of research is quantitative, with a sample of 235 students enrolled in theoretical subjects of the Faculties of Engineering, Veterinary Medicine and Zootechnics, Economic and administrative sciences. The instruments used were: the SHTQ questionnaire (Study Habits and Techniques Questionnaire) that was adapted to the use of studying techniques: underlining, summary and, the main idea; likewise, a diagnostic activity on text analysis was performed at the beginning and the end. The intervention was carried out in 10 sessions and included four phases: diagnosis, design, implementation, and data analysis and interpretation. The results reinforced the knowledge on the techniques of underlining, the main idea, and summary; likewise, it had positive and significant effects on the global comprehension of texts, with scores higher than the initial diagnosis.

Keywords: Academic performance · Comprehension of texts · Learning process · Study techniques · Study method

1 Introduction

The comprehension of texts is a fundamental capacity for the development of thought, the capacity to generate ideas, to get to grips with them and to modify previous schemes of meaning. Likewise, taking into account that in this age of almost unlimited access to information calls into question some forms of education based solely on transmission, it is increasingly necessary to teach comprehension reading skills that enable students to acquire tools for their academic, working and social life. Thus, the role of educational institutions at all levels is key to training in reading and writing skills. According to Alvarado [2], teaching reading and writing:

"has fostered the modes of reflection and knowledge production that allow access to science and theory. These modes of knowledge production are closely linked to the

H. Florez and H. Gomez (Eds.): ICAI 2022, CCIS 1643, pp. 324–337, 2022.
https://doi.org/10.1007/978-3-031-19647-8_23

deferred, distanced and controlled nature of written communication, which favors the objectification of discourse and its manipulation. For this reason, training in the production of written texts of a certain complexity, which require composition processes, has always been the task of the school (P. 31)".

In the same sense, Peña [17] points out that "What is important is not reading or writing per se, but what teachers and students do with them, the way they appropriate and use reading texts or their written productions to think and learn better". (P. 2).

However, reflection on text comprehension leads us to think about concepts such as studying and learning. In the first case, from this study it is assumed as "a term that describes a type of relationship that a subject establishes in a certain situation, making aware of the elements involved in these relationships and the type of relationship they maintain" and learning "is a word with a descriptive sense that is used to indicate an achievement, a particular result, not the actions that led to that result" Morales et al., p. 5. [15]. In this sense, it is increasingly important for students to understand how they carry out their study process for reading and for teachers to contemplate didactically elements to favor learning. According to Knorr [13] solid learning occurs when knowledge is the product of the gradual understanding and integration of topics and concepts located in the disciplinary area of training. He further notes: "Comprehensive, appropriate and effective reading of study materials is the key to achieving this goal". He then concludes: "The literature reviewed indicates that the problem of text comprehension is one of the greatest difficulties faced by university students" (P. 15).

Thus, it is increasingly common to observe students who find it difficult to carry out analysis and text comprehension activities that require them to obtain satisfactory and effective results, situations that may be associated with the use of an inappropriate study method. According to Peña [17], students entering university have difficulties to.

"understand and produce academic texts; they present their ideas in an isolated and schematic way; they do not develop a prior plan or a systematic process of textual production; they do not know the genres and conventions of academic writing; they have problems of coherence and cohesion in the development of ideas or transcribe literally from the texts they read, without critical appropriation and evaluation, and without making them an integral part of their own text".

There are many ways of dealing with these problems. For the purpose of this study, work with study techniques has been chosen as a strategy to contribute to the strengthening of comprehension.

Cedeño Meza et al., [6] argues that the low academic performance of school and university students refers to the fact that they do not know how to study or lack the appropriate skills to explain, classify information, reason, represent what they have learned, among others, and deal with large amounts of information.

This statement is related to the study by Briones Menéndez [5] associated with Study Techniques, where the sampled students do not have adequate techniques for reading and taking notes, inadequate distribution of their time and lack of concentration, with low results in reading comprehension.

Bedolla [4]. Stated that the lack of implementation of study techniques has an impact on the learning process, leading to poor academic performance, and highlights the importance of students knowing and using a procedure to favour the study task.

Study techniques are defined in the text of Monereo et al., [14] as "a process of conscious and intentional decision making, which consists of selecting the conceptual, procedural and attitudinal knowledge necessary to fulfil a certain objective, always according to the conditions of the educational situation in which the action takes place" [14].

Thus, a study technique is a tool or procedure to facilitate study and improve achievement. Specialists affirm that the study technique requires an active attitude, where the student assumes a leading role and overcomes passivity [16].

As stated by Ruiz Coello [20], Chilca Alva [7], study techniques are a resource that benefits the quality and adapts to the needs of each student, a good incorporation allows improving academic performance and making study hours profitable. These include: comprehension and reasoning, planning and time/work management, content analysis and synthesis techniques, attention and concentration techniques, memorisation techniques, motivation techniques, and relaxation techniques.

Content analysis techniques include underlining, main idea and summarising. Serafini [21] mentions that underlining is selecting certain parts of a text by assigning personal marks that subsequently allow attention to be focused on them for the purposes assigned by the reader. The main idea is annotations that express relevant information for the development of the topic being dealt with, for which key words or fragments, superordinate concepts, assigned title and topic of the text are needed. The summary is to reduce the essential, to reproduce briefly the content of a text.

Meanwhile, a survey of students from three Colombian universities: 1 Corporation of Huila CORHUILA, 2 Surcolombiana USCO, 3 Francisco Jose de Caldas, 4. EAN, shows that a significant number of university students rarely use the techniques of underlining, summary, synthesis, note-taking, preparation and development of exams, technique of schemes (Table 1).

Table 1. Table use of study techniques in three Institutions of higher education in Colombia.

Higher education institution		Underlining	Summary	Synthesis	Note-taking	Preparation exam	Schemes
1	Not use	63	59	58	43	15	40
	Use	52	56	57	72	100	75
	Total	115	115	115	115	115	115
2	Not use	33	36	30	17	23	20
	Use	17	14	20	33	27	30

(continued)

Table 1. (*continued*)

Higher education institution		Underlining	Summary	Synthesis	Note-taking	Preparation exam	Schemes
	Total	50	50	50	50	50	50
3	Not use	43	35	33	38	10	40
	Use	23	31	33	28	56	26
	Total	66	66	66	66	66	66
4	Not use	48	53	50	39	6	45
	Use	47	42	45	66	89	50
	Total	95	95	95	95	95	95

They also show a high "Not use" value for the underlining technique, the summary technique and the main idea technique with ranges of 50% and 66% for the three HEIs.

This is followed by note-taking and outline techniques with medium high values of "No use" with a range of 35% and 57%. Finally, the technique with the lowest percentage of "No use" is the technique of preparation and development of exams with University EAN with 7%, Corporation of Huila with 14%, University Distrital Francisco José de Caldas with 16% and University Surcolombiana with 46%.

This has implications for the exercise of text comprehension, due to the weaknesses of having resources that facilitate the processing of information and the incorporation of new knowledge.

On occasions, these deficiencies lead students in the first semesters to drop out of their chosen academic programmer because, according to their criteria, they feel saturated by the academic load and by the development of activities with a high level of demand.

In accordance with the above, this project aims to learn through the development of study guides the study techniques of underlining, main idea and summary in the university context, recognizing that these are acquired through practice and that they become a learning tool in the comprehension of a text.

It is important to highlight that the concept of didactic guides is related to a support and motivational tool for organizing classroom content and activities, Aguilar Feijoo [1]. For their development, objectives, initial reflection activities or prior knowledge, content selection, contextualization activities and identification of knowledge necessary for learning, knowledge transfer activities, etc., were established for their development.

2 Method

The research responds to a quantitative perspective, because it allowed the description, interpretation and analysis of numerical data in relation to the technical variables of study and analysis of student texts [11, 23]. The participants were 235 students enrolled in the course Oral and Written Communication, Expression and Communication, Research Methodology, Formulation and Evaluation of Projects, during the academic semester 2021-B of the Corporation of Huila described in Table 2. A non-probabilistic sampling by convenience was used, because the choice of the units to be investigated responds to reasons related to the characteristics and context in which the research is developed [15].

Table 2. Table Sample for each group.

Number group	Description group	Quantity
1	Communication Oral and written	134
2	Expression and communication	12
3	Methodology of the investigation	51
4	Formulation and evaluation of projects	38

The research had four phases: diagnostic, design of the guides, implementation and evaluation phase. Table 3 describes each of them with their respective pedagogical interventions.

The following instruments were used for data collection:

- Initial diagnostic test on global comprehension of texts.
- Adaptation of the Study Habits Inventory, which links study behavior with the use of the following techniques: underlining, main idea and summarizing. The answers are given as never, almost never, sometimes, often, and almost always.
- Final diagnostic test on the global comprehension of texts which allows for an analysis of the learning acquired.
- Survey of open questions to self-assess the level of learning of underlining, main idea and summary.

3   Results

The application of the initial diagnostic activity of each group showed a distribution adjusted to normality (see Fig. 1) with mean 2.585 and standard deviation 0.66, which is corroborated by the data generated in the Kolmogórov-Smirnov statistical test with a value of 0.067.

In order to graphically evaluate the distribution of the quantitative variable in the different groups (Fig. 2), a box plot of the averages of the diagnostic test before being submitted to the implementation of the study technique guides is developed, the statistical values show that the students present the same difficulties when working on global text comprehension, with averages around 2.5 and 2.6 for the four courses.

These results indicated the need to define strategies to level students and prepare them in the construction of reasoning, such as the appropriate use of study techniques.

Table 3. Table Description of the phases with the pedagogical activities.

Phase	Pedagogical interventions
Diagnostics	• To inform students about the development of the research • To find out the initial state of global comprehension of texts • Apply the instrument on the use of the techniques: underlining, main idea and summary
Design of the guides	Analyze the results of the diagnostic phase, in order to design guides with the following characteristics: They are clear and well-illustrated: ✓ The terminology is in line with the lexicon of the learners ✓ The guides had a semantic sequence, an introduction and well-defined objectives ✓ The criteria to be assessed are clearly indicated ✓ They present an initial reflection or prior knowledge ✓ Contextualizes the student on the importance of the technique ✓ Encourages attention ✓ It makes recommendations ✓ Develops group competencies
Implementation	• Train on the proper use of each technique • Develop guidelines: 1 underlining, 2 main idea, 3 summary
Evaluative	• Evaluate and give feedback on each guide • To know the final state of global comprehension of texts • To get students to self-assess the level of learning of underlining, main idea and summary

Next, the use of the techniques of underlining, main idea and summarizing was investigated through the instrument in Table 4. The students presented averages between 2.0 and 2.9 for the four groups with respect to the questions "Does it identify the subject area, subject or type of text?", "Do you ask yourself what is the aim of the assigned task or work?", "Do you underline important ideas?", "Do you underline key words?", "Do you reread the underlines?", "Do you create graphic organizers, diagrams, personal notes?", "Do you find the main idea to understand the text?", "Do you summarize to establish the global semantic structure of the text?".

Regarding the question "Do you read and reread information or texts?" there is a value of 3.0 in the Expression and Communication group, in contrast to the groups of Oral and Written Communication, Research Methodology, Project Formulation and Evaluation with averages between 2.4 and 2.5.

The values observed in Table 4 highlight the deficiencies in the use of the techniques of underlining, main idea and summary for the process of global text comprehension, due to the fact that the averages are associated with low values "sometimes".

Once the study technique guides had been developed, the final diagnostic activity was applied to check whether differences were observed in the students with respect to the scores obtained in the initial diagnostic activity.

In principle, Fig. 3 shows a normal or Gaussian distribution with a mean of 3.597 and a standard deviation of 0.719. However, the Kolmogorov Smirnov test with a value of

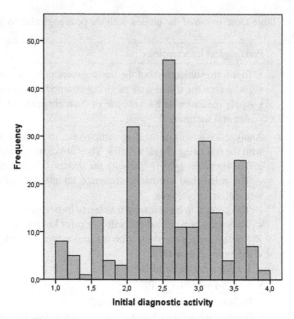

Fig. 1. Histogram of the initial diagnostic activity

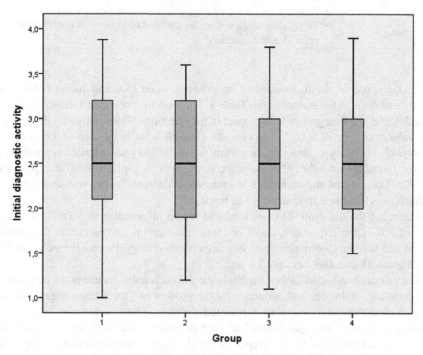

Fig. 2. Mean box plot for initial diagnostic activity

Table 4. Table average analysis of the use of study techniques.

Question	Group	N	Mean	Standard deviation
Does it identify the subject area, subject or type of text?	1	134	2,68	,469
	2	12	2,92	,289
	3	51	2,55	,642
	4	38	2,61	,547
Do you read and re-read information or texts?	1	134	2,53	,544
	2	12	3,00	,000
	3	51	2,51	,505
	4	38	2,42	,500
It asks what the objective of the task or work assigned is?	1	134	2,54	,544
	2	12	2,50	,522
	3	51	2,37	,528
	4	38	2,55	,555
Do you underline important ideas?	1	134	2,40	,613
	2	12	2,67	,492
	3	51	2,20	,693
	4	38	2,34	,534
Underline the key words?	1	134	2,25	,609
	2	12	2,25	,452
	3	51	2,16	,644
	4	38	2,32	,662
Do you reread the underlines?	1	134	2,28	,593
	2	12	2,50	,522
	3	51	2,16	,579
	4	38	2,32	,662
Do you make graphic organizers, diagrams, personal notes?	1	134	2,10	,547
	2	12	2,42	,669
	3	51	2,00	,640
	4	38	2,08	,632
Do you find the main idea to understand the text?	1	134	2,17	,655

(*continued*)

Table 4. (*continued*)

Question	Group	N	Mean	Standard deviation
	2	12	2,42	,515
	3	51	2,24	,513
	4	38	2,29	,611
Does it make summaries that allow the overall semantic structure of the text to be established?	1	134	2,36	,593
	2	12	2,58	,515
	3	51	2,25	,627
	4	38	2,47	,506

0.061, greater than 0.05, reaffirms that it is a normal distribution and that, consequently, we can apply parametric tests.

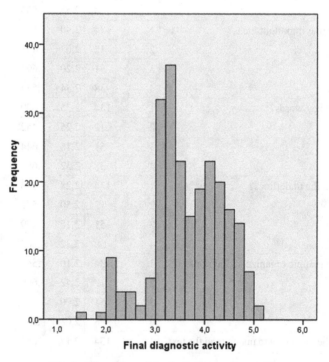

Fig. 3. Histogram of the final diagnostic activity

The results that the students had improved after the implementation of the guides show statistically significant values, as shown in Fig. 4. The group called Oral and Written Communication has an increase from 2.6 to 3.7, the Expression and Communication group had a higher increase from 2.5 to 4.1, the Research Methodology group increased from 2.5 to 3.4 and the Project Formulation and Evaluation group increased from 2.5 on average to 3.2.

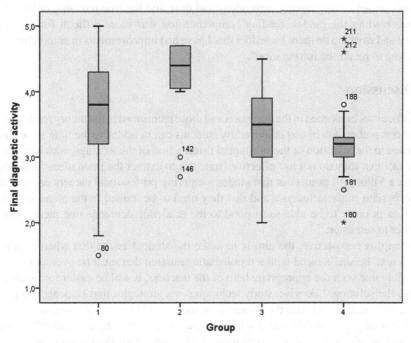

Fig. 4. Mean box plot for final diagnostic activity

It is also evident that quartile 3 of the Oral and written communication group has a maximum value of 5.0 and quartile 1 has a minimum value of 1.5.

On carrying out the test of homogeneity of variances for the initial diagnostic activity and the final diagnostic activity in the 4 groups (Table 5), the proposed null hypothesis that "The study techniques used by university students do not affect the process of global comprehension of a text" is rejected, due to the fact that Levene's statistic for the final diagnostic test is 0.001 < 0.05, which implies different variances.

Table 5. Table Average analysis of the use of study techniques.

Activity	Levene's statistic	gl1	gl2	Sig.
Initial diagnostic activity	1,478	3	231	,221
Final diagnostic activity	5,898	3	231	,001

In this sense, it is worth noting that the students' opinions on the positive effect of the study guides on text comprehension were marked with comments associated with: "It helps me to understand texts a bit more", "I broaden my knowledge about recognising key words in a text and comprehension"." By following the steps of underlining, the ideas are clearer and more precise", "The guides were a great help to strengthen the overall understanding of texts and to understand in a simpler and easier way", "I found an improvement in organising main ideas and thus find the true meaning of the text", "Before reading the guides, reading comprehension was more difficult for me, after reading and working on them I consider that I have had improvements in comprehension, managing to retain the information".

4 Discussion

The difficulties evidenced in the diagnosis and those mentioned in the theory related to the global comprehension of text in university students can be added to the little importance attributed to the selection of the substantial information of the writings, which is related to the fact that they do not use effective strategies to extract the main ideas [10]. Thus, Enriquez Villota [9] points out that students entering professional careers are unaware of appropriate study techniques and that they need to be trained in the management of resources in order to be able to respond to the academic demands that increase from semester to semester.

From this perspective, the aim is to make the student aware that when reading a written text, he/she is faced with a problematic situation that must be overcome; and it is possible that with the appropriate help of the teachers, it will be easier for him/her to assume the solution. Likewise, study techniques are strategies that students can use to obtain, analyze and deal with the information understood in a text; it is to discover local and global meanings of different discursive types, to infer the objective, to differentiate facts from opinions, it is an approximation of what the author thinks and feels [18].

Taking into account the results of the application of the diagnostic test, these show a tendency of data distribution towards low scores in the comprehension of a text, which demonstrates the need to implement strategies or resources that help improve academic performance and facilitate the process of memorization and study, exhibiting similar results in relation to the study of Bedolla Solano [4].

The use of study techniques by students is based on what they assume will bring them the greatest probability of success in learning outcomes, i.e., students are autonomous in applying a strategy for their study, and can even review the content only on the day on which the assessment will take place, which would have a direct impact on their academic performance [3, 22].

According to Pinchao Benavides [19] there are deficiencies in the use of the underlining study technique, given by the habit of marking the entire text and the non-separation of what is relevant from what is not. This technique facilitates retention, the preparation of schemes and/or summaries and makes learning an active and committed process, improves attention and facilitates revision.

Also, when comparing the results with the study done by Crispín Bernardo et al. [8] students should understand that study techniques are not learned, if they are not constantly practiced. Only in this way will they be able to observe their benefits, which are related to study efficiency, such as time and effort spent.

Through the general balance of the results achieved in a general way by the students, it is evident that the study techniques used in this project helped to improve the global comprehension of texts, becoming a significant tool for university students and at the same time of greater interest to retrieve explicit and implicit information about the texts.

University education, in this case, that of the engineer, must promote the learning of reading and writing from its epistemic function, because getting to the ideas of others, dialoguing with various sources, building and reconstructing notions always goes through the understanding of texts. Thus, speaking of understanding is analogous to critical thinking that becomes renewed and relevant knowledge.

If reading comprehension is essential in the development of educational processes, as it is the substratum of learning, then, the greater the ability of a student to read and write, the greater the capacity for the elaboration of logical reasoning, abstract thought., argumentation and creativity, among others.

Now, in the specific case of future systems engineers, the current context requires, in a demanding way, to understand the new forms of communication in digital environments: on the one hand, to understand phenomena such as the mass media era, since this context does not It only modifies oral and reading-writing practices, but also the mental processes that come from them and the very structure of knowledge. Technological advances, the incidence of the Internet and the certain presence of digital natives require an analysis of the current language supports and their different ways of reading, writing, listening and speaking. The digital age demands education for effective search on the net, ability to reveal ideological biases or dominant or exclusive positions; cyberculture requires investigating that projection of the self as a public discourse that speaks of other subjectivities (social networks); it requires knowledge of dynamism, of multimodality (text, image, sound), of speed, of the hyperlink (which can lead to loss), of the confluence of new discursive genres.

5 Conclusions

It is important to note that the design of materials such as workshops or learning guides contribute to the awareness of the importance of carrying out step-by-step procedures for underlining, identifying the main idea and summarizing. This is not least because it emphasizes the linking of the learner to his or her teaching and learning process. It is therefore essential to consider how self-assessment, for example, contributes to this purpose of making the learner aware of how he or she learns.

In this sense, it is worth highlighting the students' progress in text comprehension, through study techniques, but also the importance of the methodology and type of assessment adopted.

With respect to the hypotheses put forward, the alternative hypothesis is accepted, which indicates that there is a statistically significant relationship between the use of the underlining technique, identification of the main idea and preparation of a summary, in university students for the global comprehension of a text, so that this research opens the way for future research into the effectiveness of other study techniques in the learning processes.

In terms of text comprehension, the teaching process through learning guides provides tools not only so that students can better understand the texts of their discipline of training, reviewing the signs that these emit and transforming these signs into new content and ideas, but also help young people to interpret various texts in the different current literate roles that are multiple and complex. It should be remembered that students outside the university participate in non-academic forms of reading and writing that influence their ideas and representations.

References

1. Aguilar Feijoo, R.: The didactic guide, an educational material to promote autonomous learning. Evaluation and improvement of its quality in the open and distance modality of the UTPL. Revista Iberoamericana de Educación a Distancia **7**(2), 179–192 (2004)
2. Alvarado, M.: Writing and Invention in School. Fondo de cultura económica, Buenos Aires (2013)
3. Arrieta-Reales, N., Arnedo-Franco, G.: Sleep-inhibiting substances, study habits and academic performance in medical and nursing students from universities in the city of Barranquilla **21**(5), 306–312 (2020). Elsevier
4. Bedolla Solano, R.: Educational program of techniques and study habits to achieve sustainable learning in new students entering higher education. Revista Iberoamericana De Educación **76**(2), 73–94 (2018). https://doi.org/10.35362/rie7622959
5. Briones Menéndez, V.: Study techniques and academic performance of nursing students. Jipijapa-UNESUM, Manabí (2019). http://repositorio.unesum.edu.ec/handle/53000/1863
6. Cedeño Meza, J., Alarcón-Chávez, B.E., Mieles Vélez, J.C.: Study habits and academic performance in second level psychology students at the Technical University of Manabí. Dominio de las Ciencias **6**(2), 276–301 (2020). https://doi.org/10.23857/dc.v6i3.1218
7. Chilca Alva, M.: Self-esteem, study habits and academic performance in university students. Propósitos y representaciones **5**(1), 71–127 (2017). https://doi.org/10.20511/pyr2017.v5n1.145
8. Crispín Bernardo, M.L., et al.: Aprendizaje Autónomo orientaciones para la docencia. CLACSO Virtual Library Network, Mexico (2011)
9. Enriquez Villota, M.F.: Hábitos y técnicas de estudio en la Universidad Mariana. UNIMAR **31**(2), 81–97 (2013)
10. Guevara Benítez, Y., Guerra García, J., Delgado Sanchez, U., Flores Rubi, C.: Assessment of different levels of reading comprehension in Mexican psychology students. Acta Colombiana de Psicología **17**(2), 113–121 (2014). https://doi.org/10.14718/ACP.2014.17.2.12
11. Hernández Sampieri, R., Mendoza Torres, C.P.: Research Methodology: The Quantitative, Qualitative and Mixed Routes. McGraw-Hill, New York (2018)
12. Hernández-Sampieri, R., Mendoza Torres, C.P.: Research Methodology: The Quantitative, Qualitative and Mixed Routes, 1 edn. McGraw-Hill Interamericana (2018)
13. Knorr, P.E.: Strategies for approaching texts. In: Career: Writing and Reading Academic and Professional Texts, pp. 15–37 (2012)
14. Monereo Font, C., Castelló Badia, M., i Muntada, C., Palma, M., Pérez Cabani, M.L.: Estrategias de enseñanza y aprendizaje: formación del profesorado y aplicación en la escuela, vol. 112. Graó, Mexico (1994)
15. Morales, G., Chávez, E., Rodríguez, R., Peña, B., Carpio, C.: Studying and learning: precisions on its analytical nature and empirical research. J. Educ. Dev. (2016). https://www.cucs.udg.mx/revistas/edu_desarrollo/anteriores/37/37_Morales.pdf
16. Navarro Soria, I., González Gómez, C., Real Fernández, M.: Relationship between study techniques, academic performance and gender. Revista de Investigación Educativa Universitaria **1**(1), 1–12 (2019). http://revistas.educacioneditora.net/index.php/RIEU/article/view/15

17. Peña Borrero, L.: Oral and written competence in higher education (2008). https://www.min educacion.gov.co/1621/articles-189357_archivo_pdf_comunicacion.pdf
18. Pérez Grajales, H.: Comprensión y producciónn de texto educativos. Magisterio, Bogotá (2006)
19. Pinchao Benavides, L.E.: Una experiencia de investigación acción en educación (IAE) La glosa y el subrayado, como recursos didácticos, para favorecer la comprensión lectora. Diálogos educativos (20), 41–61 (2010)
20. Ruiz Coello, E.: Guía práctica de técnicas de estudio: Saber estudiar, la clave del éxito académico. Kindle edition (2015)
21. Serafini, M.: How to Study: The Organisation of Intellectual Work. Ediciones Paidós (1991)
22. Mendez, O., Florez, H.: Applying the flipped classroom model using a VLE for foreign languages learning. In: Florez, H., Diaz, C., Chavarriaga, J. (eds.) ICAI 2018. CCIS, vol. 942, pp. 215–227. Springer, Cham (2018). https://doi.org/10.1007/978-3-030-01535-0_16
23. Martinez-Zambrano, K., Paez, J., Florez, H.: Pedagogical model to develop virtual learning objects for people with hearing impairment. In: CEUR Workshop Proceedings Volume, vol. 2992, pp. 62–732021 (2021)

TPACK and Toondoo Digital Storytelling Tool Transform Teaching and Learning

Serafeim A. Triantafyllou[✉] ⓘ

Greek Ministry of Education and Religious Affairs, Athens, Greece
ser.triant@gmail.com

Abstract. Web 2.0 technologies transform teaching and learning and the teachers which have a positive perception of technology, they seem as the most appropriate to run technology-mediated learning projects, because they can support mature students to achieve their learning goals and to construct new knowledge based-on their previous knowledge and learning experiences. This study explores Technological Pedagogical Content Knowledge Framework (TPACK) and Toondoo, with basic aim to enhance collaboration among students and help them to understand complex learning concepts. After a careful selection of studies from literature based on specific criteria, a comparative analysis of Toondoo, Goanimate and and Fileguru edtech tools, was conducted across six basic aspects concerning students' learning progress: (i) knowledge of use of the edtech tools, (ii) teamwork, (iii) accomplishment of learning goals, (iv) creativity, (v) motivation and (vi) engagement. Emphasis is given on Toondoo because it was used systematically during the learning process to enhance students' creativity and motivation. Also, this study tries to answer two basic research questions with a statistical analysis of the data collected with a questionnaire given to mature students of 18–35 age group to answer it. The first research question tries to investigate to what extent students can participate in specific learning activities with digital storytelling, and the second research question explores the students' learning achievements by using Toondoo in a technology-enhanced learning environment. The creation of an effective learning environment where teachers have the important role of designing, training, coordinating, and monitoring the learning process, is a continuous effort that depends on teachers' will to run technology-enhanced learning environments. Toondoo and other similar edtech tools can bring the desirable learning outcomes and lead to the achievement of learning goals in a computer science course because they emphasize on how technology can best be used to support teaching and learning.

Keywords: Computer science · Educational technology · Technological pedagogical content knowledge framework · Toondoo

1 Introduction

The rapid development of Information and Communication Technology in teaching and education has led many researchers and teachers to seriously consider adopting new pedagogical approaches and not just to rest in traditional teacher-centered methods. Many

H. Florez and H. Gomez (Eds.): ICAI 2022, CCIS 1643, pp. 338–350, 2022.
https://doi.org/10.1007/978-3-031-19647-8_24

teachers argue that learning requires the introduction of a new form of pedagogical approach structured in the relationship developed between teachers and students. Traditional teacher-centered methods where the teacher plans, designs, teaches, and evaluates his/her teaching often make students passive recipients who receive accumulated knowledge and are not incentivized to develop advanced creative thinking. Each student carries his/her own learning experiences that a teacher who wants to succeed in his/her didactic work must take seriously into account, to help students develop critical thinking and ensure success in their effort to learn how to learn.

Advanced creative thinking is the result of acquisition of collaborative knowledge. Collaborative knowledge is not a stagnant process but an evolving process of collecting new ideas and information to construct new knowledge. Teachers should try to incentivize students to think about new concepts and share new ideas, because new knowledge is built only when teachers take seriously into account students' prior learning experiences to help them go to the next step and develop critical thinking [6, 16].

Creating an interactive learning environment that can bring the desirable learning outcomes is not an easy task [8]. Web 2.0 technologies in education can help students to express new ideas and actively participate in the learning process by adding digital content [26]. Therefore, students are transformed from passive receivers into planners of their own knowledge. Today, with the proper use of Internet and Web 2.0 technologies, teachers can create a powerful learning environment for research and problem analysis, thereby facilitating better access to information and collaborative learning.

2 TPACK and Web 2.0

Nowadays, teachers with basic technology skills, do not think the use of technology in class as a complex task, but try to incorporate web-based technological tools to their teaching [7, 9]. Over the past decade, students had limited access to educational resources. Web 2.0 technologies brought a new era where students have access to a digital ocean of information and should develop critical thinking to identify the educational resources that best fit to their needs. The revolution of Web2.0 over Web 1.0 was that it allowed users not to simply read the digital content of a web page, but enabled them to add digital content, share information, and collaborate online [2]. However, in order to incentivize users to properly use Web 2.0 technologies in schools, schools should have the basic technological infrastructure that ensures that all students have access to a computer with the pre-installed software needed for educational use.

Punya Mishra and Matthew J. Koehler's TPACK framework (Fig. 1), which focuses on technological knowledge (TK), pedagogical knowledge (PK), and content knowledge (CK), offers a new approach that can help teachers to enrich their teaching by using edtech tools [1, 3, 11]. According to the TPACK framework, specific technological tools are best used to give students a better understanding of the subject they study. The three types of knowledge Technological Knowledge, Pedagogical Knowledge, and Content Knowledge – are thus combined in various ways within the TPACK framework. Technological pedagogical knowledge (TPK) describes relationships and interactions between technological tools and specific pedagogical practices, while pedagogical content knowledge (PCK) describes relationships and interactions between pedagogical practices and specific learning goals; finally, technological content knowledge (TCK) describes relationships and intersections among technologies and learning goals [1, 11]. Pedagogical Knowledge (PK) describes teachers' knowledge about pedagogical practices and teaching methods. Pedagogical Knowledge focuses on the purposes, values, and aims of education, and may apply to specific domain areas including the understanding of student learning styles, classroom management skills, lesson planning, and assessments. Technological Knowledge (TK) describes teachers' knowledge to use technological tools, and associated resources. Technological Knowledge concerns understanding educational technology, considering its possibilities for a specific domain area, learning to identify when it will help learning, and continually learning and adapting to new technological advance [1, 11, 13].

True knowledge is based on experience and not disseminated from experts to learners [20]. Knowledge is not a stagnant process but continuously evolves. Many researchers suggested that students could be active receivers of knowledge and "construct" the new forms of knowledge they take on earlier forms of knowledge [5, 15, 17, 27]. Skilled teachers use their knowledge of pedagogy, content and technology (TPACK) to successfully pass their teaching and help students develop critical thinking. Therefore, the role of the teacher should be facilitating [12] and help students to create their own knowledge.

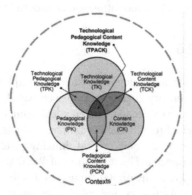

Fig. 1. Representation of the technological pedagogical content knowledge framework

3   Digital Story Telling and Toondoo

Joe Lambert and Dana Atchley as the cofounders of the Center for Digital Storytelling in late 1980s are the pioneers of the digital storytelling movement [14]. Digital storytelling can help teachers to promote innovation by introducing new pedagogical tools in classroom. [4] investigates how digital stories can be transformed into a pedagogical tool in two undergraduate psychology classes. The findings show that edtech tools such as the wikis and the digital stories constitute the basis for constructing new knowledge in classroom.

Cartoons can be an effective Web 2.0 technological tool for students to understand the teaching material of a course. Using concept cartoons in teaching helps students express their opinions and develop their questioning skills by learning to investigate and question their knowledge during the learning process [18]. ToonDoo (www.too ndoo.com) is a characteristic example of a website for cartoon and animation creation; other similar websites are Goanimate (www.goanimate.com), and Fileguru (www.fil eguru.com). Emphasis is given on Toondoo because it was used systematically during the learning process to enhance students' creativity and motivation. Toondoo (Fig. 2) is a digital storytelling tool and specifically a browser-based application that provides tools to draw, create and paint cartoons through the Internet. Students can create their digital stories by using toondoo environment [10, 19]. Toondoo is a great edtech tool to identify students' understanding of digital storytelling, as it allows them to easily design projects and create cartoons by dragging pre-installed backgrounds, text boxes, and digital characters into the cartoon panel selected by them.

Fig. 2. Toondoo edtech tool

Comics are now used in the learning process and students can be taught how to develop digital stories by developing their story writing skills and achieving learning objectives. Within minutes, students can create cartoons and they can download them, share via email or embed them to a blog or a website.

4 Methodology

This study aims to investigate students' learning outcomes after incorporating Toondoo edtech tool in a Computer Science course. Our research methodology was based on the following basic research questions:

(RQ1): To what extent can students participate in specific learning activities with digital storytelling?

(RQ2): What is the students' learning achievement by using Toondoo in a technology-enhanced learning environment?

Our research methodology is based on review of previous works and the following basic steps show our basic research plan (Fig. 3):

Fig. 3. Steps of our methodology

Step1: Initial Search in bibliographic databases

The basic aim of our research methodology was at first to direct our research to find relevant studies about digital storytelling and the use of Toondoo edtech tool in Computer Science courses. To find more publications of high scientific rigor, a detailed and focused search process was run in relevant bibliographic databases such as Scopus database, SpringerLink and Science Direct (Elsevier) (a search with "Toondoo", and "Computer Science" in the field including titles, abstracts and keywords in the Scopus, the SpringerLink and Science Direct (Elsevier) databases, accessed 20 March, 2022).

Step2: Defining Selection Criteria

To select our papers, we defined the following criteria:

1. Peer-reviewed full-text papers published in an international venue were selected for review.
2. Research methods in the papers are clearly explained.

Step3: Selected Studies

The number of selected papers is presented in Table 1:

Table 1. Selected studies

Papers type	Studies
Research articles	([10, 19, 21–23]. [24, 25])

With basic aim to examine cartoon and animation creation edtech tools, ToonDoo (www.toondoo.com), Goanimate (www.goanimate.com), and Fileguru (www.fileguru.com) were examined. With the use of a spreadsheet, comparative analysis was conducted for the three edtech tools across six basic aspects concerning students' learning progress: (i) knowledge of use of the edtech tools, (ii) teamwork, (iii) accomplishment of learning goals, (iv) creativity, (v) motivation and (vi) engagement. Within each of six aspects, specific points were awarded. The points were: 0 points, (zero result), 1 point (Weak result), 2 points (Average result), 3 points (Good result), 4 points (Very Good result) and 5 points (Excellent result). The final results are presented in the following graph (Fig. 4) and Table 2.

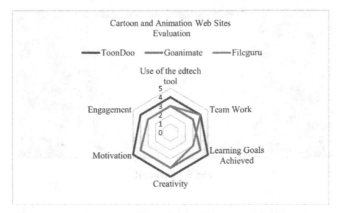

Fig. 4. Graph of the three edtech tools

Table 2. Awarded points

	ToonDoo	Goanimate	Fileguru
Use of the edtech tool	4	3	3
Team work	4	3	4
Learning goals achieved	5	4	3
Creativity	5	4	4
Motivation	5	4	4
Engagement	4	3	3

The ultimate aim of this study was to investigate the learning outcomes after the integration of Toondoo in the learning process. One of the Web 2.0 tools that have been proposed by [1], as an important teaching strategy was Toondoo. This study goes a step further to examine how Toondoo which is generally defined as a method of storytelling through multimedia, can increase students' motivation and engagement when participating on a computer science course. In a computer science course, learning tasks were organized with digital storytelling in a way to teach and promote creativity in students, which is necessary when students try to understand the practical implications of algorithms in computer science. A constructivist approach was adopted in teaching, and the teacher acted as the facilitator in the overall learning process to support students to build new knowledge. Toondoo interface was explained to students in order to understand the selected edtech tool use during the learning activities of the course. Toondoo interface contains three basic parts that are DoodleR, ImagineR and TraitR. Screenshots of these parts are presented in the following figures (Fig. 5, Fig. 6, and Fig. 7). With TraitR students could create a character, with ImagineR they could upload an image, and with DoodleR they could use drawing tools on their sketch.

Fig. 5. DoodleR

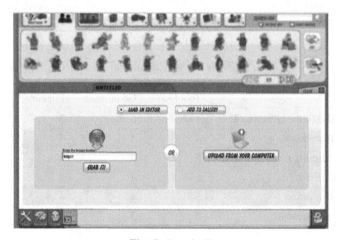

Fig. 6. ImagineR

In addition to these three basic parts, there are also features to add, delete, rotate, shape, and resize the digital objects and characters (Fig. 8). The final part of the Toon-doo interface is the inventory which contains any created, used or saved objects and characters.

The methodology used to conduct our survey and answer the basic research questions (RQ1) and (RQ2) of this study, was the construction of a questionnaire given to mature students of 18–35 age group to answer it. The completion of the questionnaire was optional and anonymous. The type of questions we finally chose to include in the questionnaire was the structured questions and in particular, (i) Rating Scales: it is about questions with a rating scale in the answers. Specifically, queries were selected on a Likert scale of five levels from 1 (Not at all) to 5 (Very much). The final questionnaire sent in response contained Likert-type questions related to digital storytelling and the use of Toondoo in technology-enhanced environments of a Computer Science course. The implementation of the questionnaire was done using Google's docs software. The

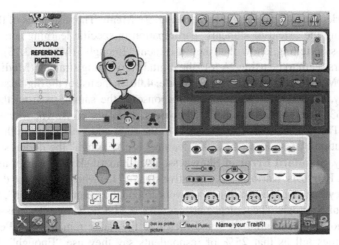

Fig. 7. TraitR for creating digital objects and characters

Fig. 8. Toolbox

collection of responses finally resulted within two months (September 2019 – November 2019) after sending the online questionnaire to a sample of 100 mature students. In order for the specific sample to be representative it was chosen at random, by random sampling. With regard to the gender of the respondents, the male population (48 men) corresponds to 48.00%, while the female population (52 women) is 52.00%.

5   Results

For the statistical processing of the results the statistical package that was selected was SPSS Statistics 20.0 (Statistical Package for Social Sciences). Next, the encoding of the (RQ1) and (RQ2) research questions is presented in detail to allow them to be entered into the SPSS database.

Question (RQ1): To what extent can students participate in specific learning activities with digital storytelling?

(1)   Name of variable:
PARTICIPATION_IN_LEARNING_TASKS_WITH_DIGITAL_STORYTELLING.
Measurement: ordinal.
Label: PARTICIPATION_IN_LEARNING_TASKS_WITH_DIGITAL_
STORYTELLING.
Values: 1 = "Not at all", 2 = "Little", 3 = "Enough", 4 = "A lot", 5 = "Very Much".

Remarks for (RQ1) (see Table 3 and Fig. 9): **Mean**: The responses of the sample regarding the extent of students' participation in specific learning activities with digital storytelling, show that they use them "Enough" (**Mean: 3.75**), **Median**: Learners seem to be using "A lot" the digital storytelling strategy (**Median: 4.00**), **Mode**: Most learners chose "A lot" (**Mode: 4.00**) in the use of the digital storytelling strategy, **Standard Deviation**: The response of the sample is from the average of 0.833 (**Std. Deviation: .833**), **Skewness**: The sign of skewness is negative (**-.033**). The distribution of responses is to the right and has its tail on the left. The distribution of responses show that learners use "Enough" the digital storytelling strategy, **Standard Error of Skewness**: The standard skewness error amounts to **24.1%**, **Kurtosis**: Kurtosis has a negative sign (**-.713**) which makes the distribution a platycyte, with concentration of answers around the mean of "Enough", **Standard Error of Kurtosis**: The typical Kurtosis error is **47.8%**, **Range**: The answers cover the whole range from 1 to 5 and therefore the range remains **3.0**, **Percentiles**: Percentiles tell us that **25%** of respondents say they use "Enough" the digital storytelling strategy, **50%** of respondents say they use "A lot" the digital storytelling strategy and **75%** of respondents say they use "A lot" the digital storytelling strategy.

Table 3. Participation in learning tasks with digital storytelling

Statistics		
PARTICIPATION_IN_LEARNING_TASKS_WITH_DIGITAL_STORYTELLING		
N	Valid	100
	Missing	0
Mean		3,75
Median		4,00
Mode		4
Std. Deviation		,833
Skewness		-,033
Std. Error of Skewness		,241
Kurtosis		-,713
Std. Error of Kurtosis		,478
Range		3
Percentiles	25	3,00
	50	4,00
	75	4,00

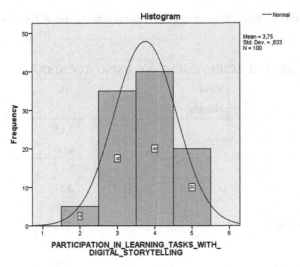

Fig. 9. Histogram

Question (RQ2): What is the students' learning achievement by using Toondoo in a technology-enhanced learning environment?
Name of variable:
STUDENTS_LEARNING_ACHIEVEMENT_BY_USING_TOONDOO.
Measurement: ordinal.
Label: STUDENTS_LEARNING_ACHIEVEMENT_BY_USING_TOONDOO.
Values: 1 = "Not at all", 2 = "Little", 3 = "Enough", 4 = "A lot", 5 = "Very Much".

Remarks for (RQ2) (see Table 4 and Fig. 10): **Mean**: The responses of the sample regarding students' learning achievement by using Toondoo in a technology-enhanced learning environment, show that they achieve "A lot" their learning goals **(Mean: 4.15)**, **Median**: Learners seem to be using "A lot" the Toondoo to achieve learning goals **(Median: 4.00)**, **Mode**: Most learners chose "Very much" **(Mode: 5.00)** in the use of the Toondoo to achieve learning goals, **Standard Deviation**: The response of the sample is from the average of 0.857 **(Std. Deviation: .857)**, **Skewness**: The sign of skewness is **negative (-.296)**. The distribution of responses is to the right and has its tail on the left. The distribution of responses show that learners use "A lot" the Toondoo to achieve learning goals, **Standard Error of Skewness**: The standard skewness error amounts to **24.1%**, **Kurtosis**: Kurtosis has a **negative sign (-1.583)** which makes the distribution a platycyte, with concentration of answers around the mean of "A lot", **Standard Error of Kurtosis**: The typical Kurtosis error is **47.8%**, **Range**: The answers cover the whole range from 1 to 5 and therefore the range remains **2.0**, **Percentiles**: Percentiles tell us that 25% of respondents say they use "Enough" the Toondoo to achieve learning goals, 50% of respondents say they use "A lot" the Toondoo to achieve learning goals and 75% of respondents say they use "Very much " the Toondoo to achieve learning goals.

Table 4. Students learning achievements with the use of Toondoo

Statistics		
STUDENTS_LEARNING_ACHIEVEMENT_BY_USING_TOONDOO		
N	Valid	100
	Missing	0
Mean		4,15
Median		4,00
Mode		5
Std. Deviation		,857
Skewness		-,296
Std. Error of Skewness		,241
Kurtosis		-1,583
Std. Error of Kurtosis		,478
Range		2
Percentiles	25	3,00
	50	4,00
	75	5,00

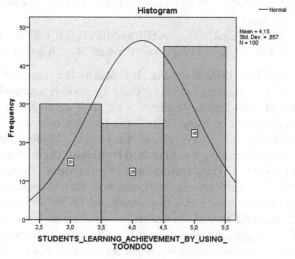

Fig. 10. Histogram

6 Conclusions

The main reasons for mature students to participate in a computer science course are motivation for learning. Inspired teachers are those who support students to take control of their learning and build new knowledge according to the previous knowledge and learning experiences. Pedagogical and technological approaches based on the basic guidelines of the TPACK framework, can promote learning and innovation in teaching. Edtech tools like Toondoo when properly implemented, can promote digital storytelling strategies in learning, and enhance students' motivation for learning. A combination of traditional teaching methods and technology-driven approaches seem as the best option to help students develop critical thinking and build new knowledge.

References

1. Angeli, C., Valanides, N.: Epistemological and methodological issues for the conceptualization, development, and assessment of ICT–TPCK: Advances in technological pedagogical content knowledge (TPCK). Comput. Educ. **52**(1), 154–168 (2009). https://doi.org/10.1016/j.compedu.2008.07.006
2. Baltaci-Goktalay, S., Ozdilek, Z.: Pre-service teachers' perceptions about web 2.0 technologies. Procedia - Social Behavioral Sci. **2**(2), 4737–4741 (2010). https://doi.org/10.1016/j.sbspro.2010.03.760
3. Bustamante, C., Moeller, A.J.: Exploring the unique case of a professional development program on web 2.0 technologies for teachers of German. CALICO J. **30**(1), 82–104 (2013). https://doi.org/10.1558/cj.30.1.82-104
4. DeGennaro, D.: Grounded in theory: immersing pre-service teachers in technology-mediated learning designs. Contemporary Issues in Technology and Teacher Education, 10(3), 338–359. Waynesville, NC USA: Society for Information Technology & Teacher Education. (2010). https://www.learntechlib.org/primary/p/32358/
5. Dewey, J.: Nationalizing education. J. Educ. **84**(16), 425–428 (1916)
6. Ghazal, S., Al-Samarraie, H., Wright, B.: A conceptualization of factors affecting collaborative knowledge building in online environments. Online Inf. Rev. **44**(1), 62–89 (2019). https://doi.org/10.1108/oir-02-2019-0046
7. Gooding, J.: Web 2.0: a vehicle for transforming education. Int. J. Inf. Commun. Technol. Educ. (IJICTE) **4**(2), 44–53 (2008)
8. Groff, J., Mouza, C.: A framework for addressing challenges to classroom technology use. AACE Review (formerly AACE Journal), **16**(1), 21–46. Waynesville, NC USA: Association for the Advancement of Computing in Education (AACE), (2008). https://www.learntechlib.org/primary/p/24421/
9. Huang, H.-M.: Toward constructivism for adult learners in online learning environments. Br. J. Edu. Technol. **33**(1), 27–37 (2002)
10. Marie, O., Robles, A.: Evaluating the use of toondoo for collaborative e-learning of selected pre-service teachers. Int. J. Modern Educ. Computer Sci. **9**(11), 25–32 (2017). https://doi.org/10.5815/ijmecs.2017.11.03
11. Mujallid, A.: Instructors' readiness to teach online: a review of TPACK standards in online professional development programmes in higher education. Int. J. Learning, Teaching Educ. Res. **20**(7), 135–150 (2021). https://doi.org/10.26803/ijlter.20.7.8
12. Ornstein, A.C., Hunkins, F.P.: Curriculum, Foundations, Principles and Issues. Allyn& Bacon, US (1998)

13. Ribeiro Silva, L., Pedro da Silva, A., Toda, A., Isotani, S.: Impact of teaching approaches to computational thinking on high school students: a systematic mapping. In: 2018 IEEE 18Th International Conference On Advanced Learning Technologies (ICALT), (2018). https://doi.org/10.1109/icalt.2018.00072

14. Robin, B.: Digital storytelling: a powerful technology tool for the 21st century classroom. Theory Into Practice **47**(3), 220–228 (2008). https://doi.org/10.1080/00405840802153916

15. Shabani, K., Khatib, M., Ebadi, S.: Vygotsky's zone of proximal development: instructional implications and teachers' professional development. Engl. Lang. Teach. **3**(4), 237–248 (2010)

16. Scardamalia, M., Bereiter, C.: Knowledge building. In Encyclopedia of Education, 2nd ed., pp. 1370–1373. Macmillan Reference, New York , USA (2003)

17. Schwebel, M., & Raph, J. (1973). Piaget in the classroom

18. Stephenson, P., Warwick, P.: Using concept cartoons to support progression in students' understanding of light. Phys. Educ. **37**(2), 135–141 (2002). https://doi.org/10.1088/0031-9120/37/2/306

19. Tahsaldar, M., Semaan, C.Y.: The impact of toondoo comics on undergraduate students taking creative writing and children literature courses at the lebanese university faculty of pedagogy. Int. J. Humanities Social Sci. **5**, 203–226 (2018)

20. Voogt, J., Fisser, P., Pareja Roblin, N., Tondeur, J., van Braak, J.: Technological pedagogical content knowledge - a review of the literature. J. Comput. Assist. Learn. **29**(2), 109–121 (2012). https://doi.org/10.1111/j.1365-2729.2012.00487.x

21. Goncalves dos Santos, C., Figueiredo, R., Nunes, M., Silva, I., Salgueiro, E., Batista Diniz da Silva, M.: Popularization of computer science: the production of educational subjectis for histories in comic books. In: 2018 XIII Latin American Conference On Learning Technologies (LACLO), (2018). https://doi.org/10.1109/laclo.2018.00078

22. Gürsoy, G.: Digital storytelling: developing 21st century skills in science education. European J. Educ. Res. **10**(1), 97–113 (2021). https://doi.org/10.12973/eu-jer.10.1.97

23. Özenç, M., Dursun, H., Şahin S.: The effect of activities developed with web 2.0 tools based on the 5E learning cycle model on the multiplication achievement of 4th graders. Participatory Educ. Res. **7**(3), 105–123 (2020). https://doi.org/10.17275/per.20.37.7.3

24. Ottenbreit-Leftwich, A., Liao, J., Sadik, O., Ertmer, P.: Evolution of teachers' technology integration knowledge, beliefs, and practices: how can we support beginning teachers use of technology? J. Res. Technol. Educ. **50**(4), 282–304 (2018). https://doi.org/10.1080/15391523.2018.1487350

25. Muamber, Y.: Impact of instruction with concept cartoons on students academic achievement in science lessons. Educ. Res. Rev. **15**(3), 95–103 (2020). https://doi.org/10.5897/err2020.3916

26. Triantafyllou, S.A.: Web 2.0 technologies in education. A brief study. GRIN Verlag, Munich (2014)

27. Triantafyllou, S.A.: The Effects of Constructivism Theory in the Environment of E-learning. GRIN Verlag, Munich (2013)

Image Processing

Fully Automated Lumen Segmentation Method and BVS Stent Struts Detection in OCT Images

Julia Duda[1,2]([✉])[iD], Izabela Cywińska[1,2][iD], and Elżbieta Pociask[1,2][iD]

[1] Department of Biocybernetics and Biomedical Engineering, AGH University of Science and Technology, Mickiewicza 30 Av., 30-059 Krakow, Poland
{juliaduda,cywinska}@student.agh.edu.pl, elzbieta.pociask@agh.edu.pl
[2] Regional Specialist Hospital, Research and Development Center, 51-124 Wroclaw, Poland

Abstract. Optical coherence tomography is a medical imaging tool that produces high-resolution images of the coronary vessels. Currently, the main step leading to the correct choice of stents used in the treatment of atherosclerotic lesions is the correct segmentation of the vessel lumen. In this article, we present a method for fully automatic vessel lumen segmentation and detection of bioresorbable stents in OCT images. This algorithm's key steps include preprocessing, which reduces noise and artifacts in images, transformation to polar and Cartesian coordinates and the segmentation method. The algorithm was validated and compared with manual segmentation. Bland-Altman's plots were made to evaluate the agreement between the two measurement methods. A confusion matrix was created to statistically evaluate the accuracy of the method for detecting bioresorbable stents.

Keywords: Lumen segmentation · BVS stent strut detection · OCT images · OCT

1 Introduction

Coronary artery disease is the most common cardiovascular disease [1,2]. It occurs as a result of myocardial ischemia, which is a consequence of atherosclerosis of the coronary arteries. Obstruction of the vessel lumen is performed by implanting stents. A stent is a cylinder-shaped vascular prosthesis with a mesh structure. They are usually made of steel or a chromium-cobalt alloy [3]. Stents prevent the vessel from collapsing and ensure a continuous blood flow. There are three generations of stents. The first is metal stents, called BMS. The second is drug-eluting stents, called DES. These are used to release drugs. The third generation is bioresorbable stents - BVS, these are self-absorbable and biodegradable, and their breakdown products occur naturally in the body [4]. They work in the same way as traditional stents, but over the time stents are absorbed by the endothelium of the treated vessel. It takes decades for BVS stents to fully resorb.

H. Florez and H. Gomez (Eds.): ICAI 2022, CCIS 1643, pp. 353–367, 2022.
https://doi.org/10.1007/978-3-031-19647-8_25

Resorption is necessary for full restoration of vessel structure and function. The ABSORB stent from Abbott Vascular (Santa Clara, CA, USA) is the best known and most advanced bioresorbable stent technology available and tested. These stents release the antiproliferative drug everolimus. They are absorbed after two years and then enable the return of vasomotor function in the treated segments [5,6].

To properly match a stent to a vessel, the vessel's lumen must be detected. By detecting the lumen of the vessel, the maximum and minimum diameter of the vessel can be calculated, and the maximum stenosis of the artery can be found. Determining the diameter of the vessel's lumen allows for the selection of a suitable type of stent. The process of vessel lumen detection is a key point leading to the quantitative analysis of arterial morphology. Unfortunately, it brings many difficulties due to artifact presence in the images such as the presence of blood clots, bifurcations and irregular surface morphology of the vessel lumen [7]. During the detection of the vessel lumen, the analysis should be performed based on the mentioned morphological features [8].

In vivo assessment of stent apposition/malapposition and neointima coverage is possible using intravascular optical coherence tomography (OCT) with micron-scale resolution [9]. Optical coherence tomography is an imaging method that uses infrared light to obtain images of tissue. This phenomenon is based on the interference between the signal coming from the test object and the reference signal. It consists of emitting a beam of infrared light inside the vessel and obtaining images from the information contained in the returning beam. IVOCT aids physicians in detecting and measuring stent apposition and neointimal coverage of coronary stents, both are linked to stent thrombosis. However, with such a huge number of struts from IVOCT, quantitative analysis may only be feasible if strut detection is automated. Even with high-resolution IVOCT usage, detecting BVS is difficult due to the interference of blood artifact and the ambiguity of stent position and size [10].

Structure of the Work. This paper is organized in 5 sections as follows: Sect. 1 presents the motivation of this work and the review of the state of art in the area of lumen segmentation and BVS stent struts detection. In Sect. 2 we describe materials and methodology according to which we proceeded. In the 3rd section we present obtained results along with statistical analysis. Discussion of the results is included in Sect. 4. The 5th section is conclusions and it closes the paper.

State of the Art. The optimal approach for detecting bioresorbable stents automatically is being explored. For example, Lu et al. [11] developed a two framework for struts analysis: first, the Adaboost detector was used to detect struts, and then dynamic programming (DP) was used to segment them. In their method detection and segmentation is correctly in 87.7% while showing 18.6% false positives. This method failed to detect struts that were irregularly shaped, as well as shadows and blood artifacts which are frequently misidentified as struts. On the other hand S. Tsantis et al. [12] proposed a method to identify lumen using Markov random field model. The strut positions of stents were determined by including each strut wavelet response across scales into a feature extraction and classification approach to improve strut position recognition. Proposed technique had high accuracy however the calculation time was long. In C. Huang et al. [13] the process of segmentation the contours of BVS stent struts is made using U-Net network. They added convolutional attention layer and dilated convolution module, and finally used weakly supervised learning strategy to further enhance performance. X. Qin et al. [14] proposed segmentation of a bioresorbable stent strut based on finding its four corners. AdaBoost classifier was used to detect the struts, after which it was possible to detect the four corners of each element. This method achived an average Dice's coefficient of 0.82 for struts segmentation areas.

Automatic lumen contour detection is a challenging task in OCT images that contain guiding shadows, motion artifacts, bifurcations, or undiluted blood inside the vessel. Different OCT technologies, image textures, diffuse and complex lesions all have a significant impact on segmentation and feature extraction results. E. Pociask et al. [16] present a similar method for detecting the vessel lumen, although they do not consider BVS stent struts detection. The most difficult challenge in detecting BVS is that their structure changes over time, so the most difficult problem in detecting them is where they are incomplete, geometrically irregular or embedded in the vessel lumen, as well as fractures within the struts.

Taking into consideration all of above mentioned methods, we propose a fully automated method to segment the lumen area in run OCT pullbacks. We included in analysis every image frame, even the frames with artifacts. Moreover we propose an automated technique to detect BVS stent struts. Poor-quality photos as well as images with sick arteries and bifurcations can be analyzed with our method.

2   Materials and Methods

The proposed algorithm for vessel lumen segmentation and bioresorbable stent struts detection consists of four main steps. The first one is preprocessing: enhancement of the image and elimination of artifacts. Then lumen segmentation and contour drawing. The final step is to find the edges of the stents struts and outline them. The software which has been used for image analysis is Python 3.9.10 64-bit with Python libaries: NumPy, Matplotlib, OpenCV, SciPy and Skimage.

2.1   Database Specification

Images used in this study were acquired by the FD-OCT system (C7-XR system OCT Intravascular Imaging System, Westford, MA) and two kinds of imaging catheters: the C7 Dragonfly and Dragonfly OPTIS catheter with automatic pull-back, drive motor optical controller. The analyzed data were obtained with the pullback speed of 20 mm/s and 18 mm/s, respectively. The images were saved in DICOM format. The data came from different patients and analysis was performed on 457 frames showing a cross-section of the coronary artery with bioresorbable stents struts present. All images, including those highlighting bifurcations and artifacts, were analyzed. Exemplary frame showing the cross-section of the coronary artery used in this work is shown in the Fig. 1.

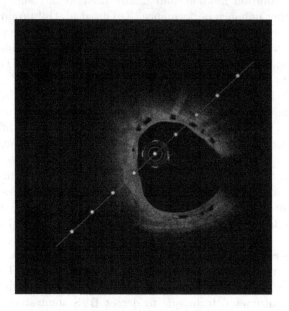

Fig. 1. OCT image of the vessel

2.2   BVS Stent Detection

OCT Image Preprocessing. An RGB image was loaded and then converted to grayscale. Then histogram equalization was performed using the CLAHE (Contrast Limited Adaptive Histogram Equalization) method which improves contrast of the image. Next step was image thresholding using OTSU method where threshold value is determined automatically. It is based on the histogram of the image and works globally. It is based on minimizing the weighted sum of the variance of two classes, which are the background and the object.

After OTSU thresholding there was an area opening process performed. That is the filter that removes from a binary image the components with area smaller than a parameter λ. Here the value was set to 64. A 3×3 mask was applied to the binary image to act as a median filter, which is a nonlinear filter that operates by selecting the median value of an ascendingly ordered sequence of pixel brightness values of the processed point and its surroundings. It is a filter used to remove noise from an image [15].

In order to avoid detecting stents struts in areas with noise and shadows we created the function that calculated the center of mass of the image and created a circle outside the vessel. In this way, the area of interest was mapped and has been analyzed. This action guaranteed the elimination of most false positives stents struts.

Struts Detection. After preprocessing stage thanks to the flood_fill Python function the values of neighbour pixels were changed to the value equal to 1. As a result, only black areas are visible in the image, which visualize stents struts. Then small holes, which are smaller than the set threshold value are being removed from image. Final step is Canny edge detection, which leaves just the outlined stents on the image.

2.3   Lumen Segmentation

OCT Image Preprocessing. The image is converted to grayscale, then CLAHE histogram equalization is applied to improve contrast of the image. Next step is to perform the binarization of the image using OTSU threshold. After binarization, the polar transform is applied [16]. The circular shape of the coronary artery shown in a cross-sectional image can be converted to a straightened structure with this transformation. Knowing the diameter of the DragonFly catheter(for this type of catheter the diameter is equal to 2 mm) and the resolution of the image, it is possible to remove a portion of the image that shows a shadow coming from the catheter, which is classified as artifact. Insufficiently flushed blood from the vessel may also affect the correct segmentation of the vessel lumen. The noise coming from the blood can be classified as tissue, which will affect the correct calculation of the vessel lumen area. A median filter with a mask size of 5×5 was then applied to the image to remove any small noise and speckles.

Lumen Segmentation and Contour Drawing. The correct segmentation of the vessel lumen is the main point for the subsequent analysis of OCT images including the detection of bioresorbable stents [17]. Yet, automatic analysis of bioresorbable structures is difficult to perform and apply due to the complexity of the images.

In the polar coordinate image, a function called findContours provided by OpenCV library was used to find the contours so that only the outline of the vessel was obtained. This allowed the most protruding ends of the vessel to be found, then marked at each end and then combined. As a result of performing this operation, the gap that was present in the image was eliminated and the entire vessel is continuous, allowing the shape of the entire vessel to be reconstructed when returning to Cartesian coordinates.

The final step was to return to Cartesian coordinates and detect the edge of the vessel lumen using Canny's algorithm. After all the above operations were performed, the maximum diameter, minimum lumen diameter and lumen area were calculated.

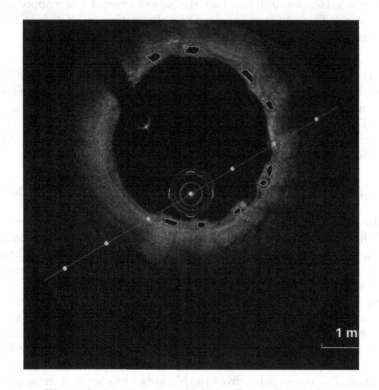

Fig. 2. Correct detection of stent struts on OCT image

3   Results

BVS Stent Struts Detection. Confusion Matrix was used to analyze the results - the data were defined as positive and negative and were subjected to classification, which appropriately assigned them to the predicted positive class (true positive) or the predicted negative class (true negative). This made it possible to calculate the precision, sensitivity and accuracy of the algorithm.

The algorithm was tested on 1726 images (split into 5 folders) from different patients of the Regional Specialist Hospital in Wroclaw. Four folders contained images of vessels into which stents struts had been implanted several months before the OCT procedure. The older the stents are, the more difficult it is to perform correct detection because their contours are less visible and more over-grown by the tissue. One folder contained images that showed newly implanted

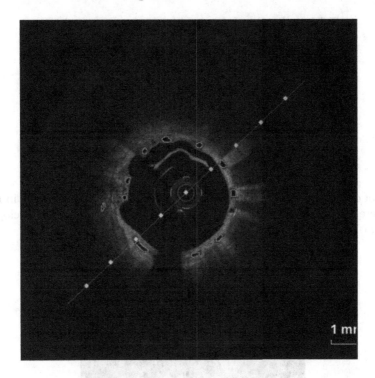

Fig. 3. Wrong detection of stent struts on OCT image

stents, but the quality of these images was poor and the visibility of the stents struts had very faint outlines of contours. 428 of these images showed a cross-section of the vessel on which the stents struts were visible. The exact number of stents visible on the image was determined by the expert. Correctly detected stents struts were marked and they are shown in Fig. 2. On the other hand, in some cases the proposed algorithm detects stent struts wrongly due to noise visible in the OCT images. Incorrect detection is shown in Fig. 3. On the left side of the image algorithm detected one strut inaccurately. The results obtained from the proposed algorithm were compared with those obtained by the expert and comparison results are shown in Table 1 as a precision, sensitivity and accuracy.

The average precision of the algorithm is 86.42%. Precision is the rate of compliance between two measurement methods. The sensitivity remains at 70.36%. It is the ability of the algorithm to correctly detect the stent strut. The accuracy is equal to 70.30%. It is the degree of exactness of a measurement compared to the expected or desired value. In our case the desired value was the value obtained by the Expert. The percentage of false positives for precision over 86% is about 14%.

Lumen Detection. The validation of the described lumen segmentation method has been performed on 234 intravascular optical koherence tomography

Table 1. Results of the algorithm performance analysis

Folder	Precision [%]	Sensivity [%]	Accuracy [%]
1	78.32	83.05	82.75
2	86.40	75.20	75.20
3	89.74	77.04	77.04
4	84.74	39.00	39.00
5	92.44	71.23	71.23

images of different patients. The result of lumen segmentation is shown in Fig. 3. Data were provided by Regional Specialist Hospital, Research and Development Center in Wroclaw, Poland.

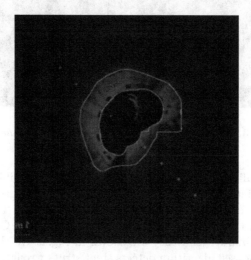

Fig. 4. Result of the described lumen segmentation algorithm

Statistical Analysis. Data for statistical analysis are acquired using our algorithm, ground truth mask and commercially available system. Manual segmentation of vessel's lumen was performed by analyst. The first and third quartiles of continuous parameters were reported as mean and median (Q1: 25%; Q3: 75%). To evaluate the agreement made between two measurement methods, the Bland-Altman analysis was performed. It is the method based on the quantification of agreement between two quantitative measurements through the use of mean difference analysis and the construction of limits of agreement.

Validation of Automated Lumen Segmentation. In order to validate proposed method we compare three segmentation methods: our algorithm, commercially available system - System I and ground truth mask. The following parameters were examined for each of the described methods: lumen area, mean lumen diameter, minimal lumen diameter and maximal lumen diameter and are summarized in Table 2.

Table 2. Calculated parameters for each of analyzed methods

	Proposed method mean	System I mean	Ground truth mean
Lumen area [mm^2]	7.60 ± 2.36	7.29 ± 2.47	7.54 ± 2.30
Mean lumen diameter [mm]	3.13 ± 0.46	3.03 ± 0.48	3.07 ± 0.44
Minimal lumen diameter [mm]	2.85 ± 0.48	2.72 ± 0.54	2.78 ± 0.51
Maximal lumen diameter [mm]	3.40 ± 0.46	3.29 ± 0.46	3.35 ± 0.41

The results of the assessed parameters are collected in Table 2 and presented by the Bland-Altman plots.

Table 3. Statistical comparison of the parameters between our methodology and manual analyses by analyst (ground truth).

	Proposed method mean	Manual analysis mean	Proposed method median (IQR)	Manual analysis median (IQR)
Lumen area [mm^2]	7.60±2.36	7.54±2.30	7.25 (6.00–8.65)	7.17 (6.16–8.56)
Mean lumen diameter [mm]	3.13±0.46	3.07±0.44	3.08 (2.83–3.35)	3.02 (2.77–3.07)
Minimal lumen diameter [mm]	2.85±0.48	2.78±0.51	2.80 (2.53–3.11)	2.69 (2.46–3.07)
Maximal lumen diameter [mm]	3.40±0.46	3.35±0.41	3.37 (3.12–3.59)	3.33 (3.07–3.54)

Table 4. Statistical comparison of the parameters between our methodology and System I.

	Proposed method mean	Manual analysis mean	Proposed method median (IQR)	Manual analysis median (IQR)
Lumen area [mm^2]	7.60±2.36	7.29±2.47	7.25 (6.00–8.65)	6.76 (5.81–15.23)
Mean lumen diameter [mm]	3.13±0.46	3.03±0.48	3.08 (2.83–3.35)	2.92 (2.75–3.30)
Minimal lumen diameter [mm]	2.85±0.48	2.72±0.54	2.80 (2.53–3.11)	2.66 (2.36–3.05)
Maximal lumen diameter [mm]	3.40±0.46	3.29±0.46	3.37 (3.12–3.59)	3.27 (3.01–3.51)

In Table 3 are visible mean values with standard deviation and median values with IQR(interquartile range) calculated for: vessel lumen area, mean, minimum and maximum vessel lumen diameter for the two measurement methods, which are the proposed method and the manual analysis performed by the expert. In Table 4 is shown comparison between our proposed method and System's I method.

4   Discussion of the Results

The best results for stent struts detection were obtained for folder 5, the precision reached 92.44% with a sensitivity and accuracy of over 72%. The images from this folder (123 images) had the best quality, the shape of the vessel in most cases was regular and resembled a circle, which influenced the best result.

Due to low quality images caused by a heavily attenuated signal the data in folder 4 has the lowest accuracy. The objects in the images were difficult to distinguish so even Expert had difficulty in identifying the number of stents struts. The outlines of the stents were blurred and there were shadow interferences in the image.

Excluding the results from the analysis of data in folder 4 (68 images) due to the low quality of the images, the obtained analysis parameters increase. Low quality of the image is interpreted as absence of stents' struts contours, image noise and not well-diluted blood from the vessel. Precision increases to 86.75%, sensitivity is 76.63% and accuracy is equal to 76.56%.

The Bland-Altman plot or the difference plot, is a graphical method to compare two measurements techniques. In this graphical method the differences between the two techniques are plotted against the averages of the two techniques [18]. Horizontal lines are drawn at the mean difference, and at the limits of agreement, which are defined as the mean difference plus and minus 1.96 times the standard deviation of the differences.

The Bland-Altman plots showed a significant positive correlation between our method and the System I (Fig. 5–8). The solid line representing the mean difference between the first and second measurements and the dashed lines representing 1.96 standard deviation. The majority of the points are plotted between the solid line (mean difference) and the dashed line which indicates high compliance.

In order to verify the correctness of the values obtained, they were compared with the results obtained from the manual and automatic analysis. From the data contained in Tables 2–4 it can be concluded that the methods are consistent with each other and the results are comparable over the entire range. The results obtained by the proposed algorithm are more similar to the manual analysis performed by the analyst than to the results obtained after the automated analysis by System I.

The mean value of the vessel lumen area for the automated analysis by the algorithm developed in the project was 7.60 mm^2 and for the manual analysis it was 7.54 mm^2. The mean value of the minimum diameter that was obtained was 2.85 mm, and for the manual analysis it was 2.78 mm. The maximum diameter value was 3.40 mm, where for the analysis performed by the analyst it was 3.35 mm. This shows that the created algorithm works very well on a large number of images. It copes with images that show bifurcations and unwashed blood from the vessel. The effectiveness of the developed method for the area of the vessel lumen was 99% and for the average diameter 98%.

Bland-Altman plots for our method and manual analysis are shown below in the 9–12 figures and they also show high correlation between these two measurement methods.

Bland-Altman diagrams for our method and commercially available system are shown below.

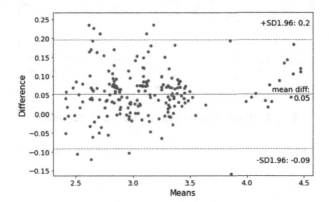

Fig. 5. Bland-Altman plot for mean diameter

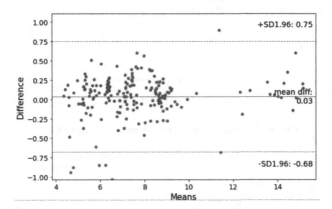

Fig. 6. Bland-Altman plot for lumen area

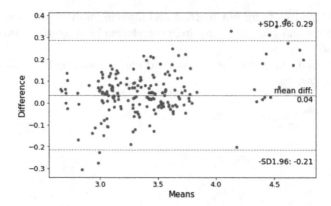

Fig. 7. Bland-Altman plot for maximal diameter

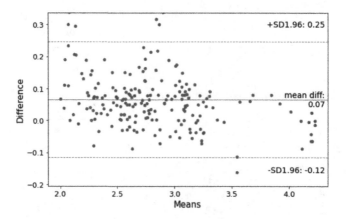

Fig. 8. Bland-Altman plot for minimal diameter

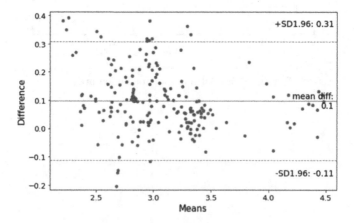

Fig. 9. Bland-Altman plot for mean diameter

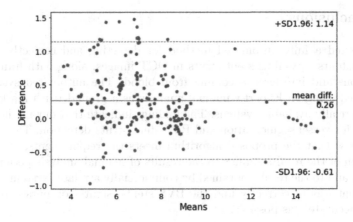

Fig. 10. Bland-Altman plot for lumen area

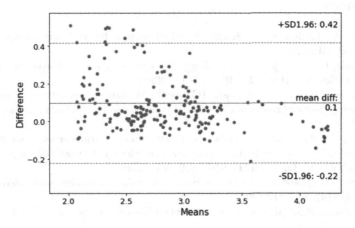

Fig. 11. Bland-Altman plot for maximal diameter

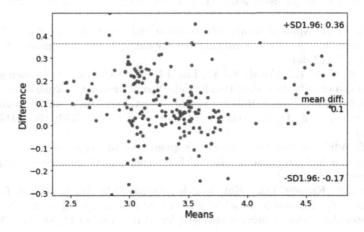

Fig. 12. Bland-Altman plot for minimal diameter

5 Conclusions

We presented a fully automated method for detecting and correctly drawing lumen contours as well as stent struts in OCT images, along with frames with bifurcations and interference coming from blood. The automated system has been tested using an Expert's manual analysis as a ground truth mask as well as commercially available systems. The findings indicate that our method could be useful for vessel segmentation and BVS stent struts detection. The obtained results show that the proposed algorithm meets the requirements, which were acquisition of the results similar to the results of manual analysis performed by an expert and to the results obtained by commercially available system. Another requirement was to correctly find the BVS stents' struts contours and outline them as accurately as possible.

References

1. Brown, J., Gerhardt, T., Kwon, E.: Risk factors for coronary artery disease. Accessed 5 Jun 2021
2. Okrainec, K., Banerjee, D., Eisenberg, M.: Coronary artery disease in the developing world. Am. Heart J. **148**(1), 7–15 (2004)
3. Paszenda, Z.: Politechnika Śląska (Gliwice) i Wydawnictwo, "Stenty w kardiologii interwencyjnej: wybrane zagadnienia". Wydawnictwo Politechniki Śląskiej, Gliwice (2013)
4. Ormiston, J.A., et al.: A bioabsorbable everolimus-elutingcoronary stent system for patients with single de-novo coronary artery lesions (AB-SORB): a prospective open-label trial. Lancet **371**(9616), 899–907 (2008)
5. Milewski, K., Tajstra, M.: Stenty bioresorbowalne—aktualny stan wiedzy. Folia Cardiol. **7**(4), 213–219 (2012)
6. Lobodzinski, S.S.: Bioabsorbowalne stenty wieńcowe. Folia Cardiol. **4**(4), 247–250 (2009)
7. Yihui, C., et al.: Automatic lumen segmentation in intravascular optical coherence tomography images using level set. Comput. Math. Methods Med. **2017**, 11 p. (2017)
8. Lu, H., et al.: Application and evaluation of highly automated software for comprehensive stent analysis in intravascular optical coherence tomography. Sci. Rep. **10**(1), 1–13 (2020)
9. Yang, S., Yoon, H.J., Yazdi, S.J.M., Lee, J.H.: A novel automated lumen segmentation and classification algorithm for detection of irregular protrusion after stents deployment. Int. J. Med. Robot. Comput. Assist. Surg. **16**(1), e2033 (2020)
10. Huang, D., et al.: Optical coherence tomography. Science **254**(5035), 1178–1181 (1991)
11. Lu, Y.: Adaboost-based detection and segmentation of bioresorbable vascular scaffolds struts in IVOCT images. In: IEEE International Conference on Image Processing (ICIP) (2017)
12. Tsantis, S., Kagadis, G.C., Katsanos, K., Karnabatidis, D., Bourantas, G., Nikiforidis, G.C.: Automatic vessel lumen segmentation and stent strut detection in intravascular optical coherence tomography. Med. Phys. **39**(1), 503–513 (2012)

13. Huang, C., Zhang, G., Lu, Y., Lan, Y., Chen, S., Guo, S.: Automatic segmentation of bioabsorbable vascular stents in Intravascular optical coherence images using weakly supervised attention network. Future Gener. Comput. Syst. **114**, 427–434 (2021)
14. Qin, X., et al.: Corner detection based automatic segmentation of bioresorbable vascular scaffold struts in IVOCT images (2018)
15. Tadeusiewicz, R., Korohoda, P.: Komputerowa analiza i przetwarzanie obrazów. Wydawnictwo Fundacji Postępu Telekomunikacji, Kraków (1997)
16. Pociask, E., Malinowski, K.P., Ślęzak, M., Jaworek-Korjakowska, J., Wojakowski, W., Roleder, T.: Fully automated lumen segmentation method for intracoronary-optical coherence tomography. Image Segmentation Techniques for HealthcareSystems (2018)
17. Wang, A., et al.: Automatic detection of bioresorbable vascular scaffold struts in intravascular optical coherence tomography pullback runs. Biomed. Opt. Express **5**(10), 3589–3602 (2014)
18. Giavarina, D.: Understanding Bland Altman analysis. Biochem. Med. **25**(2), 141–51 (2015)

Predictive Modeling Toward the Design of a Forensic Decision Support System Using Cheiloscopy for Identification from Lip Prints

Agustin Sabelli⬤, Parag Chatterjee$^{(\boxtimes)}$ ⬤, and María F. Pollo-Cattaneo⬤

Grupo de Estudio en Metodologías de Ingeniería de Software (GEMIS), Universidad Tecnológica Nacional Facultad Regional Buenos Aires, Buenos Aires, Argentina
paragc@ieee.org

Abstract. Cheiloscopy is a technique of forensic investigation with the purpose of identifying humans based on their lip prints. Analyzing the lip prints in detail, detailed characteristics could be deciphered, establishing a unique link with a specific person, thus helping in identification in persons using lip prints. Machine learning has significant applications in this forensic identification process with cheiloscopy, spanning from data collection to intelligent analysis. In this work, a design for a forensic decision support system has been proposed, aimed at identification of persons in terms of their biological sex based on cheiloscopy. In this respect, a generalized architecture for the implementation of cheiloscopy has been presented, along with the predictive modeling with lip prints using supervised algorithms, which has illustrated reasonable accuracy in identifying persons in terms of their biological sex.

Keywords: Forensic decision support system · Image processing · Cheiloscopy · Machine learning · Predictive modeling · Architecture · Lip prints

1 Introduction

Forensic identification is an application of forensic science and technology to identify specific objects from the trace evidence they leave, often at a crime scene or the scene of an accident. Modern forensic science deals with several identification techniques where digital tools play a pivotal role. Identification methods through anthropometry, fingerprints, sex determination, age estimation, measurement of height, and differentiation by blood groups, DNA and odontology are traditionally used in forensics. In this respect, biometrics play a fundamental role. Biometrics is a fundamental verification mechanism that identifies individuals based on their physiological and behavioral features. These biometric expansions are easily observable in different forensic identification areas, e.g., face, fingerprint, iris, voice, handwriting, etc. The effectiveness of biometrics system lies in different recognition processes which include feature extraction, feature robustness and feature matching. However, traditional methods face several challenges like insufficiency of available evidence, concealment of identity from traditional models, time consumption, lack of standardization and interoperability [1].

H. Florez and H. Gomez (Eds.): ICAI 2022, CCIS 1643, pp. 368–377, 2022.
https://doi.org/10.1007/978-3-031-19647-8_26

In this respect, newer techniques are being considered, coupled with the power of data science. Cheiloscopy is the forensic investigation technique dealing with identification of humans based on lip traces [6–9]. Several algorithms like top-hat transform, vote counting, time warping, and Hough transform are efficient methods to automate the process of identification from lip prints based on cheiloscopy [12]. However, recent years have seen a significant scope in this area due to lack of investigation on significant information like the sex or age apart from the identity [2, 3].

This work is aimed at designing the architecture for a Forensic Decision Support System based on cheiloscopy, using predictive modeling through machine learning. It focuses on the use of supervised learning algorithms with the aim of identifying a person in terms of their biological sex using their lip prints, illustrated through a cohort of 43 subjects, performing predictive analysis on 40 labial features for forensic identification. Subsequently, an architecture for a forensic decision support system implementing identification from cheiloscopic techniques is presented in this work.

2 Materials and Methods—Predictive Modeling and Architecture for Forensic Decision Support System

In the domain of biometrics, machine learning has illustrated its capability in the betterment of precision in the identification process [4, 9]. Biometric features collected at the first instance are not essentially the same as the subsequent samples. The use of machine learning provides a significant support in this respect. A biometric system aiming to predict the identifying information of a person based on a biometric sample automatically or check if it links to an existing information in the database usually follows the following structure (Fig. 1).

Fig. 1. Generalized pipeline of the system for biometric authentication

This study consists of 43 subjects (26 females and 17 males). The input data of lip impressions has been collected from the subjects by pressing their lips colored with lipstick against a paper.

In this respect, a generalized architecture (Fig. 2) has been designed using the Amazon Web Services (AWS) platform, aimed at a Forensic Decision Support System based on cheiloscopy.

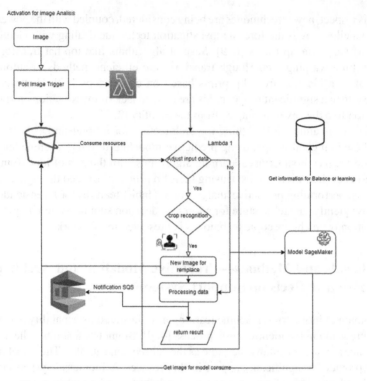

Fig. 2. Model for forensic decision support system using cheiloscopy

The architecture is based on AWS tools which are designed to follow a streamlined flow of the entire process from collection of images to solving the decision support tasks in an agile way. The principal modules of the designed architecture are as follows:

Input Image
This image is sent through a post request to an API Gateway which consists of communication with lambdas starting the analysis process. The image is uploaded to S3 prior to executing Lambda 1.

Lambda 1 (image processing):
This lambda consists of input values which will allow delimiting the treatment processes for the image to be analyzed. These values will be defined to indicate that the loaded image requires a specific crop, in which case it will generate the following processes:

a. The image will use the recognition tool generating a crop in the necessary area.
b. The resulting image will be uploaded to S3 to continue the analysis process.

Sagemaker

In case the image does not require a treatment, the execution of the processing and consumption of Sagemaker will be direct.

Modeling in SageMaker

The implementation of the model in SageMaker will allow consumption to be more distributed and its management more uniform in terms of version management. The model will receive as input the URL parameters where it must obtain the image to be processed, which generates a consumption to S3.

The model consumes its dataset from the database indicated in the architecture to balance the information and return a result to the lambda either by listening to a record in the database or as a direct response. The response to the SageMaker process obtained in the lambda will execute two processes, both the return of the response to the frontend through the API gateway and, if necessary, a notification via Amazon Simple Queue Service (SQS).

The flow diagram (Fig. 3) consists of AWS tools designed to speed up and improve the extraction and insertion of information in the consumption dataset of the model. The process consists of loading an image through the frontend which will proceed to be processed through lambdas.

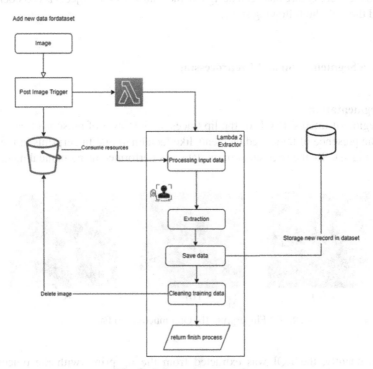

Fig. 3. Information extraction

Image upload: The upload of the image to an S3 will generate an execution of a lambda process which will give rise to the start of the process in the indicated lambda.

Lambda: Input information processing consists of receiving initial parameters to support the lambda to identify the location of the necessary image and previous processes that require treatment, such as formatting or renaming, as well as information added to specify the information itself, to extract, if necessary, subsequently.

Extraction: The extraction process will consist of the method or script used for the local extraction of information of the training image, either with a direct implementation or an alternative process to the lambda.

Storage of information: The saving of the information resulting from the previous process will be stored in the dataset of information in the database.

Cleaning: It is proposed to perform the deletion of the image uploaded to S3 for extraction, this to maintain a cleaner and more sustainable environment.

Completion notification: The lambda process will return a result, if necessary, through the API gateway to the frontend which indicate that the process was successful.

Once the architecture has been designed, the dataset of 43 subjects is considered and modeled through the following steps.

2.1 Data Segmentation and Preprocessing

Data Segmentation
In the region of interest (ROI) of the lip traces, a high level of noise is often common due to the presence of undesired elements like facial hair and fingerprints in the image sample (Fig. 4). So, the segmentation of data was performed using manual methods.

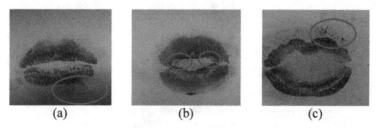

(a)   (b)   (c)

Fig. 4. (a) Fingerprint. (b) Oral mucosa. (c) Facial hair.

Subsequently, the ROI was extracted from the lip prints with the objective of separating the lower lip from the upper lip (Fig. 5).

Fig. 5. Lip prints ROI

Once the segmentation has been performed, the prints of the upper and lower lip were stored as separate files since they were treated differently by the next level of the modeling process based on whether it is an upper or lower lip.

Preprocessing
Since the algorithm for feature selection primarily considers the lower lip traces, the images of the upper lips were vertically flipped, whereas the images of lower lip traces were kept intact.

The transparent pixels (with a zero value for alpha channel) were replaced by white colored pixels (i.e. [255, 255, 255, 0] in [R, G, B, A] notation). Following that, the images have been aligned horizontally and converted to grayscale. For the horizontal alignment, the extremities and corners of the lip prints were pointed, to calculate the anchor point (the middle spot in between the corners) for the horizontal rotation (Fig. 6).

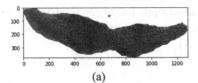
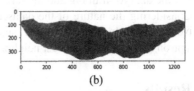

Fig. 6. (a) The corners and anchor points of the lip print. (b) Horizontal alignment of the lip print.

Following that, the minimum bounding rectangle enclosing the lip print has been calculated, and the image is cropped, taking this rectangle into account. Afterwards, the image was resized to establish a common size for all the prints, performing normalization (1500x500 pixels). Finally, the image was binarized (Fig. 7).

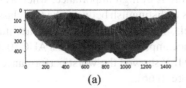
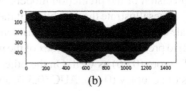

Fig. 7. (a) Removal of white space and normalization. (b) Binarized lip print.

2.2 Feature Selection

For all the lip prints of the sample set, the same set of biometric features have been determined. Each set of lip print-based features are denoted as $f_n = [f_1, ..., f_n]$ (Table 1). For using in the classification algorithms, 40 features in each side of the lips have been extracted, counting to 80 features in total for each whole lip trace, following which standardization have been performed on the features.

2.3 Classification

The first phase of feature extraction produced a substantially high number of features, leading to the need of dimensionality reduction, to preserve only the relevant ones, for a smooth modeling procedure. The dimensionality reduction was performed using Extra Tree Classifiers, also called as Extremely Randomized Trees, which is a type of ensemble learning technique consisting of many decision trees and the prediction of each tree is considered to reach the final decision. In this classifier, random selection is performed on all the features and splits, and Gini importance is used to measure the relevance of a feature. Consequently, the features are ordered in descending order of this value to fit the high-dimensional data into a low-dimensional space, selecting the top k-features (43) from the original set of 80 features. Following that, the dataset was prepared for the modeling using supervised algorithms, considering that the data is labeled, and the objective is to predict or classify the observations. The dataset was split into test and train data after different sequences of train-test data through cross-validation, finalizing 80% of the data for training and the remaining 20% for testing.

Considering the nature of the dataset, five algorithms have been used for the predictive analysis—logistic regression, support vector machine, naïve bayes, multilayer perceptron (MLP), and k-nearest neighbors (kNN).

3 Results

The results and the respective performance metrics for the classification algorithms are shown in Table 2. In each case, the optimal combination of features has been mentioned.

Across the different classifiers, the optimal number of features varies; however, an average of 25 features have been considered from the original 80 features.

Among the considered metrics, the accuracy of the classification algorithms illustrates the correctness of the algorithm classifying a data point. To analyze the recall and precision of the prediction models, the f1 score is of high importance, whereas the AUC values illustrate the capability of the models to distinguish between the two classes (female or male). Among all the considered models, k-NN provided the highest accuracy (0.82) to predict the biological sex of the person, accompanied by the highest AUC (0.80) and f1 score (0.86) as well. On the other hand, MLP showed the worst performance in terms of accuracy (0.65), AUC (0.59), and f1 score (0.66).

Table 1. Key aspects of the lip print-based features

#	Measurement metric	Feature	Visual illustration
(a)	Perimeter	$f_1 = [p]$	
(b)	Area	$f_2 = [a]$	
(c)	Solidity	$f_3 = [s]$	
(d)	Equivalent diameter	$f_4 = [ed]$	
(e)	Extent	$f_4 = [ex]$	
(f)	Main peaks and valley of the vertical projection	$f_5 = [p_1, v_1, p_2]$	
(g)	Maximum length of the horizontal projection	$f_6 = [l]$	
(h)	The distance to the outer edges from the left corner [80°, 50°, 30°, 20°, 10° and 2°]	$f_7 = [ld_1, ld_2, ld_3, ld_4, ld_5, ld_6]$	
(i)	Distance to the outer edges from the right corner [80°, 50°, 30°, 20°, 10° and 2°]	$f_8 = [rd_1, rd_2, rd_3, rd_4, rd_5, rd_6]$	
(j)	Distance to the outer edges from the upper center [2°, 10°, 30°, 60°, 90°, 120°, 150°, 170° and 178°]	$f_9 = [cd_1, cd_2, cd_3, cd_4, cd_5, cd_6, cd_7, cd_8, cd_9]$	
(k)	Distance to the inner edges from the upper center [2°, 10°, 30°, 60°, 90°, 120°, 150°, 170° and 178°]	$f_{10} = [id_1, id_2, id_3, id_4, id_5, id_6, id_7, id_8, id_9]$	
(l)	Length of the skeletonized lip print	$f_{11} = [sk]$	

Table 2. Performance metrics of the supervised models

Classifier	# Features	Accuracy	f1 score	AUC
kNN	28	0.82	0.86	0.80
Logistic Regression	23	0.79	0.80	0.75
Naïve Bayes	24	0.77	0.81	0.77
Support vector machine	25	0.70	0.77	0.78
MLP	25	0.65	0.66	0.59

4 Conclusions

This work illustrates the architectural design of a forensic decision support system through predictive modeling with supervised algorithms, aiming at identifying the biological sex of a person using their lip prints. Based on the original dataset comprising of lip prints and using five machine learning models, k-NN provided the highest performance, with all the models providing reasonably good accuracy in determining the biological sex of a person using their lip traces. However, within the forensic decision support system, the key challenge is the image segmentation module, since the presence of noise and unwanted elements in the image samples led to manual preprocessing for basic cleaning and extraction of the ROI. With respect to the supervised algorithms, scarcity of image samples was a challenge, in terms of training and test-data. Another significant challenge has been the area of feature selection for the classification models, considering the huge number of features associated with the sample, which was resolved using a hyperparameter tuning function [5].

This work provides a generalized structure for the cheiloscopy-based forensic decision support system, along with a specific module for predictive modeling. On one hand, it provides an integral structure to receive the samples, preprocess and finally predict the identifying attributes of the subjects. On the other hand, it opens the pathwat to reengineer the similar architecture for other biometric features as well, for a more comprehensive and integral identification system. However, further work on this line is aimed toward the predictive modeling using unsupervised algorithms, provided the availability of sufficiently big datasets. Subsequently, other significant information like age and other identifying attributes could be extracted from the lip prints through a comprehensive decision support system. Similarly, it might provide further information like age that could still be extracted out of lip prints.

Acknowledgements. This work was supported and financed by the Cloudgenia group through its technical and operational capabilities for the design of the decision support system architecture.

References

1. Saini, M., Kumar Kapoor, A.: Biometrics in forensic identification: applications and challenges. J Forensic Med. **1**(108), 2 (2016). https://doi.org/10.4172/2472-1026.1000108

2. Kumar, A., Prasad, S.N., Kamal, V., Priya, S., Kumar, M., Kumar, A.: Importance of cheiloscopy. IJOCR **4**, 48–52 (2016). https://doi.org/10.5005/jp-journals-10051-0012.

3. Sandhya, S., Fernandes, R.: Lip Print: An emerging biometrics technology - a review. In: 2017 IEEE International Conference on Computational Intelligence and Computing Research (ICCIC),. pp. 1–5 (2017). https://doi.org/10.1109/ICCIC.2017.8524457

4. Akulwar, P., Vijapur, N.A.: Secured multi modal biometric system: a review. In: 2019 Third International conference on I-SMAC (IoT in Social, Mobile, Analytics and Cloud) (I-SMAC),. pp. 396–403 (2019). https://doi.org/10.1109/I-SMAC47947.2019.9032628

5. Tuning the hyper-parameters of an estimator — scikit-learn 0.24.2 documentation. https://sci kit-learn.org/stable/modules/grid_search.html Accessed 23 Aug 2021

6. Caldas, I.M., Magalhães, T., Afonso, A.: Establishing identity using cheiloscopy and palatoscopy. Forensic Sci Int. **165**, 1–9 (2007)

7. Tsuchihashi, Y.: Studies on personal identification by means of lip prints. Forensic Sci. **3**, 233–248 (1974)

8. Cheiloscopy, K.J.: In: Siegel, J.A., Saukko, P.J., Knupfer, G.C. (eds.) Encyclopedia of Forensic Sciences. 2nd edi. I, pp. 358–361. Academic Press, London (2000)

9. Acharya, A.B.: Teaching forensic odontology: an opinion on its content and format. Eur J Dent Educ. **10**, 137–141 (2006)

10. Velosa, F., Florez, H.: Edge solution with machine learning and open data to interpret signs for people with visual disability. CEUR Workshop Proceedings **2714**, 15–26 (2020)

11. Sabelli, A.F., Chatterjee, P., Pollo-Cattaneo, M.F.: Predictive modeling toward identification of sex from lip prints-machine learning in cheiloscopy. CEUR Workshop Proceedings **2992**, 29–43 (2021)

Robotic Autonomy

Automotive Industry Applications Based on Industrial Internet of Things (IIoT). A Review

Luis Carlos Guzman Mendoza, Juan Carlos Amaya, César A. Cárdenas, and Carlos Andrés Collazos Morales(✉)

Universidad Manuela Beltrán, Bogota, Colombia
carlos.collazos@docentes.umb.edu.co

Abstract. The 4.0 technologies are improving all kinds of industry, including automotive factories. One of these technologies is the Internet of Things (IoT). When the IoT is applied in the manufacturing process is called Industrial Internet of Things (IIoT). Many automotive factory applications (apps) based on IIoT are limited and scattered. To provide valuable insights into technological environments and support researchers, we must understand the available options and gaps in this line of research. Thus, in this study, a review is conducted to map the research landscape into a coherent classification. The search is focused in articles related to (1) automotive factories, (2) apps, and (3) IIoT; in four major digital databases: Web of Science, Scopus, ScienceDirect and IEEE Explore. These databases contain enough literature focusing on automotive manufacturing apps using IIoT. The final dataset resulting from the classification scheme includes 16 articles divided into six classes: Intrusion detection and security software; Re- views; Framework related apps; Toolset apps; economy surveys and; analysis and designing methods.

Keywords: Industrial IoT · Automotive factory · Industry 4.0 · Automated manufacturing

1 Introduction

Internet of Things is defined as a network of interconnected devices equipped with sensors that convert physical real world magnitudes into digital data that can be sent via communication modules to be analyzed by computer systems remotely, and, at the same time receive instructions to execute control commands by triggering actuators [1]. In addition to hardware, it has embedded software or firmware to execute basic programmed routines.

When the Internet of Things is used in industrial environment it is known as the Industrial Internet of Things (IIoT). The IIoT allows machines to access information from sensors in real time and enable the application of decision-making algorithms, giving rise to Smart Manufacturing Processes.

In the automotive industry, automated mechanisms with previously programmed functions are used, by equipping them with networks of interconnected sensors (IIoT),

H. Florez and H. Gomez (Eds.): ICAI 2022, CCIS 1643, pp. 381–393, 2022.
https://doi.org/10.1007/978-3-031-19647-8_27

these functions can be reprogrammed in real time without human intervention, increasing the efficiency and speed of the processes, positively impacting the productivity of the factory.

Automotive sector has had excellent automation dynamics it in recent decades, which is why it becomes an appropriate platform for the deployment of industry 4.0 enablers, taking advantage of the inertia of technology adoption managed from culture of innovation and application of agile methodologies open to new challenges.

Another aspect that plays in its favor is the economic growth of the sector, which allows the maintenance of investments in new technologies with the aim of reducing costs and increasing profits [23]. Except for the crises generated by external factors such as the real-estate bubble in 2008 or the fall in oil prices in 2014, the growth of the sector has been sustained last decade [2].

Additional factor driving the sector is the advances in research about autonomous vehicles to put them on the market, as well as the boost that electric vehicles have had, which are already beginning to have significant market shares. Then it is observed how the automotive sector is the ideal one to carry out research on the adoption of new technologies, especially the industry 4.0 enablers. This article addresses the adoption of the Industrial Internet of Things in the automotive sector. A systematic review is conducted in the largest digital databases: IEEE, Scopus, ScienceDirect and Web of Science.

This paper is organized in five sections: in Sect. 1 IIoT and its automotive applications are introduced; in Sect. 2 is presented the methodology of research, scope and filter options to select the papers; in Sect. 3, the results of final set articles are showed. In Sect. 4 a discussion is performed and finally, in Sect. 5, the conclusions are presented.

2 Methods

The keyword in this survey is "Industrial Internet of Things (IIoT)" and its applications (apps) in the automotive industry. It's excludes other non IIoT based industrial automotive apps, also other apps non applied to automotive manufacturing process. The scope was limited to English literature but all IIoT apps in automotive factory automation were consider. Four web-based databases were consulted in order to get the articles with high quality level: Scopus, ScienceDirect, Web of Science (WoS) and IEEE Explore [3].

The conducted survey includes a search for target articles and 3 scanning and selection iterations. First one, duplicated articles were removed; second, all unrelated articles were excluded; and finally, the remained articles were full text reviewed. The search was realized in August 2020 using the databases search tools. To get related articles, a query used was: (IIoT OR "Industrial Internet of Things") AND (Automotive) AND (factory OR manufacturing). Filtering tools were used to choose only English articles and only Article and review document types. After download the articles from databases and apply filtering selection iterations, exclusion criteria were applied to the full text reviewed articles: (1) The article is not focused on IIoT apps; and (2) the article is not related to automotive manufacturing.

The read articles were classified into an Excel table to get the main topics and a comprehensive organization. Text were categorized depending on how the IIoT is used.

Redondo et al., [17] obtain a dataset of variables from a cutting machine located in an automotive factory. The machine cuts using water. 3 parts of the machine are analyzed: The intensifier pumps and the vacuum cyclone.

Riel et al., [18] explore and explain Signal Flow Analysis (SFA) and Axiomatic Design (AD) concepts and its application to a particular case study: automotive electric power steering system (EPS), where they integrate the proposed design method with current standards.

Kamath et al., [15] develop a robust experimental setup and data analysis for manual grinding, testing the setup with grinding experiments, where an initial empirical model to correlate relevant operator-controlled variables and process information variables with the process outcomes, namely surface roughness and material removal rate (MRR).

3   Results

The initial search results include 44 papers: 15 from Scopus database, 12 from WoS, 11 from IEEE Explore, and 6 from ScienceDirect. The articles were published from 2016 to 2020. 19 papers were duplicated in various databases. In the full-text read were excluded 9 articles, for a total 16 paper in the final set. Figure 1 shows the number of papers published by year.

Papers were organized in six categories: Reviews (3/16), intrusion detection and safety software (3/16), Framework (5/16), tool set (2/16), economy survey (1/16) and analysis and designing methods (4/16). Figure 2 shows the number of articles by topic.

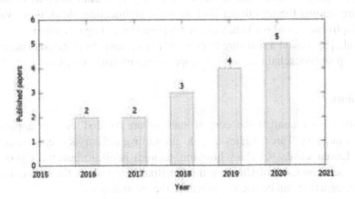

Fig. 1. Published papers by year.

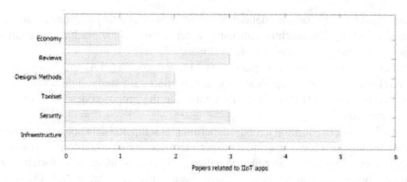

Fig. 2. Articles by topic.

3.1 Intrusion Detection and Safety Software

Arshad et al., [1] performs a design of an intrusion detection system in an IoT network. It is divided into two parts: Detection in the modem/router and detection in the connected devices. They carry out a design validation by simulating the system in the Contiki operative system, where they analyze a network of 5 devices connected to a modem and 3 external sources that try to enter the network. In the simulation, they perform calculations of the electrical power consumed by the network and the overload of the RAM memory of the devices when performing the intrusion detection routine.

Boudagdigue et al., [4] propose a dynamic model for industrial environments. A comparative study is conducted to show the energy efficiency benefits of the H-IIoT architecture against the traditional IIoT network architecture. Also, they evaluate the ability, adaptiveness, and resiliency of the proposed model against others.

He et al., [5] present a software to protect IIoT systems from external attacks, using the peer-to-peer blockchain network to improve monitoring systems.

3.2 Reviews

Review articles summarize the current state of art on IIoT and its applications in automotive industry. Three studies include automotive industry systems based on IIoT:

Fraga-Lamas et al., [6] show how the vehicles begin to become Cyber-Physical systems, where the Control-Unit and the On-Board Unit allow the collection of large amounts of data that can be used to diagnose the car status.

Cronin et al., [7] present integration with Big Data and Machine Learning methods required to smart manufacturing in the automotive sector that can only be made possible through the support of IIoT.

Vitturi et al., [8] show an assessment of future perspectives including next-generation Ethernet, software-defined networking (SDN), IIoT, and 5G, for automotive apps.

3.3 Framework

Five papers related to framework applications were included. [9] It uses smartphone as a gateway to send data to the cloud to be analyzed by the manufacturer. An App installed on the cell phone receives the data from the On-Board Diagnostics (OBD) and sends it to a web server. OBD has Bluetooth support. It communicates with the Engine Control Unit (ECU) via CAN, SAE J1850 PWM, SAE J1850 VPW, ISO 9141–2 and ISO 14230 KWP2000) to obtain the relevant data.

Pease et al., [10] use a microcontroller and dedicated sensors that allow to measure the variables of interest (electrical energy, active, reactive and appar- ent power, motor speed (RPM), operating frequency, etc.) and report them in a local user interface with access from the cloud. System validation is carried out by simulating the parameters in multi-physics software such as Matlab-Simulik and Labview.

Krugh et al., [11] present a Wireless Sensor Network (WSN) that allows to establish the useful times of the machines and the operators in a production line. It uses sensors with Bluetooth connectivity to determine the movement of workers and pressure sensors. The working times of the machines are measured with sensors built into them.

Segura Velandia et al., [12] use RFID antennas to identify different parts of the Crankshaft and obtain its history, to later store it in databases and achieve traceability of the parts during the manufacturing process.

Yerra et al., [13] provide a thought-provoking application of IIoT in automotive composites body shop. With IIoT application to the material handling system, the smart material flow and interconnected grid layout has significantly improved the productive time.

3.4 Tool Set

There are two papers that describe application tools to use into an automotive factory.

Minnetti et al., [14] present a design and implementation of a portable device that allows measuring the gap and flush of surfaces in different places of a vehicle, during the assembly process. The device performs the measurement using laser triangulation. High resolution camera is used to capture the reflections of the laser on the surface. The captured image is sent wirelessly to a Smartphone where it is analyzed by CNN algorithms that determine the values of interest. Laboratory and field validations are carried out, where better uncertainty results are obtained than with traditional measurement devices.

Kamath et al., [15] present an experiment to determine the correlation between interest variables in the process of final finishes (cutting and polishing) using hand tools. It uses an accelerometer controlled by an app installed into a smartphone.

3.5 Tool Set

Arnold et al., [16] present a quantitative study on the impact of IIoT on the business models of different sectors, including the automotive. They analyze business models through a survey of industrial executives, including 17 from automotive industry.

The influence of IIoT on business models is analyzed, showing how the relationship between suppliers and consumers has improved significantly with the implementation of IIoT.

3.6 Analysis and Designing Methods

Redondo et al., [17] present a visual tool for analyzing possible failures and their use in predictive mainte- nance. It uses exploratory techniques such as: Classical Multidimensional Scaling (CMDS), Sammon Mapping (SM) and Factor Analysis (FA). A real case study is ana- lyzed in a water cutting machine in an automotive factory.

Riel et al., [18] present a design method that applies some standards and complements them where they find gaps.

4 Discussion

This work presents the most relevant articles on state-of-the-art industrial automotive applications based on IIoT. This review aims to highlight the research trends in this area and to get a general overview.

Table 1 shows a relative comparison between the articles that implement security and intrusion detection software for IIoT systems. It is observed that none use mobile applications for their operation. [1] and [4] perform measurements of electrical energy consumption using variables such as voltage, current, power. Only [4] evaluates the execution times of its algorithms. [1] describes the use of the 6LoWPAN standard (IPv6 over Low power Wireless Personal Area Networks). In [5], the use of Blockchain as a tool to protect IIoT networks stands out. In the reviewed works, it is proposed to increase the inclusion of cryptography as an aspect that allows improving the security levels of protected systems.

Table 1. Relative comparison of existing approaches for intrusion detection.

Article	Description	Physical variables	Communication standard
[1]	Design of an intrusion detection system in an IoT network	Power [mW], Supply voltage, Current consumption	6LoWPAN
[4]	Propose a dynamic trust management model suitable for industrial environments	Energy consumption	-
[5]	Software to protect IIoT systems from external attacks, using Blockchain	-	-

Table 2 shows the comparison of the papers related to the toolsets developed for the automotive industry based on the IIoT. Both tools include applications for mobile devices and use 4G and WIFI connectivity to link to the network, allowing to store data in the cloud to be consulted and analyzed later.

Table 2. Relative comparison of existing approaches for Toolset.

Article	Description	SmartApp	Physical variables	Communication standard
[14]	Device to measure the gap and flush of surfaces in different places of a vehicle, during the assembly process	Yes	Gap and flush measurement	USB, WIFI
[15]	This is an experiment to determine the correlation between the variables of interest in the final finishing process (cutting and polishing) using hand tools	Yes	Material removal rate (MRR), grinding force, feed rate, wrist acceleration, workpiece vibration	WiFi

Additionally, in [15] one of the sensors is controlled from the app installed on the smartphone. In the case of [14], the USB standard is also used. In [15] the energy consumption is evaluated by measuring the active power. The two applications are implemented in the automotive sector, as part of the automation of processes.

Table 3 compares the papers related to applications for the infrastructure of automotive factories, where only [9] has a mobile application and only (Pease et al., 2018) evaluates energy consumption by measuring variables such as active, reactive and apparent power. [9] and [10] measure physical variables such as travel speed, distance traveled, motor rotational speed, torque, and time. [11] Considers the distance traveled by workers in a section on an assembly line. In [12] the operating frequency, distance, area and coverage angle are evaluated.

The communication standards used include: CAN, WIFI, 4G, WSN, Bluetooth and RFID. In [13] the IIoT is used to improve the production of an assembly line connecting the entire body-shop to the network, increasing its production per unit of time, however, it is not specified what type of standard is used to make the connection.

Table 3. Relative comparison of existing approaches for framework

Article	Description	SmartApp	Physical variables	Communication standard
[9]	It uses smartphone as a gateway to send data to the cloud to be analyzed by the manufacturer	Yes	Speed, time elapsed and distance	CAN, WIFI, 4G
[10]	Industrial energy monitoring	No	Speed, RPM and torque; Active, reactive and apparent power	WSN
[11]	WSN that allows determining the spatial location coordinates and the movements of workers on the assembly line	No	Distance	Bluetooth
[12]	Combine RFID antennas to identify different parts of the crankshaft and obtain their history	No	Operating frequency, distance, area and angle of coverage	RFID
[13]	All units of the body-shop are connected with IIoT to evaluate their performance	No	-	-

5 Main IIoT Applications on Automotive Industry

IIoT systems allow to monitor physical variables of interest and convert them into dig- ital data that can be interpreted, organized and analyzed by Big Data algorithms that generate information from datasets, allowing decision-making and the prediction and optimization of digitized systems, resulting in efficient processes and high quality standards. IIoT scheme system in a factory is shown in Fig. 3.

Based on these technologies, different applications have been proposed in the automotive industry that can be categorized depending on the beneficiary: On the one hand applications for the end user and on the other hand we have applications aimed at vehicle manufacturers.

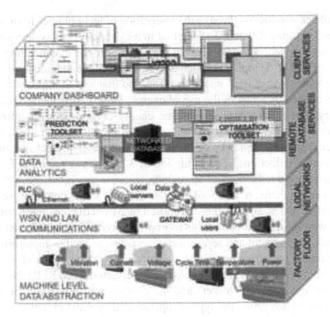

Fig. 3. Articles by topic.

5.1   Car Owner Oriented Applications

Applications of the industrial internet of things in the automotive industry can be categorized according to who is the beneficiary of the application. On the one hand, there are applications that provide information to the driver of vehicles about the status of different mechanical car components, obtaining information from the OBD and specialized sensors (e. g. engine status, its temperature, RPM, among others).

The driver can also receive information about traffic status using Global Positioning System (GPS) sensors. These applications use artificial intelligence algorithms to determine the best routes to help the driver reach his destination, also relying on social networks with information from other drivers. Sadiq et al. [19] proposes a system to share information between vehicles using a wireless communication system known as Vehicular Ad-hoc Networks (VANETs).

Another application is the use of video cameras to identify the driver's facial gestures, recognizing when he is alert or distracted and even if he is falling asleep. Akhtar et al. [20] proposes a WIFI based system to perform the driver fatigue recognition.

5.2   Vehicle Manufacturing Applications

On the other hand, there are applications that are aimed at generating useful information for vehicle manufacturers. These applications allow factories to obtain feedback on automobile performance, distances traveled, fuel consumption efficiency, and engine behavior stability [9], among others. These applications allow the manufacturer to determine if a vehicle model requires any modification in real time, as well as the type of modification necessary to satisfy the requirements of the end user.

This feedback is achieved through the integration of technologies from Industry 4.0, namely: Manufacturing 4.0 and IIoT applied in a cyber-physical system such as a car. Figure 4 shows the feedback scheme from the end user to the manufacturer.

Another type of IIoT application that also has the vehicle manufacturer as a beneficiary are the tools that are used inside factories and that aim to improve the quality of processes, increase efficiency in the use of energy, reduce costs and production times, among others. Pease et al. [10] propose an energy consumption monitoring system using sensors connected wirelessly to a LAN network, with which they characterized the energy consumption behavior of the machines, to later predict and optimize the process, obtaining reductions in consumption of 3.35%, however, other factories have reported consumption reductions of up to 25%.

In this category there are also tools for the use of workers that improve the quality of production processes, such as those proposed by Minnetti et al. and Kamath et al.,

[14, 15] who design and build tools to improve production and precision in taking measurements of alignment and separation of surfaces, as well as monitoring and controlling the process of cutting and polishing surfaces, reducing material waste by 22%. Krugh and Segura Velandia [11, 12] proposes using Bluetooth and RFID wireless sensors to monitor the movement of workers and the components to be assembled in a work station, in order to determine the type of operation they must execute, generating the instructions that allow to optimize the process and reduce human errors, at the same time that the working times of the machines associated with the activity are monitored. Syafrudin, et al., [21] propose a monitoring system for physical variables (Temperature, humidity, vibration and gyroscope), information analysis (Big Data) and prediction of operating conditions (Normal or failure) using Machine Learning, with which they identify the main failure conditions in different production processes within the automobile factory, mainly in assembly lines.

Another type of IIoT application that also has the vehicle manufacturer as a beneficiary are the tools that are used inside factories and that aim to improve the quality of processes, increase efficiency in the use of energy, reduce costs and production times, among others [22, 24]. Pease et al. [10] propose an energy consumption monitoring system us- ing sensors connected wirelessly to a LAN network, with which they characterized the energy consumption behavior of the machines, to later predict and optimize the process, obtaining reductions in consumption of 3.35%, however, other factories have reported consumption reductions of up to 25%.

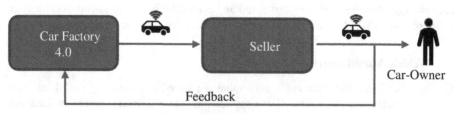

Fig. 4. Customer feedback using IIoT [9].

In this category there are also tools for the use of workers that improve the quality of production processes, such as those proposed by Minnetti et al. and Kamath et al., [14, 15] who design and build tools to improve production and precision in taking measurements of alignment and separation of surfaces, as well as monitoring and controlling the process of cutting and polishing surfaces, reducing material waste by 22%. Krugh and Segura Velandia [11, 12] proposes using Bluetooth and RFID wireless sensors to monitor the movement of workers and the components to be assembled in a work station, in order to determine the type of operation they must execute, generating the instructions that allow to optimize the process and reduce human errors, at the same time that the working times of the machines associated with the activity are monitored. Syafrudin, et al., [21] propose a monitoring system for physical variables (Temperature, humidity, vibration and gyroscope), information analysis (Big Data) and prediction of operating conditions (Normal or failure) using Machine Learning, with which they identify the main failure conditions in different production processes within the automobile factory, mainly in assembly lines.

6 Conclusions and Future Work

A recent disruptive trend has emerged in the use of IIoT and applications in automotive industry. Research on this trend is ongoing, although related descriptions and limitations remain vague. Obtaining insights into this emerging trend is important. This article aims to contribute such insights by surveying works related to automotive industry apps based on IIoT. These works are divided into six classes: Intrusion detection and security software; Reviews and surveys; Framework related apps; Toolset apps; economy surveys and analysis; and designing methods.

Most of the articles are related to applications for the infrastructure of the automotive factories, while the economic studies present the fewest studies. Security against external attacks or intrusions also has a significant number of papers, however, important gaps are identified in the precision of the security systems proposed to detect and block attacks of greater scale and complexity. The effectiveness in the detection of attacks can be improved by applying Machine Learning techniques. Another important aspect to improve regarding security is encryption and access control to IIoT systems networks.

The developments of hand tools denote important advances, however, greater research efforts and integration of IIoT type technologies are required in this type of applications for the automotive sector. Difficulties are identified evaluating the designs implemented in large-scale systems. Integration of Big Data and Machine Learning analysis methods to identify patterns in collected data should be consider in future works.

RFID has been well received in IIoT applications in the automotive sector, however, there are still gaps that do not allow the full adoption of RFID technology as a solution for the identification of parts and their tracking.

As a future work, [9] propose the addition of the instant fuel consumption algorithm, enabling pollution levels to be measured; to analyze the State of Charge (SOC) of the vehicle batteries and the use of Big Data and machine learning techniques to detect patterns from the collected data.

References

1. Arshad, J., Azad, M.A., Abdeltaif, M.M., Salah, K.: An intrusion detection framework for energy constrained IoT devices. Mech. Syst. Signal Process. **136**, 106436 (2020)
2. Wagner, I.: Motor vehicle sales worldwide 2005–2019. statista.com (2020). https://www.statista.com/statistics/265859/vehicle-vehicle-worldwide/ Accessed 3 Mar 2021
3. Alaa, M., Zaidan, A.A., Zaidan, B.B., Talal, M., Kiah, M.L.M.: A review of smart home applications based on Internet of Things. J. Netw. Comput. Appl. **97**, 48–65 (2017)
4. Boudagdigue, C., Benslimane, A., Kobbane, A., Liu, J.: Trust management in industrial internet of things. IEEE Trans. Inf. Forensics Secur. **15**, 3667–3682 (2020)
5. He, S., Ren, W., Zhu, T., Choo, K.K.R.: BoSMoS: a blockchain-based status monitoring system for defending against unauthorized software updating in industrial internet of things. IEEE Internet Things J. **7**(2), 948–959 (2020)
6. Fraga-Lamas, P., Fernández-Caramés, T.M.: A review on Blockchain technologies for an advanced and cyber-resilient automotive industry. IEEE Access **7**, 17578–17598 (2019)
7. Cronin, C., Conway, A., Walsh, J.: Flexible manufacturing systems using IIoT in the automotive sector. Procedia Manuf. **38**(2019), 1652–1659 (2019)
8. Vitturi, S., Zunino, C., Sauter, T.: Industrial communication systems and their future challenges: next-generation ethernet, IIoT, and 5G. Proc. IEEE **107**(6), 944–961 (2019)
9. Silva, M., Vieira, E., Signoretti, G., Silva, I., Silva, D., Ferrari, P.: A customer feedback platform for vehicle manufacturing compliant with industry 4.0 vision. Sensors (Switzerland) **18**(10), 1–24 (2018)
10. Pease, S.G., et al.: An intelligent real-time cyber-physical toolset for energy and process prediction and optimisation in the future industrial Internet of Things. Futur. Gener. Comput. Syst. **79**, 815–829 (2018)
11. Krugh, M., et al.: Measurement of operator-machine interaction on a chaku- chaku assembly line. Procedia Manuf. **10**, 123–135 (2017)
12. Segura Velandia, D.M., Kaur, N., Whittow, W.G., Conway, P.P., West, A.A.: Towards industrial internet of things: Crankshaft monitoring, traceability and tracking using RFID. Robot. Comput. Integr. Manuf. **41**, 66–77 (2016)
13. Yerra, V.A., Pilla, S.: IIoT-enabled production system for composite intensive vehicle manufacturing. SAE Int. J. Engines **10**(2), 209–214 (2017)
14. Minnetti, E., et al.: A smartphone integrated hand-held gap and flush measurement system for in line quality control of car body assembly. Sensors (Switzerland) **20**(11), 1–17 (2020)
15. Kamath, A.K., Linke, B.S., Chu, C.H.: Enabling advanced process control for manual grinding operations. Smart Sustain. Manuf. Syst. **4**(2), 210–230 (2020)
16. Arnold, C., Kiel, D., Voigt, K.I.: How the industrial internet of things changes business models in different manufacturing industries. Int. J. Innov. Manag. **20**(8), 1–25 (2016)
17. Redondo, R., Herrero, Á., Corchado, E., Sedano, J.: A decision-making tool based on exploratory visualization for the automotive industry. Appl. Sci. **10**(12), 4355 2020
18. Riel, A., Kreiner, C., Messnarz, R., Much, A.: An architectural approach to the integration of safety and security requirements in smart products and systems design. CIRP Ann. **67**(1), 173–176 (2018)
19. Sadiq, A.S., Khan, S., Ghafoor, K.Z., Guizani, M., Mirjalili, S.: Transmission power adaption scheme for improving IoV awareness exploiting: evaluation weighted matrix based on piggybacked information. Comput. Networks **137**, 147–159 (2018). https://doi.org/10.1016/j.comnet.2018.03.019
20. Akhtar, Z.U.A., Wang, H.: WiFi-based driver's activity recognition using multi-layer classification. Neurocomputing **405**, 12–25 (2020)

21. Syafrudin, M., Alfian, G., Fitriyani, N.L., Rhee, J.: Performance analysis of IoT-based sensor, big data processing, and machine learning model for real- time monitoring system in automotive manufacturing. Sensors (Switzerland) 18(9), 2946 (2018)
22. Hernandez, J., Daza, K., Florez, H., Misra, S.: Dynamic interface and access model by dead token for IoT systems. In: International Conference on Applied Informatics, pp. 485–498 (2019)
23. Morante, A., Villamil, M.P., Florez, H.: Framework for supporting the creation of marketing strategies. International Information Institute (Tokyo). Information 20(10A), 7371–7378 (2017)
24. Rabelo, L., Ballestas, A., Valdez, J., Ibrahi, B.: Using delphi and system dynamics to study the cybersecurity of the IoT-based smart grids. ParadigmPlus 3(1), 19–36 (2022)

Implementation of an IoT Architecture for Automated Garbage Segregation

Angel Antonio Rodríguez Varela[✉], Germán A. Montoya, and Carlos Lozano-Garzón

Universidad de Los Andes, Bogotá, Colombia
{aa.rodriguezv,ga.montoya44,calozanog}@uniandes.edu.co

Abstract. Recycling can be up to six times cheaper for a nation than not doing proper waste management at all. That is why the government of Colombia set out to take advantage of over 40% of the waste produced in the country by 2030. Therefore, it is particularly important to develop tools and mechanisms that enable proper recycling. The effort of this paper resulted in an IoT architecture that allows for the identification of users and separation of bags while enabling the analysis of the entire process. This was achieved by using RFID tags, for user recognition, object detection models, for classifying the bags, bands with ultrasound sensors, a robotic arm and a cloud analytics system.

Keywords: Architecture · IoT · Detection · Cloud · Analytics · Robotic

1 Introduction

Colombia is responsible for producing over one million tons of garbage every year. From those million tons, 85% of these are deposited, without any major separation, in huge landfills or open sky communal dumps. In retrospective, this implies that only 15% of the waste generated is being used for recycling [10]. This becomes a problem, not only because landfills are responsible for 8% of the greenhouse effect, but because discarding waste, regardless of the new use that it can be given, turns out to be over six times more expensive for a country (as stated previously on the abstract) than doing the proper management of garbage [12]. That is why the National Government of the country established, since January 1 of 2021, a unique code for classifying and separating waste in the whole territory. This was intended to be done from the source; every household in the country should be responsible for following the recycling laws, to start generating the consciousness needed to solve the problem of waste management [8]. However, having control over the source renders itself useless if the process is not coherent from start to finish and everything is just thrown into a communal dump.

In Bogotá alone, the Doña Juana landfill reaches over six thousand tons of garbage every year [10]. This is where the problem of controlling the entire process begins to take its shape. The model of waste management for an apartment complex goes as follows: every tower has its own garbage shut. When a family needs to deposit a garbage bag, they just go to the common trash shut and dump the bag right in there. There are no bins for each color that the government established (black, white or green). Some administrations define that the garbage that can be recycled (white) needs to be left to the side for "special pickup" but, then again, there is no actual guarantee that those bags will get the proper treatment, or that even if they are separated, at first, that they will not end up in the same communal dump. Given that over 60% of households in the capital of Colombia live in apartments and that, as stated previously, there is no control over recycling after the garbage leaves a home for these forms of housing, there is no actual guarantee that this will be useful throughout the whole lifecycle of waste management if everything just goes into the same container. Even if there are penalties for households that do not comply with recycling laws (penalties that can go up to sixteen minimum wages), this type of reinforcement will not have an effect, either, because there is no actual way of telling who is doing the proper separation of garbage or when in the process is the recycling lost to remedy the situation [11].

For 2030, the Government of Colombia established as a goal to take advantage of more than 40% of the waste produced. This comes as no surprise, because, other than being cost efficient for the nation, it is also one of the main components of what is known as "circular economy" for the optimized exploitation of resources that can go back into the value chain and the productive lifecycles of incorporations.

Recycling also allows for, among other things, reducing the energy consumption. For example, to produce aluminum, more than 90% of the energy needed can be saved when discarded aluminum is used again, as compared to working with the metal element from scratch. Just the recycling of a glass bottle alone represents the saving of energy needed to light up an old lightbulb for more than four hours, and to light up a new LED one even more. Besides, it is also important to note that, for example, paper and Wood production from exploitable waste implies less deforestation, contributing, this way to the health of the environment. Lastly, the task of recycling, and reaching the target established by the government, can increase the number of jobs generated for the citizens. This is critical given that for 2021 the unemployment rate was over 10,5%, and one of the reasons for riots and protests in the country [13].

The paper presented here posits a solution for classifying and separating bags effectively, that could potentially be implemented in apartment complexes or even industrial buildings. It leverages a MobileNet V1 SSD object detection model, manually trained (in a Nano Jetson computer for faster AI processing), and a UR3 robotic arm to deposit bags according to their color, along with band mechanisms and other sensors (such as ultrasound and RFID antennas) that complement the architecture and makes for a complete and robust system, able to identify users and mobilize bags. Finally, a visualization dashboard was built on Data Studio for analyzing the process in terms of trends for colors, days, and users.

2 Requirement Gathering

The requirements for this solution involved:

- A User Recognition system was required for the analysis of the process to be complete end-to-end. This system was assumed to be remote, as the garbage containers in buildings are usually far away, in closed rooms on the lowest levels. This would also mean the first step in the garbage disposal system, the first component that would initialize the process of detecting and depositing bags. This is how the RFID server was conceived.

- A central processing unit was required to detect garbage bags and coordinate depositing them with the band system and the robotic arm. This server would receive the signal from the user recognition system to start up all the other components. This would also imply having the object detection model to communicate to the robotic arm the correct position of the container to deposit the bags. This is how the Nano Jetson Server came to be.
- Development of an Analysis Engine was also required for the process to be supervised. This could potentially mean having insights as to when pickup of the garbage should be scheduled or any other decisions that may improve the overall process.

3 Architecture Design

3.1 Theoretical Framework

Internet of Things for Waste Management

Internet of Things (or IoT, as it is vastly known) is the expansion of software beyond the boundaries of computers and networks. It entails the integration of sensors and other components such as industrial artifacts or common domestic home appliances to further improve what technology can do for humankind. IoT has applications in various fields such as the automotive industry, health, and security [1].

Said applications, also, include waste management as a benefactor from IoT systems. As it can be seen in [2], object detection models can be used to even go as far as detecting individual waste (not just garbage bags) and classifying them as glass, metal, cardboard, paper plastic or general trash. The work also references the use of radiofrequency identification (RFID) in monitoring of solid waste and grey level co-occurrence matrixes for trash separation that can be seen in [3].

MobileNet v1 SSD for Object Detection

Conceived, first, for embedded applications and mobile environments, MobileNet serves as an improvement in performance and efficiency for computer vision. While the architecture itself is composed of 28 layers, the basis behind the model is a depth-wise convolution with a 1x1 pointwise convolution for reducing computation and model size [4]. After that, every layer finishes with a batch normalization and ReLU applied for optimization purposes. SSD Stands for "Single Shot Detector" and it is included as the last layer in MobileNet for Object Detection models. This algorithm places an already predefined number of boxes in the whole image with both a class and a score for each class that helps detect where the objects are placed [5].

3.2 Implementation

The following image depicts the overall design of the architecture defined for the solution needed. In this section a discussion about what each element represents, the responsibilities and dynamics that come to play can be found.

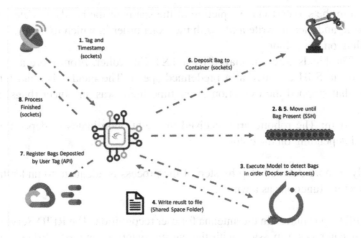

Fig. 1. Architecture design representation

In Fig. 1, at the top left corner, an image of an antenna is shown, this is to represent the RFID module of the architecture. Next, at the bottom left corner icons of the Google Cloud Platform and Data Studio can be seen, this is to represent the analytics engine which was built with said technologies. Furthermore, at the centre of the figure, there is a CPU icon that represents the Nano Jetson server used for processing and core orchestration of the entire IoT architecture. Next, at the bottom right corner there is a compound icon of Pytorch and Docker, to represent the object detection module. At the centre right side of the image there is a long band that represent where the bags go before being deposited. Finally, at the top right corner is the representation of the robotic arm, which, for this paper, was a UR3.

Now, it is relevant to mention a deep dive on each component and the responsibility that it holds in the architecture:

– RFID Antenna: This sensor was used for the recognition of users in the system. Its job was to detect when a tag was placed between the two receivers. From there the information of the tag was sent, to a connected PC via USB, to serve as the first input of the model.
– RFID Server: The laptop connected to the RFID Antenna oversaw receiving the tag information to be sent to the Nano Jetson, along with the datetime registered when the RFID tag was detected.
– Nano Jetson: This is where the orchestration took place. The Nano Jetson oversaw calling for the bands to move, run a Docker subprocess with the object detection model was and get the information needed to send for the robot to deposit the bags detected where they belonged. Not to mention, also, that this server was also in charge of sending out all the information to the Analytics Engine for further visualization of the process.
– Object Detection Model: The model, built with Pytorch, ran on a Docker container inside the Nano Jetson as a subprocess. Its job was, upon execution from the core

program in the server, to take a picture of the status of the bands, to detect the bags to deposit, and then to write a file with the exact order in which to deposit each bag, depending on the colour.

- Bands: The bands where managed by a TXT Controller. From there a.py file was executed via SSH to move at a predefined speed. The bands also had ultrasound sensors that stopped the execution every time there was an object (bags) between them.
- Robotic Arm: The robotic arm received the right coordinates to deposit each bag detected depending on the colour.

Finally, a more detailed step by step of the process is adequate to understand how the architecture functions as a whole:

1. An RFID tag is placed in the antenna for user recognition. The RFID Server gets the tag, concatenates a message with the current datetime and establishes connection with the Nano Jetson via Sockets to send said message.
2. The Nano Jetson receives the message and splits it to send the user and datetime information appropriately to the Analytics Engine. Then it executes the.py file in the Bands via SSH to move them a first time. This is to get some initial separation of the bags to take the picture and detect them.
3. Once the bags detect the first bag, and it is in place to be deposited, the bands stop and the process in the core program of the Nano Jetson continues. Now, the Object Detection model can be executed. Next, the program inside the Docker container takes the picture of the status of the bands, detects the bags present and writes a file with the order of colours that need to be deposited. The order is established in relation to the proximity with the robotic arm.
4. Now that the bags are detected, the core program in the Nano Jetson server proceeds to read the file that the Docker program wrote to coordinate bands and robot movement.
5. For each colour detected the Nano Jetson commands the bands to move. The bands move until the ultrasound sensors are interrupted. Afterwards execution in the band ends and continues in the Nano Jetson.
6. Once the bag is placed into position, a command to the robot is sent via Sockets to be moved to the location of the specific container for the colour.
7. Then, when steps 5 and 6 have been repeated for all the colours detected, the Nano Jetson sends all the information to BigQuery through an API. One row for each colour detected with the information of the user and datetime registered by the RFID Server.
8. Lastly, the Nano Jetson establishes a connection, via Sockets, with the RFID Server that sent the signal to enable it for more tags to be received.

4 Results

This section intends to show the final deliverables that were made, based on the architecture design and the results of the executions of the paper.

4.1 Pseudocode

All the following programs were made in Python, a list of the links to all the real implementations can be found in Annex A. However, the following figures serve as an overview of the overall behavior, in a more technical sense than the step by step listed in the architecture design. Every external method find within the procedures explains code that is specific to connection or sensor management, i.e., code for initializing and binding sockets, that was found irrelevant to explain the functioning of the architecture.

Pseudocode for Nano Jetson Server

The code below corresponds to the core orchestration made by the Nano Jetson with all the other systems in the architecture. Lines 1–3 correspond to the initial steps needed to define the table schema in BigQuery. Line 2 describes the columns that are used for the main analysis table: RFID Tag, the color of the bag, how many bags for this color were deposited on one full execution and the datetime of this execution. Line 4 is crucial to identify the Docker container that will run the object detection model. Line 5 establishes SSH connection with the bands to order them to start the motion. After that, in line 6, the server-like behavior begins (infinite loop, as an infinite number of users can use the architecture for garbage disposal) (Fig. 2).

```
Procedure Nano_Jestson_Final_Integration (Bands_File_Run_Until_Sensor_Interrupted,
Docker_Objetc_Detection_File, Shared_File_Docker, Robot_IP, Bands_IP)
   1.  Bigquery_API.Establish_Connection_Bigquery()
   2.  Column_Schema = [RFID_TAG, Bag_Color, Bag_Count, Date_Registered]
   3.  Bigquery_API.Create_Table_If_Does_Not_Exist(Column_Schema)
   4.  Docker_ID ← Subprocess.Run(Find ID of Current Docker Running)
   5.  Bands_API.Establish_ SSH _Connection _Bands(Bands_IP)
   6.  Repeat (Server Type Behavior: Always Running)
   7.      Socket.Set_Socket_On_Listenning_Port()
   8.      RFID_IP, Message ← Socket.Accept_Message_Close_Connection()
   9.      RFID_TAG, DATE ← Message.Split()
   10.     Base_Dictionary ← {'RFID': RFID_TAG, 'DATE_REGISTERED': DATE}
   11.     Subprocess.Run(Run Docker_Object_Detection_File in Docker With Docker_ID)
   12.     Bags_Colors_Ordered ← Read_Resulting_File_As_Array(Shared_File_Docker)
   13.     Bag_Color_Count = {'Black':0, 'White':0, 'Green':0, 'Undefined':0,}
   14.     Robot_API.Establish_Connection(Robot_IP)
   15.     For Bag_Color in Bags_Colors_Ordered Do
   16.         Bands_API.Execute_Command(Bands_File_Run_Until_Sensor_Interrupted)
   17.         Robot_API.Deposit_Bag(Bag_Color)
   18.         Bag_Color_Count[Bag_Color] =+ 1
   19.     Endfor
   20.     Robot_API.Close_Connection()
   21.     For Color in Bag_Color_Count_Dict Do
   22.         Bag_Color_Registry ← Base_Dictionary.copyWith(Color=Bag_Color_Count[Color])
   23.         Bigquery_API.Register_New_Row(Bag_Color_Registry)
   24.     Endfor
   25.     Socket.Connect(RFID_IP)
   26.     Socket.Send_And_Close_Connection('STATUS:OK')
   27. End
   28. End Nano_Jestson_Final_Integration
```

Fig. 2. Pseudocode for Nano Jetson server

Lines 7–9 correspond to the initial connection with the RFID Module. First the Nano Jetson waits for the message, then it stablishes it with the RFID Server that wants to communicate, annotates the IP to respond later and separates the message received to use for uploading the table info. Line 10 is intended for creating a base dictionary, this is the way that rows are sent through the BigQuery API, one copy of this dictionary will be created later for every color deposited. Line 11 starts the Object Detection program as a subprocess in the Docker container identified earlier in line 4. Once that program has run and written the order of the bags detected in a shared folder, the Nano Jetson server reads it in line 12. The results are read as an array, which is already ordered depending on the closest colors to the robotic arm. Line 13 creates a counter for each garbage bag color possible, to later create the row dictionaries that will be sent to BigQuery. This serves the purpose of keeping a number in memory, rather than sending a request to the Analytics engine for every bag deposited in the next loop. Line 14 represents connecting with the UR3 Robot through Sockets. Lines 15–19 represent the actual garbage disposal behavior. For each bag color, the bands are moved to place it for the robotic arm to grab it, the robot goes to the container of that specific color and then the counter for that specific color is increased. Line 20 closes connection with the Robot. Lines 21–24 are about creating a copy of the Base Dictionary from line 10 with the color count from line 13 to insert a row in BigQuery for each color. Lines 25 and 26 are about connecting with the RFID Server that sent the request to enable it again for more tag reception.

Implementation of the Nano Jetson Server: https://github.com/aa-rodriguezv/AIA-robot-project/blob/master/communication_trials/nano_jetson_final_integration.py.

Pseudocode for the Docker Container with the Object Detection Model

The figure presented above holds the representation for the Docker container with the Object detection model, implemented in PyTorch. In line 1 a variable to find the best loss possible among the trained epochs of the model. Line 2 initializes a variable to find this best model in the files. Lines 3–8 iterate over the trained models and finds the best possible one depending on the loss it had. This allows for retraining, and using in the architecture automatically, the detection model to improve performance. For line 9 the program reads the labels for this model. Line 10 initializes the Convolutional Neural Network (CNN) with the model found in line 6, for this paper the Mobilenetv1 architecture was used to detect the objects. Line 11 creates the predictor to read the camera input and detect objects based on the CNN of line 10. Line 12 specifies to take a picture. Line 13 detects the labels present in the bands. Then, at line 14 the labels are sorted depending on the proximity, of the X axis, regarding the robot. Line 15 represents writing the file, with the labels ordered, in the shared spaced folder between the Docker container and the Nano Jetson itself (Fig. 3).

Implementation of the Object Detection Model: https://github.com/aa-rodriguezv/pytorch-ssd-modified-AIA-thesis/blob/master/inside_docker_container_final.py.

```
Procedure Docker_Object_Detection_File (Shared_File_Docker, Camera, Detection_Model_Directory,
Labels_Path)

    1.  Best_Min_Loss = 1000
    2.  Best_Model_Path
    3.  For Resulting_File in Detection_Model_Directory do
    4.      Current_Loss = Read_Loss(Resulting_File)
    5.      If Current_Loss < Best_Min_Loss then
    6.          Best_Model_Path = Resulting_File
    7.      EndIf
    8.  EndFor
    9.  Class_Labels ← Read_As_Array(Labels_Path)
    10. SSD_MobileNet ← NVDLI_API.Create_Mobilenetv1_SSD(Best_Model_Path,
        SizeOf(Class_Labels))
    11. Predictor ← NVDLI_API.Create_Mobilenetv1_SSD_Predictor(SSD_Mobilenet)
    12. Image ← OpenCV.VideoCapture(Camera).read()
    13. Labels_Present_In_Camera ← Predictor.Predict(Image)
    14. Labels_Present_In_Camera.Sort(Closest to Robot Arm on X axis)
    15. Write_Labels(Shared_File_Docker)
    16. Return
    17. End docker_controller_API
```

Fig. 3. Pseudocode for the docker container.

Pseudocode for the RFID Server

The following code is much more straightforward, since its main concern is communication, and the user recognition part is simplified by the RFID antenna that detects the tags. It is always in an infinite loop since an infinite number of users can deposit bags indefinitely. Line 2 begins with the reception of the RFID tag in the antenna. Line 3 registers the current date and time. Line 4 creates the message that needs to be sent to the Nano Jetson server to start depositing bags. Line 5 creates the connection and in line 6 the message is officially sent. Line 7 sets the RFID module to listen until it receives a message from the Nano Jetson in line 8 to continue receiving tag signals (Fig. 4).

```
Procedure RFID_module_communication(Nano_Jetson_IP)

    1.  Repeat (Server Type Behavior: Always Running)
    2.      RFID_Tag ← Received Input Signal from Antenna
    3.      Date_Registered ← DateTime.Now()
    4.      Message_To_Nano ← Concatenate(RFID_Tag, Date_Registered)
    5.      Socket.Connect(Nano_Jetson_IP)
    6.      Socket.Send_And_Close_Connection(Message_To_Nano)
    7.      Socket.Set_Socket_On_Listening_Port()
    8.      Continue ← Socket.Accept_Message_Close_Connection()
    9.  End
    10. End RFID_module_communication
```

Fig. 4. Pseudocode for the RFID server

Implementation of the RFID Server: https://github.com/aa-rodriguezv/AIA-robot-paper/blob/master/communication_trials/RFID_module_communication.py.

Pseudocode for the Bands Mechanism

The figure above describes the behaviour of the bands, which is simple. As the title denounces it, the bands move until the sensor is obstructed by an object which, in this case, are bags. Line 1 initializes the sensor. Line 2 declares the loop to stay attentive to changes in it. Line 3 declares a condition. If the distance in the sensor is reduced, the bands stop in line 4 and the program finishes in line 5 so that the program in the Nano Jetson can keep the execution going. Otherwise, the bands keep moving at the determined speed in line 7 (Fig. 5).

```
Procedure Bands_File_Run_Until_Sensor_Interrupted(UltraSound_Sensor_Max_Distance, MaxSpeed)

 1.  UltraSound_Sensor
 2.  Repeat(OnTimer Continuously Check Band Status)
 3.      If UltraSound_Sensor.Distance < UltraSound_Sensor_Max_Distance
 4.          MoveBandsAtSpeed(0)
 5.          ExitWithStatus(0)
 6.      Else
 7.          MoveBandsAtSpeed(MaxSpeed)
 8.      EndIf
 9.  End
10.  End  Bands_File_Run_Until_Sensor_Interrupted
```

Fig. 5. Pseudocode for the bands mechanism

Implementation of the Bands Behavior: https://github.com/aa-rodriguezv/AIA-robot-project/blob/master/miscellaneus/OneStopUltraSound/one_stop_ultrasound.py.

The code listed above may use other libraries and specific APIs, but these can be found in the projects that contain them. The modularity design was intended for the code to be as representative of the behavior of each component as possible, leaving connection-specific commands in separated files.

The following repositories were used to leverage the PyTorch and BigQuery technologies in the paper:

- https://github.com/dusty-nv/pytorch-ssd
- https://github.com/tylertreat/BigQuery-Python

4.2 Test Case

The first step for the development of the solution was to establish a communication model between the RFID server and the Nano Jetson. To establish an on-going, dynamic, and simple protocol the decision was to use Sockets for this task. As it was defined before in the pseudocodes, the RFID first waits for the input of the Antenna. Once it gets it, it connects to the Nano Jetson, and sends a message with the tag and datetime. Conversely, the Nano Jetson always starts listening, then when the RFID server wishes to communicate, it connects and gets the message.

On Fig. 6, displayed below, is the visualization report created to analyze the data of the process (sent by the Nano Jetson server, through an API).

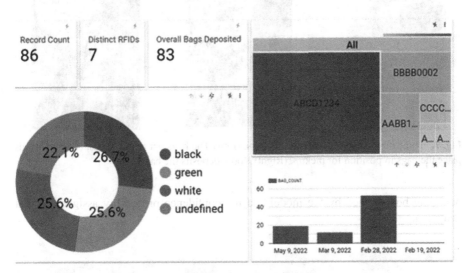

Fig. 6. Analysis report of the waste management process.

Once the behavior of the RFID Module was finished, and there was progress for both the Nano Jetson and the Analytics Engine, it was time to integrate the movement of the Robotic Arm and moving the bands to place the bags in pickup position. Figure 7 represents three moments of the deposit process. First, the bags reach the bands (Image on the left), after the RFID sends the tag to the Nano jetson server. The communication is established via SSH through the Paramiko library. It allows for the connection with the TXT controller of the bands, and it enables sending shell commands. This is how the Nano Jetson can execute the Python file that orders the bands to move until there is an object. Once it finishes execution, because a bag interrupts the ultrasound sensor (image on the center), the Nano Jetson commands the robot to pick up the bag, then, depending on the color, it tells it to go to a specific container to deposit the bag. If there are more bags, the process continues, until all the bags have been deposited.

Up until this point, a full execution can be made, and the architecture would appear to be working as expected. But the configuration of the bags was already predefined, it would only work for a specific number of bags and colors, in a particular order. So, it was necessary to implement the final component of the architecture: the object detection model.

The first step for this was to train and test the model. The sample consisted of 300 pictures with all four types of bags that could be detected: black, white, green and undefined (for bags not compliant with the color-coding schema determined by the Government of Colombia). Every picture with a small variation, i.e., lighting, placement of the bags and order in which they were placed on the bands. With this configuration, only 3 epochs were needed to get the results found below in Fig. 8. Each box has the

Fig. 7. Three moments of the deposit process. (Left) The bags get to the bands, (Center) bands place the bags in position for pickup. (Right) Robot deposits the bag.

bounding box defined by the model and the confidence probability assigned to that detection.

Fig. 8. Results of the object detection model on live feed.

The image above corresponds to a screenshot of the detection model running on a live camera stream on the Nano Jetson server. Table 1, shown below, lists the configuration of the detection model that led to the results in Fig. 8.

Table 1. Configuration and performance of the object detection model.

	Metric	Measure
Train	Images Sample	300
	Manually Drawn Boxes	1200
	Box/Class	300
	Epochs Ran	3

(continued)

Table 1. (*continued*)

	Metric	Measure
Result	Best Loss Acquired	1.28
	Best Epoch	#3
	Avg. Inference Time	109s

It is worth reminding that the model was implemented using PyTorch, using the SSD Mobilenet V1 CNN Architecture. The process of shooting the photos, labeling and effectively training, and validating, the model took approximately 8 h.

Though having the object detection model made for great progress, having a standalone model would make no impact on the architecture without communication. The next, and last step, in the paper was to establish a way in which the model could be used, based on the status of the bands, and the core program running in the Nano Jetson could read the detection to proceed with depositing the bags. For this to be achieved, first it was necessary to identify the Docker container running on the Nano with the detection model. Figure 9 below shows an execution where the Nano Jetson, running a subprocess, identifies the container.

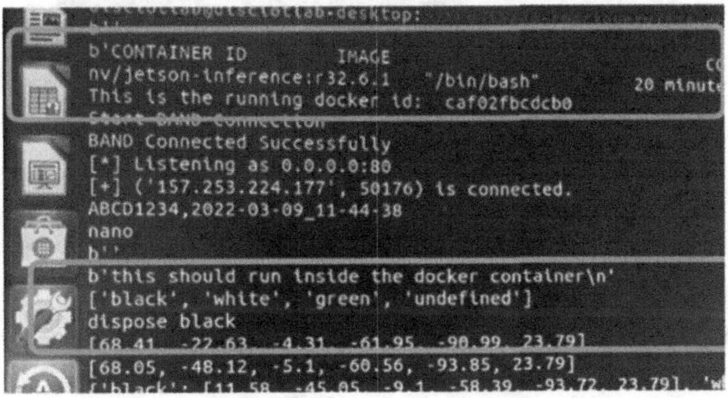

Fig. 9. Nano Jetson server running.

Once the communication was possible, it was time to start using the object detection model in the architecture. Figure 10 shows an execution of the program inside the Docker container that loads the model (red rectangle), takes a picture, detects objects (yellow rectangle) and writes the result to a file in a shared space folder (green rectangle).

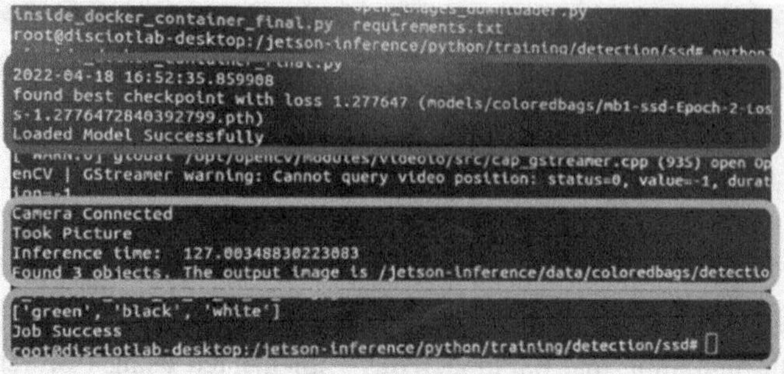

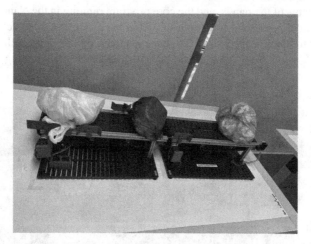

```
inside_docker_container_final.py  requirements.txt
root@disclotlab-desktop:/jetson-inference/python/training/detection/ssd# python
2022-04-18 16:52:35.859908
found best checkpoint with loss 1.277647 (models/coloredbags/mb1-ssd-Epoch-2-Los
s-1.2776472840392799.pth)
Loaded Model Successfully
[ WARN:0] global /opt/opencv/modules/videoio/src/cap_gstreamer.cpp (935) open Op
enCV | GStreamer warning: Cannot query video position: status=0, value=-1, durat
ion=-1
Camera Connected
Took Picture
Inference time:  127.00348830223083
Found 3 objects. The output image is /jetson-inference/data/coloredbags/detectio
['green', 'black', 'white']
Job Success
root@disclotlab-desktop:/jetson-inference/python/training/detection/ssd# []
```

Fig. 10. Execution on the docker container inside the Nano Jetson server. (Color figure online)

The execution above resulted from the picture shown below in Fig. 11.

Fig. 11. Status of the band for the execution in Fig. 10.

Finally, as a bonus for the paper, to verify the performance of the model in the architecture itself (not just on a live camera stream running independently, like in Fig. 8) the program running inside the docker container writes the captured image with the bounding boxes and the confidence probability for the bags detected.

Fig. 12. Model performance evidence in the architecture.

Figure 12 shows the captured image in one of the executions made and it is worth noting that these images, like the result file the Nano Jetson reads, were also placed in a shared spaced folder for persistence.

5   Conclusions

From the results the main conclusion drawn is that it is possible to implement an IoT architecture that allows for the automation and analysis of the process for classifying and separating garbage bags. The solution presented, as evidenced in Sect. 4.2, is resilient and robust enough to serve its purpose well and allows for improvements and incremental developments to be built on top. Another conclusion that can be drawn from the paper is that, building an object detection model for similar elements that only differ in color does not require a great and significant effort (in this case it took a day's work in time and a small sample of images). However, for this paper to be a solution ready to be launched to the public and implemented in real buildings there are some considerations and further implementations that need to be considered.

Currently, there is a need for the RFID antenna to be connected to another server, but this could increase the price of implementation unnecessarily, as its only job is to communicate the date of registry and the incoming tag to the Nano Jetson. Another problem that arises with users is related to the concurrency. For now, the architecture can hold one user at a time. But, virtually, an infinite number of users could deposit bags at the same time. With it, not only it becomes a problem to receive multiple users at the same time, but identifying which bags belong to each user becomes another challenge. Furthermore, there are some improvements that can be made related to connection. For instance, every IP on the architecture is pre-defined, but there could be mechanisms that can be developed for the Nano Jetson to identify the Robot and the Bands within the same network. Additionally, there could be more advanced developments regarding the interaction with the Robotic Arm and the bags. The robot could optimize the placement of the grip to grab the bags and automatically find the container that matches with the color of the bag. Finally, testing different detection models and increasing the sample to improve performance could be of significant help to reduce the inference time and make the process run faster.

References

1. ORACLE Corp. (N.D.) What is IoT?. https://www.oracle.com/co/internet-of-things/what-is-iot/
2. Mitra, A.: Detection of Waste Materials Using Deep Learning and Image Processing (2020). https://scholarworks.calstate.edu/downloads/gx41mn74q
3. Arebey, M., Hannan, M., Begum, R., Basri, H.: Solid waste bin level detection using gray level co-occurrence matrix feature extraction approach. J. Environ. Manage. **104**, 9–18 (2012)
4. Howard, A.G., et al.: Mobilenets: Efficient convolutional neural networks for mobile vision applications (2017). http://arxiv.org/abs/1704.04861
5. Suharto, E., et al.: J. Phys. Conf. Ser. **1524**, 012105 (2020)
6. Pineda, J.: El problema Ambiental de la Basura (2017). https://encolombia.com/medio-ambiente/interes-a/problema-ambiental-basura/

7. Vera, K.T.: Año nuevo con nuevo código de colores para separar residuos. Pequisa Javeriana (2021). https://www.javeriana.edu.co/pesquisa/ano-nuevo-con-nuevo-codigode-colores-para-separar-residuos-en-colombia/

8. VIDA: Se usarán tres colores para reciclar en todo el país. El Tiempo (2019). https://www.eltiempo.com/vida/medio-ambiente/blanco-negro-y-verde-nuevo-codigo-decolores-para-reciclar-447228

9. S.A.: Manejo de Basuras, Una problemática en Colombia. Medio Ambiente (2021). https://www.kienyke.com/medio-ambiente/manejo-de-las-basuras-una-problematica-encolombia

10. S.A.: Problemática por basuras: voces de expertos, testimonios y cifras. RTVC Noticias (2021). https://www.rtvcnoticias.com/basuras-colombia-toneladas-manejo-reciclaje

11. S.A.: La mayoría de los colombianos todavía prefieren vivir en casas que en apartamentos. La República (2019). https://www.larepublica.co/economia/la-mayoriade-los-colombianos-todavia-prefieren-vivir-en-casas-que-en-apartamentos-2903583

12. Friends of The Earth. 7 Benefits of Recycling. Disponible en (2018). https://friendsoftheearth.uk/sustainable-living/7-benefits-recycling

13. S.A.: Tasa de desempleo en Colombia fue de 10,8 % en noviembre del 2021. Portafolio (2021). https://www.portafolio.co/economia/empleo/tasa-de-desempleo-en-colombia-en-noviembredel-2021-560102

Software Architectures

Architecture on Knowledge Management Systems: Its Presence in the Academic Literature

Luciano Straccia[✉], María F. Pollo-Cattáneo, Matías Giorda, M. Gracia Bongiorno, and Adriana Maulini

Grupo de Estudio en Metodologías de Ingeniería de Software (GEMIS), Universidad Tecnológica Nacional Facultad Regional Buenos Aires, Buenos Aires, Argentina
`{lstraccia,fpollo,mgiorda,mbongiorno}@frba.utn.edu.ar`

Abstract. Knowledge management allows managing not only the information possessed by people, but also the experiences, judgments, cognitive beliefs adapted and empowered by an individual's mind. The concrete implementation of knowledge management in organizations requires considering diverse views (or approaches), including the technological aspects and their structure in a software architecture. This paper proposes a Scoping Study based on the following research questions: how many papers associated with knowledge management deal with software architecture? what types of architectures are presented in the papers found? and what information about these architectures are presented in the papers?

Keywords: Knowledge management · Architecture · KMS

1 Introduction

The changes in organizational practices in the last decades, the incorporation of information technologies, the identification of the importance of the collaborative knowledge building and the attention on the staff turnover that affects some industries, have increased the concern for knowledge management, understood as an emerging instance from the experiences that workers produce in their daily actions, the decisions they make, the interactions with other individuals, etc. Thus, knowledge management is already an indispensable practice for organizations. However, despite the maturity in the awareness of the relevance of knowledge management aspects, it is still difficult to implement a complete process and a Knowledge Management System (KMS) since there have been no significant advances in the research of technological aspects that support the processes and practices, and there is no clarity in the theoretical frameworks regarding the technological architecture to be used. This paper seeks to review the academic literature to identify proposals related to knowledge management architecture in order to contribute to the construction of a conceptual framework and to identify the different types of possible architecture models and what information (and technologies) about these architectures are presented in the papers.

© The Author(s), under exclusive license to Springer Nature Switzerland AG 2022
H. Florez and H. Gomez (Eds.): ICAI 2022, CCIS 1643, pp. 411–423, 2022.
https://doi.org/10.1007/978-3-031-19647-8_29

This work presents the concepts of Knowledge (Sect. 2.1), Knowledge Management (Sect. 2.2), architecture (Sect. 2.3) and architecture for KM (Sect. 2.4). In Sect. 3, it presents the method. Then, it shows the scoping study (Sect. 4) and the study selection (Sect. 5). Finally, Sect. 6 presents the results and Sect. 7, the conclusions.

2 Background

2.1 Knowledge

Knowledge is part of a hierarchy, called DIKW (see Fig. 1) proposed by Ackoff [1] constituted by data at the lowest level, information in a next level and knowledge in the third level of the hierarchy; finally, wisdom constitutes the upper level.

Fig. 1. DIKW hierarchy

Traditionally, data has been defined as a symbol that has not yet been interpreted [2] or as a simple observation of the state of the world [3]. Information is understood by Davenport and Prusak [4] and Nonaka and Takeuchi [5] as a set of messages; while Bollinger and Smith [6] define it as processed data [7]. Information can be defined as a function of data [8, 9], for containing both the data and their context, as specified in Li's Equation:

$$Information = f(Data) = Data + Context_d$$

where f (Data) represents the function that makes sense of Data and returns Information, and $Context_d$ indicates the context of Data.

For Díaz and Millán [10], knowledge is defined as: "the mixture of cognitive and contextualized beliefs, perspectives, judgments, methodologies, information, experiences and expectations made about an object, which are adapted and potentiated by the mind of an individual (knower)". Cornella [11] argues that "the 'metabolization' of information, its conversion into mental structures, generally permanent, leads to the creation of knowledge in our minds," which becomes facts with meaning and structure [12]. In Li's equation is:

$$Knowledge = p(Information) = Information + Context_i + Insight$$

where p(Information) denotes the processing function that returns Knowledge by making sense of Information under its context, i.e. $Context_i$.

2.2 Knowledge Management

Knowledge management (KM) is a theoretical notion attributed to Etzioni Amitai and defined as "how to create and use knowledge without undermining the organization" [13]. It is an integrated field of multiple disciplines that allow the development of initiatives at different levels of the company [14], with a multidisciplinary approach aimed at a comprehensive and systematic view of information assets [15].

Perez Gonzalez and Darín [16] define it as "an agglutinating process of information management, technology and human resources whose execution is focused on the improvement of high-impact processes, the optimization of knowledge based on these processes and their dissemination throughout the organization".

As regards Knowledge Management there are five views. A view describes the concepts, elements and characteristics of an integrated knowledge management system from the perspective of a set of related concerns. For KM, the views are: a) people (role, responsibilities, etc.); b) organizational aspects (including structure and culture); c) process (or activities); d) knowledge representation and technologies; and e) governance [17, 18]. But to identify the technological components without defining a comprehensive architecture is incomplete and difficult to implement. Vasconselos [19] says that "it is essential to derive the technological component in which the main technologies that will be used for the design of the information systems implementation infrastructure are specified".

2.3 Architecture

The origin of software architecture is attributed to Dijkstra, who proposed a structuring for software systems in 1968 [20]. Later, Wirth [21] defined the concept of "stepwise refinement" (the software must be developed considering the decomposition of tasks into subtasks and data into data structures) and DeRemer and Kron [22] introduced the notion of "programming-in-the-large" (design a larger system as a composition of a smaller part). However, these highest-level abstractions as a discipline correspond to the 80's through the work of Mary Shaw [23] and the appearance of "software architecture" as a term by Perry and Wolf [24].

The software architecture of a system is the set of structures needed to reason about the system. It comprises software elements, relationships between them and their properties [25, 26, 49, 50]. For IEEE, software architecture is the fundamental organization of a system, formed by its components, the relationships between them, the context in which they will be implemented, and the principles that guide their design and evolution [27]. The architecture "constitutes a relatively small and intellectually accessible model of how the system is structured and the way in which its components work together" [25].

A survey of the different concepts of software architecture according to various authors can be found in CMU [28], most of which emerged between 1992 and 1995. These concepts are presented in Table 1.

The notion of software architecture can be used at different levels of abstraction, from a general architecture level of an information system (regardless of its computerization) to the architecture of low-level classes. The Open Group's reference framework

Table 1. Definition of software architecture

Author	Definition
Clements et al.	The set of structures needed to reason about the system, which comprises software elements, relations among them, and their properties
Bass et al.	Structures of the system, which comprise software elements, their externally visible properties, and their relation
IEEE	Fundamental organization of a system, embodied in its components, their relation and the environment, and the principles governing its design and evolution
Kruchten [29]	The set of significant decisions about the organization of a software system, the selection of the structural elements and the interfaces in the system, together with their behavior as specified in the collaborations among those elements, the composition of these structural and behavioral elements into progressively larger subsystems, and the architectural style guiding this organization

[30] presents an enterprise architecture that can be viewed as a set of the following architectures: information architecture, business architecture, technology architecture and application architecture. The last two architectures are more related to this work. The technological architecture describes the hardware, software and communications structure required to support the implementation of information systems [31] and the application architecture defines "the applications required for information management" [32].

This paper uses the technological architecture and the application architecture as the scope of the architecture and explores how both aspects constitute Knowledge Management Systems.

2.4 Architectures for Knowledge Management System

According to Medina García et al. [33], the architectures for Knowledge Management Systems can be divided into two approaches: classical architectures and proprietary architectures. Proprietary architectures are structured with a strong component of agents and are related to proprietary software with their consequent integration and dependency. Classical architectures are considered generic and can be applied to all types of Knowledge Management System and their architectural style is N-Layered, organized by layers that communicate to complete the required functionality; each layer has a well-defined scope and functionality. However, there are architectures that, even if they were generic, might not have an N-Layer architectural style. Therefore, the following types of architectures can exist: generic N-layer, generic without N-layer (called Non Layer in this paper) and proprietary [51].

3   Method

This work proposes a Scoping Study (also known as Systematic Mapping Study). It's is a type of Literature Review. While the Systematic Literature Review makes it possible to identify, evaluate and interpret all available research relevant to a particular research question, or topic area, or phenomenon of interest, Systematic Mapping Studies are designed to provide a wide overview of a research area. Their main differences are the depth of the study and the rigorous application of the method and definition of inclusion and exclusion criteria. Shows details about the differences.

Scoping studies "aim to map rapidly the key concepts underpinning a research area and the main sources and types of evidence available and can be undertaken as standalone projects in their own right, especially where an area is complex or has not been reviewed comprehensively before" [34]. It is possible to identify at least four common reasons why a scoping study might be undertaken: to examine the extent, range and nature of research activity; to determine the value of undertaking a full systematic review; to summarise and disseminate research findings and to identify research gaps in the existing literature [34].

Arksey & O'Malley [35] propose the following method for the scoping study: identifying the research question; identifying relevant studies; study selection; charting the data; and collating, summarising and reporting the results. The phase of study selection is important because the initial outcome examination from the search protocol may pick up a number of irrelevant studies [35]. This is related to the importance of defining terminology at the beginning of a scoping study, and sometimes reflects some specific difficulties, such as the use of terminology in different countries, different contexts or different countries. The phase of charting describes a technique for synthesising and interpreting qualitative data [36].

4   Scoping Study

4.1   Identifying the Research Question

This paper is based on the following research questions:

- How many papers associated with knowledge management deal with software architecture?
- What types of architectures are presented in the papers found?
- What information about these architectures are presented in the papers?

4.2   Identifying Relevant Studies

For the identification of relevant studies, this study includes 3 searches (see Table 2). The first searches (Search 1 and Search 2) are conducted on Latin American repositories. The last search (Search 3) is wider in geographic scope and more specific in search terms.

Table 2. Search criteria

Criteria	Search 1	Search 2	Search 3
Source	La Referencia Redalyc SciELO SEDICI SNRD	Idem Search 1	ACM DBLP IEEE Mendeley Springer
Period restriction	2019–2020	2021	2019–2021
Keywords	"gestion del conocimiento"	Idem Search 1	Keyword 1: "knowledge management" architecture Keyword 2: "knowledge architecture"
Keywords in	All	Only Title	All
Inclusion criteria	Publications in Spanish, Portuguese or English		
Exclusion criteria	non-accessible publications publications of authors of this paper		

4.3 Study Selection

The search, whose criteria were defined in Sect. 4.2, returned 1132 papers. In the detailed analysis of the papers, 3 criteria for the selection of studies were considered:

1. papers that match the term search but use the concept of KM with a different scope than the one presented in this paper were excluded. Generally, these papers refer to topics related to pedagogy;
2. papers related with KM, but which do not make specific reference to any of the views presented in Sect. 2.2 were excluded;
3. papers related with KM, but which do not present any technological architecture as presented in Sect. 2.3 were excluded.

The results of the searches and the application of the selection criteria presented above yielded the results presented in Table 3.

As presented in Table 3, for search 1 there are 837 results and 60% of them do not match the Knowledge Management topics according to the definitions established in the present work. However, differences are observed between those papers that have the search term in the title (group 1) and those that do not have the search term in the title (group 2): while in the first group only 21% (out of a total of 479) are excluded, in the second group 88% are excluded (out of a total of 358 works). These differences are presented in Table 4. Therefore, in search 2, the search criteria are redefined and only papers that include the search term in their title are considered.

Comparing search 1 and search 2 and considering the same search criteria (search 1 group 2 and search 2), even considering that search 1 corresponds to 2 years (2019 and 2020) and search 2 to only 1 year (2021), there is a decrease in the number of

Table 3. Study selection

	Search 1	Search 2	Search 3
Results	837	130	163
Exclusion criteria 1	499 (60%)	16 (12%)	134 (82%)
Subtotal 1	*338*	*114*	*29*
Exclusion criteria 2	164 (49%)	71 (62%)	1 (3%)
Subtotal 2	*174*	*43*	*28*
Exclusion criteria 3	166 (95%)	43 (100%)	19 (68%)
Total	*8*	*0*	*6*

Table 4. Study selection. Differences in search 1.

	Search 1	Group 1	Group 2
Results	837	479	358
Exclusion criteria 1	499 (60%)	423 (88%)	76 (21%)
Subtotal 1	*338*	*56*	*282*
Exclusion criteria 2	164 (49%)	29 (52%)	135 (48%)
Subtotal 2	*174*	*27*	*147*
Exclusion criteria 3	166 (95%)	26 (95%)	140 (95%)
Total	*8*	*1*	*7*

papers found (from 358 to 130). If the years of the first search are analyzed, a decrease is observed too: for the year 2019 there are 203 papers; for 2020, 155; and finally, for 2021, there are 130.

The papers found related to knowledge management architecture are presented in Table 5 and are detailed in Sect. 5.

Table 5. Papers found.

Search 1	Search 3	Both
Zavala Zavala (2019)	Tadejko (2020)	Moscoso-Zea et al. (2019)
Jofré et al. (2019)	Liu (2019)	Ruiz et al. (2020)
Moscoso-Zea (2019)	Ting Su et al. (2019)	
Gutierrez Bogota (2020)	Haitao et al. (2020	
Pastrana Cruz (2020)		
Sanchez Valencia (2019)		

4.4 Charting the Data

As presented in Sect. 2.4., according to Medina García et al. [33], the architectures for Knowledge Management Systems can be divided into two approaches: classical architectures and proprietary architectures. For Medina et al., classical architectures are considered generic and can be applied to all types of Knowledge Management Systems and their architectural style is N-Layered. However, there are architectures which, even if they were generic, might not have an N-Layer architectural style. Therefore, the following types of architectures can exist: generic N-layer, generic without N-layer (called Non Layer in this paper) and proprietary.

Considering the research questions "what types of architectures are presented in the papers found?" and "what information about these architectures is presented in the papers?", this paper aims to identify the following characteristics of each architecture presented:

a. Type of architecture: generic N-Layer; generic Non Layer; proprietary;
b. Whether it defines components (technologies and applications);
c. Whether it presents the relationships between components;
d. Whether it presents the relationships between components of the same layer (only for N-Layer architecture)
e. Whether it presents the relationships between components of different layers (only for N-Layer architecture)

4.5 Collating, Summarising and Reporting the Results

The data collation, summary and report are presented in Sect. 6.

5 Study Selection

This section present details about the findings for each knowledge management architecture in the scoping study.

Zavala Zavala [37] presents a technological integration model of Kerschberg and makes a proposal for a knowledge management software with a component model structured in layers and a computer model for analysis and automation. The proposed layered model preserves the 3 layers proposed by Kerschberg: presentation, knowledge management and information sources. However, it does not present technologies or technological processes associated with the first two layers, reserving the presentation of technology only for the information sources layer.

Jofré et al. [38] defines an architecture organized according to the architecture of De Freitas and Yaber, who classify knowledge management tools according to the activity to which they are associated: knowledge acquisition, discovery and creation, use and development and its dissemination and present architectures of Tiwana, Woods and Sheina and Kerchsberg. None of the architectures presented have a higher level of detail than the high level of architectural definition (i.e. its layers and some tools).

Moscoso-Zea [39] and Moscoso-Zea et al. [40] proposes a framework for knowledge management, presenting the necessary people and processes, Business Intelligence activities (analysis and ETL) and their relationship with Enterprise Architecture, and presents the following technologies: data warehouse, EA repository and a knowledge management system, also including OLTP Databases, OLAP Tools, Educational Data Warehouse and Educational Data Mining. However, it does not propose further details associated with technological architecture.

Gutierrez Bogota [41] proposes a layered architecture: vision, communities, access channels, applications, knowledge repository, infrastructure and enabling environment. It can be observed that some of the layers do not correspond to technological architecture but they are associated with enterprise architecture; in the remaining layers the author does propose any specific technologies.

Pastrana Cruz [42] proposes a knowledge management architecture with layers of information sources, knowledge management and presentation, without defining any specific technologies for each layer.

Ruiz et al. [43] presents a detailed architecture for knowledge management. However, it seems to be a description of processes with some references to the architecture, with identification of some components.

Sanchez Valencia [44] seeks to determine the incidence of ITIL (a set of concepts and best practices for technology service management) in knowledge management in the application support area of an IT consultancy. He presents a web architecture for a knowledge management system, though very basic, defining the need for a metadatabase and a FileSystem.

Tadejko [45] presents a Cognitive Services subsystem in Knowledge Management IT System Architecture as well as Cognitive Services functions in relation to the DIKW Pyramid.

Liu [46] conducted a research work on Knowledge Management Technology of Aerospace Engineering Based on Big Data and shows the Hadoop architecture. Hadoop is a distributed system infrastructure developed by the Apache Foundation and implements a Distributed File System. Liu shows a framework model of Knowledge Management with activities and technologies. Although the framework includes more activities than technologies, some technologies can be found in the creation and storage stage.

Ting Su et al. [47] presents a tool that captures and provides visualization of the usage data of SA artefacts, in particular the usage data of software architecture documents (ADs) called KaitoroCap, a plug-in for the Atlassian Confluence. This tool supports document creation and dynamic restructuring; annotation; exploration path capturing, visualisation and searching. The paper shows a high-level design of KaitoroCap.

Haitao et al. [48] propose an architecture of a pathological Knowledge Management System. It shows a Browser/Server structure with 3 layers: user interface, application layer and storage layer. The application layer mainly includes some modules such as structured pathological knowledge management, semi-structured knowledge management, pathological knowledge network, and pathological knowledge mining modules In turn, the storage layer includes two components: database and knowledge base. The knowledge base "stores knowledge of pathological diagnostic criteria data and clinic pathological diagnosis results obtained by summarizing, filtering and reviewing the data in the pathological database". No integration between components is observed.

6 Results

Each of the papers presented in Sect. 5 is analyzed according to the characteristics indicated in Sect. 4.4. And the results are presented in Table 6. The analysis is performed considering the following:

a. Type of architecture: generic N-Layer; generic Non Layer; proprietary;
b. Whether it defines components (technologies and applications);
c. Whether it presents the relationships between components;
d. Whether it presents the relationships between components of the same layer (only for N-Layer architecture)
e. Whether it presents the relationships between components of different layers (only for N-Layer architecture)

Table 6. Results

Model	A	b	c	d	e
Zavala-Zavala	Generic N-Layer	Yes	Yes	No	No
Jofré et al.	Generic N-Layer	Yes	Yes	Yes	No
Moscoso-Zea	Generic Non Layer	Yes	Yes	N/A	N/A
Moscoso-Zea et al.	Generic Non Layer	Yes	Yes	N/A	N/A
Gutierrez Bogotá	Generic N-Layer	Yes	No	No	No
Pastrana Cruz	Generic N-Layer	No	No	No	No
Ruiz et al.	Generic N-Layer	Yes	Yes	Yes	Yes
Sanchez Valencia	Generic N-Layer	Yes	No	No	No
Tadejko	Generic N-Layer	Yes	Yes	Yes	Yes
Liu	Generic N-Layer	Yes	Yes	Yes	Yes
Ting Su et al.	Propietary	Yes	Yes	N/A	N/A
Haitao et al.	Generic N-Layer	Yes	Yes	No	No

Although the Moscoso-Zea architectures are considered in this paper, they are higher level architectures (Enterprise Architecture Software), even though they present some proposals that could be used in the architecture for Knowledge Management System. Similarly, Gutierrez Bogota's architecture is also an Enterprise Architecture and proposes layers associated with the business aspect and others linked to knowledge and software. Ting Su especially analyzes a proprietary architecture of a software called KaitoroCap.

The remaining works, oriented to generic architectures, present a layered architecture. This is related to Medina García's statement regarding the relationship between generic architectures and their presentation with a layers style.

The architectures of Zavala-Zavala, Jofré and Haitao are based on Kerchsberg's proposals and consider the traditional layers of software production: presentation layer, knowledge management layer (similar to the logical layer or software business layer) and data source layer. The models of Pastrana Cruz and Sanchez Valencia present their architectures with these same layers.

The proposals of Ruiz, Liu and Tadejko are very different from those mentioned above. Ruiz and Liu present architectures based on the different knowledge management activities, although they also consider them in a layered format and propose some specific applications, while Tadejko proposes an architecture based on the constructivist vision of knowledge and the DIKW pyramid.

7   Conclusions

The architecture of knowledge management is a poorly investigated topic in the bibliography of knowledge management in the sources consulted in this work. In future works, it is planned to carry out a wide search (like those carried out in searches 1 and 2) in the sources used in search 3 (non-Latin American repositories), which will involve an analysis of about 800 papers.

In the works found, the architectures can be categorized as proprietary or generic and can be observed with (or without) the application of the layered architectural pattern. Most of the knowledge management architectures found are layered architectures, with 3 styles for defining the layers: the first is a traditional way associated with software production and based on Kerschberg's architectures (presentation, knowledge management or logical layer and data layer); the second, defines one layer for each knowledge management activities; and, the last associated each layer with the levels of the DIKW pyramid.

References

1. Ackoff, R.: From data to wisdom. J. Appl. Syst. Anal. **16**, 3–9 (1989)
2. Spek, R., Spijkervet, A.: Knowledge Management: Dealing Intelligently with Knowledge. Kennis-centrum CIBIT, Utrecht (1997)
3. Davenport, T.: Information Ecology: Mastering the Information and Knowledge Enviroment. Oxford University Press, New York (1997)
4. Davenport, T., Prusak, L.: Working Knowledge: How Organisations Manage What They Know. Harvard Business School Press, USA (1998)
5. Nonaka, I., Takeuchi, H.: The Knowledge-Creating Company. Oxford University Press, Oxford (1995)
6. Bollinger, A., Smith, R.: Managing organisational knowledge as a strategic asset. J. Knowl. Manag. **5**(1), 8–18 (2001)
7. Aristizabal Boero, C.: El dato, la información, el conocimiento y su productividad en empresas del sector público de Medellín. In: Semestre Económico. Universidad de Medellín (2011)
8. Kaipa, P.: Knowledge architecture for the twenty-first century. Behav. Inf. Technol. **19**(3), 153–161 (2000)
9. Li, Z.: On a factorial knowledge architecture for data science-powered software engineering. In: Proceedings of the International Conference on Software and e-Business, Osaka, Japan (2020)
10. Díaz, M.; Millán, J.: Gestión del Conocimiento y Capital Intelectual, a través de modelos universitarios. Económicas CUC (2013)

11. Cornella, A.: Infonomia! La empresa es información, Deusto, Bilbao, España (2000)
12. Chekland, P., Holwell, S.: Information, Systems and Information Systems. John Wiley & Sons, Chichester, UK (1998)
13. Farfán Buitrago, D., Garzon Castrillón, M.: La Gestión del Conocimiento. Editorial Universidad del Rosario, México (2006)
14. Wiig, K.: Enterprise Knowledge Management (2007)
15. Geisler, E., Wickramasinghe, N.: Principles of Knowledge Management Theory, Practice, and Cases. Routledge, New York, USA (2015)
16. Perez Gonzalez, Y.; Darin, S.: El diagnóstico como proceso esencial para implementar la gestión del conocimiento: prácticas del Centro de Estudios Martianos (2013)
17. Straccia, L., Ramacciotti, C., Pollo-Cattáneo, M.F.: Una visión de la tecnología para la Gestión del Conocimiento. Resultados en la literatura latinoamericana. In: Serna, E (ed) Desarrollo e Innovación en Ingeniería, Editorial Instituto Antioqueño de Investigación, pp. 135–142 (2020)
18. Milton, N.: The 4 legs on the Knowledge Management table (2015)
19. Vasconcelos, A.; Sousa, P.; Tribolet, J.: Information system architectures: representation, planning and evaluation. In: Proceedings of International Conference on Computer, Communication and Control Technologies (2003)
20. Dijkstra, E.: The structure of the multiprogramming system. Commun. ACM **26**(1), 49–52 (1968)
21. Wirth, N.: The programming language Pascal. Acta Informatica **1**, 35–63 (1971)
22. DeRemer, F., Kron, H.: Programming-in-the-large versus programming-in-the-small. In: Proceedings of the International Conference on Reliable Software, vol. 10, pp. 114–121. Association for Computing Machinery (1975)
23. Shaw, M.: Larger-scale systems require higher-level abstractions. In: Proceedings of the Fifth International Workshop on Software Specification and Design, pp. 143–146 (1989)
24. Perry, D., Wolf, A.: Foundations for the study of software architecture. ACM SIGSOFT **17**(4), 40–52 (1992)
25. Bass, L., Clements, P., Kazman, R.: Software Architecture in Practice, 2nd edn. Addison Wesley (2003)
26. Clement, P., Bachmann, F., Bass, L. Documenting Software Architectures: Views and Beyond, 2nd edn. Addison Wesley (2010)
27. IEEE Std. 1471-2000
28. CMU What is Your Definition of Software Architecture? Carnegie Mellon University (2017)
29. Kruchten, P.: The Rational Unified Process: An Introduction (1999)
30. The Open Group: The Open Group Launches the TOGAF® Standard, Version 9.2 (2018)
31. Ledesma Alvear, J.: Frameworks de Arquitectura Empresarial, Trabajo de Especialización en Ingeniería de Software, Facultad de Informática, Universidad Nacional de La Plata, La Plata (2017)
32. Cabrera, A., Carrillo, J., Abad, M., Jaramillo, D., Romero, F.: Diseño y validación de arquitecturas de aplicaciones empresariales. In: Revista Ibérica de Sistemas e Tecnologias de Informação (2015)
33. Medina García, V., Perez, P., Rolón, J.: Arquitectura de un sistema de gestión del conocimiento basado en agentes inteligentes (2008)
34. Mays, N., Roberts, E., Popay, J.: Synthesising research evidence. In: Fulop, N., Allen, P., Clarke, A., Black, N. (eds.) Studying the Organisation and Delivery of Health Services: Research Methods, pp. 188–220. Routledge, London (2001)
35. Arksey, H., O'Malley, L.: Scoping studies: towards a methodological framework. Int. J. Soc. Res. Methodol. **8**, 19–32 (2005)
36. Ritchie, J., Spencer, L.: Qualitative data analysis for applied policy research. In: Bryman, A., Burgess, R. (eds.) Analysing Qualitative Data, pp. 173–194. Routledge, London (1994)

37. Zavala-Zavala, E.: Propuesta de software de gestión del conocimiento para la optimización de la orientación al contribuyente. Tesis de Maestría en Ingeniería en Sistemas. Universidad Nacional Federico Villarreal (2019)
38. Jofré, N., Rodriguez, G., Alvarado, Y., Fernandez, J., Guerrero, R.: Plataforma para repositorios digitales 3D de colecciones biológicas. En: XXV Congreso Argentino de Ciencias de la Computación. Río Cuarto, Argentina (2019)
39. Moscoso-Zea, O.: A Hybrid Infrastructure of Enterprise Architecture and Business Intelligence & Analytics to Empower Knowledge Management in Education. Tesis Doctoral. Universidad de Alicante (2019)
40. Moscoso-Zea, O., Castro, J., Paredes-Gualtor, J., Luján-Mora, S.: A hybrid infrastructure of enterprise architecture and business intelligence & analytics for knowledge management in education. IEEE Access **7**, 38778–38788 (2019)
41. Gutierrez Bogota, W.: Diseño de un Sistema de Gestión del Conocimiento para la Empresa de Servicios Petroleros Sonoma Colombia S.A.S. (2020)
42. Pastrana Cruz, A.: Proyecto piloto para la implementación del sistema de gestión del conocimiento (KMS) para el área de Help Desk en Berlitz Colombia (2020)
43. Ruiz, M., Tabatabaeimehr, F., Velasco, L.: Knowledge management in optical networks: architecture, methods and use cases. J. Opt. Commun. Netw. **12**, 70–81 (2020)
44. Sánchez Valencia, G.: ITIL en la gestión del conocimiento en el área de soporte de aplicaciones en consultora de TI. In Tesis de Maestría. Universidad César Vallejo. Lima, Perú (2019)
45. Tadejko, P.: Cloud cognitive services based on machine learning methods in architecture of modern knowledge management solutions. In: Poniszewska-Marańda, A., Kryvinska, N., Jarząbek, S., Madeyski, L. (eds.) Data-Centric Business and Applications. LNDECT, vol. 40, pp. 169–190. Springer, Cham (2020). https://doi.org/10.1007/978-3-030-34706-2_9
46. Liu, J.: Research on knowledge management technology of aerospace engineering based on big data. In: Proceedings of the 2019 3rd High Performance Computing and Cluster Technologies Conference. Association for Computing Machinery, New York, NY, USA, pp. 172–176 (2019)
47. Su, M.T., Grundy, J., Hosking, J., Tempero, E.: Leveraging usage data of software architecture artefacts. In: Proceedings of the 2nd International Workshop on Establishing a Community-Wide Infrastructure for Architecture-Based Software Engineering, pp 13–21 (2019)
48. Haitao, Z., Shu, O., Hailan, W., Jieping, X.: Research on the construction of pathological knowledge management system based on web. In: Proceedings of the 2020 The 2nd World Symposium on Software Engineering, Association for Computing Machinery, New York, NY, USA, pp. 42–45 (2020)
49. Florez, H., Sánchez, M., Villalobos, J.: A catalog of automated analysis methods for enterprise models. Springerplus **5**(1), 1–24 (2016). https://doi.org/10.1186/s40064-016-2032-9
50. Florez, H., Sánchez, M.E., Villalobos, J.: Embracing imperfection in enterprise architecture models. In: CEUR Workshop Proceedings (2013)
51. Straccia, L., Pollo-Cattaneo, M.F., Maulini, A.: Knowledge management technologies for a n-layered architecture. In: CEUR Workshop Proceedings (2021)

Software Design Engineering

Automatic Location and Suppression of Calcification and Atheromas by Gradient Change in the Pattern of Intensities Inside the Carotid Artery

Fernando Yepes-Calderon[1,2,3]([⊠]) [iD]

[1] Science Based Platforms, 405 Beach CT, Fort Pierce, FL 34950, USA
[2] GYM Group SA, Cra 78A No. 6-58, Cali, Colombia
[3] Universidad del Valle - Facultad de Medicina, Cl. 4b #36-00, Cali, Colombia
`fernando.yepes@strategicbp.net`

Abstract. Atherosclerosis is associated with the first cause of death worldwide. However, early diagnosis is now feasible with sophisticated imaging methods called angiographies that produce 3D representations. From the images, it is possible to see the degree of stenosis that atheroma and calcifications produce within arteries. But yet, after locating and visualizing the abnormality, quantification of blockages is cumbersome due to the randomly intricate trace that arteries take. To overcome this difficulty, scientists trace the center line of the conduit to create parallel planes that serve as a basement to accurately define the geometries in health and disease. Unfortunately, the correct determination of the center line in blockages boycotts the accurate determination of parallel planes. This work presents an algorithm to automatically detect obstructions in the arteries and clean the path to facilitate the estimation of arteries' center lines. The developed algorithm managed to clean the images with high precision and can adapt itself to the contrast regardless of the intensity profiles present in the images. Therefore, this method is suitable for any laboratory and is unsensible to differences in scanning setups.

Keywords: Carotid artery imaging · Artery lumen intensity · Artery calcification intensity · Computer tomography imaging · Atherosclerosis

1 Introduction

In theory, computer tomography (CT) images produce image intensities reproducible among scanners [6]. This claim is partially valid because, in addition to configuration parameters accessible by technicians, the distances and physical setup also influence ionizing radiation absorption [7]. According to our testing, up to 93% of the pixels in CT are well classified with local ranges of thresholds that Gaussian statistics can yield. However, there are two situations where the statistical study is insufficient. One is when 7% of uncertainty manifests itself,

© The Author(s), under exclusive license to Springer Nature Switzerland AG 2022
H. Florez and H. Gomez (Eds.): ICAI 2022, CCIS 1643, pp. 427–439, 2022.
https://doi.org/10.1007/978-3-031-19647-8_30

and the other occurs when trying to work with data series from laboratories out of those listed in the statistical studies [2]. These two reasons are more than compelling to think about the need to create an automation that generalizes the segmentation problem and can work in any CT study independently of the setup or acquisition protocol.

The proposal described in this work aims to reach more than 93% of accuracy in segmenting calcifications and atheroma in CT images of arteries, regardless of their origin or setup. This approximation begins by transforming each cut's matrix pattern of intensities into a vector. Once the image is transformed, we identify the geometric characteristics of the resulting vector and relationships between the found phenomena as it appears in the vector and how it is manifested in the original image. Then, we use digital signal processing techniques to determine boundaries automatically. Finally, we move the vector back to the image domain. The modifications performed in the one-dimensional algorithm are presented as segmentations that separate the pixels corresponding to atheroma and calcifications. The signal processing is executed in the time domain, which is faster regarding computational load.

2   Materials and Methods

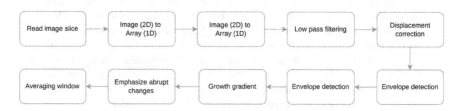

Fig. 1. Proposed pipeline for automatic segmentation of calcifications and atheroma inside the carotid artery

The method depicted in Fig. 1 aims to eliminate calcifications and atheroma using the intensity change rate that occurs between the different areas of the image. The procedure moves the 2D representation of each slice in the volumetric study to the vectors. To assert standardization, the vectorization reads all columns first before changing the row and starts in the upper left corner of the image. Then, we apply a low pass filter on the vectorized image to eliminate high-frequency changes [10]. This filter ensures that the imaging system generates the most abrupt changes in the resulting vector when finding transitions from one zone to another and are not the consequence of digitalization. We run an envelope detection algorithm on the filtered vector and recover the overall form in a polynomic function [4]. Most abrupt changes are emphasized, while smooth ones are obviated after affecting the vectors with a power-of-two function. Finally, a sliding window integral [11] covers the peaks of the vectorized signal identifying the regions where the intensities correspond to abnormalities.

A second pass of the same algorithm will start picking the areas where the intensity is hierarchically lower than calcifications, such as atheroma.

2.1   Domain Change, Smoothing Filter and Delay Correction

On every slice I_z, a pixel $p_{(x,y,z)}$ is taken to the 1D domain by applying Eq. 1.

$$X_{(x+y)}(T) = p_{(x,y,z)} \; \forall p \in I_z \tag{1}$$

Note that it is always possible to go back to the image domain since the X index is a function of the position of the intensity in the original 2D domain. The existence of z-axes says that there will be an array X for each slice I in the volume.

Once the vector representing the intensity profile is obtained, the high frequencies are eliminated with Eq. 1.

$$Y(nT) = 2Y(nT-T) - Y(nT-2T) + X(nT) - 2X(nT-6T) + X(nT-12T))/36 \tag{2}$$

where Y is the output signal, X is the input signal, n is the sample number, and T is the sampling, which is synthetically assigned since the array is not a digitalization product.

The filter has a delay of six samples, so the Eq. 3 performs the required correction:

$$Y(nT-6) = X(nT) \tag{3}$$

2.2   Envelope Detection

The array $Y_n(T-6)$ has a low-frequency signal being modulated in amplitude by a high-frequency signal. Judging by the original image, the low-frequency signal provides information about image boundaries; therefore, the data of interest is found in the envelope of the vector. The envelope detection process seeks to recover the low-frequency signal. The problem is similar to retrieving messages in an Amplitude Modulation (AM) radio system. There are efficient envelope detector filters like the one described in [5]. This filter uses the Hilbert transform [1], and the discrete Fourier transform to compute each sample. Then the inverse Fourier transform must be applied to return to the original domain. We designed the filter for a telecommunications environment where recovering the message is critical, and the quality of the receiver depends on the fidelity of the detection system. Although highly sophisticated, the described filter is not used in real-time transmissions because it is computationally exigent [3]. If the algorithm is discarded for real-time systems in telecommunications, it is because of its extensive execution time. The best option for envelope detection was sought in terms of computational loads, such as the one is described in [3], This method requires precise information about the sampling frequency and its relation to the carrier. Our information vector is not the result of a modulation process in amplitude, and the objective is not to recover a message. Still, the carrier must be as faithful as possible to maintain the intensity levels of the original image. This algorithm works in the time domain. For this reason, no transforms are required to transport the information from one domain to another, this represents an advantage at runtime. The Eq. 4 performs the required envelope detection in the time domain:

$$Y(nT) = \sqrt{X(nT)^2 + \left[\frac{X(nT-T)}{sin(\omega)} - \frac{X(nT)}{tan(\omega)}\right]^2} \tag{4}$$

To apply Eq. 4, one must know the relationship between the frequency of the carrier signal and the frequency sampling rate ω. It must then be defined where this information is found when the signal of AM comes from an unconventional source, such as the intensity pattern of a CT image. The high-frequency signal is the cut product of a row; that is, the carrier frequency is known; it is assumed that there is a cycle for each row change so that the carrier signal could have a frequency 1 Hz. In that order of ideas, the sampling frequency is equal to the number of samples in a row; this data is variable and depends on the width of the ROI. All of the above suggests an adaptive implementation whose only variable is the width of the ROI; the height only modifies the extension of the vector. Still, neither its frequency nor the number of samples per line; the window's height does not change the sample rate. With these relations, it is always possible to determine the parameter ω. A threshold function is applied to the envelope vector. This threshold is not critical and was selected as the minimum value for calcification among four laboratories. The function consists of taking to a negative level all the values in the vector that are above the threshold. This operation is done to reduce the execution time of the following routines since all of them are applied only to the vector indices whose values are negatives in the envelope vector under the threshold.

2.3 Calculation of Growth Gradient, Emphasis on Significant Changes and Averaging Window

After thresholding, all sections corresponding to negative values are selected in the resulting vector. The gradient function presented in Eq. 5 is applied to the thresholded vector Y.

$$Y(nT) = X(nT - T) - X(nT) \tag{5}$$

The gradient vector transforms the steeper slopes appearing in amplitude peaks in the filtered vector of intensities. Then, to emphasize abrupt changes and include downhill slopes, the nonlinear function in Eq. 6.

$$y(nT) = y(nT)^2 \tag{6}$$

Finally, an averaging window is applied to wrap the peak areas in the original vector, as shown in **Equation**.

$$y(nT) = \frac{1}{N}\left[X(nT) + \sum_{M=1}^{N-1} X(nT - (N-M)T)\right] \tag{7}$$

where N is the window size and M is a summation index. The value of N is selected with 5% of the samples included in a row.

3   Results

This section presents the results of every step listed in Sect. 2 and how the proposed method performs in clinical images.

3.1   Transfering Data from Matrix to Array

The graphical representation of the domain transfer is presented in Fig. 2. The data image equivalent to the array – in blue – is shown in the top right corner.

It is expected that regions of similar intensities are encompassed by abrupt changes since pixels belonging to a region in the image are neighbors.

3.2   Array Filtering

The array filtering presented in Fig. 3, is performed to eliminate the highest frequency introduced by the imperfection of the digital-to-analog conversion.

The blue line in Fig. 3 is a filtered version of the intensity profile that is convenient for the envelope detection algorithm.

3.3   Envelope Detection

In Fig. 4, envelope detection is performed to recover the low-frequency signal that encompasses the changes between intimately related regions in the image.

The envelope vector in Fig. 4, ignores strong variations in the intensity profile array.

3.4   Noncritical Session over Envelope Signal

This noncritical step depicted in Fig. 5 presents thresholding that does not significantly affect the method's performance but accelerates its execution.

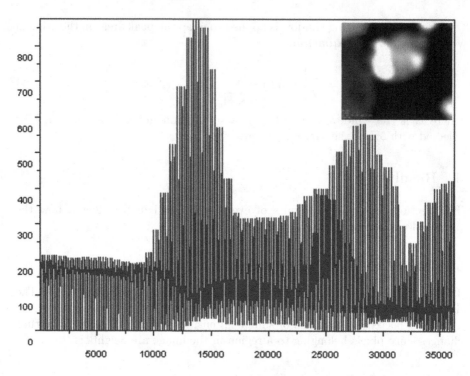

Fig. 2. The image is converted to an array, and the position index is kept by indexing with $(x + y)$. The images are always swept from the left top corner and columns first fashion.

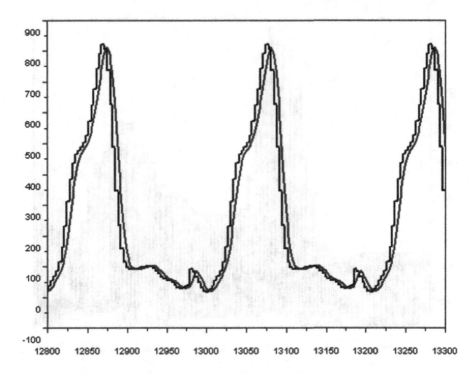

Fig. 3. The array of intensities profile (black) and array after filtering (blue). The subsequent procedure works on the filtered version of the intensities profile. This figure shows a part of the signals to enhance visualization. (Color figure online)

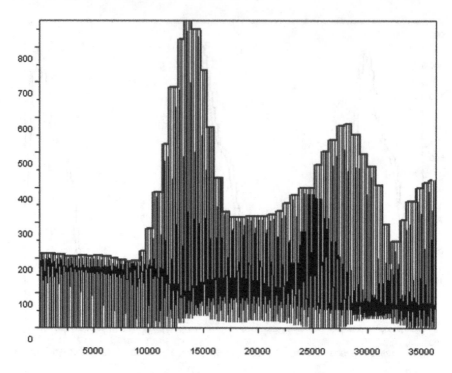

Fig. 4. The envelope array (blue) and the intensity profile (black) (Color figure online)

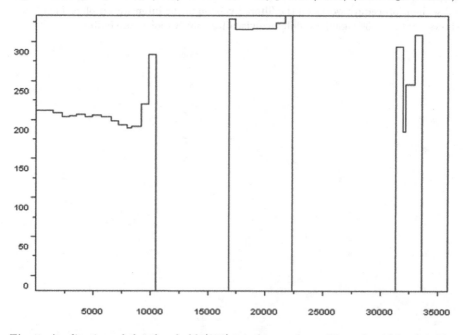

Fig. 5. Application of the threshold (350) on the envelope. The selected level is the lower level of the statistically defined range for calcification. This step is optional and included only to increase the execution speed of the method

3.5 Growth Gradient, Emphasis on Sharp Changes and Averaging Window Functions

The Fig. 6 shows the results of all functions referred to in the section title. These functions are only executed on the regions where the profile are zero in Fig. 5.

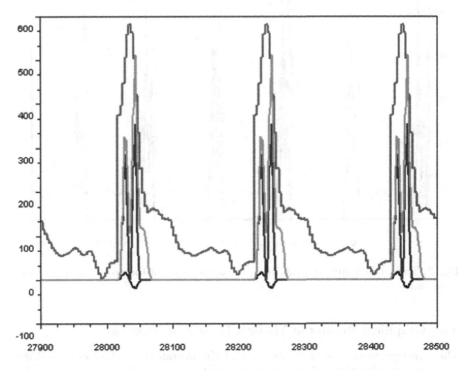

Fig. 6. Filtered array of intensities (red), gradient (black), emphasis in sudden changes (blue), averaging window array (green). (Color figure online)

The results shown in Fig. 7 is the one used to pick the indexes that should be set to lumen color so abnormalities disappear within the artery.

The data indexes covered by the blue line will be taken back to the original domain, and the selected pixels will be taken to zero level, so the selection is visible to the readers. In the medical scenario, the selected regions will be set to levels of intensity corresponding to the lumen; therefore, the central line algorithms can traverse the artery without the perturbing elements represented by atheroma and calcifications.

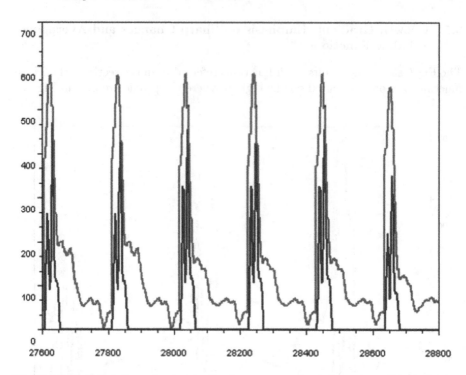

Fig. 7. The original filtered array (red), the array result of the process (blue). (Color figure online)

3.6   Graphical Results in Medical Images of Arteries

The envelope worked with accuracy, and the overall method picked the high-intensity areas in Fig. 8 the envelope worked precisely. This strategy complies with the dual purpose of cleaning the artery, facilitating central line algorithms, and characterization and quantification of blockages. In the placebo, structures of high intensity outside the lumen (lower area right of the last row) caused the method to be applied and consume time; however, the lumen was not touched by the automation as expected.

4   Discussion

A method was created for the location of severe pathologies in the carotid artery based on the intensity change rate from one zone to another. The steps described in the method involve simple procedures validated and implemented in telecommunications. The reported equations can be directly implemented in a Digital Signal Processor (DSP) to accelerate the process and have it done during image acquisition [8]. Handling envelope detection is convenient because the resulting vector defines a tendency that filters the substantial variations that generate the island effects-something almost impossible to handle with simple thresholding.

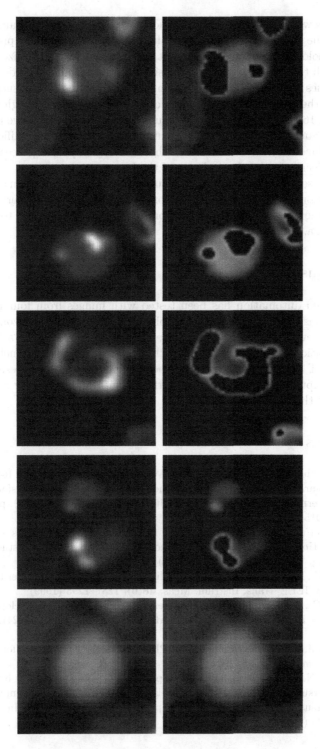

Fig. 8. The results are presented in pairs per row. On the left is the original image. On the right, the image with calcifications and atheroma is automatically detected and taken to zero level of intensity. The last row includes a placebo where the artery was clean.

Although we try to reduce the execution time by restricting the analysis zones by the middle of the envelope, the method is slow compared to preprocessing using thresholds. The execution time not only increases with the size of the ROI but also with the presence of high-intensity structures found outside the lumen.

Techniques on native slices that attempt to improve resolution, such as resampling, affect the execution time of the described method [9]. Although the image's resolution is 16 bits, the calcification values are not presented above the decimal value 2047. Such a finding suggests a cutoff of the four most significant bits of the image since they are always zero. This not only improves processing speed, but it also decreases the size in bytes of the image.

One can use the proposed method recurrently in the same section after removing calcifications to obtain only lumen zones. In this case, when there are no calcifications, the abrupt changes appear only from the background to the lumen and vice versa.

5   Conclusions

The presented automation has been tested with images from four institutions where previous research showed overlapping ranges along the four zones found in the field of view of carotid arteries. Since the automation requires a high degree of generalization, we propose an algorithm to clean up the channel inside the arteries of CT images. The testing has been exhaustive, and the results suggest that this adaptive implementation performs with high accuracy regardless of the origin of the images.

References

1. Chanwimalueang, T., von Rosenberg, W., Mandic, D.P.: Enabling R-peak detection in wearable ECG: combining matched filtering and Hilbert transform. In: 2015 IEEE International Conference on Digital Signal Processing (DSP), pp. 134–138. IEEE (2015)
2. Free, J., et al.: The effect of different CT scanners, scan parameters and scanning setup on Hounsfield units and calibrated bone density: a phantom study. Biomed. Phys. Eng. Express **4**(5), 055013 (2018)
3. Fritsch, C., Ibanez, A., Parrilla, M.: A digital envelope detection filter for real-time operation. IEEE Trans. Instrum. Meas. **48**(6), 1287–1293 (1999)
4. Gianto, G., Salzenstein, F., Montgomery, P.: Comparison of envelope detection techniques in coherence scanning interferometry. Appl. Opt. **55**(24), 6763–6774 (2016)
5. Honiball, J.R.: The development of a PPG and in-ear EEG device for application in fatigue measurement (2021)
6. Nerlekar, N., et al.: Poor correlation, reproducibility, and agreement between volumetric versus linear epicardial adipose tissue measurement: a 3D computed tomography versus 2D echocardiography comparison. JACC Cardiovasc. Imaging **11**(7), 1035–1036 (2018)

7. Oh, J.H., Choi, S.P., Wee, J.H., Park, J.H.: Inter-scanner variability in Hounsfield unit measured by CT of the brain and effect on gray-to-white matter ratio. Am. J. Emerg. Med. **37**(4), 680–684 (2019)

8. Robelly, J., Cichon, G., Seidel, H., Fettweis, G.: Implementation of recursive digital filters into vector SIMD DSP architectures. In: 2004 IEEE International Conference on Acoustics, Speech, and Signal Processing, vol. 5, pp. V–165. IEEE (2004)

9. Samuelson, F.W., Petrick, N.: Comparing image detection algorithms using resampling. In: 3rd IEEE International Symposium on Biomedical Imaging: Nano to Macro, pp. 1312–1315. IEEE (2006)

10. Shaikh, M.S., Choudhry, A., Wadhwani, R.: Analysis of digital image filters in frequency domain. Int. J. Comput. Appl. **140**(6), 12–19 (2016)

11. Wei, Y.Q., Liu, D.Y., Boutat, D., Liu, H.R., Wu, Z.H.: Modulating functions based model-free fractional order differentiators using a sliding integration window. Automatica **130**, 109679 (2021)

Introducing Planet-Saving Strategies to Measure, Control, and Mitigate Greenhouse Gas Emissions and Water Misuse in Household Residences

Ronald S. Marin Cifuentes[2,4], Adriana M. Florez Laiseca[3,5],
and Fernando Yepes-Calderon[1,2,3(✉)] ⓘ

[1] Science Based Platforms, 405 Beach CT, Fort Pierce, FL 34950, USA
[2] GYM Group SA, Cra 78A No. 6-58, Cali, Colombia
[3] Bosque Biodiverso SA, Calle 19N No. 18-68, Armenia, Colombia
`fernando.yepes@strategicbp.net`
[4] Institución Universitaria Antonio José Camacho, Av. 6 No. 29N-25, Cali, Colombia
`rsmarin@estudiante.uniajc.edu.co`
[5] Economy Department, Universidad del Quindio,
Cra 15 No. 12 N, Armenia, Colombia
`amflorez@uniquindio.edu.co`

Abstract. After several attempts to get world nations in agreement about the global warming menace and how the topic required immediate attention, the COP21 held in France (2015) ended with a clear pipeline to measure warming emissions after executing production processes. Although the strategy is full of flaws regarding mechanisms to assure the integrity of the reported data, it seems like consciousness has emerged in the head of leaders and entrepreneurs. Yet, in COP21, the warming emissions continue to be considered the sole responsibility of massive production, and the need to care for the planet has not spread to citizens. Such perspective leads the individuals to a passive role that, due to the growing number of humans globally, results in unnoticed individual emissions that conglomerate to reach enormous proportions. This paper describes an early implementation of ISO 14064 and ISO 14046 regulations that involve individuals in the care of the planet and is intended to cover a need with worldwide implications.

Keywords: Greenhouse gases control · ISO 14064 · ISO 14046 · GHG measurement · Sustainable homes

1 Introduction

The growing concern for the environment, particularly global warming, is the consequence of failed attempts to create international agreements on the generation of greenhouse gases (GHG) [22]. Global warming brought together world

The original version of this chapter was revised: The Figure 5 has been corrected. The correction to this chapter is available at
https://doi.org/10.1007/978-3-031-19647-8_33

H. Florez and H. Gomez (Eds.): ICAI 2022, CCIS 1643, pp. 440–454, 2022.
https://doi.org/10.1007/978-3-031-19647-8_31

leaders for the first time in Kyoto-1997 [6]. By then, industrialized societies committed to stabilizing GHG emissions at 5% below their baseline read in 1990 [19]. However, commitments claimed then only turned into real administrative actions by February 2005, and the implementation period was extended until 2020. Unfortunately for the planet and life, it has never been possible to give these agreements a binding status; instead, countries are expected to voluntarily adopt the necessary measures to optimize their processes and mitigate emissions. [7,21,24]. Proof of the laxity and ineffectiveness of the strategies presented to date in terms of emissions is evident in the progression of the increasingly more ambitious commitments made by the countries in the recent summits for the environment [15]. e.g., Paris COP21 (2015) [11], and ratified in subsequent sessions, COP22 - Morocco 2016 [14] until COP 26 - Glasgow [2]. Currently, countries have made reduction commitments of up to 40%, and peremptory proposals have been approved for abandoning fossil fuels [31], something unthinkable just a decade ago.

Global warming is an induced phenomenon secondary to Green House Gases (GHG) generation [23]. The GHG causes part of solar energy that the planet must reflect to remain trapped in the atmosphere. This captured radiation, mostly infrared, rises the temperatures exacerbating climatic events [13]. According to the international panel for climate change (IPCC), an increase in global temperature of 1.5 °C in the present century will have severe consequences on ecosystems and life as we know it will be unfeasible [16].

The ISO 14064 regulation introduces the ton of carbon equivalent (TCo2e) as a unit of measurement for the GHG inventory. The IPCC also defines emission factors for each activity to present a service or create a product [5]. Naturally, CO_2 is not the only shielding gas nor the one with the highest caloric potential, even more so if it is the most abundant. That is why the unit of measure standardizes the global inventory, and the emission factors take the consumption made in various measuring units – e.g., gallons, liters, cm3, among others – to TCo2e.

The regulation divides consumption/GEI (C-GEI) generation into three groups. The C-GEI that results from activities directly associated with the main product or service rendered by a company belongs to scope 1. The used electricity goes in scope two. Finally, C-GEI generated by providers goes in scope 3 [27]. This regulation is aimed at companies and corresponds to the GHG manager and his work team to systematically keep records of C-GEI and operate these values with the emission factors to report the inventory in TCo2e.

It is prudent to note that ISO 14064 is the main instrument of the global strategy; therefore, companies are the entities in charge of reducing emissions to levels compatible with life. By forcing reports in TCo2e, states can aggregate and dispatch their numbers to the IPCC on an equal basis, verifying whether commitments have been met and enabling comparison among nations for the planet's sake [8].

ISO 14064 is a regulation that has associated markets with which companies and countries can monetize the effort to implement the standard. The carbon credit markets [3] trade billions of dollars. Although they motivate the adoption of the regulation, they also open the possibility of disguised reports that, in principle, improve the image of the companies and increase their participation in the markets. However, since there are no adequate controls on what is reported [9], fraud in the medium and long term reduces confidence and the price of green bonds in the places where inconsistencies are detected. But without a doubt, the most negative impact is presented in the affectation on the environment. For this reason, it is prudent to involve technology capable of granting confidence in what is measured and reported.

The IPCC recently reported that, in the best of cases, humanity's efforts so far would lead us to planet-warming by $1.8\,^{\circ}C$ in the current century [17]. The optimistic estimate makes most of the commitments made by the world's countries, based on studies of space for improvement, insufficient.

For this reason, we enlighten the need to involve the most abundant production units, households, in caring for the planet. And with it, keep track of each individual's contribution to global warming.

If caring for the planet is the goal, water consumption is another mandatory aspect to control in residential units. Water is essential for living metabolisms but also plays a crucial role in global warming since the absence of the liquid, or the deterioration of its quality precludes the generation of wetlands, mangroves, and peatlands to protect us from flooding and erosion. Watery formations also capture carbon emissions [25].

The need to care for the water has forced humanity to create standards to measure the footprint in the ISO 14046 [20], and the audit of strategies to use the liquid efficiently worldwide are presented in the ISO 46001. Again, these regulations assume that only companies affect the vital compound through their production processes.

For this aim, a system must be developed that measures emissions and water footprint without requiring additional and exhaustive day-to-day work for household members. We envisaged a solution implemented in low-cost technology that automatically reports to an intelligent system capable of presenting home consumption in TCo2e. Concerning water footprint, we propose an approach complying with ISO 14046, while directives to certify ISO 46001 compliance will be considered in further developments. The proposed plan must be easily scalable to summarize the real-time TCo2e emissions and water consumption of blocks, neighborhoods, cities, and nations.

This document presents the construction details of a system capable of implementing the standards ISO 14064 and ISO 14046 in residential homes using low-cost electronics and centralizing software that allows for fast reporting scalability.

2   Materials and Methods

The following are the driving directives for the presented implementation.

- Low-cost of components yet, acceptable accuracy in the measurement
- Fully automatic intakes and reporting

- Low-maintenance and configuration to free household members of additional responsibilities
- Intuitive configuration interfaces to set up limits to C-GEI
- On-line data centralization and scalability

The designed architecture consists of a core system that can allocate a theoretically unlimited number of modules. The modules could be sensors, actuators, or both; therefore, the communication paths are bidirectional among all connected devices (See Fig. 1).

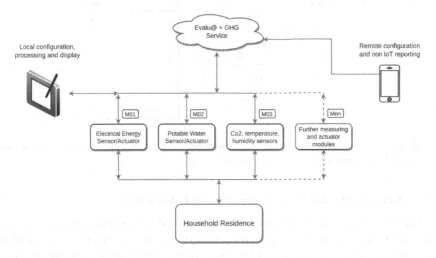

Fig. 1. Evalu@ + GHG. General diagram of an implementation for monitoring GHG and water footprint in residential households

Although the modular flexibility of the system allows for unlimited inclusion of modules, we prioritized three modules in the prototyping stage:

- The M01 module encompasses measures of electrical variables and actuators for loads on—off, and dimerization [1]. The use of electrical energy is listed in scope 2 of the ISO 14064 [27].
- The M02 module registers water consumption and controls dosing. Water consumption and opportunities to dose are not part of ISO 14064 but are regulated in ISO 14046 – water footprint – a crucial aspect of environmental management.
- The M03 measures CO_2 generation due to human activities, mostly respiration. It also includes temperature and humidity sensing to correct the CO_2 value. This scope is not included in ISO 14064 and is purely experimental. Only after massive use of this module will we know how significant the contribution of human respiration and animal breeding activities to GHG is.

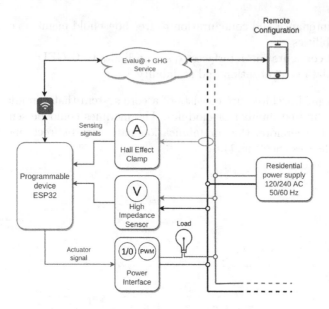

Fig. 2. Diagram of components and signals in M01 for measuring energy consumption and controlling the use of electrical energy.

2.1 M01. Electrical Energy Sensor and Actuator

The electrical module can measure the two main electrical signals in magnitude and form. Furthermore, it can control the power provided to any load in the electrical network. These two functions of the M01 module are independent and can be coupled/decoupled at will.

Electrical Measuring System. The low-cost electrical measuring module uses a high impedance voltage (V) detector and a hall effect clamp to measure alternate current (AC). These sensors work in parallel and feed their signals to an ESP32 chip. The read signals are digitized with a 10-bits analog-to-digital using a voltage reference (V_{ref}) of 3.3 V; therefore, the system has a resolution of 322 uV. The signals are sampled 20 times in a signal cycle – nearly ten times above the Nyquist theorem –; thus, a tuple value (Voltage, Current) is created every 833 us. This system reads 10 AC cycles of the residential supply signal. After a timer set to one second raises the interruption flag, it computes the RMS values and phase displacement and creates signal forms.

Electrical Actuator. The electrical module can operate on/off devices. We have added a TRIAC-based power, an optocoupled interface, and developed the required code in the ESP32 that switches the power supply up to 2000 VAC. The system holds a Pulse Width Modulation (PWM) adjustable by the developed automation, which modifies the duty cycle from 0 to 100% after detecting the residential power signal's zero-crossing.

2.2   M02. Water Sensor and Actuator

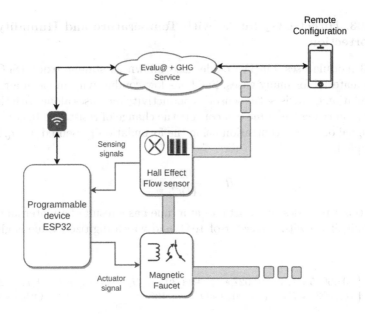

Fig. 3. Diagram of components and signals in Module 02 for measuring water consumption and controlling its use.

Similar to M01, M02 can measure and control the sensed variable. It consists of a hall effect container with a rotating turbine set into motion when the water moves through the sensor's case. This simplistic hardware requires firmware programming to transfer the pulsating pattern into the caudal. Furthermore, the module has a water faucet that closes and opens electronically when a programmed condition is met.

Water Measuring System. The water measuring device has a hall effect flow sensor capable of measuring caudals in the range of 1 to 60 l/min with a resolution of 1380 pulses/L. The sensor feeds the pulsating signal to an ESP32 module [4], where pulses are translated to volume in the lapse time of reading. In the ESP32, we have activated the edge interruption every time the flow sensor produces a low-to-high transition. We save the elapsed time between pulses and aggregate it in every interruption; therefore, the caudal is always available and suitable to be presented in real time.

Water Supply Actuator. The electronic actuator consists of an electromagnetic faucet that needs 12V in its terminals to open a normally closed gate. The on/off system is driven by low consumption and a fast response transistor configured in cut and saturation mode. This actuator uses the less expensive configuration for the aim.

2.3 M03. Direct CO_2 Intake with Temperature and Humidity Correction

The M03 module uses Tin(IV) oxide, also known as stannic oxide (SnO2), as sensitive material for many gases. Sn02 has low conductivity in clean air. When target pollution gas exists, the sensor's conductivity increases along with the CO_2 concentration rising [18]. One can convert the change of resistance to correspond output signal of gas concentration using the formulation presented in Eq. 1–4 for each sample i.

$$R_i = \frac{1023}{ADC_i} * 10 \tag{1}$$

Equation 1 provides the resistance at a time i as a result of an internal voltage divider built it up with a resistor of $10\,\Omega$, and which digitized value is given by ADC_i

$$CF_i = \begin{cases} (0.00035 * T_i^2) - (0.027 * T_i) + (1.39 - ((H_i - 33) * 0.0018) & \text{if } T_i < 20°C \\ (0.00035 * T_i) + (-0.0019 * (H_i - 1.130)) & \text{Otherwise} \end{cases} \tag{2}$$

The CF_i in Eq. 2, corresponds to the correction factor which is created with the instant temperature and humidity (T_i) and (H_i) respectively. We use a different CF_i depending on whether the temperature surpasses the 20°C level.

$$RCo_i = R_i/CF_i \tag{3}$$

With the yielded resistance R_i and the correction factor CF_i, we can estimate the corrected resistance (RCo_i) for sample i as shown in Eq. 3.

$$CO_i^2 = 116.60 * \left(\frac{RCo_i}{76.63}\right)^{-2.769} \tag{4}$$

Finally, we calculate the CO_i^2 magnitude in parts per million (PPM) using Eq. 4.

2.4 Evalu@ Configuration and Scalability

Evalu@ is the web centralizer aimed at Artificial Intelligence implementations [29]. The system is agnostic and can be configured to suit the specific necessities through excel files, as demonstrated in several published implementations [28, 30]. The Fig. 5 shows the configuration steps for a testing household residence, the setup files of every presented module (M01 - M03), and the web display for a system allocating one home of possibly many.

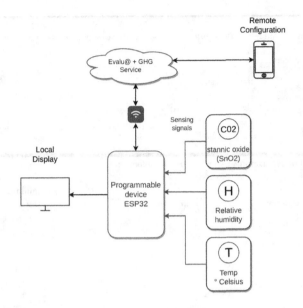

Fig. 4. The Module M03 uses a SNO^2 based sensor that varies its electrical resistance with the CO_2 saturation. The systems corrects the CO_2 reading with the temperature and humidity as shown in Sect. 2.3

3   Results

Once the modules are integrated into the flexible architecture presented in Fig. 1, the Evalu@ API is used to insert the sensor's data with a frequency that can be configured by the user. Furthermore, the user can set thresholds to activate the actuators. In the following sections, we present the graphics displayed by Evalu@ with the data pushed by each sensor.

3.1   Data from M01 Sensor. Electrical Variables

The RMS values presented in Fig. 6 are the results of analyzing ten AC signal cycles which correspond to 166 ms of computational effort (60 Hz) to estimate the consumption in the analyzed second. Since the loads in residence are connected in parallel, the variation in the voltage magnitude is minimal. Nevertheless, a measuring system of this nature can not assume the values of variables that can suffer cuts and slight variations due to overloads in the distribution network. Furthermore, the electrical signals are measured in magnitude, form, and relative displacement to estimate indexes such as power factor and consumption of reactive energy.

The Fig. 7 presents the report in the units stipulated by ISO 14064 regulation in its scope 2. The IPCC factor has transformed the power consumed in this household residence to equivalent CO_2 in Tons. The red line is the baseline

Item a evaluar	Descriptor	↑ (Imágenes deben decir: photo. Fechas deben decir DD/...
Residencias		
	Dirección	Cra 78A No. 6-58 — **A**
	Responsable	Ronald Santiago Marin
	Área	180 m²
	Estrato	5
	Barrio	Ciudad Capri
	Ciudad	Cali, Medellin, Bogota, Bucaramanga, Barranquilla, Pasto
	Departamento	Valle, Bogota DC, Atlantico, Antioquía, Nariño
	País	Colombia, Ecuador, Panama, Perú

Nombre evaluación Electricas - Home Automation
Nombre corto Electricas – HA

Categoría	Subcategoría	Opciones cuantitativa	
		Valores	Unidades
			B
Variables electrícas		sum	
	Voltaje	m	Volts
	Corriente	m	Ampers
	Desface	m	ms
	Onda voltaje (lista)	m	Amplitud
	Onda corriente (lista)	m	Amplitud

Nombre evaluación Agua Consumo – Home Automation
Nombre corto Agua Consumo – HA

Categoría	Subcategoría	Opciones cuantitativas	
		Valores	Unidades
			C
Consumo de agua		sum	
	Caudal	m	Lt/min
	Tiempo de uso	m	us

Nombre evaluación Ambientales - Home Automation
Nombre corto Ambientales – HA

Categoría	Subcategoría	Opciones cuantitativas	
		Valores o rango	Unidades
			D
Ambientales		sum	
	Humedad	m	%
	Temperatura	m	Celcius
	CO_2	m	ppm

E

Fig. 5. Evalu@ configuration. Panel A is the template for registering household residences. The excel in Panel B teaches E@ to follow the electrical variables. The excel in Panel C setups E@ to track water footprint variables. The excel in panel D tells E@ how to follow environmental variables. Finally, panel E shows the interface provided by E@ once the setup is completed.

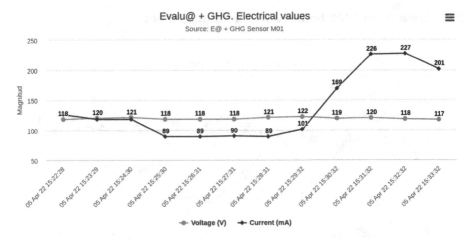

Fig. 6. Current (mA) and Voltage estimations as received by Evalu@ during 12 continuous seconds

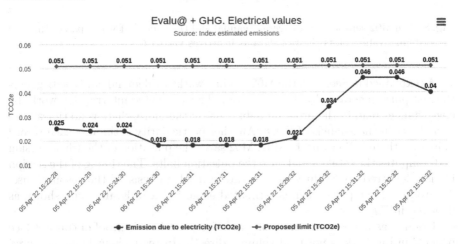

Fig. 7. CO₂ equivalent to the power consumed during the measuring time shown in Fig. 6. The red line is the baseline of the reference level that is mandatory in the ISO14064 regulation

or reference required in the regulation and plays a dual role in this implementation. Since M01 has an actuator, the sensor can be programmed to turn off the system or dimmer the load, secondary to using pulse with modulation (PWM) signals. The PWM is connected to an optocoupled Triode for Alternating Current (TRIAC), which is rapid, efficient, durable, and more silent compared to its mechanic counterpart (the relay).

3.2   Data from M02 Sensor. Water Management

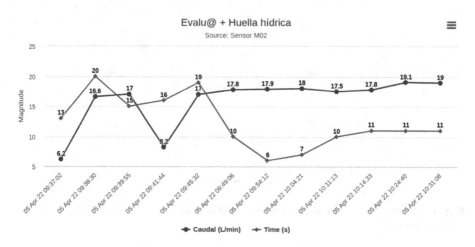

Fig. 8. The M02 sensor reports average caudal and the time that water passes through the system. Evalu@ plots the raw data as it arrives via API.

As explained in Sect. 2.2, the M02 module works by demand, and the trigger is the first pulse generated by the flow sensor. The associated interruption works by edge changes read in the programmable device; therefore, there is no timestamp periodicity in the x-labels of Fig. 8. Another particularity is the way each record point is gathered. Contrary to M01, M02 saves the pulsation of the whole session and computes the total caudal once the pulsation halts. The timing of the session is also delivered to Evalu@ to facilitate crucial analysis of the resource use. The total volume per session is estimated as an index in Evalu@ and shown as depicted in Fig. 9.

Evalu@, as it was configured for water footprint in this proof of concept (see panel C in Fig. 5, does not read volumes directly. Instead, the volume measured is created as an index that computes the variables shown in Fig. 8 to report the utilized water per session in liters. Then, the limit set (also in liters) will trigger the near-to-the-limit alarms and shut off the faucet when the limit is reached.

3.3   Data from M03 Sensor. Direct CO$_2$ Measurement

The M03 module reads CO$_2$ directly, and the two other captured variables (humidity and temperature) are provided to correct the CO$_2$ measurement. There was no need to generate traffic with the two variables; however, several events depend on these two basic measurements. Since our team is planning to use artificial intelligence tools to predict environmental outcomes, having more factors is desirable, which is the main reason to keep the temperature and humidity records. The Fig. 10 shows the intakes read with the designed sensor in the presented proof of concept.

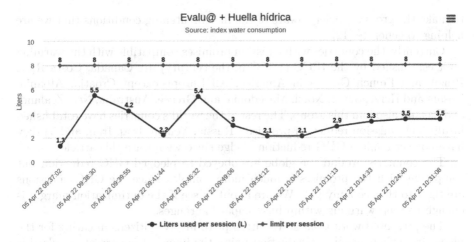

Fig. 9. The caudal and time provided in each gathered point – see Fig. 8 – is converted to total volume by the centralizer through a pre-configured index.

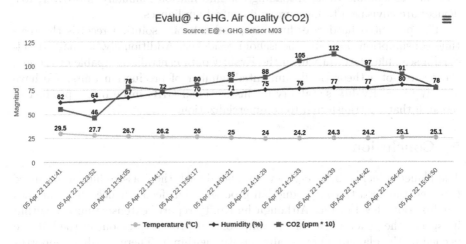

Fig. 10. The M03 module reads CO_2 in parts per million (ppm). It could use present this information in mg/mm^3. The humidity and temperature are initially read to correct the CO_2 but are propagated through the system to augment data in anticipation of intelligence implementations.

4 Discussion

The care for the environment and climate change has gained relevance due to the magnitude and exacerbation of natural climate events that the globe has experienced recently [26]. Such circumstances call humanity to give attention and take the necessary actions to stop a progressively growing menace. Scientists have been captured and judicialized for perturbing the order in a desperate attempt to make the gross of society aware of the life-threatening conditions that we are helping to generate [12].

Currently, the countries with emission promises compatible with the warming limit established by the IPCC (1.5 °C in the century) are Canada, Costa Rica, Brazil, and French Guiana in America. All Europe except Croatia, Albania, Bosnia and Herzegovina, North Macedonia, and Greece. Australia, New Zealand, and Iceland also join this group. The rest of the world's countries have established insufficient emission reduction promises. Russia, Yemen, Iraq, Iran, and Turkey have not yet made a GHG reduction pledge since we release this article.

The countries around the globe are obeyed to pledged GHG reduction but complying with the promises is much more complex since the GHG emissions are tight to the economy [10]. We are about to see if the optimization margin is enough to keep warming within life-compatible ranges.

The presented work is an active attempt to involve citizens in caring for the planet from their primary production unit - the home - the current standard is still used. Still, the level of automation sought frees the operator of the tedious and time-consuming tasks of loading the information manually. Moreover, IoT devices are envisaged to measure and control appliances.

The presented hardware, firmware, and software solution records the real-time consumption done in a household residence. Additionally, we have developed a scalable platform within the Evalu@ data centralizer capable of keeping the records of a theoretically unlimited number of production units. We have already tested Evalu@'s stability for institutional GHG inventory, a product of research that we transferred to commercialization.

5   Conclusion

The planet is facing an emergency associated with the massive human presence here and the need to run production processes that feed our necessities besides our luxurious level of life. Although humanity reports extensive misery within its specie, the general level of consumption has proven to be out of the balance needed by the planet and other alive entities within it. There is still an opportunity behind the optimization concept, and this work is devoted to pragmatically exploiting that opportunity even when most of the members of the vast societies still do not understand the magnitude of the menace we are facing.

References

1. Al Abshari, T.A., Suyuti, A., Ahmad, A., Salam, A.E.U., et al.: Control of light intensity via microcontroller for the efficiency of electrical energy. In: MATEC Web of Conferences, vol. 331, p. 06006. EDP Sciences (2020)
2. Alexander, M., et al.: COP26: looking forward from Glasgow by placing health at the center of climate action (2022)
3. Anjos, M.F., Feijoo, F., Sankaranarayanan, S.: A multinational carbon-credit market integrating distinct national carbon allowance strategies. Appl. Energy **319**, 119181 (2022)

4. Babiuch, M., Foltýnek, P., Smutný, P.: Using the ESP32 microcontroller for data processing. In: 2019 20th International Carpathian Control Conference (ICCC), pp. 1–6. IEEE (2019)

5. Bastianoni, S., Marchi, M., Caro, D., Casprini, P., Pulselli, F.M.: The connection between 2006 IPCC GHG inventory methodology and ISO 14064-1 certification standard – a reference point for the environmental policies at sub-national scale. Environ. Sci. Policy **44**, 97–107 (2014)

6. Böhringer, C.: The Kyoto protocol: a review and perspectives. Oxford Rev. Econ. Policy **19**(3), 451–466 (2003)

7. Chidiak, M.: Lessons from the French experience with voluntary agreements for greenhouse-gas reduction. J. Clean. Prod. **10**(2), 121–128 (2002)

8. den Elzen, M.G., Lucas, P.L.: The FAIR model: A tool to analyse environmental and costs implications of regimes of future commitments. Environ. Model. Assess. **10**(2), 115–134 (2005). https://doi.org/10.1007/s10666-005-4647-z

9. Frunza, M.C.: Aftermath of the vat fraud on carbon emissions markets. J. Financ. Crime (2013)

10. Gillingham, K., Stock, J.H.: The cost of reducing greenhouse gas emissions. J. Econ. Perspect. **32**(4), 53–72 (2018)

11. Habib, R.R.: Thinking through climate change & health post-COP21 (2016)

12. Kalmus, P.: https://www.theguardian.com/commentisfree/2022/apr/06/climate-scientists-are-desperate-were-crying-begging-and-getting-arrested

13. Kweku, D.W., et al.: Greenhouse effect: greenhouse gases and their impact on global warming. J. Sci. Res. Rep. **17**(6), 1–9 (2018)

14. Leggett, J.A.: The united nations framework convention on climate change, the Kyoto protocol, and the Paris agreement: a summary. UNFCC, New York 2 (2020)

15. Markolf, S., Azevedo, I., Muro, M., Victor, D.: Pledges and progress (2020)

16. McDonald, J., Telesetsky, A.: Disaster by degrees: the implications of the IPCC 1.5 C report for disaster law. Yearbook Int. Disaster Law Online **1**(1), 179–209 (2019)

17. Meinshausen, M., et al.: Realization of Paris agreement pledges may limit warming just below 2° C. Nature **604**(7905), 304–309 (2022)

18. Noroña, L.C.S., Aimara, F.A.A., Martínez, K.A.L., Arrobo, Y.A.A.: Implementation of a quadrupedo robot for monitoring temperature, soil humidity and gases, in tomato crops in greenhouses. Polo del Conocimiento: Revista científico-profesional **7**(4), 11 (2022)

19. Olivier, J., et al.: Sectoral emission inventories of greenhouse gases for 1990 on a per country basis as well as on 1× 1. Environ. Sci. Policy **2**(3), 241–263 (1999)

20. Pfister, S., Ridoutt, B.G.: Water footprint: pitfalls on common ground. Environ. Sci. Technol. **48**(1), 4 (2014)

21. Price, L.: Voluntary agreements for energy efficiency or GHG emissions reduction in industry: an assessment of programs around the world (2005)

22. Rosen, A.M.: The wrong solution at the right time: the failure of the Kyoto protocol on climate change. Polit. Policy **43**(1), 30–58 (2015)

23. Sivaramanan, S.: Global warming and climate change, causes, impacts and mitigation. Central Environmental Authority 2 (2015)

24. Storey, M., Boyd, G., Dowd, J.: Voluntary agreements with industry. In: Voluntary Approaches in Environmental Policy, pp. 187–207. Springer (1999). https://doi.org/10.1007/978-94-015-9311-3_11

25. Szwedo, P.: Water footprint and the law of WTO. J. World Trade **47**(6), 1259–1284 (2013)

26. Ummenhofer, C.C., Meehl, G.A.: Extreme weather and climate events with ecological relevance: a review. Philos. Trans. R. Soc. Lond. B Biol. Sci. **372**(1723), 20160135 (2017)
27. Wintergreen, J., Delaney, T.: ISO 14064, international standard for GHG emissions inventories and verification. In: 16th Annual International Emissions Inventory Conference, Raleigh, NC (2007)
28. Yepes-Calderon, F., Giraldo Quiceno, A.F., Carmona Orozco, J.F., McComb, J.G.: The Bio-I capsule. Preventing contagion of aerial pathogens with real-time reporting in Evalu@. In: Florez, H., Misra, S. (eds.) ICAI 2020. CCIS, vol. 1277, pp. 116–128. Springer, Cham (2020). https://doi.org/10.1007/978-3-030-61702-8_9
29. Yepes-Calderon, F., Yepes Zuluaga, J.F., Yepes Calderon, G.E.: Evalu@: an agnostic web-based tool for consistent and constant evaluation used as a data gatherer for artificial intelligence implementations. In: Florez, H., Leon, M., Diaz-Nafria, J.M., Belli, S. (eds.) ICAI 2019. CCIS, vol. 1051, pp. 73–84. Springer, Cham (2019). https://doi.org/10.1007/978-3-030-32475-9_6
30. Yepes Zuluaga, J.F., Gregory Tatis, A.D., Forero Arévalo, D.S., Yepes-Calderon, F.: Evalu@ + sports. Creatine phosphokinase and urea in high-performance athletes during competition. a framework for predicting injuries caused by fatigue. In: Florez, H., Pollo-Cattaneo, M.F. (eds.) ICAI 2021. CCIS, vol. 1455, pp. 290–302. Springer, Cham (2021). https://doi.org/10.1007/978-3-030-89654-6_21
31. Zhongming, Z., Linong, L., Xiaona, Y., Wangqiang, Z., Wei, L., et al.: COP26: promises 'ring hollow' when fossil fuels still receive trillions in subsidies; UN chief calls on negotiators to pick up the pace (2021)

Team Productivity in Agile Software Development: A Systematic Mapping Study

Marcela Guerrero-Calvache[1](✉) and Giovanni Hernández[2](✉)

[1] Universidad de Nariño, San Juan de Pasto, Nariño, Colombia
marcela1396@udenar.edu.co
[2] Universidad Mariana, San Juan de Pasto, Nariño, Colombia
gihernandez@umariana.edu.co

Abstract. The culture of agility has been incorporated into the software industry, offering various benefits such as increased team productivity. However, this indicator is addressed in a limited way in the literature and its measurement continues to be a great research challenge. The purpose of this article is to characterize the conceptions of team-level productivity in agile software development (ASD) through a Systematic Mapping Study (SMS) where 616 studies were identified, of which eight were included applying of the protocol described in this text. As a result of the SMS, it is possible to establish the sense and meaning of team productivity in ASD, which is revealed as an abstract, relevant concept, composed of a set of factors, which function as an indicator of compliance with goals and continuous improvement. The review revealed 63 factors that contribute to the measurement of team productivity in ASD, categorized as: meaning, impact, flexibility and high performance. The main contribution of this work is to present a systematic and repeatable way to make an approximation to the definition of team productivity in ASD, identifying factors that can be measured, which were organized into four categories.

Keywords: Agile software development · Productivity factors · Team productivity

1 Introduction

The use of agile methods generates different benefits within the organizations that adopt them. One of them is the increase in team productivity as stated in the Fifteenth Annual State of Agility Report [1] in the year 2021.

There is a paradox to formally define the term productivity due to the positions found in different fields of action [2]. Productivity is not only the potentiality with which an activity was carried out to achieve a goal, it is necessary to demonstrate its applicability within organizations, which must be managed in a standardized way and using a measurement [2].

In Software Engineering, the term productivity has its origins in the late seventies [3]. From that moment on, the study of this topic has been centralized in positions oriented

H. Florez and H. Gomez (Eds.): ICAI 2022, CCIS 1643, pp. 455–471, 2022.
https://doi.org/10.1007/978-3-031-19647-8_32

to the estimation and planning of projects for organizations, sectors and industries. However, productivity brings with it the interaction with people, the individual and group vision and the characteristics inherent to the job; which in this area reduced information is evidenced [3].

Team productivity is a serious concern in the software industry, it is essential for the achievement of successful projects in ASD [4–6] and it is estimated objective the performance of each of its participants. Therefore, studying this topic is interesting [6].

Although the measurement of this indicator has been addressed in the literature in a very limited way [7, 8], knowing the relevance of team productivity metrics for professionals who use agile methods can establish a guide for the measurement process. of the effort in delivering value [9].

Therefore, the motivation of this research is to investigate through a Systematic Mapping Study (SMS) what is the conception that exists about team productivity in ASD and what factors, metrics or models exist for its measurement. Eight primary studies were included that focused on addressing this topic and answered the research questions posed in Sect. 3.

The article is organized as follows: Sect. 2 presents related works to Productivity in ASD. Section 3 presents the methodological design used in this research. Section 4 shows the results and finally the conclusions are detailed in Sect. 5.

2   Related Works

Team productivity in Agile Software Development is a topic that has been gaining relevance in recent years, as shown by the studies presented below.

In [7] conceptions of productivity at the team level from an ASD perspective are contrasted with the perceptions of professionals in the software industry. As a result of the study, it is evident that the concept of team productivity in ASD exposed in the literature is categorized in three dimensions: input, process and output; emphasizing the software development team; while the responses of the professionals focus on a general perception associated with the fulfillment of an objective or the delivery of a software product, leaving aside activities inherent to teamwork.

The main similarity with this study is that both address the issue of team productivity in ASD throughout the literature. However, the background makes use only of the Scopus search engine and its results do not show measurement factors for this indicator, as this research does.

In [8], through a Systematic Literature Review (SLR), 21 productivity metrics were found for work teams in ASD, which are associated with early and frequent delivery of software, measuring organizational performance and assessing effectiveness. And efficiency of the team. The study found no metrics to measure team motivation.

The previous study is similar to this research by addressing the issue of team productivity in ASD in the literature considering a search protocol. However, it only works with two sources of information; the research questions proposed by the author only emphasize metrics and not a formal definition of team productivity in ASD. In addition, the study does not show a categorization of the factors that may influence it.

In [5] the factors that can influence productivity in ASD equipment are identified. To achieve this, the research combines an SLR and the application of an online questionnaire to 52 software development companies in Pakistan. The results showed that all team factors (team member and leader role, inter-team relationship, handling requirements, team velocity, conformance quality and team vision) are correlated favor productivity; and leadership meetings, as well as unit and regression tests, are negatively correlated with productivity.

In [10] the factors that influence work productivity in an agile software development team and how they are related are explored. The research included 60 participants from 18 Bangladeshi software companies. Two phases stand out within the methodological process. The first is the development of an SLR and conducting interviews and surveys with members of agile teams; to identify productivity factors. In the second phase, the construction of a qualitative system dynamics model (causal loop diagrams) is proposed based on the findings found in the first stage. The results obtained were the identification of factors such as motivation, effectiveness and team management.

The main similarity of the studies [5, 10] with the present investigation is related to the fact that it is based on a literature review on team productivity in ASD. However, the search string they use does not include the terms models or evaluation metrics. In addition, a classification of the identified factors is not made.

In [11], research carried out on the subject of productivity in ASD teams is investigated, to identify the factors, methods, levels, agile methodologies and the use of the most used metrics. The authors carry out an SMS in which they include 25 primary studies where they identify the most important factors that affect productivity in ASD teams, highlighting that most of them were related to teamwork. In addition, productivity can be seen from three levels: project, team and from a general vision focused more on agile software development. Finally, they highlight that the metrics analyzed are related to the quality of the product and do not consider customer satisfaction.

The similarities with this research lie in the fact that they start from an SMS on the topic of team productivity in ASD and consider the concept of *'performance'* in the search string. The differentiating aspect is related to the search time of [11] which is between 2007 and 2016; and within their search criteria they do not relate the concept of *'productivity evaluation model'*.

3   Research Method

To carry out the Systematic Mapping Study (SMS) on team productivity in ASD, the present study is guided by the systematic, orderly, methodical and replicable process proposed by [12], which contains a series of fundamental steps for obtaining information. The adoption of this protocol in the investigation is detailed in Fig. 1.

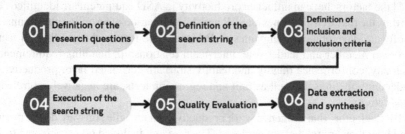

Fig. 1. Systematic mapping process. Source: self-made.

3.1 Defining Research Questions

The research questions selected for the SMS on team productivity in ASD (as shown in Table 1) allow defining the scope of the research process, which will contribute to a clear objective, considering the particular interests of the study.

Table 1. Research questions for the SMS

RQ	Research questions	Justification
1	How many primary studies describe the concept of team productivity/performance in ASD?	Determine the number of current studies detailing the concept of team productivity/performance in ASD
2	What types of study do the articles found refer to?	Determine the types of study of the selected articles
3	Where do primary studies belong?	Determine the country of affiliation of the selected studies
4	What is the publication frequency of studies that describe the concept of team productivity in ASD?	Check how often studies related to team productivity are being conducted in ASD and determine if it is a current research topic
5	In what context are the conceptions of team productivity in ASD?	Find in which contexts research related to team productivity in ASD is being developed
6	What methods of agile software development are contemplated in primary studies?	Determine the most representative ASD methods within the primary studies
7	How do primary studies define team productivity in ASD?	Determine the concept of team productivity in ASD
8	How is team productivity measured at ASD?	Establish how the productivity measurement of the ASD team is being carried out

3.2 Defining Search String

In this phase, a search string is built in line with the previously defined scope and the research questions. The string includes the terms shown in Table 2 and makes use of Boolean operators (OR and AND) to connect them. The bibliographic databases consulted were IEEE Xplore, ACM Digital Library, Scopus, Compendex, Web of Science and Springer Link. It should be noted that depending on the database, the query parameters were adjusted.

Table 2. Search string

Operator	Parameters
	"Model" OR "Method" OR "Framework" OR "Technique" OR "Process"
AND	"Evaluation" OR "Assessment" OR "Measurement" OR "Appraisal"
AND	"Productivity" OR "Performance"
AND	"Team" OR "Group" OR "Teamwork" OR "Collaborative team"
AND	"Agile" OR "Scrum" OR "Extreme Programming" OR "Kanban" OR "Lean" OR "Crystal"
AND	"Software Development" OR "Software Creation" OR "Software Construction" OR "Software Management" OR "System Development" OR "System Creation" OR "System Construction" OR "System Management"

3.3 Defining Inclusion and Exclusion Criteria and Search Filters

The classification scheme was based on the application of the inclusion and exclusion criteria (See Table 3) and the defined filters (See Table 4) in order to select the most relevant studies.

It is important to mention that the columns called "Applied Inclusion Criteria" and "Applied Exclusion Criteria" shown in Table 4 are related to the criteria that shown in Table 3 were applied by each filter.

Table 3. Inclusion and exclusion criteria

ID	Inclusion criteria	Exclusion criteria
1	Studies published between 2001 and 2021	Studies published before 2001
2	Complete studies published in journals, conferences or congresses with peer review	Technical reports and discussion or discussion articles or non-peer-reviewed material
3	Studies published in English	Studies written in a language other than English
4	Studies related to productivity in agile software development	Studies that do not involve productivity in agile software development
5	Studies that are reported as primary studies	Secondary or tertiary studies that report results of other investigations
6		Studies not available in full text
7		Duplicate studies

The present investigation decided to consider studies from the year 2001 due to the fact that, from that date, the current of agility began to take shape together with the consolidation of the Manifesto for Agile software development [13], generating a new approach in Software Engineering.

Table 4. Selection strategy

Step	Description	Applied sinclusion criteria	Applied exclusion criteria
1	Review the articles applying the search string in the reference managers. The parameters included in the search were the publication rank of the articles, the type of publication and the language	1, 2 y 3	1, 2 y 3
2	Read the title, keywords and abstract of the article	2, 3, 4 y 5	2, 3, 4 y 5
3	Remove duplicate studies	-	7
4	Read the introduction, results and conclusions of the article	3, 4 y 5	3, 4, 5 y 6
5	Read the full article	3, 4 y 5	3, 4, 5 y 6

3.4 Search Execution

Searching in Bibliographic Databases Using Search String. It should be noted that in addition to the search string detailed in Table 2, the publication date (2001–2021), the type of content or publication and the language (English) were applied as the first filter in each of the bibliographic databases. However, in IEEE Xplore and ACM Digital Library it was not possible to filter by language since this functionality was not built-in.

In the case of Springer Link, the discipline and sub-discipline were also taken into account, which was different for each type of content. For example, for the studies whose classification was **Conference Paper**, the selected discipline was "Computer Science" and the Subdiscipline was "Software Engineering"; while for the studies whose type was **Article**, the selected discipline was "Computer Science" and the Subdiscipline was "Software Engineering/Programming and Operating Systems".

Reviewing of Title, Abstract and Keywords. In this phase, the title, abstract and keywords of each of the selected studies are read. It should be noted that in the case of keywords, related terms were considered, which varied according to each search engine. This information is shown in Table 5.

Table 5. Concepts in keyword review

IEEE xplore	ACM digital library	Scopus	Compendex	Web of science	Springer link
Author keywords	Keywords	Author keywords, index keywords	Controlled/Subject terms, uncontrolled terms	Author keywords	Keywords

Removing Duplicate Studies. Once filter 2 is applied, duplicate studies continue to be eliminated, considering that Scopus, Compendex and Web of Science collect information from various digital libraries including ACM digital Library and IEEE Xplore.

Reading the Introduction, Results and Conclusions of the Article. Once filter 3 has been applied, we continue to read the introduction, results and conclusions of each of the selected articles considering the inclusion and exclusion criteria set out in Table 3.

Reading the Full Article. The last filter of the systematic mapping is related to the reading of the complete article considering the rest of the structural elements, such as the background framework, the study design or methodological design, and the discussion of results.

Figure 2 summarizes the number of studies found after the application of each of the filters discriminated by each bibliographic database.

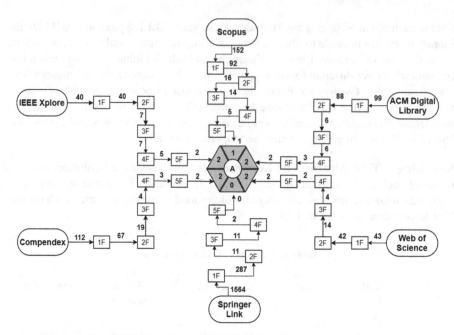

Fig. 2. Results of the systematic review. Source: self-made.

3.5 Quality Evaluation

After the selection process, a new task related to quality assurance of the articles found is carried out, which corresponds to inspecting a set of criteria shown in Table 6.

Table 6. Quality evaluation criteria

ID	Criteria	Category
C1	The research objectives and questions are explicitly described, clear and relevant	Report quality
C2	The research presents a methodological design that allows you to achieve the objectives	Rigor
C3	The data collection procedure is consistent with the methodological design	Rigor
C4	The results presented are clear and consistent with the proposed methodological design	Credibility
C5	The study is valued by other researchers	Relevance

To evaluate the quality of the articles, a scale was established to inspect the level of compliance with the criteria, as follows: High (2 points), Medium (1 point) and Low (0 points).

For the Relevance criterion related to the evaluation given by other researchers to the study, the number of citations it has was taken into account, considering that:

- Greater than or equal to 10 citations: High (2 points)
- Between 1 and 9 citations: Medium (1 point)
- No citations: Low (0 points)

The articles that met with a score equal to or greater than 80% of the total possible points are what were finally chosen. At the end of the quality evaluation process, of the 9 studies, 8 articles exceeded 80%. In Table 7, the selected ones are presented.

Table 7. Primary studies included. Source: self-made.

ID	Paper title
S1 [14]	Productivity, Turnover, and Team Stability of Agile Teams in Open-Source Software Projects
S2 [15]	A Statistical Model to Assess the Team's Productivity in Agile Software Teams
S3 [16]	How Do Software Developers Experience Team Performance in Lean and Agile Environments?
S4 [17]	Group Hedonic Balance and Pair Programming Performance: Affective Interaction Dynamics as Indicators of Performance
S5 [18]	A case study of using the hybrid model of scrum and six sigma in software development
S6 [19]	An empirical study of WIP in Kanban teams
S7 [20]	Understanding lack of trust in distributed agile teams: A grounded theory study
S8 [21]	Decision support technology for sprint planning

3.6 Data Extraction and Synthesis of Results

In this stage, data extraction is carried out considering the research questions defined in the first phase of the mapping. The review allowed the information debugging considering the following metadata per article: title, authors, bibliographic database, type of study, name of the publication, institution and country of affiliation, year of publication and keywords.

After the previous phase, the information provided by each of the studies was organized according to each variable and answering the research questions. The results obtained are presented in the following section.

4 Results and Discussion

The results found in relation to the research questions formulated are presented below.

For the analysis of the information extracted from the articles that were selected, the "ID" column of Table 7 is taken as a reference.

4.1 General Aspects (RQ1-RQ6)

The number of studies that met the filters set forth in Table 4 and the quality criteria was eight (8). This allows us to affirm that there is limited information on team productivity in ASD in the literature and how to measure it [8], making this topic a challenge [22, 23] within research.

The studies found belong to the selected information sources (See Fig. 3) with the exception of Springer Link, of which no study classifies in the final selection. The main reasons are due to the fact that the results obtained after applying the search string were extensive (287 articles with the first filter) and the information generated did not have the same level of precision as the other engines.

It should be noted that two studies were found in Compendex, one of them refers to the IEEE Xplore library and the other to the ACM Digital Library. The above shows that 75% of the selected articles belong to these bibliographic data managers (See Fig. 3).

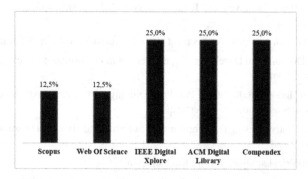

Fig. 3. Classification of studies found by search engine

According to the type of study of the selected articles, it is found that 62.5% are studies presented at a Conference or in a Journal. Regarding the country of affiliation to which the articles correspond, 50% of the investigations are from the European continent and 25% from the Asian continent. Similarly, the absence of studies from Latin America is evident and only 12.5% corresponds to North America.

Regarding the frequency of publication of the articles, it was found that, between 2018 and 2021, 67.5% of the articles addressed team productivity in ASD, which shows a growing interest on the part of the academic community about this theme.

Regarding the context in which the articles are addressed, 100% are developed in the field of the software industry. The foregoing allows us to reveal that productivity in ASD is an indicator within software companies and its measurement could contribute to knowing the team's performance in carrying out each of the activities at a given moment.

Keyword analysis was also performed on the selected studies. It was decided to form categories based on the level of similarity between them and the recurring ones were selected. Table 8 shows the results found and allows us to affirm that the selected categories are closely related to the search string proposed in Table 2 and, in turn, are aligned with the objective of the study.

Table 8. Categories identified with keywords

Category	S1	S2	S3	S4	S5	S6	S7	S8	FO	% FO
Agile development method	X	X	X		X	X			5	62,5%
Team productivity	X	X				X		X	4	50,0%
Team performance	X		X	X				X	4	50,0%
Behavioral factors	X		X	X					3	37,5%
Development method					X		X		2	25,0%
Agile practices				X				X	2	25,0%

Regarding the agile software development methods contemplated within the primary studies (See Table 9), it stands out that the most used was Scrum with 50.0%, followed by Extreme Programming with 37.5% and Kanban with 25%.

Table 9. ASD methods of primary studies

ASD method	S1	S2	S3	S4	S5	S6	S7	S8	FO	% FO
Scrum		X			X		X	X	4	50,0%
Extreme programming		X	X				X		3	37,5%
Kanban		X				X			2	25,0%
Six sigma					X				1	12,5%
Lean			X						1	12,5%
Agile UP		X							1	12,5%
Unspecified	X								1	12,5%

On the other hand, in 62.5% of the jobs analyzed, the concept of team performance was used more than team productivity.

4.2 Concept of Team Productivity in ASD (RQ7)

The definitions of ASD team productivity exposed in the selected primary studies allow establishing the most relevant categories associated with this indicator. Table 10 summarizes this information.

The definition of team productivity in ASD in the literature is an abstract concept [14, 15], its meaning is still being studied and is under construction.

For software organizations, team productivity in ASD plays a fundamental role [14, 15] because they consider it as an indicator of improvement within their processes [16, 18] and it helps teams achieve better results [15]. In most of the studies analyzed [14–17, 19–21], team productivity is composed of a set of factors of various types (context, socio-human, organizational, project, among others) that generate an impact within the team,

Table 10. Conceptions of team productivity in ASD in primary studies

ID	Concept of team productivity in ASD	Category
S1 [14]	Productivity in software development has been extensively studied in the same way as the factors that compose it, considering that these must be reevaluated according to the new needs of the software industry. In the context of agile software development in open-source projects, there is still very little information on this indicator	Relevance
		Factors
		Abstract concept
S2 [15]	The productivity of the software team has become one of the most important challenges to control, predict and improve the projects of software companies. Likewise, for agile software teams it is essential to increase performance in software development. Knowing the level of productivity of the team can contribute to obtaining better estimation results in the time and cost of projects, as well as generating greater customer satisfaction. There is no particular definition regarding team productivity in the literature, existing studies have emphasized identifying factors and possible impacts, rather than consolidating a mathematical equation to evaluate this indicator	Relevance
		Factors
		Abstract concept
		Impacts
		Compliance with client goals
S3 [16]	Performance is a concept that can be approached and evaluated from different points of view within an organization. To achieve good performance, the intervention of a series of factors that come from different contexts is necessary. For software development companies, performance is a key indicator that must be constant and aligned with market trends. The concept of team performance is associated with two important axes. The first is related to the perception that professionals have about performance, which can start from an individual vision guided by the understanding of work roles, to a more global vision associated with the team, the market or the stakeholders themselves. The second axis is associated with the fulfillment of the objectives and expectations coming from a client through adequate work planning together with the need for interaction and communication in which the software teams can play a relevant role	Factors
		Improvement indicator
		Compliance with client goals

(continued)

Table 10. (*continued*)

ID	Concept of team productivity in ASD	Category
S4 [17]	The performance of a team does not depend so much on the individual intelligence of its members, but rather on their social sensitivity. In the case of pair programming groups, the group hedonic balance is a relevant indicator for performance	Factors
S5 [18]	Software development companies continually seek to implement new alternatives to improve the performance of a team when producing software in order to generate greater customer satisfaction. It should be noted that the use of ASD methods such as Scrum and Six Sigma can contribute to considerably increasing this aspect	Improvement indicator
		Compliance with client goals
S6 [19]	Productivity is a function of how much is produced, of what quality, in what period of time, and using a certain number of resources. Productivity is linked to various factors and one of the most important is related to the size of a team	Factors
S7 [20]	Trust is a factor that contributes to a team being cohesive, effective and high performing. The performance of a team refers to how well the team has achieved the results collectively agreed with the client. Team performance can lead to the success or failure of a software development project	Factors
		Compliance with client goals
S8 [21]	Performance management is the process that helps measure and improve team performance to achieve IT business goals. Team performance can be determined by a set of key performance factors	Compliance with client goals
		Factors

the organization and even the market. It also makes it possible to visualize customer satisfaction through the functional and quality delivery of a software product [15, 19] according to their expectations and needs [15, 16, 18, 20, 21].

4.3 Measurement of Team Productivity in ASD (RQ8)

For the measurement, the factors that determine, influence and impact the productivity of the team in ASD are taken into account. The factors are classified considering some concepts exposed in [16], consolidating the following categories: a.) **Meaning**. Within this category are grouped the factors that are related to the perception that the members of the development team have about productivity, which can be seen from an individual approach or from a general perspective. Understanding performance helps to understand what the team hopes to achieve; b.) **Impact**. The factors that affect within the team and that generate a negative, positive or even neutral influence on its behavior are considered;

c.) **Flexibility**. In this category are grouped the factors that affect the performance of a team when it is subjected to conditions that imply changes, that is, adapt to change; and d.) **High performance**. Factors related to capabilities that consolidate the identity of the team and contribute to achieving higher levels of performance are grouped together.

The present investigation identified in the selected studies sixty-three (63) factors that influence the measurement of team productivity in ASD (See Fig. 4), which were organized into the four categories mentioned above. As a result, it is obtained that, for the *Meaning* category (19%), the most recurrent factors can be grouped into: Velocity, Work Capacity and Customer Satisfaction. In the *Impact* category (36.5%) the following factors stand out: Collaboration, Communication and Quality.

For the *Flexibility* (17.5%) and *High Performance* (27%) categories, there is no evidence of recurrence of the productivity factors among the articles, that is, a factor only appears in one article.

Figure 4 summarizes the factors identified in the literature with the respective established categories.

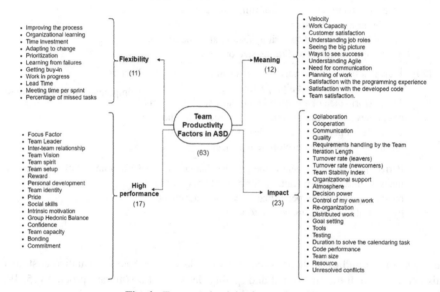

Fig. 4. Team productivity factors in ASD

Subsequently, the definitions of the team productivity factors in ASD were extracted for each category. For example, for the Meaning category, the Velocity factor is found, which according to the articles corresponds to: *Amount of work that a team has completed during an increment and iteration.*

The definitions of all the factors can be consulted in the link https://docs.google.com/spreadsheets/d/1cDtpXQAqrJg742m0tRrIKS6PSZ_0gS6G/

On the other hand, in the studies analyzed, only one of them [15] used a statistical model to evaluate team productivity in agile teams, showing that productivity depends precisely on team effectiveness factors.

5 Conclusions

The Systematic Mapping Study carried out in six information sources (IEEE Xplore, ACM Digital, Scopus, Compendex, Web of Science, Springer Link) allowed the identification of eight primary studies with 63 factors to measure team productivity in agile software development.

Based on the studies analyzed, an approximation is made to the definition of team productivity in ASD, highlighting that it is an abstract concept, of great relevance for software organizations since it functions as an indicator of continuous improvement. In addition, team productivity in ASD is made up of factors that generate an impact and that allow the achievement of the objectives associated with the expectations coming from a client.

The identified factors were classified into four categories: *Meaning, Impact, Flexibility* and *High performance*. It is highlighted that in the category of Meaning there were recurring factors such as Team Speed, Work Capacity and Customer Satisfaction, and in the Impact category it was perceived that Collaboration, Communication and Quality were the most frequent.

Although the selected systematic path included the keyword "model" in the search string for the period between 2001 and 2021, it was not possible to identify elements with a higher level of abstraction that integrate and interrelate categories and factors to measure team productivity in ASD.

The main limitation of this study was that bibliographic sources of information such as Wiley or Science Direct were not considered. It would be interesting to replicate the research including these search engines.

As future work, it is intended that the conceptualization of team productivity in ASD together with the factors for its measurement established in this SMS, be contrasted with the appreciations obtained by the members of ASD teams. This will allow proposing a measurement process through the construction of a team productivity evaluation model for this context.

References

1. Annual State of Agile Report. 15th Annual State of Agile Report I Digital.ai. State Of Agile Report (2021). https://digital.ai/resource-center/analyst-reports/state-of-agile-report
2. Ghobadian, A., Husband, T.: Measuring total productivity using production functions. Int. J. Prod. Res. **28**(8), 1435–1446 (1990). https://doi.org/10.1080/00207549008942803
3. Hernández-López, A., Colomo-Palacios, R., García-Crespo, Á.: Medidas de productividad en los proyectos de desarrollo de software: una aproximación por puestos de trabajo. Carlos III de Madrid (2014)
4. Fatema, I., Sakib, K.: Factors influencing productivity of agile software development teamwork: a qualitative system dynamics approach. In: Proceedings of the 2017 24th Asia-Pacific Software Engineering Conference (APSEC), pp. 737–742 (2017). https://doi.org/10.1109/APSEC.2017.95
5. Iqbal, J., Omar, M., Yasin, A.: An empirical analysis of the effect of agile teams on software productivity. In: Proceedings of the 2019 2nd International Conference on Computing, Mathematics and Engineering Technologies (iCoMET), pp. 1–8 (2019). https://doi.org/10.1109/ICOMET.2019.8673413

6. Iqbal, J., Omar, M., Yasin, A.: Defining teamwork productivity factors in agile software development. Int. J. Adv. Sci. Eng. Inf. Technol. (2022). https://doi.org/10.18517/ijaseit.12.3.13648

7. Guerrero-Calvache, S.-M., Hernández, G.: Conceptions and perceptions of software industry professionals on team productivity in agile software development: a comparative study. Rev. Fac. Ing. **30** (2021). https://doi.org/10.19053/01211129.v30.n58.2021.13817. http://www.scielo.org.co/scielo.php?script=sci_arttext&pid=S0121-11292021000400104&nrm=iso

8. Hernández, G., Martínez, Á., Jiménez, R., Jiménez, F.: Métricas de productividad para equipo de trabajo de desarrollo ágil de software: una revisión sistemática. TecnoLógicas **22**, 63–81 (2019). https://doi.org/10.22430/22565337.1510

9. Hernández, G., Navarro, A., Jiménez, R., Jiménez, F.: Cómo los profesionales perciben la relevancia de las métricas de productividad para un equipo ágil de desarrollo de software. Rev. Ibérica Sist. e Tecnol. Informação (E32), 596–609 (2020)

10. Fatema, I., Sakib, K.: Using qualitative system dynamics in the development of an agile teamwork productivity model. Int. J. Adv. Softw. **11**(1), 170–185 (2018)

11. Ramírez-Mora, S.L., Oktaba, H.: Productivity in agile software development: a systematic mapping study. In: Proceedings of the 2017 5th International Conference in Software Engineering Research and Innovation (CONISOFT), pp. 44–53 (2017). https://doi.org/10.1109/CONISOFT.2017.00013

12. Petersen, K., Feldt, R., Mujtaba, S., Mattsson, M.: Systematic mapping studies in software engineering. In: Proceedings of the 12th International Conference on Evaluation and Assessment in Software Engineering, pp. 68–77 (2008). https://dl.acm.org/doi/10.5555/2227115.2227123

13. Cockburn, A., Highsmith, J., Jeffries, R.: Manifiesto por el Desarrollo Ágil de Software. Agilemanifesto.Org (2014). https://agilemanifesto.org/iso/es/manifesto.html. Accessed 12 Jul 2022

14. Scott, E., Charkie, K.N., Pfahl, D.: Productivity, turnover, and team stability of agile teams in open-source software projects. In: Proceedings of the 2020 46th Euromicro Conference on Software Engineering and Advanced Applications (SEAA), pp. 124–131 (2020). https://doi.org/10.1109/SEAA51224.2020.00029

15. Mashmool, A., Khosravi, S., Joloudari, J.H., Inayat, I., Gandomani, T.J., Mosavi, A.: A statistical model to assess the team's productivity in agile software teams. In: Proceedings of the 2021 IEEE 4th International Conference and Workshop Óbuda on Electrical and Power Engineering (CANDO-EPE), pp. 11–18 (2021). https://doi.org/10.1109/CANDO-EPE54223.2021.9667902

16. Fagerholm, F., Ikonen, M., Kettunen, P., Münch, J., Roto, V., Abrahamsson, P.: How Do Software Developers Experience Team Performance in Lean and Agile Environments? (2014). https://doi.org/10.1145/2601248.2601285

17. Jung, M., Chong, J., Leifer, L.:Group hedonic balance and pair programming performance: affective interaction dynamics as indicators of performance. In: Proceedings of the SIGCHI Conference on Human Factors in Computing Systems, pp. 829–838 (2012). https://doi.org/10.1145/2207676.2208523

18. Sarpiri, M., Gandomani, T.J.: A case study of using the hybrid model of scrum and six sigma in software development. Int. J. Electr. Comput. Eng. **11**, 5342–5350 (2021). https://doi.org/10.11591/ijece.v11i6.pp5342-5350

19. Sj\oberg, D.I.K.: An Empirical Study of WIP in Kanban Teams (2018). https://doi.org/10.1145/3239235.3239238

20. Dorairaj, S., Noble, J., Malik, P.: Understanding lack of trust in distributed agile teams: a grounded theory study. In: Proceedings of the 16th International Conference on Evaluation Assessment in Software Engineering (EASE 2012), pp. 81–90 (2012). https://doi.org/10.1049/ic.2012.0011

21. Melnyk, K., Hlushko, V., Borysova, N.: Decision support technology for sprint planning. Radio Electron. Comput. Sci. Control, 135–145 (2020). https://doi.org/10.15588/1607-3274-2020-1-14

22. García-Crespo, Á., Hernández-López, A., Colomo-Palacios, R.: Productivity in software engineering: a study of its meanings for practitioners: understanding the concept under their standpoint. In: Proceedings of the 7th Iberian Conference on Information Systems and Technologies (CISTI 2012), pp. 1–6 (2012). https://ieeexplore.ieee.org/document/6263205

23. Hernández-López, A., Palacios, R.C., García-Crespo, Á., Cabezas-Isla, F.: Software engineering productivity: concepts, issues and challenges. Int. J. Inf. Technol. Proj. Manag. **2**, 37–47 (2011)

Correction to: Introducing Planet-Saving Strategies to Measure, Control, and Mitigate Greenhouse Gas Emissions and Water Misuse in Household Residences

Ronald S. Marin Cifuentes, Adriana M. Florez Laiseca,
and Fernando Yepes-Calderon

Correction to:
Chapter "Introducing Planet-Saving Strategies to Measure,
Control, and Mitigate Greenhouse Gas Emissions
and Water Misuse in Household Residences" in: H. Florez
and H. Gomez (Eds.): *Applied Informatics*, CCIS 1643,
https://doi.org/10.1007/978-3-031-19647-8_31

In the originally published version of chapter 31 the Figure 5 was processed improperly. The Figure 5 has been corrected.

The updated original version of this chapter can be found at
https://doi.org/10.1007/978-3-031-19647-8_31

Item a evaluar	Descriptor	(Imágenes deben decir: photo. Fechas deben decir DD/?
Residencias		
	Dirección	Cra 78A No. 6-58
	Responsable	Ronald Santiago Marin
	Área	180 m²
	Estrato	5
	Barrio	Ciudad Capri
	Ciudad	Cali, Medellin, Bogota, Bucaramanga, Barranquilla, Pasto
	Departamento	Valle, Bogota DC, Atlantico, Antioquía, Nariño
	País	Colombia, Ecuador, Panama, Perú

A

Nombre evaluación	Electricas - Home Automation		
Nombre corto	Electricas – HA		
		Opciones cuantitativa	
Categoría	**Subcategoría**	**Valores**	**Unidades**

B

Variables electrícas		sum	
	Voltaje	m	Volts
	Corriente	m	Ampers
	Desface	m	ms
	Onda voltaje (lista)	m	Amplitud
	Onda corriente (lista)	m	Amplitud

Nombre evaluación	Agua Consumo – Home Automation		
Nombre corto	Agua Consumo – HA		
		Opciones cuantitativas	
Categoría	**Subcategoría**	**Valores**	**Unidades**

C

Consumo de agua		sum	
	Caudal	m	Lt/min
	Tiempo de uso	m	us

Nombre evaluación	Ambientales - Home Automation		
Nombre corto	Ambientales – HA		
		Opciones cuantitativas	
Categoría	**Subcategoría**	**Valores o rango**	**Unidades**

D

Ambientales		sum	
	Humedad	m	%
	Temperatura	m	Celcius
	CO2	m	ppm

E

Fig. 5. Evalu@ configuration. Panel A is the template for registering household residences. The excel in Panel B teaches E@ to follow the electrical variables. The excel in Panel C setups E@ to track water footprint variables. The excel in panel D tells E@ how to follow environmental variables. Finally, panel E shows the interface provided by E@ once the setup is completed.

Author Index

Printed in the United States
by Baker & Taylor Publisher Services

Printed in the United States
by Baker & Taylor Publisher Services